Musical Semiotics in Growth

Musical Semiotics in Growth

Edited by

Eero Tarasti

Assistant Editors

Paul Forsell
Richard Littlefield

Indiana University Press
International Semiotics Institute
Imatra　•　Bloomington　1996

ACTA SEMIOTICA FENNICA
IV

Editor
Eero Tarasti

Assistant Editors
Paul Forsell
Richard Littlefield

Editorial Board

Indiana University Press
International Semiotics Institute
Imatra • Bloomington

Printed by Gummerus Printing, Jyväskylä, Finland, 1996

Library of Congress Cataloging-in-Publication Data

Musical semiotics in growth / edited by Eero Tarasti ; assistant editors, Paul Forsell, Richard Littlefield.
    p. cm. — (Acta semiotica Fennica, ISSN 1235-497X : 4)
Includes bibliographical references.
ISBN 0-253-32949-3 (alk. paper). — ISBN 0-253-21009-7 (pbk. ; alk. paper)
    1. Music—Semiotics. 2. Music—Philosophy and aesthetics. 3. Musical analysis.
I. Tarasti, Eero. II. Forsell, Paul. III. Littlefield, Richard. IV. Series.
ML3845.M9755 1996
781'.1—dc20   96-21230

1 2 3 4 5 01 00 99 98 97 96   MN

Contents

Philosophical approaches

Principles and concepts of music analysis

Semiotics as "social psychology"

Vocal music

Instrumental music

Forewords

The international research project on Musical Signification, since its founding over ten years ago, has sought to win new scholars to musical semiotics. To that end, the Department of Musicology at Helsinki University has, since 1991, organized international doctoral and postdoctoral seminars. At these seminars, musicologists from all over the world receive advice and tuition in their studies. Altogether five seminars have taken place, and by now they have become something of a tradition. Can anyone become a semiotician through training and education? Which avenues lead a young music scholar to semiotic analysis? This anthology suggests a positive answer to the first question, and attempts to elucidate the latter.

The teaching of musical semiotics has not yet been incorporated into mainstream curricula of conservatories and music schools worldwide with an efficiency comparable to, say, Schenkerian methods. This is understandable, inasmuch as musical semiotics has never constituted *one* monolithic approach or analytic method. The Musical Signification project has nurtured this ecumenical spirit, which goes beyond the semiotic "schools" proper. For who can say definitely what semiotics is, and especially musical semiotics? Our seminars, to which representatives from a worldwide scientific community have come during these five years to Helsinki or Imatra, constitute one answer: musical semiotics is precisely what we are doing right now.

To describe the Musical Signification project to an "outsider", one might list the following traits: 1) Many of its scholars take certain forebears as their starting-points; that is, musical semiotics is the *application* to music of the ideas of certain semioticians. Thus if names such as Peirce, Greimas, Eco, Lotman, and Sebeok appear in their studies, the latter obviously belong to the field of musical semiotics. 2) Musical semiotics in a broader sense is involved when a study engages problems generally conceived as semiotical; these may include issues of musical communication and signification, the methodology and epistemology of music analysis, the essence of musical language, the relationship of musical discourse to other discourses, intertextuality, and the like. 3) A study may qualify as musical semiotics if any problem related to music,

musical concepts, or musical behaviour is examined in the spirit of semiotics. I purposely leave this "spirit" without closer definition. For it is
any impression, reaction, intuition, or instinct of a competent music
scholar who says, "Indeed, this is semiotics!" It is of the utmost importance that semiotics not become mired in any one particular phase, and
thereby canonize a prevailing method as the "official" or "one and only"
semiotics, whether it be the cognitive approach, the generative course, or
any other "canonized" theoretical outlook. Only such an attitude legiti-
mizes the title of our anthology: Musical Semiotics in *Growth*.

The working method of the seminars was simple but efficient, and the
average number of participants was about twenty active students and
visiting scholars. This anthology consists of papers given in the first
three seminars. The essay by Dr. Dinda L. Gorlée was added later
because of its special interest for the project. My co-director and invalu-
able supporter in these seminars was Dr. Raymond Monelle of Edinburgh University. The seminar has already seen useful results. For one,
it has enabled many a post-graduate student to find the appropriate
university at which to realize his/her doctoral project. For another, a
good number of doctoral theses has already been completed in connection
with our seminars. Also, many young scholars were able to give their
first professional presentations, and to a sophisticated international
audience. Finally, thanks to these seminars the Musical Signification
project has gained more members and has grown into a group of about
two hundred scholars.

Dissertations, as such, may vary greatly as to their level in many
European countries and elsewhere in the world. In some places the
doctoral thesis is not yet considered to be independent scientific work,
whereas in other countries it is almost a life-long task, often not completed till one reaches the age of fifty. Yet dissertations in musical semiotics usually prove exceptional, no matter where they are written. For
this particularly demanding field of studies is entered only by those
whose nature compels them to experiment with new methods and who
display a certain intellectual vigilance. Since the area is relatively young,
a kind of avant-garde of musicology, all findings in the field are innova-

tions and thus strategically crucial. It is in this groundbreaking aspect where this anthology finds its justification.

The articles are grouped under various headings, though with no strict rule guiding their categorization. **Philosophical Approaches** begin with my own overview of various sign practices and theories in our music history since the last century. It is followed by Raymond Monelle's discussion of the postmodern project in music theory. Monelle focuses on the present state of music and music analysis, rationalism, myths of organicism, the scientificity of musical discourses and music's essence as a metonymic, allegoric and deconstructive activity. The essay by Cynthia Grund examines from a philosophical standpoint the applications of Bentham's and Vaihinger's theory of fiction to arts and music. Her thesis is: "In order for a sequence of sounds to be music, it must be apprehended *as if* it were something else. This idea coincides with that traditional musical aesthetic view which believes that 'music' does not lie in the tones, in the signifiers, but 'behind' them, in what they express." The Polish scholar Maciej Jabłoński researches the sources of Peircean semiotics and considers the axiological aspects of pragmatism. Thus far in our seminars, ethnomusicologists have unfortunately been a minority; and for some contributions it is impossible to say whether they represent anthropology, philosophy, or semiotics. Such is the case with the Brazilian José Luiz Martinez, who combines Western thought, represented by Charles Sanders Peirce, with the oriental tradition of so-called *rasa* aesthetics and Indian music theory. The dialogue between these two worlds is staged in a fascinating and challenging way in Martinez's article.

The next group, **Principles and Concepts of Music Analysis**, begins with Alfonso Padilla, who ponders the epistemological prerequisites of any musical research, be it ethnomusicological or "general", and the relationship of that research to history, modernity, and universality. He responds to these issues with a pluralistic method of analysis, which he has already applied, among other places, in his treatise on Boulez and dialectics. The Italians Michele Ignelzi and Paolo Rosato develop an original theory of homeostasis in music, which joins ideas from Nattiez's paradigmatic method to the semiotics of Eco and the systems theory of

Fulvio Delli Pizzi. Intuitively, mathematics and musical semiotics seem to have much in common, and the essay by the German Thomas Noll convincingly demonstrates this closeness. He starts with Roland Posner's linguistic model and ends with the mathematical music theory of Guerino Mazzola. In her essay on semiotic terminology in music analysis, the Hungarian-born Márta Grabócz, currently teaching in Strassbourg, elucidates terms from Greimassian semiotics — semes, isotopies, narrative programs and schemes — and various ways they are articulated. The Swiss Raphaël Brunner discusses the epistemological status of musical semiotics and sketches a theory of narrativity in music; for this task, he draws upon Barthes, Jauss, Monelle, and the "ostensive-inferential" model of Sperber and Wilson. In his second paper, Raymond Monelle examines the suitability of the concept of "text" as a unit of music analysis; to illustrate, Monelle examines Mahler's conception of a textual subject, both in his music (the finale of the Third symphony) and in his verbal comments.

In the section on **Semiotics as "Social Psychology"** Jean-Marie Jacono, from Aix-en-Provence, investigates the institutionalization of art works and compositions in a broader sociosemiotic context. His doctoral thesis some years ago was a remarkable study of various versions and stagings of *Boris Godunov*. Olga Danilova and Yelena Pokorskaya report on work done at the Moscow Art Studies Institute on the style development of various arts. This development seems to be guided historically by oscillations between oppositions in the social-psychological climate of rationality/emotionality, openness/isolation, democracy/authoritarianism, and others. The theory is supported by extensive statistical research on the history of arts. Jarmila Doubravová applies the so-called interpersonal hypothesis to problems of musical semantics and shows how certain musico-cognitive models, which she analyzes in psychological terms, are close to, among other things, the Greimassian modalities. One group of studies in musical signification has always been computer-assisted approaches. A primary center in this field is the Musicology Department at Florence Conservatory, run by Lelio Camilleri. Francesco Giomi and Marco Ligabue, from that institution, look at ways to correlate semiotic research and analysis with composition.

As far as a truly "semiotic" spirit manifests in studies in the **Interrelationships of Arts** (e.g., between literature and music), the essay by Michael Spitzer is one of the most topical in the whole book. He connects Proust and Beethoven, and as a skilful music theoretician is also able to prove his hypothesis by revealing structural isomorphisms between the works of the two artists. Greimas's semiotics seems to be the starting-point for many a scholar. It is adopted here by Ennio Simeon, who deals with the narrative grammar of film music — certainly a most fascinating area for a semiotician. Sarah Menin, in turn, examines the relationship between architecture and music. The connection between buildings designed by Alvar Aalto and symphonies written by Jean Sibelius is intuitively quite evident to anyone who is familiar with both, but how to prove it scientifically? Sarah Menin's essay offers an answer to this question.

Many studies have been done on **Vocal Music**. One of the most systematic applications of Greimas's generative course to music is doubtless Willem Marie Speelman's study of liturgical music of the Dutch church. Combining early Greimas with Hjelmslev's notions of content and expression, Speelman aims at creating a sophisticated metalanguage by which one might analyze any monodic vocal music. (Speelman's dissertation has been published by the University of Tilburg.) Did you know that Charles S. Peirce was a Wagnerian and translated many of Wagner's librettos into English? This amazing aspect of the life of the great American semiotician was recently discovered by Dinda L. Gorlée and is presented in detail in her contribution. Fabienne Desquilbé shows, in her analysis of Monteverdi's *Orfeo*, how well certain Greimassian concepts (such as semeanalysis and isotopies) fit into the intertextual field. Patrick Farfantoli, also from the "Aix School", elucidates intersemiosis, paying particular attention to the presence and absence of significations in a discourse. This is illustrated by his analysis of Mozart's *Don Giovanni* and Berlioz's *Symphonie fantastique*.

Opera is indeed a verdant field of signs. Anneli Remme, in her analysis, shows how Benjamin Britten utilizes iconicity, symbols, and conventional signs in his opera *Death in Venice*. The strong ties with folk traditions, which the Soviet regime was not able to destroy completely, are also reflected in Baltic musicology. Urve Lippus draws a profile of the Estonian composer Veljo Tormis on the basis of his ballet-cantata, *Estonian Ballads*, with emphasis on musical symbols. Lippus's doctoral thesis, "Linear Thinking", published last year, focused on Baltic folk songs and musical structures. Lithuania has given Greimas to semiotics, and to music the fascinating composer Brunius Kutavicius (who, unfortunately, is still relatively unknown in the West). Departing from such Greimassian notions as the actant model, Inga Jankauskienė studies the role of written text in Kutavičius's music, which is highly "semiotic" in nature.

The last, but not the least interesting, section of the anthology is dedicated to **Instrumental Music**. In her essay, Isabelle Servant unites her knowledge of French Baroque clavichord music with a theory of "temporal environments". The result is an impressive and articulate overview of temporal techniques in Baroque music, probably also gener-alizable to other musical genres of the period. Christine Esclapez, also from Aix, likewise studies issues of time. Her monumental thesis on temporality in Beethoven was some years ago brilliantly defended in France. (Hers is also a good example of work done under the guidance of professor Bernard Vecchione.) It is well known that in the Soviet Union the arts were so controlled that artists had to create hidden sym-bols and sign languages by which to express the real content of things. The music of Dmitri Shostakovitch is full of such hidden meanings, and as such represents a challenge to any semiotician. This challenge has been taken by Esther Sheinberg, who studies the composer's "yurodivy" image in his string quartets. In Russian musicology the notion of "mo-dality" is used in many senses, as the article by Svetlana Bauer shows, in her applications of that concept to the Fourth Symphony of Alfred Schnittke. Serial music has received relatively little semiotic analysis, since it has been taken for granted that repetition is the only starting-point for style analysis. Nevertheless, Anne Sivuoja-Gunaratnam demon-strates that semiotic mechanisms are functioning even in serial music, in her study of the orchestral piece *Arabescata* by Finnish composer Einojuhani Rautavaara.

Special thanks are owed to my faithful assistant editors, Paul Forsell in Helsinki, and Richard Littlefield in Texas. Mr. Forsell has prepared the layout, gathered materials, and done other technological work with the book, while Mr. Littlefield has devoted all his skills to improving the English and style of the articles. I am very grateful to both of them. My thanks are also due to Ms. Minnakaisa Kuivalainen for help in typing and to Mr. Andrew Chesterman for revising the English of some of the essays. Likewise, I want to thank Professor Thomas A. Sebeok for his genuine interest in musical semiotics and all his warmhearted encouragement for many years. The Finnish Academy of Sciences provided a grant to cover part of the printing costs of the book.

Helsinki, January 20, 1996

Eero Tarasti

PHILOSOPHICAL APPROACHES

Music history revisited
(by a semiotician)

EERO TARASTI

A semiotic interpretation of the two last centuries in the history of Western art music is in many respects a challenging enterprise. For it often has been said about the application of semiotic methods to various stylistic eras of music that "semioticians of music are kings as long as one moves within the values of nineteenth-century music." But as soon as we come to the musical avant-garde of our own time, we notice that semiotic interpretations are as bound with the epistemes of the Romantic period as musicology was when it was born at the end of the nineteenth century.

However, it is justified to scrutinize the musical development of both the nineteenth and the twentieth centuries in the same chapter insofar as many musical concepts of Romanticism are still vigorously alive, such as the view of musical communication with the composer as center, the stress upon the national isotopy, and the like.

On the other hand, when interpreting music history semiotically we deliberately put upon it the network of our own semiotical metalanguage in order to pick up the aspects relevant for us. But what then is this metalanguage, which kind of conception about music history does it represent and to which or whose semiotics do its tools belong?

In what follows I take the liberty to use all those semiotic concepts which prove useful in the explanation of music history. Therefore, I dare to use side by side concepts from Greimas, Peirce, and Lotman, believing in the opinion of the last-mentioned that the contradiction between the two first-mentioned theories about the structure of a sign — a musical one in our case — is no longer the most crucial matter but rather the problem of its relation to the universe of signs surrounding it, to its semiosphere — or here to its *tonosphere*.

Characterization of Musical Forms in Nineteenth-Century Music History

A musicologist who belongs to those who have in the most profound way investigated the musical language of Romanticism, is Ernst Kurth (1922: 149) — whom we also have to consider a presemiotician of music in the same sense as Boris Asafiev about a rhythmic-symmetric and lied-like melodic thinking which is based upon groups of two, four, and eight measures (Example 1).

Example 1. W. A. Mozart: Sonata for Piano, K. 576 — Beginning of 3rd movement.

This kind of grouping is one of the basic types of rationality inherent in Western art music. Any deviation from it in favour of asymmetry has always been experienced as a break against the musical logic itself. If the symphonic thinking of Anton Bruckner was still basicly rooted in these kinds of unit, the formal thought of, let us say, Jean Sibelius is very asymmetric, non-schematic, and perhaps due to this feature not easy to make fit with this rationality and logic into which Central-European music listeners have grown and become educated.

On the other hand, this formal concept also fulfils one of the most central aesthetic ideas in Western art music in the nineteenth century, namely the actorialization (Greimas 1979: 8–9) of music through the concept of theme. The musico-theoretical criteria of theme are namely: a theme has to contain sufficiently characteristic musical features — let them be called phemes and/or semes; it must have a relatively simple chordal background; and it has to be of a certain length. These criteria, which hold true for a theme in Beethoven among others, display the functioning of three semiotic categories determined by Greimas: actorial, spatial, and temporal. By the actorial category in music I mean all those elements which make a musical text or a part thereof — even the smallest one — anthropomorphic; that is, such as to be grasped by the music listener and to be identified with in some way by him. (As to the musico-psychological conditions for the actorialisation of these musical traits or figures are experienced as musical actors or 'personages', this is a problem not to be dealt with here, but would certainly belong to the area of cognitive musicology.)

The chordal or harmonic background of a theme in turn refers to its position in the tonal space or in the spatial category. The requirement about its length concerns the temporal category, in that a musical theme-actor has to consist in rhythmic units of a given size. For one musical actor — which could be any theme in a Classico-Romantic piece — all these three categories are functioning and forming a balance with each other. As a whole this phenomenon might be called the *actorialization* of music, which is one of the most striking sign processes in nineteenth-century music. It exceeds the limits of different musical genres (for example, Schubert might use the same theme actors in his lieder as in his instrumental works; e.g., the lied "Der Wanderer" and the main theme of the *Wanderer Phantasy*) as well as different arts (the leitmotifs of Wagner as musical, poetic, and scenic units) and in the context of one theme trespassing the various parts of one piece (e.g., the so-called cyclic form in César Franck and other Romantics; i.e., the return of the same theme actor at the end of a work).

A good deal of expression and subjectivity in the aesthetic of musical Romanticism becomes manifest precisely through the concept of a theme or actor, which was also conceptually noticed by many composers in their writings about music (such as Berlioz and Liszt). Nevertheless, as with so many other features of musical form, even actoriality developed as early as in the period of Classicism. Charles Rosen (1980: 8–15) elucidated from a music-sociological point of view upon which factors the triumph and incomparable success of the Classical style in music history was based. For Rosen, these factors arose from the multi-levelled nature of this style. On the deepest level of tonal structures a specialist could, when listening to a Beethoven or Haydn symphony, distinguish a certain simple pitch structure — such as the *Stufen* in an *Ursatz*, to follow the idea of Heinrich Schenker (1956) — while in the more superficial structures an ordinary music listener without any particular musical competence could discern menuettos, marches, hunting calls, etc.; that is, elements coming from everyday social life. These repeated stylistic features have been called topics by Leonard Ratner (1980: 9–24) who discusses galant, military, *Empfindsame*, *Sturm und Drang*, and other styles and topics in the Classical era. From a semiotic standpoint the topics are musical icons borrowed from social reality and practises external to music. (One has to recall that an icon is a sign in a relation of similarity with its object. Hence, in a broader sense, there exists an iconic relation between two similar musical signs whether they originated from two different musical universes — as in the case of a hunting signal and its occurrence in a Haydn symphony — or with the same musical piece and universe of signs — as with a theme and its variations.)

Thus, we might analyze the following beginning of the C minor Phantasy of Mozart with the aforementioned topics of Ratner, and at the same time note the tonal-spatial structure holding these topics on the surface level (Example 2).

Although this beginning quotes many topics from the Classical style, as to its general expression, it clearly betokens Romanticism, to which such musemes as the key, the usage of a broad range, dynamic contrasts in timbre and tempo. In fact, this brief example displays Immanuel Kant's notion of "how a genius gives a rule to art" or how a Classical and Romantic composer differ in their ways of creation: if a classicist produces within the limits of the rules, a romanticist rather creates outside rules by violating them. In the view of Guido Adler, the Romantic style was characterized by an inclination to underline the contents at the cost of the form.

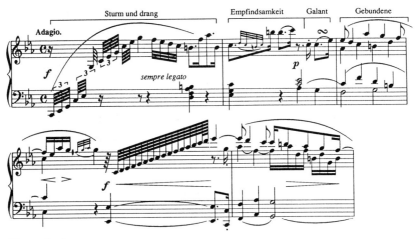

Example 2.

With these sign conceptions referring to nineteenth-century music, we have, without noticing it, come to one central idea in musical semiotics. Namely, as a kind of minimum level of musical semiotics there should be at least two levels of articulation: (1) the level of expression, the concrete physical-aural stimulus and (2) the level of content or emotions, associations, values and meanings joined to music. These two levels are inseparably united with each other — precisely as Saussure presumed that every sign has two aspects: signifier and signified, which are like two sides of the same sheet of paper. Therefore the semiotical analysis of music requires that one pay simultaneous attention to both expression and content. Most interesting is that even this axiom, which has been often posed as the universal of musical semiotics, is itself if not a straightforward product of a certain musico-historical period, that of Romanticism (as early as the eighteenth century, musical aesthetics in France knew the distinction between *musique imitative* — a kind of programmatic music — and *musique naturelle*, a purely mathematic, non-programmatic music), then at least a view strongly emphasised and evaluated by it.

Accordingly, if in this sense the last 'Romantics' in twentieth-century musicology, Boris Asafiev and Ernst Kurth found music to be a semiotic sign process — the former as intonations expressing emotions, values and world views, the latter as *Bewegungsphasen* and *Linienzüge* (Kurth 1922: 1–32) conveying kinetic energies — then they were already pre-semioticians of music. A critical mind might argue against this starting point by asking whether such strongly historical concepts can at all be sufficiently universal to depict such musical texts as pieces by John Cage or Anton Webern? Anyway, we must try in our musical semiotics not to fulfil any systematic theory at the cost of violating empirical facts. A musico-semiotical view of history has to be, above all, flexible.

If we still return to the problem of the topics, it is clear that later the period of Romanticism developed topics of its own. Marta Grabócz (1986: 121–123) has analysed the whole pianistic output of Franz Liszt and remarked that it is based upon seven basic topics or 'isotopies', as she says, which are: 1) the macabre interrogation, the *lugubre* search, the Faustian question, the 'why'; 2) the pastorale; 3) the heroic; 4) the macabre or tempestuous, demoniac fight; 5) sorrow; 6) the religious; and 7) the pantheist. Every composer develops his own characteristic isotopies according to his musical education, background, environment and general aesthetico-social context. At the same time, one may notice the emergence of topics common to all Romantic composers. Among the most common groups are the so-called mythical topics, in correlation with and due to the general orientation of the era to temporally and spatially distant spheres of culture.

Thus it is astonishing that composers could at the same time and without knowing it come to use similar musical topics when expressing the same mythical content. In this way, for example, G minor conveys the balladic in Wagner (the Ballade of Senta in the Flying Dutchman; in the forging song of Siegfried in *Siegfried*), in Glinka (the Monologue of the Head from *Russlan and Ludmila*), in Brahms (G minor Ballade), in Schumann (*Im Legendenton* in the C major Phantasy), etc. Or the use of the English horn may be related to something mythical both in Sibelius (*The Swan of Tuonela*) and in Berlioz (*L'amour l'ardente flamme* in *La Damnation de Faust*), E flat major and horns are signs for the heroic-mythical as early as the *Eroica* of Beethoven until the *Heldenleben* of Richard Strauss (see Tarasti 1979: 66–129).

One can even distinguish a network of this kind of mythical topic (or seme, in that we are only defining their content) manifesting a particular aesthetics of mythicism in music. This kind of network can be considered as a chain of interpretants similar to the series of transformations of myths studied by Lévi-Strauss, for which the narrator does not know for any individual myth that he is repeating a fragment from a larger whole — as little as a Romantic composer is aware of his belonging to a broader stylistic paradigm.

Particular Musical Sign Processes of the Romantic Period

How can one semiotically characterize certain musical practices of Romanticism? We may examine separately different musical parameters as to how they carry semiotic sign processes.

As to melody, it is typical of Romantic melody that its ambitus grows. What takes place is thus some kind of spatial (in the external sense) *débrayage* disengagement) (Greimas 1979: 79) and great interval leaps are provided with a strong expressive function; they become indexes of emotion and passion in precisely the sense that Vladimir Karbusicky (1986: 59–71) has defined indexical signs in music. On the other hand, melodies also become clearly distinguishable theme-actors whereupon formal articulation takes place. As the best illustration one can point to the symphonic poems and piano works of Franz Liszt, which are often based on monothematicity, i.e. on one musical theme-actor (see, for example, *Vallée d'Obermann*). In many cases melodies assume, due to their frequent repetition, the function of a leitmotif, beginning as early as in Berlioz's *Symphonie Fantastique*. All this makes it possible to apply to these works Greimas's actantial model, with its articulation of *actant/negactant/anti-actant/neganti-actant*. In the same sense, one may even speak about helper themes and opponent themes. On the narrative surface level compositions are constructed in such a way that the listener is persuaded to follow the fortunes of these few theme actors throughout the piece until the final victory (the Fifth Symphony of Beethoven, *Les préludes* by Liszt or the Second Symphony of Sibelius) or ultimate loss (the finale of Tchaikovsky's *Symphonie Pathétique*).

In some cases the relation of a melody to its musical surroundings, or to that which is normally called an accompaniment (the Greimasian categories *englobé/englobant*), proves to be exceptionally unclear: the theme and its environment have been, for example, derived from the same thematic texture, which does not give the impression of theme and its different tonal 'landscape' (wherein Beethoven was master — one may think of the variations of the slow movement of the Fifth Symphony, where the theme actor appears in always varied sound fields and by all this constitutes a kind of narrative process). This is illustrated by the beginning of Schumann's Phantasy in C major.

The mere timbre of a melody can be as decisive as its other musical substance, beginning from the Finale of Beethoven's *Waldstein* Sonata, which employs the whole keyboard and its sound vibrations, until the opening theme in the *Vyšehrad* by Smetana, whose tone colour imitates an old harplike gussli instrument, and until the Prelude to the *Rheingold* by Wagner or Scriabin's *Vers la flamme*, in which cases the melodic passage entirely consists of timbre to the extent that it causes a kind of de-actorialisation. Moreover, it is typical of Romantic melody that it also contains so-called *intertexts* or allusions, among others, from instrumental melodies into vocal ones. The resemblance between Chopin melodies and Italian operas, particularly Bellini's vocal lines is most obvious (whereas Mozart's instrumental music, such as his piano concertos, may evoke the dramatic dialogue structure of an Italian opera). In some cases the melodic structure is determined by the principle of iconic similarity and imitation between the instrument, player, and music itself.

They represent so-called *Spielfiguren* (Besseler 1957), i.e. figures idiomatic to some instrument, but which may be moved to another instrument (such as the piano paraphrases of Liszt based upon Paganini *Etudes* or his arrangements of the Beethoven symphonies, the imitations of organs in the wind sections of orchestras, etc.) It was precisely the cult of virtuosity that strongly underlined the level of *Spielfiguren* in music. The technical qualities and the physiology of a player adapted to these figures began to appear as iconic signs in the music itself, even ruling over the harmonic and melodic tonal articulation (for example, through the choice of a certain key because it fits the hand or of a given register that sounds well in an instrument). Hence, we may interpret the virtuoso culture of Romanticism as a manifestation of iconicity.

Sometimes melody in the Romantic period becomes a long continuous line breaking the rhythmic-symmetric organisation mentioned by Kurth. Then it may consist of a wide range with large, sweeping motion and many leaps. It can be strongly based on and generated by harmonic content, with much use of triadic arpeggiation, extensive embellishment of fairly simple lines, by means of grace notes, passing and neighboring tones, etc. But it can also be chromatic, usually conjunct, employing larger intervals for dramatic passages, with a wide range sometimes covering as much as three to four octaves (for instruments), highly motivic with motives developed through extension and manipulation. In this way, we might characterize the melodies of Chopin and Wagner. In the semiotical sense, this description naturally moves at the level of musical signifiers. In the sense of Greimasian theory, what is involved is the disengagement of the external spatiality while the inner spatiality remains strongly and keenly centripetal, engaged (*embrayé*). By external spatiality is meant simply the use of different registers (see, for example, Cogan and Escot who in their treatise *Sonic Design* (1976: 88) expressly identify the language-likeness of music with its space) while the inner spatiality means the events in the functional harmony of a piece; for example, the movement towards, away from, and against the tonic or dominant.

In other words, in a harmonic sense Romantic music maintains the principle of one tonal center, a principle established as early as two hundred years earlier; while in terms of melody and other parameters, Romantic music may do all it can to weaken the external spatiality with a maximal and often irreducible *débrayage*.

A good illustration for this is provided by the Introduction to the Third movement of Berlioz's *Symphonie Fantastique*, *Un bal*. The tonal and harmonic content, i.e. the inner spatiality, involves simply a transition from A minor to A major, while in the external tonal space occurs the expansion from the middle into the extreme register; this is supported by the transformation of the instrumental colour from dark, mystic timbres into bright and light colouring in the orchestral tutti. Notice particularly the two ways of using the harp at the beginning in order to increase obscurity and at the end brightness (Example 3).

Example 3. Berlioz: "Symphonie fantastique" — 3rd movt. "Un bal": harmonic reduction of the beginning.

Here we enter into the semiotic investigation of the *harmonic* aspects of Romantic music. Romantic melody depends heavily on the harmony, which the above observations on spatiality in music have already confirmed. In addition to this, one has to see more particularly how a composer is enabled by these tools to create a smaller narrative program even within a given theme — and all this by purely musical means, i.e., without programmatic references. This becomes obvious especially in more extensive thematic constructions. The broad opening theme of the Adagio movement in Bruckner's Eighth Symphony gives us a good illustration of this kind of smaller narrative program. One may distinguish there seven sub-actors altogether (Example 4).

1st phrase (mm. 1–6): the 'overall impression is that of a restful neighbour-note character and alternation between major and minor; the modality of "being";

2nd phrase (mm. 7–10): towards a dysphory, the lack of the "value object," a descending, lamenting melodic passage or *Linienzug*, dissonant harmony; notice the enharmonic change from D flat minor to C sharp minor, which references the forthcoming climax in A major, the *Rausch* element (a term used by Friedrich Nietzsche, as well as that of *Traum*);

3rd phrase (mm. 11–14): a transition with the oscillating motif from the beginning, which now carries the spatial change preparing,

Example 4. Bruckner: Eighth Symphony — beginning of 3rd movt.

premodalizing", and indexicalizing the next phrase, i.e. what is involved is modalisation through anticipation of that which is coming;

4th phrase (mm. 15–18): the *Rausch* element, A major, the use of the upper register, the sudden elevation in height, i.e. the external spatial disengagement;

5th phrase (mm. 19–21): a still more sudden return to the dysphoric character, *lugubre*, mourning music, and at the same time to the darkened key of B flat minor;

6th phrase (mm. 22–23): the *Traum* motif, G flat major;

7th phrase (mm. 24–25): the elevation, *das Erhabene* (a very general topic in the Classic-Romantic tradition, in Beethoven, among others; the melodic line is not so much experienced as linear as like changing harmonies; the result is a joint effect of linear and harmonic (syntagmatic and paradigmatic) aspects;

8th phrase (mm. 26–31): the sinking, the renunciation; notice the timbre of the orchestra.

Some details of our small analysis need further clarification. First, when we quote some concept from the German literary and philosophical tradition (such as *Traum* and *Rausch* or the Apollonic and Dionysiac from Nietzsche, which terms played a central role in his early work *Die Geburt der Tragoedie aus dem Geiste der Musik*) we adopt the so-called emic approach. In other words, we attempt to describe music with terms immanent to its own cultural context or semiosphere (as a contrast to the so-called etic or eticist analysis, which uses external categories). We have also used the concepts of modalities and modalization. They do not refer in this context to the so-called church modes, but should be understood in a philosophical and linguistic sense as the ways in which a speaker or enunciator expresses his attitude to what he is enunciating.

According to Greimas (1979: 144) there are two basic modalities, those of "being" and "doing", which in music would simply mean the principles of stasis, rest, non-tension, and consonance for the former; and action, tension, dynamism and dissonance for the latter. In addition there are modalities such as 'will', 'can', 'know', 'must', and 'believe'. All these are also transferable into musical 12. discourse, although they have not yet been explicitly used in the analysis above. Usually music is only then experienced as music when in the performance something is added to it, i.e., when it is interpreted or modalized, as we say. On the other hand, the modalisation can also be written in the text itself — in its *"niveau neutre"* — to use Jean-Jacques Nattiez's term (1975: 52) — when it represents kinetic energy, which according to Kurth appears as the original and deepest source of all music. Furthermore, since music is a process occurring in time, we may say that a certain phrase is as it were *pre-modalised*, i.e. anticipated by its preceding section, while it, on the other hand, can also be *post-modalised* by the consequent section. In these cases we notice how the kinetic energy of a given motif, theme, phrase or section is, as it were, stronger or weaker compared to its neighbouring sections and is thus either subordinated to them or dominating them. Third, the categories dysphoria/euphoria mean the so-called thymic aspect and its articulation, i.e., the negative and positive value of an emotional attitude (terms employed by Greimas). In music the simplest illustration would be that major, consonance = euphoria, minor, dissonance = dysphoria. Yet, in the age of Romanticism these emotional values, which held true for the Classicists, change. We know ever since Wagner's *Tristan* that a dissonance in music can also be pleasing. A continuous, unresolved tension can be experienced as a constant, stable state, as a musical "being", following the principle of *"Wonne der Wehmut"*. Theodor Adorno (1952: 62) paid particular attention to this aspect in Wagner.

This phenomenon is naturally connected, at the level of expression (signifiers) to the increase of chromaticism and altered harmonies, the growth of dissonances leading ultimately to the break-down of the whole inner spatial system of the musical discourse. When the normal syntagmatic course in the musical texts of Romanticism remains, in general, the same, and their paradigmatic alterations are likewise constant:

1st group of chords	I	IV	V
2nd group of chords		II	VII
3rd group of chords	VI		
4th group of chords			III

In the Romantic era, composers start to use quick modulations, secondary dominants and altered harmonies, which render the harmonic interpretation of musical texts ambiguous or bi-isotopic. Also the harmonic rate of change grows dramatically with the chromaticism. Moreover, the harmonies begin to loose their syntagmatic function and to assume a new task of conveying colours. They become autoreflexive musical signs, to use the term in introduced by Umberto Eco and Roman Jakobson. As a classical example one may take the scene of Boris's coronation in *Boris Godunov*, in which the enharmonic alteration of F sharp into G flat causes an impressive change of the color in the chord. This stylistic device strongly influenced Debussy and other Impressionists.

In the temporal or rhythmic respect the period of Romanticism means a rupture in the dominance of the rhythmic-symmetric rationality principle determined by Kurth. It is replaced by a freely pulsating rhythm which follows no meter and which may contain improvisatory interpolations (like the cadenzas in solo concertos). Particularly, the rhythmic rubato has often been written in the musical text itself. Romanticism is the age of ritardando — recall even how the Piano Sonata Op. 31 No. 2 in E flat major by Beethoven starts with an immediate, great ritardando. In other words, even in the temporal sense the rhythmic focus looses its power and music becomes metrically *debrayé* or disengaged.

Programmatic and Narrative Aspects of Romantic Music

The place of music, in general, in the whole formed by various texts of a culture, changes in the era of Romanticism. On one side, it comes closer to other arts but at the same time remains as the leading art form (at least in Germany). Compositions start to depict both the life of an artist and the content of a literary text. The motto of Schumann's C major Phantasy is a verse from Friedric Schlegel: *"Durch alle Töne tönet im bunten Erdentraum/Ein leiser Ton gezogen für den der heimlich lauschet"* (Through all tones sounds a soft tone in the coloured sleep of earth/for the one who listens to it secretly). If a scholar starts to find out where in the musical piece itself that "soft tone" appears, he may search for it in vain, getting only trivial answers (e.g., it is a descending fifth, with which it is known that Schumann made allusions to his wife, Clara Wieck). If one thinks of nineteenth century music at the level of its musical signifiers, the dispute between the supporters of program and absolute music seems to be almost without any basis.

The thesis by Eduard Hanslick, that music is only *"tönend bewegte Formen"* (moving sound forms) and nothing else, was later repeated in the aesthetics of the music of this century, notably by Stravinsky — and in a sense also in that of Lévi-Strauss (1971: 579) (*"La musique, c'est le langage moins le sens"*); but if we take, for example, Brahms's Piano Sonata in F minor, we notice there very Wagnerian topics and even a literary quotation from Hebbel. And this composer was supposed to represent absolute music. It is evident that there also runs throughout the nineteenth century a Classicist line — as represented by Chopin, who was not overtly inspired by literary programs but who in turn himself inspired many others to fabricate literary hermeneutics (poetic programs) for his works. The Romantic tradition of poetic hermeneutics was at the beginning of this century ripe enough to be crystallized into a musicological method, whose main representative was Arnold Schering (1936). In his mind all the absolute instrumental pieces of Beethoven were united with certain literary works (the Adagio from the Seventh Symphony = the funerals of Mignon in Goethe's *Wilhelm Meister*; Piano Sonata Op. 110 in A flat major = *Maria Stuart* by Schiller; etc.). In Finland, as late as the 1920s, Ilmari Krohn — more famous for his method of classifying folk songs (adopted by Béla Bartók, among others) — still wrote literary interpretations to all the symphonies by Jean Sibelius, such as each musical theme-actor depicting some personage in Finnish mythology or history. In the semiotic regard we consider these interpretations as having very trivial connections with musical signifiers and thus not representing any pre-semiotic thought in musicology. Rather, they were literary speculations which taken as a whole can be considered as an interesting manifestation of the Romantic culture.

Nevertheless, it is true that Schering did not think of the presentation of poetic programs as having any absolute aim, but serving only as an animating impulse, a verbal support to the structure and development of a musical work, which occupied the thoughts of a composer only as long as the work to be written was under its influence. When the composition was completed, the program had fulfilled its task in the generative process and could then sink into darkness.

In any case, the programmatic quality of Romanticism also expressed a general narrative principle or model which was applied as much to the lives of artists as to the writing of musical histories and to music itself. As an illustration of how the first mentioned and the last case could mix with each other, one may take Berlioz's *Symphonie Fantastique*. It is obvious that, when Berlioz writes as a subtitle of his work *"Episode d'une vie d'un artiste"*, the artist of the work is depicting is not necessarily himself. In other words, the distinction between the subject of the enunciate and that of enunciation has to be made here, as well as for the themes of Mahler's symphonies, about which Adorno argued that they are like faded protagonists of a novel and others that the composer put himself into them (psychoanalytic interpretations).

The main theme of Berlioz's symphony is in fact epistemic since it depicts the relation of the hero , the subject of the enunciate, to reality using categories of "being" (*être*) and "appearing" (*paraître*). The symphony consists in five movements: 1) *Rêveries — Passions*, 2) *Un Bal*, 3) *Scène aux Champs*, 4) *Marche au supplice*, and 5) *Songe d'une nuit du Sabbat*. The three first movements illustrate how the subject searches for the object and the two last movements his frustration when he is definitely disconnected from the object (according to the Greimasian narrative formula: F[S $\vee$ O]). In a sense the three first movements represent a real search and action while the last two depict unreal escape into illusions.

There is another problem connected with the programmatic quality of music — namely, how music can function as a realistic art describing the outer world. Even in such cases where music seems to be its most programmatic, it has a tendency to "internalize" the signs originally referring to the outer reality into the inner processes of the musical discourse itself, in other words, to transform exteroceptive into interoceptive signs.

A good example is provided by the *Pictures at an Exhibition* by Mussorgsky, a work that was inspired by the paintings by Viktor Hartmann. However, the essential point is that Mussorgsky was able to change the external icons, indexes, and symbols into inner, interoceptive signs in his work. By inner iconicity and indexicality I do not mean merely the promenade sections of the piece that hold it together — their task is (a) to serve as inner indexical phases that take the narration from one scene to another, and (b) to furnish the piece with sufficient consistency by producing a series of iconic transformations of the same subject. I also refer to what happens in each picture as to its iconic and indexical signs: namely, the embedding of realistic elements borrowed from the external reality into the kinetic and energetic texture of the music. In other words, what is involved is an unnoticeable gliding from the programmatic quality into the absolute. As soon as the musical icons of Mussorgsky — the Old Castle, the Jews, the playing children, Bydlo, the chickens, etc. — have been introduced to the listener and their immediate representative character has been uncovered, they become signs for entirely other kinds of semiotic processes.

As early as in the reception of the piece as at the level of *Firstness*, certain passages may make an immediate impression upon the listener, at least a competent one. Nevertheless, only a subsequent analysis on the level of *Thirdness* is able to clarify the factors upon which these impressions are based. One phase of this kind occurs in the Gate of Kiev when we hear a sudden shift to a gloomy, clock-like atmosphere, in the inner spatial sense into the tonal field of A flat minor and, in the outer sense, into a lower and darker register. The section is a musical symbol in the sense that it is a self-quotation from *Boris Godunov*, from the clocks related with Boris. Amidst the triumph it is the reminder of the dysphoria of death, thus throwing a shadow onto the festival atmosphere. In the aesthetic sense, it is one of the most impressive moments of the whole piece. But it is effective also for those who do not recognize this symbolic value. If one pays attention to the structure of the first promenade, it is striking by its modality (now "modality" in a musical sense), i.e., by the fact that the leading tone A (in B flat major) is avoided. When it finally appears in the subordinate section it occurs as a lowered A flat. In the same way, at the beginning of the Gate of Kiev this A flat note is deliberately avoided in order to be spared as an impressive understatement for this point.

Accordingly, as early as at the beginning of the piece, in the first promenade this particular point of the tonal space has been marked and provided with a special value due to the fact that it is used only there where it is needed for a strong expression. Moreover, the A flat note is also an allusion to the tonality of the Old Castle, which is G sharp minor (enharmonically A flat minor). This phenomenon can be designated with the term used in the musical semiotics of Robert S. Hatten (1987: 412): markedness.

Nationalism in Music

In the Romantic period an important phenomenon emerges in music history, which can be called the birth of national music styles. How to interpret this still central musical phenomenon in the semiotic terms? The use of folk music in art music appears most often as "quotation" embedded in the composition, as another text, whose limits against its surrounding text can vary according to the three-phase model by Béla Bartók (1957: 161–164) from a complete fusion ("the composer has learnt the musical language of the peasant and applies it as perfectly as a poet his mother tongue") to the mere harmonisation of a folk tune, to surrounding it with elements offered by art music. The Greimasian category *englobé/englobant* (surrounded/surrounded) would fit here very well, indeed.

From the point of view of Lotman's theory (1976) what is involved is the quoting of an alien text from a sphere experienced as non-culture or anti-culture, and which even has to be taken as "alien", "exotic", "distant", "original" in order to function in the role allotted to it. Yet even in cases where a composer has totally assumed the language of a folk music, his work remains as an artificial, stylized text and is not a solution dictated by "nature" — as the national ideology attempts to legitimize the use of folk music. Carl Dahlhaus has remarked that they are great master composers who first create the national tonal language, and only thereafter do the "people" identify itself with that language and adopt it as its own. In the semiotical respect we have here a kind of "inner" iconicity; i.e., a relation of iconic similarity prevails between the original folk tune and its variant in a work of art music. The same folk melody can serve as a legisign for several art music sinsigns with a folkmusical nature. For example, the hymn of the German emperor is this kind of iconic sign as it appears in a string quartet of Haydn and in the finale of Brahms's F minor Sonata for Piano, or a Finnish folk tune arranged by Ferruccio Busoni or Jean Sibelius. In these cases what matters most is precisely the new "tonosphere", into which the element borrowed from elsewhere has been embedded and which provides it with a new flavour and a "secondary" meaning.

Some composers, musical enunciators, want to make their works of this kind look like (*faire/paraître*) completely original, non-motivated sign complexes (Sibelius), denying that they ever used any direct folk tunes, although later studies have clearly revealed direct iconic relations with the primary, folkmusical texts. Others in turn want to appear as national, as "iconic" composers as possible, while subsequent research has shown that their melodies were purely invented, arbitrary products (Heitor Villa-Lobos).

On the other hand, the supposed foundation of art music upon folk music has been exploited as an ideological *devoir* far into this century, with the argument that folk music is a natural language of music, a kind of primary modelling system, upon which any artistic composition (the secondary modelling systems) should be based. Among others, the intonation theory of Boris Asafiev has been used for these kinds of un- or almost anti-semiotical inferences, as much as his theory may in other respects look like an implicitly semiotical approach.

The Emergence of Musicology as a Particular Semiotic Consciousness of Music

The term "musicology" was first used in 1863 by the German musicologist, best-known as the writer of a Händel biography, Friedrich Chrysander. Yet it would be wrong to imagine that musicology was born all at once, since, in fact, there are texts *about* music in such abundance as early as the seventeenth and eighteenth centuries that it is not difficult to find among them their own "presemioticians". One need only think of such a long series of musical histories upon varied titles as those written by Praetorius (1605–21), Athanasius Kircher (1650), Jacques Bonnet (1715), Padre Martini (1757–82), John Hawkins (1776), Charles Burney (1776–89), etc.; or famous music dictionnaries starting with Brossard and Rousseau, up to the music-aesthetical tracts from that by Descartes onward.

The formidable amount of texts dealing with music was as late as at the beginning of this century given a clearcut organisation — in a somewhat similar way as de Saussure elucidated different views about language with his famous dichotomy *langue/parole* — when the Austrian musicologist Guido Adler divided music research into two branches: the systematic, which dealt with the musical *langue*, its constant, immutable and general regularities; and the historic, which examined the musical *parole*, the varied practices of music with their different conceptual systems over the course of time.

Each period of music history was to be examined, following methods of style criticism developed by Adler, from its own starting points, even if his theory like other music theories at the beginning of the century was extremely normative and limited mostly to the isotopies of German music. On the other hand, there were also signs of a broader musico-semiotical consciousness taking shape in the consideration of extra-European musical reality, as in the *Histoire générale de la musique* by Joseph Fétis (1869–1876). Still, far into this century the extra-European musical reality was seen through the isotopies of Western art music. One illustration can be found in the first volume of the music history written by August Wilhelm Ambros (1887) — one of the first holders of a chair in musicology in Prague beginning in 1869 — who consecrated it to the music of Greece and Orient and also introduced music of the Far East with many examples. He gives a sample of the so-called Djungel-Tuppah melody harmonised by himself, i.e., interpreted according to Western tonal isotopies (Example 5).

Ambros is totally convinced of the correctness of his harmonisation:

Hier wie in allen folgenden Proben indischer Melodik ist die Harmonisierung von mir beigefügt. Sie ist ein Beweis wie sehr diese Melodien im Sinne europäischer Musik erfunden sind, da sie eine reiche harmonische Behandlung nicht nur gestatten sondern beinahe verlangen. (Ambros 1887: 237)

Example 5.   A harmonisation of an Indian melody by August Wilhelm Ambros.

Nevertheless, the harmonisation in question undeniably produces a phenomenon of *méconnaissance* (Jankélévitch 1974) of the original melody; i.e., it is provided with wrong, incompatible isotopies.

The methods of style analysis developed by Guido Adler were based upon binary oppositions between various stylistic genres. The most important opposition for him was the contrast between the Classical and Romantic styles; other dichotomies were vocal/instrumental, great/small style, music for home/church, and so on. Regarding music history, one may in the way of Lévi-Strauss (1958: 347–348) speak about two kinds of models: either we have a so-called *thought-of-model* which a scholar, writer of musie history, constructs in order to create continuity and coherence in a series of musical events, which would otherwise look detached and illogical. Or it is a *lived-in-model*, i.e., a model functioning in and influencing the acts of musical subjects themselves, where we would ask whether there are in the musical data themselves something which would justify a certain order among them. One might in other words ask if there is anything such as "musical progress" — a term used by Charles Burney (1789/1935). Or do we follow the view given by the thought-of-model, according to which such an order is always introduced by external consciousness, always brought there by ourselves. In this case the term used by Carl Dahlhaus (1977: 80), *Erzählbarkeit*, would be a key concept of music history, and that history as a whole has to be seen as a special case of human narrative activity. Music histories are texts whose actors are composers and which are organized according to their own narratological laws. (One may apply the Greimasian categories inchoativity/durativity/terminativity: the creation of a new musical work/the development of some musical genre or form/the decline and oblivion of some work in the "memory" of musical culture.)

In fact, our speech and texts about music follow certain principles of the narrative model which were generalized precisely during the age of Romanticism and which persistently continue to exist. Attempts and efforts of musical modernism and "scientific" discourse throughout the twentieth century have sought to annihilate the narrative model in the general consciousness, without any convincing success. If modernism has any common denominator in this century it is absolutely its anti-narrativity. By the narrative model we understand nearest the model articulated by the *parcours-génératif* of Greimas (1979: 160), which articulates both music and texts about music from a deep level until the surface on two parallel lines, those of expression and content, signifier and signified, syntax and semantics. The narrative model is therefore a model articulating both music and discourse about music, but it can happen that not all the phases of the generative course are realized and exploited in an individual piece or text. Altogether it is a useful tool in musical semiotics. One species of music texts generalised in the age of Romanticism were the composer biographies, which set the musical enunciator as the focus of attention and often according to the emotive function defined by Roman Jakobson (1963: 214). Composer biographies often take a form analysable in the way of Vladimir Propp (1922/1970: 35–80) into functions such as the childhood of a composer, his musical influences, anecdotes depicting his early exceptional gifts, fight for success, illness, travels, premature death, glorification, etc. Not all of these functions need to occur in one biography, but they constitute a kind of ideal paradigm from which one may then realize various types of biographies according to a self-destruction model (Mozart, Wolf, Schumann, Mussorgsky, Schubert, etc.), a glorification model (Wagner, Liszt, etc.), an emigrant model (Stravinsky, Rachmaninov, etc.), a national hero model (Sibelius, Grieg, Dvořák, Paderewski, Villa-Lobos, etc.) etc. As in folktales, alongside a hero appears a false hero who is later unmasked, in the same way an original and true genius can be juxtaposed with a false or would-be genius. The mythical actor model of Greimas is suitable in some cases for the articulation of actors in a composer biography, as in Hildesheimer's Mozart biography (or in the drama *Amadeus* by Schaffer): sender — Leopold Mozart, receiver — Humanity, subject — Mozart, object — music, helper — Baron v. Swieten, opposer — Salieri.

Musical Modernism in the Light of Semiotics

The emergence of modernism in the history of music means above all a revolt against the earlier narrative model of Romanticism. The temporal, spatial, and actorial categories of the Classic-Romantic period lose their centers and music becomes non-periodic, atonal; i.e. without a tonal center in the sense of inner spatiality, and athematic, i.e. without musical theme-actors. In its most complete form what is involved in a musical work of the Schoenberg school is a total *débrayage*, disengagement, although this is very difficult to realize simultaneously on all levels since even the slightest allusion to the preceding model makes the old, inbred listening habits and mechanisms function. The development has therefore been that of a gradual distanciation from the narrative model of Romanticism, just as Charles Rosen has said: if Stravinsky's neoclassic music is like Bach with wrong bass notes, then the case of Boulez is much more difficult since in his music all notes are wrong.

Nevertheless, even in the most recent experimental music at least one level of discursivisation may evoke narrativity; even in the case of the so-called spectral music, represented in France by Tristan Murail and Charles Grisey actoriality may suddenly emerge: e.g. in Grisey's work

Partiels, which is based on an atemporal and a-spatial construction using the smallest parts of the harmonic series, at the end actoriality enters in the shape of conductor, a musical enunciator who pulls from his pocket a red handkerchief and starts to mop his brow before the end of the piece. This also shows how modern music subordinates all the aspects of musical work, both of musical enunciate and enunciation, to transformation.

Are there any common features for all modernism in our century, i.e., concepts which could be defined by a semiotic metalanguage? The question seems to be difficult to answer if we think like Helmut Kirchmeyer (1958: 222) that the twentieth century in European art and music is an endless succession of modernist manifestos. Even before the 1920s one finds at least the following isms: "... atonalism, bruitism, chromaticism, dadaism. debussysm, eroticism, expressionism, folklorism, formalism, futurism, impressionism, intellectualism, classicism, conservatorism, constructivism, cubism, lyrism, machinism,. mecanicism, modernism, motorism, mysticism, naturalism, neoclassicism, neoprimitivism, neoromanticism, orientalism, orphism, primitivism, progressism, romanticism, scriabinism, stravinskysm, superchromaticism, symbolism, vitalism, wagnerism..."

For many of the isms mentioned above it was characteristic to have a belief in a kind of grammar of art, which could be formulated with almost axiomatic precision. Oftentimes these models were also interartistic in nature — even when dealing with music. The principal theoretician of the Bauhaus school, Wassily Kandinsky, attempted to create in his works *Über das Geistige in der Kunst* (1912) and *Punkt und Linie zu Flache* (1926) a grammar and vocabulary the plastic arts. He sought to construct a method applicable to all the arts. The first problem he met was the same that later crystallized into the common starting point for all structuralists: the search for the smallest units of signification, from which one could through some kind of ars combinatoria arrive at more extensive texts and their meanings. In Kandinsky's view there were three units of this kind: point, line, and plane, which applied equally to architecture, dance, and music. In Kandinsky's structuralism the very concept of an "element" was determined in two ways. From an external point of view any form can be an element, but from an inner point of view the form itself is not an element but the inner living tension animating it. External forms never define a work of art; rather it is made by the forces and tensions that live in these forms. Yet neither is it a chaos of forces, but a consciously planned whole of intended tensions. If these tensions suddenly disappear or weaken, then with them the living art work itself is lost. Kandinsky's aesthetics is related to the semiotic aesthetics formulated later by Umberto Eco (1971: 116) in his work *La struttura assente*. There Eco says that a structure consists in inner tensions, and he compares a work of art with a magnetic field in which the relations among different parts are as it were magnetised, pulling and pushing each other according to a certain code. Even in musical semiotics the line we may form from the energetism of Henri Bergson in the turn of century through Ernst Kurth and Boris Asafiev to the music applications of the semiotics of A. J. Greimas touches also the dynamic structuralism of Kandinsky, due to its emphasis on the temporal, kinetic, and continuous nature of music. In Kandinsky's view, line and plane are therefore also the smallest units of dance and music; he depicts the second theme from the first movement of Beethoven's Fifth Symphony in the following way (Example 6).

Also interesting is Kandinsky's system of correspondences of arts, i.e., between lines, pictures, and colours. It evokes as well some interrelational diagrams concerning colours and keys made at the turn of the century, such as those elaborated by Rimsky-Korsakov and Scriabin. Different arts formed in the period of Symbolism a common intertextual semiosphere in which any sign could refer to any other sign, according to Baudelaire's doctrine of correspondences.

Another figure from the Bauhaus school, the architect Le Corbusier, developed his own system of architecture in a structuralist way, from the smallest units which the mathematics inherent in the human body offered. He called them moduls, but in this theory he was more particurly inspired by music, which provided him with a model showing how to proceed even in other areas.

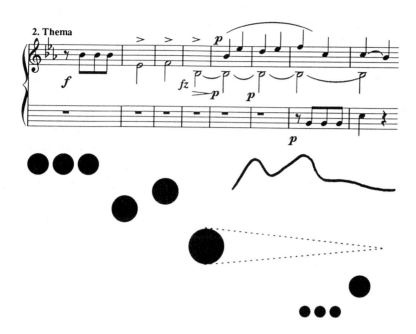

Example 6.   The subordinate theme from the 1st movement of the Fifth
              Symphony by L. van Beethoven and its graphic analysis by W.
              Kandinsky.

With musical semiotics we can understand both the *research* of the
semiotic object itself and the inner organisation and order of this *object*.
These two orientations get fused within the music of this century. Thinking of the structuralist phase in semiotics in the 1960s, one notices how
composers become interested in structural linguistics precisely in order
to produce new musical works. Luciano Berio and Pierre Boulez study
information theory, de Saussure, and structuralism; people start to speak
of serial thought not only as the analysis of already existing structures
but also as the production of new structures. The *Sinfonia* by Berio is
partly based on texts from *The Raw and the Cooked* by Lévi-Strauss.
Even in those cases in which semiotics and structuralism do not form a
direct starting point for yielding, one may at least say that both the

avant-garde music of our time and the development of semiotic go side by side, enlivened by the same spirit.

Particularly the progress of modern technology has opened new possibilities for the elaboration of musical substance, the sound. This would not have been possible without the advancement of such supporting background factors of semiotics as linguistics, information theory, cybernetics, and cognitive sciences. It is not without reason that Carl Dahlhaus has characterized the phase of modernism in music as formalism and structuralism. In the musical aesthetics of this period the central factor is no longer the composer but the composition itself and its structure. This idea had its roots in nineteenth century aesthetics and in the theory of Eduard Hanslick, which has been already mentioned, and which Igor Stravinsky continues with his theses about the incapacity of music to express anything other than itself. Structure is thus the key word of modernism. For example, Pierre Boulez (1971: 18) has fixed as a point of departure for any musical research the following attitude: "Let us define what may be considered the indispensable constituents of an 'active' analytical method: it must begin with the most minute and exact observation possible of the musical facts confronting us; it is then a question of finding a plan, a law of internal organisation which takes account of these facts with the maximum of coherence".

On the other hand, even composers admit that the phenomenon of music itself has turned out to be more and more complicated, and this fact is now also influencing the process of composing itself as well as musical performance. Pierre Schaeffer has examined the changes in the musical communication chain due to this development, in his work *Traité des objets musicaux* (1966: 129–130). He considers a musical event to be a chain with seven members: a) there is first the visual origin of the sound at the level of an instrumental gesture: we meet the performer; b) in the next phase, vibrations of instruments, which are the purely acoustic result of the activity of the performer; c) this traditional course has become more complicated nowadays: there are microphones, magnetophones, amplifiers, etc. placed between the performer and the listener, in other words the whole electro-acoustic chain; d) when the sound arrives in the ear we enter the area of the physiology of aural sensations; e) thereafter musical impressions are raised in the listener and we move into the area of psychophysiology; f) the listener recognizes a musical work which the composer has sent to him, and we come to the musical psychology and aesthetics; g) we are now at the point from which we could have started as well, namely, at the intentions of a composer, in the field of a "pure art", as Schaeffer says.

Depending on which phase of this chain of musical communication we emphasize, we get different definitions of what is music or the concept of a note or tone. Ingmar Bengtsson (1973: 17) has suggested the following notations: $tone_f$ = a tone in the physical sense, $tone_\varphi$ = a tone as a phenomenal, experienced unit, $tone_n$ = a tone as notated. To this we might add a further category: $tone_g$ = a tone which means a certain gesture when the tone is performed.

Nevertheless, at the same time as scientific inquiry reveals the nature of the musical phenomenon to be more and more complicated, and this new musical knowledge (*savoir*) is reflected also in the heightened complexity of composing itself to such an extent that it can be accomplished only by computers, there is also another tendency in twentieth century music, which contrarily aims to reject maximal control of music. If the most perfect control of all musical parameters was the aim of the serial school, then such trends as *musique pauvre* (beginning with Erik Satie), minimalism, and the music philosophy of John Cage represent an entirely different attitude. Cage believes that the more one controls the musical structure, the more it controls the man. This goes against his philosophy of freedom inherited from the American transcendentalists Thoreau and Emerson and about which Daniel Charles (1976: 66) has used the apt expressions of *musique du non-vouloir* and *musique indéterminée*. On the other hand, there looms in the background of the apparently simple musical structures of minimalists the philosophy of *musique pauvre* on one side (Arvo Pärt) and, on the other, a musical technique which is only possible for people living in the electronic age. Some minimalist compositions, with their repetitive structures, sound as if they were Kafka-like, swollen musical tests to whose innocent objects the listeners are subordinated. Among others, Diana Deutsch has investigated how simple musical figures, like those used by minimalist composers, get synthesized in the brain. Although all music is based upon repetition — except serial music, where it is expressly prohibited —

repetition has in minimalism the particualr function of serving as the basic substance of a musical work. When a deviation from repetition occurs in a work by Reich or Glass, this deviation forms the true *différance* of the text. Earlier, this principle of repetition itself — was the *différance* of an artistic text (in the sense of Derrida).

The dream of the modernists was a work of art that was totally disengaged, *debrayé*. This represented also a deep change in the epistemes of Western culture, a transition to a world view in which man as an acting and desiring subject was hurled from the center of his own existence. If atonal music was in the spatial sense completely disengaged, it was not so in the temporal sense for some time, but was articulated often following the same kind of temporal models as the preceding tonal music. It was only later in this century when avant-garde music found that which might be called, using the term by Daniel Charles, zero-time (see for example *Die Soldaten* by Berndt Alois Zimmermann).

Nevertheless, it seems that we moved with the minimalism of the 1980s to a safe *embrayage* of temporal, spatial, and actorial categories. This is only partly true: some extremely scarce works by John Cage, like his *Music of Changes*, consist in a series of musical points, chords, and knockings which are separated from each other by long pauses. What is involved is precisely the idea of activating the listener's modalization in such a way that he is tempted to modalize each musical point in a different way. Therefore musical modernism has inherited the Romantic narrative model and utilizes it in many ways and forms, while at the same time it has also created an abundant diversity of musical languages. There remains the problem for the listener of how to receive simultaneously message and code. On the other hand, the activation and continuous growth of the semiotic research of music from the 1970s to 1990s must also be taken as the sign of an effort to form a common view on the extremely heterogeneous and pluralist musical reality towards the end of the twentieth century.

References

Adler, Guido (1911). *Der Stil in der Musik*. Leipzig: Leipzig & Härtel.
Adorno, Theodor W. (1952). *Versuch über Wagner*; citation from the Suhrkamp Taschenbuch edition 1974. Frankfurt am Main: Suhrkamp.
Ambros, August Wilhelm (1887). *Geschichte der Musik*. Leipzig: Verlag von F. E. Keuckart.
Asafiev, Boris (1976). *Musical Form as a Process*. Transl. and Comm. by J. R. Tull. Diss. Ohio state University.
Bartók, Bela (1957). *Weg und Werk. Schriften und Briefe*. Zusammengestellt von Bence Szabolcsi. Budapest: Corvina.
Bengtsson, Ingmar (1973). *Musikvetenskap. En översikt*. Stockholm: Esselte Studium (Scandinavian University Book).
Besseler, Heinrich (1957). "Spielfiguren in der Instrumentalmusik" *Deutsches Jahrbuch für Musikwissenschaft*, 12–37. Leipzig.
Boulez, Pierre (1971). *On Music Today*. Cambridge, Massachusetts: Harvard University Press.
Burney, Charles (1935). *A General History Of Music. From the Earliest Ages to the Present Period*. 2 vls. London: G. T. Foulis & Co. Ltd.
Cage, John & Daniel Charles (1981). *For the Birds*. John Cage in conversation with Daniel Charles. London: Marion Boyars Publishers.
Charles, Daniel (1978). *Gloses sur John Cage*. 10/18. Paris: Union Generale d'Editions.
Le Corbusier (1951 and 1958). *Modulor I-II*. Faber & Faber and M.I.T Press.
Dahlhaus, Carl (1977). *Grundlagen der Musikgeschichte*. Köln: Musikverlag Hans Gerig.
Doubravová, Jarmila (1982). *Hudba a výtvarné umení*. Praha: Ceskoslovenska Akademie Véd.
Eco, Umberto (1971). *Den frånvarande strukturen*. Original title *La struttura assente* (1968). Lund: Bo Cavefors Forlag.
Greimas, A. J. and Joseph Courtés (1979). *Sémiotique. Dictionnaire raisonné de la théorie du langage*. Paris: Hachette.
Hatten, Robert S. (1987). "Style, Motivation and Markedness", *The Semiotic Web 1986*, Thomas A. Sebeok and Jean Umiker-Sebeok (eds.). Berlin, New York, Amsterdam: Mouton de Gruyter.
– (1994). *Musical Meaning in Beethoven. Markedness, Correlation, and Interpretation. Bloomington & Indianapolis: Indiana University Press*.
Jakobson, Roman (1963). *Essais de linguistique générale*. Paris: Editions de Minuit.
Jiranek, Jaroslav (1985). *Zu Grundfragen der musikalischen Semiotik*. Berlin: Verlag Neue Musik.
Kandinsky, Wassily (1970). *Point, ligne, plan. Pour une grammaire des formes*. Original title *Punkt und Linie zu Fläche*. Paris: Editions Denoel.

Karbusicky, Vladimir (1986). *Grundriss der musikalischen Semantik.* Darmstadt: Wissenschaftliche Buchgesellschaft.

Kirchmeyer, Helmut (1958). *Igor Strawinsky. Zeitgeschichte im Persönlichkeitsbild.* Regensburg: Gustav Bosse Verlag.

Kurth, Ernst (1922). *Grundlagen des Linearen Kontrapunkts.* Berlin: Max Hesses Verlag.

Lévi-Strauss, Claude (1958). *L'Anthropologie structurale.* Paris: Plon.

– (1971). *L'Homme nu. Mythologiques IV.* Paris: Plon

Lotman, Juri et al. (1975). "Theses on the Semiotic Study of Cultures (as Applied to Slavic texts)", *The Tell-Tale Sign: A Survey of Semiotics,* ed. by T. A. Sebeok. Lisse

Mäkelä, Tomi (1989). *Virtuosität und Werkcharakter.* Berliner Musikwissenschaftliche Arbeiten, Band 36. München/Salzburg: Musikverlag Emil Katzbichler.

Monelle, Raymond (1992). *Linguistics and Semiotics in Music.* Edinburgh Harwood Academic Publishers.

Nattiez, Jean-Jacques (1975). *Fondements d'une sémiologie de la musique.* 10/18, Paris: Union Générale d'Editions.

Nietzsche, Friedrich (1964). "Die Geburt der Tragoedie", *Sämtliche Werke in zwölf Bänden,* Band I, Stuttgart.

Propp, Vladimir (1970). *Morphologie du conte.* Collection Poétique. Paris: Seuil. (Original title *Morfologija skazki,* Leningrad, 1928.)

Ratner, Leonard G. (1980). *Classic Music. Expression, Form and Style.* New York: Schirmer Books.

Rosen, Charles (1976). *The Classical Style. Haydn, Mozart, Beethoven.* London: Faber & Faber.

– (1980). *Sonata Forms.* New York, London: W. W. Norton & Company.

Samuels, Robert (1995). *Mahler's Sixth Symphony. A Study in Musical Semiotics.* Cambridge, New York: Cambridge University Press.

Schaeffer, Pierre (1966). *Traité des Objets Musicaux.* Paris: Seuil.

Schenker, Heinrich (1956). *Neue musikalische Theorien und Phantasien. Der freie Satz.* Wien: Universal Edition.

Schering, Arnold (1936). *Beethoven und die Dichtung.* Berlin: Junker und Dünnhaup Verlag.

Stefani, Gino (1982). *La competenza musicale.* Bologna: Cooperativa Libraria Universitaria Editrice Bologna.

Tarasti, Eero (1979). *Myth and Music. A Semiotic Approach to the Aesthetics of Myth in Music, especially that of Wagner, Sibelius and Stravinsky.* Approaches to Semiotics 51. The Hague, Paris, New York: Mouton Publishers.

– (1983a). "De l'interpretation musicale", *Actes sémiotiques: Documents* 5/42: 1–16.

– (1983b). "Sur les structures élémentaires du discours musical", *Actes sémiotiques: Bulletin* 6: 6–13.

– (1984). "Pour une narratologie de Chopin", *International Review of the Aesthetics and Sociology of Music* 15(1): 53–75.

– (1985a). "Music as Sign and Process", *Analytica. Studies in the description and analysis in honour of Ingmar Bengtsson,* 97–115. Stockholm: The Royal Swedish Academy of Music, no. 47.

– (1985b). "A la recherche des 'modalités' musicales", *Exigences et perspectives de la sémiotique: recueil d'hommages pour A. J. Greimas,* 649–659. Amsterdam: John Benjamins.

– (1986). "Music Models Through Ages: A Semiotic Interpretation", *International Review of the Aesthetics and Sociology of Music* 17(1): 22–32.

– (1987a, ed.). "Semiotics of Music", special issue of *Semiotica* 66/1–3.

– (1987b). "Basic Concepts of Studies in Musical Signification: A Report on a New International Research Project in Semiotics of Music", *The Semiotic Web 1986,* Thomas A. Sebeok and Jean Umiker-Sebeok (eds.), 405–581. (Approaches to Semiotics 78.) Berlin, New York, Amsterdam: Mouton de Gruyter.

– (1987–1988, ed.). "La musique comme langage I–II", *Degrés* 52 and 53. Bruxelles.

– (1988). Ed. together with Veikko Rantala and Lewis Rowell. *Essays on the Philosophy of Music.* (Acta Philosophica Fennica 43.) Helsinki: Akateeminen kirjakauppa.

– (1994). *A Theory of Musical Semiotics.* Bloomington & Indianapolis: Indiana University Press.

– (1995, ed.). *Musical Signification. Essays in the Semiotic Theory and Analysis of Music.* Berlin, New York: Mouton de Gruyter.

– (1995). *Heitor Villa-Lobos.* Jefferson: McFarland.

The postmodern project in music theory

RAYMOND MONELLE

Many of us can remember when the primary imperative for a music theorist was to be modern. Modernity meant being on the leading-edge, being enlightened, being international, being smart. But curiously, modernity no longer feels like the leading-edge of music theory; about the time of structuralism and positivist semiotics, the modern tendency settled down and became dated. Everyone now talks about being postmodern, and the most challenging philosophical writers are now using this term, albeit reluctantly in some cases (for example, Lyotard, 1984).

Perhaps the main difficulty with postmodernism is the fact that its unifying factor is, specifically, a rejection of unification, of manifestoes, of centralizing and totalizing forces. It is both a return to pluralism after the modernist experiment and — its true novelty — an embracing of pluralism as a fundamental tenet.

Modernism was born during the Enlightenment. Where classical rationalism and Cartesianism involved the rational scrutiny of traditional notions, the project of the eighteenth century was to universalize rationalism, to develop "total discourses" which in principle embraced all contingencies. This meant the destruction of many long-held beliefs and the "desacralization" of knowledge, and thus a new kind of rationality; not the rationalization and clarification of tradition, but a break with tradition, based on progress and an all-embracing theory. The authority of post-Enlightenment ideologies, including science, is legitimated by encyclopedism. This kind of radical theory led, of course, to destruction as well as creativity, as can be seen in many ancient cities like Mannheim that were knocked down in the eighteenth century to make way for rationalistic layouts.

Encyclopedic rationalism proved ineffectual in the moral field. Its attempts at social reform — notably the French Revolution — led to tyranny and reaction. Industrialism and capitalism were the de facto destiny of European society, aided by the morally uncommitted skills of technology. The metanarratives of rationalism engaged with everything except the contingent subject; they depended, in fact, on an idealized subject, the *speaker* of rationality whose words are infallible and whose authority is total. The rationalist philosopher did not write for himself; he was the public orator of rationalism, the Aaron to rationalism's Moses. Rationalism, he declared, had absolute authority; all must submit and obey. Unfortunately, he was tempted to assume his master's cloak. Thus, the undeniable authority of abstract rationalism turns imperceptibly into the tyrannical authority of the rationalistic speaker. For all discourse must proceed from a subjectivity. I speak high-mindedly on behalf of rational objectivism, but nevertheless it is I who speak; and my moral judgement will tend to arise from custom and prejudice, however rational I sound.

Habermas has shown that the postmodern predicament arose from Hegel's imperfect critique of subjective rationalism. In the Cartesian-Kantian view, reason is determined by a sovereign rational subject who is super-moral and super-linguistic, but this ideal figure tends always to be embodied in the rationalistic thinker herself and thus to lead to authoritarianism and tyranny. Subjectivity is "puffed up into a false absolute", transforming reason's powers of liberation into "just so many instruments of objectification and control" (Habermas, 1987, p. 56). Hegel saw this difficulty but he tried to replace subjectivity with a theory of Absolute Knowledge, which had to be modelled on subjectivism itself; and thus his followers fell again into the centralizing tenets of subjectivism. The step was bold, but not bold enough. A world of plural subjectivities was still out of Hegel's grasp. It is this world which we must now lay claim to; the nineteenth century lived on "spiritual capital" (Wordsworth's phrase, though he applies it differently), but our capital has run out this century. The paraphernalia of custom and prejudice, bourgeois respectability, national selfconsciousness and the canon of great artworks — now seem like broken toys in a world of violence, starvation and environmental destruction.

If we are to summarize the postmodern message, the message of Habermas, Lyotard, Harvey, and to a large degree Foucault, Lacan and Derrida, we must refer first of all to an opposition to meta-narratives, an acceptance of heterogeneity and multifariousness in preference to uniformity and unity. The Enlightenment devotion to the totalizing discourse and the meta-narrative was disingenuous. It was connected with authoritarian control and political centralization; it was part of the impulse to create a standardized world that could be dominated by an elite, and which gave no regard for the people who had to live in it. The example of Le Corbusier's Pavillon Suisse is given; the architect would not allow the student residents to instal blinds because these were not part of his conception, and in summer the poor inhabitants were fried alive (Harvey, 1990, p. 36). I am told that the architect's famous Unité d'Habitation in Marseille is known nowadays, in local parlance, as "la maison du fada" — the madman's house. It is scarcely surprising that Marx's total narrative of political economy, which was meant to be liberating, turned out in practice to ground yet another authoritarian regime. The rationalized and science-dominated world of the modern city is, potentially, a world in which everything is decided by "them", by a team of distant bureaucrats, on behalf of a race of helpless proles whose very entertainment and cultural engagement is served up to them ready-cooked in the form of television programmes.

The divisive character of meta-narratives is typified by their exclusiveness, their creation of an excluded world of all that is not part of the theory, not orthodox, not obedient — the world of the "Other". The transcendent legitimation of my meta-narrative gives me licence to persecute, punish and dispossess the Other, whether it be doctrine, practice or person. Classical logic was designed to exclude an intellectual Other, the Other of falsehood, superficiality, deceit. Meta-rationalism extended this to a universal Other, which included blacks, homosexuals, Jews, proletarians and women. Its style of discourse is polemic and disputational, the style of the white male.

Postmodernism turns away from this view and so brings into being an infinite range of others. Though they are apart from me, they stand beside me with an equivalent and irrevocable legitimation of their own. In place of a principle of sameness as the pivot of intellectual activity, we have a principle of otherness; our concern is with "the multiple forms of otherness as they emerge from differences in subjectivity, gender and sexuality, race and class" (Huyssens, 1984, p. 50).

But returning to modernism, the legacy of the Enlightenment: the centralizing and standardizing effect of meta-narratives transformed our ideas of space and place, and the relation of space and time. Space is full of temporal narratives (for example, my house may contain a place for the morning, a place for the evening, a place for the night), and time extends and embraces space (thus two places a mile apart are encompassed in terms of the time taken to travel between them). Space and time are contingently related in a fructifying dialogue, and one explicates the other. Yet the modern world hinges on a compression of space into no time (as when we make a telephone call to Australia) or of time into no space (in the portrayal, on a map, of the road between two towns as a single black line, or the feeling that a symphony is contained all at once in a score). The result is that we find ourselves in no-place; contemporary ideology identifies us as bourgeois, socialist, salaried, heterosexual — all states of totalized understanding rather than places. Internationalism was construed as homogeneity and uniformity rather than an acceptance of infinite variety; a German movement before War 1 proposed a "world office" which would "unify all the humanitarian tendencies that run in parallel but disorderly directions, and bring about a concentration and a promotion of all creative activites" (quoted in Tafuri, 1985, quoted by Harvey, 1990, p. 270). Such well-meaning enterprizes, like the rebuilding of Mannheim, were fundamentally destructive. The contingent subject finds the centre where she happens to be, not in some totalized, generalized, political or cultural place. Certainty is a local matter; it is merely a kind of accidental "local determinism" (Lyotard, 1984, p. xxiv). "The centre is where I am" was replaced, in modernism, by "the centre is London, Helsinki, the Aryan race, great masterpieces, socialism, the market economy".

The effect was to alienate the individual, for the first locus of life and culture is the body. People have their own lives in their own unique places, and so they are alienated from themselves by the concentric ideology of modernism. For to be sure, art and culture are physical first and foremost, physical and psychological in the best contingent sense;

the body cannot be generalized. Postmodernism turns ironically to the artistic world of modernism and says that "Flaubert is to the library what Manet is to the museum" (Foucault, in Harvey, 1990, p. 272). Where is Flaubert? Modernist culture wishes us to find him out of space in time; in the great history of the French novel. But he is really to be found here, and here, wherever his books are located, just as Manet is to be found, not in the history of realist painting, but in the Musée d'Orsay and the National Gallery. Instead of the great tradition, the non-spatial canon of great art divorced from the contingent reader or listener, we now have music therapy, community music projects, creative musical education. Yet music theory has been left behind; theorists still swarm to analyze Beethoven sonatas.

Rationality is a good servant but a bad master. It was Nietzsche who first radically distrusted the idealized subjectivity of reason; he perceived that every subject is, in fact, located in the bosom of time and space; no longer can we overlook "the influence of the unconscious on the conscious, the role of the preconceptual and conconceptual in the conceptual, the presence of the irrational — the economy of desire, the will to power — at the very core of the rational" (Thomas McCarthy in Habermas, 1987, p. ix). Our desires, our needs, our cruelty find their way into language as rhetoric, and philosophy has to be written in that same rhetoric-infested language. Philosophy cannot escape being an agent of the will to power, and reason, Foucault says, is "a thing of this world".

In place of reason and absolute truth Habermas evokes "legitimation". Certain narratives and discourses, formerly legitimated by divine or authoritarian decree, are now legitimated by the consensus of the people; and there are several master-discourses of legitimation, the chief of these being "science". Jean-François Lyotard gives us a distressing pragmatics of science. For every scientific utterance there must be a sender, an addressee and a referent. As we see it, the truth of science depends on certain language games, but scientific knowledge is characterized by its limitation to one language game only, that of *denotation*, the sort that depends on the truth-value of the proposition. This means that the sender, the *destinateur*, of scientific discourse, must seem to vanish; the referent is not an expression of a subjectivity, but an observation about the world, objectively related to physical fact and inwardly consistent. *Objectivity* and *consistency* are the special marks of denotative discourse, the rhetoric, if you will, of the disappearance of rhetoric, the present signs of the vanished speaker. "One is a scientist if one can produce verifiable or falsifiable statements about referents accessible to the experts" (Lyotard, 1984, p. 25). So my rhetorical game is to make an expert of my reader — or, more likely, to make her feel like an outsider.

We seem to have strayed away from art and from music (though this is not the case, as will shortly be seen). To talk about art we surely need a discourse that concerns itself with the speaker and the receiver; that abandons objectivity, responsibility, consistency and deduction for fantasy, persuasiveness, sensuality; in short, an *aesthetic* discourse. Let us turn, therefore, to a Marxist bedtime story.

> Imagine a society sometime in the indeterminate past, before the rise of capitalism, perhaps even before the Fall, certainly before the dissociation of sensibility, when the three great questions of philosophy — what can we know? what ought we to do? what do we find attractive? — were not as yet fully distinguishable from one another. A society, that is to say, where the three mighty regions of the cognitive, the ethico-political and the libidinal-aesthetic were still to a large extent intermeshed. Knowledge was still constrained by certain moral imperatives — there were certain things you weren't supposed to know — and was not viewed as sheerly instrumental. The ethico-political question — what are we to do? — was not regarded simply as a matter of intuition or existential decision or inexplicable preference, but involved rigorous knowledge of what we were, of the structure of our social life; that there was a way of describing what we were from which it was possible to infer what we should do or could become. Art was not sharply separated from the ethico-political, but was one of its primary media; and it was not easily distinguishable from the cognitive either, because it could be seen as a form of social knowledge, conducted within certain normative ethical frameworks. It had cognitive functions and ethico-political effects.
>
> Then imagine, after a while, all this changing. The snake enters the garden; the middle classes start to rise; thoughts fall apart from feelings, so that nobody thinks through their fingertips any more; and history starts out on its long trek towards Mr George Bush. The three great areas of historical life — knowledge, politics, desire — are uncoupled from one another; each becomes specialized, autonomous, sealed off into its own space. Knowledge burst out of its ethical constraints and began to operate by its own internal autonomous laws.

Under the name science, it no longer bore any obvious relation to the ethical or aesthetic, and so began to lose touch with value. About this time, philosophers began to discover that you could not derive a value from a fact. For classical thought, to answer the question "what am I to do?" involved making reference to my actual place within the social relations of the *polis*, . . . Now, however, the answers to why we should be moral become non-cognitivist. Either: you ought to be moral because doesn't it feel nice to be good? Or: you should be moral because it is moral to be so. Both of these responses utilize, in very different ways, the model of the aesthetic, which at about this time was also floating adrift into its own autonomous space, and so could be drawn upon as a kind of model of ethical autonomy. The moral and the aesthetic, both in deep trouble, could thus come to one another's aid. The cultural system had detached itself from the economic and political systems, and thus came to figure as an end in itself. Indeed art had to be an end in itself, because it certainly didn't seem to have much else of a purpose any more (Eagleton, 1990, pp. 366–7).

In this way Terry Eagleton summarizes his book, *The ideology of the aesthetic*. The aesthetic, according to this interpretation, is a different and much easier way of being good. Art is where you find delight, *jouissance*, eloquence, reassurance, sensuality. Wouldn't it be lucky it it contained a kind of goodness as well? Let us detach it, therefore, from any kind of practical responsibility, any commitment to kindness, fairness, unselfishness and peace, and find its legitimation in beauty, refinement and sublimity. The beautiful must be good; come to think ot it, it may be true as well, so aesthetics is able to do the job of cognition as well as morality. To act well is to be elegant, gentlemanly, refined; factual truth is all very well, but within art there is a truth that is more profound.

In art itself, the effect of this was to produce undirected individualism and "self-expression", what Walter Benjamin called "auratic" art, art legitimated by an aura of creativity, "dedication to art for art's sake, in order to produce a cultural object that would be original, unique, and hence eminently marketable at a monopoly price" (Harvey, 1990, p. 22). In place of culture there was the "work of art" which, ostensibly personal, was nearly always the work of somebody else and represented, not priceless unique experience but economic value.

This heavy load of intellectual baggage came along at the same time as the totalizing discourse — during the Enlightenment, with Baumgarten's *Aesthetica* of 1750. It was bound to distort the nature of art, as well as to create an easy option for morality and knowledge. Since aesthetics was ideology, designed to hide the moral decay of an acquisitive society, it must develop a myth of sanctity, which it did by inventing the canon of *great works*, prating that the moral guarantee of the aesthetic universe reposed in the great tradition of Michelangelo, Shakespeare, Goethe and Beethoven. When artists eventually turned on the moral with obscene gestures — as did James Joyce and Egon Schiele — their moral value was still mysteriously guaranteed by their executive ability, by the *artistic* quality of their art. And to be artistic meant to communicate truth as well as to be moral, for the aesthetic was also propping up the cognitive at this time.

Much aesthetic writing about music invites us to consider the question of beauty; it presents itself, apparently, as truly *aesthetic* writing. We must seek for "the beautiful in music"; but that very phrase, which is the English title of Hanslick's masterwork, reminds us that aesthetics was being used as an underpinning for cognitive truth as well as morality. For Hanslick instructs us to listen, not with our feelings but with our cognitive attention. The faculty of listening is called "contemplation"; any emotional effect is extraneous to the fruits of this intelligent search. The musical event was a coherent discourse, united in the expression of a single idea, and this idea was a lofty truth, the product of "creative genius".

The characterization of music as discourse began with the baroque theorists. Music, according to Mattheson, Riepel and Koch, was a kind of rhetoric, coherently expounding its non-referential sense in *exordium, propositio, confirmatio* and *peroratio*. Or perhaps the sense was not even non-referential; the theory of topics related the rhetorical syntagmata to extra-musical themes (as Ratner and Agawu assure us) (see, on rhetorical theory, Bonds, 1991).

The mastering virtue of music-discourse was coherence and persuasiveness. But the hallmark of the new vision was "organic unity". With the turn of the twentieth century, there came a doctrine of totalizing unity in the visual arts, accompanying a movement of universal formalism. Roger Fry (in *Vision and Design*, 1909) based value in visual art on unification and order in the overall form and Clive Bell (in *Art*, 1914) spoke of "significant form", the eloquence of formal coherence which grounded the signification of a painting. Heinrich Wölfflin told the history of art in terms of forms (in *The Philosophy of Art History*). At the same time, Heinrich Schenker deplored the preoccupation of analysts with the *Vordergrund* of a musical piece, where apparent diversity is to be found, and directed their attention to the *Hintergrund* of uncompromising unity. Hugo Riemann, Rudolf Réti, Arnold Schoenberg all had similar ideas of musical legitimation.

Let us turn to a quite recent text on music theory, written by one who clearly speaks for Modernism. The essay of Pierre Boulez, "Idée, réalisation, métier", published in the collection *Jalons* of 1989, is a rewriting of a lecture delivered at the Collège de France in 1978. Here Boulez describes the function of the composer. Apart from a few rather sheepish nods in the direction of "personality" this is a highly cogent account of the activity of a selfconscious, subjectivist, selfjustified and unpopular composer of the mid-century.

The artist must first learn professionalism, what Boulez calls "métier". This he may do by analyzing the works of others, but mere inventorization is not enough: "Defining multiple relations of intervals according to a catalogue. . . is this a prelude to the *essential*? [His emphasis]. But what *essential*? . . . Formal means are not enough to define the work, but analysis cannot get beyond them. They are the way from idea to realization . . . Analysis is the tracing of the labyrinth joining idea and realization" (Boulez 1989, pp. 36–7).

What one must learn is not merely a routine of work, but the fact that past works make some decisions unavoidable. Every *œuvre* of a significant composer is a new synthesis of possibilities, rendering for ever this same synthesis impossible for his successors. The solution, which was hard to achieve for the predecessor, becomes data for the successor. Thus, musical style must evolve steadily, each stage being superseded by the next. It could hardly resemble more closely the experimental progress of scientific thought, from hypothesis to experiment and experiment to law, from law to refutation and to further hypothesis.

There is, of course, an element of chance, an "élément aléatoire", in each composer's choice of the available possibilities. But this choice is not really random: "On a oublié cette donnée fondamentale du langage qui est la responsabilité de tout élément par rapport à un autre dans un système cohérent. Déduire un motif d'un autre, déduire la dimension verticale de la dimension horizontale. . . un intervalle d'un autre, telles me paraissent les conditions absolument indispensable à la cohérence, et donc à la *nécessité* du langage" (Boulez 1989, p. 49; again, his emphasis). This word "responsibility" means the observation of "one note's responsibility with regard to another, of one line with regard to another". "A melodic line, to whichever period it belongs, obeys unavoidably this necessity of responsibility. . . (which) establishes the coherence, the validity, the very sense of this phrase" (pp. 50–51).

Continuing with Boulez's text: "La nécessité implique dans l'invention l'art de la déduction. . . Ce qui frappe le plus. . . c'est la relation profonde entre nécessité, responsabilité et déduction. . . Il y a des lois de déduction que l'on apprend. . . L'invention. . . est la profusion *dans la déduction*. . . L'œuvre ne peut exister que par cet échange pour aller du connu vers l'inconnu" (pp. 52–54).

An invention, guided by the professionalism of the expert, which discovers objective relations by a deductive process; thus, a vanishing of the speaker in favour of the facts of the referent, objectively followed by self-effacing responsibility — this is the narrative of *science*.

It must be stressed, however, that Boulez is talking here about composition, not about theory. It has often been said that music theory should be scientific. Even music theorists realize that the scientific narrative is the only one that can be legitimated nowadays. Yet here is music itself being characterized as an objective and deductive process; this is theory not metatheory, hanging around music's neck an albatross of ideal subjectivity and totalizing rationalism. If the composer is the ideal speaker of rationalism he will become a dictator. And so it is with Boulez and his subterranean hordes.

"Organic unity" arrived with a musical style that communicated neurasthenia, suspicion, alienation and detachment. It is well known that Anton Webern's doctoral thesis was on Heinrich Isaac, a Flemish composer of the fifteenth century, a period when music theory, following the late Greek writings of Boethius, connected music with the natural sciences — with astronomy, geometry and mathematics. This view was associated with the Pythagorean tradition, of course; writers apparently meant the theory of music when they wrote *musica*, music itself being regarded as purely phenomenal and thus ruled by scientific laws. The theoretical stance of Boulez is remarkably close to that of the Greek and medieval theorists, except that they were writing discourse about music, and he cannot free himself from the view that music is its own discourse; just as music is built on logical relations, so it is a narrative of logical relations. If music is phenomenon only, there can be no epistemology of music but only an epistemology of music theory. But if we add the baroque view of music as discourse, together with the modern view that this discourse is objective, then the music of the moderns becomes scientific and thus denotative. The Greek writers found eternal laws in music: Boulez conceived that music expounded scientific truth.

If music is scientific discourse, as Boulez seems to say, then it must be legitimated by its referent, like a scientific theorem. By implication, you ought to be able to prove or demonstrate it. Much contemporary writing on serial music seems to take this view. Oddly, this contradicts the popular view that modern music is "abstract", like modern painting (Xenakis says this in *Musique, architecture*); in reality, it is not abstract but denotative, at least in terms of its own theory.

Why is musical unity called "organic"? What sorts of unity are not organic? The implication seems to be that this unity is not contrived but grows naturally, in spite of the fact that the most obviously organic repertoire, Bartók's golden-section music, is also the most contrived. Music is a demonstrative discourse of the universal essence, rather than being merely an artifact; the referent of this discourse is nature itself, growing according to its own principles. This is the claim of science, of course, the archetypical referent-legitimated discourse.

If this account is correct, the first task of postmodern theory is to dismantle the referent-centredness of modernism. A musical work is not absolutely true because of its faithfulness to some aspect of nature, but is simply an opportunity for a good and beautiful action. Composers must put aside their claim to speak for truth, for in doing so, Stockhausen may serve imperialism and Boulez elitism. The musical performance has a place and a time and every event has just one chance of communicating. It is not validated by its radical detachment from the world of social encounter, but by its functionality within that world.

Modernism has said: there is one truth, and one function for music, namely to define that truth. The message is justified by its referent, and the sender and receiver disappear into the shadows. But this article is meant to be a programme of action for the postmodern theorist, not merely an identification of the legitimating narratives of Modernism. How are we to rescue music from totalizing discourses, and from being legitimated by a narrative of totalized rationality?

Adorno and Benjamin are seen as the prophets of postmodern music theory; Alastair Williams, for example, shows that Adorno found in music, not reconciled and generalized oppositions but heterogeneities, contradictions, unresolved antagonisms. Alan Street finds the idea of organic unity a myth of the German/Austrian tradition, designed to reconcile imaginatively the destructive contradictions of capitalist society. Joseph Kerman quips that analysis "exists for the purpose of demonstrating organicism, and organicism exists for the purpose of validating a certain body of works of art" (Kerman, 1980/1, p. 315).

Craig Ayrey (1991) attacks the "dogmatic allegories" of music analysis, suggesting that analysis is always allegorical and metonymic rather than essential and metaphorical. The analyst seeks a path through the music which listeners may choose to follow, and is legitimated by the dialogue between them. Her legitimacy does not arise from authority or from general truth.

Robert Samuels places music within the world of the text, following Jacques Derrida's notion of the "general text". Texts are about other texts, not about life or the world. "I am merely the confluence of texts without origins and without comfortingly reliable referents. . . the text is simply where I find myself" (Samuels, 1991, p. 2). Derrida had said, "A 'text' is henceforth no longer a finished corpus of writing, some content enclosed in a book or its margins, but a differential network, a fabric of traces referring endlessly to something other than itself, to other differential traces. Thus the text overruns all the limits assigned to it so far, . . . everything that was to be set up in opposition to writing (speech, life, the world, the real, history and what not. . ., " (Samuels, 1991, pp. 2–3).

This view of the "general text" suggests that theoretical discussion must locate the musical work within a world of texts, which may be literary, historical, social and scientific as well as musical. Intertextuality replaces indexicality.

The text defines what is outside itself, and thus draws attention to everything it ignores, but which is necessary for its existence. The interpretation of what is within the frame must depend on what is outside the frame. Samuels illustrates this by showing how Mahler, in his Fourth Symphony, writes music "in the past tense". Adorno had said that this symphony's sense was to say, "Once upon a time there was a sonata." The extraordinary cessation of movement and pause just before the second subject of the first movement, a deceptively uncomplicated and *Biedermeier* tune, though it creates never a ripple in a Schenkerian view, presents a problem through the very fact that it is so unproblematic. Mahler is speaking, ironically no doubt, of a nostalgia for *Die gute alte Zeit*.

This kind of intertextuality views the work in its context of a culture, musical and extramusical. A second kind of intertextuality respects the hyper-work, the corpus of works by a single composer, or a group of composers, which represent a continuum. Composers sometimes assert that their works are not separate at all, but parts of a continuing enterprise. Ideas, both musical and associative, carry across from one work to the next. Again, musical motives can attach themselves to associative ideas and can recur, as when the *Hallelujah chorus* is quoted in the "Et excelsis" of Mozart's C minor Mass and in a fugue from Haydn's *The Creation*, or when Peter Maxwell Davies self-confessedly, but unconsciously, echoes "Der kranke Mond" from Schoenberg's *Pierrot Lunaire* when the text makes reference to the moon in the *Leopardi Fragments*, and hints at Debussy's *La Mer* in the Cello Concerto, which he admits to be associated with the sound of the troubled sea across the Pentland Firth.

Another, much-ignored kind of intertextuality concerns the embeddedness of classical works in the world of the people at large. This is strongly stressed by Asafiev and his followers (see Monelle, 1992, pp.

274–303), and appropriately Tchaikovsky, a composer analysed by Asafiev, illustrates it clearly with a quotation from a Paris café song in the First Piano Concerto. It is the basis, too, of transculturation, the transference of a corpus or a style from one social level to another, as when the street serenade and *Harmonie* of baroque Vienna formed the basis of the classical string quartet, which thus seemed to spring from nowhere. The echoing of social dance, admirably described by Wye Jamison Allanbrook (1983), is an essential feature of classical style.

I return to the views of Craig Ayrey. In attacking music's dogmatic allegories, he follows many past writers in claiming that music ought to be a better guide for theorists — not a worse one than other sorts of utterance, because it cannot, by its nature, lead to essentialist interpretations. One recalls the feelings of Schopenhauer, Walter Pater, Verlaine and Susanne Langer about music as the true pattern for theories of utterance.

Deconstructionism teaches that every assertion implies its own reverse, that every enclosure points to what is outside, the every text subverts itself with a necessary subtext. This was a thread that began with Nietzsche, too (if one disregards its earlier forebears in Burke and Hegel and perhaps in Vico), and led through Heidegger's idea of *presence*, the illusory notion that in every dividing of signification one pole of the opposition was to be preferred because it was nearer to present "reality", to a concrete and extra-semiotic object. The only reality, Derrida concluded, was *différance*, a neologism which, replacing the E with an A, tried to convey the very thing which language cannot convey, because it is the basis of language. Rousseau looked back to the origin of language and music in the "natural cry" (in the *Essai sur l'origine des langues*) in which he imagined he had found a point where signified and signifier were not divided, but the signification was a natural expression, and thus a part, of the signifier. But there was never any such time; signifier and signified were "always already" divided, for there can have been no world without signification.

I should like to defend this insight of Derrida against vulgar criticism. It is imagined that the philosopher discredits all signification and vitiates every assertion, since all statements necessarily contain their own opposites. This would be nihilism indeed. But this was not Derrida's intention; he is a thinker of much gaiety and wit, with a lively engagement in culture. His theory liberates signification rather than vitiating it. In the dual branching of *différance* traditional thought posited a "reality" for one branch only and thus identified the Other. The Other was false, illusory, unorthodox, unsocial, unscientific and superstitious. The effect was to create a stultified world of static significations, an unbending tree which the first gust of wind would bear down. But in practice, the simplest text offered alternatives, side-routes and subtexts. Language did not function in an essentialist way and it was better not to pretend that it did. Deconstruction opens up the blocked alternative; and since every stopping-point must divide again, the universe of purport is envisioned as a network or honeycomb of infinitely dividing significations, to which every sign yields admission. If a sign must mean just one thing, it means nothing. Yet every sign means everything, having its own habitation in the network. The object of deconstruction, and the proper task of the critic, is to open up the blocked channels of signification and bring every text into communication with the universe of purport; in so doing she will subvert each "essential" meaning as it arises.

Now, the point is that music is bound to demonstrate this because no musical utterance can ever be bound, even falsely, to a single essential signified. Language seems constantly to arrest itself at "true meanings", and it is the function of literary critics to release its flow of signification. There is no need for musical critics to do this; like the gesture of Mahler, music's problem is its very unproblematic quality. Musical theorists, instead of accepting graciously the infinite plurivalence and significative flow of music, have tried to arrest it, like language, at points of presence and essentiality.

Just as, in ordinary language, denotation is the site of essential meaning, in rhetorical and literary language we must look in the direction of metaphor. Comparison of a literary and a musical metaphor will be instructive. Proust defined the metaphor as the "coming together of two varied ideas such that each is illuminated by their common qualities, enclosed in a fine style". This is so often the case in music that we overlook its deconstructive force. Musical works often begin with two inconsistent ideas, either played together or consecutively, which are compared metaphorically in a syntagm that seems to make a new truth out of them. Analysts have always proceeded, either as though there were no inconsistency, or by showing that one is rationalized and thus obliterated by the other.

Thus, the Prelude to *Die Meistersinger*, that quintessentially diatonic opera, begins with a triad of C major followed by a quite remote augmented chord in which the note written as F natural may have to be analyzed as E sharp (I am indebted to Denis Matthews for pointing this out). After all, this opera is an uneasy work in which Sachs's emotions are left uncomfortably in mid-air, just as the chromaticism of the initial syntagm, later clinched by a quotation from *Tristan*, articulates a problem which is never resolved. Bach's A flat fugue from the second book of the "48" (BWV 886) combines a diatonic subject in the style of a trio sonata with a chromatic countersubject that turns out to be an immemorial sign of lamentation. At first the two figures seem to explain each other, like a metaphor; but finally they are revealed to be metonymic when the harmony and tonal structure disintegrate into grotesque chromaticisms (see Monelle, forthcoming b). Debussy's *Prélude à l'Après-midi d'un Faune* presents a chromatic figure on flute followed by a bi-pentatonic syntagm on two horns; it illustrates, not a poetic unity but the duality of Verlaine's "nuance", which "joins dream to dream and flute to horn".

Music, then, is fundamentally allegorical, metonymic and deconstructive. It ought to be easy for music theory to take this path; the time has come to abandon resistance. It may be that the central theme of postmodern theory will be the search for multifariousness, for the untidy and marginal, for the excluded and the intertextual. A tiny unique event may open the piece to a different semiotic dimension, as when Brahms inserts a few bars of chorale into the introduction of the finale of the First Symphony, speaking momentarily of the world of Bach and of his own retrospective historicism. Or such an event may be the key to nothing, as when Beethoven quotes a theme from a juvenile string quartet early in the first movement of his Piano Sonata, Op. 2 No. 3.

If there are codes of signification, there must be many codes, some in dialogue, some conflicting, some simply related metonymically. Samuels shows how a variety of codes must be consulted to get what is going on in the Scherzo of the Sixth Symphony of Mahler (Samuels, 1989). Do not pursue organic unity, for you will find that music is always in the business of subverting its own unity.

There are certain popular movements in music theory at present which do not seem reassuring. The mania for analysis has given the impression, sometimes, that music theory is nothing more than analysis, and that analysis is preoccupied with questions of structure. Palisca began his *Grove* article by saying, "Theory is now understood as principally the study of the structure of music." The most important theoretical departure of yesterday, Nattiez's "tripartition", was discredited because people imagined it was a method of analysis, and found the results rather meagre. Much of the theoretical work in our universities is concentrated in the areas of Schenkerism and pitch-class set theory, disciplines which proclaim their essentialism whenever possible. Interval contents are "the sole objective basis for whatever connections one may wish to establish between pitch collections" according to George Perle (1977, p. 172), and Allen Forte feels that pitch-class set theory reveals the "fundamental components of structure" (Forte 1973, p. ix). The ideas of Babbitt and Forte constitute a true body of theory of great elegance, but like all analytical theories, it is compelled to essentialize itself.

The darling theory of today is that of cognitive science. This, like tripartitionism, makes claims of objectivity, derived not now from philosophical positivism but from psychology. Here, perhaps, the error is epistemological and the cognitivists cannot be blamed. If cognitive theory sets out to describe "how musical structure is represented in cognition" (Howell, West & Cross, 1991, p. ix), then there is no reason why music theory should pay attention to it, except to give it fraternal acknowledgement. Unfortunately, many have assumed that a theory of cognitive engagement with music is itself a theory of music, and the strictly empirical and falsifiable methods of cognitive science have been imported into musical science. A theoretical standpoint not endorsed by psychology is called a "figment of our theoretical imaginations" (Fred Lerdahl in Howell, West & Cross, 1991, p. 273). The masterly — if totalizing — theory of Forte is clearly such a figment; thus, with luck, the two dominant theories of today may consume each other.

The postmodern programme of theory must set out to open doors and liberate music from tyranny; empirical psychology will clearly close doors with lugubrious finality, and pitch-class set theory, dissatisfied with its evident nobility (it was called "consistently high-minded" in *PNM*), longs to be king.

It is necessary to return to Eagleton's view of aesthetics, for up till now this account has seemed to be preoccupied with masterworks. The overwhelming emphasis on a canon of masterworks will not do, however. Max Weber decries the *Wertästhetik*, the domination of music theory by a machinery for determining the value of the artwork, and Habermas doubts the post-Nietzschean privileging of the extraordinary, "limit-experiences of aesthetic, mystical or archaic provenance" (Thomas McCarthy in Habermas, 1987, p. xvi). Again, the canonic view of music is quite recent; it is part of the world of modernism, if modernism can be traced to the end of the eighteenth century, as Habermas believes.

The legitimation of the masterwork, pace Boulez, is generally conceived along Eagleton's aesthetic lines. If the canon of masterworks enshrines our identification of morality with refinement and exquisiteness, then it is also the emblem of bourgeois exploitation, imperialism and colonialism. "Stockhausen serves imperialism", wrote Cornelius Cardew in his famous title, thus enthroning the composer rather uncomfortably in the canon. To put it shockingly, Bach is starving the Sudan and Beethoven is shooting people in Somalia.

We shall not at once abandon our immersion in the great canon, but there is a need for "music for people"; theorists must turn away from the masterwork towards music therapy, infant music, music in the community, creative music for prisoners, the sick, the young and the elderly, to popular music, women's music, ethnomusicology and even the music of animals, if François-Bernard Mâche is followed (see Mâche, forthcoming). These musics need no extra-moral doublethink for their legitimation, and they are not enclosed in "works", but are ongoing, functional activities that unite instead of dividing, that create no Other, that point to a more fundamental unity, that of cognition, ethics and feeling, which our bodies find in a still uneasy union.

I have scarcely sketched the programme for a non-organic music theory. First of all we must remember that theories of unity were parts of the emic landscape for the composers who respected them, just as

Brahms consciously invented "second subjects" after theorists identified them. Beyond that, analysis ought to proceed heterogeneously, moving freely between narrative, rhetorical, symphonic and social codes. There are so far very few examples of such a nondoctrinal approach, since analysis has recently been a tool for expounding theories, rather than the reverse. One thinks of the intuitive analyses of Tovey, the type of writing which Nattiez calls "explication de texte"; but this kind of thing is pre-theoretical. One thinks also of the fashion for comparative analysis, which resembles a lottery; enough throws of the dice, and you are sure to get the right answer. But there is no reason why postmodern analysis should not be theoretically rigorous, provided it passes freely from theory to theory and from code to code.

As for theory in general, the pretence of scientificity will not stand, because it implies the legitimation of music by its referent, and therefore demonstration and proof, as I have suggested. Music is always legitimated by the speaker and listener; theory must engage with its persuasiveness, its effectiveness, its cogency and well-formedness and honesty, rather than its truth. And even theory is a kind of rhetoric. Nattiez shows some consciousness of this in his recent *Musicologie Générale*, where it is admitted that the neutral level is necessarily examined aesthesically because the analyst engages interpretatively. If music is effective and cogent, then music theory must be so *a fortiori*, because it does not even offer the sensual delight that will sustain music when the last theorist has fallen silent.

References

Allanbrook, Wye Jamison (1983). *Rhythmic Gesture in Mozart: Le Nozze di Figaro and Don Giovanni*. Chicago: University of Chicago Press.
Ayrey, Craig (1991). Diversity and method: some prospects for the 1990s. Unpublished paper delivered at the City University, London.
Bonds, Mark Evan (1991). *Wordless Rhetoric: musical form and the metaphor of the oration*. Cambridge, Mass.: Harvard University Press.
Boulez, Pierre (1989). *Jalons (pour une décennie): dix ans d'enseignement au Collège de France (1978–1988)*. Paris: Bourgois.
Eagleton, Terry (1990). *The Ideology of the Aesthetic*. Oxford: Blackwell.

Forte, Allen (1973). *The Structure of Atonal Music*. New Haven: Yale University Press.

Habermas, Jürgen (1987). *The Philosophical Discourse of Modernity*. Translated by Frederick Lawrence. Cambridge: Polity Press.

Harvey, David (1990). *The Condition of Postmodernity*. Cambridge, MA: Blackwell.

Howell, Peter, West, Robert & Cross, Ian (1991). *Representing Musical Structure*. London: Academic Press.

Huyssens, A. (1984). "Mapping the post-modern", *New German Critique*, 33, pp. 5–52.

Kerman, Joseph (1990/1). "How we got into analysis, and how to get out", *Critical Inquiry* 7.

Lyotard, Jean-François (1984). *The Postmodern Condition: a Report on Knowledge*. Translated by Geoff Bennington & Brian Massumi. University of Minnesota Press.

Mâche, François-Bernard (forthcoming). "Syntagms and paradigms in zoomusicology", *Musica significans: proceedings of the Third International Congress on Musical Signification, Edinburgh 1992*, R. Monelle (ed.). Chur: Harwood Academic Press.

Monelle, Raymond (1992). *Linguistics and Semiotics in Music*. London: Harwood Academic Publishers.

– (forthcoming a). "A semantic approach to Debussy's songs", *The Music Review*, 51/3: 193–207.

– (forthcoming b). "BWV 886 as allegory of listening", *Musica significans: proceedings of the Third International Congress on Musical Signification, Edinburgh 1992*, R. Monelle (ed.). Chur: Harwood Academic Press.

Perle, George (1977). *Twelve-Tone Tonality*. Berkeley: University of California Press.

Samuels, Robert (1989). Deconstruction/reconstruction: some recent theory and music analysis. Revised form of unpublished paper delivered to the Royal Musical Association, November 1989.

– (1991). Music as text. Unpublished paper delivered to City UMAC (Analysis Conference, City University).

Tafuri, M. (1985). *USSR-Berlin 1922: from populism to constructivist international*. Princeton Architectural Press.

Jeremy Bentham's theory of fictions:
some reflections on its implications for musical semiosis and ontology

CYNTHIA M. GRUND

Jeremy Bentham (1748–1832), the father of utilitarianism, produced work which has had a profound impact upon moral, political and legal philosophy. He is not, however, a philosopher to whom either philosophers of art or semioticians have directed their attention. As the following twentieth-century comment by Bentham afficionado and scholar C.K.Ogden indicates, however, this state of affairs is perhaps one which deserves correction:

> If the Theory of Linguistic Fictions is to take the place of Philosophy, as he [Bentham, CMG] undoubtedly intended that it should, it must be developed as the nucleus of a complete theory of symbolism in every branch of human thought; from the first mnemic reaction, through all forms of perception, interpretation, and eidetic projection, to the final achievements of grammatical accessories, abbreviations, and condensations in notations as yet unborn (Ogden 1932, cxlix).

The 1932 publication in which this remark appears, *Bentham's Theory of Fictions*, is a work whose approximately 300 pages are almost equally divided between a long introductory commentary by Ogden and Bentham's original material. The writings in which Bentham's theory of linguistic fictions is developed are spread throughout his voluminous works, so regardless of what one might think of Ogden's section of commentary, his editorial work in collecting together all of this material from so many disparate locations within Bentham's production is of great value in itself. Although Ogden's prefatory comments serve to provide some perspective on what is to come, the ensuing collection of

Bentham's writings on fictions consists of such dense and complex material that there is need for much more explication and analysis.

The present paper has as its aim such explication and analysis of Bentham's theory of fictions as would arouse the interest of those philosophers and semioticians who are interested in questions of musical semiotics and/or ontology. It is a work-in-progress which, in turn, is part of a larger ongoing study which has as its goal an understanding of how fictionalism may contribute to theoretical examination of several problems of ontology, epistemology and signification which are raised by aesthetic objects. Since the purpose of this paper is primarily that of providing a suggestive overview, many points which deserve further discussion and explication will not receive the treatment which they both require and deserve, but if the reader is able to receive an idea as to how Bentham's theory may provide a philosophical framework in terms of which at least some problems relevent to musical ontology and signification may be discussed, the principal aims of the paper have been met.

Much of what Bentham says provides both theoretical and historical support for a view which I have previously proposed and discussed (please see list of references at conclusion of this article). Expressed in somewhat cursory fashion, this view is that *music* cannot exist for/in a group of individuals without the preexistence of a language in the group which is sophisticated enough to enable the expression of counterfactual thinking: (+) IN ORDER FOR A SEQUENCE OF SOUNDS TO BE *MUSIC*, IT MUST BE APPREHENDED *AS IF* THEY WERE SOMETHING ELSE, i.e., SOMETHING WHICH ITSELF IS NOT A SEQUENCE OF SOUNDS. Two crucial points regarding the demand for the "preexistence of a language in the group which is sophisticated enough to enable the expression of counterfactual thinking:" (1) "The group" for whom the sound sequence is music, may, indeed, be a group of agents *external* to those who are *producing* the sound sequences in question; and (2) some might question the stress on such a language, asking if it were not, indeed, enough to require only the counterfactual thinking. This is neither the time nor the place to open *that* particular philosophical can of worms, so all that I wish to say here is that I cannot seriously imagine this sort of thinking occurring in any meaningful way *without* such a language. Now, *if* we can provide inducement for enter-taining either the view that *music* wholly or partially has the ontological status of *fiction*, or the view that components the presence of which are necessary for the "constitution" of music are themselves fictions, Bentham *undergirds* my contention ($+$), as is evidenced by the following remark: "To language, then — to language alone — it is, that fictitious entities owe their existence; their impossible, yet indispensable existence" (Bentham 1932, 15). And, since, as we soon shall see, fictions themselves are the products of a species of contrary-to-fact thinking, the reader can clearly see why, given the above thoughts regarding language, counterfactual thinking and music, a closer look at Bentham's theory of fictions is a relevant project for this writer.

As we soon will see, the Benthamite method is full of moves which require contrary-to-fact thinking. It is perhaps not all that remarkable that Bentham's work has been ignored in semiotics and signification studies when one discovers that Bentham's theory of fictions is not even mentioned in recent philosophical treatments of counterfactual thinking and reasoning. The latter appear to completely ignore Bentham's effort to explicate and study the role which contrary-to-fact assumptions and reasoning play in our attempts to bring conceptual organization into our experience of the world. For example, no mention is made of Bentham in Nelson Goodman's *Fact, Fiction and Forecast* (Ist ed. 1954), David Lewis' *Counterfactuals* (1973) or Igal Kvart's *A Theory of Counterfactuals* (1986), works all three of which are central within the canon of contemporary philosophical treatment of counterfactuals.

It should be noted, moreover, that Bentham's work with the theory of fictions predated the appearance of the philosophical movement known as *fictionalism* by half a century or so. At the center of this movement was the investigation of the role which contrary-to-fact thinking and reasoning plays in our ongoing epistemological game of give-and-take with our world; interestingly enough, this movement seems to be just as throughly ignored as Bentham is within the context of recent philosophical treatments of counterfactuals.

One of the central figures within fictionalism proper was German philosopher Hans Vaihinger (1852–1933), whose monumental *Die Philosophie des Als Ob (The Philosophy of "As if")* was first published in 1911. Interestingly enough, it is C.K.Ogden who is responsible for the easier accessibility of Vaihinger's work to an English-speaking public, his translation — *The Philosophy of "As if"* first appeared in 1924. In the 1935 edition of this translation, Vaihinger sums up the fictionalist program as follows, and, in the main, these remarks may be considered to hold for Bentham as well:

> The principle of Fictionalism, . . . , or rather the outcome of Fictionalism, is as follows: "An idea whose theoretical untruth or incorrectness, and therewith its falsity, is admitted, is not for that reason practically valueless and useless; for such an idea, in spite of its theoretical nullity may have great practical importance. (Vaihinger 1935, viii).

This remark is interesting in the light of the prominent role which pragmatism — thanks largely to the achievements of C.S.Peirce — has played in semiotics and signification studies, compared with the manner in which fictionalism has been virtually ignored. Neither Bentham nor Vaihinger devoted any significant effort to explaining the centrality of fictionalism in aesthetic contexts, although some of Vaihinger's Swedish followers, particularly Alf Nyman and Rolf Ekman, did, the former, for example, in his 1922 article "Metafor och fiktion" ("Metaphor and fiction"), and the latter in his 1949 doctoral dissertation *Fiktionerna i det estetiska livet* (The Fictions of Aesthetic Life).

Let us now turn our attention to Bentham's theory. First, we will look at what fictions are, and then we will consider a suggestion for how this theory might provide a philosophical grounding for our thinking with regard to both the ontology of music and the mainsprings of musical signification.

In order to understand what sort of thing a *fiction* is, we are perhaps best served by a study of the following outline of the Benthamite ontology, which I have reconstructed on the basis of Bentham's description on pp. 7–18 in *Bentham's Theory of Fictions*, as well as on the basis of what Bentham writes in the ensuing pages of material which has been collected from his work. The reconstruction has been made with an eye to rendering an interpretation of Bentham which is both charitable and consistent, since inconsistencies do crop up here and there when one regards the fragments of Bentham's work which have been collected together as a whole. For example, he states in the Summary on p. 137 that "Entities are either *real* or *fictitious* . . . ," whereas on p. 17 he states: "To distinguish them from those fictitious entities, which, so long as language is in use among human beings, never can be spared, *fabulous* may be the name employed for the designation of the other class of unreal entities." As is shown below, I have chosen to maintain this finer distinction, in which *real* is placed in opposition with *unreal*, and the latter is divided into *fabulous* and *fictitious*. This is more ontologically elegant and is also conceptually useful (examples of selected entities appear in italics followed by the page in Bentham 1932 or Ogden 1932 on which they are explained:

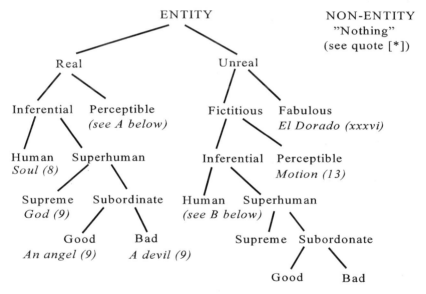

Diagram 1. Outline of the Benthamite ontology.

A. Under the head of perceptible real entities may be placed, without difficulty, individual perceptions of all sorts: the impressions produced in groups by the application of sensible objects to the organs of sense: the ideas brought to view by the recollection of those same objects; the new ideas produced under the influence of the imagination, by the decomposition and recomposition of those groups: — to none of these can the character, the denomination of real entities be refused (Bentham 1932, 10).

B. Faculties, powers of the mind, dispositions: all these are unreal; all these are but so many fictitious entities. When a view of them comes to be given, it will be seen how perfectly distinguishable, among psychical entities, are those which are recognized in the character of real, from those which are here referred to the class of fictitious entities. (Bentham 1932, 10)

An *entity* is a "denomination in the import of which every subject matter of discourse, for the designation of which the grammatical part of speech called a noun-substantive is employed may be comprised" (Bentham 1932, 7). A clarifying point which is necessary at this point in the presentation is the following:

Of fictitious entities, whatsoever is predicated is not consistently with strict truth, predicated (it then appears) of anything but their respective names.

But forasmuch as by reason of its length and compoundedness, the use of the compound denomination *name of a fictitious entity*, would frequently be found attended with inconvenience; for the avoidance of this inconvenience, instead of this long denomination, fictitious entity, will commonly, after the above warning, be employed (Bentham 1932, 17).

It is crucial to the understanding of Bentham's program that the distinction between *non-entity* and *fictitious entity* be very clear. The following quote provides perhaps the clearest idea as to why Bentham takes this ontological stance:

(*) In the house designated by such a number (naming it), in such a street, in such a town, lives a being called the Devil, having a head, body, and limbs, like a man's, horns like a goat's, wings like a bat's, and a tail like a monkey's. Suppose this assertion made, the observation naturally might be, that the Devil, as thus described is a non-entity. The averment made of it is, that an object of that description really exists. Of that averment, if seriously made, the object or end in view cannot but be to produce in the minds to which communication is thus made, a serious persuasion of the existence of an object conformable to the description thus expressed. Thus much concerning a non-entity. Very different is the notion here meant to be presented by the term fictitious entity. By this term is here meant to be designated one of those sorts of objects which in every spoken language must, for the

purpose of discourse, be spoken of as existing — be spoken of in
the like manner as those objects which really have existence, and
to which existence is seriously meant to be ascribed, are spoken
of; but without any such danger as that of producing any such
persuasion as that of their possessing, each for itself, any separate,
or strictly speaking, any real existence (Bentham 1932, 16).

Entities are classified by means of several levels of binary classification,
Bentham's method of preference for any sort of classificatory endeavor.
Entities may be divided into *real* and *unreal*.: "A real entity is an entity
to which, on the occasion and for the purpose of discourse, existence is
really meant to be ascribed " (Bentham, 10). Real entities then divide
into *inferential* and *perceptible* ones: "An *inferential* entity which, in
these times at least, is not made known to human beings in general, by
the testimony of sense, but of the existence of which the persuasion is
produced by reflection — is inferred from a chain of reasoning"
(Bentham 1932, 8). On the other hand: "A *perceptible* entity is every
entity the existence of which is made known to human beings by the
immediate testimony of their sense, without reasoning, *i.e.* without
reflection. A perceptible entity is, in one word, a body" (Bentham 1932,
7). It is at the binary classification of those entities which are unreal that
we arrive at the distinction between *fabulous* and *fictitious*. With reference to the above diagram, note that fictitious entities may either be
perceptible or inferential, but they are *always unreal*. For the sake of
clarity in this matter, it is very instructive to regard the following:

> A fictitious entity is an entity to which, though by the grammatical
> form of the discourse employed in speaking of it, existence be as-
> cribed, yet in truth and reality existence is not meant to be ascribed.
> Every noun-substantive which is not the name of a real entity,
> perceptible or inferential, is the name of a fictitious entity (Bentham
> 1932, 17).

As indicated in the above, this second occurrence of "fictitious" needs to
be modified to read "unreal" if we are to unambiguously incorporate a
distinction which is introduced by Bentham later on: "To distinguish
them from those fictitious entities, which, so long as language is in use
among human beings, never can be spared, fabulous may be the name

employed for the designation of the other class of unreal entities"
(Bentham 1932, 17). Continuing,

> Every fictitious entity bears some relation to some real entity, and
> can no otherwise be understood than in so far as that relation is per-
> ceived — a conception of that relation is obtained.
> Reckoning from the real entity to which it bears relation, a ficti-
> tious entity may be styled a fictitious entity of the first remove, a
> fictitious entity of the second remove, and so on.
> A fictitious entity of the first remove is a fictitious entity, a con-
> ception of which may be obtained by the consideration of the relation
> borne by it to a real entity, without need of considering the relation
> borne by it to any other fictitious entity.
> A fictitious entity of the second remove is a fictitious entity, for
> obtaining a conception of which it is necessary to take into consider-
> ation some fictitious entity of the first remove (Bentham 1932,
> 12–13).

Earlier, I agreed with Bentham when he asserted that: "To language,
then — to language alone — it is, that fictitious entities owe their existence; their impossible, yet indispensable existence." Bentham's work
supports my contention that music cannot exist for/in a group of individuals without the preexistence of a language in the group which is sophisticated enough to enable the expression of counterfactual thinking: In
order for a sequence of sounds to be music, the sounds must be apprehended as if they were something else. A contention which might be
raised immediately, however, is: "Could one not just as justifiably claim
that fictitious entities need to be countenanced in some form before
language can get off the ground and reach any reasonable level of sophistication? Bentham also acknowledges this fact:

> What will, moreover, be seen is, that the Fiction — the mode of
> representation by which the fictitious entities thus created, in so far as
> fictitious entities can be created, are dressed up in the garb, and
> placed upon the level, of real ones — is a contrivance for which
> language, or, at any rate, language in any form superior to that of the
> language of brute creation, could not have existence (Bentham 1932,
> 16).

Do we truly have a chicken/egg problem here? If we are to follow Bentham's and my way of thinking, are we caught in a vicious circle in which a reasonably sophisticated language must be in place for fictions (and thus music), to be possible, and, at the same time, fictions (and thus music) must be countenanced in order for a reasonably sophisticated language to be in existence? Actually, the problem is only a problem as long as we stay on the *surface* of both language and fictional contructs. The problem is a familiar one for anyone who has pondered the problem of mathematical induction, or any other phenomenon which is dependent upon recursive definitions and procedures. (A glance at Diagram 2 might prove helpful here.) The hallmark of such procedures is that they "refer back to themselves." There is a very important reason why they are not circular, however, and that is that the structure is parsed into levels, so that when one object refers back to another object of the same kind within the context of a definition, circularity is not present, because the object so referred to for the purposes of definition is on a "lower" or "previous" level, and in such fashion, has already been defined. It is, however, crucial that such a system have a "bottom rung" or 0–level at which objects are taken as primitive, viz., without need of definition. In this fashion, some objects must, indeed, be "bootstrapped" to the meaning which they have, namely these base-level ones, and the other remaining objects in the system can, then, thanks to these "ur" objects and operations may by definition in terms of these "ur"-elements obtain meaning and a place within the levels of the system. That such an approach to Bentham's work is justified is made clear by the way he discusses the "removes " of fiction which are given birth to by language.

It is immediately clear that such a hierarchical structuring allows us, to a great extent, to both have our cake and eat it, too. Once certain — perhaps only partially analyzable — bootstrappings have occurred, so that a base level set of objects along with attendant meanings are at hand — in this case, some level of language and fictions — it may very well be the case that subsequent levels of language "superior to that of the language of the brute creation" (Bentham 1932, 16) are, indeed, not possible, without previously "expounded" fictions. Let us further suggest that the codifiable process for continued "construction" of both linguistic and fictional elements is one which employs some combination/operation upon previously constructed/expounded linguistic and fictional elements. Bentham gives clear indications as to how such operations might look. Considering that he was working long before the notion of recursion was even given clear definition within philosophical and logical circles, it is fascinating to see the way his analysis permits of a faithful reformulation in terms of it. First, a schematic representation of the mechanics of recursion (Diagram 2).

SYSTEM/SET S RECONSTRUCTED RECURSIVELY

Level n: Elements contructed/defined by means of operations applied to level n–1, level n–2, . . . level 0.

Level 3:   Elements contructed/defined by means of operations applied to level 2, level 1 and level 0.

Level 2:   Elements contructed/defined by means of operations applied to level 1 and level 0.

Level 1:   Elements contructed/defined by means of operations applied to level 0.

Level 0:   Base elements of S.

Diagram 2. The bare bones of recursion.

Before proceeding to the nuts and bolts of Bentham's method, a diagram which relativizes Diagram 2 to Bentham's approach is helpful (Diagram 3).

Level n+k: Entities "created"/expounded by means of operations applied
             to level
             n+k–1, level n+k–2, . . . level 0.

                              ^

                              ^

                              ^

                              ^

                              ^

                              ^

Level n: Entities "created"/expounded by means of operations applied to
             level n–1, level n–2, . . . level 0.

⟹   Our *proposed* example: Music

                              ^

                              ^

                              ^

Level 2:   Entities "created"/expounded by means of operations applied to
             level 1 and level 0.
             Examples: Quality, Modification.

                              ^

Level 1:   Entities "created"/expounded by means of operations applied to
             level 0.
             Examples: Matter, Form, Quantity, Space.

                              ^

Level 0:   "Real" entities: "A real entity is an entity to which on the occasion
             and for the purpose of discourse, existence is really meant to be as-
             cribed."

             ∿∿∿∿∿∿∿∿∿∿∿∿∿∿∿∿∿∿∿∿∿∿∿∿∿∿∿∿∿∿

Operations: Examples: Reverse Archetypation, Phraseoplerosis, Paraphrasis

                          ****

Diagram 3. Bird's-eye view of Benthamite "recursive fictions".

Let's take a closer look at Diagram 3, beginning with the operations.
Bentham provides a clear exposition of the use of the operations of

Archetypation, Phraseoplerosis and Paraphrasis, one which is informative enough to justify the rather extensive quote which follows. Note that the "operation" of reverse archetypation is the one given in Diagram 3. This is for the technical reason that the operations in the recursive diagram must proceed from bottom to top, from a lower level to a higher one, and as is evident from the following, archetypation goes in the other direction. Here Bentham applies and explicates his approach to the word "obligation:"

> 1. The exponend, or say the word to be expounded, is an obligation.
> 2. It being the name not of a real, but only of a fictitious entity, and that fictitious entity not having any superior genus, it is considered as not susceptible of a definition in the ordinary shape, *per genus et differentiam*, but only of an exposition by way of paraphrasis.
> 3. To fit it for receiving exposition in this shape, it is in the character of the subject of a proposition, by the help of the requisite complements, made up into a fictitious proposition. These complements are (1) the predicate, *incumbent on a man*; (2) the copula *is*: and of these, when thus added to the name of the subject, viz. *obligation*, the fictitious proposition which requires to be expounded by paraphrasis, viz. the proposition, *An obligation is incumbent on a man*, is composed.
> 4. Taking the name of the subject for the basis, by the addition of this predicate, *incumbent* on a man, and the copula is, the phrase is completed — the operation called *phraseoplerosis*, i.e. completion of the phrase, is performed.
> 5. The source of the explanation thus given by paraphrasis is the idea of eventual sensation, as expressed by the names of the different and opposite modes of sensation — viz. pain and pleasure, with their respective equivalents — and the designation of the event on the happening of which such sensation is being about to take place.
> 6. For the formation of the variety of fictitious propositions of which the fictitious entity in question, viz. obligation, or an obligation, is in use to constitute the subject, the emblematical or archetypal image, is that of a man lying down, with a heavy body pressing upon him; to wit, in such sort as either to prevent him from acting at all, or so ordering matters that if so it be that he does act, it cannot be in any other direction or manner than the direction or manner in question — the direction or manner requisite (Bentham 1932, 89–90).

Having come thus far, a few comments are in order:

(a) This is an approach to the issues of ontology which begins with sense perceptions and then proceeds to construct just about everything of which we speak, and does so in terms of the operations discussed in the paragraphs of the preceding section. The sweep of this approach may be too grand for some who would prefer to regard many of the entities included among Bentham's long list of fictions as being entities which are not fictional in nature. This does not, however, undermine the relevance of this approach as a suggestion for a view of the ontology of music, as long as the entities from which it is "constituted" by the operations are, as before, either real or fictions which have already received exposition by means of the operations.

(b) Why not just define these fictional entities in the Aristotelian genus and differentia manner which had been used for centuries? Bentham explains:

> The only mode of exposition commonly understood by the word 'Definition' is that which by the Aristotelians was called definition *per genus et differentiam*: an exposition which is performed by naming a class or genus of objects within which that which is designated by the term thus undertaken to be defined is included, and thereupon, some circumstance or other by which the contents of this lesser class are considered as being distinguished from all the other contents of the greater and containing class.
>
> This being the case, if so it happens, as it most commonly does, that the word thus undertaken to be defined is the name not of a class of real but of a class of fictitious entities, what commonly happens is that, the word not having belonging to it that sort of relation which is the principal object of research, namely, a word significant of a superior, i.e. more extensive and containing genus, the thing thus undertaken to be done belongs to the category of impossibles. What he gives for the name of the superior genus, coupled with words designative of some differential character, is at best no more than a synonym by which no ulterior information is given, and which itself stands in as much need of exposition as the word for the exposition of which it is employed (Bentham 1983, 77–78).

In order to clarify things to an even greater degree, Ross Harrison writes:

Definition by genus and differentia only works if someone understands the genus. Of course, such understanding might be provided by another definition; but eventually, another method must be used because we shall come to terms having no superior genus. As long as we are acquainted with examples, we can have understanding of this genus, and this will be the method. If, however, we are not dealing with real entities, then we cannot be acquainted with examples; hence there is no way of achieving or conveying understanding of the superior genus. Hence another method is needed than that of definition, the method of paraphrasis (Harrison 1983, 56).

(c) A final comment to reassure the anxious reader that the notion of "recursive fiction" is not foreign to the spirit of Bentham's work: In addition to the quoted material (Bentham 12–13) which has appeared previously in this paper, Ogden provides us with the following editorial "aside:"

The manuscript of this section finishes at this point, but the marginal note in pencil is: "Go on, bring to view the several other fictitious entities of the second remove, those of the third remove, if any, and so on" (Bentham 1932, 14).

*****

Now that a survey and reconstruction of the nuts and bolts of the Benthamite method of "fictional recursion" are in place, we conclude with some brief reflections regarding the relevance of all of this to philosophers and semioticians who ponder questions of musical semiotics and/or ontology:

1. Aren't the prospects for the characterization of music as a "recursive fiction" tantalizing? What sorts of choices would we allow for archetypes, what products of paraphrasis and phraseoplerosis would we accept? Given Bentham's own examples of low-level fictitious entities, as are seen in Diagram 3, it is obvious that music has many components which are fictitious in a basic, meat-and-potatoes sort of philosophical sense. For example, it is clear that much of what constitutes music is indeed, fictional in nature: take, for example the idea of musical motion. There is no "thing" which moves within the music, but we talk as if there were. This sort of motion is, obviously, dependent upon whatever

notions we have of motion *simpliciter*, but this only makes musical motion a fiction of an even higher order, since physical motion itself is regarded as a fiction, at least in the systems of both Bentham and, indeed, Vaihinger. But what higher-level entities, both real and fictitious, would we choose as part of the accretive, recursive constitution of music regarded from this fictional point of view? (This question is particularly relevant if one chooses not to buy Bentham's sweeping ontological program — see comment (a) a few pages back.) Depending on one's point of view, entities connected with the emotions might appear sooner or later in the process, or perhaps not at all. Given the dogged, bottom-to-top constructive nature of the enterprise, however, we may be forced to reconsider constructive constituents which are often ridiculed as too base for proper inclusion in a discussion of the ontology of aesthetic objects, such as our likes and dislikes with regard to food or sex.

2. Given the hierarchical structure which has just been suggested, there is no contradiction inherent in the avowal that some level of linguistic sophistication must have been reached in a group of individuals in order for it to be meaningful to ascribe the presence of music in and for that group. Alternatively, in order to reach even greater levels of linguistic sophistication, certain musical fictions must be part of the "ladder" of linguistic/fictional entities which have been reached within the group.

3. In many ways, Bentham inherited the ontological outlook of the empiricist tradition, a tradition which has exercised an enormous influence over Anglo-American philosophy, particularly in the way that philosophy has dealt with the philosophy of logic and language. One needs only look at Russell's doctrine of sense data and his work with contextual definitions. The formulation of Bentham's explications in terms of archetypes, paraphrasis, etc., and his acknowledgement of the *indispensability* of fictions allow him to both espouse *ontological parsimony*, while providing an escape hatch to provide for *ontological plenitude* as well. *Ontological parsimony* is a watchword of the hardfisted Anglo-American logico-analytic tradition, a tradition which has preferred to deal with mathematical and scientific entities. A little afterthought reveals that *ontological parsimony* is perhaps not the attitude most conducive to studies involving artistic and creative endeavors, in which, if anything, an attitude of *ontological proliferation* would seem to

be the most natural. After all, *ontological parsimony* is to be desired in a world where that which is, will, indeed, have to be cleaned out of a closet eventually, taken to a junkyard, mowed with a lawnmower, or the like. But such drudgery is hardly foisted upon us by the existence of yet another symphony, play or poem, except in the prosaic sense in which anyone who reads this occasionally feels powerless when trying to put his or her LPs, tapes, CDs, scores and books in order. *Ontological plenitude* would thus seem to be the most appropriate desideratum for a philosophy of art and music. And it is in this respect, among others, that Bentham's views are refreshing.

References

Bentham, Jeremy (1932). *Bentham's Theory of Fictions*, edited by C.K. Ogden, 1–150. London: Kegan Paul, Trench, Trubner & C., Ltd.
– (1983). *The Collected Works of Jeremy Bentham*. J.R. Dinwiddy (ed.). Deontology together with A Table of the Springs of Action and The Article on Utilitarianism, edited by Annon Goldworth. Oxford: Clarendon Press.
Ekman, Rolf (1949). *Fiktionerna i det Estetiska Livet*. Lund: C.W.K. Gleerup.
Goodman, Nelson (1983). *Fact, Fiction and Forecast*. 4th ed. Cambridge: Harvard.
Grund, Cynthia M. (1988). "Metaphors, Counterfactuals and Music", *Essays on the Philosophy of Music*, Veikko Rantala, Lewis Rowell and Eero Tarasti (eds.), 28–53. (Acta Philosophica Fennica 43.) Helsinki: Akateeminen kirjakauppa.
– (1995). "How philosophical characterizations of a musical work lose sight of the 'music' and how it might be put back", *Musical Signification: Essays in the Semiotic Theory and Analysis of Music*, Eero Tarasti (ed.), 63–79. Berlin/New York: Mouton de Gruyter.
Harrison, Ross (1983). *Bentham*. London: Routledge and Kegan Paul.
Kvart, Igal (1986). *A Theory of Counterfactuals*. Indianapolis: Hackett.
Lewis, David (1973). *Counterfactuals*. Cambridge: Harvard.
Nyman, Alf (1922). "Metafor och fiktion", *Lunds Universitets årsskrift*, 3–81. Avd. 1. Bd 18. Nr 6. Lund: C. W. K. Gleerup.
Ogden, C. K. (1932). *Introduction to Bentham's Theory of Fictions*, C.K. Ogden (ed.), ix–clii. London: Kegan Paul, Trench, Trubner & C., Ltd.
Vaihinger, Hans (1935). *The Philosophy of 'As if'*. Trans. by C. K. Ogden. 2nd ed. London: Routledge and Kegan Paul Ltd.

Some semiotic problems of Krzysztof Penderecki's sonoristic style

DANUTA MIRKA

1. The Polish sonoristic style of the 1960s arose as a reaction against serialism. In contrast to the hyperformalist intellectual orientation of serialism, commonly held to be influenced by structuralism, sonorism has been considered as devoid of interest in intellectually organized form and as concerned only with exploration of formless sound matter. Accordingly, in sonoristic compositions the material has been viewed as of primary importance, whereas the form, instead of underlying on a deeper level the manifestation of matter, has been seen as constituting a secondary resultant of the fluctuation of free sound.

Founded on such a reversed hierarchy of textual levels, the musical world of sonorism has been considered chaotic; and since explanation of chaos is unthinkable, no explanatory analysis of sonoristic music has ever been elaborated. Traditional musicology, which is based, either explicitly or implicitly, on the above-mentioned theoretical presumptions, has thus attained only the descriptive analysis of sonoristic sound effects. Most times, such description is merely verbal repetition of what can easily be seen on the score.

Such theoretical presumptions do not hold true in the case of Krzysztof Penderecki's sonorism. Careful examination of the earliest and most representative examples of his sonoristic style—works such as *Threnody*, *Polymorphia*, *Fluorescences*, and others—allows one to formulate the following hypothesis: in spite of the commonly held view, the sound material of those works is secondary to the form. Indeed, it is the form that underlies the atemporal inventory of sound effects as well as their succession in the temporal course of musical narration. In reality, the contrast between serialism and Penderecki's sonorism lies not in the strict formal organization of the former and its lack in the latter, but rather in a different application of equally strict formal orders in each of those compositional modes. Whereas in serial composition the order rules relationships between single tones, in the sonoristic works of Penderecki order governs distinct states of sound matter taken *en masse*.

If the above hypothesis is right, the universe of Penderecki's sonoristic style constitutes not chaos, but cosmos, within which an explanatory analysis should be possible. Or the converse: the construction of an explanatory analysis based on an explicit generative grammar is an indispensable condition, if the hypothesis in question is to be confirmed.

2. Elementary structures of the required grammar are binary oppositions in the four parameters of the sound universe: pitch, duration, dynamics, and colour. These oppositions establish the basic categories in Penderecki's sonoristic style and are comparable to phemic categories of a linguistic system, their opposite terms being, in turn, equivalent to phemes.

	+	−
categories of pitch	spatial continuity spatial mobility highest register	spatial discontinuity spatial immobility lowest register
categories of duration	temporal continuity temporal mobility (rhythm)	temporal discontinuity temporal immobility (lack of rhythm)
categories of dynamics	loud	silent
categories of sound colour	string instruments arco etc.	wind instruments non-arco etc.

Table 1.

2.1. On the paradigmatic axis, the above-listed oppositions account for the morphology of the generative grammar. Just as in language, in Penderecki's sonorism a combinatory of a few of these musical phemes generates a large number of units forming the inventory of sonoristic sound effects: clusters, glissandi, and atypical articulations on several instruments. Each of these effects, perceived as a simple unit by traditional descriptive analysis, appears now to be a complex configuration comparable to a linguistic phoneme and explainable as an arrangement of several distinctive features. In this way the new analytical perspective proposed here allows one to replace the mere specification of Penderecki's sonoristic sound effects with a taxonomy of the same, a taxonomy based on musical phemes.

A cluster, one of the most typical effects in Penderecki's sonoristic pieces, can be defined as an arrangement of the following four phemes taken from phemic categories of pitch and duration: spatial continuity, spatial immobility, temporal continuity, temporal immobility. Occurring in a given work as a concrete sound effect, however, a cluster is always endowed with all the sound parameters and, as such, determined additionally by phemic categories left outside its definition. For example, the cluster from rehearsal number 6 of *Polymorphia* (1961), includes the following, "extra" phemes: the lowest register, the hushed dynamics, and the colouristic value of bowed strings.

2.2. The same set of binary oppositions, which on the paradigmatic axis underlies the morphology of generative grammar, on the syntagmatic axis determines syntax. This is so because phemic categories generate not only a taxonomy of musical phonemes, but also a logic of their sequences in a musical narration. This logic, closely related to the "logic of contradictions" investigated in mythical narration by Claude Lévi-Strauss, is based on two mechanisms: exposition and mediation of oppositions included in phemic categories. Such a logic thus operates on the four terms of a semiotic square, which arise from an expansion of each opposition (Figure 1).

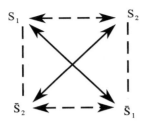

Figure 1.

The exposition of a given category thus involves its single contrary terms: positive (s_1) and negative (s_2). Mediation, instead, makes use of the contradictory axes of this square; that is, of the complex term "both s_1 and s_2 " ($s_1 + s_2$) as well as of the neutral term "neither s_1 nor s_2" ($\bar{s}_1 + \bar{s}_2$), which otherwise is also complex, as A. J. Greimas points out.

exposition:	s_1	$(+)$
		$(-)$
mediation:	$s_1 + s_2$	$(+-)$
	$\bar{s}_1 + \bar{s}_2$	(0)

Ruled by such a logic, the syntax of Penderecki's sonoristic style admits only those sequences of musical phonemes whose component phemic sequences take shape as of one of the following trajectories:

exposition:

$$s_1 \rightarrow s_2 \qquad (+ \rightarrow -)$$

$$s_2 \rightarrow s_1 \qquad (- \rightarrow +)$$

mediation:

$$s_1 \rightarrow s_2 + s_2/\bar{s}_1 + \bar{s}_2 \rightarrow s_2 \ (+ \rightarrow +-/0 \rightarrow -)$$

$$s_2 \rightarrow s_1 + s_2/\bar{s}_1 + \bar{s}_2 \rightarrow s_1 \ (- \rightarrow +-/0 \rightarrow +)$$

This kind of syntax can be traced easily in the initial fragment of *Polymorphia*. The particular phemic trajectories of this fragment are as follows:

spatial continuity/discontinuity
(+)   1: a single point-like pitch (E) as an example of discontinuity;
(+-)   2–4: mediation by means of a transition from a discontinuous single tone to a continuous cluster;
(-)   5: spatial continuity of the cluster;

lowest/highest register
(+)   1–9: lowest register of contrabasses and cellos (C-B);
(+-)   10: complex term arising through the introduction of the highest register (highest possible tones of the violins);
(0)(+-)   11: combination of a previous complex term with the neutral one, resulting from the introduction of the middle register of violas;
(0)   22: middle register as a neutral term of opposition;

spatial mobility/ immobility
(+)   1–7/16: lowest tones spatially immobile;
(+-)   8/17–15/19: a particular case of mediation through a complex term, where a mobility of single instruments (glissandi) results in the overall effect of immobile clusters;
(-)   16/20–24: movement of both single tones of individual instruments and the resulting clusters;

arco/non-arco
(+)   1–23: arco;
(-)   24: con dita (with fingers) and pizzicato as articulations "non-arco";

temporal continuity/discontinuity
(+)   1–23: long-lasting tones and glissandos as temporally continuous phenomena;

(–)   24: discontinuity of point-like impulses of pizzicato and con
             dita articulation;

temporal mobility/immobility
(–)   1–24: because temporal mobility is considered as a
             phenomenon of perceivable temporal relations (rhythms)
             between sound phenomena, both long–lasting tones (1–23)
             and maximally dense impulses (22–24) are temporally
             immobile;

loud/soft dynamics
(–)   1–24: several shades of soft dynamics (ppp-p).
Results of the analysis are condensed in the following diagram (Figure
2).

3. The generative grammar described above not only confirms our
hypothesis about the "cosmic" character of Penderecki's sonoristic
universe. Further, it shows that the plainly structural organization of this
grammar leads to the conclusion—paradoxical as it may seem from the
common musicological viewpoint—that Penderecki's sonoristic style
forms a musical equivalent of structuralism. Still more paradoxically, his
sonoristic style most likely constitutes the only true example of a
structuralist attitude in music; since, if "serial" and "structural"
thoughts are different, as Claude Lévi-Strauss and Umberto Eco claim
(thereby calling into question another commonly held view), the
manifestation of structuralism in music is to be sought not among the
French compositions of the 1960s, composed at the center of the
structuralist movement and in the period of its most spectacular
triumphs, but—most unexpectedly—in the music of a Polish composer
who had not even heard of structuralism when he started to elaborate his
structuralist compositional method in the late 50s and early 60s. No
better example of the structuralist concept of "episteme" can even be
imagined than this one, which refers to structuralism itself.

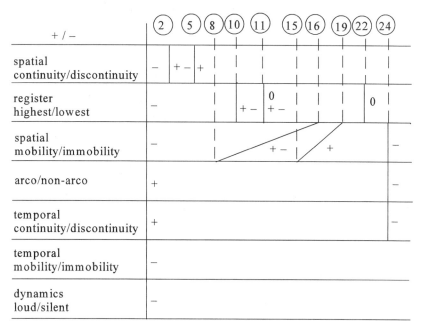

Figure 2.

4. All the above observations concern the expression plane of Pende
recki's sonoristic style. Yet a semiotic approach would try to expand the
perspective of this study onto the content plane as well and, in this way,
to view signification as a junction between expression and content of the
musical phenomenon under discussion.

The solution to this problem depends on our first answering a more
general question: what is the nature of the reciprocal relationship
between expression and content in music as such? There are two possible
options here.

4.1. The first option assumes a similarity between musical and linguistic
semiotic systems in this respect. According to this assumption, the
relationship between content and expression in music is, as in language,
indirect; that is, the said relationship constitutes a correlation in which
both planes, though analogically organized as hierarchies of levels (with

phemes, phemic categories and phonemes on the plane of expression; and semes, semic categories and sememes on the plane of content), are displaced with respect to each other. Consequently, what is assigned to the elementary level of content is one of the higher levels of expression, consisting of recurrent sequences of elementary units—words, in the case of language—whose distribution is governed by syntax. The elementary level of expression—in the case of language, that of phonemes—is devoid of any content at all.

In Penderecki's sonoristic works, however, sound effects constituting musical equivalents of phonemes are not joined into recurrent sequences of a higher level that would be ruled only by syntax. On the contrary, as has been shown, the syntax of such effects is applied immediately to phonemes, the order of which is governed by phemic trajectories. Since the works in question contain no higher level of the expression plane, the semiotic situation of Penderecki's sonorism is comparable to the situation of a linguistic system without words or of an alphabet without a dictionary.

In the framework of the first option, the case of Penderecki's sonoristic music is thus exceptional. Yet its interpretation can still be twofold. First, it can be seen as an expression without content. In terms elaborated by Umberto Eco, such a phenomenon is called an "s-code" or structure, and not a code properly speaking, the latter being defined as a reciprocal assignment between two structures. Seen from this angle, the exceptional nature of Penderecki's sonoristic derives from the fact that it constitutes a unique musical system of expression, an expression consciously unconnected with any system of content.

In contrast, in the second interpretation of the same first option, the unique position of Penderecki's sonoristic music issues not from the lack of content, but rather from the atypical relationship between content and expression established here. While normally this relationship is that of correlation, in Penderecki's sonorism it assumes the shape of a direct assignment, that is, of identity. In this view, just as the "meaning" of the single phoneme "d" from Jakobson's famous example is nothing but the set of its distinctive features, the meaning of any given musical phoneme from Penderecki's sonoristic works would be nothing more than the set of all its musical phemes. Consequently, syntactic and semantic categories would interchange here, phemes being tantamount to semes, phemic categories to semic categories, and phonemes to sememes.

Both interpretations in fact give the same result. Whether the content does not exist or is identical with expression, the only self-dependent plane in Penderecki's sonoristic music is the expression plane. Mathematically speaking, the expressions /a/ and /a=a/ do not differ, the latter being a tautological expansion of the former.

4.2. The identification of content and expression, treated as exceptional by the first option, can, however, be assumed as a normal state of music, a state which distinguishes it from the linguistic semiotic system. Obviously, such a second option for the junction between the content and the expression plane in music does not affect the interpretation of Penderecki's sonoristic style. Yet, viewed from this new angle, his sonorism, which identifies expression with content, would no longer be an exceptional case in the area of music, but, on the contrary, the most typical one.

Notes

1. Colour is here described not in its phenomenal aspect as the most complex sound parameter, but in the aspect of production, as a resultant of orchestration and articulation. The number of possible categories of sound colour is very high, much higher than the two simplest categories given in the table.
2. Transition forms a particular case of mediation, not discussed in this paper. Because of their temporal character, transitions are not fully explainable in the atemporal terms of the semiotic square; the interpretation of transition as complex term (+-) is given here for the sake of simplicity only.
3. Asynchronic changes of phemes in the layers of different registers (such as the passage from a negative [-] to a complex term [+] between rehearsal numbers 8 and 16 or from complex [+-] to positive term [+] between 15 and 19) are examples of a topological conception of time that is characteristic of Penderecki's sonoristic works.

Values and their cognition in the semiotic theory of Charles S. Peirce

MACIEJ JABŁOŃSKI

Preliminary remarks

Complying with the useful postulate of cohesion between the title of the paper and its content, I wish to make some small supplementations in reference to this text. My objective is to show the possibilities of carrying out such an interpretation of some threads in Peirce's theory of signs that will reveal the aesthetic involvement of some semiotic categories constituting the stem of this theory. The inquiry oriented in this way, based on the hypothesis of the aesthetico-semiotic function of the interpretant category, will refer to the comparative material consisting of solutions arrived at by John Dewey (1934, 1935) in his work dealing with axiological matters. At the same time, these solutions present at several points an interesting example of the "general philosophic convergence" that can be shown in reference to two philosophic systems that fundamentally differ in their assumptions.

Peirce's avoidance of direct reference to the category of "values" makes it difficult to recognize the areas of his semiotic reflections that "suggest" the problem of values. However, when we analyze penetratingly the group of questions associated with the philosophic premise fundamental for the pragmatists and articulated as the thesis about the unity of cognition ("thought") and action, particularly the practically-involved action, we find in consequence some threads revealing the axiological dimension of the Peirce's philosophic system. The statement about the axiological involvement of the philosophic thought of pragmatists does not seem to be very revealing, if we take into consideration that almost all protagonists of this orientation refer to the connections of their views with the problems of "values" or themselves created some interesting conceptions of this field.

Pragmatists' *novum*

The essence of the philosophic novum of the pragmatists lies certainly in the formulation of the assumption about the basic role of the sphere of action in human life. It outstrips all other activities, and furthermore it constitutes the foundation of this activity. The discarding of the traditional dichotomy "action/cognition" resolves itself into several consequences on the epistemological, ontological, and finally the axiological planes. The reductionism characteristic of this type of reflection is revealed basically in the absolutization of the idea of the normative character of cognition, i.e., such that it is essential to turn to the "practically perceptible consequences" as being the basis of all rules and directives of action. This thesis, as we know, was outlined for the first time by the creator of pragmatism, Charles Peirce. It has also a direct connection with his "pragmatic maxim". According to Peirce, from the concept of the unity of cognition and action it follows that the description of a phenomenon is important only when it is the basis for determining the directives of action. Furthermore, the function of the pragmatic maxim is combined, on the basis of Peirce's philosophic system, with the leading premise of this system about the mediation of signs in all cognitive acts. In this way, this principle becomes at the same time a universal rule defining the meaning of signs (= "thoughts", since each thought is a sign) and this determination is done in the process of cognitive semasiological interpretation (Hill 1930).

Speaking about "practical consequences" understood as a particular type of meaning, Peirce has in mind a general, universal directive that is free of any references to particular situations. The semiotico-cognitive function of the pragmatic maxim is defined also by its role in the solution of one of the main problems of Peirce's semiotics, namely, the regress ad infinitum of the relation of sign interpretation by another sign, which precludes unequivocal determination of the "earliest beginnings" or first anchorage of the relational sequence. In this understanding, the definitely interpreted sign requires the existence of an interpreting sign that can be "translated" into a rule of action, and this in turn would constitute in the final result the proper meaning of the sign. The indication of an objectively important meaning, which in consequence can be translated into a rule or a set of rules of a practical character, causes the introduction of a definite element into the interpretative sequence. The pragmatic principle is therefore able to serve the function of a metaprinciple adjusting the interpretative activity and to define the way of understanding the meanings of the signs included in the range of all kinds of semiotic processes.

"Interpretation" and cognition

From the gnoseological point of view, the most significant for the philosophic system of Peirce is the category of "interpretation". The act of interpretation is an act of cognition, always scientifically mediated, and in its effect, the meaning of the sign, i.e., the interpretant, is constituted. In order to avoid the objection of solipsism, with regard to the ideal sphere where the acts of the semasiological interpretation creating signs "are realized", Peirce introduces a sphere of reality accessible to subjective experience. The difference between both spheres is based primarily on the fact that the meanings of signs subjected to interpretation and created in the second sphere have the status of degenerated meanings (signs). This has a significant importance for our further considerations, since the degenerated interpretants, among others due to their reference to the sphere of experiences and emotions, can be defined as axiological (aesthetical) categories, i.e., as values with a psychological sense. The role of experience as the source of cognition is strongly accentuated more than usual by the creator of pragmatism, whereas, as mentioned before, it can be an experience whose result is evoked in the subject by an emotional state (e.g., the perception of a musical work). Of course, it is one of many possible interpretations of the complex problem of the nature of the interpretant. However, a number of remarks made in this regard by Peirce himself, primarily the reference to the "experience" of a musical work, justifies the proposal of the above thesis.

The semasiological function of the interpretative act gains in expressiveness particularly when we realize its place and role in the "synechistically" understood process of cognition (Murphy 1967: 76). According to Peirce, the particular acts of cognition (interpretation) are not specific "atoms", isolated and partial moments of the cognitive process, but being interdependent they create one continuous and inseparable sequence. Therefore, each of these acts should be analyzed not only on with respect to its own features, but also in a comparative way in reference to the type of relation connecting it with the preceding or the following act. In this connection, the act of cognitive interpretation gains a particular value constituted by the force of having fulfilled the function of a relevant partial moment of this process, due to the preservation of the "synechisticity" of the cognitive process. I propose to define this situation as an *axio-functional* one.

The act of interpretation, however, being itself axiologically characterized, is in the first place a semiotic act, i.e., such an act that aims to determine the meaning of the sign that is the object of interpretation. Therefore, the fulfillment of the act of interpretation depends primarily on the realization of the stated aim. At the same time, as indicated earlier, the act can be referred both to the sphere of ideal meanings, genuine signs, and can also be engaged in the sphere of degenerated meanings (subjective relativization).

The interpretant plays a particularly important role in the degeneration of partial moments of the triadic relation, i.e., taking place on three planes — of the sign understood ideally as a triadic unity of the transferring medium, the object of reference, and the meaning. According to many investigators (Greenlee 1973; Buczyńska 1981; Zeman 1988), a precise definition of this category (interpretant) is the most difficult one because of the unusually unclear and obscure statements made by the creator of pragmatism himself. Characteristic of the tendency to extend the meaning- ranges of notions is one of Peirce's definitions of the interpretant category: "Taking the sign in its widest sense, its interpretant is not necessarily a sign. . . . But we can take a sign in such a wide sense that its interpretant will be not a 'thought' but an 'action' or 'experience', or we can extend the notion of a sign to such an extent that its interpretant will be only a quality of feeling" (Buczyńska 1981: 132).

It follows from the above quotation that Peirce admits in principle three possible types of sign-interpretants; they are: conscious experience understood as a type of passive perception (emotional interpretant), active action (energetic interpretant), and finally another sign (logical interpretant, called also the intellectual interpretant).

The interpretation that discovers the logical interpretant of the sign refers only to the sphere of signs. The emotional and energetic interpretants are effects evoked by the sign "in somebody" who perceives and interprets these signs; at the same time, it is a type of interpretation completely different from that which decides about the form of the translation within the relation inside the universum of signs. These interpretants are thereby the external results of the existence of sign, while the interpretative act is done by reference to the external, extra-sign reality of the world of signs.

The theory of interpretant, or rather of many interpretants, shows a multi-aspectual meaning, and at the same time the possibility of its many-sided analysis. In each process of thinking (acting), including the process of the cognition of value (value– fact), there coexist and overlap all interpretants of a sign. This coexistence is connected with the fact that each sign, being the object of a definite empirical "perception" (meaning is an empirical meaning since, as justly noticed by Quine, the idiom "to have a practical meaning" should be interpreted according to the pragmatic principle as "to be observable"), and constituting the immediate sense of the observed sign in the form of one of two possible degenerated interpretants, contains at the same time the substitute of a "general" ideal sign (Quine 1986: 153). According to this conception, our understanding of the particular and empirical situation appears as a preliminary stage, followed as a rule by an unrealized act of the generalization of the content of a definite sign and abstraction from it of the quality or qualities that function by force of the objective "law" and that have decided on the creation of this and not another type of sign situation. Hence, the essential role of the category of interpretant, which permits uncovering of the character of the type of connection linking the reference elements of the objective sign.

Since, as mentioned before, the most essential aim of the interpretative act in the semiotic sense is the constitution of an interpretant (in the ideal triad, it is the final interpretant; in the degenerated forms, the direct or indirect one), I propose, according to the discussed relation between the act of interpretation and the synechistic nature of cognition, to introduce the notion of a semiotic *axio-teleological* situation for the determination of the connection between the interpretative act and the interpretant. At this point it is obvious that, though the "occurrence" of the interpretative act and the "creation" of the interpretant are in a feedback relation with each other in the sense that the interpretation act cannot be fulfilled without the constitution of the final effect of this act, i.e., the meaning (interpretant), and the meaning cannot be "discovered" without the participation of the interpretation, there is no doubt that the primary function in this system is played by the act of interpretation.

The constituted interpretant can assume the degenerated or the final form. At the same time, in the second case it is defined as a logical interpretant (the interpretant of a sign is another sign) in differentiation from the other two remaining interpretants discussed above (emotional and energetic interpretants) created in the first case. However, as follows from a number of remarks made by the author of the pragmatic maxim, there exists a certain type of link connecting all three types of interpretant; since each of them "has" in some way its "immediate element", although in this respect the emotional interpretant is particularly distinguished being the most "directly" given in comparison to the remaining ones.

Axiological clues to Peircean pragmatism

The characterization of the axiological threads of Peirce's pragmatism should be carried out on the basis of their connection with the evidently anthropocentric traits of this philosophy. Since in essence, as stressed by Buczyńska, on the ground of pragmatism, the category of value proves to have a specific, particular character (1970: 320). In this fact, similarly as in many other places, the reductionistic "leitmotif" of pragmatic philosophy is equally strongly revealed, determining the value only in categories of occasional utility. The cancellation of distinguishing between value and fact reduces in consequence the former to the role of an element of the world of experience; and by force of the main thesis about the primacy (also from the "axiological" point of view) of the purposeful action of man over all his other activities, it decides about its situational relativity. This situation finds its particularly striking substantiation in John Dewey's concepts of instrumental value (value as the result of experience-action), in C. I. Lewis's notion of cognition as valuation (cognition is always relativized due to values which are to be realized by action), or the axiologically and semiotically characterized concept of Charles Morris's "preference behaviours" (Buczyńska 1975).

In this place, one should certainly consider Peirce's conception of "truth", whose axiological dimension was revealed by indicating the teleologico-rational selections dictating or inspiring the behavior of man in life. This understanding refers obviously to the pragmatic principle which should be interpreted in terms of "confirming experience" (Quine 1986: 155).

The hypothesis of the aesthetico-semiotic function of the category of interpretant is based on the analysis of the thesis according to which aesthetics, in the understanding proposed by Peirce as one of three normative sciences, has on the one hand the status of a basic science in reference to the two remaining domains (logic and ethics); on the other hand, it is founded on the theory of "category" constituting the nucleus of Peirce's ontology. According to the views of the creator of pragmatism, aesthetics is defined as a science about phenomena, objects in their "direct presence", existence, and expressed in semiotic terminology as signs "as such", as signs "in themselves". From the point of view of ontological classification, Peirce assigns to these "objects" the category of Firstness. And it is essential that the author of the pragmatic maxim connects with this category the notion of "feeling" defined as a pre-reflexive, timeless quality "given directly" in the cognitive act. A separate and certainly difficult problem is the justification of any "speaking" about Firstness (interference of reflection), since at the moment when we realize the fact that "something" is "first", that "something" ceases being "first" and becomes "second", i.e., "something" that has come into existence in the most rudimentary form in our consciousness. While Secondness introduces the element of "discreteness" to our consciousness. Thirdness refers to relations characteristic of events, phenomena, objects. Therefore, Thirdness is a category of "law", "relativity", "rule". Referring here to the earlier mentioned example (adduced by Peirce) of a musical work, we can state that in a direct, pre-reflectional perception it appears as a category of Firstness. Then, after a definite existence of the particular sound in "time and space", it is seen as Secondness; while in the from of an identifiable structure of morphological elements it is a category of the Thirdness.

This reference to the theory of "category", although carried out in a rather superficial and abbreviated form, facilitates and in some degree "softens" our passing into the sphere of connections between Peirce's conception of aesthetics and his theory of signs. Defining the interpretant as the "proper effect of the meaning" of the sign, Peirce made two significant triadic divisions of the category of meaning, developing particularly the analysis of one of them, namely, the logical interpretant. According to the classification based on the ontological categories, the interpretant is defined as the category of Thirdness. At the same time, we obtain three types of interpretants: the direct, the dynamic, and the final interpretant. By means of the second of the proposed divisions — emotional, energetic, and logical interpretants[1] — and its usability for further considerations, I shall focus my attention on the direct and dynamic interpretants.

The first of the above-mentioned types of interpretant refers to the sign "itself" (medium of transfer in the terminology of Bense) and is defined as the ". . . effect evoked by the sign without carrying out any reflection on it" (Bense 1980: 43). The second type, the dynamic interpretant, is "the real effect that the given sign exerts" (Buczyńska 1975: 133). It consists in the "direct effect factually exerted by the sign on its interpreter" (ibid.). Utilizing again the classification of interpretants on the basis of ontological "categories", we find in reference to the second of the above-mentioned triadic divisions that the emotional interpretant understood as "the primary semantic effect of a sign", i.e., "feeling", is the correspondent of Firstness. So, on the one hand, Firstness is the direct interpretant semiotically defining the modus of the existence of these "qualities" given pre-reflexively; on the other hand, it is the emotional interpretant referring to the category of "feeling". In turn, the energetic interpretant is connected with the category of Secondness; it is a kind of "superstructure" over the emotional interpretant, and constitutes its supplementation, which is the real effect of a sign — the observable "action" of the sign on the subject who perceives that sign. According to Peirce, the reactions of the subject can have the character of definite psychical states evoked by the sign (by the emotional interpretant of the sign) or physiological reactions.

Analyzing closely and penetratingly the category of logical interpretant, Peirce makes a number of significant remarks, which without affecting the architectonics of the his semiotic system can be extrapolated into the area of reflection on the remaining types of interpretants. Although from the point of view of the hierarchy of normative sciences, logic is "subordinated" to aesthetics, it had absorbed the author of the pragmatic principle much more than aesthetics. According to Peirce, the "first" logical interpretant should be identified with the "preliminary", "rudimentary", "instinctive" experience, or it should be defined as a type of an usually unconscious "doubt" (Peirce 1931–1935, vol. 5: 480). At the same time, both formulations constitute a distinct parallel to the way of understanding a direct interpretant.

In the next phase, the subject undertakes a number of actions that, due to the convictions and motives steering them, constitute attempts at "neutralizing" the "doubting" attitude in relation to the inner world (ibid.: 481). This constitutes the phase of logical dynamic interpretants (according to Zeman, the appearance of a logical dynamic interpretant is connected with the "conscious restructurization of elements which emerged in the phase of direct logical interpretants"; 1988: 249). The subject realizing these actions, on the basis of the criterion of having achieved the desired results, creates in himself some kind of a "habit", a "disposition" to actions that have the status of conscious "habits", being the effect of "self-analysis" of the subject. Therefore, these dispositions are the final logical interpretants.

Now, coming back to the problem of the relation between both triadic divisions of interpretants, we notice that the emotional interpretant has the most "direct" character of all the interpretants. The experience constituting the energetic interpretant "creates" also, besides the direct one, its dynamic dimension, while in the case of the logical interpretant we have additionally to do with the third, final dimension.

The central category of experience obtains in this moment a new meaning. On the one hand, it is the primary, irreducible modus of our perception of the world; and on the other hand, from the semiotic point of view, it "organizes" the complex network of the interdependent interpretants discovered in the process of cognitive interpretation. This ordering presented in the form of a sequence of sign-mediated acts of experience leads therefore to the creation of a specific hierarchy of "meanings", starting with the emotional, through the energetic, and concluding with the logical interpretant. Also the aesthetic experience proves to have its localization in this semiotico-cognitive continuum. At the same time, it is just the emotional interpretant that decides about this placement. Such understanding of the interpretant proposed by Peirce, where it is identified with the aesthetic category of "feeling" being constitutive for emotively understood aesthetic experience, brings the conception of the author of the pragmatic principle closer, at least in this point, to a number of theses advanced by another representative of American pragmatism, John Dewey.

The remarks of Peirce made both in relation to aesthetics as well as to ethics are limited to those occasions in which he discusses their connections with logic. Hence, and it has to be openly admitted, a considerable part of his views referring to aesthetic problems are revealed only through the comparison of these views with the undoubtedly "parallel" style of thinking represented by the pragmatic conception of instrumental values. I am particularly interested in those considerations of Dewey that deal with the notion of experience, including aesthetic experience, as well as those that point to the important role of the "emotional dimension" of experience. According to Dewey, the emotional part, the constitutive "quality" of experience, decides about its ". . . fullness, unity, it makes it specifically complete" (1934: 41).

This formulation corresponds completely to the main premise of Peirce's understanding of the function of the prereflexive "emotional quality" (emotional interpretant) that unifies and forms the nucleus of the experience. Peirce writes: ". . . that quality is the unmediated presence in the experience' (1931–1935, vol. 2: 199). This "quality", as we remember, has a corresponding ontological category of Firstness. Continuing his considerations, Peirce stresses that Firstness has a universal and basic character and that it defines "the way of existing in itself" (1931–1935, vol. 1: 531).

A fragment of the views referring to the relation of the universal category of Firstness and the emotive dimension of experience is most frequently quoted by Dewey in his analysis of Peirce's ontological categories. Dewey, in his references to the solutions of Peirce in this field, accentuates particularly strongly the convergences that can be shown between his (Dewey's) conception of experience and the theory of "category" formulated by Peirce (Dewey 1935: 210).

The cardinal element of Dewey's aesthetics is the category of "experience" understood in some specific way. This thinker distinguishes the experience constituted thanks to the "presence" of the "directly given emotional quality" from the experience that he defines as "incomplete", "incoherent", that is, as we might guess, an experience deprived of this unifying "quality". The notion of "present unmediated quality" in the sense of "given directly" connects the category of experience with another central notion in the philosophical reflection of Dewey, namely, the notion of "context" or "situation" (1934: 199). Our experiences, as noted by Dewey, never refer to objects or events analyzed in isolation, but are always within the frames of some "contextual entirety". The context gives precisely the "situation" where, as Dewey writes, it is essential that it is "totally infiltrated" by "quality", which in turn decides about its coherence or "contextual entirety". The "presence" of this "quality" is therefore a relevant distinguishing factor defining the relation of experience (in the first of the above-mentioned meanings) to the situation. Therefore, the experience is understood as an "experience of situation". It happens thanks to the "quality" common to both categories, which permits one to distinguish the particular individual "experience", defined by the specific organization of elements and relations creating a "contextual entirety", from "experience in general" (in the second sense mentioned above). This is the consequence of constitutive properties that in the cognitive act appear to us as "directly given" and independent of the discourse. In this way, aesthetic experience resolves itself, in the understanding proposed by Dewey, into the variant of the direct cognitive act. This moment determines the first contact point between Peirce's and Dewey's conceptions of aesthetic experience.

Conclusions

Following from the above remarks, we can state that the "contextual entirety" or "situation" is experienced, according to Dewey, as an undeniable whole. We perceive here a distinct parallel to the formulation of Peirce, where experience understood as a cognitive act is "part" of a semiosis and as such through interpretation it constitutes the interpretant (which is the result of experience regardless of what kind of experience it is). Since this type of the discussed experience is identified with the category of Firstness, we still remain in the sphere of interpretants classified as "the first ones". In this connection, on the one hand we deal with the emotional interpretant contrasted with energetic and logical ones; on the other hand, we have the direct interpretant (next to the dynamic and the final one) appearing in turn as a constitutive co-member of the emotional interpretant, as a consecutive co-member, next to the dynamic co-member of the energetic interpretant, and as the constitutive co-member, next to the dynamic and final ones, of the logical interpretant.

The phases of experience distinguished by Dewey, defined as aesthetic, practical, and intellectual, bring to mind the classification and articulation of the interdependence of categories and interpretants. The aesthetic phase of experience corresponds to Peirce's category of Firstness; the practical phase indicates a definite action, and behavior is equivalent to the category of Secondness; and the intellectual phase corresponds to Thirdness (here, the analogy is more than obvious). Continuing our comparison, we perceive that the aesthetic dimension of

Dewey's experience can be interpreted as Peirce's emotional interpretant, the practical moment of experience as energetic interpretant; and finally the intellectual moment is connected with the logical interpretant. This "structural" correspondence of Dewey's aesthetics and Peirce's theory of interpretants determines the first stage of the comparison of both conceptions.

The second stage, discussed earlier, is defined by the thesis of a homogeneous treatment by both philosophers of the category of emotive, unmediated experience, which from the aesthetic point of view is the most desired moment, generating further phases of experience that may but do not have to occur. According to Dewey, what is "direct in experience" is revealed by the fact that it is not verbalizable, it cannot be determined or defined, it can only be "shown". In Peirce's system of interpretants, this situation corresponds to the function of a direct interpretant.

So, the aesthetic thread of Peirce's theory of interpretants refers in fact to two problems. Firstly, the aesthetic experience in its most pure form takes place in the act of cognition that constitutes the emotional direct interpretant. This conclusion is backed up by: (a) the primary function of the direct interpretant connected with (b) the category of "feeling" (emotive moment). On the other hand, what is "aesthetic", the first phase of experience, organizes in some way the further stages of experience, constituting thereby the energetic and logical interpretants. It is obvious, as follows from the remarks above, that each of these types of experience have semiotic status, although they refer to different organizational levels within the universum of signs.

The *axio-teleological* situation of the semasiological interpretation is always determined by reference to the realized aim, that is, the "discovery" of the interpretant; yet each time it is determined by the type of experience. Due to subjective relativization, the experience imparts to the interpretation a degenerated character since in its result "there appear" sign-defining meanings anchored in extra-sign reality.

Concluding, one must stress that as a result of the para-aesthetico-semiotic view of the creator of pragmatism there appears a clear, though maybe not very attractive, picture of the discussed problems. We obtain a conception with a distinctly emotive inclination, accentuating aesthetically the fundamental role of direct experience. Yet according to Peirce's epistemological pansemiotism, in order to become "final and valid" the experience must be mediated by a sign (cancellation of the moment of directness). This gives in effect a conception of cognition as a continuum whose stages, inseparably connected with each other, create on the one hand the "horizontal" dimension in compliance with the synergistic nature of any cognition; and on the other hand, they form the "vertical" dimension "created" by the overlapping but "holistic" cognitive acts and their semantic "effects" (interpretants), having at their foundation the aesthetic cognition (emotional interpretant respectively) understood here as the most rudimentary and prereflexive form of cognition-experience.

Note

1. Buczyńska refers to the logical interpretant as the "intellectual interpretant" (1975: 132).

References

Bense, M. (1980). *World as the Prism of Signs* [in Polish], trans. J. Garewicz. Warsaw.
Buczyńska, H. (1970). *Values and Fact: Considerations about Pragmatism* [in Polish]. Warsaw.
– (1975). *Sign, Meaning, Value* [in Polish]. Warsaw.
– (1981). "The notion of a degenerated sign" [in Polish], *Studia Semiotyczne* 11, 121–140.
Dewey, John (1934). *Art as Experience*. New York.
– (1935). "Peirce's theory of quality", *Journal of Philosophy*.
Greenlee, D. (1973). *Peirce's Concept of Sign*. The Hague: Mouton.
Hill, W.H. (1930). *Peirce's Pragmatic Method* (= Philosophy of Science).
Murphy, M. (1967). "Peirce", *The Encyclopedia of Philosophy*, vol. 6, P. Edwards (ed.), 76–77.
Peirce, Charles S. (1931–1935). *Collected Papers of Charles S. Peirce*. Vols 1–6, C. Hartshore and P. Weiss (eds.). Cambridge, MA: Harvard University Press.

Quine, W. V. (1986). "The place of pragmaticists in empiricism" [in Polish], *Limits of Science and Other Philosophic Essays* 1, trans. B. Stanosz. Warsaw: n.p.
Zeman, J. (1988). "Peirce's theory of sign", *A Perfusion of Signs*, Thomas A. Sebeok (ed.). Bloomington, IN: Indiana University Press.

Musical semiosis and the *rasa* theory

JOSÉ LUIZ MARTINEZ

> Her breast adorned with saffron, embraced by her man of
> expert taste in music, so shines Āsāvarī, in the minds of
> the sages.
>
> (*Catvariṁsacchatarāganirūpaṇa* 22,
> in Danielou 1980: 164)

Indian aesthetic theories have dealt with matters related to perception
and signification for at least two thousand years. Although the variety of
approaches, in time and space, leads the several outlasting Sanskrit treatises into inconsistencies (if compared without a proper historical view),
musical practice, especially in North India, persists in relating musical
structures to categories of sentiment, proper performance times of the
day, Indian myths, deities, seasons and festivals. It seems to me that a
semiotic study — based on the semiotic theory developed by the
American logician and philosopher Charles Sanders Peirce (1839–1914)
— can help listeners, musicians, and scholars to understand better those
forms of semiosis.

Peircean semiotics has often been seen, at least in the last twenty
years, as a possible theory on which to base musical signification
studies. Attesting to this fact is the work of Coker (1972), Oliveira
(1979), Fischer (1985), Tarasti (1987, 1994a, 1994b), Lidov (1987),
Karbusicky (1987), Santaella Braga (1988), Hatten (1989) Monelle
(1991), Dougherty (1993), Mosley (1995) and Mirigliano (1995). Still,
applications of Peircean semiotic concepts to music have usually been
limited to short references or odd interpretations (with a few good
exceptions). Such applications are usually brief and undeveloped, and
most of them fail to realize that Peirce designed his work as intermingled
theories. His classification of signs, a powerful analytical system, could
easily be misunderstood without deep knowledge of its grounds. Joseph
Ransdell has warned: "As important as this classification system is, its

effective use is necessarily limited by the extent to which one understands something of the philosophical ideas at its basis" (1977: 158).

To achieve a theory of musical signification of this kind, it is necessary to build on a thorough Peircean semiotic foundation, little by little (the subject is too broad), and under the critical eye of a community of researchers. One objective of my research is to develop part of such a project. My first step (master's thesis) was to apply to music the well-known Peircean semiotic concepts of icon, index, and symbol. Dealing with the question of reference, my thesis analyses how signs in music can stand for their objects (musical or non-musical). In that study, I verified that Peircean semiotics is quite apt to ground signification analyses, ranging from absolute music to every kind of program music; to musical metalanguage; to systems such as *Affektenlehre*, *Figurenlehre*, leitmotifs; contextual references (cultural, historical, etc.); and also aspects of musical cultures from the East (see Martinez 1991, 1994, 1996).

Concerning the investigation of South Asia culture, there are already anthropological studies grounded on Peirce's semiotics. Milton Singer (1984) is a pioneer in this respect. Peirce, in Singer's work, far from clashing with the Indian rationale, helps us to understand better a society full of ambiguities and overlapping categories. Amazingly, Singer even thinks that "Peirce's world view is much closer to the Indian than to the Western" (1984: 184). It seems to me that ethnomusicology would benefit from a Peircean semiotic theory of music. In the first part of this article, I will present the semiotic foundations, which support the second part, the study of *rasa* in Hindustani classical music.

The concept of musical sign and semiosis

In Charles Sanders Peirce's architectural classification of the sciences (see Kent 1987), phenomenology is the science that supplies elementary conceptions to the group he called normative sciences: aesthetics, ethics and semiotics (or logic). In this sense, phenomenology — the study of phenomena as immediately present — precedes semiotics. The object matter of Peirce's phenomenology is the *phaneron,* "the collective total of all that is in any way or in any sense present to the mind, quite regardless of whether it corresponds to any real thing or not" (CP 1.284). The *phaneron* can be understood and analyzed by means of the Universal Categories: Firstness, Secondness and Thirdness. Peirce wrote a paper, in early 1888 (completed just after his famous *A Guess at the Riddle),* ironically titled *Trichotomic,* in which he describes in simple terms his categories: "First is the beginning, that which is fresh, original, spontaneous, free. Second is that which is determined, terminated, ended, correlative, object, necessitated, reacting. Third is the medium, becoming, developing, bringing about. A thing considered in itself is a unit. A thing considered as a correlate or dependent, or as an effect, is second to something else. A thing which in anyway brings one thing into relation with another is a third or medium between the two" (Peirce 1992:280). Another important point is that Peirce's categories are not isolated spheres. Their logical rule of interdependency states that firstness is independent; secondness encompasses firstness; and thirdness encompasses secondness and firstness.

From the phenomenological categories of Peirce one can infer that every musical *phaneron* can present itself as mere acoustical qualities (firstness), as particular existents (secondness), or as habits, laws, or signs (thirdness). There are many other possibilities for musical classifications based on Peirce's universal categories, obviously because they were thought out as *universal:* "a category is an element of phenomena of the first rank of generality" (CP 5.43). It is important to bear in mind that his categories manifest themselves in a multitude of aspects of Peircean semiotics and in its classification of signs. The very idea of Semiosis, "the triadic nature of the operation of a sign" (CP 5.484), is a genuine triadic process, in which three relata take part:

> a sign endeavours to represent, in part at least, an Object, which is therefore in a sense the cause, or determinant, of the sign even if the sign represents its object falsely. But to say that it represents its Object implies that it affects a mind, and so affects it as, in some respect, to determine in that mind something that is mediately due to the Object. That determination of which the immediate cause, or determinant, is the Sign, and of which the mediate cause is the Object may be termed the Interpretant. (CP 6.347)

The Sign is a First that is determined by a Second, its Object, to a Third, its Interpretant which is usually another sign. The object can also be a semiotic object, that is, a previous sign. Therefore, the triadic nature of semiosis is essentially dynamic. It could be understood as a chain, or web of signs, since semiosis is a continuous interpretation process.

The structure of the sign and the nature of its action unfold through sign classification. In 1903 Peirce conceived it as three trichotomies (CP 2.243), based on the relations between the three semiosis relata: the sign in itself; the sign related to its object; and the sign related to its interpretant. Each trichotomy encompasses three kinds of sign (CP 2.244–252), which are submitted to the logical architecture of firstness, secondness, and thirdness (see Table 1). Then, upon the basic trichotomies, follows the logical combination of these nine kinds of sign, establishing ten sign classes (CP 2.254–263).

	FIRSTNESS	SECONDNESS	THIRDNESS
THE SIGN IN ITSELF	qualisign	sinsign	legisign
THE SIGN RELATED TO ITS OBJECT	icon	index	symbol
THE SIGN RELATED TO ITS INTERPRETANT	rheme	dicent	argument

Table 1. Peirce's basic trichotomies.

Anything, acoustical or not, could be a musical sign if somehow related to some kind of musical semiosis. The first rank of musical signs are acoustical phenomena, of course. But there are other possibilities such as scores, recordings, musical instruments, musical cultures, etc. One can find simple Indian musical examples for the three basic trichotomies. Concerning the sign related to itself: qualisign, a sound quality (e.g., the timbre of a tāmbūra); sinsign, an individual existent (e.g., a live performance of Tānsen's *rāga Myāṅ kī Toḍī*); legisign, a musical structure as a law or convention (e.g., the *kāyadā,* a tablā solo form). Concerning the sign related to its object: icon, a sign that represents its object by the fact that there is qualitative likeness to it (e.g., the heavy pakhāvaj drum strokes in a composition, representing the steps of Gaṇeśa, the elephant headed god); index, a sign that represents its object by means of dynamic relations to it (e.g., a *Nagasvaram* solo, as a sign of South Indian music); symbol, a sign that is interpreted as representing its object merely by habit or convention (e.g., a national anthem, such as the *Bande Mataram;* or a certain śahnāī melody, in *rāga Mālakauńsa,* played at weddings in North India). Concerning the relations sign-interpretant: rheme, a sign of possibility to its interpretant (e.g., an accompanist drummer, trying to figure out the *tāla* from the very first beats, when the soloist starts singing or playing the metered section); dicent, a factual sign to its interpretant (e.g., recognition of a certain composition at a concert); argument, a sign that represents its object as a sign to its interpretant (e.g., the *rasa* of a *rāga,* for an expert).

To achieve more accurate semiotical analysis, however, it is necessary to take semiosis into more precise account. Peirce divided the concepts of object and interpretant (which increases sign classification to ten distinct trichotomies, left by Peirce to future explorers; see CP 8.344). These finer divisions of object and interpretant are necessary in musical analysis since they reveal important features of semiosis.

Peirce envisioned the concept of object as twofold: immediate object and dynamical object. The immediate object is the object as represented in the sign. It is the inner part of the sign and conditioned by the representation. The dynamical object is the object in itself, and it determines the sign (see CP 8.183; also Ransdell 1986: 679–680). Musically, the immediate object of a composition (as sound construct) or a musical performance will be those very acoustic qualities. The dynamical object of the same kinds of sign will depend on each particular case. For example, take the *Bande Mataram,* mentioned above, as a sign: its acoustic features are the immediate object. If, for a certain listener, only those very acoustic features are meaningful, then the dynamical object is identical to the immediate object. The sign is an icon (pure music). However, if the cultural context of India is taken as the dynamical object of the sign, from this point of view, the *Bande Mataram* is an index of India. Further, taking into account the political situation in India at the beginning of the twentieth century, when the song was often performed concluding classical music recitals with a political tinge, the *Bande Mataram* represents the struggle for independence. In that case, the dynamical object is an idea related to the sign's immediate object (the same acoustic features of the above mentioned cases) on the basis of habit. The sign is a symbol.

The interpretant was divided by Peirce into three concepts: immediate, dynamical, and final. The interpretant, in general, is a process, a chain of sign translations. But there are important features revealed through division and subdivision. As the immediate object, the immediate interpretant is part of the sign. According to Ransdell (1986: 682), it is "the range — always vaguely circumscribed — of the interpretant-generating power of the sign at a given time." Music offers a wide range of possible interpretants, which can be actualized from emotional or energetic to logical, according to another of Peirce's divisions (CP 5.475).

The action of a sign leads to the dynamical interpretant or "the actual effect produced upon a given interpreter on a given occasion in a given stage of his consideration of the sign. This again may be 1st a feeling merely, or 2nd an action, or 3rd a habit" (Peirce MS. 339d: 546–547, in Johansen 1985: 247). Thus, an actual listener could dynamically interpret a musical sign as (first) pure sound qualities (or qualities of feeling), as (second) inner action (mental or endosomatic) or body movement (dancing or working), or as (third) intellectual construction (analysis or any kind of rational listening).

The term final interpretant refers to "the manner in which the Sign tends to represent itself to be related to its Object" (CP 4.536 and also 8.315, 8.414). Ransdell considers the final interpretant as "the totality of all that the sign-powers of a given sign would have manifested when it had shown all that it could be — all it could *do* — as a sign" (1986: 682). But the real accomplishment of this idea, especially in music, would be very occasional, since sign development could be infinite. It would be better to think of final musical interpretants as a continuous process of interpretation fulfillment. That is, if signification is, in the immediate interpretant, at a potential level and, in the dynamical interpretant, at an actual level, it is in the final interpretant that the sign manifests its tendency to grow, or better, its teleology. Consider the remote sign chain that nourished the idea of *rāga* as a flavor to be tasted by the mind (via the theory of *manorasaromaka*, explained bellow), which is hardly known by Westerners, even though they may listen to and enjoy Indian art music in concerts in Europe and America. Consider the possibility that the multitude of existing musical phenomena are simultaneously unfolding and converging upon a tomorrow that will never come. Only examples of such magnitude can account for final interpretants in music.

Fields of musical analysis

From the idea of sign action as a triadic process it becomes clear that musical signification studies can be broadly divided according to the relations between the three relata in the Peircean conception of semiosis; that is, Sign, Object, and Interpretant. Musically, three broad analysis fields can be inferred from: (1) the musical sign in relation to itself, (2) the musical sign in relation to its possible objects, and (3) the musical sign in relation to its interpretants. This division, also supported by the three elementary sign trichotomies (CP 2.243), and by the ten derived classes of signs (CP 2.254 to 2.264), opens the possibility of working with: (First) Intrinsic Musical Semiosis, (Second) Musical Reference, (Third) Musical Interpretation.

Intrinsic Musical Semiosis, or the study of the musical sign in itself, deals with internal musical signification. It constitutes the semiotics of musical materiality. Acoustics and the several music theories (according to the various musical systems) may be supplemented here by semiotic analysis. This field could study issues such as musical qualities or qualisigns (timbre and melodic, rhythmic, formal qualities, etc.), individualities or sinsigns (works, performance differences, replicas or actualization of legisigns, etc.), and laws or legisigns (musical systems, genres, forms, improvisation or development rules, imitation, variation, recurrence, cadences, etc.). In this field, the immediate and dynamical objects of a musical sign are always of an acoustic nature. There is material identity between the two relata.

Musical Reference, or the study of musical signs related to their possible objects, deals with the question of reference to a broad class of objects. Acoustical immediate objects can be related either to sonorous dynamical objects or to non-acoustic objects. This field would investigate issues such as how a musical sign refers to an object, the possible relations between a dynamical object and the immediate object as represented in the sign, and the possible dynamical objects in music and their modes of being. This extensive range of topics can be organized according to different schemes.

As early as 1897 (*On a New List of Categories*), Peirce stated that there are three kinds of representations:

> First. Those whose relation to their objects is a mere community in some quality, and these representations may be termed *likenesses* [later called icons].

> Second. Those whose relation to their objects consists in a correspondence in fact, and these may be termed *indices*. . . .

> Third. Those the ground of whose relation to their objects is an imputed character, which are the same as *general signs*, and these may be termed *symbols*. (CP 1.558)

Later (1903), the three kinds of representations were conceived as the second of three basic trichotomies. This second trichotomy is set "according as the relation of the sign to its object consists in the sign's having some character in itself, or in some existential relation to that object, or in its relation to an interpretant" (CP 2.243). From this point of view, musical representations spread firstly as pure acoustic reference (the question of musical icons) and reference by quality likeness (musical hypoicons); then as existents or signs of existents (index and indexical signs); finally as habitual or conventional reference (symbols). A detailed classification of musical signs is useful and reveals features of musical composition, performance and interpretation that usually go unnoticed or badly explained in musicological studies (see Martinez 1991, 1994, 1996). However, it is necessary to keep in mind the interdependence of signs. Peirce wrote that: "the most perfect signs are those in which the iconic, indicative, and symbolic characters are blended as equally as possible" (CP 4.448). Musical symbols, for instance, manifest themselves by means of replicas, that is sinsigns, which can function as indices, and certainly have iconic qualities.

Musical Interpretation (in a Peircean sense), or the study of the musical sign related to its interpretants, deals with the action of musical signs in an existing or potential mind. It seems that musical interpretation questions can be divided into three sub-fields: (First) musical perception (or "modes of hearing" as suggested by Brazilian music critic J. Jota de Moraes, 1983: 63–70); (Second) performance (or modes of playing, singing, or conducting), and (a double Third) musical scholarship (analysis, criticism, teaching, theorizing and, of course, musical semiotics) and composition (as intellectual elaboration based on all three fields).

At first, it seems possible to apply this framework to every kind of musical phenomenon or musical system, since Peirce's semiotic theory was conceived to be applied to every kind of sign. But, of course, each musical system will determine its own semiotic theory (for the object determines the sign), which will be more a theoretical translation than a rigid model intended to rule over all types of music. However, it is of the greatest importance to notice that this possible semiotic theory of music constitutes an interrelated, flexible structure. There is no isolation between the fields, which could also be organized in different ways. Actually, it is very difficult (and undesirable) to think about one field without referring to the other two. On the other hand, Peirce's later ten trichotomies could expand musical semiotics to hitherto unthought-of limits.

Hindustani music and the *rasa* theory

The classical music of India can be classified as modal, based on the simultaneous development of *tāla* (rhythmic axis) and *rāga* (melodic axis) as materialized in several vocal and instrumental genres. *Tāla* and *rāga* are concepts that refer to both musical structure and particular musical entities, such as *Ektāla* and *rāga Yaman*. The Sanskrit term *rāga* itself points to the aesthetic question, and can be translated variously as coloring, affection, feeling, passion, charm. The word comes from the roots *rāj* or *rañj* and could also be understood as "to be colored" (red in particular), "affected with a strong feeling", "to be delighted with." The purpose of a *rāga*, according to Ravi Shankar (1969: 20), is to fill the listener's mind with color, that is, feeling.

In the *Nātyaśāstra*, a dramaturgy treatise written in the early centuries a.d., attributed to Bharata, we find the earliest available information about early Indian music and aesthetics. Its chapters on music do not take on the concept of *rāga* as understood today (which was a later development), but the *Nātyaśāstra* grounds the subsequent theoretical corpus that concerns musical theory and aesthetics.

The essence of the aesthetical process lies in the concept of *rasa*. According to Prof. Prem Lata Sharma, the word *rasa* has three distinct meanings: "1. Of being the object of perception by the sense of taste — *Rasana*, 2. Of being the essence of anything or any being; the earth is known as *Rasa* as it holds the essence of life for all creatures — vegetable, human or animal, 3. Of being something liquid or dynamic, as opposed to being solid or static" (Sharma 1970: 57). *Rasa,* as a taste to be relished, brings also the idea of immediacy between the experience of tasting and the object of it. However, *rasa* as aesthetical experience is not an instance of transient tasting but a process of enjoying a relish. This is specially clear in Indian music, a musical quality of feeling nourished and relished in a long span of time. The last meaning of the word *rasa* can be translated as sap, that is, a liquid with dynamical properties, the fluid that moves inside the plants.

Rasa, as aesthetic experience, originates from Indian drama theory, frequently explained with food savoring analogies. According to the *Nātyaśāstra:*

> Just as flavour (*rasa*) comes from a combination of many spices, herbs and other substances, so *rasa* (in a drama) comes from the combination of many *bhāvas* [emotions].

Further:

> (It is called *rasa*) because it can be savored (*āsvādyatvāt*). How is *rasa* savored? As gourmets (*sumanas*) are able to savor the flavor of food prepared with many spices, and attain pleasure etc., so

sensitive spectators (*sumanas*) savor the primary emotions suggested (*abhivyañjita*) by the acting out of the various *bhāvas* and presented with the appropriated modulation of the voice, movements of the body and display of involuntary reactions, and attain pleasure, etc. (NŚ 6.31, Masson & Patwardhan's translation 1970:46)

Rasa, in the aesthetic sense, is not just to be experienced. Rather, it should be relished. Abhinavagupta, in his eleventh-century commentary on the *Nātyaśāstra*, states that, at the theater, "One's heart becomes like a spotless mirror, for all of one's normal preoccupations have been completely forgotten, and one is lost in aesthetic rapture, listening to the fine singing and music" (in Masson & Patwardhan 1970: 33). But more than availability is required for aesthetic relish. It is necessary to have aesthetic sensitivity (Firstness), experience (Secondness) and knowledge (Thirdness), since *rasa* are categories of sentiment. The word *rasika* means connoisseur. On the other hand, perfection is required from the performer. The work of art must be *saṃskṛta*, that is, must be conceived as that classical language of India is: refined and masterfully accomplished.

The *Nātyaśāstra* lists eight *rasas* (6.15):

Śṛṅgāra	(the erotic)
Hāsya	(the comic)
Karuṇa	(the pathetic)
Raudra	(the furious)
Vīra	(the heroic)
Bhayānaka	(the terrible)
Bībhatsa	(the odious)
Adbhuta	(the wondrous)

Later, one more was accepted, *Śānta* (tranquillity). Abhinavagupta argued for it, not only as the ninth *rasa*, but also as the main one (see Masson & Patwardhan 1969).

Another term in aesthetic relish is *bhāva*, emotional fervor. It produces the outcome of a *rasa* and thus is directly related to the technical features of the performance. The word comes from the root *bhū:* become, arise, happen. In classical Indian theater theory *bhāva* are the emotions resulting from situations to be acted out; these are divided into two classes: *sthāyibhāva*, main and permanent emotions; and *vyabhicāribhāva*, complementary, but transitory emotions. There are eight *sthāyibhāvas* that, with the help of the thirty-three *vyabhicāribhāvas*, produce the *rasas*. The relationships between the *sthāyibhāvas* and related *rasas* are quite direct:

Sthāyibhāva:	Rasa:
(arouses)	
Rati (love)	*Śṛṅgāra* (the erotic)
Hāsa (laughter)	*Hāsya* (the comic)
Śoka (sorrow)	*Karuṇa* (the pathetic)
Krodha (anger)	*Raudra* (the furious)
Utsāha (energy)	*Vīra* (the heroic)
Bhaya (fear)	*Bhayānaka* (the terrible)
Jugupsā (disgust)	*Bībhatsa* (the odious)
Vismaya (wonder)	*Adbhuta* (the wondrous)
Tattvajñana (knowledge of the truth)	*Śānta* (tranquillity)

Musical expression of the *rasa* in early Indian music concerns emphasis on a special scale degree. It is from the modal function called *aṁśa* that the *charm* (*rāga*) of the song depends (NŚ 28.76). For example, to express *śṛṅgāra* a *jātī* (mode) is indicated, in which the fourth or the fifth is the *aṁśa*, the sonant note, the main modal function of the early Indian musical system. This idea extends to the other seven *rasas*. Therefore, each *jātī* with its own musical structure and inner musical qualities represents a *rasa* and is ascribed to a certain dramatic situation (NŚ 29.1–16).

The *jātī* tradition has long been obsolete, though. Contemporary Indian music follows the *rāga* tradition. But, especially for Hindustani music, *bhāva* still has an important meaning, not explicitly related to note emphasis but to the inner technical and aesthetic qualities of the several *rāgas*.

Each *rāga*, as a musical structure, has its own *rāgabhāva*. As stated by Wim van der Meer (1980: 110), "Every *rāga* represents a musical entity, a tonal complex, pervaded by its own atmosphere. This is called *rāgabhāva* by the musicians." Thus, the relishing of a *rāga* depends on it. During the course of a certain *rāga* performance the *rāgabhāva* emerges and, little by little, causes a particular *rasa* in the mind of the listeners. The realization of these three elements as an aesthetic whole could be received by the audience euphorically, uttering expressions of approval such as: *vāh, vāh, vāh!*

The process, of course, succeeds with a learned audience, since the relation between *bhāva, rāga,* and the related *rasa* is a matter of tradition. One such tradition, which started between the seventh and eleventh centuries with the *Saṅgītamakaranda* treatise, classifies musical entities as male and female, later named *rāga* and *rāgiṇī.* According to Kaufmann (1965: 276), "male *rāgas* represent the *rasa* of passion and heroism, the female ones represent love and humor, and a third, neutral type represents fright, loathsomeness and peacefulness." From the sixteenth century onwards, treatises also translated the aesthetical features of *rāga* to poetry (called *dhyāna*) and miniature paintings. These books are called *rāgamālā* (garland of *rāgas*). Nowadays, scholars consider these traditions as obsolete, yet it is clear that the aesthetic core of contemporary Hindustani *rāga* rests largely on those old traditions.

Analyzing *rasa* semiosis

There are three terms that could be considered the main links in the sign chain that bears the aesthetic process in Hindustani art music: *rāga, bhāva,* and *rasa.* As a whole, these terms are engaged as the three relata of the semiosis: *rāga* is the sign, the entity that represents an object, the *bhāva,* and determines an interpretant, the *rasa.* In an actual performance, a *rāga* is sung or played. If performed correctly, it refers to the *rāgabhāva* and is interpreted, by the attuned audience, as a *rasa.* This kind of representation is only possible for learned listeners, since the relation that grounds the *rāga-bhāva-rasa* process requires knowledge of traditions. Here, the *rāga* will be interpreted as a sign that represents its object as a representamen *per se*, despite any relation of likeness or contiguity that it may have to its object. Therefore, the

Peircean idea of symbol can be applied to understand the semiosis in the aesthetic enjoyment of classical Indian music.

The *rāga-bhāva-rasa* process has many features similar to the idea of semiosis itself and, more particularly, to semiosis as symbol action. There is a rule of interpretation that connects the three elements. For Peirce, "A *Symbol* is a Representamen whose Representative character consists precisely in its being a rule that will determine its Interpretant" (CP 2.292). The meaning produced by *rāga-bhāva-rasa* was the result of a long cultural process that established an association of general ideas as an interpretative habit. The idea of *rasa* is certainly general. What is meant by *rasa* is not particular feelings but prevailing ones. Indeed, the *rasas* are universal categories of emotions. This was very clearly stated by V. Raghavan: "An emotion is recognized as *Rasa* if it is a sufficiently permanent major instinct of man, if it is capable of being delineated and developed to its climax with its attendant and accessory feelings and if there are men of that temperament to feel imaginative emotional sympathy at the presentation of that *Rasa*" (1975:17).

The origin and development of *rāgas,* a continuous cultural process, grows as symbols grow: "A symbol, once in being, spreads among the peoples. In use and in experience, its meaning grows" (CP 2.302). In the case of a performance, the *rāga-bhāva-rasa* semiosis is progressive, brought to interpreters' minds little by little. The growth of the *rāga-bhāva-rasa* process tends to a gradual unveiling of the meaning, which is proper of a symbol interpretant: an infinite and pervasive process of semiosis. It shares some of the same properties that life has. In fact, the idea of continuity is one of the most important elements in Indian culture. It is directly related to Indian cosmology through the concept of *nāda*, primordial, cosmogonic sound. Continuity is thus a common feature for *nāda* and *rasa* (see Rowell 1988: 329).

But the continuous and progressive development of a symbol is goal-oriented. There is a tendency towards a certain direction of meaning, that which is determined by the interpretative rule grounding the symbol. An actual *rāga-bhāva-rasa* entity only exists in order to be interpreted as such, which presupposes listeners able to comprehend it. Paradoxically, the relishing of an emotion in Indian music is a rational process.

Of course, this is not the only way to listen to Indian music. Everyone who recognizes a performance of a *rāga* as a sign of the music of India is interpreting the sign-object relation as a dynamic fact. Hence, the sign is an index. The Indian musical culture is the object to which the sign refers, but the reference here is existential. There would be no Indian music if Indian culture did not exist.

Unlike verbal languages, music can be appreciated as pure sonorous qualities. In this case, a *rāga* does not represent a *bhāva* or musical culture; instead, its object is the musical materiality of the sign. There is material identity of sign and object. Thus, the *rāga* is an icon. It is important to notice that a sign could bear all these three kinds of representation (icon, index, and symbol) at the same time.

From another point of view, *rāga* as a sign in itself should be analyzed according to the first trichotomy. As pure music, a *rāga* is just a flux of acoustical qualities, a qualisign. An actual performance of a *rāga*, as a real existent, is a sinsign or a replica, that is, an actualization of a general musical structure: the *rāga* as a legisign (encompassing all technical features that bear the concept of *rāga*).

The third trichotomy — the relationship of the sign to its interpretant — according to J. Ransdell, "concerns the extent to which the sign limits what its actual interpretant *can* be" (1986: 689). If a *rāga* can only be interpreted as qualitative possibilities, in the instance of listening to it as pure music, then the *rāga* is a rheme and can only be contemplated. If the same sign determines an interpretant of concrete existence, such as a particular culture, performer, style, etc., then it is a dicent and can be either urged or contemplated. Finally, if the meaning of a *rāga* specifies by itself its own interpretant, that is, a particular *rasa*, then the sign is an argument (in a broad sense) that could be submitted (to analysis), urged (by insistence), or contemplated by an actual interpretant (CP 8.338). Notice the cumulative possibilities for the interpretation of an argument.

At this point a cycle of analysis is closed. The basic, direct relationships are shown in Figure 1. They are not exclusive and many other lines and paths could be drawn, according to the ten classes of sign (see CP 2.254–63). The connections between object and interpretant are the result of the mediation of the sign in a triadic cooperation that can not be reduced to simpler dyadic relations. The relations shown by the paths are

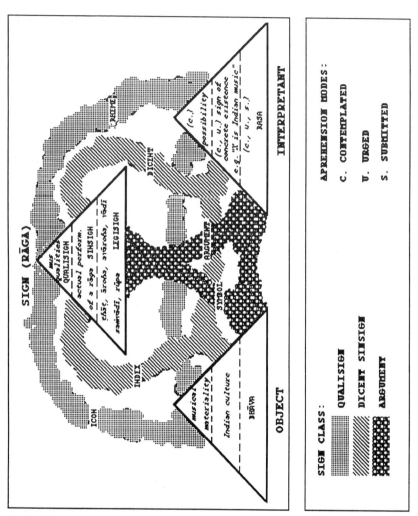

Figure 1. Semiosis in Indian music. Elementary relations.

just the three classes' extremes; that is, qualisign (CP 2.254), dicent sinsign (CP 2.257), and argument (CP 2.263). It is important to realize that signs operate as do Peirce's universal categories: Thirdness encompasses Secondness, and Secondness encompasses Firstness. This is the reason for the pyramidal diagrams. Actually the three pyramid relata (sign, object, and interpretant) are not separate, but join in a multidimensional complex, perhaps similar to a Klein bottle or many bottles simultaneously.

In connection with this semiosis interdependency, the idea that "aesthetic distance" is necessary (Rowell 1992: 328–329) to experience *rasa* seems not to be very precise. It is similar to Wilson Coker's statement about aesthetic emotion: "our deliberate inhibition of the immediate felt tendency affords us a critical contemplative moment in which the rational and affective dispositions blend together in the aesthetic present" (1972: 231). Although "contemplative moment" might apply to very different listening instances concerning Indian or Western music, it is important to remember that rationality does not exclude the category of sentiment. As much as Thirdness encompasses Firstness, the symbol comprehends the icon, and logical reasoning also has its own quality of feeling. In the case of science, it is clear that quality of feeling is a by-product (as the feeling of a superb logical demonstration), although in the *rasa* theory it is the main element. The feeling produced by inference of a *rasa* is not a separate entity but rather a complex whole, of such generality (a distinctive feature of rational thought) as to be shared by all listeners. Feeling and reasoning are joined when one savors *rasa*.

Indeed, at the same moment one could be relishing *śānta rasa*, listening to *rāginī kedāra* performed by Lakshimi Shankar, and enjoying the rich *tāmbūra* timbre of her ensemble. At the other side, on the stage, the *rāgabhāva* could be shown or hidden by the performer. One resource of the great musicians is the ability to display straightforward features of the *rāga* (*āvirbhāva*) masterfully merged with some false musical phrases (*tirobhāva*). Wim van der Meer describes this process of hiding and unveiling as "an almost sensual game of creating confusion ('a cloud covering the moon'), resolved again by a clear statement of the *rāga* (*āvirbhāva*), which as a result stands out even more luminously than before" (1980: 111). This, of course, can not be perceived by an uncultivated audience. Nonetheless, if the interpretation of a symbol, on the one hand, is conditioned by the knowledge of the interpreter, then on the other, it opens plenty of possibilities for aesthetic enjoyment. It encompasses all the other semiotical levels. Thus, there is no paradox about conceptualizing *rasa* as a rational emotion.

The *rāga*, as to its general capacity of coloring or affecting minds, is generous. The Sanskrit expression *manorasaromaka* — relishing an emotion by the mind — refers to its highest instance. Nevertheless, to achieve the relishing of *rasa*, either by means of inference, familiarity, or contemplation, one must be experienced in classical Indian music. As a *gourmet* must know *cuisine*, to enjoy the taste of a *rāga* it is necessary to know *sangīta* (music), Indian mythology, metaphysics, and perhaps the 64 gallant arts that Vātsyāyana listed in the *Kāmasūtra*. Semiosis in Indian art music encompasses the material qualities, existential references, and interpretative rules, which by means of the semiotical body of a *rāga* constitutes the traditional conception of aesthetic emotion.

However, that is not all. According to Abhinavagupta, who established the final form of the *rasa* theory, the ultimate experience of *rasa* is a state of delight — "aesthetical rapture" — whose prevailing feeling is *śānta*. In the *Abhinavabhāratī*, the commentary on the *Nātyaśāstra* written by Abhinavagupta, *śānta* is compared with the white thread of a necklace:

> What is the nature of its true relish? It is the following: The nature of the soul is tinged by *utsāha*, *rati*, etc., which are capable of imparting their (peculiar) tinges to it. It is like a very white thread that shines through the interstices of sparsely threaded jewels. It assumes the forms of all the various feelings like love, etc., (which are superimposed on it), because all these feelings are capable of imparting their tinges on it. Even then it shines out (through them), according to the maxim that once this *Ātman* [self or soul] shines, (it shines forever). (in Masson & Patwardhan 1969:142)

In this analogy, or rather, diagram, Abhinavagupta compares the *bhāvas* with precious stones. Each of them have their different colors, or qualities. Their projection on the white thread, which stands for the spectator's consciousness, represents the *Nātyaśāstra's* eight *rasas*. Although the colors tinge the continuous thread, its essence remains constant, shining clear between the jewels. The Indian philosophies recognize tranquility as the core of mind. For Abhinavagupta, who was also a philosopher and a Tantric yogi, the aesthetical experience is akin to that of a mystic. In its ultimate stage, the spectator reaches the deepest sources of all mental activities. By means of poetry, drama or music, a *rasika* is able to experience, at least for a while, the same bliss achieved by the yogi after years of training and disciplined meditation.

Rasa is not limited to the *bhāvas* or *rāgabhāva* presented on the stage. Those are signs which, once the inference process necessary to their intellectual absorption is achieved, allow the semiosis processes still to proceed. This time, arguments fade away in favor of their qualities of feeling, which by their own nature, resonates sympathetically (iconically) with the deep level of a consciousness. There, in the *Ātman,* the substratum of all mental activities, where resides the instinctual basis of *rasa,* the *rasika* founds the "pleasure of knowing Brahman as being of the form of the resonance of a bell (*ghaṇtyanuraṇana*)" (Masson & Patwardhan 1969:28). For Abhinavagupta, all *rasas* correspond to variations, colors, on a white screen, whose fundamental form is *śānta.* Several Indian philosophies endorse the idea that *śānta* is the state of mind connected to the highest of human aspiration: *mokṣa,* liberation. Further, the "poetic delight called *Rasa* is always of a non-worldly (*alaukika*) character, shorn as it is of all mundane associations, a limitless, unbounded and ineffable bliss, and hence is of the form of *Śānta*" (Raghavan 1975:198). Is there any feeling that is more apt than *śānta* to represent the essence of Indian music? Yet, other Indian aestheticians thought differently. For Bhoja (eleventh century), it is *śṛṅgāra* that constitutes the rasa synthesis; and for the Vaiṣnava rhetoricians of Bengal, it is rather *bhakti* (devotional love).

But I am diverging of the main question: what is the semiotic constitution of the highest stage of *rasa?* Considering the Abhinavagupta paradigm, it seems to be the reverse of semiosis. The ultimate aesthetic experience is not a logical interpretant — the generality and convention of *rāga-bhāva-rasa* symbolic relation. Following the sensuality of a hide-and-seek intellectual game, the performance leads semiosis in Indian music into a vertiginous dive: the formalized feeling loses its personal character, the *rasika* ignores the actual circumstances of a concert, and the enjoyment of music gives birth to a special state of mind: *ānānda* (peacefulness). At this point, the limit of the *rasika's* ego is overcome. The spectators' mind overflows and blends, as Abhinavagupta writes. A particular *rasa* is also transcended, as well as time and space. Still, there is delight and bliss. The only semiotic idea that matches with such a state of consciousness is that of Firstness. Signification in Indian music looks like a multidimensional labyrinth. The doorways of feeling, existence and knowledge are on different levels, but at the same time they overlap. The ultimate aesthetic experience in Indian art music is a pervasive quality of feeling.

Rasa and *rāga*

To give an outline of some *rāgas* and expressed *rasas*, as well as to show some of the Indian scholarship discrepancies in time and space, I selected some Hindustani *rāgas* (Examples 1–7) and their related poetic texts, called *dhyāna* (contemplation, reflection), from *rāgamālā* treatises (according to Danielou 1980). The indicated *rasa* were inferred abductively from the *dhyāna* contents. The tradition which related music, poetry and painting flourished during the sixteenth and seventeenth centuries. Only the words and images survived, and it is not possible to relate with certainty the mentioned *rāgas* with their contemporary forms.

Danielou quotes those *dhyānas* in connection to the contemporary *rāgas* he describes. Each *rāga dhyāna* I have chosen has a musical illustration transcribed roughly to the musical staff. The basic technical features of the *rāga* are: scalar configuration, both ascending (*ārohana*) and descending (*avārohana*); tonic and main modal functions (*vādī* and *samvādī*); and essential melodic motives (*rūpa*). I also present, when available, the contemporary interpretation about the *rasa* connected to each *rāga*.

1. *Rāginī Āsāvarī,* that is, a female *rāga*, represents *śṛṅgāra* (the erotic), according to the following *dhyāna*. It has to be performed in the morning. In contemporary practice, the eroticism gives place to a quiet and gentle mood (Kaufmann 1968:463). A *gentle mood* is not a classical *rasa*. Yet it can still be a complementary emotion related to *śṛṅgāra*.

> I remember *Āsāvarī,* all clad in red, eating pomegranates. Fair, with lovely nails, her arm supports heavy breasts. Holding a cushion she

bends her body and shows her face, loosening her garments in her eagerness for pleasure. (*Rāgasāgara* 3.65, in Danielou 1980:164)

Example 1. Śṛṅgāra, Rāginī Āsāvarī, morning.

2. *Rāginī Dhanāśrī* represents *Karuna* (the pathetic). Its performing time is the afternoon. Nowadays, Indian musicians think that this *rāginī* expresses a light and cheerful mood (Kaufmann 1968:365). It is hardly performed, except for its composite form: *Pūriyā Dhanāśrī.*

Charming is *Dhanāśrī*, her body sombre like the *durvā* grass. Her cheeks are pale with the torment of separation. The tear drops falling on her breast, she is writing to her beloved. (*Saṅgītadarpana* 2.70, in Danielou 1980:220)

3. *Rāga Kalyāna* represents *raudra* (the furious). Its performing time is the evening (sunset). According to Walter Kaufmann, contemporary

Example 2. Karuna, Rāginī Dhanāśrī, late afternoon.

Indian musicians believe this *rāga* brings luck, blessing and soothing feelings (1968:62). In its current form, it is called *Yamana kalyāna*.

> Blood-red, sword in hand, his forehead marked with sandal paste, he enters the battle robed in gold. The sages speak of *Kalyāna* as the embodiment of fury. (*Sangītadarpana* 2.82, in Danielou 1980:269)

Example 3. Raundra, rāga Kalyāna, early evening.

4. *Rāga Mālakauñsa* represents *vīra* (the heroic). It must be performed at night. According to Ustad Amjad Ali khan (personal communication), this *rāga* still express *vīra,* as the medieval treatises state. Kaufmann mentions seriousness (1968:535).

> His mace running with blood, garlanded with the skulls of heroes, *Mālakauñsa*, surrounded by braves, and bravest of the brave! (*Sangītadarpana* 2.52 in Danielou 1980:324)

Example 4. Vīra, rāga Mālakauñsa, night.

5. *Rāgiṇ ī Kāmodī* represents *bhayānaka* (the terrible). It has to be performed in the evening. Kāmodī is obsolete in Hindustani music. Its contemporary form, kāmoda, refers to the happiness of springtime.

> In the forest, dressed in yellow and with lovely hair, *Kāmodī* looks about on every side in terror. Thinking of her lover, even the cuckoo's happy cry fills her with desperation. (*Saṅgītadarpaṇa* 2.68, in Danielou 1980:272)

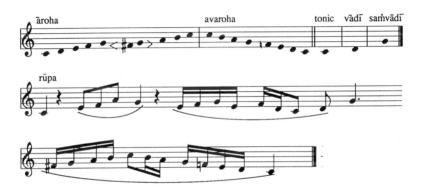

Example 5. Rāga Kāmoda, evening.

6. *Rāga Bhairava* represents *adbhuta* (the wondrous). Its proper performing time is sunrise. *Bhairava* is one of the most important *rāgas,* considered "the first among them", in the medieval treatises. *Bhairava* is a form of the god Śiva. According to Dr. Ritwik Sanyal (personal communication), this *rāga* is poignant and sublime. Kaufmann writes that it expresses an awesome grandeur (1968:233).

> Upholding Ganga, the crescent moon upon his brow, three-eyed, wrapped in the skin of an elephant and adorned with snakes, his scarf white, his garland of human skulls, armed with a burning trident — so triumphs Bhairava, the first of *rāga*. (*Saṅgītadarpaṇa* 2.46, in Danielou, 1980:125)

Example 6. Adbhuta, rāga Bhairava, dawn.

7. *Rāginī Kedāra* represents *śānta* (tranquility), It is to be performed at sunset. Kaufmann mentions the belief that *Kedāra* has magical properties (1965:289, 1968:88), which is something also found in yogic lore.

> Her matted locks are crested with the silver moon, her breast and shoulders wreathed with snakes. Wearing the veil that Yogis use in meditation, her mind immersed in contemplation of the Lord of Sleep [Śiva] upholder of the Ganges. (*Saṅgītadarpaṇa* 2.65, in Danielou 1980: 277)

Example 7. Śānta, rāginī Kedārā, sunset.

These few *rāgas* (among the existing two or three hundreds), of course, can not illustrate the complex web of significations implicit in Indian musical aesthetics. They should not be taken as one to one reference, since there are divergences within the several traditions and sources. As indicated by the poems, some *rāgas* have had their *rasas* modified through the centuries. Nowadays, musicians often refer to *rasas* that do not correspond to the classical nine. Missing are two *rasas* not employed in classical music: *hāsya* (the comic), and *bībhatsa* (the odious). Other *rāgas* were later developed by great musicians who did not use the *rāgamālā* system. Indeed, Indian art music is not a frozen tradition. It has been and still is in transformation, and in this century has gained more and more new adepts abroad. On the one hand, the constant transformation and addition of new followers help to preserve the tradition, which is perhaps the oldest musical culture in the world. On the other hand, new followers rejuvenate the purely musical aspects of Indian music (especially as regards instrumental virtuosity), as well as its cultural and aesthetic representations.

References

Bharata (1967). *Nātyaśāstra,* trans. by Manomohan Ghosh, 2 vols. Calcutta: Manisha Granthalaya. [References as NŚ (chapter).(verse)].

Coker, W. (1972). *Music and Meaning.* New York: Free Press.

Danielou, A. (1980). *The Rāgas of Northern Indian Music.* New Delhi: Munshiram Manoharlal.

Dougherty, W.P. (1993). "The Play of Interpretants: A Peircean Approach to Beethoven's Lieder", *The Peirce Seminar Papers: An Annual of Semiotic Analysis,* M. Shapiro (ed.), vol. 1, 67–95. Oxford: Berg.

Fischer, G. R. (1985). "How Music Communicates", *Semiotica* 53(1/3), 131–144.

Hatten, Robert (1989). A Peircean Perspective on the Growth of Markedness and Musical Meaning. Paper presented at the C. S. Peirce Sesquicentennial International Congress, Harvard University.

Johansen, J. D. (1985). "Prolegomena to a Semiotic Theory of Text Interpretation", *Semiotica* 57(3/4), 225–288.

Karbusicky, V. (1987). "The Index Sign in Music", *Semiotica,* Eero Tarasti (guest ed.) 66(1/3), 23–35.

Kaufmann, W. (1965). "Rasa, Rāga-Mala, and performance times in North Indian rāgas", *Ethnomusicology* 9 (3), 272–291.

– (1968). *The Rāgas of North India.* New Delhi: Oxford and IBH.

Kent, B. (1987). *Charles S. Peirce — Logic and the Classification of the Sciences.* Kingston and Montreal: McGill University Press.

Lidov, D. (1987). "Mind and Body in music", *Semiotica*, Eero Tarasti (guest ed.) 66(1/3), 69-97.

Martinez, J. L. (1991). Música e Semiótica: Um Estudo Sobre a Questão da Representação na Linguagem Musical [Music and Semiotics: a Study on Musical Representation]. Unpublished M. A. dissertation, Pontifícia Universidade Católica de São Paulo (Catholic University of São Paulo, Brazil).

– (1994). "Practicing Musical Semiotics", *Musiikkitiede* 6(1/2), 158-163.

– (1996). "Icons in Music: a Peircean Rationale", *Semiotica* 110(1/2).

Masson, J. L. & Patwardhan, M. V. (1969). *Śāntarasa and Abhinava-gupta's Philosophy of Aesthetics*. Bhandarkar Oriental Series 9. Poona: Bhandarkar Oriental Research Institute.

– (1970). *Aesthetic Rapture*, 2 vols. Poona: Deccan College.

Meer, W. van der (1980). *Hindustani Music in the 20th Century*. New Delhi: Allied Publishers.

Mirigliano, R. (1995). "The sign and music: A reflection in the theoretical basis of semiotics", *Musical Signification,* E. Tarasti (ed.), 43-61. Berlin, New York: Mouton de Gruyter.

Monelle, Raymond (1991). "Music and the Peircean Trichotomies", *IRASM* 22(1), 99-108.

Moraes, J. J. de (1983). *O que é Música*. São Paulo: Brasiliense.

Mosley, D. L. (1995). "Peirce's 'ground' and the 19th-century Lieder", *Musical Signification,* E. Tarasti (ed.), 413-421. Berlin, New York: Mouton de Gruyter.

Oliveira, W. C. de (1979). *Beethoven Proprietário de Um Cérebro*. São Paulo: Perspectiva.

Peirce, C. S. (1938-1956). *Collected Papers*, C. Harshorne, P. Weiss, and A. Burks (eds.). Cambridge: Harvard University Press. [References as CP (volume).(paragraph)].

– (1992). *The Essential Peirce,* N. Hauser and C. Kloesel (eds.), vol. 1. Bloomington: Indiana University Press.

Raghavan, V. (1975). *The Number of Rasas,* 3rd. ed. Madras: Adyar Library and Research Centre.

Ransdell, J. (1977). "Some Leading Ideas of Peirce's Semiotics", *Semiotica* 19(3/4), 157-178.

– (1986). "Peirce, Charles Sanders", *Encyclopedical Dictionary of Semiotics*, T. Sebeok (ed.), 673-694. The Hague: Mouton.

Rowell, L.(1988). "Music in India and the Ancient West", *Essays on the Philosophy of Music*, V. Rantala, L. Rowell, and E. Tarasti (eds.), 323-342. Helsinki: Philosophical Society of Finland.

– (1992). *Music and Musical Thought in Early India*. Chicago: University of Chicago Press.

Santaella Braga, M. L. (1988). "For a Classification of Visual Signs", *Semiotica* 70(1/2), 59-78.

Shankar, R. (1969). *My Music, My Life*. New Delhi: Vikas.

Sharma, P. L. (1970). "Rasa Theory and Indian Music", *Sangeet Natak Academy* (journal) 16, 57–64.

Singer, M. (1984). *Man's Glassy Essence — Explorations in Semiotic Anthropology.* Bloomington: Indiana University Press.

Tarasti, E. (1987). "Some Peircean and Greimasian Semiotic Concepts as Applied to Music", *The Semiotic Web 1986,* Thomas Sebeok and Jean Umiker-Sebeok (eds.), 445–459. Berlin/New York/Amsterdan: Mouton de Gruyter.

– (1994a). "Can Peirce be Applied to Music?", *Peirce and Value Theory: On Peircean Ethics and Aesthetics,* Herman Parret (ed.), 335–348. Amsterdam/Philadelphia: John Benjamins.

– (1994b). *A Theory of Musical Semiotics.* Bloomington: Indiana University Press.

PRINCIPLES AND CONCEPTS OF MUSIC ANALYSIS

Vers une conception pluraliste de l'analyse musicale

ALFONSO PADILLA

Dans cette article notre propos est de traiter d'une manière générale les fondements de ce qui peut être une conception pluraliste de l'analyse musicale. La notion d'analyse musicale porte ici une double signification; d'un côté la recherche musicale dans un sens très ample: c'est la recherche de la musique entendue comme un réseau complexe de relations de caractères très différents: intrinsèques, externes, sociologiques, anthropologiques, esthétiques, psychologiques, pédagogiques, linguistiques, idéologiques, etc. Comme l'a dit Molino, "le fait musical est un fait social (et anthropologique) total" (1973: 49). Dit d'une autre manière, on peut aborder la musique dans sa relation à tout ou partie de tout de ce qui l'entoure tout aussi bien qu'en elle même. D'un point de vue étroit et spécifique, l'analyse musicale veut dire que la musique peut être étudiée en tant qu'entité fermée et enfermée en soi même, comme une unité formée par des relations intrinsèques spéciales, comme une réalité mise en rapport seulement avec elle même. C'est-à-dire, qu'on peut étudier le texte musical — écrit ou oral — d'une manière *relativement* indépendante de son contexte, quel que soit ce contexte.

La conception pluraliste de la recherche (analyse) musicale se fonde sur le fait que la musique joue un rôle essentiel dans la société humaine de tous les temps et de toutes latitudes. Alan P. Merriam l'a signalé tout en remarquant la différence entre l'*usage* et la *fonction* de la musique: toute musique — n'importe où et quand elle se produit — est fonctionnelle. La musique joue un rôle multiple dans la société, dès la satisfation des nécessités esthétiques jusqu'à celles du divertissement; elle est un élément unificateur de la communauté sociale, et même un facteur essentiel de son identité culturelle.

La recherche musicale, en son sens moderne, a été en charge principalement de deux branches des sciences humaines: la musicologie (générale) et l'ethnomusicologie (autrefois connue sous le nom de musicologie comparée). Cette séparation stricte des deux disciplines à une base *historique* — la musicologie, à l'origine, étudie la musique dite classique ou artistique occidentale (1) — et, d'un autre côté, il y a une raison *socio-politique:* la musicologie comparée se préoccupe de la musique des colonies des pays européens (particulièrement de l'Afrique, de l'Asie et du Prôche et du Moyen Orient), la musique des ethnies indigènes (comme dans toute l'Amérique) ou de certaines régions rurales et appauvries de l'Europe (comme en l'Hongrie et en Finlande). Tant la musicologie que l'ethnomusicologie ont leur point de départ dans une perspective occidentale, comme l'a précisé Nettl (1983: 25). La séparation de la recherche du "fait musical total" s'appuie, pourtant, sur une notion ethnocentriste — eurocentriste — du monde et une attitude colonialiste, deux aspects d'un même phénomène. La persistance aujourd'hui d'une telle séparation des disciplines a des fondements similaires — nous dirions maintenant néocolonialistes –, auxquels s'ajoute un simple besoin de commodité (2).

Les raisons de l'existence de deux disciplines sont, donc, historiques et socio-politiques, mais non scientifiques. À partir de Guido Adler la musicologie s'est centrée dans l'étude de la musique d'art occidentale du point de vue historique, de la théorie musicale (dans un sens large), philosophique, esthétique, organologique et de la pédagogie musicale, et plus tard, psychologique, sociologique et de la technologie du son. La musicologie comparée, devenue à partir des années cinquante ethnomusicologie, étudie toute la musique restante, en mettant l'accent sur les considérations anthropologiques. Cette distinction entre deux disciplines est arbitraire, premièrement, parce que la musique étant un phénomène social total, tous les aspects traités en musicologie générale se retrouvent *dans tous les cultures musicales du monde.* En outre, comme il est connu et même accepté!, il y a des cultures musicales au delà de l'Occident qui ont des systèmes théoriques, philosophiques et esthétiques complexes, y compris des codes de notation et d'écriture très développés. L'ordinateur a été aussi utilisé largement dans des recherches ethnomusicologiques, par exemple, le projet bien connu du *Cantometrics* de Alan Lomax.

L'objet de la musicologie et l'ethnomusicologie

Dans un sens plutôt traditionnel, la musicologie a comme objet d'étude la musique d'art occidentale tandis que celui de l'ethnomusicologie étude "tout le reste", surtout les musiques non-européennes et le folklore musical occidental. Pendant les deux dernières décades on s'est beaucoup intéressé à l'étude de la musique populaire occidentale, avant tout le rock, le pop, le jazz et ces dernières années, la musique connue sous le nom de "the world music". Cette séparation de l'objet d'étude est aussi capricieuse. Edward Elgar et Paul McCartney, par exemple, ont entre eux plus d'éléments communs qu'il n'y en a entre le dernier nommé et la musique classique arabe ou coréenne. D'autre part, Elgar est plus proche de la musique classique japonaise ou du gamelan balinais que Jimmy Hendrix, des cultures musicales d'Orient. Cependant, la musique populaire occidentale — *le dernier grand bastion de la musique tonale* — est étudiée à côté de cultures musicales qui ont des propos, des structures et des significations très différentes. D'autre part, les cultures musicales classiques de l'Orient — par leur systèmes théoriques, philosophiques, esthétiques, pédagogiques, de compositions, d'écriture et d'analyse très élaborés — sont plus proches de la musique d'art occidentale que de la musique africaine tribale ou de la musique indigène de l'Amérique du Sud.

La conception pluraliste de la recherche musicale propose de dépasser cette dichotomie artificielle en postulant l'existence d'une seule science musicale, intégrée, dont l'objet d'étude est, simplement, toute la musique que la société humaine a produite. Certes, un champ aussi étendu exige une spécialisation, comme n'importe quelle branche scientifique, mais a l'avantage de travailler avec des outils méthodologiques communs. Il n'est pas nécessaire de trouver un nouveau nom pour cette science, celui de musicologie est bien suffisant. Il est nécessaire de réintégrer l'ethnomusicologie dans la musicologie générale, ainsi que la recherche de la musique populaire occidentale, qui ces dernières annés, a pris un chemin à peu près distant de l'ethnomusicologie. Cette idée n'est pas nouvelle: dans les années cinquante déjà Charles Seeger avait proposé une chose de ce genre.

Un mythe qui a soutenu, comme une éminence grise, ce divorce des disciplines, c'est l'idée que la seule musique de caractère artistique c'est la musique dite d'art occidentale. Non seulement l'existence millénaire de certaines cultures orientales dément un tel préjugé, mais aussi le fait que beaucoup de membres des différentes cultures musicales du monde, parmi lesquelles la musique folklorique et populaire d'Occident, octroyent à leurs musiques ou à une partie de celles-ci un caractère artistique ou au moins la reconaissance qu' elles sont porteuscs de certaines valeurs esthétiques. L'idée que l'art musical est seulement possible dans le cadre de la musique artistique occidentale, n'est pas uniquement la preuve d'une conception ethno(euro)centriste, mais aussi est un cas de paresse intellectuelle — on répète une vérité immuable par habitude, par commodité, "par tradition" — et, finalement, c'est une situation d'ignorance.

L'idée que c'est seulement dans le cadre de la musique d'art occidentale que peut exister la musique de caractère artistique — thèse si insoutenable que presque jamais on ne l'exprime explicitement, mais qui circule *sotto voce* dans les milieux musicaux et entre les autorités culturelles d'Occident — a un effet qui dépasse le cadre des discussions scientifiques et se manifeste froidement dans la définition et la mise en œuvre des politiques culturelles officielles. Quelques exemples en Finlande: le mot "musique" (sans adjectifs) est réservé à la musique d'art occidentale à la Radio Nationale (YLE) et dans le principal journal du pays (*Helsingin Sanomat*) s'en tient. Selon certaines études (Hurri 1983: 12–13), 95% des ressources de l'État et des municipalités destinées à la musique sont consacrés à soutenir la musique dite "cultivée" ou "artistique" occidentale. Une situation de ce genre se retrouve très probablement dans tous les pays occidentaux et occidentalisés.

Texte et contexte

La deuxième idée qui justifie l'existence de deux branches disciplinaires a un caractère double. D'une part, on définit la musicologie comme une science qui se préoccupe avant tout de l'étude de la structure de la musique (d'art occidentale), c'est-à-dire, du texte musical, tandis que l'ethnomusicologie ferait essentiellement des recherches sur le contexte socio-anthropologique de la musique nèo-occidentale. D'autre part, à partir de ces prémisses, quelques uns affirment que la musique folklorique (le terme est très ambigu) a une structure si simple qu'elle ne présente aucun intérêt immanent, mais seulement sociologique et anthropologique. Examinons ces deux arguments.

Quelques ethnomusicologues ont défini avec une certaine ironie la (supposée) différence méthodologique essentielle entre la musicologie et l'ethnomusicologie: la musicologie étudierait "des notes, partitions"; en revanche, l'ethnomusicologie concevrait la musique "dans la culture", "comme partie de la culture", "en fonction de la culture qui l'entoure" (3). D'un autre côté, quelques musicologues définissent la musicologie comme la science qui étudie le texte musical (la partition). Ces points de vue sont des simplifications grossières de ce qui arrive dans la réalité des deux disciplines. A notre avis la préoccupation *essentielle* (pas unique) de la musicologie aussi bien que de l'ethnomusicologie c'est l'étude du texte musical (4): il s'agit de trouver les lois internes, les traits stylistiques d'une œuvre, pièce, répertoire, d'un corpus musical déterminé (d'un musicien, genre, groupe social, région, pays, époque, etc.). L'analyse du texte musical exige l'étude du contexte culturel-historique d'une musique. La conaissance du contexte socio-culturel n'est pas seulement une nécessité de l'ethnomusicologie, mais également de la musicologie; la différence c'est que dans les études sur la musique d'art occidentale il n'est pas besoin de "partir de zéro" dans l'exposition du contexte, qu' on suppose connu du lecteur.

Si nous observons le contenu des articles dans les plus importantes revues musicologiques nous constatons que dans une forte proportion ils abordent la musique de points de vue très différents (historique, ses relations avec d'autres arts, ses liaisons avec l'idéologie, la philosophie, l'esthétique, la religion, etc.) (5). À l'inverse, dans nombre de publications ethnomusicologiques nous trouvons des articles qui analysent principalement non le contexte culturel, mais le texte musical (6).

Si "musique folklorique" veut dire la tradition musicale de tous les peuples, communautés et sociétés du monde, cette musique traditionnelle présente bien sûr beaucoup d'intérêt "musicologique", c'est-à-dire, d'intérêt pour le texte musical lui-même. Debussy, Stravinsky, Bartók, Villa-lobos, de Falla, Cowell, Messiaen et plus récemment Cage, Ligeti, Berio, Stockhausen, Boulez, Eloy, Reich, Nancarrow, Bergman ont pris aux cultures de divers endroits du monde quelques idées, principes de composition et théoriques, notions musicales, instruments ou façons de jouer de certains d'entre eux, etc. L'intérêt de ces créateurs n'est pas orienté en premier lieu vers les aspects anthropologiques, mais envers la musique elle-même et ses principes de fonctionnement.

Modernité des musiques traditionnelles

À vrai dire, une connaissance profonde et répandue de nombreuses cultures musicales extra-européennes aurait épargné à l'Occident beaucoup de discussions, de recherches et de justifications dans les années 1945–65, période où l'on voit se faire jour les principaux courants de la musique contemporaine, en suite de quoi la musique occidentale a pu innover très peu. Plusieurs des techniques de composition, des conceptions musicales, l'élargissement de la palette sonore caractéristique de la période indiquée, entre autres, existaient déjà, à tout le moins sous la forme de principes ou d'idées sinon comme large mise en practique, en de nombreuses cultures musicales des cinq continents. Nous osons affirmer que — mise à part la musique tonale, phénomène proprement occidental — sauf la musique stochastique (Xenakis) et les apports au monde sonore de l'informatique (par exemple Grisey, Saariaho, Lindberg), question éminement technique, tous les autres principes de composition de la musique contemporaine occidentale ont existé dans les différentes cultures musicales du monde, quelquefois même pendant des siècles et des millénaires. Nous voudrions énumérer quelques unes des idées ou des conceptions de l'utilisation de l'espace sonore dans diverses cultures musicales traditionnelles et qui ont été la préoccupation centrale de nombreux compositeurs contemporains.

– concevoir le champ musical comme illimité, non dépendant d'un système fixe comme, par exemple, l'affination tempérée du piano ou d'instruments similaires;

– existence de modules d'organisation de l'espace sonore autres que l'octave;

– la division de l'octave en intervalles égaux, mais différente de l'échelle chromatique occidentale;

– l'utilisation de microintervalles;

– l'existence d'échelles en nombre illimité;

– des polyphonies formées de parties vraiment indépendantes;

– indépendance dans l'utilisation simultanée de différents paramètres musicaux;

– l'existence de polyrythmique développé;

– le répétitivisme, le "minimalisme";

– des notions de composition circulaires, cycliques;

– la variation constante;

– de conceptions temporelles riches et complexes ;

– l'utilisation diversifiée des ressources vocales;

– incorporation du *bruit* au matériau musical;

– un très riche monde de sonorités, dû à l'utilisation de milliers d'instruments de musique;

– diverses formations musicales, entre autres, des groupes d'instruments à percussion;

– un emploi très diversifié des instruments de musiques;

– l'existence d'une musique "écologique" ou qui utilise dans un sens musical l'environnement naturel (la montagne, l'eau, les forêts, etc.);

– la transposition des conceptions religieuses et cosmologiques en termes musicaux;

– l'existence de manifestations musicales aléatoires;

– l'existence d'événements musicalaux où se trouvent d'autres manifestations artistiques (théâtre, par exemple) d'une manière plus ou moins aléatoire, comme une espèce de "happening";

– la notion "d'œuvre d'art total": musique, danse, théâtre, poésie, arts plastiques, mise en scène, etc.

Universalité de la musicologie et de la sémiotique musicale

La connaissance approfondie des cultures musicales "exotiques" est d'un grand intérêt pour le développement de la musique contemporaine occidentale. Pour le musicologue traditionnel et surtout pour le compositeur, la musique traditionnelle d'autres cultures les obligent à penser la musique selon des critères nouveaux. Quant à l'ethnomusicologue, la connaissance approfondie de la musique occidentale contemporaine lui sera très profitable, par exemple, en utilisant l'écriture moderne, avec laquelle est possible de refléter les complexes phénomènes sonores si fréquents dans les cultures musicales non-européennes.

La musicologie doit aspirer à être une science universelle au sens strict du terme. Elle doit inclure dans son objet d'étude tout le phénomène musical existant et de toutes les époques et latitudes du monde. La linguistique en offre un très bon exemple: c'est une science universelle parce qu'elle a compris le caractère général, universel du phénomène linguistique et l'a assumé en conséquence. De la même façon, si la sémiotique (ou sémiologie) musicale se réclame d'un caractère universel, elle doit aussi essayer d'élargir son objet d'étude et d'arriver à une vision méthodologique globalisante, mais non unique. À la différence de la linguistique, la musicologie (et la sémiotique musicale) n'a pas besoin de concevoir des méthodes analytiques uniques: la si grande diversité des cultures musicales et le caractère très riche de beaucoup d'entre elles, exigent plutôt l'utilisation d'outils analytiques différents.

La conception pluraliste de la recherche musicale envisage l'existence d'une seule science musicale dont l'objet d'étude serait tout le spectre musical de toute l'humanité. Le "fait musical" étant un complexe réseau de relations, la musique peut s'étudier sous des angles très divers et selon diverses méthodes. La vision pluraliste — ou dialectique — n'exclut a priori aucune approximation valable, ne postule pas de voie analytique unique. Tout dépend du matériau à étudier et de ce qu'on veut analyser. Notre vision est méthodologiquement pluraliste. Dans l'ethnomusicologie on discute encore le fait de savoir si la recherche doit être diachronique ou synchronique, être réalisée d'un point de vue émique ou étique et si l'on doit fixer l'attention sur le texte musical ou sur le contexte socio-anthropologique. En musicologie la question est de savoir si l'œuvre d'art musicale est autonome ou non et, selon la réponse donnée, si elle doit être envisagée comme une réalité isolée, absolue, autosuffisante, ou bien dans ses relations avec le monde environnant, le propre monde musical compris.

Le pluralisme méthodologique

À les questions possés auparavant le pluralisme méthodologique — le terme méthode est ici utilisé dans une acception générale et une autre plus particulière — essaye de répondre d'une manière dialectique, créatrice, ouverte à la complexité de l'objet étudié. En accord avec une vision pluraliste, la recherche musicale peut être diachronique et/ou synchronique; l'analyse peut être historique ou non-historique (cependant pas anti-historique). Observons que diachronique n'est pas synonyme d'historique; le diachronique porte l'idée de chronologique, mais pas nécessairement d'historique, c'est-à-dire, dans une relation avec une situation historique déterminée. De la même façon, synchronique n'a pas le sens de non-historique, car une étude peut être synchronique — l'analyse d'un phénomène à un moment donné — mais en conservant ses relations historiques concrètes. De ces deux oppositions (diachronique/synchronique et historique/non-historique) résultent quatre cas possibles: l'analyse peut être diachronique et historique, diachronique et non-historique, synchronique et historique et, enfin, synchronique et non-historique. Tout dépend de ce qu' on veut étudier. L'analyse peut se focaliser sur le texte ou bien sur le contexte; elle peut aussi prendre en compte les deux, organiquement liés ou non; elle peut étudier le texte DANS le contexte ou aussi bien le contexte DANS le texte. En tout cas, il n'est pas possible de faire une étude valable qui exclut absolument l' un ou l'autre aspect: une analyse textuelle comporte, de toute manière, une analyse contextuelle et vice-versa. Or, le texte ne doit pas être confondu avec la musique, le texte musical (oral ou écrit), et le contexte être confondu avec ce qui l'entoure (les condi-tions socio-culturelles et historiques). La musique peut être aussi bien contexte d'un texte discursif sur la musique. Texte et contexte ne sont pas des *choses* dissemblables, mais des *fonctions* distinctes et des moments différents de l'analyse. Comme Mikko Heiniö l'a remarqué avec précision (1992: 10), ce qui est texte dans un sens, peut être contexte dans un autre.

La dichotomie émique/éthique est elle aussi fausse: toute analyse est éthique; elle se fait du point de vue du chercheur, même quand celui-ci est membre de la culture étudiée. L'investigateur n'est pas une personne physique, mais un rôle, une fonction, une perspective. La problématique émique/éthique est trop souvent liée à la situation d'un (e) chercheur occidental qui étudie la musique d'une culture "exotique". Mais, bien sûr, tel membre d'une culture peut étudier certains phénomènes musicaux de sa propre culture. C'est le cas habituel du musicologue dans la culture occidentale: ici on fait la recherche de perspectives à la fois émiques et éthiques. C'est pour cela que la discussion sur l'émique/l'éthique se pose surtout dans le cadre de l'ethnomusicologie. Dans l'ethnomusicologie (et en musicologie aussi) il ne peut y avoir d'analyses valables que si l'on prend en compte les deux optiques. D'une otre part, il est pas justifiable de donner au point de vue émique une valeur absolue; l'investigateur doit toujours maintenir une certaine distance scientifique par rapport à l'objet étudié. La recherche, l'analyse est, essentiellement, selon Jay Rahn, une question d'*interprétation* (1983: 3). Nous partageons la conception dialectique de Nattiez sur la question émique/éthique (1987: 88–89 et 227–244).

A notre avis, l'œuvre d'art n'est pas strictement une entité ontologique absolue. L'œuvre d'art a un conditionnement historique et culturel précis, elle se situe dans l'espace et le temps d'une manière concrète; elle n'existe pas hors de ses coordonnées spécifiques. Cependant, l'œuvre d'art — et nous comprenons par là non seulement celles produites dans des sociétés qui ont un concept d'œuvre d'art — transcende les cadres qui l'ont vue naître et elle peut être considérée, du point de vue de l'analyse de sa structure interne, comme une entité autonome, avec ses propres lois internes qui la renvoient à elle-même. Cette autonomie relative permet l'analyse immanente *comme un moment* d'une analyse plus large et globale. L'isolement du phénomène étudié est une abstraction scientifique comme n'importe quelle autre; c'est une nécessité du processus de la recherche scientifique. Il n'est pas possible d'aborder minutieusement tous les aspects de l'objet étudié, pas même de quelquns d'entre eux, d'une façon simultanée.

L'enquête d'un certain corpus musical, pourtant, historique, sociologique, anthropologique, théorique, analytique de la structure musicale, psychologique, fait d'un point de vue de la réception et de la perception de la musique; la recherche peut être cognitive, sémiotique-sémiologique ou faite de n'importe quel autre point de vue global. La recherche peut embrasser plusieurs perspectives ou même aspirer à une vision totalisante, globalisante, étant dans ce dernier cas extrêmement difficile, pour ne dire pas impossible. Comme Molino l'a souligné, "l'analyse du fait musical est interminable" (1975: 58).

La méthode pluraliste

En tant que formulation théorique générale, nous faisons nôtre le modèle analytique de la tripartition sémiologique, exposé par Molino (1975: 47–48) et développé par Nattiez (1975: 45–89 et 1987: 25–64), qui prit en compte l'existence de trois niveaux du phénomène musical: la dimension poïétique, la dimension esthésique et l'objet musical lui-même, le niveau "neutre". À notre avis ce modèle *général* d'analyse permet de surpasser les impasses méthodologiques que la musicologie et l'ethnomusicologie ont affrontées tout au long de leur histoire, à condition que la tripartition soit appliquée dialectiquement et d'une manière créatrive et conséquente. Des modèles analytiques proches de la tripartition sémiologique dans les grandes lignes ont été offerts par Mantle Hood (7) et particulièrement par María Ester Grebe, dont le modèle anthropologique peut être appelé aussi "dialectique". Pour Grebe:

> L'aspect décisif c'est d'arriver à la fusion organique entre la Musicologie et l'Anthropologie, ce qui permet une vision en profôndeur de l'interaction dynamique entre des catégories musicales, culturelles et sociales d'un univers d'étude particulier à travers tant d'une analyse musical contextellement sensitive que d'une analyse socio-culturel musicalment sensitive (1981: 60).

Malgré certain excès sociologiques, le concept de totalité dynamique *(dynamic totality)* de Ballantine — le *tout*, entendu comme se produisant dans un processus perpétuel de changement — peut être utile dans les études sur la musique:

> Very briefly, it is a view of human activity as something wich belongs to a greater whole, wich extends both spatially and in time and wich thus embraces the totality of our social, physical, economic, historical, and cultural world (1988: 21).

L'analyse musicale culturelle de John Blacking (1976), le modèle anthropologique d'Alan Merriam (1978) et les apports d'autres chercheurs (8) constituent des contributions importantes à une vision globale de la recherche musicale. La musicologie cognitive offre de nombreux points communs avec notre conception pluraliste. Quelques représentants de la sémiotique musicale (Chenoweth, par exemple) ont fait des apports significatifs sur certains aspects méthodologiques centraux de la musicologie.

Dans le champ de la musicologie traditionnelle, il nous semble que la philosophie de l'histoire de la musique de Carl Dahlhaus coïncide pour l'essentiel avec une vision dialectique et pluraliste de l'analyse musicale. Particulièrement intéressante pour notre proposition est la conception dialectique qui est à la base de la pensée philosophique, esthétique et théorique de Pierre Boulez, dont nous avons fait l'analyse dans des divers travaux (1988 et 1989). Quelques uns comme Bloch (1985: 183-194), Asafiev (voir McQuere 1983: 222), Adorno (9), Ballantine (ibid.: XV-XVI et 30-48), Thoresen (1987: 222-224), Aho (1988), Supicic (1971) et Shepherd (1991: 1-18), entre beaucoup d'autres, ont écrit sur le caractère dialectique de la musique et du processus musical et ont tenté d'appliquer la méthode dialectique à l'analyse musicale ou à la réflexion sur la question de la relation de la musique avec le monde qui l'entoure et sur la définition de l'objet d'étude de la sociologie de la musique.

L'analyse du texte musical

Dans un sens très restreint, on peut dire que l'analyse musicale s'applique à révéler la structure interne d'un corpus musical, ses lois et principes formels, les techniques de composition utilisées, sa logique de structure et de fonctionnement. C'est l'analyse immanente du niveau neutre, pour utiliser la terminologie de Molino-Nattiez (10). Cette analyse répond à la question de savoir quel est le contenu musical d'un corpus donné, quelle est sa structure, comment sont sa conception et sa réalisation. Ian Bent exprime cela ainsi:

> Musical analysis is the resolution of a musical structure into relatively simpler constituent elements, and the investigation of the functions of those elements within that structure (1987: 1).

À partir de la connaissance des *pourquoi* et *comment* il est possible de faire une analyse qui essaye d'interpréter l'œuvre ou le corps musical dans des perspectives plus larges et plus profondes que les seules perspectives structurales et l'on peut établir des généralisations et relations avec des phénomènes plus amples. C'est alors qu'une intervention valable est possible, par exemple, des stratégies narratives greimasiennes, telles que celles développées par Tarasti (1989: 4–46). En d'autres termes: une analyse de cette nature n'est pas alternative ni exclusive par rapport à celle qui découvre la réalité immanente du discours musical.

Boulez a signalé avec précision le caractère et l'itinéraire de l'analyse musicale dans un sens restreint, qu'il a nommée "méthode analytique active":

> ...l'on se doit de partir d'une observation aussi minutieuse et aussi exacte que possible des faits musicaux qui nous sont proposés; il s'agit ensuite de trouver un schéma, une loi d'organisation interne qui rende compte, avec le maximum de cohérence, de ces faits; vient, enfin, l'interprétation des lois de composition déduites de cette application particulière. Toutes ces étapes sont nécessaires; c'est se livrer à un travail de technicien tout à fait secondaire que de ne pas poursuivre jusqu'à l'étape capitale: l'interprétation des structures; à partir de là, et de là seulement, on pourra s'assurer que l'œuvre a été assimilée et comprise (1964: 14).

La méthode exposée par Boulez est avant tout inductive. On ne doit pas oublier que ses mots s'appliquent principalement à l'analyse de la musique contemporaine, qui exige que chaque œuvre soit étudié à partir de ses propres coordonnées spécifiques. L'idée boulézienne de l'analyse peut aussi être appliquée à une méthodologie plus générale, valable aussi bien pour les recherches dans le champ de l'ethnomusicologie. Le fait que cette méthode boulézienne soit inductive ne veut pas dire que c'est la seule possible. Nous envisageons que l'analyse peut être inductive et/ou déductive, descriptive, analytique à proprement parler, synthétique et même comparative.

Du point de vue de l'analyse du texte musical, il n'existe pas une méthode analytique particulière qui soit *universelle* et *totale*, c'est-à-dire, d'une part, applicable à toutes les cultures musicales et, d'autre part, qui embrasse tous les aspects du phénomène musical et les épuise. Jay Rahn a essayé d'établir une méthode analytique *"for all music"* qui est explicitement non-historique, et ne rend pas compte des facteurs culturels ni de facteurs sociologiques et psychologiques de la production, perception et réception de la musique ni des stratégies compositionnelles. Il s'agit seulement d'analyser le phénomène sonore "pur" à partir de trois dimensions basiques, à savoir, la hauteur, le "moment" (durée) et l'intensité du son. Pour Rahn tous les autres éléments musicaux (timbre, tempo, forme, harmonie, contrepoint, etc.) sont secondaires, et ne méritent pas d'être étudiés (1983: 52–53). Son système analytique n'est pas universel, malgré sa prétention, parce qu'il'existe des musiques qui ne peuvent être analysées du point de vue de la hauteur du son ou du rythme, comme celles basées en glissandos continus, en sons très larges, sans structuration temporelle traditionnelle (sans "rythme"). La méthode de Rahn n'est pas non plus totale, parce que, explicitement, elle ne prend pas en compte les autres éléments qui forment la réalité du corpus musical.

Une autre méthode d'analyse qui tente d'être universelle, c'est la paradigmatique de Ruwet-Nattiez. Il s'agit cette fois de segmenter le discours musical en les plus petites inités possibles en se basant sur les principes d'identité et de répétition. Pour les mêmes raisons que dans le cas précédent, ce système analytique n'est pas universel et total: il y a beaucoup de musiques (par exemple la musique tibétaine, certains chants de moines bouddhistes japonais, des indigènes Kamayurá du Brésil ou certaines œuvres de Ligeti, Xenakis ou Saariaho, la musique électronique (11)) qui refusent d'être segmentées sur des critères aussi simplistes que ceux de l'analyse paradigmatique. D'un autre côté, le système ne considére pas tous les paramètres musicaux. À notre avis, l'analyse paradigmatique, telle que Nattiez la présente, est en flagrante contradiction avec tout l'esprit du projet tripartite sémiologique de Nattiez lui-même. La tripartition essaye de rendre compte des *découpages culturels* de la musique, c'est-à-dire, de son contexte historique et socio-culturel, mais l'outil analytique spécifique du niveau neutre (la segmentation paradigmatique) est non-historique, se situe au delà des conditionnements culturels de la musique. Avec l'analyse paradigmatique, Nattiez contredit totalement l'esprit de son projet global tripartite. Nattiez affirme que "... il faut admettre la nécessité d'aborder les phénomènes musicaux à la fois d'un point de vue anthropologique, tout en ayant recours aux outils de l'analyse du niveau neutre" (1987: 88), cependant, pourquoi restreindre "les outils de l'analyse du niveau neutre" à la seule analyse paradigmatique? Molino — le créateur du modèle tripartite — se demandait si "cette analyse peut (--) se faire dans le cadre d'un formalisme unique". Voici sa réponse:

> Il n'y a pas, et il ne saurait y avoir, de formalisme unique qui épuise les propriétés d'un domaine de l'existant, d'un vécu découpé et reconnu comme tel par la pratique sociale: un formalisme unique serait-il capable de rendre compte de toutes les propriétés d'une table, d'une montagne, ou d'un organisme vivant? S'il n'y a pas de procédure unique d'étude dans les sciences physiques et biologiques, comment y en aurait-il une pour le langage, la musique ou la religion? Il ne suffit pas de poser des niveaux abstraits de représentation, liés par des règles: rien ne permet d'assurer que les niveaux correspondent toujours et partout, dès que le nombre de niveaux dépasse deux. Car il ne faut pas confondre découpage de l'objet et structuration réelle du monde (1975: 58–59).

Relativité de l'analyse musicale

S'il n'existe pas de méthodes analytiques universelles, l'analyse du corps musical est nécessairement relative. Puisque toutes les cultures musicales sont historiques et culturellement déterminées, les outils analytiques doivent s'adapter à ce fait. L'universalité de l'analyse est une utopie. D'autre part — comme l'a souligné Molino — aucune méthode n'est capable de rendre compte de tous les aspects de la musique. Chaque méthode concrète donne quelque lumière sur un certain type de musique ou certains paramètres musicaux.

L'analyse ne peut pas être anti- ou non-historique. L'analyste et l'analyse sont eux aussi historiques et culturellement déterminés. D'un autre côté, le phénomène musical est un processus en changement constant, et pourtant les outils analytiques doivent aussi se modifier. Dans le cas de la musique d'art occidentale où il existe la notion d'œuvre d'art, chaque époque peut estimer, envisager, percevoir une œuvre de manière différente. Cette perspective multiple d'une œuvre peut exister dans un même moment historico-culturel entre divers chercheurs et même dans l'estimation d'un analyste, dont la vision change aussi avec le temps. L'ambiguïté et la multiplicité des significations de l'œuvre d'art permettent cette approximation si riche et diversifiée.

La relativité de l'analyse entraîne qu'elle n'est pas universelle, mais culturellement déterminée, qu'elle n'est pas totale, mais nécessairement partielle; enfin, qu'elle n'est pas immuable, mais changeante. Un quatrième élément à considérer est que, malgré l'opposition ouverte, et même contradictoire entre des méthodes analytiques hétérogènes, elles ne sont pas exclusives l'une de l'autre, mais *complémentaires*. Par exemple, la théorie de la croissance et du développement organiques de A.B. Marx et du processus thématique de Réti, l'analyse fonctionnelle de Keller, les systèmes analytiques de Riemann et Schenker et l'analyse harmonique de De la Motte, sont tous des points de vue divers qui mettent l'accent sur l'un ou l'autre aspect de la musique tonale occidentale, à savoir, sur la forme, la mélodie, le principe d'identité et de contraste, le rythme et l'harmonie (12). Ces approximations à l'œuvre musicale, si divergentes entre elles qu'elles soient, jettent une lumière sur certains traits sans qu'aucune ne l'épuise, ni même toutes ensembles. Si l'on observe à distance, ces visions sont plus complémentaires qu'exclusives. Dans le cas de l'ethnomusicologie, la grammaire générative de Chenoweth, la notion de consonance et dissonance de Kolinski, la méthode ethno-théorique de Zemp, l'analyse culturellement sensitive de Blacking et la *cantométrique* de Lomax peuvent donner des aspects divers d'un même corpus musical d'une manière complémentaire, intégrée et logique.

Notre point de vue est éclectique en ce sens qu'il n'exclut pas a priori ni adopte aucune méthode particulière. Pour nous, une bonne méthode analytique est celle qui *respecte* l'intégrité de la musique, se subordonne à elle en ce sens qu'elle essaye de refléter de la manière la plus fidèle possible — le subjectivisme ne peut être totalement éliminée — la structure et les principes de fonctionnement du corpus musical. Le but de l'analyse musicale n'est pas de démontrer l'efficacité d'une théorie ou d'une méthode quelconque, mais de donner une vision le plus proche, large et profonde de la réalité de l'œuvre musicale. La méthode doit être au service de la musique et non le contraire. L'emploi de telle ou telle méthode spécifique est donné par le caractère du corpus musical, ses coordonnées historique-culturelles, sa spécificité et par ce qu'on veut étudier. Quelle que soit la méthode, elle doit obéir aux critères scientifiques que la philosophie de la science a établis.

Mikko Heiniö a critiqué, ou du moins mis en question, le pluralisme méthodologique parce qu'il comporte le danger imminent de dispersion et de manque de logique et d'unité de l'analyse. Il se prononce plutôt pour le monisme méthodologique et conçoit le chemin pluraliste seulement dans des cas très spéciaux, par exemple quand elle est utilisée par des musicologues "du calibre de Carl Dahlhaus". Notre projet est à l'abri de cette critique, car nous concevons aussi que l'analyse soit faite sous un seul angle. Ces études monistes sont non seulement possibles, mais aussi valables et très importantes, parce qu' elles éclairent un ou plusieurs aspects d'un phénomène musical. Ce à quoi nous nous opposons c'est présenter une seule méthode déterminée comme l'unique possible, valable et vraie.

L'analyse musicale se trouve dans une phase synthétique. À la séparation et à la "lutte interne" des courants analytiques succède une période de synthèse, de visions plus globales, riches et ouvertes. Dans ce sens, la sémiotique (sémiologie) musicale ou la tendance cognitive, par exemple, ne sont pas une alternative, en bloc, à la musicologie: elles font partie d'elle.

Notes

1. Malgré l'*Histoire générale de la musique* de Fétis qui, selon Harrison
   "was the first attempt at a history of the music of all peoples, regarding
   the music of the West as the expression of one culture among many"
   (1963: 30), la musicologie (historique), à partir d'Adler, a été orientée
   vers la recherche de la musique d'art occidentale. Hood précise que
   "[the] ethnomusicology embraces all kinds of music not included by
   studies in historical musicology, i.e., the study of cultivated music in
   the western European tradition" (1963: 217).
2. A titre d'exemple il suffit de lire la première partie (Objets et méthodes
   en musicologie) du livre d'Édith Weber, professeur à l'Université dc
   Paris-Sorbonne (1980: 11–27).
3. Alan Merriam nous dit: "for me ethnomusicology is to be defined as
   "the study of music in culture" (1978: 6).
4. Nous sommes dans la même ligne de pensée que Mantle Hood: "One of
   the basic precepts of ethnomusicology — *the study of music in terms of
   itself* — represents a challenge the very nature of wich is insufficiently
   understood." (1963: 240). Pour de nombreux sémioticiens de la
   musique ce problème est aussi un défi.
5. Ici quelques exemples parus récemment dans des publications
   musicologiques: Simon Miller, *Instruments of Desire: Musical Morphology in the Early Work of Picasso* (The Musical Quarterly, vol. 76,
   N° 4, 1992, pp. 443–464); Fred Everett Maus, *Hanslick's Animism*
   (The Journal of Musicology, vol. X, N° 3, 1992, pp. 273–292); Andrew Wathey, *The Marriage of Edward III and the Transmission of
   French Motets to England* (Journal of the American Musicological
   Society, vol. XLV, N° 1, 1992, pp. 1–29); Robin Engelman, *Percus-
   sionists in the West. Coping with Change* (Contemporary Music Re-
   view, vol. 7, part 1, 1992, pp. 5–13); Judith K. Delzell & David A.
   Leppla, *Gender Association of Musical Instruments and Preferences of
   Fourth-Grade Students for Selected Instruments* (Journal of Research in
   Music Education, vol. 40, N° 2, 1992, pp. 93–103); Bernard Brauchli,
   Christian Baumann's Square Pianos and Mozart (The Galpin Society
   Journal, vol. XLV, 1992, pp.29–49); Pierre-Albert Castanet, Roger
   Tessier: *L'artisan de l'Itinéraire. L'Itinéraire de l'artisan* (La Revue
   Musicale N° 421–424, 1991, pp. 125–148); et même dans Current
   Musicology, revue spécialisée dans l'analyse du texte musical, nous
   trouvons l'article de Shai Burstyn, *The "Arabian Influence" Thesis
   Revisited* (N° 45–47, 1990, pp. 119–146).
6. Quelques exemples de publications ethnomusicologiques des dernières
   années: Terry E. Miller, *The Theory and Practice of Thai Musical
   Notations* (Ethnomusicology, vol. 36 N° 2, 1992, pp. 197–221); Lisha
   Li, *The Symbolization Process of the Shamanic Drums Used by the*

Manchus and Other Peoples in North Asia (Yearbook for Traditional Music, vol. 24, 1992, pp.52–80); Francis Katamba and Peter Cooke, *Ssematimba ne Kikwabanga: The Music and Poetry of a Ganda Historical Song* (The World of Music, vol.XXIX, Nº 2, 1987, pp.49–66); Keith Howard, *Why do it that way? Rhythmic Models and Motifs in Korean Percussion Bands* (Asian Music, vol XXIII, Nº 1, 1991–92, pp. 1–59); *Divergence and Intricacies in the Compositional Techniques of the Different Baaj/Gharane in Tabla Vadan* (Journal of the Indian Musicological Society, vol 21, Nº 1 & 2, 1990, pp. 72–96); Wim van Zanten, *Malawian Pango Music From the Viewpoint of Information Theory* (African Music, vol. 6, Nº 3, 1983, pp. 90–106); Gerhard Kubik, *Drum Patterns in the Batuque of Benedito Caxias* (Latin American Music Review, vol. 11, Nº 2, 1990, pp. 115–181); Rob van der Bliek, Wes Montgomery: *A Study of Cohe-rence in Jazz Improvisation* (Jazzforschung, vol. 23, 1991, pp. 117–178); Stan Hawkins, *Prine: Harmonic Analysis of "Anna Stesia"* (Popular Music, vol. 11, Nº 3, 1992, pp. 325–335).

7. Hood propose un schème global d'analyse interdisciplinaire qui'l appelle "la ligne G-S", c'est-à-dire, un *continuum* qui va du général au spécifique (1971: 296–312).

8. Par exemple, Nettl (1964, 1983), Rice (1987) et Koskoff (1987).

9. Adorno utilise ou tente d'utiliser la méthode dialectique dans tous ses écrits de philosophie, d'esthétique et de sociologie de la musique. Voir spécialement Philosophie de la nouvelle musique, Théorie Esthétique et Impromptus.

10. "Qu'est-ce donc que l'analyse de la musique? C'est cette dialectique du travail scientifique qui, partant de l'analyse «neutre» du matériau sonore transcrit par une pratique sociale qui est déjà une analyse, progresse en définissant, au fur et à mesure, de nouvelles strates d'analyse, soit en intégrant des données empruntées aux autres dimensions (production et réception), soit en mettant en question les instruments utilisés pour l'analyse et en essayant d'en forger de nouveaux" (Molino 1975: 58). Pour Nattiez, l'analyse du niveau neutre *"c'est un niveau d'analyse où on ne décide pas a priori si les résultats obtenus par une démarche explicite sont pertinents du point de vue esthésique ou poïétique. Les outils utilisés pour la délimitation et la dénomination des phénomènes sont exploités systématiquement jusqu'à leurs ultimes conséquences, et ne sont remplacés que lorsque de nouvelles hypothèses ou de nouvelles difficultés conduisent à en proposer de nouveaux. «Neutre» signifie à la fois que les dimensions poïétiques et esthésiques de l'objet ont été neutralisées et que l'on va jusqu'au bout d'une procédure donnée, indépendamment des résultats obtenus "* (1987: 35–36).

11. L'analyse que Gilles Naud a fait de *Nomos Alpha* de Xenakis (1975: 63–72) ne rend compte de tous les aspects de l'œuvre, par exemple, de la syntaxis. D'autre part, elle est principalement descriptive; elle omet l'interprétation, la dernière phase de la conception analytique proposée

par Boulez. L'analyse paradigmatique a été appliquée avant tout à des cas de musiques monodiques. Nous avons utilisé l'analyse paradigatique dans des études de musique folklorique et populaire du Chili et de l'Amérique du Sud.

12. Un exemple d'analyse méthodologiquement pluraliste dans le cadre de la musicologie générale, c'est la thèse de doctorat de Murtomäki sur Sibelius (1993), où íl utilise des systèmes analytiques "traditionnels", l'analyse paradigmatique et celle de Schenker. La thèse de doctorat de Moisala est elle aussi pluraliste, à partir d'une conception cognitive.

Bibliographie

Aho, Kalevi (1988). *Einojuhani Rautavaara as Symphonist*. Helsinki: Sibelius Akatemian julkaisusarja 5.

Ballantine, Christopher (1988 [-58]). *Music and its Social Meanings*. Glasgow: Gordon and Breach Science Publishers.

Bent, Ian (1987). *Analysis*. London: Mcmillan.

Blacking, John (1976). *How Musical is man?* London: Faber and Faber.

Bloch, Ernst (1985 [-74]). *Essays on the Philosophy of Music*. London: Cambridge University Press.

Boulez, Pierre (1963). *Penser la musique aujourd'hui. Le nouvel espace sonore*. Paris: Éditions du Seuil.

Dahlhaus, Carl (1983 [-77]). *Foundations of Music History*. Bath: Cambridge University Press.

Grebe Vicuña, María Ester (1981). "Antropología de la música: nuevas orien-taciones y aportes teóricos en la investigación musical", *Revista Musical Chilena*, vol. XXXV, N° 153-155, 52-74.

Harrison, Frank Ll. (1963). "American Musicology and the European Tradition", *Musicology*, F. Harrison, M. Hood and C. Palisca (eds.), 10-85. Englewood Cliffs: Prentice-Hall.

Heiniö, Mikko (1992). "Konstekstualisoiminen taidemusiikin tutkimuksessa", *Musiikki* 1: 1-78.

Hood, Mantle (1963). "Music, the Unknown", *Musicology*, F. Harrison, M. Hood and C. Palisca (eds.), 215-326. Englewood Cliffs: Prentice-Hall.

- (1971). *The Ethnomusicologist*. USA: McGraw-Hill Book Company.

Hurri, Merja (1983). "Vero- ja raha-arpajaisvarojen käyttö musiikin edistämiseen", *Suomen Musiikin koko kuva*, 12-13 et 16.

Kimmey, John A., Jr. (1988). *A Critique of Musicology. Clarifying the Scope, Limits, and Purposes of Musicology*, Lewiston. New York: The Edwin Mellen Press.

Koskoff, Ellen (1987). "Response to Rice", *Ethnomusicology,* vol XXXI, N° 3, 497-502.

McQuere, Gordon D. (1983). "Boris Asafiev and Musical Form as a Process", *Russian Theoretical Thought in Music,* Gordon D. McQuere (éd.), 217–252. Michigan: UMI Research Press.

Merriam, Alan (1978 [–64]). *The Antropology of Music.* Northwestern University Press.

Moisala, Pirkko (1991). *Cultural Cognition in Music. Continuity and Change in the Gurung Music of Nepal.* Jyväskylä: Suomen etnomusikologisen seuran julkaisu 4.

Molino, Jean (1975). "Fait musical et sémiologie de la musique", *Musique en Jeu* 17: 37–62.

Murtomäki, Veijo (1993 [–90]). *Symphonic Unity. The development of formal thinking in the symphonies of Sibelius.* Helsinki: Studia musicologica Universitatis Helsingiensis.

Naud, Gilles (1975). "Aperçus d'une analyse sémiologique de Nomos Alpha", *Musique en Jeu* 17: 63–72.

Nattiez, Jean-Jacques (1975). *Fondements d'une sémiologie de la musique.* Paris: Union générale d'Éditions.

– (1987). *Musicologie générale et sémiologie.* Paris: Christian Bourgois Éditeur.

Nettl, Bruno (1964). *Theory and Method in Ethnomusicology.* New York: Schirmer Books.

– (1983). *The Study of Ethnomusicology.* Urbana-Chicago-London: University of Illinois Press.

Padilla, Alfonso (1988). "Partons pour l'inconnu, avec passion". Acerca de las concepciones filosóficas, estéticas y teóricas de Pierre Boulez, Mémoire de maîtrise, manuscrit. Université d'Helsinki.

– (1989). "Partons pour l'inconnu, avec passion. Pierre Boulezin estetiikasta I", *Musiikkitiede* 2: 147–163.

Rahn, Ray (1983). *A Theory for All Music: Problems and Solutions in the Analysis of Non-Western Forms.* Canada: University of Toronto Press.

Rice, Timothy (1987). "Toward the Remodeling of Ethnomusicology", *Ethnomusicology,* vol. XXXI N° 3: 469–488.

Shepherd, John (1991). *Music as Social Text.* Worcester: Polity Press.

Supicic, Ivo (1971). *Musique et société. Perspectives pour une sociologie de la musique.* Zagreb: Institut de Musicologie, Académie de Musique.

Tarasti, Eero (1989). "Chopinin g-molli balladin narratiivinen kielioppi", *Musiikkitiede* 2: 4–46.

Thorensen, Lasse (1987). "An auditive analysis of Schubert's Piano Sonata Op. 42", *Semiotica,* Eero Tarasti (éd.), 66/1–3: 211–237.

Weber, Édith (1980). *La recherche musicologique. Objet, méthodologie, normes de présentation.* Paris: Beauchesne.

Semiotic processes in music:
Systemics and modelization in paradigmatic analysis

MICHELE IGNELZI AND PAOLO ROSATO

(Rosato)

1. Processes in musical fact: The neutral level with respect to studies on musical signification

1.1.1. All scholars acknowledge that musical phenomena are complex facts. This complexity requires a manifold approach that includes Molino's tripartition of the total musical fact into poietic, neutral, and aesthesic levels; the relationships between these three levels and their sub-levels; the linguistic functions of musical objects; the diverse modalities of communication of these objects; the parametrical subdivision of the musical object into melodic, harmonic, rhythmic, and other levels; the systemic aspect of these parameters; the general and local rules of the musical object; the analytic methodology for studying all these phenomena.

1.1.2. The complexity of the total musical fact does not hinder us from isolating inside it a *musical object*, by which we mean the investigative field of Molino's and Nattiez's analysis of the neutral level. It signifies both a phonic event and the translation of that event into a score. In fact, if every word-like object is always a mental representation, there is no great difference between the mark on the paper and that mark in a brain. Consequently, prescriptive and descriptive scores may be studied through an analysis of the neutral level. Both include those elements and relationships through which we construct external objects. In a natural language we can say "I'm going home", and we can write or think that, even if we have a sore throat. In music we may play on a trombone "A, B♭, A, G, F", and we can also write or think that, even if we cannot play trombone.

1.1.3. Ruwet's and Nattiez's analyses produce a static complexity that depends on criteria of structuralist origin, such as repetition and length. In our opinion, the musical object may be analyzed from the point of view not only of different parameters and levels, but also by processual and functional criteria.

1.2. To clarify this interpretative course, we introduce some concepts drawn from Umberto Eco.

1.2.1. He says that a code can operate as a language not only with a double articulation, it can also signify in the presence of a single articulation, mobile articulation, or no articulation at all. As Eco says, in a recognizable melodic sequence that changes timbre with every tone, a simple sequence of timbres is heard; the tone ceases to be a pertinent trait and becomes a facultative variant (1968: 137–140).

1.2.2. Eco distinguishes between analytic and synthetic codes. The most general elements in a lower code (syntagms or significative units) may become basic units (pertinent traits) in a higher code. For example, the set "the hero leaves" is a syntagm in a linguistic code, and a distinctive trait in a narrative code. In the same way, phonemes /h/, /i/, /r/, /u/, etc. are distinctive traits in a linguistic code, and significative units in a phonological code (Eco 1968: 141–143).

1.2.3. Finally, Eco admits the existence of more musical codes: formalized semiotics, onomatopoeic, connotative and denotative systems, stylistic connotations which have different modalities of signification (ibid.: 398–399). Figure 1 shows our subdivision of these codes.

1.3.1. We can study the musical fact from two different points of view: The syntactic, which concerns the operating of patterns and functions of musical objects; and the semantic, which involves poietic and aesthesic processes working on the neutral level.

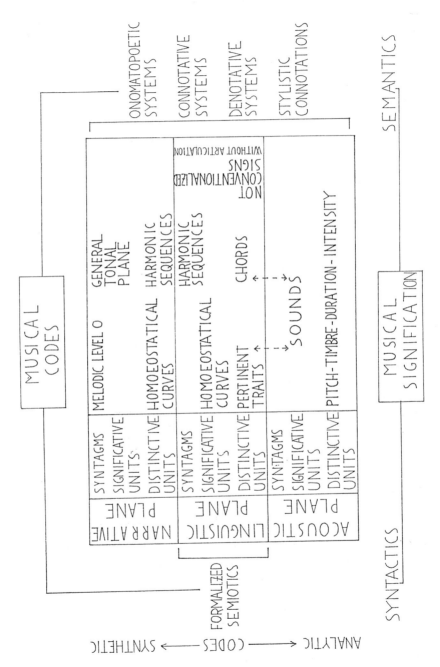

Figure 1.

1.3.2. In parallel to our preceding division of synthetic and analytic codes into three planes, we may distinguish between acoustic, linguistic, and narrative planes in a musical object. The linguistic plane, explainable through formalized semiotics, is articulated in various ways, depending on the analyzed musical parameters and on the criteria for segmentation. Melodies and harmonies may be variously articulated into more levels. The most general levels may be described by means of external narrative approaches. The acoustical plane is studied, for example, by analysis of electro-acoustic music. Other parameters such as dynamics, timbre, and agogics have no double articulation; they can however constitute a system of significative oppositions on the linguistic plane. By contrast, on the acoustical plane, timbre is articulated into a system of distinctive units.

1.3.3. A musical object may undergo manifold interpretations in accordance with its contextual position. For example, the same distinctive unit may assume different functions depending on its placement in a homeostatic curve. Contrarily, in Figure 2 you can see that the typology, profiles, and functions of curves are not changed by different tones.

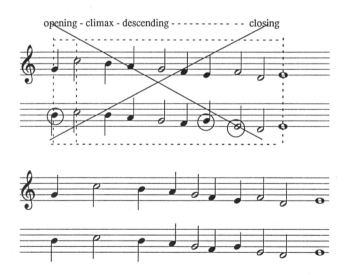

Figure 2.

1.4. Musical communication can take place in accordance with two different modalities: *semantic* communication concerns processes external to the musical object. On their basis any musical object can enter into a communicative system thanks to conventionalization and naturalization by usage. On the other hand, *syntactic* communication concerns the internal nucleus of the musical object.

1.5. In a jazz performance, a listener may be interested in the social, cultural, or political aspects of this music; he can feel different emotions and confront them with other members of his community. Another listener may wish to reproduce that kind of music; then he will record, transcribe, and analyze it in order to understand its functioning. The first behavior is external to the musical object and concerns the musical fact in its complexity. The second behavior is internal to it, and chooses the way of a neutral approach to the fact.

1.5.1. Relationships between poietics, aesthesics, and the neutral level cannot be reduced to mere projection of strategies of composer and listener. Some attributions of signification to musical objects — becoming in this case signifiers — are motivated, as happens in a natural language for onomatopoeia and derived words. The process of "communication", however, cannot be univocal, as Nattiez says, because those projections are imbued with linguistic elements too.

Such elements are considered linguistic because they are organized in a system, though they do not necessarily have a conventionalized referent. That systemic aspect makes it so that the signifying attributes of curves are transported from composer to listener through the musical object, in accordance with Eco's model. It is also true that, because of the absence of conventionalization, the musical fact gives more place than a verbal communicative system to those projections which lie at the basis of Nattiez's conception. The dialectic of musical signification and the role of object in a semiotic system can be synthesized as shown in Figure 3. The model we propose (Figure 3c) is dynamic, capturing manifold relationships between the three levels. In particular, the dashed arrow emphasizes the autonomous role of the neutral level. The articulation takes place in two phases:

1. The composer "produces" the piece through his "strategies". Those strategies, however, lose their autonomy as the piece grows; the internal legality (as Adorno says) of the piece, which the composer started, now guides his hand.

2. The listener, through the "produced" piece, goes back to strategies of composing, which are part of a linguistic system. (Ignelzi & Rosato 1992)

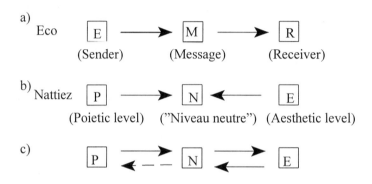

a)

Eco   E ⟶ M ⟶ R

(Sender)   (Message)   (Receiver)

b)

Nattiez P ⟶ N ⟵ E

(Poietic level)   ("Niveau neutre")   (Aesthetic level)

c)

P ⇄ N ⇄ E

Figure 3.

1.5.2. On symbolic communication, Cesare Segre (1985: 10–11) writes that, confronted with a literary work, a reader "is between two poles: comprehension and variation. He can try to comprehend the meanings the work gives, or abandon himself to fantastic associations... I speak of *poles* because there is no reading that can marginalize freedom of imagination (which is often rife with interpretative proposals), and no reading that can totally suppress what the text says."

1.5.3. It is evident that a process that moves from analysis to synthesis is necessary for studying every musical fact.

1.6.1. In our view, aesthesics and semantics are not coincident. Semantics studies relationships between mental representations and signs; aesthesics concerns not only what a musical object means for a listener, but especially how perception projects onto the musical objects.

1.6.2. The endowment of a musical event with sense may occur in two different modalities. We can attribute an *a posteriori* sense on the basis of our experiences, which are external to the musical object; or with an *a priori* synthesis we can extract from this object its properties, without referring to its environment or context.

1.7. For these reasons it is important to study separately the linguistic plane of a musical fact. Currently many scholars are applying semiotical categories to the musical fact without having adequate knowledge about it. In conclusion:

1.7.1. It is possible to attend to musical signification from a mere semantic point of view, but this approach covers only a part of aesthesics and, in parallel, of poietics.

1.7.2. It is possible to separate the semantic plane from the narrative, linguistic, and acoustic planes, without giving up a semiotic approach to the musical fact.

1.7.3. It is possible to study separately the linguistic and acoustic planes, but not the narrative plane, which presupposes linguistic study.

1.7.4. The linguistic plane cannot be investigated with traditional instruments of analysis nor considered as a mere taxonomy or catalogue of musical objects.

(Ignelzi)

2. Processes in the musical object: Systemics and paradigmatic analysis

2.1. The systemics of musical parameters

Following Delli Pizzi, we believe that musical parameters are definable in terms of a systemic model.

2.1.1. Western tonal harmony is a system as far as its objects (which we can individuate through taxonomic analysis) are connected in a complex of relations that can be described by combinatory rules. Such relations are established in consequence of attractive forces existing between one harmonic object and the others. The rules of prescriptive and descriptive syntaxes are founded, consciously or not, on that network of forces.

2.1.2. Taxonomy cannot individuate melodic objects that have a level of distinction comparable to harmonic levels. In our view, it is not possible to attribute fixed levels of interpretation to melodic significative and distinctive units. The lack of a taxonomy, however, does not affect the systemic character of melody. Units can of course be isolated on grounds of intervallic and rhythmic characteristics, as Ruwet and Nattiez have shown. Nevertheless, to speak of a systemic level of melodic events, we must study the relationships between melodic units not only in terms of mere repetition, but through networks of forces and balance.

2.2. A linguistic category

Harmonic and melodic patterns are explainable by means of the linguistic category called homeostasis. Drawn by Delli Pizzi from the physical sciences, it represents the principle regulating the process of breaking off from an original and of subsequent restoration of balance. Homeostasis makes possible the articulation of a musical object into levels of signification.

2.3. Analysis of processes in musical objects

Nowadays, analysis of the neutral level is identified with structuralist and synchronic studies, which exclude interpretation and hermeneutical approaches to the musical object. In our opinion, it is possible to individuate processual and dynamical aspects in musical works through a parametric analysis of the neutral level.

2.3.1. This kind of analysis subdivides the musical object into the parameters of harmony, melody, rhythm, timbre, dynamics, agogics, and other elements, which can constitute significative oppositions. Some of these parameters may be organized into units of different levels of articulation. This is valid primarily for harmony and melody. A global vision of the musical object demands subsequent reintegration of these manifold levels and parameters.

2.3.2. One of our main purposes is to give to paradigmatic analysis of the neutral level a new role in determining dynamic and tensional processes. This is possible by applying criteria such as homeostasis, tension, detension, significative and distinctive units, transformation, etc.

2.3.3. Our paradigmatic analysis "modelizes" inasmuch as it allows us to individuate traits of the musical object which have an "initiating" character — a genetic blueprint for subsequent processes.

2.4. Melodic analysis

This involves a reformulation of Ruwet's and Nattiez's type of melodic analysis, in order to engage not merely repetitions, but also dynamic and processual phenomena.

2.4.1. Applying the homeostatic criterion to a melodic event, it is possible to map linear processes to curves, which can be reduced to typologies and classified. They are observable from the point of view of their contour or of their intervallic structure.

2.4.2. Melodic traits serve different functions according to their position in a curve. Linear functions include opening, climax, closing, tension, detension, and so forth.

2.4.3. The key-word in our studies on melodic processes is *significative unit*, a concept borrowed by Delli Pizzi from André Martinet. Our paradigmatic analysis separates out units on the grounds of tensive, functional, and homeostatic principles. This furnishes the units with their signification: a unit receives signification in so far as it is homeostatic, tensive, and so on. The distinctive unit is a subsection of a significative unit. Unlike its linguistic analogue (by Martinet), it does have signification, though only contextual. Repetition and length are not the only means for identifying equivalences. Through the foregoing criteria it is possible to define transformations that occur between significative and distinctive units, so that we obtain a dynamic and processual view of melodic patterns in a musical object.

2.5. Harmonic analysis

2.5.1. In the study of harmony, taxonomy provides the initial analytic objects that constitute, in our opinion, a level of second articulation for a linguistic approach. This represents a provisional stage in our investigation; these objects could be further subdivided, without moving onto a merely acoustic plane. Harmonic functions, as melodic functions, can be studied through a homeostatic criterion that develops as a path departing from and then returning to the tonic. This course of tension-detension generates harmonic sequences, which we consider as units of first articulation, assuming that sequences ending with the tonic are significative units. The presence of regional tonics and different planes of harmonic tension forces us to use a subdivision whose hierarchization is higher than that which we apply to the study of melody.

2.5.2. The differentiation of possible sequences leads us to a simultaneous setting of units into more levels; such "telescopic" paradigmatization makes necessary both previous explanation of all levels of harmonic stratification and an adequate metalanguage.

2.5.2.1. We can find a tonal plane on very different levels of analysis: sonata expositions/developments/recapitulations, movements, entire symphonies, operas, etc. Unfortunately, we do not have a distinct terminology for everyone of these harmonic stratifications.

2.5.2.2. At the level of syntagms, tonic may represent different stages of homeostatic attraction, depending on temporal and rhythmic factors, root position or inversion of chords, texture, and instrumentation.

References

Delli Pizzi, Fulvio (1982). "Analisi e psicanalisi nello studio della 'poietica'?", *Musical Grammars and Computer Analysis*. Florence.

Eco, Umberto (1968). *La struttura assente*. Milan.

Ignelzi, Michele and Rosato, Paolo (1992). Signification in Music between Structure and Process: A "New" Role of Paradigmatic Analysis. Paper given at the Third International Congress on Musical Signification, Edinburgh, 1–5 September 1992.

Nattiez, Jean-Jacques (1987). *Musicologie générale et sémiologie*. Paris.

Rosato, Paolo (1990). "Su un madrigale di Andrea Gabrieli", *Eunomio* 17: 26–32.

Ruwet, Nicolas (1972). *Langage, musique, poésie*. Paris.

Segre, Cesare (1985). *Avviamento all'analisi del testo letterario*. Torino.

Music as a subject of semiotic analysis

THOMAS NOLL

Introduction

Characteristic of most activities in the field of musical semiotics is the application of semiotic concepts, models, and theories to musicological tasks and problems. These concepts, models, and theories function more or less as new tools within music theory, musical sociology, ethnomusicology, music history, etc.; and the existence of music itself is regarded as a matter of course. There is, however, another aspect of musical semiotics, namely the definition of its own position within the different fields of cultural semiotics and semiotics in general. In this respect, an elaborated theory of musical semiotics may prove a valuable contribution to the linguistics-dominated contemporary semiotic science. Traditional music theory as well as musical esthetics must then be considered as subjects of pure theory as well, inasmuch their descriptive codes became prescriptive in musical practice.

This article represents the current state of my research, which is still incomplete. The considerations on pragmatics (first section) and the remarks on semantics (last section) contain many questions and hypotheses; the main (middle) section presents a powerful metalanguage for musical syntactics and an outline of its application to a nontrivial example: Western harmony. I could have presented only this paragraph without relating it to the widely unstructured fields of musical semantics and musical pragmatics, but the aim of my work is not to understand Western harmony. I chose harmony as a phenomenon on which the general theory should be tested. According to Morris (1946), syntactics is embedded in semantics which itself is embedded in pragmatics. Following this architecture of semiotics, the aim of my further work will be an embedding of the syntactic theory into comprehensive semantic and pragmatic theories. It is my strategy to approach the central processes of musical sign-production involving highly elaborate code systems from two different sides: the middle section considers the syntactic theory as the main part of this article; the first section presents the sketch of a pragmatic approach following Posner (1991, 1992, 1992a). At the end a few suggestions, remarks, conditions, and questions concerning a possible semantic theory are formulated.

1. A pragmatic approach to musical semiotics

Doubtless there is a difference between human communication and phenomena occurring when people perform and experience music. Thus we have to find out how this difference can be described. The problem leads us to pragmatics, which investigates the relations between sign vehicles and their users and the processes involved in sign interpretation. According to Posner (1991), the components of a semiosis are given as follows (Figure 1).

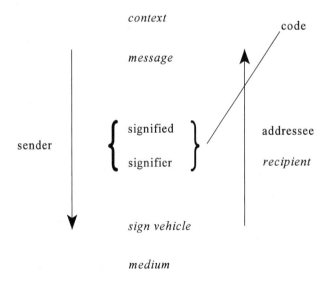

The terms denoting the components whose presence is necessary and sufficient for semiosis to take place are italized. The left hand arrow indicates the sequence of choices in the sender, the right hand arrow that in the addressee.

Figure 1. Components of semiosis.

There are two types of processes involved:
(1) code-related sign processing; (2) situation-dependent inference

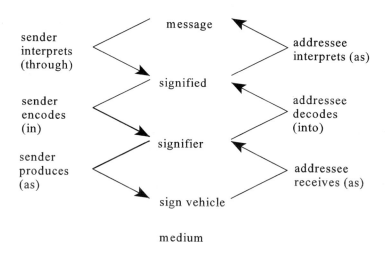

Among these six processes only the sender's and addressee's interpretation activities are pragmatic processes in the narrow sense

Figure 2. Pragmatic processes.

Levels of reflection

Investigating the complexity of the interpretation processes using three main concepts from intensional logic, namely causing, believing, and intending, Posner (1992) gave a formal description of the reflection levels in semiosis up to communicating and derived the five types of speech acts: declaration, directive, assertive, expressive, and commissive. In order to discover the position of music, we have to look at a brief summary of this theory. Posner (1992: 220) considers sign processes as special cases of causal processes:

Causal processes can be described by the formula E(f) → E(e), where "f" and "e" are terms denoting events, "→" is a two-place sentence operator denoting the cause-and-effect relation and "E" is a one-place predicator denoting the property that the event denoted by its argument term occurs (at a certain time and place).

He considers four basic sign types in hierarchic order, each being a special case of its predecessor: signal, indicator, expression, gesture.

Signal processes can be described by the formula E(f) → T(a,r), where "a" is a term denoting a behavioral system, "r" is a term denoting its behavior and "T" is a two-place predicator denoting the relation of performance that holds between the behavioral system (denoted by its first argument term) and the behavior (de-noted by its second argument term). In this constellation, a is called a reacting system, T(a, r) is called its response or interpretant, and f is called a signal for a to do r. (Ibid.: 221)

Think of a dog *a* lying near the piano, where his master's playing makes a noise occur — E(f), which functions as a signal for the dog to disappear immediately — T(a, r) being the interpretant of this signal process.

Indicator processes can be described by the formula E(f) → G(a, p), where "p" is a sentence denoting a proposition and "G" is a two-place operator having a behavioral system as its first argument and a proposition as its second, and denoting the relation of belief that holds between the behavioral system and the proposition. In this constellation, a is again called a reacting system, G(a,p) is called its response or interpretant, p is called the message of f for a, and f is called an indicator for p. (Ibid.)

Again think about our dog *a* as not having recognized that his master has come home because it was sleeping somewhere in the house. The noise of the piano playing E(f) will then function as an indicator of the fact that his master is present p; that is, the noise causes his belief G(a, p) that his master is present, being the interpretant of this indicator process.

Expression processes can be described by the formula E(f) → G(a, Z(b)), where everything is as in the formula for indicator processes except that p is replaced by Z(b); "b" is a term denoting a behavioral system and "Z" is a one-place predicator denoting the property of its argument being in a certain state. In this constellation, b is called an acting system, a is called a reacting system, G(a,Z(b)) is called a's response or interpretant, Z(b) is called the message, and f is called an expression of b's state for a. (Ibid.: 222)

Think about our dog's master *b* closing the piano with a loud bang f, the occurrence of which makes the dog believe that his master is angry Z(b).

Gesture processes can be described by the formula E(f) $\rightarrow$ G(a, I(b, T(b, g))), where everything is as in the formula for indicator processes except that p is replaced by I(b, T(b, g)). Here "I" is a two-place operator having a behavioral system as its first argument and a proposition as its second, and denoting the property of the behavioral system having the intention to realize the proposition. "T(b, g)" is to be interpreted in a way analogous to "T(a, r)", with "T" as a two-place predicator, and "g" as a term denoting the behavior of the first argument of T. In this constellation, b is called an acting system, a is called a reacting system, G(a, I(b, T(b, g))) is called a's response or interpretant, I(b, T(b, g)) is called the message, T(b, g) is called the gestured behavior, and f is called a gesture of b's intention for a. (Ibid.: 223)

Let us imagine our dog's master *b* approaching the piano — E(f) — which makes the dog *a* believe, that he (b) intends to play (g) the instrument — G(a, I(b, T(b, g))). These types define the first reflection level of semiosis with respect to the perspective of the receiver and is denoted by Ia.

If a behavioral system *b* makes an event f occur with the intention, that the occurrence of f causes the occurrence of another event e, then we have an action:

T(b, f) and I(b, E(f) $\rightarrow$ E(e))

Applying this definition to the basic sign concepts, we get signaling, indicating, expressing and gesturing as special cases of actions. As an example let us look at the structure of expressing: T(b, f) and I(b, E(f) $\rightarrow$

G(a, Z(b)). This is the reflection level Ib; that is, the first level with respect to the sender's perspective.

If the message p of an indication is an action, then we reach the second reflection level IIa with respect to the receiver's perspective. As special cases we get indications of signaling, indications of indicating, indications of expressing, and indications of gesturing. Intended indications of actions lead us to reflection level IIb with respect to the sender's perspective. Here we have indicating an action and especially indicating a signaling, indicating an indicating, indicating an expressing, and indicating a gesturing.

Posner (1992: 226) defines the five types of communicating as follows:

> – declarational communicating, which consists in acting by indicating that action,
> – directive communicating, which consists in signaling by indicating that signaling,
> – assertive communicating, which consists in indicating by indicating that indicating,
> – expressive communicating, which consists in expressing by indicating that expressing,
> – commissive communicating, which consists in gesturing by indicating that gesturing.

Ceremonial sign use

According to the number of reflection levels, which is of course theoretically unlimited, a number of conditions have to be fulfilled such as: sincerity, unmistakenness, seriousness, felicity, the success of the involved actions, etc. Varying the different combinations of their possible realizations or non-realizations, one gets a classification of all types of manipulation (presuming that at least level Ib is involved) where communicating is only a special type. We do not go into details here, but note that many examples of indirect communication, such as type switching, involve at least two interpretation processes, one of them often based on signification, the other being a situation dependent inferencing (Posner

1991 and 1992). Code-related sign processes in particular support the possibility of fake indicating.

Let us consider a series of indication processes starting with a tool (see Posner 1989 and 1992a). In contrast to arbitrary instruments, tools are artifacts and signify their purpose. If $p = E(f_t) \to E(e_t)$ is the causal process intended by the tool user, it can be considered as a token of the signified purpose. Here $E(f_t)$ denotes the event of use of that tool at a certain time t, while $E(f)$ denotes the occurrence of the tool at the moment when the receiver a recognizes its tool-ness.

indicator of tool-ness:
$E(f) \to G(a, T(b, f)$ and $I(b, p))$

indicator of bad tool-ness:
$E(f) \to G(a, T(b, f)$ and $I(b, p)$ and not p)

indicator of fake tool-ness:
$E(f) \to G(a, T(b, f)$ and $G(b,$ not p) and $I(b, E(f) \to G(a, p)))$

indicator of indicating fake tool-ness:
$E(f) \to G(a, I(b, G(a, T(b,f)$ and $G(b,$ not p) and $I(b, E(f) \to G(a, p)))$

indicator of openly fake tool-ness
(openly fake tool-ness = fake tool-ness + indicating of it):
$E(f) \to G(a, T(b, f)$ and $G(b,$ not p) and $I(b, E(f) \to G(a, p)$
and $I(b, G(a, T(b ,f)$ and $G(b,$ not p) and $I(b, E(f) \to G(a, p)))$
or shorter: set $q = T(b,f)$ and $G(b,$ not p) and $I(b, E(f) \to G(a, p))$, then
we have $E(f) \to G(a, q$ and $I(b, G(a, q)))$.

Ceremonial tools can be considered as special cases of openly fake tools, namely if there is a secondary purpose. These formulas, of course, present only one of several different possibilities.

We can use the same idea to describe ceremonial action. Therefore we have only to insert $p = E(f) \to E(e)$ in the above formulas instead of $p = E(f_t) \to E(e_t)$. While fake indicating of an action includes reflection level IIb, and openly fake indicating includes level IIIb.

The sender intends that the addressee recognize, that the sender intend, that the addressee recognize, that the sender does not believe himself what he intends to make the addressee believe. And he intends that all this lead to a certain effect e´:

$T(b, f)$ and $I(b, (E(f) \rightarrow G(a, q$ and $I(b, G(a, q)))) \rightarrow E(e´))$ with q as above.

In this case we say that a ceremonial sign use (by ceremonial acting) takes place. For example, take initiation rites as being declarations through ceremonial acting. The awkward question arises as to what degree the sender must be aware of the intended effect e´.

As special cases of ceremonial acting we have ceremonial signaling, indicating, expressing and gesturing. Ceremonial sign use is mainly based on already established signification processes, and frequent repetition will lead to new automatization, that is, to a change of the original codes, or to new codes or new sign systems. The interplay of automatization and "innovative" sign use, such as indirect or ceremonial, should be well understood. Roughly speaking, the more automatization takes place, the less the originally involved reflection levels occur; but the better the conditions for new indirect and ceremonial sign use become. So the search for ceremonial use of already coded musical signs in a developed musical practice is closely connected with semantic questions.

Raymond Monelle (1992) compares two compositions of J.S. Bach: the Fughetta in F BWV 901 and the A♭ major Fugue from Book II of the *Well-Tempered Clavier*:

> The later piece is twice as long as the earlier. Since the subject and countersubject of both versions are opposed in signification (modern/ancient, chamber/church, abstract/symbolic etc.) the original counterpoint may be viewed as a metaphor, and the later extension of the piece as a deconstruction of this metaphor...

In my view we have here an excellent example of ceremonial sign use. The involved inference processes may be characterized by meta-abduction (see Eco 1985: 316) leading to the code itself.

Prehistoric music

Because there is as yet no suitable metalanguage for the description of musical codes, one can try to reconstruct the conditions of their constitution. The question of the phylogenesis of music was very popular in the first half of our century, but it went out of fashion, perhaps because of its speculativeness.

According to Walter Wiora it is possible to reconstruct several facts about the music of the late paleolithic era, supposing that it was embedded as an integral part of hunting ceremonies and other ceremonies, so that one can interpret petroglyphs referring to those ceremonies. Also one can compare the music and the myths of living tribes that had no contact with each other for thousands of years. Following some arguments of Carl Stumpf and Walter Wiora, I intend to correlate their hypotheses to the concept of ceremonial sign behavior.

The fundamental dimensions of musical sign vehicles are rhythm and melody, which may have been established separately from ceremonial acting (in the narrow sense) and ceremonial signaling. So the first dances were based on openly fake indicating of body movements signifying their already coded purposes, for example the openly fake indicating of hunting.

> Aufschlußreich ist besonders der Hinweis, da die Verwendung der Zaubertrommel bei Lappen, Samojeden und anderen nordasiatischen Völkern auf die Verwendung des Bogens zurückgeht, mit dem einst der Zauberer den Geistern drohte und auf sie schoß. . . (Wiora 1961a).

Thus the prehistoric drum is nothing but a ceremonial bow, and the noise of its plucked tendon, which signifies /shouting/, was performed as ceremonial shouting. Remember that Apollo, with the bow as an attribute, is known as the god of music.

Carl Stumpf claims that the first long notes with fixed pitches and also the first simultaneous and succeeding intervals occurred as sign vehicles for long-distance signaling. In this case it should not be considered as a phenomenon of music. In such use it also signifies /long distance of the addressee/. Thus ceremonial use can occur when all members of the group are nearby.

In that sense, such "premusic" does not presuppose an already elaborated language, but of course the melodic and rhythmic sign behavior (as introduced above) once invented could have been applied in order to perform ceremonial speech acts. The acoustic sign vehicle, produced within a speech act, has two components corresponding to two involved sign processes, one of them being an expressing of a state of the utterer through intonation. Any code may offer itself for ceremonial use, providing its users are able to enter reflection level III. My hypothesis on the phylogenesis of music might therefore be formulated as follows:

The origins of rhythmic and melodic behavior consist in ceremonial acting and signaling. The accomplishment of the phylogenesis of language singing has developed as a ceremonial expression of certain intentions. The possibility of ceremonial sign behavior in general depends entirely on the cognitive equipment, which leads to genetic questions.

An interesting study on the acoustics of chanted texts was carried out by Jaan Ross and Ilse Lehiste (Ross 1992). Here Karelian and Estonian lamenting has been characterized as a performance half-way between speech and music, but "half-way" according to acoustic properties. One may ask which kind of pragmatic processes might correspond to this fact.

We did not say much about possible intended effects within the ceremonial processes discussed above. Our notion of "music" therefore remains very weak. Even if the hypothesis is acceptable, only a classification of the intended effects can solve the problem, whether it is correct to assume a general subject matter "music" or not.

If we proceed to historic times, the hypothesis finds some new arguments. As already mentioned, there are two messages combined within a speech act: a basic coded message and the sender's changing intention. Posner (1988) shows how this structure is related to the simultaneous development of alphabetic writing and abstract Western music:

> But why did man develop two complementary sound systems instead of one? The answer becomes evident when we consider the abstractions necessary for the development of alphabetic writing

systems. In the Semitic language group, just as in the Indo-European, the timbre of an utterance conveys its lexical and grammatical structure, i.e. its semantic content. Duration of sounds, volume and pitch mostly carry pragmatic information regarding the relationship between speaker and addressee, the speaker's general intentions, and his appraisal of the communication situation.

By focusing on the timbre of the utterances to be transcribed and neglecting sound duration, volume, and pitch, alphabetic writing systems foregrounded semantic content at the expense of pragmatic information. . . .

Urban life in Western societies has since become even more highly organized. No wonder that the neglected dimensions of language and the abstracted kinds of information were taken up and elaborated in a complementary sound system: music. But then, of course, music developed its own automatizations in order to counteract language.

Western harmony is a special result of this unique development and its investigation should be of great interest to cultural semiotics. The concept of ceremonial sign use has to be accomplished by other concepts in order to formulate a pragmatic theory. For the moment a syntactic metalanguage shall be tested in order to approach the semantic dimension from the other side in this special case.

2. A syntactical approach to musical semiotics

Mathematical music theory as a syntactic metalanguage

It is an interesting fact that classical theories of syntax, such as Rudolf Carnap's *Logische Syntax der Sprache* (1934) have been greatly influenced by the central ideas of a mathematical program initiated by Felix Klein in his famous lecture known as "Das Erlanger Programm" (1872; and see Posner 1986):

A generalisation of geometry raises the following problem: Let there be a multiplicity of elements and a group of transformations defined on them; now the configurations of elements in that multiplicity should be studied with respect to those properties that remain unchanged when transformations of that group are applied to them. . . . The task is to develop the theory of invariants for that group.

The most important developments in twentieth-century mathematics and mathematical physics are related to this program. In the last ten years a mathematical music theory has been developed by Guerino Mazzola (1985, 1990), which follows this program within a very successful tradition, namely algebraic geometry and category theory. There are three types of syntactic studies (Posner 1986):

Syntactics$_1$ as the study of the formal aspects of signs
Syntactics$_2$ as the study of the relations of signs to other signs
Syntactics$_3$ as the study of the way in which signs of various classes are combined to form complex signs.

While mathematical music theory basically gives a framework for syntactics$_1$ and syntactics$_2$, which can be and (partly has already been) operationalized, Mazzola also developed axiomatic models for complex sign production; for example, classical counterpoint (1989) and modulation theory (1985). As a short introduction to this theory we will look at how the two fundamental types of relations between signs — paradigmatic and syntagmatic relations — can be described by mathematical music theory.

Paradigmatic relations

Mazzola distinguishes two kinds of objects, which he calls *local* and *global compositions*. They are objects of suitable categories (in the sense of mathematical category theory), which also include (possibly empty) sets of *morphisms* for any pair of objects. Those morphisms are descriptions of *paradigmatic relations* of sign vehicles, while the sign vehicles are described by the local and global compositions. The construction of the categories themselves can therefore be considered as a task for syntactics$_1$ (for the general definition see Mazzola 1985 or 1990). The construction of such a category starts with a decision about a coordinate domain due to the considered subject matter. Let us look at a simple example:

The "natural" tuning which is based on the addition of octaves, perfect fifths, and major thirds to a certain fundamental pitch leads to a 3–dimensional lattice generated by log2, log3, log5 over the ring of integers Z. So the fundamental coordinate domain in this case is Z. In some cases one wants to take into account the fact of octave identification. The considered lattice will then be two dimensional. The objects are the finite subsets of the lattice. A morphism f: A → B is a usual map of the sets A and B, which is induced by a transformation of the lattice; i.e., morphisms of objects respect the lattice structure, where they are embedded according to the initial decision in syntactics₁.

As an example we look at the C major and c minor scales as local compositions in the two-dimensional situation (Figure 3). In the natural tuning with respect to octave identification we get G and D by adding fifths to C and F by subtracting a fifth. The notes A, E, and B we get by adding thirds to F, C, and G respectively; we get A♭, E♭, and B♭ by subtracting thirds from C, G, and D. This is how Hindemith (1940) derived the tonal system in which he considered notes as "sons" and "grandsons" of a given fundamental note.

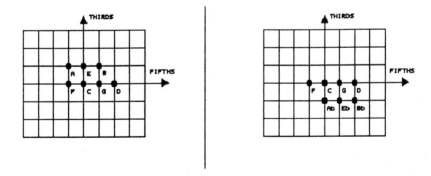

Figure 3. Major and minor scales in natural tuning.

Hindemith compares two relations between major and minor, which he calls "Spiegelung" (mirage) and "Trübung" (tarnishing), giving preference to "Trübung" as being non-symmetric. Mazzola mentions that there are exactly two lattice-transformations of the fifth-third lattice, which map the C major scale on the c minor scale and vice versa (Figure 4). The "Trübung", as induced by a lattice-transformation, is symmetric as well! There is, however, a qualitative difference between these two paradigmatic relations, which is important for the understanding of musical paradigmatics in general. While the lattice transformation describing the mirage is composed of two 1–dimensional transformations along the horizontal fifth-axis and the vertical third-axis respectively, the tarnishing is described by a transformation which mixes up the fifth- and third-dimensions. Of course, Hindemith was not aware of these geometrical facts, but perhaps his intuitive decision is involved here.

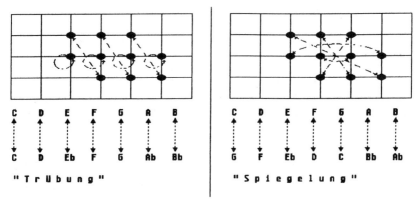

Figure 4. Paradigmatic relations between the major and minor scales.

This may suggest an even more general strategy. If one considers melodic motives, then from a naive point of view they are series of pitches together with certain rhythmic patterns. It would be a mistake to consider only the relations between motives, which are composed of relations of their pitch series and relations of their rhythmic patterns. Numerous significant examples in Mazzola's papers show that there are many more nontrivial paradigmatic relations; e.g., the analysis of Beethoven's Op. 106, first movement (Mazzola 1985) or of Schubert's song "Auf dem Wasser zu singen" Op. 72 (1990).

Syntagmatic relations

The global structure of composed signs in music is much more complicated than in language. The theory has to solve two problems: (1) to
describe different views on complex objects as being composed of local
objects in a category of global compositions; (2) to compare different
global views on the same or on different local objects in a precise manner. The fact of polysemy in musical object language must not lead to
polysemy in the metalanguage of the observer! (For definitions, again
see Mazzola 1985 or 1990.)

In a similar manner as geographers study the globe using local maps
collected in an atlas, we can study global compositions through a collection of local compositions, which are glued together. To reconstruct the
globe out of an atlas requires exact knowledge of how the single maps
overlap. Mazzola here applies the theory of manifolds, where this principle has been formalized. Instead of giving the definition, let us look at an
example:

Global structures are also of interest in the study of musical material. So the diatonic scale of seven notes can be considered as a global
composition with an atlas of seven maps (with three notes each). These
maps will be the seven fundamental steps: I, II, III, IV, V, VI, VII. To
understand how the maps are glued together, one looks at the nerve of
the global structure. Any global composition defines a *nerve*, which is
the formal description of its *syntagma*. We reach the nerve of the step
interpretation of the diatonic scale as follows:

For each map i = I, ... , VII we fix a point P_i. For each pair (i, j) of
maps we choose the connection line between the points P_i and P_j if there
is a nonempty intersection of the two maps. For each triple (i, j, k) we
choose the triangle spanned by the points P_i, P_j, and P_k, if there is a
nonempty intersection. The procedure stops here in our case, because
there is no intersection of four maps, but in general one gets higher
dimensional simplices. The nerve or syntagma for the diatonic scale with
respect to the step interpretation is going to be a Moebiusian ribbon

(Figure 5) consisting of 7 triangles, 14 lines, and 7 points (see Mazzola 1985, 1990).

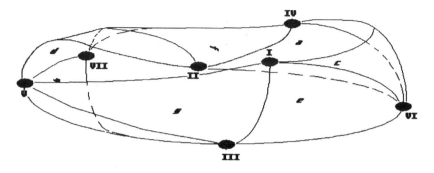

Figure 5. Nerve of the step interpretation of the diatonic scale.

(The notion of a harmonic ribbon was already used by Schoenberg in his *Harmonielehre*. Some difficulties in Riemann's conception of harmony can be explained by the fact that the Moebiusian ribbon has no orientation.)

A classification of all global compositions with respect to a given coordinate domain is theoretically possible by applying highly nontrivial methods from algebraic geometry (the corresponding theorems are given in Mazzola 1985). There might be some esthetic relevance for these classifications. Mazzola shows how Molino's and Ruwet's approaches can be formulated in a precise manner and even operationalized. Nevertheless there is some reason for me not to follow strictly this conception. For the understanding of musical macrosigns, such as whole songs or pieces, another conception of categories must also be taken into consideration, which is the conception of prototypes (see Stefani 1992). While categories in Mazzola's sense are defined through necessary and sufficient conditions of membership (in terms of isomorphisms), the categories in Stefani's sense, are defined through centrality of good examples. The borderline of the category is weakly characterized through bad examples and non-examples for the category. Here we have the confrontation of formal syntactics and empirical semantics. We shall return to this problem at the end.

Interval fields as interior structures of chords

The 12–note system, as considered in a cyclic finite lattice (with respect to well-tempered tuning), we denote by the symbol Z_{12}, while the notes C, C♯, D, ... B we denote by the numbers 0, 1, 2, ... 11. The lattice Z12 is the product of two smaller lattices, according to the fact that any note belongs exactly to one of the 3 fully-diminished seventh chords {0,3,6,9}, {1,4,7,10}, {2,5,8,11} and to one of the 4 augmented triads {0,4,8}, {1,5,9}, {2,6,10}, {3,7,11}. Thus we have a torus generated by two lattices of (tempered) minor and major thirds.

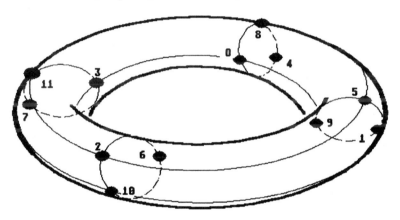

Figure 6. The geometric structure of Z_{12} — a torus.

We are interested in the paradigmatic relations induced by transformations of this torus. There are 48 invertible lattice transformations, called automorphisms, and another 96 non-invertible ones, so that there are 144 lattice-mappings, which we call endomorphisms. (Note that these 144 mappings, which follow the lattice-structure, are only a very few among nearly 9 thousand billion combinatorially possible mappings of a set of 12 elements into itself.) To get an impression of these endomorphisms, I give a list of their conjugation classes, which can be considered as types of endomorphisms. (There exist 28 such types. 15 of them are classes of automorphisms, while 13 are classes of noninvertible endomorphisms [see Figure 7]; for simplicity one representative of each endomorphism class is drawn within a circle each instead of a torus.)

Musical chords are not only sets of notes, but beyond that also sets of interrelated notes. Any chord of n notes contains n^2 intervals. To define a (reflexive) interval field on a chord means to choose n relevant intervals out of all possible n^2, one starting from each note. So there are n^n possible interval fields on a chord of n notes. The chord itself then is called the support of the interval field. For musical paradigmatics it seems to be useful, as I intend to show, to consider only interval fields that are induced by endomorphisms of their supports (i.e., restricted endomorphisms of the lattice, which map the chord into itself). We call such objects *graphic interval fields*, because they are graphs of endomorphisms. The idea is, following Mazzola's work on classical counterpoint, that the harmonic syntax is based on *dichotomies* of interval fields, as is the case with consonances and dissonances. Mazzola showed that the following dichotomy of intervals (Figure 8)

K = {0,3,4,7,8,9} — prime, thirds, fifth, and sixths

D = {1,2,5,6,10,11} — seconds, fourth, sevenths

is in a excellent geometrical position among all possible interval dichotomies, and in opposition to another one, namely:

I = {2,4,5,7,9,11} — melodic intervals in the ionic scale

J = {0,1,3,6,8,10} — complement of I

(Here the integers denote interval types instead of notes, but the lattice structure will be the same.)

Note that the consonances and dissonances are well distinguished on the torus, while the intervals of the I/J dichotomy are extremely mixed up. Both K/D and I/J have autocomplementary functions, which relate the two halves to each other (Figure 9).

Investigations of the electrical activity (depth EEG) of the human brain in relation to consonant and dissonant musical stimuli have been carried out by a group of Swiss scientists (see Mazzola 1989). One of the main results is, that "the EEG of the hippocampus reflects the consonance-dissonance-dichotomy in a predominant way". Even evidence of the autocomplementary function has been observed. As only one consequence of these observations, one should consider that in Western music the acoustic properties of sign vehicles are less relevant

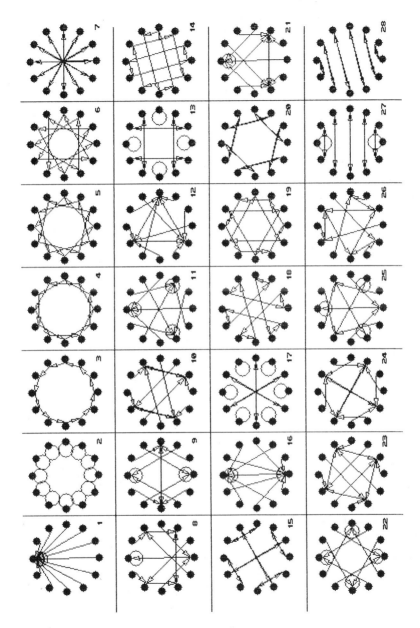

Figure 7. Conjugation classes of lattice endomorphisms.

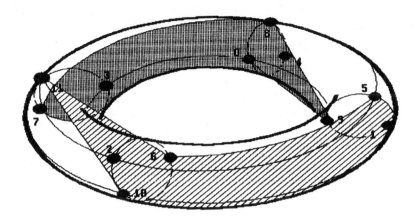

Figure 8. The K/D dichotomy.

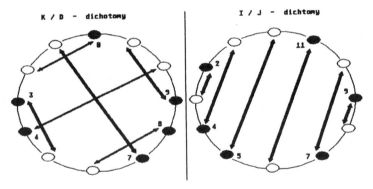

Figure 9. The autocomplementary functions of K/D and I/J.

than traditional music theory and musicians themselves assume.

The first step as a task of syntactics$_2$ is to calculate all possible graphic interval fields. The surprising result is that the most "popular" musical chords are in an excellent position among the others. Interval fields split into classes of isomorphic interval fields, which may be considered as different types of interval fields. I give a brief explanation of this, but without touching the technical details. All 4,095 chords (i.e., nonempty subsets of Z_{12}) fall into 157 isomorphy classes. The first 88 classes have class indices according to the number of notes and to the lexicographic order of their representants (here I follow the lists in Mazzola 1985 and 1990). The remaining 69 classes consist of chord-complements from already counted classes and have the index: 100 + index of the complement. (So the numbers 89–101 are not used as indices, and there are also gaps between 163 and 188, because some of the 6–note chords are isomorphic to their complement and others not.) Within the set of all 157 chord classes, we have:

1 class, which contains only one element: Z_{12} (class index 1)
1 class of 1–chords, i.e., of single notes (class index 2)
5 classes of 2–chords (class indices 3, 4, 5, 6, 7)
9 classes of 3–chords (class indices 8–16)
21 classes of 4–chords (class indices 17–37)
25 classes of 5–chords (class indices 38–62)
34 classes of 6–chords (class indices 63–88, 165, 166, 169, 172, 173, 179, 181, 185)
25 classes of 7–chords (class indices 138–162)
21 classes of 8–chords (class indices 117–137)
9 classes of 9–chords (class indices 108–116)
5 classes of 10–chords (class indices 103, 104, 105, 106, 107)
1 class of 11–chords (class index 102)

Some of the facts about reflexive graphic interval fields only depend on the chord class of their supports. There are two "natural" definitions of isomorphy possible between interval fields (natural with respect to the decisions in syntactics$_1$), one of them being a refinement of the other. The more isomorphisms there are, the fewer classes occur. In the one case we have an equivalence between classes of interval fields and chord classes. The coarse isomorphy concept then leads to a refinement in the structure of field classes. (The corresponding classification theorems have been formulated and proved by Mazzola and myself, and will be published soon.) The interplay of these two classifications seems to be the key to an understanding of paradigmatic relations within harmony. The following list gives the numbers of interval fields and the numbers of their isomorphy classes according to the coarse isomorphy concept for each chord class.

The representatives denote members of the corresponding classes. There are 12 coordinates within a 12–tupel equal to x or o, where x in the k'^{th} position means, that the note k belongs to the chord; i.e., the 12–tupel refers to the cycle of ascending semitones and its first position to the note $0 = C$. But by changing the cycle into descending semitones or ascending or descending fourths and varying the corresponding note for the first position, one can also read all members of the chord class out of the coordinates of the representative. For example: xxoxooooooxoo will be the chord $\{0,1,3,9\}$ out of class 26; but it can also be read as $\{0,11,9,3\},\{0,5,3,9\},\{0,7,9,3\}$ or any transposition of these four chords simultaneously.

1 — C H O R D S

representative	chord class index	number of interval fields	number of field classes
xooooooooooo	2	1	1

2 — C H O R D S

representative	chord class index	number of interval fields	number of field classes
xxoooooooooo	3	4	3
xoxooooooooo	4	4	3
xooxoooooooo	5	4	3
xoooxooooooo	6	4	3
xoooooxooooo	7	4	3

3 — C H O R D S

representative	chord class index	number of interval fields	number of field classes
xxxooooooooo	8	5	4
xxoxoooooooo	9	4	4
xxooxooooooo	10	8	8
xxoooxoooooo	11	5	4
xxooooxooooo	12	7	5

xoxoxooooooo	13	5	4
xoxoooxooooo	14	8	8
xooxooxooooo	15	7	5
xooooxoooxooo	16	9	4

4 — CHORDS

representative	chord class index	number of interval fields	number of field classes
xxxxooooooooo	17	6	4
xxxoxooooooo	18	5	5
xxxooxoooooo	19	5	5
xxxoooxooooo	20	7	7
xxxooooxoooo	21	10	7
xxoxxooooooo	22	8	6
xxoxoxoooooo	23	6	5
xxoxooxooooo	24	8	6
xxoxoooxoooo	25	10	10
xxoxooooxoo	26	12	12
xxoxooooooxo	27	8	5
xxooxxoooooo	28	8	6
xxooxooxoooo	29	12	10
xxooxoooxooo	30	14	11
xxooxooooxoo	31	16	9
xxoooxxooooo	32	10	7
xxooooxxoooo	33	16	7
xoxoxoxooooo	34	8	6
xoxoxoooxooo	35	14	11
xoxooooxoxooo	36	16	9
xooxooxooxoo	37	16	7

5 — CHORDS

representative	chord class index	number of interval fields	number of field classes
xxxxxooooooo	38	7	5
xxxxoxoooooo	39	6	6
xxxxooxooooo	40	8	8
xxxxoooxoooo	41	8	8
xxxoxxoooooo	42	6	6
xxxoxoxooooo	43	8	8
xxxoxooxoooo	44	9	7
xxxoxoooxooo	45	16	16
xxxoxoooxoo	46	7	5

xxxoxooooxo	47	11	8
xxxooxxooooo	48	8	8
xxxooxooxooo	49	10	10
xxxooxoooxoo	50	13	9
xxxoooxxoooo	51	11	9
xxxoooxoxooo	52	13	7
xxoxxoxooooo	53	10	10
xxoxxooxoooo	54	14	14
xxoxoxxooooo	55	11	8
xxoxoxoooxoo	56	19	16
xxoxooxxoooo	57	14	12
xxoxooxooxoo	58	22	18
xxoxoooxoxoo	59	21	13
xxooxxooxooo	60	17	11
xxooxooxxooo	61	19	14
xoxoxoxoxooo	62	17	11

6 — C H O R D S

representative	chord class index	number of interval fields	number of field classes
xxxxxxoooooo	63	8	5
xxxxxoxooooo	64	9	9
xxxxxooxoooo	65	9	9
xxxxxooooxooo	66	16	12
xxxxoxxooooo	165	9	9
xxxxoxoxoooo	67	10	6
xxxxoxooxooo	68	9	9
xxxxoxoooxoo	69	15	15
xxxxoxooooxo	70	10	6
xxxxooxxoooo	71	11	11
xxxxooxoxooo	72	12	8
xxxxooxooxoo	73	20	13
xxxxoooxxooo	74	12	7
xxxoxxxooooo	166	10	6
xxxoxxooxooo	75	17	17
xxxoxxoooxoo	76	14	10
xxxoxxoooxo	169	11	11
xxxoxoxxoooo	172	12	10
xxxoxoxoxooo	77	22	14
xxxoxoxoooxo	78	23	23
xxxoxooxxooo	181	20	18
xxxoxooxooxo	79	22	15
xxxoxoooxxoo	80	16	1
xxxooxxoxooo	81	14	10

representative	chord class index	number of interval fields	number of field classes
xxxooxxooxoo	82	17	17
xxxoooxxxooo	83	20	12
xxoxxoxxoooo	173	16	9
xxoxxoxooxoo	84	24	14
xxoxxoxoooxo	179	22	11
xxoxxooxoxoo	85	28	15
xxoxoxxooxoo	185	30	23
xxoxooxxoxoo	86	32	20
xxooxxooxxoo	87	36	12
xoxoxoxoxoxo	88	36	12

7 — CHORDS

representative	chord class index	number of interval fields	number of field classes
xxxxxxxooooo	138	11	7
xxxxxxoxoooo	139	10	10
xxxxxxooxooo	142	16	16
xxxxxoxxoooo	140	12	12
xxxxxoxoxooo	143	20	20
xxxxxoxooxoo	153	20	20
xxxxxoxoooxo	147	21	14
xxxxxooxxooo	148	18	18
xxxxxooxoxoo	155	15	8
xxxxoxxxoooo	141	12	12
xxxxoxxoxooo	144	13	9
xxxxoxxooxoo	154	26	26
xxxxoxxoooxo	146	17	12
xxxxoxooxxoo	149	18	18
xxxxooxxxooo	151	15	11
xxxxooxxoxoo	157	23	16
xxxoxxxoxooo	145	22	22
xxxoxxxooxoo	150	19	13
xxxoxxooxxoo	160	25	19
xxxoxxooxoxo	156	25	16
xxxoxoxxxooo	152	27	17
xxxoxoxxoxoo	159	33	29
xxxoxoxoxoxo	162	43	19
xxxooxxoxxoo	161	25	14
xxoxxoxxoxoo	158	33	23

8 — CHORDS

representative	chord class index	number of interval fields	number of field classes

xxxxxxxxoooo	117	14	8
xxxxxxxoxooo	118	19	19
xxxxxxxooxoo	122	28	20
xxxxxxoxxooo	119	19	19
xxxxxxoxoxoo	123	20	13
xxxxxxoxooxo	127	24	13
xxxxxxooxxoo	128	26	14
xxxxxoxxxooo	120	23	23
xxxxxoxxoxoo	124	24	17
xxxxxoxxooxo	126	31	31
xxxxxoxoxxoo	125	31	31
xxxxxoxoxoxo	134	42	17
xxxxxooxxxoo	132	24	15
xxxxoxxxxooo	121	18	9
xxxxoxxoxxoo	129	30	23
xxxxoxxooxxo	131	36	19
xxxxooxxxxoo	133	32	14
xxxoxxxoxxoo	130	30	19
xxxoxxxoxoxo	135	46	19
xxxoxoxxxoxo	136	56	28
xxoxxoxxoxxo	137	64	21

9 — C H O R D S

representative	chord class index	number of interval fields	number of field classes
xxxxxxxxxooo	108	23	14
xxxxxxxxoxoo	109	30	30
xxxxxxxoxxoo	110	36	36
xxxxxxxoxoxo	113	43	18
xxxxxxoxxxoo	111	29	20
xxxxxoxxxxoo	112	35	29
xxxxxoxxxoxo	114	51	31
xxxxxoxxoxxo	115	45	32
xxxoxxxoxxxo	116	63	20

10 — C H O R D S

representative	chord class index	number of interval fields	number of field classes
xxxxxxxxxxoo	103	40	23
xxxxxxxxxoxo	104	54	25
xxxxxxxxoxxo	105	50	19

xxxxxxxoxxxo	106	60	31
xxxxxoxxxxxo	107	68	28

11 — C H O R D S

representative	chord class index	number of interval fields	number of field classes
xxxxxxxxxxxo	102	71	31

From this information we may observe the following:

(1) The largest number of field classes does not occur at the chord consisting of all 12 notes, but at a chord class with chords of 9 notes (class index 110), which contains the complements of the major and minor chords. The number of field classes is actually 36, while the full chord of 12 notes has only 28 classes of interval fields, corresponding to the 28 conjugation classes of lattice endomorphisms.

(2) Among all 3–chord classes, the classes of index 10 and 14 are in excellent position with 8 field classes each. Class 10 contains all major and minor chords, class 14 contains chords like {G, F, B} or {F, A, B}. (Remember that {G,B,D} and {G,F,B} can be combined to the dominant seventh-chord {G, B, D, F}.)

(3) Among the 4–chord classes most field classes occur at a class of index 26, which contains the dominant seventh-chords as well as the half-diminished seventh-chords like {D, F, A, B}. The number of field classes is 12.

(4) Among all 5–chord classes the maximal numbers of interval fields and field classes occur at a class of index 58 containing the dominant ninth-chords such as {G, B, D, F, A♭}. (22 interval fields fall into 18 classes.)

(5) Among the 6–chord classes there are two with 23 field classes each. One of them (with class index 78) contains the famous "Prometheus" chord {G, D♯, A, C♯, F♯, B}, a central paradigm in Scriabin's *Prometheus: Le poème de feu* Op. 60.

The number of field classes of a chord should also be compared with the number of its interval fields. While the latter counts endomorphisms of a chord, the former counts them up to automorphisms of this chord. For a further evaluation of chords, it is useful to compare them with respect to their automorphisms. Among the 4–chord classes there are 5 classes without nontrivial automorphisms: 18, 19, 20, 25, 26. Such chords without inner symmetries are better able to function as distinctive units than symmetric chords such as {G, B♭, D♭, E}. The class of index 25 has 10 field classes as well as 10 interval fields and it contains chords like {G, F, B, E}, which I would like to call the "Chopin dominant". In my view the number of field classes together with the type of automorphism group of a given chord somehow measures its syntactical usability. But this statement has to be formulated within a generative theory using the microscopic perspective on concrete interval fields. Here are just two suggestive remarks concerning the major chord:

(1) There is a hierarchy within all interval fields on a given chord according to the number of "beginnings", which we call key-notes. (The choice of this notion is related to the hypothesis that the actual distributions of notes of a chord in concrete musical situations embody the traces of certain interval fields.) At the top of the hierarchy for the major chord there are two interval fields, with only one key-note each (Figure 10). We call them circle fields (one can consider them as very simple "fractals").

(2) There is a "nontrivial" 2–dimensional paradigmatic relation between these two circle fields in the sense of the refined isomorphy concept. This relation is important within our harmonic "grammar". In precise analogy to the concept of markedness in linguistics, and following our conception of paradigmatic relations, we can describe the opposition of these two circle fields: the 5/3 chord being unmarked, the 6/4 chord being marked, a relation akin to the deictic expressions "here" and "there" in English.

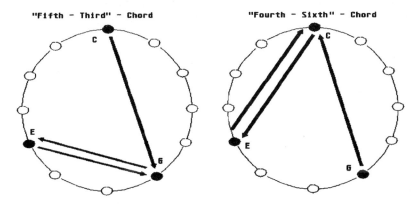

Figure 10. Circle fields on the C major chord.

My hypothesis is that in general the evolution in Western harmony can be described in terms of paradigmatic relations of interval fields according to the geometric structure of Z_{12}. This would be a task for syntactics$_3$.

An algebraic speculation on the 12–note system

Now back to syntactics$_1$. We saw that for the consideration of the tonal system it is sometimes useful to work with Z^2; other times its better to choose Z_{12}. This is acceptable within syntactics$_2$. The tonal systems (natural tuning, well-tempered tuning, and mixed forms) are historically related and one may ask: how?

The traditional answer, also given by musicians themselves, was that of an acoustic compromise, which made the Pythagorean comma mostly disappear.

Doubtless this was an important factor, but let me conclude by saying that I believe there was another, perhaps more important reason for this development.

What counts here is only the fact that the natural tuning is based on a two-dimensional lattice. Instead of examining the lattice, we should concentrate on its transformation group. This is what the "Erlanger Program" suggests and what also inspired the classical approach to syntactics$_1$ in language. In our case we deal with the group SL(2, Z), which has been investigated by many mathematicians.

Greimas — metaphorically, but with good intuition — used the notion of homologization in order to describe the mechanism of "reasoning by analogy" within structural semantics. We are now in a situation where we are examining the structure of a chosen metalanguage, which seems to be a suitable one, but of course at first sight this has little to do with Greimas's subject matter. Nevertheless it should come as a surprise that the first homology group of the infinite group SL(2, Z), which measures its commutativeness, is a cyclic group of order 12, such as the group of transpositions in Z_{12} or even the group Z_{12} itself.

Concluding remarks on a semantic theory

In general, one distinguishes between pure semantics and descriptive semantics (Morris 1938). While there are many activities in descriptive musical semantics, we must admit that there exists no pure semantic theory of music. The characterization of the difficulties within semantics of natural languages given by Morris in 1938 seems to be highly relevant for musical semantics in 1992 as well.

Without an elaborated syntactical metalanguage there is no access to pure semantics and hence no systematisation of the various activities in descriptive semantics. The mathematical theory now has to be tested. One of the main tasks consists in the development of a dynamic model, combining the two complementary conceptions of categories in order to describe the "life" of codes. From a naive point of view it seems that the two conceptions are related to different "ages" of a code: the prototypes to "young" codes and the well defined ones to elaborated "old" codes, which are characterized by standardization and which are often governed through prescriptive metacodes. In my opinion the problem leads to topology, which might provide a common language to speak about "distance" between two examples of a prototype and about its "center" and "boundary". The interesting problem, which requires the unification of the two concepts, is that even the "youngest" prototypes in Western music are in an excellent position according to systematic theory, which has obviously not been a prescriptive code for musicians. The latter will of course change very soon — perhaps more quickly than sleepy musicology will recognize the theory itself.

References

Brown, Kenneth S. (1982). *Cohomology of Groups*. New York: Springer.

Carnap, Rudolf (1934). *Logische Syntax der Sprache*. Wien: Springer.

Eco, Umberto (1985). "Hörner, Hufe, Sohlen", *Der Zirkel oder Im Zeichen der Drei*, Eco and Sebeok (eds.). München: Wilhelm Fink.

Greimas, A. Julien and Courtés, J. (1979 and 1986). *Sémiotique: Dictionnaire raisonné de la théorie du langage*. Paris: Hachette

Hindemith, Paul (1940). *Unterweisung im Tonsatz*. Mainz: Schott.

Mazzola, Guerino (1985). *Gruppen und Kategorien in der Musik*. Berlin: Heldermann.

– (1986). "Die Rolle des Symmetriedenkens für die Entwicklungsgeschichte der europäischen Musik", *Symmetrie*, vol. 1: 405–416. Darmstadt: Institut Mathildenhöhe.

– (1987). *Mathematische Betrachtungen in der Musik*. Lecture notes, University of Zürich.

– (1990). *Geometrie der Töne*. Basel: Birkhäuser.

Mazzola, Guerino et al. (1989). "A symmetry-oriented mathematical model of classical counterpoint and related neurophysiological investigations by depth EEG", *Computers and Mathematics* 17: 534–594.

Monelle, Raymond (1992). BWV 886 as allegory of listening. Paper presented at the *Third International Congress on Musical Signification*, Edinburgh; quotation from author's abstract.

Posner, Roland (1986). "Syntactics", *Encyclopedic Dictionary of Semiotics*, T.A. Sebeok (ed.). Berlin: Walter de Gruyter.

– (1988). "Balance of complexity and hierarchy of precision: Two principles of economy in the notation of language and music", *Semiotic Theory and Practice*, 909–919. Berlin: Walter de Gruyter.

– (1989). "What is culture? Toward a semiotic explication of anthropological concepts", *The Nature of Culture*, Walter A. Koch (ed.), 240–295. Bochum: Brockmeyer.

– (1991). "Research in pragmatics after Morris", *L'homme et ses signes*, M. Balat and J. Deledalle-Rhodes (eds.). Berlin: Mouton de Gruyter.

– (1992). "Believing, causing, intending: The basis for a hierarchy of sign concepts in the reconstruction of communication", *Signs, Search, and*

communication: Semiotic Aspects of Artificial Intelligence, Jorna, van Heusden, and Posner (eds.), 215–270. Berlin: Walter de Gruyter.
– (1992a). A general typology of signs from the distant past. Paper presented at the workshop on *Semiotics and Archeology*. Third official meeting of the research group on prehistoric pictographs and petroglyphs at the NASS/sffs Congress of Semiotics.
Ross, Jaan (1992). Interface between language and music: A study of rhythm in spoken and chanted texts. Paper presented at the *Third International Congress on Musical Signification*, Edinburgh.
Stefani, Gino and Marconi, Luca (1992). Melody: Prototypes, family airs, types of sign production. Paper presented at the *Third International Congress on Musical Signification*, Edinburgh).
Stumpf, Carl (1911). *Die Anfänge der Musik*. Leipzig: Johann Ambrosius Barth.
Wiora, Walter (1961a). "Musikgeschichte und Urgeschichte: Särtryck ur Studier tillägnade Carl-Allan Moberg", *Svensk tidskrift för musikforskning*, 375–396.
– (1961b). "Die Natur der Musik und die Musik der Naturvölker", *Journal of the International Folk Music Council* 13: 43–49.

The role of semiotical terminology in musical analysis

MÁRTA GRABÓCZ

Semes

In my system of analysis applied to Liszt's piano compositions (1987), the smallest semantic unit is called the *seme*. On the syntagmatic axis of musical analysis, semes correspond to *motifs* found either in musical mottos (Example 1) or elsewhere in the texture, as in the accompaniment figuration (Example 2); they also correspond to the *illustrative-associative figures* and to the *symbols* used by Liszt in transitional sections, introductions, and sometimes in developments (Example 3).

In a wider sense, the semes correspond to musico-historical "symbolism", as enacted by a melodic motif, by a characteristic feature of harmonic concatenation, or by a musical texture. This is the case of the onomatopoeia as used by the madrigalists of the sixteenth century, and of the "rhetorico-musical" figures in Bach's cantatas and Passions, where a single interval, a relation of harmonies, or a change in register can carry symbolic or descriptive onomatopoeic expression concerning the outer world, nature, human gestures, the expression of different moods, and so on.

Musical symbolism and association are discussed by József Ujfalussy in his book *The Logic of Musical Signification* (1962: 64) and elsewhere (1968, 1978). He describes these phenomena as follows:

> Musical action takes place within the network, the system created by the sounds. The image of things, or at least their place, their position appears on this screen, on this system of coordinates, in a manner permitting many-sided comparison. The individual musical sounds, in themselves, are not as rich in their immanent determination as are objects or individual people. Yet they can be related to one another in

Example 1. Semes (Mottos of Liszt).

Example 2. Semes (Pastoral and pantheist figures).

1.*a)* Sonetto 123 del Petrarca

b) Bénédiction de Dieu dans la solitude

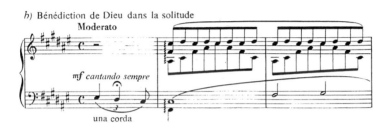

c) Vallée d'Obermann

d) Grosses Konzert-Solo

e) Bénédiction de Dieu dans la solitude

f) Au lac de Wallenstadt

g) Au lac de Wallenstadt
　　Andante placido

h) Bénédiction de Dieu dans la solitude

Example 3.   Semes (Onomatopoeic figures: semes of storm, semes of heroic fanfares).

so many subtle ways that by their relationships, by their being inter-
linked with one another from the outside, they come — at a certain
point — close to the character of objects. The sounds are discrete,
qualitatively separated, displaying their characteristics in their relation
to the others. This is why the individual movements are interrelated
with a certain objectivity and discreteness and do not produce something inarticulated and blurred in music. This is what the objectivity
of musical reality consists of. This objectivity, however, differs from
the objectivity of other arts inasmuch as the elements of objectivity
are determined by their correlation and not immanently. This degree
of objectivity is referred to by György Lukács as undetermined objectivity.

When the sounds give up the discrete pitch order and merge, they
again come closer to the sphere of tactile sense, of direct motion. The
glissandos have the same association as if one were slipping and
unable to find some support in the tonal system, some place to get a
foothold. Grace notes that attain their pitch swiftly, with a sweep,
definitely conjure up the image of the energetic and emphatic motion
of gestures. All musical phenomena blurring the relative and the
absolute pitch distinction refer back to the sphere of touch and movement. The system of distinctive and relative pitches outlined above is
what enables us to remember a formation, a structure, to recall the
correlation of the different elements thereof.

Jaroslav Jiránek (1979: 149) calls these smallest meaningful units
"initial semantic elements", and characterizes them as follows: ". . .
segments of human life . . . enter every work of art as social and com-
municable semantic elements. S. Šabouk called them initial semantic
elements. An artist draws these initial semantic elements in the whole
breadth of their connotations into the general system of the semantic
process of his work on the basis of the individual form of his work"
(1985). Jiránek describes the initial semantic elements as originating in
nature, in "the anthropological layer", or in the activities of "man in
society" (1985: 153–154).

It will be useful to recall some definitions of semes, as found in the
Analytical Dictionary of Greimas and Courtés (1982: 278):

The nature of semes is purely relational and never substantial, and the
seme cannot be defined as the end-term of the relation that one sets up
or grasps with at least one other term of the same relational network.
Thus, we acknowledge that semic categories [semantic categories that
constitute the content plane] are logically anterior to the semes that

can make up these categories and that semes can be apprehended only within the elementary structure of signification. It is by giving a precise logical status to constituent relations of such a structure (contradiction, contrariety, implication) that the concept of seme can be determined and made operational.

The *Dictionary* distinguishes several classes of semantic categories, and two of these seem to correspond entirely to our typology of figures and symbols; we have in mind the *figurative semes* (Greimas & Courtés 1982: 279):

> They are entities on the content plane of natural languages, corresponding to elements of the expression plane of the semiotics of the natural world, i.e., corresponding to the articulations of the sensory classes, to the perceptible qualities of the world; b) *abstract semes* are content entities that refer to no exteriority, but which, on the contrary, are used to categorise the world and to give it meaning: for example, the categories relation/term, object/process;...

In my study on Liszt I distinguish four major types of signified carried by mottoes, associative-symbolic figures, symbols of accompaniment, and sections of transition or evolution. These provide four major types of semes: (a) *pastoral semes* (Examples 1 and 2); *"storm" semes* (Example 3c); (c) *heroic semes of fanfares for fight* (Example 3a, no. 1); (d) *macabre semes* (Example 1: b, d, f, h, i).

Classemes-sememes-intonations

The second level of semantic units will be referred to as the category of *classemes*. The *Analytical Dictionary* describes them as follows (Greimas & Courtés 1982: 29–30):

> A. J. Greimas uses this term in a slightly different sense. He designates contextual semes as classemes, that is to say, those semes which are recurrent in the discourse and which guarantee its isotopy. . . It is difficult at present to define the limits of the semantic domain covered by classemes. At the moment, we can make only a few suggestions:
> (a) As recurrent semes, classemes, theoretically, must constitute very general categories: it is in the list of classemes that the concepts

that are not defined in semiotic theory (such as "religion", "term", etc.) should be found, as well as the so-called grammatical semes (which serve to constitute grammatical categories or classes). The problem of language universals is linked to the classematic inventory...

(c) If the grammatical semes guarantee the permanence of communication insofar as it concerns ordinary language the secondary systems which develop within natural languages (such as poetic discourse) can set up classematic categories which are peculiar to them, thereby freeing — at least partially — speech from its syntactic constraints.

For the term *semanteme*   a kindred notion, seldom used since the Prague School of musical semiotics — the *Dictionary* gives the following definition (ibid.):

In B. Pottier's terminology, the *sememe* is defined as the set of semes identifiable within the minimal sign (or morpheme). This unit of signification thus delimited is composed of three semic sub-sets : the classemes (generic semes), the *semanteme* (specific semes) and the virtueme (connotative semes). . . Whereas Pottier attributes to the sememe the totality of investments of the signified of a morpheme, the sememe for us — corresponds to what everyday language calls an "acceptation" or "particular meaning" of a word. Pottier's sememe, then, corresponds to our lexeme, the latter being made up of a set of sememes. . . that are held together by a common semic kernel.

In the history of musical aesthetics, Boris Asafiev was perhaps the first to try to attribute specific meanings, taken from a common musical language assumed in every epoch, to certain musical units which he called "intonations". Since Asafiev's theory of intonation was inspired by research conducted by Russian structuralists in the literary sciences, it might be interesting to quote András Pernye's interpretation of the roots of Asafiev's theory (1962: 21):

His reasoning is simple, indeed. When Asafiev speaks of orchestral music or chamber music or when he analyses an opera overture or an instrumental interlude, every line tells of the question not raised: why should a composer making music without words be obliged to stop being a realist and to enter the sphere of abstractions where none of the sounds can be traced back to its origin, to inspiring reality? In a long series of concrete analyses he gives the answer to this question.

The gist of his answer is as follows: there is no substantial difference between music based on text and music without words. The intonations of the latter — and consequently its spiritual basis — can be traced back to the common musical language existing in the collective mind just as much as those of music based on text except that the procedure of tracing them is more complicated, requiring keener attention, a wider view of the whole, and one has to be more aware of the danger of popularization which is invariably there.

In Hungarian musical aesthetics of the sixties, Ujfalussy developed intonation theory to the point where this category became a key to analyzing structure and content, applied mainly to classical music to demonstrate the existence of the same types of musical compositions written with and without words. While analyzing in this manner the semantic references of some Beethoven's symphonies, Ujfalussy established a parallel between Beethoven's thoughts, which can be detected in the Fifth and Sixth Symphonies, and the revolutionary ideology of the times and Kantian philosophy (1978: 136–137).

The materialist tradition of musical aesthetics uses the term intonation for denoting the sound expressions of a social milieu, of a human attitude, of a type of man and of a definite situation. This term derives from vocal music, from the traditional interpretation of music which, since Antiquity, has tried to find in music an equivalent of human attitudes and sentiments expressed in the intonations of spoken language. Nevertheless, in the current practice of musical aesthetics the category of intonation represents inflections of the spoken language rather than simple melodic and rhythmic imitation. In the present terminology of [Marxist] musical aesthetics intonation means formulaic types of specifically musical sounds that transmit a human-social message, that represent definite characters in the totality of a composition; their fate is shaped in the large musico-dramaturgical units, like that of the characters we can observe in dramas, and help reveal the image of the entire world of the artist.
It is through the concept of intonation that music assumes contact with a central, important category of general aesthetics: the typical.

Resorting to the theories of Asafiev and of Ujfalussy, Jiránek classified the term intonation among the semiotic units called "semantemes", in order to perform a complex analysis of Alban Berg's Concerto for Violin, with a view to the structural and semantic interpretation of the work. In the introductory chapters of his book *The Basic Questions of Musical Semiotics*, he outlines all historical aspects of musical aesthetics dealing with meaning. In his typology of semantic units he characterizes the second basic semantic element, the semanteme, as follows (1979: 154):

> In music the function of semantemes is fulfilled by a specific musical semantic unit: intonation, which can be defined as a plurality of the smallest concrete sound contexts which for a certain historically determined social subject (social class, stratum, environment) have relatively the same meaning (they point to the same social and life situations and to the same circle of extra-musical reality). This meaning is characterized by a certain concrete . . . structure of relations within all the components of sound expression, i.e., melody, rhythm, harmony, timbre, dynamics, tempo.

Jiránek distinguishes *intonations of genre* (e.g., music of ceremonies and rites, such as dance, march, lullaby, religious music); *intonations of instruments; tectonic intonations; and intonations of musical styles.*

Another typology appears, though under a different semantic denomination, in the category of "sème mythique", suggested by Eero Tarasti (1978), who classifies the principal types of Romantic themes of music called "mythic" as follows: mythical nature, the mythical hero, the magical, the fabulous, the balladic, the legendary, the sacred, the demonic, the fantastic, the mystic, the exotic, the pastoral, the tragic, the primitivistic, the national-musical, the sublime, the gestural.

Among the terms of the *Dictionary*, the category of the classeme — and that of the sememe with a certain degree of reserve — is what best corresponds to the level of the musical phrase and period, i.e., to the dimensions of musical themes. Since intonation also conforms to the level of themes, it seems necessary to adhere to the thesis according to which the concept of the classeme coincides with the term of musical aesthetics: "intonation" used to denote units having exact meanings, having crystallized and accumulated in the course of the history of music. Once this thesis is accepted, it becomes clear how, in the course of the syntagmatic and "programmatic" analyses undertaken in my research, I could demonstrate the existence of *sixteen major types of classemes*:

1. appassionato — agitato
2. march
3. heroic
4. scherzo
5. pastoral
6. "religioso"
7. "folkloric"
8. bel canto — singing
9. bel canto — declamatory
10. "recitativo"
11. lamenting, elegiac
12. citations
13. the "grandioso", "triumfando" (going back to the heroic theme)
14. the "lugubrious" type deriving at the same time from "appassionato"
and "lamentoso" ("lagrimoso")
15. the "pathetic", which is the exalted form of "bel canto"
16. the "pantheistic", an amplified variant of either the pastoral theme or
of the religious type

Two of these sixteen major groups of classemes are demonstrated in
Examples 4 and 5.

Semantic isotopy

To define isotopy we shall rely on the terms and explanations of A.J.
Greimas:

> Isotopy is a redundant complex of semantic categories permitting a
> uniform reading of a narration resulting from the partial readings of
> the utterances and from the solution of their ambiguities which is
> guided by the unique reading (1970: 188).

> Isotopy is generally understood to be a cluster of redundant semantic
> categories underlying discourse. Two discourses may be isotopes but
> not isomorphous (ibid.: 10).

.a) Lyon

b) Chapelle de Guillaume Tell

c) Invocation

d) Aux Cyprès de la Villa d'Este - II

e) Après une lecture du Dante

f) Ballade Nr.2.

g) Grosses Konzert - Solo

h) Sonate H - moll

Example 4. Classemes (Heroic themes).

Example 5. Classemes (Pastoral themes).

> As an operational concept, isotopy at first designated iterativity along a syntagmatic chain of classemes which assure the homogeneity of the utterance-discourse (Greimas & Courtés 1982: 163).

Distinguishing the different isotopies with regard to the generative level of the discourse, the *Dictionary* defines *semantic isotopy* as quoted above. Greimas will later distinguish thematic isotopy from figurative isotopy; but as far as analysis of the content is concerned, at the level of formal sections or sometimes even of an entire musical form, the definition of semantic isotopy is entirely satisfactory. By "semantic musical isotopy" we shall understand the categories of the signified comprising several classeme-intonations to put into relief an essential and recognizable semantic category, in several works and in different forms, with the help of intonations and different semes.

Semantic isotopies

Having examined a large number of Liszt's compositions for piano we can discern the following isotopies, subject to realization, by choosing among the different possible semantemes and intonations.

1. The isotopy of the macabre and sinister interrogation, the Faustian question, the anguished "why" of existence.

It appears most frequently at the beginning of the compositions and sometimes also at the end. It can be materialized in the following classeme-intonations: funeral march, lamento-lagrimoso, recitativo, lugubrious. Among the semes (i.e., among the associative-symbolic figures) we find the figures of storm ("tempestuoso") and the different macabre symbols which may contribute to their materialization. The works where this isotopy recurs include the following: the Étude "Il lamento", No. 10 of the *Transcendental Etudes*, "Funérailles", "Tombez larmes", "Pensée des morts", "Orage", "Chapelle de Guillaume Tell" (coda), *Vallée d'Obermann* (first thematic complex), *Le mal du pays*, *Lyon*, *Sonetto 104 del Petrarca*, *Canzone*, *Dante Sonata* (the first form of the first theme plus refrain), the Ballade in B minor (first form of the first theme), *Aux Cyprès de la Villa d'Este* I and II (motto), *Grand solo de Concert* (first thematic complex), Sonata in B minor (refrain, first and last forms of the mottoes).

2. Pastoral isotopy

I have elsewhere shown (1987) that entire works take place under the sign of this isotopy. Among them: *La leggierezza, Waldesrauschen, Paysage, Harmonies du soir, Au lac de Wallenstadt, Les cloches de Genève*. It also occurs among the isotopies within one work: *Aux Cyprès de la Villa d'Este* I, *Dante Sonata*, the Ballade in B minor, *St. François d'Assise, St. François de Paule...*, *Grand solo de Concert*, Sonata in B Minor. It may surface in themes of "scherzo", "folkloric", "bel canto", and in pantheistic figures.

In certain works this pastoral isotopy may acquire a connotation of "amoroso", as in *Un sospiro, Cantique d'amour*, Nos. 47 and 104 of the *Petrarch Sonnets*. It received the indication "con amore" in the first version of the *Vallée d'Obermann*, and could be interpreted in the same manner in the *Dante Sonata*, in the second thematic complex of the Sonata in B minor, and in other pieces.

3. Heroic isotopy

It becomes manifest through such classemes as "agitato", "marche", "héroique", "recitativo", "grandioso-triumfante", and by using semes called "figures of fanfare for fight" as well as figures "tempestuoso-eroico". This isotopy can be detected, for instance, in *Mazeppa, Vision, Eroica, Wilde Jagd, Chapelle de Guillaume Tell, Lyon*; and in certain sections of *St. François de Paule...*, the *Dante Sonata*, the *Grand solo*, the Ballade in B minor, and the sonata in the same key.

4. Religious isotopy

This is revealed by such classemes as "religioso", "bel canto chantant", "recitativo", pantheistic and "pastoral-pantheistic" semes. It recurs, for instance, in *Ave Maria*, *Angelus*, *Bénédiction de Dieu*, *Invocation*, *Sposalizio*, *St. François d'Assise*, *Tombez larmes*, the *Dante Sonata*, Sonata in B minor, *Vallée d'Obermann*, and *Pensée des morts*.

5. Pantheistic isotopy

In some works — including *Vallée d'Obermann*, the *Dante Sonata*, *St. François de Paule...*, and *Bénédiction de Dieu* — the exalted, intensified form of the religious or pastoral isotopy assumes a specific character, which could be called "pantheistic".

6. Isotopy of mourning

This comes to the fore in themes with qualities of "appassionato", "marche funèbre", "lugubrious", "recitativo-parlant", and macabre symbols (semes), as in *Funérailles*, *Tombez larmes*, *Pensée des morts*, *Il penseroso–La notte*, *Grand solo de concert*, *Aux Cyprès de la Villa d'Este* I, *Les jeux d'eaux à Villa d'Este*, *Lyon*, *Chapelle de Guillaume Tell*, and others.

7. Isotopy of the macabre fight; stormy, demoniac.

In some works the appearance of the search filled with alarm in an exalted, agitated, heroic and combatant form corresponds to sections Liszt designates as "tempestuoso", "energico", "agitato", or "stringendo". We find them in almost all works with a heroic isotopy (see no. 3, above). This isotopy manifests itself with the help of figures of storm and of fanfare.

These seven isotopies are clearly expressed by indications Liszt writes at the head of the scores. The quotations from Byron and Sénancour express the search, the spleen, the most sinister questions; the quotations from Michelangelo refer to mourning; the quotation from Sénancour corresponds to the description of pantheist feelings and of love of nature; quotations from Lamartine are expressions of pantheistic-religious feelings.

On the basis of the typology of isotopies, one can regroup Liszt's compositions according to their semantic substance by examining the number of underlying isotopies. In most cases we find works with a single isotopy, mainly those built around the pastoral isotopy (see no. 2, above), the religious isotopy (no. 4, above), or the isotopy of mourning (no. 6).

Two isotopies occur in *Lyon* (heroic and of mourning), *Orage* (heroic and search), *Tombez larmes* (mourning and religious), *Pensée des morts*, and *Mal du pays* (search and pastoral).

Three isotopies can be detected in the following: *Chapelle de Guillaume Tell* (religious-heroic, heroic, and macabre fight), *Invocation* (religious, search, and religious-heroic), *Bénédiction* (pantheistic-religious, search, pastoral), *Les jeux d'eaux* (pastoral, heroic, mourning), *Aux Cyprès* II (search, heroic, pastoral), *St. François de Paule* (pastoral-pantheist, heroic, macabre fight), *Sunt lacrimae rerum* (mourning, pastoral-amoroso, heroic).

We can discern four isotopies in: the *Grand solo de concert* (search, pastoral-amoroso, heroic, mourning), the Ballade in B minor (search, pastoral-amoroso, heroic, pantheistic), *Vallée d'Obermann* (search, pastoral-amoroso, macabre fight, pantheistic), and Scherzo and March (pastoral, search, mourning, heroic). Five isotopies appear in the *Dante Sonata* (search, pastoral-amoroso, lugubrious fight, heroic, religious). Seven isotopies are contained in the Sonata in B Minor (search, pastoral-amoroso, heroic, macabre fight, religious, pantheistic).

We shall rely on these three major types of semiotic and semantic units — seme, classeme, and isotopy — to build a system for the narrative interpretation of Liszt's works. We shall also resort to other terms from the *Dictionary* Greimas and Courtés for carrying out the semantic analysis of the compositions.

Narrative program

In our typology of formal sections, the narrative program corresponds to thematic complexes of syntagms made up of two or more isotopies. For instance, the *Dante Sonata* comprises the isotopy of macabre search and the heroic isotopy (outcome of the last thematic complex). This applies to all works starting with a sonata exposition (e.g., *Invocation*, *Lyon*, the *Grand solo*) or from its transformation into a thematic complex having several subjects (as in the Sonata in B minor and Ballade in B minor). In those narrative programs we always find an "énoncé de faire", which materializes with the help of some transitional part and which, in most cases, transforms the first subject into a second subject having an "object of disjunctive or conjunctive value". Greimas and Courtés have this to say (1982: 245):

> According to the *Dictionary*, the *narrative program* is an elementary syntagm of the surface narrative syntax, composed of an utterance of doing governing an utterance of state. It can be represented under the following forms:
>
> NP (henceforth: PN) = F [S1 $\rightarrow$ (S2 $\cap$ Ov)]
>
> PN = F [S1 $\rightarrow$ (S2 $\cup$ Ov)]
>
> Where: F = function
> S1 = subject of doing
> S2 = subject of state
> O = object . . . , V = value, semantic investment
>
> [] = utterance of doing
> () = utterance of state
> $\rightarrow$ = function of doing. . . .
>
> $\cap\cup$ = junction (conjunction or disjunction) indicating the final state, the consequence of the doing.
>
> . . . The narrative program is to be interpreted as a change of state effected by any subject (S1) affecting any subject (S2). On the basis of the utterance of state of the PN, considered as a consequence, figures such as text, gift, etc., can be reconstituted on the discursive level.

When the thematic complex advances in a teleological manner one obtains a "positive" face of the first theme or some other theme (first theme-complexes in *Invocation*, the *Dante Sonata*, Sonata in B minor, and others); this is the case of conjunctions. But if the complex results in an alienated variant (the exposition of *Lyon*, third thematic complex in the Sonata in B minor, in the *Dante Sonata*, *Vallée d'Obermann*, *St. François de Paule*) you can recognize disjunction.

Thus the only criterion for having a narrative program is the presence of two syntagms possessing two different semantic investments, that is, two different isotopies that appear in the form of a seme (motto, refrain, figure of transition) or a classeme (musical theme) or in a form where two units make a simultaneous appearance.

To come back to the question of "narrative trajectory", its presence can be ascertained in those works of Liszt that carry several thematic complexes, each with two different subjects. The simplest cases or, let us say, the most traditional ones, are obviously the sonata forms transformed with the help of the principle of evolution: *Invocation* and *Chapelle de Guillaume Tell* — 2 PNs; *Lyon* — 3 PNs. *Aux Cyprès* II shows a 3PN structure yet deviating from the principle of sonata form. We have already spoken of the number of thematic complexes (that is, of the number of PNs) in complex structures having several structural functions: the *Dante Sonata* — 4 PNs; *Grand Solo* — 5 PNs; Ballade in B minor — 6 PNs; Sonata in B Minor — 7 PNs.

Narrative strategy and Narrative trajectory

Narrative strategy seems to comprise, on the one hand, programming in the broad sense of the term (that is, the establishment of complex narrative programs that bear on the construction, circulation, and destruction of objects of value, as well as the institution of delegated subjects, responsible for executing annex narrative programs and, on the other hand, manipulation in the strict sense of the term . . .). In these two directions, strategy encroaches on the domains of narrative syntax, dealing with the setting up and functioning of narrative trajectories. (Greimas & Courtés 1982: 312)

As to form, three basic types were found to exist in the construction of Liszt's composition for the piano.

1. "Figurative" strategy

The recapitulation, the renewal of the form called enumerative (*Reihenform* or serial form); that is, the use of the arch form and of traditional variation coupled with one of the types of evolutional form (*Entfaltungsform*), namely with the formal variation of a theme or of a thematic complex, indicates a purely figurative musical narrative strategy, a strategy that only exists on the plane of "expression" (surface). In all three ways of creating a form, the strategy — often based on duplication, triplication, and, in general, on multiplication for the sake of emphasis — is determined by repetition. This emphasis may be situated in the middle (arch form) or at the end of the work (form of evolution). We have already enumerated and analyzed pieces that correspond to these structurations, so now we shall only recall some titles: *Ab irato*, *Ricordanza*, *Harmonies du soir*, *Bénédiction*, *Cantique d'amour*, *Vision*, *Paysage*, *Sposalizio*, *Il penseroso*, *La notte*.

2. "Simple" strategy (or trajectory)

The second large group of narrative strategies may be called simple strategy or simple trajectory. It is based on a single subject (musical theme) and evolves different semantic functions of the latter through the succession of different isotopies which materialize in classeme-intonations. In our typology of forms in Liszt, this strategy covers the concept of the form of evolution built on the variation of characters from a theme or a thematic complex possessing a single isotopy. The compositions falling under this category are: *Orage*, *Tombez larmes*, *Vallée d'Obermann*, *St. François de Paule*, *Pensée des morts*, *Sunt lacrimae rerum*, and *Les jeux d'eaux*.

In the first four of these works a single theme fulfills different functions; in the three compositions mentioned last the series of the different isotopies is represented by a thematic complex. Since monothematicism allows a very concise and clear realization of the imaginary program (i.e., of the underlying narrative scheme), it is by no means accidental that the "architecture" of the succession of the most important semantic functions can be recognized for the first time in the *Vallée d'Obermann*, inspired by Sénancour's "spleen" of 1803. This composition shows already the series of four semantic functions (search, love, macabre fight, and pantheism) while all the other works determined by this variation of character incorporate only two or three of them.

3. Complex narrative trajectory achieved by several narrative programs

The third type of strategy used by Liszt resorts to narrative programs composed from the very start of two or three isotopies (semantic functions) of different character. It is the fighting or confrontational isotopy that engenders various new "subjects" — the different isotopies emerging in the sequence of varied thematic complexes. In the succession of the different PNs we are aware of the dramaturgy of the latent program revealed in the *Vallée d'Obermann*, although here it is not always the semantic function of the "search" introduced at the beginning of the work but the very conflict of two functions that elicits later, different responses. The works having a complex narrative trajectory are: *Invocation*, *Lyon*, *Chapelle*, the Ballade in B minor and Sonata in B minor, the *Grand Solo*, and *Aux Cyprès* II.

Narrative Scheme

> It could be said that it is the narrative strategy which orders the arrangements and intertwinings of narrative trajectories, whereas the *narrative schema* is canonic as a reference model, in relation to which deviations, expansions, and strategic localisations may be calculated (Greimas & Courtés 1982: 206).

About the trials being narrative recurrent syntagms, Greimas says:

Indeed, the narrative schema constitutes a kind of formal framework within which is recorded "life meaning" with its three essential domains: the qualification of the subject, which introduces it into life; its "realisation", by means of which it "acts"; and finally the sanction — at one and the same time retribution and recognition — which alone guarantees the meaning of its actions and installs it as a subject of being (ibid.: 204).

With Liszt the succession of the above-mentioned four semantic functions, concerning the narrative strategy in the simple courses, will be considered as a canonic narrative scheme. In *Vallée d'Obermann*, as mentioned, the first thing sought is "the meaning of life". Then the composer tries to outline the possible answers: love or the peace of nature, a disappointed fight and a desperate heroism, an answer found in the religion of nature, in pantheism and, before the end, a short recapitulation of the interrogation. In other compositions Liszt uses a variable number of functions or different PNs, and a variable number of this canonic scheme is modified either by reducing the functions or by enlarging the succession of the "responses" with the help of the most complex PNs in themselves, by changing the place of the functions mentioned above, or by investing their succession with another initial "problem" — with other possible dénouements, with another definitive solution. Example 6 examines at close quarters the various ways in which the narrative scheme is realized.

Article finished in 1989

References

Grabócz, Márta (1987). *Morphologie des œuvres pour piano de Liszt: Influence du programme sur l'évolution des formes instrumentales*. Budapest: MTA, Institute of Musicology of the Hungarian Academy of Sciences. (Second and completed edition: Paris, Ed. KIMÉ, 1996.)

Greimas, A.J. (1970). *Du sens*. Paris: Seuil.

Greimas, A.J. and Courtés, J. (1982). *Semiotics and Language: An Analytical Dictionary*. Bloomington: Indiana University Press.

Jiránek, Jaroslav (1979). *Tajemství hudebního výzamu* [The Secret of Musical Semantics, English summary]. Prague.

	Quête macabre	Héroique	Pastorale-amoroso	Lutte macabre	Deuil	Religieuse	Panthéiste
Vallée d'Obermann	Fonction sémantique/1		Fonction sémantique/2	Fonction sémantique/3			Fonction sémantique/4
Invocation	PN1 b PN2b		PN 1 a PN 2 a			PN 1 c	PN 2 c
Lyon		PN 1 a PN 2 b		PN 2 a	PN 1 b		
Chapelle de G. Tell		PN 1 b PN 2 b		PN 2 a	PN 3	PN 1 a	
Tombez, larmes...			FS 2		FS 1	FS 3	
Pensée des morts			PN 2		PN 1		PN 3
Sonate de Dante	PN 1 a	PN 1 b PN 4 b	PN 2	PN 3		PN 4 a	
St. François de Paule marchant sur les flots	PN 4	PN 3	PN 1	PN 2			PN 5
Aux Cyprès de la Villa d'Este–II	PN 1 a PN 3	Pn 1 b	PN 3		PN 2		
Sunt lacrimae rerum		PN 3	PN 2		PN 1		
Grand solo de Concert	PN 1 a PN 4 a	PN 1 b PN 3 PN 5	PN 2		PN 4 b		
Ballade in B minor		PN 4 a	PN 1, 2, 3 b	PN 1, 2, 3 a			PN 5
Sonate in B minor	PN 1 a PN 5 PN 7 b	PN 1 c PN 5 b PN 6 a	PN 2 PN 6 b	PN 3 a	PN 3 b	PN 4 a PN 7 a	PN 4 b

Example 6. Various realisations of the narrative scheme.

– (1985). *Zu Grundgragen der musikalischen Semiotik* [On the Basic Issues of Musical Semiotics] (= translation of 1979). Berlin: Verlag Neue Musik.

Pernye, András (1962). "Aszafaev intonációelmélete" [Asafiev's theory of intonation], *Az orosz zene mesterei* [Masters of Russian Music]. Budapest: Zenemukiadó.

Tarasti, Eero (1979). *Myth and Music*. Approaches to Semiotics No. 51. Berlin: Mouton de Gruyter.

Ujfalussy, Jószef (1962). *A valóság zenei képe* [The Logic of Musical Signification]. Budapest: Zeneműkiadó.

– (1968). *Az esztetika alapjai és a zene* [The Foundations of Aesthetics and Music]. Lecture notes, Budapest.

– (1978). "Zeneesztétika" [Aesthetics of music], *Bevezetés a marxista-leninista ágazati esztetikába* [Introduction to Marxist-Leninist Aesthetics]. Lecture notes, Budapest.

Modélisation ostensive-inférentielle de l'œuvre musicale moderne:
la résistance au langage et au texte

RAPHAËL BRUNNER

L'œuvre musicale moderne, en mettant en crise le *stile rappresentativo* traditionnel, n'a pas seulement développé une résistance au langage en tant qu'intersubjectivité stable ainsi qu'une résistance accrue à la réduction historique; dans son approche scientifique, elle développe également une résistance à une théorie du signe basée sur le modèle du code et à un formalisme dépourvu d'épaisseur sémantique. A la suite du déchirement des langages, issu lui-même de l'éclatement des classes, cette résistance a pu devenir projet actif et nouvelle exigence de modernité. Dès lors, les modèles d'étude peuvent intégrer de telles données, notamment lorsqu'ils se calquent sur l'œuvre musicale affrontant la condition moderne et qu'ils cherchent à en décrire la spécificité sous des aspects viables épistémologiquement. La portée pragmatique du modèle de l'inférence — qu'il vaut mieux préférer ici au modèle du code — favorise de nouvelles descriptions, notamment en ce qui concerne l'interaction entre les divers niveaux langagiers de l'œuvre musicale et les divers rapports d'intentionnalité qu'elle entretient avec son contexte de production. La question très large du rapport au textuel et son seuil supérieur, la question de la narrativité, peuvent acquérir de la sorte une place privilégiée et servir d'illustration à un modèle dynamique approchant les logiques multiples et le caractère hétérologique d'une manifestation artistique demeurant particulière.

Evidemment, le cadre restreint de ma présentation me contraint à proposer des ouvertures sommaires. Je suggérerai ici que la musicologie peut bénéficier de certaines propositions récentes des méthodologies à disposition en sciences humaines, notamment en linguistique pragmatique et en sciences cognitives. Comme exemplification de mon cadre conceptuel, j'aborderai la question de la narrativité en essayant de la poser au regard des deux exigences apparentées que j'aurai précédemment dégagées (exigence de *secondarité*, exigence d'*oblicité*); ce faisant, j'aimerais aussi souligner — et c'est là peut-être le point central d'une communication dans le cadre des *musical semiotics* — comment les conceptions à la base des méthodologies appliquées au musical précèdent parfois leur mise en œuvre dans l'activité compositionnelle. Je me contenterai au cours de cette communication d'appeler quelques œuvres et projets significatifs qui heurtent la situation de l'art et je donnerai en note les compléments nécessaires au regard de la problématique complexe abordée.

Le langage et l'œuvre musicale en condition de modernité

L'œuvre musicale moderne convoque des approches renouvelées, notamment en ce qui concerne les conditions de modernité qui heurtent tout langage. En effet, l'éclatement des normes sociales et esthétiques ne garantit plus la compréhension de la musique moderne selon un principe d'intersubjectivité. Theodor W. Adorno la condamne ainsi à la « négation déterminée » (1958/79: 30), sans pouvoir cependant esquiver la question de la nécessité de l'œuvre d'art (cf. Jauss, 1967/78: 127). Pour le musicologue allemand Carl Dahlhaus, l'œuvre musicale moderne pose le principe d'une « subjectivité manifeste » (1980/89: 175). Les incidences sur les conceptions langagières de l'œuvre musicale — le langage étant considéré ici, dans un premier temps, comme intersubjectivité — peuvent être dès lors replacées dans un cadre épistémologique approprié.

C'est cette inquiétude sur le langage que la linguistique et la critique littéraire ont cherché à affronter, de manière légitime puisqu'elle ne peut guère être pensée qu'à partir d'une conception du langage et par le langage même. Mais la rapidité avec laquelle certaines théories ont été appliquées à la manifestation littéraire puis à l'œuvre musicale parle sans doute en faveur d'un questionnement réactualisé. De même que la première linguistique (linguistique des énoncés) s'ouvrait à une pragmatique interactionnelle (théorie de l'énonciation) et soumettait ses propositions à la philosophie du langage, les conceptions musicales issues des théories du langage et de la communication peuvent elles aussi se démarquer des positions crispées dans lesquelles elles se confinaient sous l'influence du structuralisme dans ses propositions les moins fines.

De la référence à l'inférence (brève archéologie critique des méthodologies issues des théories du langage et appliquées au musical)

Les méthodologies, accompagnées de leurs traditionnels discours normatifs, ont souvent réduit l'œuvre au concept ou à son empreinte sociale par des attitudes qui reviennent respectivement à surestimer ou à sous-estimer, voire à nier les contraintes langagières qu'affronte inévitablement l'œuvre musicale, ne serait-ce que du point de vue de sa réception.

Raymond Monelle (1992) a proposé récemment un panorama des méthodologies issues de la linguistique et de la sémiotique. Je me suis moi-même penché sur ces méthodologies, en notant l'interaction entre œuvres et méthodes, ainsi qu'en cherchant à actualiser leur portée sur divers projets compositionnels du XXème siècle (1993a). Cet aperçu critique, au regard des préoccupations avenues en sciences humaines, a rapidement porté le soupçon sur des méthodologies appliquées de manière unilatérale à la manifestation artistique et, plus particulièrement, à l'œuvre musicale du XXème siècle.

Les méthodologies à disposition en sciences humaines, notamment celles issues de la linguistique, ont progressivement élargi leur champ d'investigation à des données pragmatiques et contesté la prédominance du modèle du code en l'élargissant au modèle de l'inférence. La première sémiologie appliquée à l'œuvre musicale moderne, a souvent ramené l'œuvre à des systèmes de correspondances en faisant appel de manière unilatérale à une théorie du langage basée sur le modèle du code et aboutissant par divers assouplissements à la sémiologie tripartite. Dans le même temps, la musicologie se trouvait réduite, soit à écarter l'œuvre musicale moderne de son champ d'investigation, soit à l'assimiler aux empreintes sociale et historique ou encore à l'aborder par un formalisme difficilement viable épistémologiquement parce que manquant l'œuvre par une reproduction tautologique des stratégies compositionnelles. Les visées normatives de l'époque, provoquées entre autres par les mouvements « avant-gardistes » et par les multiples réactions qui les ont accompagnés, n'ont pas favorisé une prise en compte pragmatique du musical alors même que de nombreux projets compositionnels se démarquaient très tôt des inévitables idéologies pour les dépasser ou les précéder dans un véritable souci esthétique.

La typologie sémiotique de Charles S. Peirce et la sémantique développée par Algirdas-Julien Greimas peuvent peut-être apporter des outils théoriques dans la description concrète de l'œuvre musicale. Mais il faut procéder ici à quelques réorientations en raison des exigences de modernité qui heurtent non seulement les langages esthétiques mais aussi les discours sur ces langages — ce qui paraît évident mais semble néanmoins d'une réalisation difficile si l'on observe les positions apparemment inconciliables des discours exclusifs sur la modernité musicale et contre elle.

Cependant, la linguistique pragmatique et les théories de la cognition disposent d'un modèle relativement récent qui semble faciliter une conception dynamique de l'œuvre musicale suite à la mise en crise du *stile rappresentativo* ainsi que des particularités de la « communication artistique ». Le modèle prédominant du code ne parvient en effet qu'à restituer les éléments de correspondance stables entre deux niveaux articulatoires (les liens) alors que l'appel à une théorie de l'*interprétance*, élaborée par la sémiotique, ou à celle de l'*inférence*, élaborée par la pragmatique, favorise une compréhension des langages sous leur manifestation la plus dynamique (les effets, l'interaction entre les particules langagières).

Hans Robert Jauss (1967/78), avant même le *Plaisir du texte* (1973) de Roland Barthes, avait déjà proposé une lecture esthétique des négations frappant la théorie sur l'art; il réhabilitait de la sorte une dimension seconde, aux risques, assumés, d'éloigner l'art contemporain de sa réflexion et de soumettre l'œuvre d'art à un contexte de réception qui ne réceptionnerait que la fonction de l'art. La critique y est portée contre le marxisme et contre le formalisme au profit d'une première conciliation entre l'approche historique et l'approche structurale. La distinction entre la notion d'*effet* (*Wirkung*) *de l'œuvre* et celle d'*esthétique de réception* (*Rezeptionsästhetik*) permet de bénéficier de telles propositions (la notion d'*effets* peut être retenue ici en ce sens qu'elle se rapproche de la conception pragmatique du modèle de Dan Sperber et Deirdre Wilson et des notions d'*indices communicationnels* et d'*indices intentionnels*). Dans le même temps qu'Umberto Eco parle d'une « semiosis *in progress* », en précisant que ce fonctionnement sémiotique ouvert ne s'oppose pas à celui des systèmes fermés et rigoureusement structurés (1968/72: 405), Jauss parle lui, dans son approche de l'œuvre littéraire et de l'expérience esthétique lui étant liée, de l' « expansion d'un système sémiologique » (1967/78: 50). Cependant, si l'on considère le signe comme unité doublement articulée, il devient difficile d'accepter l'application *stricto sensu* d'une conception sémiotique au musical et à la théorie lui étant appliquée. Force est de constater que la musique présente rarement des unités délimitées de l'ordre du signe mais plutôt des profils délimitants (suprasegments). C'est ce que soulignait Françoise Escal, à la suite d'Emile Benvéniste, en se rapprochant ainsi de la critique adressée par Sperber et Wilson à la prédominance du modèle du code et en relativisant son application à la musique. Selon Françoise Escal, la musique s'oppose au langage verbal par le fait qu'elle ne saurait *produire* de signes et donc relever du sémiotique; elle produit des discours et relève donc du sémantique (1979: 37).

En reprenant les vecteurs dynamiques comme l'*interprétance* et la notion d'*index*, les *musical semiotics* se sont réapproprié le système sémiotique de Peirce, au risque de faire peser sur une théorie la notion de *trace* et ses implications métaphysiques: « If a sign-system, to be such, need not be shown to have a particular content but only to be capable of having a content, then music would clearly be a sign-system. » (Monelle, 1992: 45).

Si le modèle linguistique permettait dans un premier temps de souligner les éléments de concordance formant le niveau informationnel des énoncés, aujourd'hui, par l'élargissement de la linguistique aux aspects les plus dynamiques de la production du sens, on assiste donc un peu au mouvement inverse[1]. La pragmatique interactionnelle s'éloigne d'une description référentielle ou dénotative pour s'ouvrir à une dynamique connotative et inférentielle; elle prend en compte les discrépances, l'interaction (les *effets*) entre des éléments, jusque-là appelés de manière unilatérale parce que reliés au modèle normatif du code. Aussi le modèle ostensif-inférentiel peut-il favoriser une conception *oblique* et *seconde* de la communication propre à circonscrire la manifestation artistique et l'expérience esthétique lui étant liée sous un jour dynamique.

Le modèle ostensif-inférentiel pour une conception du musical

Le modèle de l'inférence développé par Sperber et Wilson (1986/89) — à la suite notamment des contraintes conversationnelles théorisées par Paul Grice —, favorise en effet une critique tant du formalisme que du sémiologique qui ont souvent répondu et qui répondent parfois encore de manière unilatérale aux dimensions multiples des manifestations langagières et artistiques, en étant incapable de rendre compte des enjeux dynamiques d'une œuvre ou en donnant parfois une exhibition forcée des contenus: ces approches univoques ne peuvent que manquer ce qui fait des œuvres d'art une manifestation artistique et non des logiques appliquées (qu'elles portent sur le sémantique ou sur le formel). Parce qu'il permet de rendre compte non seulement des fonctions référentielles du langage (ce qui ne semble guère productif suite à la mise en crise du *stile rappresentativo*), mais surtout de ces fonctionnements ostensifs-inférentiels, le modèle de Sperber et Wilson devient un appareil conceptuel bien plus approprié à une application aux langages esthétiques que celui autorisé par la traditionnelle *semiosis* et par le modèle du code. La question de la narrativité elle-même ne saurait être abordée sur le seul plan d'un temps extérieur comme ultime référence (voir *infra* ma description).

Rappelons qu'Eco avait introduit dans la conclusion de *La Structure absente* le concept d'une « semiosis *in progress* » et qu'il l'avait accompagnée de la notion pragmatique de la *circonstance*: « Puisque la circonstance contribue à faire découvrir les codes, grâce auxquels on pratique le décodage des messages, alors la sémiotique peut nous montrer comment, *au lieu de modifier les messages ou de contrôler les sources d'émission, on peut altérer un processus de communication en agissant sur les circonstances de réception du message.* » (Eco, 1968/72: 409) Jauss avait quant à lui décrit la constitution d'un « horizon d'attente » (*Erwartungshorizont*) motivant l'expérience esthétique de la réception de l'œuvre d'art (1967/78: notamment 49–63) et Barthes apportait la notion-clé d' « ancrage » (1964: 44). En se penchant sur les éléments pragmatiques qui guident l'expérience esthétique des œuvres littéraires ou qui servent de support idéologique aux messages publicitaires, ils ne pouvaient manquer d'annoncer la conception ostensive-inférentielle et son application aux particularités langagières des manifestations artistiques.

Confrontés à des situations concrètes où les mythes et les œuvres littéraires communiquent plus que leur sens linguistique, où les rites et les coutumes communiquent sans supports prédéterminés, Sperber et Wilson relèvent immédiatement qu' « une meilleure compréhension des mythes, de la littérature, des rituels, etc., montre que ces phénomènes culturels ne servent pas, en général, à communiquer des messages précis et prévisibles. Ils orientent l'attention des destinataires dans certaines directions; ils aident à structurer leur expérience » (1986/89: 20). Dès lors — notons la portée de ces propos sur une conception du musical —, « comprendre comment s'effectue la communication est encore plus important que savoir ce qui est communiqué » (1986/89: 12).

Rendre compte de la manifestation artistique sur la base d'un théorie informationnelle (donc sur un modèle de correspondances servant souvent de prétexte à l'extension des modèles informatiques fonctionnels) ne semble donc guère pertinent ici: la communication n'est pas uniquement, ni essentiellement, ce qui permet de transmettre de l'information et des messages, mais bien plus ce qui permet de désambiguïser un code implicite ou — ce qui semble plus pertinent dans ma conception du musical — de pallier à l'absence de code stable préexistant[2]. Conséquence langagière immédiate: le langage n'est plus appréhendé comme « inter-subjectivité », mais comme « inter-rogation » appelant la capacité inférentielle et affrontant le péril du questionnement[3].

Le modèle favorise ainsi les descriptions portant sur l'œuvre musicale comme objet *potentiellement* médiateur (c'est là sa « textualité »). Il permet également de conceptualiser les inévitables discrépances entre le poïétique et l'esthésique, selon la terminologie proposée par Paul Valéry et reprise par la sémiologie tripartite de Nattiez/Molino, c'est-à-dire: « comment un stimulus physique produit par un individu et perçu par un autre peut-il rendre certaines pensées du second individu semblables à celles du premier, alors qu'il n'y a pas la moindre ressemblance entre le stimulus et les pensées qu'il met en correspondance ? » (Sperber et Wilson, 1986/89: 93). On peut dès lors se demander pourquoi le modèle de la tripartition ne se réclamerait pas d'une pragmatique interactionnelle plutôt que d'une sémiologie aux colorations fortement structuralistes (je ne devrais pas avoir à expliquer ici ce que la recherche forcée de liens artificiels entre les catégories de la tripartition peut présenter comme dangers pour la création). La seule question — d'ailleurs mal posée — entre écriture et perception, est invalidée par les données pragmatiques de la réception et par les exigences de *secondarité* et d'*oblicité* du musical (l'écriture est le contraire de la perception en ce que l'œuvre musicale donne à entendre ce qui est vierge d'écoute; c'est cet inaudible, par l'audible prenant sa place, qui précède et motive l'écoute). Seule une théorie des *effets* autorisant la réception à partir de l'objet médiateur, approchée ici selon le modèle ostensif-inférentiel, et non selon le modèle exclusif du code, permet d'affronter l'euphorie, et de cet *Ur-code* « institutionnel », et de ce code génétique primaire et « naturel », conceptions encore à l'œuvre dans les questions portant sur des archétypes dépouillés de toute épaisseur culturelle (et des artifices liés à la pratique de l'écriture). Inutile même de revenir sur l'impossibilité épistémologique de ce Code dont la pseudo-existence conduit inévitablement au discrédit de la création contemporaine (Eco, 1968/72: 382 sq.) ou à sa fonctionnalisation.

Si la conception inférentielle parvient à rendre compte des inévitables discrépances entre conception et réception, entre les « circuits courts » et « circuits longs » de la communication décrits par Nattiez (notamment 1988: 24) et la diagonale entre les deux catégories de mémoires posées par Pierre Boulez, « mémoire *a priori* », « mémoire *a posteriori* » (v. Brunner, 1990), c'est notamment parce qu'elle ne vise pas le lien d'association mais l'interaction pragmatique entre les éléments et leur attribution *première impertinente* (rupture de contiguïté) réinvestie par *secondarité — et seulement par secondarité* dans un concept d'écriture non aliéné — d'une *pertinence*. Il devient dès lors possible de réhabiliter, par cette notion, le rapport dérivé avec une valeur esthétique, ce qui permet de s'éloigner, si ce n'est de l'interaction tout à fait naturelle et même souhaitable entre théorie et pratique, du moins de l'application forcée d'une correspondance entre activité « structurelle » et activité « structurale », confusion qui conduit inévitablement à l' « incompatibilité entre le structuralisme et les procédés de l'art contemporain » (Eco, 1968/72: 327–28) ou à la soumission de l'activité artistique aux diktats d'un langage devenu institution, c'est-à-dire jamais réalisé comme langage[4].

La résistance au langage: exigences *premières*, exigences *secondes* de modernité

Une application au musical d'un modèle issu des théories du langage, mais démarqué de la prédominance du modèle du code et libéré de ces liens étroits avec une conception du langage verbal, n'est pas sans bénéfices. Parce qu'il permet de mettre en évidence le caractère *interactionnel par un objet médiateur* de la communication, le modèle ostensif-inférentiel permet de cerner une conception du musical au regard de sa condition moderne et de se rapprocher des propositions d'une musicologie viable épistémologiquement.

Il devient dès lors aisé de concevoir pourquoi l'œuvre musicale convoque, *dans le même temps*, les deux *contraires*: l'écriture et l'expressivité (Célestin Deliège reprenant Yves Bonnefoy, 1988: 64; 1991: 137). Aisé également de concevoir que l'écriture tend au formalisme et à l'extériorité du sujet alors que l'expressivité peut conduire à la fonctionnalisation, et d'éléments prédéterminés, et du sujet, c'est-à-dire la négation de l'expressivité en tant que telle. Hegel notait déjà qu' « une plus grande profondeur exige qu'également dans la musique instrumentale le compositeur porte son attention des deux côtés, et sur l'expression d'un contenu assurément indéterminé et sur la structure musicale » (cité par Adorno, 1958/79: 26–27). C'est là le caractère dialectique de la musique et, en ce qui concerne sa « textualité », son exigence d'*oblicité*.

Dahlhaus souligne également la complémentarité dialectique entre le concept d'œuvre — parallèle ici à la notion du Texte décrite par la critique littéraire — et le concept du dialogue qu'il emprunte à Friedrich Schleiermacher — proche des contraintes conversationnelles de Grice et du principe de *pertinence* — : « La relation avec la catégorie de l'œuvre refermée sur soi, qui revendique d'être là pour elle-même, n'est toutefois, comme on l'a dit, pas aussi simple qu'elle ne le paraît dans la dichotomie qui oppose un concept d'œuvre aliéné et un concept de communication abstrait, c'est-à-dire confronte deux extrêmes figés, plutôt que de rechercher les médiations, qui sont à portée de main. [...] Elle [la musique] a de toute évidence besoin, pour être substantielle, d'un *objet servant d'intermédiaire dans l'interaction* entre les sujets qui recherchent la communication; et c'est par une concentration commune sur une chose — une chose certes qui en vaille la peine — plutôt que par la tentative de la produire dans une immédiateté sans objet que l'on aboutira à une intersubjectivité qui rende aussi justice au sujet comme personne, et non pas simplement comme titulaire d'une fonction. » (1980/1989: 182; c'est moi qui souligne) Il en découle la notion de « médiation interactive par un objet », notion parallèle aux propositions de Sperber et Wilson: « Toujours est-il qu'entre l'illusion qu'un texte parle de lui-même — on devrait donc uniquement adopter ce qu'il dit, en s'effaçant soi-même — et le coup de force qui veut que le seul sujet de l'auditeur ait en réalité la parole lors de la réception, il existe une médiation qui ne paraît pas impensable. [...] Si l'on part du fait qu'un concept d'œuvre non aliéné, qui autorise la possibilité d'une réception d'après le modèle du dialogue, et un concept de communication concret, qui évite les guet-apens de l'abstraction et admet en son principe la nécessité d'une *médiation interactive au moyen d'un objet commun*, ne s'excluent pas, on peut alors circonscrire la conception qui est à la base de la relation actuelle, dégagée de toute crispation sur des positions extrêmes, entre l'idée restituée de l'œuvre et l'idée malgré tout conservée de la communication. » (1980/89: 183; c'est moi qui souligne)

A la suite de ces conceptions et distinctions, il semble évident que tant l'approche sémiotique que l'approche formaliste, menées de manière unilatérales, sont non avenues lorsqu'elles portent sur l'œuvre musicale moderne puisqu'elles conduisent à l'exhibition de contenus « assurément indéterminés » ou nous privent de l'expression sensible par l'introduction du concept aboutissant à une « intériorité vide » selon la terminologie hégélienne. Sans doute vaut-il mieux se rapprocher d'un *itinéraire second* qui ne sous-estimerait pas l'exigence d'*oblicité* à la fois de l'œuvre et du discours tentant de cerner les particularités de sa manifestation.

Sur la base de ces deux contraintes opposées mais convoquées dans le même temps — écriture et expressivité chez Deliège et Bonnefoy, concept d'œuvre non aliéné et concept de communication concret chez Dahlhaus —, j'aimerais distinguer diverses *épistemè* de modernité: des exigences *premières* et des exigences *secondes*, (*secondes* parce que en relation de dérivation par rapport aux dimensions *premières*). Ces deux exigences opèrent traditionnellement en synchronie, mais l'histoire musicale moderne, par ses extrêmes opposés (les mutations successives et les refus du donné qu'elles ont provoqués), par les discours critiques conceptualisant les œuvres et allant jusqu'à s'y substituer, a largement contribué à donner pour dissociées, voire même inconciliables. De la sorte, elle nous éloignait de l'expérience esthétique pourtant appelée par les projets compositionnels ayant conservé quelque valeur culturelle. Les notions d'écriture et de Texte apparues en littérature et la conception d'œuvre renvoyant à elle-même ont amené les notions apparentées d'autographie et d'auto-signifiance (cf. la notion de *formal iconism* apportée par David Osmond-Smith) alors que l'expressivité de l'œuvre marque le renvoi au sujet — considéré ici comme référence à soi dans la référence au monde. Ces deux exigences contraires appelées simultanément impliquent dès lors la réapparition de notions de valeur accompagnant l'aspect purement formel de la manifestation artistique. Certes, les mutations d'écriture frappant les langages mettent en crise justement ce qui leur donnait capacité langagière, mais dans un mouvement *second*, que les mutations de langage, en tant que donné absolu, contribuent à diachroniser, surviennent l'élargissement pragmatique, en contexte, du langage et son inquiétude immédiate sur sa propre capacité langagière[5].

Introduire cette dimension *seconde* permet ainsi d'interpréter la négativité de l'œuvre musicale moderne comme « inversion du positif » ou comme « négativité positive » — selon les termes de Ralph Heyndels (1985: 57–98) — et de les accompagner d'une notion de valeur comme celle d'*esthétique de la réception* chez Jauss ou de *pertinence* développée dans le cadre du modèle de la communication ostensive-inférentielle. L'œuvre musicale en condition de modernité nous convie dès lors à l'histoire de la « transgression analogique », du passage du mode de la linéarité au discontinu, non pas en tant qu'abolition de la représentation et pure négativité, mais en tant qu' « effet rupteur » (Heyndels) en ce sens précis que le résultat demeure lié par *secondarité* à ce qu'il a transgressé par le travail même de déréalisation et de transgression. Cette conception dynamique est dès lors propre à relativiser toute notion exclusive de « progrès » musical et la compréhension absolue des « mutations d'écriture » telles qu'elles peuvent être motivées par une conception historiciste de l'évolution de la musique, attitudes figées se heurtant à la première théorie langagière à disposition et aux mouvements contradictoires de l'histoire.

La résistance au langage par la résistance au texte: déréaliser la textualité de l'œuvre musicale

Caractériser de manière concrète l'inquiétude de l'œuvre musicale moderne sur ses propres capacités langagières peut revenir à approcher son rapport actif et plurivoque au texte. En effet, le statut langagier de l'œuvre musicale apparaît simplement mieux lorsqu'il se confronte à un autre langage, comme le langage doublement articulé de la langue, ou lorsqu'il se confronte aux langages musicaux préexistants en vue de leur intégration dialectique au cœur de l'œuvre (ce qu'une description *a posteriori* révèle dans de multiples projets compositionnels du XXème siècle et ce qui permet l'approche historique). De manière plus large, ce sont les fondements de la « textualité » musicale qu'il peut s'agir d'ébranler.

La question peut être abordée de manière suffisamment large pour aboutir, non seulement à des correspondances son/verbe sur le modèle épistémologique des années 50–60 et de la première sémiologie, mais aussi à des aspects bien plus dynamiques faisant intervenir l'*inférence*, comme la narrativité en tant que travail sur le discontinu et recherche de *pertinence* temporelle. C'est au premier type de relations que se sont attaqué d'abord les méthodologies héritées de la linguistique (par exemple une revue comme *Musique en jeu*), au risque de se livrer quelques fois à des excès provoqués par l'application trop immédiate des premières linguistiques au fait musical, ce qui risquait de conduire au discrédit de la musique contemporaine (par exemple chez Lévi-Strauss), ou à la légitimation de l'œuvre en tant qu'objet débarrassé de liens d'intentionnalité avec l'extérieur (par exemple chez Nicolas Ruwet), finalement de toute intentionnalité (cf. la problématique de l'*intentional fallacy*). Dans mon approche historique et critique, il serait cependant erroné de sous-estimer les mouvements parallèles de ces méthodologies et des projets compositionnels, mouvements certainement révélateurs d'une situation épistémologique spécifique (il est d'ailleurs possible de décrire la réception interactive des œuvres et des théories sur cette base).

Il peut être ainsi révélateur de passer en revue les projets compositionnels qui affrontèrent les exigences *premières* frappant les mouvements « avant-gardistes » à la sortie de la deuxième guerre mondiale, puis de chercher par une lecture *a posteriori* de ces divers projets, à réinvestir le territoire formaliste d'une notion de valeur: les exigences *secondes*, celles-là mêmes auxquelles s'affrontaient les grands projets à la sortie de la guerre, révèlent des préoccupations devenues centrales aujourd'hui. La compréhension figée d'une époque comme celle de « Darmstadt » traduit bien l'exacerbation des exigences *premières* de modernité accompagnées souvent de l'occultation des préoccupations esthétiques des grands projets de l'époque dont les lignes de force sont établies parfois avant, comme celui de Boulez, des projets refusant l'utopie d'un an zéro (*das Jahr null*), comme celui de Luigi Nono (Brunner, 1991: notamment 8–15) ou éloignés d'une modernité exclusive comme celui de Klaus Huber.

La conception que je tire du modèle inférentiel me conduit à distinguer assez sommairement deux aspects. En premier lieu, la question de la *circonstance* et des données pragmatiques (l'environnement textuel, par exemple) permettant l'approche de la *textualité musicale exteroceptive*, « Musik und Text » (voir mes descriptions, 1993b: 71–93). La deuxième, dont je vais brièvement soulever les enjeux, porte sur l'effet du texte *in absentia*, la *textualité musicale interoceptive*, « Musik "als" Text », conception où il s'agira encore de distinguer une conception à proprement parler « temporelle » du temps (temps *exteroceptif*) et une conception « spatiale » (temps *interoceptif*) en abordant la question de la narrativité ainsi que son seuil, celle de l'utilisation de l'espace à fin de signification[6].

La narrativité comme seuil de la question du texte et comme recherche de pertinence temporelle

Jann Pasler (1989) propose dans son article sur les « narrative and narrativity in music » une typologie prenant en compte la relation à une temporalité *exteroceptive* (c'est-à-dire où la temporalité est l'ultime référence) mais sous-estimant la dimension spatiale de l'écriture dans un premier essai de classification[7]. Au regard du principe de *pertinence* que j'ai développé, la *narrativité* sera également envisagée ici *comme notion seconde* — je tiens à le souligner —, de manière à prendre en compte des projets compositionnels qui neutralisent les oppositions catégorielles *premières* en posant, par exemple, les bases de l'émergence narrative; la narrativité qualifiera dès lors le travail de continuité (de pertinence temporelle) portant sur le discontinu (comme rupture de contiguïté). De même, la notion d'*isotopie* se doit d'accéder à la *secondarité* de manière à ne pas réduire l'œuvre à sa surface de perception négligeant la profondeur d'écriture. Eero Tarasti proposait ainsi de traiter la notion d'isotopie sur un plan sémantique et de l'élargir à une dynamique spatiale et actantielle: « Insofar as in music isotopies are equated merely to some 'time-span', which is delineated according to gestalt-theoretical surface criteria, it would seem that the *depth dimension* of the signification would be entirely neglected. Still, music undeniably possesses this depth dimension, and is able to create meanings of meanings with several superimposed levels. It would thus seem that one should maintain the concept of isotopy in music in its particular *semantic meaning*, which refers to signification, since it is broader than the gestalt-theoretical definition based merely on surface perception. [...] Hence, in the definition of an isotopy one should take into account not only the temporal strategy, but other 'shifters' (i.e., spatial and actorial) as well. » (1987: 452; v. cependant *infra* mes réserves concernant la fonctionnalisation actantielle des projets compositionnels portant sur des éléments prédéterminés).

Je vais donc essayer brièvement de dégager quelques aspects de la question au regard des exigences que j'ai préalablement posées. Je me contenterai de survoler quelques projets compositionnels significatifs en me concentrant sur le cadre théorique qui motive mes descriptions.

La narrativité comme travail sur le discontinu

Il est peut-être bon de préciser ici que la première mutation d'écriture du siècle intervient aux alentours de 1908 (climax en 1923) et la deuxième mutation d'écriture — la généralisation de la première — atteint son climax aux alentours de 1950. La crise provoquée par la mutation est dénoncée par Iannis Xénakis dès 1955 dans un article célèbre, « Crise de la musique sérielle », alors que le *Marteau sans maître* (1953–55, rév. 1957) de Boulez et le *Gesang der Jünglinge* (1956) de Karlheinz Stockhausen en donnent des dépassements à la même époque, le premier par l'instauration de champs harmoniques et par l'écriture oblique, le deuxième par sa logique de continuité qui n'est pas étrangère à l'utilisation d'un matériau verbal restreint et de techniques électro-acoustiques imposant une certaine matérialité et continuité « analogiques » (la mutation d'écriture est déjà lue dans ces projets comme « inversion du positif » et recherche nouvelle de *pertinence*).

Il est vrai que la prise en compte immédiate des projets musicaux dans ce qu'ils ont de plus extrémiste n'était pas pour éviter la séduction d'une approche première et directe. En effet, l'histoire musicale retient comme illustration du sérialisme généralisé les *Structures Ia* (1951–52) de Boulez, à la suite du *Mode de valeurs et intensités* (1949) d'Olivier Messiaen. Seule l'approche formaliste peut rendre compte de l'isotopie de la composition: le sérialisme intégral provoque ici l'atomisation du discours musical, c'est-à-dire l'appel unilatéral à la « mémoire *a posteri-*

ori » et conduit à la proximité d'un « degré zéro de l'écriture » que Barthes avait noté en littérature (1953). L'urgence historique relègue les exigences *secondes* à quelques choix de registres (dimension spatiale *interoceptive*) et conduit le sujet à l'expérience terrorisante du dehors (cette expérience trouvera chez Jean Barraqué une manifestation des plus symboliques). En plus de cette exigence de discontinuité, apparaît dans les œuvres vocales bouléziennes l'éloignement de tout effet lyrique (c'est sans doute pourquoi Boulez dirige ses choix de textes et son esthétique vers les auteurs de la déconstruction langagière comme Stéphane Mallarmé et James Joyce, mais aussi vers la littérature métaphorique par excellence, le surréalisme). Dans *Le Marteau sans maître* sur les textes de René Char, de même que dans les *Structures*, tout demi-ton conjoint est évité, pour éviter de se rapprocher de la représentation lyrique du demi-ton et son pathos expressif tels qu'on les trouve chez Claudio Monteverdi, chez Jean-Sébastien Bach, dans l'harmonie chromatique wagnérienne, etc.

Stockhausen donne également une paraphrase du *Mode de valeurs et intensités* de Messiaen dans *Kreuzspiel* (1951) où se trouvent les fondements de la *Momentform* et d'une « esthétique de la désagrégation » privilégiant les exigences *premières*. (cf. Pasler 1989: 244.245). Il y met en œuvre un projet narratif « où le travail sur la discontinuité se borne à une élision des liens syntactiques » (Dufourt, 1991: 122).

A la même époque, Nono donne *Incontri per 24 strumenti* (1955), paraphrase du *Mode de valeurs et intensités* au même titre que les compositions de Boulez, Stockhausen ou Milton Babbit. Cependant, l'œuvre du compositeur vénitien ne trahit pas seulement l'impact du sérialisme, mais aussi un souci de hiérarchisation des masses sonores et un agencement assurant une certaine logique de la continuité par l'utilisation de l'espace orchestral. Ici, les exigences *premières* engendrant la discontinuité et la fragmentation atomique du discours sont relayées par un souci de continuité comme exigence *seconde*. Chez Nono, la dimension « politique » de l'œuvre ne se décèle pas seulement par le choix des textes et les jeux paratextuels et intertextuels, mais aussi par la soumission du sériel au non sériel, c'est-à-dire de l'écriture à l'expressif, de l'instrumental pur au lyrisme généralisé et, dans *Incontri*, par exemple, du discontinu au continu. Cette logique de continuité apparaît particulièrement bien dans une œuvre avec texte comme *Il Canto sospeso* (1955–56): les procédés de spatialisation du texte et d'ouverture du signe linguistique permettent de mieux comprendre la logique de continuité musicale appuyée ici par la continuité imposée par les couches verbales. Aussi la musique accède-t-elle à un espace intertextuel dont elle n'est qu'un élément et s'ouvre-t-elle à l'engagement, comme dans les *Epitaffi per Federico García Lorca* (1951–53) (Brunner, 1991: 141–155). Notons que cette logique de continuité n'a jamais été rompue, quoi qu'on ait pu affirmer, bien que le risque d'une musique confrontée au silence ait été poussé à l'extrême, par exemple dans le quatuor à cordes *Fragmente, Stille — an Diotima* (1979–80). L'utilisation constante d'une *Musikdramaturgie*, bien que difficile à approcher dans les œuvres de la maturité, favorise une « mise en scène » du temps et de l'espace.

Pour revenir au projet boulézien, le sérialisme généralisé conduisant au discontinu apparaît particulièrement dans le découpage séquentiel des *Structures Ia* ou de manière plus relative dans *Eclat* (1965), mais l'exigence *seconde*, telle qu'elle apparaît de manière particulièrement claire dans *Multiples* (1970) est une exigence de continuité polyphonique (les titres des œuvres sont significatifs). L'ensemble aboutit à la forme-spirale, c'est-à-dire à un univers harmonique relatif en expansion, par exemple dans *Répons* (1980–...). C'est à ce titre que le travail de Boulez cherche à « *lier le discontinu* selon un système de différences et de variations » (Dufourt, 1991: 90; je souligne).

On comprend mieux dès lors comment le temps musical est le produit d'une attribution première impertinente réinvestie d'une nouvelle pertinence. Une figure du discours oblique comme la métonymie hérite de la relation de contiguïté entre les éléments de la même *cotopie*; en revanche, la métaphore opère elle une rupture du lien de contiguïté (l'impertinence de la figure) entre les deux éléments appartenant ainsi à des *cotopies* différentes et rapprochées *secondairement* par analogie; l'inférence est dès lors rendue possible par l'attribution d'une valeur seconde de pertinence. C'est en ce sens que les mutations d'écriture appellent dans un premier temps une rupture de contiguïté et réinvestissent ensuite le lien par le principe de *pertinence* guidant l'inférence. C'est également en ce sens que l'écriture musicale est

« métaphorique », qu'elle est aussi, selon le terme boulézien, une « déréalisation » du matériau et selon le terme de Hugues Dufourt, une « transgression analogique ».

Il est un projet qui répond à la condition moderne et à la mutation d'écriture par le passage à une méta-musique, celui de Iannis Xénakis. Inutile de souligner ici les éléments de continuité provoqués par la technique globalisante de ce qu'il est difficile de traiter comme « écriture musicale » dans le sens que j'ai posé plus haut: la *pertinence* est parfois extérieure à la composition. En ceci, son œuvre précède la mise en crise du concept d'écriture par les réactions aux musiques de l'abstraction sérielle, notamment le spectralisme et le minimalisme américain (tous deux empruntent, ne serait-ce que partiellement, les relations de contiguïté inhérente au matériau sonore pré-compositionnel ou à la continuité perceptive).

L'émergence narrative

A la suite des conceptions que je viens de développer brièvement, comment donc approcher l' « inversion » du rapport écriture/son et les partis-pris entre non-narrativité et narrativité provoquant par saturation des espaces temporels *virtuels* ? Du point de vue de la narrativité, on ne peut manquer ici d'approcher l'émergence narrative et l'essai de neutralisation des catégories *premières* de la narrativité telles qu'elles apparaissent, par exemple, dans la typologie de Pasler (1989).

Le passage d'une musique de complexes de sons à une musique du son complexe, par exemple dans l'univers « bruitiste » (un premier essai de *continuum* harmonicité/inharmonicité) chez Edgar Varèse ou dans les micropolyphonies de Gyôrgy Ligeti (par exemple dans le *Kammerkonzert* (1970)) peut être abordé sur la base des liens de contiguïté — plus ou moins rompus — entre les éléments pré-compositionnels.

Les précurseurs d'une « musique de son » ne manquent pas. On s'est réclamé tour à tour de Giacinto Scelsi (Klaus Huber, etc.), de la conception formelle de Claude Debussy (Boulez, etc.), de l'orchestration « intégrale » d'Hector Berlioz, de l'univers d'Edgar Varèse, et plus récemment, en ce qui concerne la musique spectrale, de Jean Sibelius, de sa conception du temps et de la couleur orchestrale qui conduisent à une esthétique « naturaliste » du son (par exemple chez Kajia Saahriaho).

La mutation actuelle porte ainsi sur la capacité d'écriture elle-même mise en crise par le renversement possible du rapport traditionnel écriture/son en rapport son/écriture — sans parler du renversement historique pouvant lui être lié. Opérant directement sur le matériau et conservant par rapport à lui une relation de contiguïté, le travail d'écriture peut être invalidé au risque de se rapprocher d'un vide d'intention (*art of sounds* dans la terminologie de Cynthia Grund développée dans ce même volume) si elle ne parvient pas à imposer une relation *seconde* au matériau et à retrouver un poids intentionnel, un geste (*music* selon Grund et selon la conception phénoménologique de Roman Ingarden). Divers projets compositionnels illustrent particulièrement bien cette situation paradoxale, celui de Hugues Dufourt, par exemple, où l'écriture se donne comme résistance à l'entropie du langage musical par une dialectique harmonie/timbre (l'harmonie et la combinatoire des complexes de son favorisent l'écriture; le timbre et le son complexe entraînent une dépendance analogique par rapport au matériau[8]). C'est en cela que la mutation actuelle inverse la relation de transgression (*d'un point de vue langagier*, la mutation se doit d' « échouer pour réussir », de la même manière que Boulez réinvestissait une poétique dans son *Marteau* à la suite de ses propres *Structures Ia*, comme les membres de l'Ecole de Vienne résistaient au monde relatif qui se présentait à eux).

La proxémique comme seuil de la question de la narrativité

Puisque ces conceptions héritent des rapports de contiguïté spatiale à l'intérieur même des constituants du son, qu'en est-il donc de la *proxémique* compositionnelle, c'est-à-dire de l' « utilisation de l'espace à fin de signification » ?

Il s'agit ici bien évidemment de distinguer plusieurs champs catégoriels. Si le temps musical est *exteroceptif*, il y a possibilité de dialectiser temps et espace (la caractéristique même de la notion d'écriture musicale), de rechercher la diagonale entre les deux types de mémoire décrits par Boulez (la mémoire *a posteriori* est spatiale; la mémoire *a priori* est temporelle) et de poser les bases d'une narrativité comme effort de pertinence temporelle portant sur le discontinu.

Lorsque le temps est en rapport de contiguïté avec l'espace intérieur du son (par exemple par la dépendance timbre/durée mise en évidence par les nouvelles techniques de traitement du son), il y a entropie langagière et mise en crise du concept d'écriture, car la composition conserve les rapports de contiguïté avec le matériau et court le risque de s'éloigner des exigences apparentées de *secondarité* et d'*oblicité* de l'écriture musicale.

Il est aisé de concevoir que l'œuvre musicale ne puisse être ouverte dans sa réception que par l'utilisation de l'espace permettant la co-occurence de fragments mobiles: c'est en ce sens que l'ouverture *a lieu*. Les conceptions traditionelles de l'ouverture (sous-programmée par l'introduction du hasard, comme dans le *Klavierstück XI* (1956) de Stockhausen, programmée comme dans la *Sonate n° 3* (1956–57) de Boulez, sur-progammée comme dans la conception de la complexité chez Ferneyhough) investissent le poïétique; l'interprète se confronte ici à proprement parler au texte musical. La mise en scène des interprètes et des groupes instrumentaux, par exemple dans *Domaines* (1968–69) de Boulez cherchait à présenter visuellement l'ouverture. La sur-programmation de Ferneyhough présente la particularité de donner à l'écoute la multi-existence spatiale (*interoceptive*) des éléments (l'ouverture peut donc être signifiée par l'utilisation non seulement de l'espace de lecture du texte musical, mais aussi de l'espace acoustique). Chez Nono, chez Emmanuel Nuñes, chez le Boulez de *Répons*, etc., c'est par la « mise en scène » du son (investissant à la fois l'espace de l'écriture et l'espace physique), dans ses déplacements et sa fragilité mobile que l'ouverture peut désormais y faire figure et figurer un monde relatif en expansion.

La narrativité comme fonctionnalisation sémiotique d'éléments prédéterminés

Finalement, j'aimerais noter ici quelques exemples non pas d'interprétation *a posteriori* d'une œuvre existante, mais de processus de sémiotisation mis en œuvre *a priori* dans l'acte compositionnel même (il ne m'intéresse guère ici de savoir si cette attitude est consciente ou non). Umberto Eco reprochait à Claude Lévi-Strauss la confusion entre langage-objet et métalangage (1968/72: 356), amalgame dont on voit l'apparition aujourd'hui dans de multiples œuvres musicales. Si Monelle notait: « The intention is to discover hidden structures, not to impose a new conformism. » (1992: 56), comment donc interpréter et décrire de multiples esthétiques musicales qui jouent sur des éléments prédéterminés et comment ne pas noter le rapport direct qu'elles entretiennent avec la conception sémiotique ?

L'inscription de la « distance esthétique » au coeur de l'œuvre et non pas dans sa périphérie provoque des ruptures d'isotopies formelles et l' « écriture » revient à opérer sur des classes d'objets prédéterminés et présentés fonctionnellement dans le cadre de l'œuvre elle-même. L'horizon d'attente (*Erwartungshorizont*) n'est plus le produit d'un fait culturel, jugé incertain en l'absence de l'expérience esthétique, mais est pris en compte directement par la composition se voulant gratifiante.

Dans l'*Offertorium* (1980) de Sofia Gubaidulina, on reconnaît la citation initiale du thème de l'*Offrande musicale* de Bach dans une orchestration similaire à celle que réalisa Webern dans son orchestration du *Ricercar à six voix*. Plus loin, la composition présente une rupture d'isotopie formelle qui devient dynamique actantielle et « mise en scène » de langages fonctionnalisés (un épisode traumatisant, un épisode sécurisant); les apparitions « thématiques » sont parfois réduites à leur fonction expressive (qui est la contradiction de l'expressivité elle-même).

Exemple parallèle dans les *Variations on "Es ist genug"* d'Edison Denisov. Le compositeur utilise le choral de Bach — qui apparaissait également dans le *Concerto de violon* d'Alban Berg. La co-occurence de l'élément prédéterminé et de son accompagnement discrépant marque la *distance esthétique* (Jauss, 1967/78: 53–54) à l'intérieur même de la composition introduisant des ruptures d'isotopies formelles, mais l'effort de contiguïté entre les deux éléments.

Il est peut-être bon d'évoquer ici des exemples beaucoup plus ambigus dans leur interprétation. Une œuvre du compositeur suisse Klaus Huber présente des éléments particulièrement significatifs: dans la pièce intitulée *Senfkorn* (1975), insérée dans l'oratorio *Erniedrigt-geknechtet-verachtet-verlassen* (1975–78/81–82), apparaît ce que l'on pourrait appeler une « émergence thématique ». Huber reconstruit progressivement au cours de la composition l'aria « Es ist vollbracht » de la cantate de Bach, *Sehet, wir gehn hinauf gen Jerusalem* (BWV 159). Le thème de Bach sert d'ancrage à la composition de la même manière que le texte qui y est récité. Cependant, la cantate de Bach, pour laquelle Huber a choisi un nouveau texte d'Isaïe, se donne ici comme citation et légitime de la sorte la rupture isotopique *en conservant* une distance énonciative entre les énoncés. En ce sens, la musique de Klaus Huber semble par instants apte à produire ses propres images du passé (et non à les reproduire). On retrouve semblables attitudes dans une pièce récente de Huber, *Agnus Dei cum recordatione* (1990), hommage à Jehan Ockeghem, dans certaines compositions de Heinz Holliger (notamment dans le *Scardanelli-Zyklus*) ou dans certains gestes compositionnels de Helmut Lachenmann (notamment dans *Accanto*). Il est bon également de rappeler les attitudes d'Igor Stravinsky et de John Cage: s'ils jouent sur des éléments prédéterminés, c'est en cherchant à leur ôter, respectivement, toute subjectivité ou toute intentionnalité.

Cependant, dans de multiples projets récemments apparus, ce n'est pas la distance énonciative qui est recherchée et le jeu sur des éléments préconstitués vidés de leur contenu expressif ou du geste intentionnel: ils sont justement utilisés pour leurs contenus dont ils empruntent l'expressivité en la fonctionnalisant (elle n'est dès lors plus *seconde* mais *première* au même titre que le matériau !). Ainsi, dans le même temps que la *sémiotique* aborde les œuvres, des projets compositionnels « sémiotisent » leur propre discours, c'est-à-dire développent un art de transition, d'association et de superposition portant sur des éléments prédéterminés et fondent un art polystylistique (notamment chez Alfred Schnittke). Sur ce terrain-là, nul doute que la sémiotique musicale opérera sans difficultés, mais par ailleurs sans grands bénéfices puisqu'elle s'éloignerait de l'exigence d'*oblicité* des discours sur la musique en répétant tautologiquement les parcours narratifs *premiers* des compositions.

Terme provisoire

Dans le moment où la modernité semble s'épuiser, dans le moment où les échappatoires se multiplient, il n'est peut-être qu'une voie sans fin pour le compositeur: affronter l'inquiétude inguérissable sur le langage et les mouvements contradictoires de l'histoire, s'y affronter le plus loin possible. Attitude qui me semble également requise pour une étude active qui affronte elle aussi les conditions multiples de modernité et le manque propre à tout travail par le langage, sur le langage et sur le musical. Les bouleversements épistémologiques constants exacerbent le caractère hétérologique de la manifestation musicale qui retrouve sa nécessité dans le péril du questionnement symbolique; ils lui restituent finalement l'espace de silence inaccessible dont elle entend encore plus bénéficier.

Yves Bonnefoy notait ainsi le désarroi qui prélude à l'œuvre: « Puisque l'on ne peut se trouver qu'au moment de se perdre, et dans l'effacement de toute route: le désarroi est une chance. Aucune intelligence classique ne le connaît encore. Il convient de le grandir aux dimensions d'une méthode. En lui seul peut se réaliser l'*ordalie* que la pensée ruinée impose. Car on ne peut passer les négations qu'en se chargeant du poids de leur nuit, en l'aggravant. Le désarroi sera cette nuit, ordalie immanente où éprouver sa force et prouver sa vérité. » (« Sur le concept du lierre »)

Notes

1. Cf. « This is to speak of signifiance in the most fundamental sense, not in the lexical or referential sense which still pervades Saussure and has passed over into some writers on music. [...] "Wo die Sprache aufhört,

fängt die Musik an"; where language can no longer offer the clue to structure of the sign, music must step in. » (Monelle, 1992: 58)

2. La capacité inférentielle est à la fois en co-occurence et en concurrence avec l'apport informationnel dans le langage verbal; ce qui permet de qualifier la production de sens par interaction entre énoncé et énonciation. Le code n'est que rarement explicite en langue naturelle quoiqu'un énoncé puisse porter sur une discussion du code lui-même (la fonction « métalinguistique » chez Roman Jakobson). — S'opposent ici deux conceptions: une conception diachronique sédimentaire du langage (le code doit précéder l'énonciation qui ne fait que l'oblitérer) et une conception diachronique axée sur l'énonciation variable d'un code gelé historiquement. La conception synchronique porte sur la production du sens par interaction entre énoncé et énonciation. Précisons que la vision diachronique semble accompagner les conceptions musicales historicistes pouvant conduire à l'institutionnalisation des langages (leur virtualisation) et les conceptions pouvant conduire à la fonctionnalisation langagière (c'est là notamment la thèse d'Adorno concernant la musique de Stravinsky (1958/79: 187); Stravinsky avait au moins cherché à vider le contenu subjectif des musiques qu'il utilisait en conservant une distance énonciative par rapport aux « énoncés » empruntés, ce qui n'est pas forcément l'attitude de divers projets plus récents).

3. Cf. « Car l'autre fraternel n'est pas *d'abord* dans la paix de que l'on appelle l'inter-subjectivité, mais dans le travail et le péril de l'interrogation; il n'est pas d'abord certain dans la paix de la *réponse* où deux affirmations *s'épousent* mais il est appelé dans la nuit par le travail en creux de l'interrogation. » (Derrida, 1979: 49)

4. Walter Benjamin a, quant à lui, sérieusement critiqué le structuralisme qui conduit à l' « intériorité vide » dont parle Hegel; il dénonce ainsi la réduction structurale qui contraint le langage à être le simple véhicule de la raison instrumentale. Cf. « C'est quand l'écrit est *défunt* comme signe-signal qu'il naît comme langage; alors il dit ce qui est, par là même ne renvoyant qu'à soi, signe sans signification, jeu ou pur fonctionnement, car il cesse d'être *utilisé* comme information naturelle, biologique ou technique, comme passage d'un état à l'autre ou d'un signifiant à un signifié. » (Derrida, 1979: 23–24)

5. L'opposition Schönberg/Berg, toute réductrice qu'elle puisse être, me semble ici significative. Alors que l'un tend à restituer à la technique compositionnelle une objectivité, le second confronte ce nouveau langage à des langages préexistants, pour en éprouver la capacité langagière et intersubjective. L'utilisation de formes à texte est ici pleinement significative (Brunner, 1993b: 77–80).

6. Les termes d'*exteroceptivité*, d'*interoceptivité* et de *proxémique* sont proposés dans le dictionnaire de Greimas et Courtès (1979: 141, 191, 300); ils ont été repris dans des applications musicales par Eero Tarasti (1987: 448) et par Ivanka Stoianova (1987: 68–85) — Tarasti propose l'hypothèse suivante qualifiant l'interaction entre les catégories

greimasiennes de l'*interoceptivité* et de l'*exteroceptivité:* « One might almost formulate the following hypothesis (the validity of which has yet to be proven): the more music functions as an outer sign, the *less* we can experience its possible functioning as an inner sign. » (1987: 448)

7. Pasler (1989) distingue notamment des musiques « narratives » (la musique à programme, etc.), des musiques « anti-narratives (par exemple la *Momentform* chez Stockhausen), des musiques « non-narratives » (musiques minimalistes) et des musiques sans narrativité (les expériences de Cage et la notion de présence indépendante du rôle de la mémoire).

8. Cf. la figure de la « métaphore diégétique » (métaphore à fondement métonymique donné par la seule contiguïté spatio-temporelle) introduite dans le méta-discours cinématographique et reprise dans l'approche des images proustiennes par Gérard Genette: « L'emploi de ce terme [la métaphore diégétique] ne doit pas cependant dissimuler, tout d'abord, que le fait même de la métaphore, ou de la comparaison, comme de toute figure, constitue en soi une intervention extradiégétique de "l'auteur"; ensuite, que le véhicule d'une métaphore n'est en fait jamais, de façon absolue, diégétique ou non diégétique, mais toujours, selon les occurrences, *plus* ou *moins* diégétique [...]. » (1972: 48)

Références

Adorno, Theodor (1979). *Philosophie de la nouvelle musique*. Paris: Gallimard (éd. orig. en 1958: *Philosophie der neuen Musik*).

Barthes, Roland (1964). ”Rhétorique de l'image”, *Communications* n° 4, 40–51. Paris: Seuil.

– (1953). *Le Degré zéro de l'écriture*, Paris: Seuil.

Brunner, Raphaël (1990). ”Au-delà de la stérilité. Une Lecture de deux ouvrages de Pierre Boulez”, *Revue musicale de Suisse Romande* n° 2, 43ème année, 81–87. Yverdon: Henri Cornaz.

– (1991). A l'écoute d'un sens. Une Analyse critique des Epitaffi per Federico García Lorca de Luigi Nono. Mémoire de licence [ms], Fribourg (Suisse): Institut de musicologie.

– (1993a). Contribution à une modélisation ostensive-inférentielle de l'œuvre musicale moderne. Mémoire de DEA [ms], Paris: Formation Doctorale Musique et Musicologie du XXème Siècle (Ecole des Hautes Etudes en Sciences Sociales — Ecole Normale Supérieure — IRCAM — Centre National de la Recherche Scientifique).

– (1993b). ”La Parole en portée. Absence et Disparition du texte dans l'œuvre musicale moderne”, *Des Lettres dans la musique*, revue de sciences humaines *Equinoxe* n° 9, Raphaël Brunner et Françoise Zay (éd.). Lausanne: Arches Association.

Dahlhaus, Carl (1989). "Rejet de la pensée du matériau ?", *Musiques en création*, revue *Contrechamps* éditée à l'occasion du Festival d'automne à Paris, 173–183. Paris: Maulde et Renou (éd. orig. en 1980: *Abkehr vom Materialdenken* ?).

Deliège, Célestin (1988). "Moment de Pierre Boulez", *Répons/Boulez*, 45–69. Paris: Actes-Sud papiers/PUF.

– (1991). "Mutations et Traces, Essai sur l'expressivité", *InHarmoniques* n° 8/9, 111–142. Paris: IRCAM/Centre Georges Pompidou.

Derrida, Jacques (1979). *L'Ecriture et la Différence*. Paris: Seuil (éd. orig. en 1967).

Dufourt, Hugues (1991). *Musique, Pouvoir, Ecriture*. Paris: Bourgois Editeur.

Eco, Umberto (1972). *La Structure absente. Introduction à la recherche sémiotique*. Paris: Mercure de France (éd. orig. en 1968: *La Struttura assente*).

Escal, Françoise (1979). *Espaces sociaux, Espaces musicaux*. Paris: Payot.

Genette, Gérard (1972). "Métonymie chez Proust", *Figures III*, 41–63. Paris: Seuil.

Greimas, Algirdas-Julien et Courtès, Joseph (1979). *Sémiotique. Dictionnaire raisonné de la théorie du langage*. Paris: Hachette Université.

Heyndels, Ralph (1985). *La Pensée fragmentée*. Bruxelles: Mardaga.

Jauss, Hans Robert (1978). *Pour une esthétique de la réception*. Paris: Gallimard (éd. orig. en 1967: *Literaturgeschichte als Provokation*).

Monelle, Raymond (1992). *Linguistics and Semiotics in Music*. London-Chur: Harwood Academic Publishers.

Nattiez, Jean-Jacques (1988). "Répons et la Crise de la "communication" musicale contemporaine", *Répons/Boulez*, 23–43. Paris: Actes-Sud papiers, diffusion Presses Universitaires de France.

Pasler, Jann (1989). "Narrative and Narrativity in Music", *Time and Mind. Interdisciplinary Issues*, 233–257. Madison: International University Press.

Sperber, Dan et Wilson Deirdre (1989). *La Pertinence. Communication et Cognition*. Paris: Minuit (éd. orig. en 1986: *Relevance. Communication and Cognition*).

Stoianova, Ivanka (1987). "Texte/musique/sens des œuvres vocales de Luigi Nono dans les années 50-60", *Luigi Nono* (= *Contrechamps*), 68–85. Paris: L'Age d'homme.

Tarasti, Eero (1987). "Some Peircean and Greimasian Semiotic Concepts as Applied to Music", *The Semiotic Web 1986* (Approaches to Semiotics 78.) T.A.Sebeok & Jean Umiker-Sebeok (eds.), 445–459. Berlin, New York, Amsterdam: Mouton de Gruyter.

What is a musical text?

RAYMOND MONELLE

Paul Ricoeur wrote a famous article entitled, "Que'est-ce qu'un texte?"
It is a question that problematizes its own answer, for no one would ask
it if they thought the answer obvious. Literary writers have to struggle
through the apparent layer of reference which usurps the place of verbal
signification, and consequently they have been preoccupied with problems that should not trouble the musician; the questions of intention and
interpretation, for example, seem material when one envisions a "true"
meaning for the text. Does the text determine its meaning, or is the
meaning produced by the reader? Stanley Fish, Wolfgang Iser and
Richard Rorty have debated questions like this see Culler, 1983, pp.
73–78). In a medium like ours, that is supposed to be self-referential or
to have no meaning at all, the discernment of a text will seem less dependent on intention or interpretation. In music, the meaning is simply
whatever the music means; the question of "true" meanings is no more
than empty talk. It ought to be *easier* to define the text in music.

Regrettably, musicians have wasted effort on pseudo-questions. For
example, is the score the text? Or even more fruitless: is the score the
work? A recent article by Nicolas Meeus summarizes this issue. He
quotes Mesnage's view that the score is merely a coded representation of
the musical work, a "maquette" which the performance realises "in its
true grandeur", and Estreicher's comparison of the score with "a Chi-
nese shadowplay, the outline, without relief or colour, of a living being"
(Meeus 1991: 19). Or perhaps the score is a prescriptive matrix: it is "a
system of imperative symbols . . . determining . . . indirectly how the
musical work is to be played", according to Ingarden (ibid., p. 20).
Meeus sees that music has two sides, one sonic, the other graphic: "The
score, in other words, constitutes, at least in our Western music, an
essential and indispensable link in the semiotic chain."

The score is, perhaps, the text. This would seem to match the traditional musicological view, in which scholars try to establish an authoritative *text* for music of the past. By this, they mean the musical aspects that can be written, and indeed were written by the composer. Of course, the realization of this score requires much cultural knowledge; but this study, called "performance practice", is not considered a textual study.

Somewhat surprisingly, literary commentators are much less willing to identify the text with the "score", that is, the printed record. Rodolphe Gasché proposes three possible understandings of the literary text:

> 1. A text can be determined as the sensibly palpable, empirically encounterable transcription of an oral discourse . . .
> 2. A text can be determined as an intelligible object. According to this conception, which is indeed the prevailing one, a text is thought to correspond to the signifying organization of diacritically or differentially determined signifiers and signifieds . . . (Gasché 1986: 278–279).

Gasché's third meaning must wait for a while. Apparently, his first version corresponds to the musical score; it is "palpable", a "transcription", a material thing. On the other hand, most musicians are extremely reluctant to grant freely the status of *score to* the material record of a piece like Cardew's *Octet* 61, or LaMonte Young's *Piano Piece for David Tudor* (the first of these is a page of meaningless quasi-musical fragments in no special order; the second, a line of English nonsense). Thus, there is a tendency, even for musicians, to regard the score as an "intelligible object", a "signifying organization of differentially determined signifiers and signifieds".

There is here an apparent distinction which need not impede us, though it is of considerable interest. While the reader of the literary text is looking for "meanings" rather than simply phonological forms, the reader of the musical score is seemingly only in search of the oral form of the signifier, that is, the performance; any "meanings" that may ensue will follow from the sonic realization of the score. This is a pseudo-problem, connected with the chimerical view that linguistic signification is arbitrary, present and hypostatized, while musical signification is subjective. The phonology which the literary reader finds in a printed text is a signifying phonology, a union of phoneme, pheme and sememe, not the noise of a chattering ape. The same oral level is present in the realization of the musical score; the score is understood as a score because it signifies whatever music signifies.

It is perfectly clear that the score is accepted as the text in the same way as the book or the page. It is a text because it is intelligible; because it is understood to signify something that signifies. But this was only the second of Gasché's interpretations. His third view is the most profound, yet like the others, it raises certain difficulties.

> Another . . . concept conceives of *text* as the dialectical sublation, either as "form" or "content", of both its sensible and ideal determinations. . . the dialectical determination of text is its reasonable or rational concept. All those analyses that link a text's sensible and intelligible constituents, as well as the etymologies, allusions, implications, and *sousentendues* of all sorts, within one totality of either form or content, understand *text* within the limits of speculative philosophy. . . By exhibiting the text as the totality of a positioning and reciprocal annihilation of oppositions, as the play of a mutual limitation of self and Otherness, the text is determined as the milieu, the element of *Aufhebung,* or, which is the same, of the dialectical exposition of that which is implied in its very concept (Gasché 1986: 279).

A text, then, is not the pattern of signifiers or signifieds, or even the patterned relation between them; on the contrary, it is the annihilation of opposition, the stage of resolution or fruition of the opposition of sign and meaning which constitutes the action of signification. In the text, dialectics overcomes itself. "The text excludes dialectics," according to Derrida (1981: 122).

The text is not form plus content, but the overcoming of form and content. Now, it is at this point that the task of the musicologist ought to be much easier than that of the linguist. The division of form and content, of signifier and signified, has always been to some degree problematic in music. Where, for the linguist, the presence of a signified has seemed the pledge of the signifying character of language, music presents no such reassurance. This apparent deficiency has led musicians off into theories of formalism and into analytical nominalisms that have proved peculiarly fruitless. But as well as seeming "abstract", music behaves strangely with regard to its structure; it resembles, not the syntactic level of language but its semantic level, in that it generates sequence and coherence by systems of repetition, like the semes, sememes and isotopies of language (on this property of music, see Monelle, 1991; 1995; also 1992, pp. 232–242). The syntactic and semantic levels of music live in a kind of inextricable mix 'n' match.

The musical text is clearly a text in this third sense; it is the score, not as performed, but as understood, its dialectics resolved into intelligibility — if we are to speak of the score. This is a text, *a fortiori*, in which dialectics has been overcome; Hjelmslev requires of a semiotic that its expression and content planes be non-conformal (Hjelmslev 1961: 112), but the kind of non-conformality which makes dialectics, and therefore semiotics, possible is not necessary to envisage in a semiotic which overcomes dialectics at its very source.

Still, a difficulty remains with this interpretation. If the text is that boundary where dialectics is resolved into a monism, where self and Otherness confront each other, what is to be found on that boundary? Does it exist? Can it be known or interpreted? Like so many deconstructive ideas, this merging point of the text seems to be just nothing at all, an evanescent line, without breadth, size, motivation or potency. This confusion is aggravated by the passing backward and forward accross the line of many aspects of signification; some parts of the "outside" may turn up inside, as when Beethoven reflects theoretical comments on "second subjects" by writing them into his String Quartets, Op. 18 (second subjects had been discussed by G. J. Vogler and Francesco Galeazzi, for example; see Monelle, 1992, p. 309). Derrida ends by invoking the "general text", the text not closed on itself such as to define inside and outside; it is merely "that border itself, from which the assignment of insides and outsides takes place, as well as where this distinction ultimately collapses" (Gasché 1986: 280).

If you are hell-bent on finding a presence, a hypostatized meaning for your signs or your texts, then indeed the text will be nothing for you. For indeed, nothing can be said about it in the way of interpretation, and it cannot be understood as an essence or an ideality. But musicians have always known this; musical interpretation always sounds like a kind of shaggy-dog story, infinitely less serious than cold analysis, and thus the preserve of the journalist and the secondary-school teacher. The *absence* of musical signification, its dissolving under the studious eye, is not a limitation of music, but on the contrary its very life and beauty. As the linguist finds himself encumbered with the baggage of motivated "meaning", its apparent arbitrariness and independence, its semantic rules, its logical structuring, its demand for primacy, the musician is carried smoothly onward into an open universality of metonymy, a meaningfulness without meaning, a semiosis unburdened with truth-references or metaphysics or the spectre of hypostasis. If the linguist wishes to know what a text is like, in this final sense in which dialectics is overcome, he should listen to music.

One thing is certain: the text, whether literary or musical, is profoundly abstract. It is not the score, not a performance, not an intention. It is also — and this is vitally important — not the *work*. The musical work is something somebody has made; it is a *poiesis*, Nattiez might say. It is perfectly legitimate, therefore, in connection with the work, to enquire about the composer's intentions, her history, her psychology, her limitations. Such enquiries have little bearing on the musical text, though they are related to some part of the text. But the text does not merely occupy a space defined by the composer's work. Its space is chiefly defined by certain other factors: in particular, by the universe of texts, which is to say by *intertextuality*.

This is brilliantly illustrated by Robert Samuels in relation to Mahler's Fourth Symphony. It would be easy to cite straightforward similarities between musical works, or indeed dissimilarities, to show that texts define each other. Samuels goes further than this; he shows that signification depends on textuality and authoriality so radically as to cause ruptures in musical syntax. Mahler's music cannot be "analyzed" in the traditional sense because the pattern of sender-message-addressee has been subverted and there can no longer be a "finished work".

Just before the recapitulation (in the first movement of the Fourth Symphony) there is a sudden arrest, marked by a pause over the bar line (at rehearsal figure 18). When the orchestra continues, we find ourselves already in the second phrase of the first subject, and this turns out to be an amalgam of both first and second subjects; the first phrase had been played just before by clarinet and oboe, at a point where the rather crabbed semiquavers of the development section had twisted the tonality towards F sharp minor. The dénouement after the pause is a relief, a parting of the clouds, the closing flourish of a successful conjuring trick. As Samuels comments, "a traditional form of analysis would have no problems here"; the development has shown how all is derived from the first subject, and the recapitulation has been slightly overlapped. However, the disjunction caused by the pause and by the extraordinary difference in tone between the tortuous development and the simple melody have come from a different level of the text.

Both subjects (the first was at the beginning, the second high in the cellos at rehearsal figure 3) are song-like, old-fashioned and "Biedermeier" in flavour, an intrusion from another age. Adorno finds the second subject "far too self-contained" (in *Mahler: ein musikalische Physiognomik,* quoted by Samuels, p. 154), as though "within quotation marks"; the music is (Samuels's phrase) "in the past tense". "Once upon a time," thus goes Adorno's motto for the Symphony, "there was a sonata" (Samuels, p. 154). But the two charming, unbelievably cosy and unthreatened subjects are not the only archaic features. The whole movement is in a sonata form that makes a great fuss about itself, about transitions, modulations, thematic developments, tonal structures. The composer of this movement is a busy, self-satisfied tunemonger, a lovable and slightly comic figure from Schubert's Vienna. Yet the music also stands outside this conception, sufficiently for us to recognize its irony and "modernism". Another, more sophisticated voice is speaking, another level of authoriality.

Who is the composer of Mahler's Fourth Symphony? The music does not pass judgement on the Biedermeier composer of the beguiling subjects, but it dislodges him so that he stands a little "proud" of the surrounding masonry. It will be recalled that the narrator of A *la recherche du temps perdu is* not Marcel Proust, though his name may (or may not) by "Marcel" and he is somewhat like Proust, fastidious, snobbish, intellectual (but not gay or Jewish). The old-fashioned composer — "Gustav", perhaps — of these charming themes and this busy structure is similarly a visitor from some related level of authoriality, by no means all his characteristics being those of Mahler, but on the contrary features of other texts, other eras and other composers. Another composer, perhaps Mahler, but not without help from others, points a finger at this first composer when he interrupts his tune with a pause.

It is well-known that Jacques Derrida said, "Il n'y a pas de hors-texte" (Derrida 1974: 158). Ordinary intertextuality cannot explain this statement of the French theorist; we must move yet further from the composer. The listener usually hears, in a musical work, not only what the composer made and controlled but also a great deal of which she had no inkling. Indeed, the understanding of a musical message is dependent on hearing this world of what is not meant, not said, not heard, not "in the text". If this were not so, it would be intolerable (for example) to hear music of another age; to put up with Bach's "sewing machine rhythm" or Wagner's unrelenting *Ernst*.

Ordinary criticism involves taking a stance in this space outside the text. The question is, where is the *signification* to be found? If we follow tradition in locating signification within the text (which will leave us wrestling with "intentions") then the interpretive and exegetic functions of criticism are denied. We are prevented from refining signification in terms of what it is not; and this may be what it more truly is, for this is where the dialecticity of the text is operative. Just as signification is defined by what is not said, so text is defined by what is not-text. This is simply illustrated by those drawings which can be seen two ways according to whether one observes the endotopic or the exotopic form, the form enclosed by the outline or that outside it.

The text defines what is inside and what is outside; and thus, there is nothing outside, for whatever is outside is also text-defined. Criticism observes exotopically. (Here I must stress that *hors-texte* does not merely mean "outside the music", that is, extramusical, as when we say that Mahler's music is about cosmic sadness.) Indeed, critical judgements that survey the text as endotopy and exotopy will go further than Schoenberg's famous essay on Brahms, which is already outside the text in that it finds in Brahms a progressiveness that the composer did not mean or think of. They will also be outside of whatever is outside of the text, concerned not only with what the musician did not say or intend but also with what she could not have said. Furthermore, these far reaches of signification are necessary to intelligibility, they are not mere critical extravagances. For the *hors-texte is* in a dialectical opposition to what is inside the text, and the text overcomes dialectics, as Derrida has said.

How, then may we define the text? The text is *whatever criticism observes,* whatever analysis expounds. And again: the text is a discipline, holding us back from temptations to dogmatize, sacralize, hypostatize, appropriate.

If you are a modernist, and thus subject to some of these temptations, seeing music as a cognitive symbol that speaks its own truth, you will tend to observe only the score and thus to treat the score as text (Adorno propounds this kind of modernism, but does not fall into the temptation). This is a dogmatism that wants to appropriate the text for its own purism. Sometimes, of course, the score cannot be taken as text in any meaningful way; but these scores are ignored by modernists.

This obvious point may be illustrated by a reference to the fifth movement of Mahler's Third Symphony, which I choose because I have been reading Peter Franklin's superb little book on this work. The surrounding movements are expressive and rhetorical, the fourth a setting for alto solo of Nietzsche's "Was spricht die tiefe Mitternacht" from *Also sprach Zarathustra,* the finale one of Mahler's famous adagios, considered by Franklin to be "a beatified version of the alto's gesture of supplication" in the fourth movement (Franklin 1991: 71). The fourth and final movements are in D; the fourth movement ends on A, the finale begins on A as though there were direct continuity between them.

Both these expressive movements evince the Romantic idea of composer-as-orator; this is persuasive music which contemplates its own emotional content, which presses forward a speaker whose heart is full, who is a tragic seer. Thus the composer (that is, Gustav Mahler) writes over the finale, "Slow; peaceful; felt (empfunden) . . . very expressively sung" (originally he wrote, "with the most intimate feeling"— see the facsimile of his manuscript on page 72 of Franklin's book). He urges on us the subjective intensity of his fictional orator; the fourth movement was "very slow and mysterious".

Who is this speaker whose intensity Mahler so anxiously describes? He is, perhaps, Zarathustra, the orator invented by Nietzsche to give voice to his aphorisms on the state of post-Christian man. But he is also the Viennese *Lieder* composer; his intensity is that of Schubert's "Junge Nonne", and he repeats the opening words "O Mensch" halfway through the Nietzsche setting to furnish a rough-and-ready strophic form. Mahler's symphonies have dual roots, in the German symphony and in Viennese song. They are full of a dramatized and projected subjectivity.

In between these heartfelt utterances comes the notorious fifth movement, a setting for women's and children's chorus of the *Wunderhorn* poem "Es sungen drei Engel". It lasts four minutes and is in F. The children imitate bells: "Bimm, bamm, bimm, bamm" with the notes prolonged on the final "m" phoneme, and the marking is "happy and cheeky" ("lustig im Tempo und keck im Audsruck"). "The sheer cheek of the childlike angels may have more to do with Germanic Christmas carols . . . but they would soon wreck any production of *Parsifal*" (Franklin 1991: 70). There is no need to read the words of the poem, a conventional paean to "heavenly joy" with no projected orator except the voice of the alto soloist in the middle section, weeping for her transgressions against the Ten Commandments. She is summarily told to fall on her knees and pray if she wants eternal bliss.

A score-analysis of this movement would be utterly brainless, and Franklin does not attempt it. The textual analyst must intervene. During the time when he was composing the Third Symphony, Mahler was reading certain works of Nietzsche, notably *The Birth of Tragedy from the Spirit of Music, Also sprach Zarathustra* and *The Gay Science (Die fröhliche Wissenschaft)*. The last of these titles was originally the Symphony's epigraph; in this book Nietzsche finds in himself the whole of "reality", of human and cosmic history, culture, consciousness, reaching a nexus in which the future is created as though by a dreamer or somnambulist, or in another analogy, by a dancer whose dance prolongs man's knowledge of the world and itself. The world is a dream of the artist; in semiotic terms, the world is not "reality" but signification. This led Mahler to his famous comment, recorded by Adorno (and quoted by Franklin 1991: 12):

> Imagine such a *great work,* in which in fact the *whole world is* mirrored ... one is, so to speak, no more than an instrument on which the Universe plays, I tell you, in some places it strikes even me as uncanny; it seems as if I hadn't written it at all.

The work is not production or utterance but manifestation; just as the "subjective" utterances of the fourth and sixth movements are the manifestation of an impassioned speaker, so now another part of the speaking universe is manifested, the singing of children and the chiming of Christmas bells.

In spite of Mahler's feeling that he "hadn't written it", these things are firmly within the text. Their signification is primary; without them the music has no meaning. This Nietzschean message represents a reaction against Wagner's view that the revolutionary, reanimating power of the symphony has been taken over by the music drama. But certain aspects of Wagner's conception remain, notably his nationalism; just as the composer of *Die Meistersinger* believed in the healing power of *die holde, deutsche Kunst so* Mahler, in spite of his Jewish race and Czech origin, was attracted to the revolutionary pan-Germanism of the group around Engelbert Pernerstorfer and Victor Adler. This expressed itself in a devotion to German folk art, especially in the case of the Saga Society of Richard von Kralik and Siegfried Lipiner, at whose meetings Mahler was known to play the *Meistersinger* overture (all of this is summarized by Franklin, 1991, pp. 9–10 and 13–14). The "objective" singing of "Es sungen drei Engel" signifies, as well as the universal creativity of the artist's soul, an ideological conviction about the German *Volk*.

There is no need to describe in detail the many other facets of signification. In principle, the movement is in strophic form, though the soloist interjects with another melody taken from the children's song *Das himmlische Leben*. The noisy climax, at any rate, is not the culmination of a developmental form. The disunity implied by this music's intrusion between the closing movements of the Symphony may also be connected with the programmatizing of the symphony, the level of *portrayal* rather than expression in some of the Romantics. Its schizophrenia may have something to do with the German-speaking Czech and the Christianized Jew, for whom a certain elusiveness has become a habit. For whatever we conclude, this cannot be seen as an example of "structural unity" or philosophical idealism; this music does not persuade us, by any univocal organicism, that the universe is transcendentally intelligible. Just as its composer is a listener to the voices of its speakers—the impassioned tragedian of the previous movement and afterwards a bunch of noisy kids—so is he a reader of its subversive message, an ironic dissenter from the transparency of the cosmos. There is no univocal clarity to this message; it sets a question mark on all artistic expression.

But is this final composer, the problematizer and pessimist, Gustav Mahler? It looks as though we have been shunted into this signification, which is no-signification, by taking Mahler and Nietzsche at their word, and more at their word than their word could ever signify; it is *implied* by their sayings, implied because the Symphony eventually forces you out into this country of the impossibility of signification. Yet this country is also signified by the Symphony.

What, then, is signified by this movement? Viewed intertextually, the music is located at the centre of a textual network, a network of texts. One of these texts is Mahler himself, the German-speaking Christianized Czech Jew, the provincial who has made it big in the great city, the outsider struggling to get inside; this is the "composer" in the ordinary sense, the maker of the "work". In Figure 1 some of the other texts can be seen, together with a few that occurred to me while I was drawing it; and there are further subtexts beyond the texts, a generative genealogy of texts that stretches infinitely in all directions.

Each intersection of this network has been given a name as though it were an object, an objectified essence independent of the system, and this has given the whole thing an air of interpretation, a whiff of the extramusical. But the Symphony is not an object in this way; there is nothing in the Symphony which is simply itself, unrelated to other texts, intelligible without reference to what is outside it. The music is simply an epistemic nexus, the product of its significations as well as their producer, active as well as passive. The same goes for all the other intersections in the system. There are "only differences, without real terms". The signification of this masterpiece is better represented without apparent hypostasis; it is a network, but not a network of named terms (Figure 2).

The musical text, then, is a boundary between inside and outside, rendered problematic by the flow across the boundary and the interdependence of inside and outside. It is also an epistemic nexus, the meeting point of all its significations, indexical, iconic and symbolic. It is not a transcendent essence, an abstract pattern, an object, an "experience".

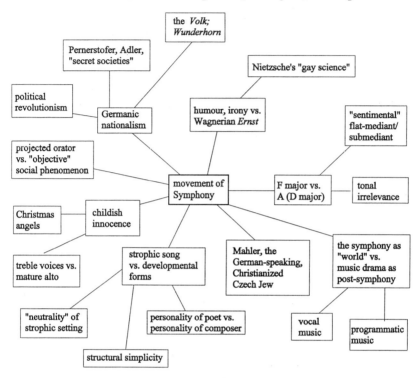

Figure 1.

The network of significations is infinite, but this does not mean that there is nothing that can be said about the music. On the contrary, it means that discourse about the music is infinite, and that no particular discourse can appropriate it, no ideology can claim the music as its own privilege. At present, there are certain analytical ideologies which would restrict discourse such that this particular symphonic movement would be almost impossible to address. This unfortunate state of affairs must be over-come.

But there is one more dimension to this analysis, obvious in the case of Mahler's Symphony, less obvious—but nevertheless present—in other

Figure 2.

music. As I have already hinted, the Nietzschean theme which led to this intrusion in the Symphony was itself a semiotic programme, a view of signification. If we examine it, it comes to resemble the very analysis of text which I have presented. The artist stands at the focal point of all history and cosmology, an active/passive dreamer who re-creates the world and ensures its continuity. Hence, the symphonic composer, having created an impassioned orator who gives voice to tragic omens, must now dream a common, jolly scene of children and Christmas carols. Outside of the world of tragic rhetoric, you could say, lies an outside-world of carefree children. But it is also inside because, textually, it defines what is inside by being outside. The artist, then—the textual or epistemic artist, not the man or woman—is an intersection in an active network of creative forces; from the world and its histories and discourses comes every signification, and each is refocussed and empowered by the artist's genius. Thus, the symphonic movement is a "reading" of the artistic or semiotic process, or, since it is not "real", an "allegory of reading". The Symphony allegorizes itself, it is its own listener; it seems to open up its own inward textures, as though Figure 2 were moving out into three dimensions. Elsewhere I have referred to music as an "allegory of listening", echoing Paul de Man's famous judgement about literature (Monelle, forthcoming).

Musicians are practical people, and they are apt to question the usefulness of philosophical investigations in their own art. If music is indeed text, what difference does it make? Since the text is whatever criticism observes, any *ideology of the text,* any objectification or hypostasis will represent a limitation of criticism. It will become improper to envisage discourse along certain lines; improper for Réti to look for motivic unity in Bach's B minor Mass because the movements were not all written at the same time, improper for Stravinsky to refer to Webern's serial compositions as "precious diamonds" because they are not meant to be anything other than music, improper for Boulez to find numerical operations in the rhythm of the *Rite of Spring* because integral serialism hadn't been invented in 1913, improper to suggest that all musical traditions, including the abstract constructivisms of the early twentieth century, are infinitely rooted in signification, literary, philosophical, cultural, social, political and existential (I refrain from giving references for each of these well-known views). Such a hamstrung version of criticism also leads to judgements of value; Berg's Violin Concerto was once thought to present a miraculous union of serial practices with pre-existent tonal material, the original tone-row eventually generating a Bach chorale, but this view cannot now be held, according to Arnold Whittall:

> The introduction of the chorale melody actually enhances the tension between the separate, potentially tonal components of the set and its general comprehensive atonality (Whittall 1987: 9).

Similarly, though *Lulu is* apparently a work of scrupulous unity, on closer examination we find that its coherence is elusive and cannot be defined in detail, according to Anthony Pople:

It must be doubted whether we yet have analytical techniques which can represent (as opposed to misrepresent) the status of . . . local and global tonalities, and the relationship between them, in the detail which is expected of serious analysis (Pople 1983: 49).

The "detail which is expected of serious analysis" is a *syntactic* detail, we may be sure; the opacity of tonal structures in *Lulu* cannot itself be a signifier because unless it can be analyzed in sufficient detail it is not yet even a syntactic unit. Of course, I stress one aspect—a mere tone of voice—in the articles of Whittall and Pople, which are much more rich and subtle than this. Nevertheless, value judgements may sometimes proceed from critical ideologies, from beliefs in "real" meanings, "true" compositional methods, "unified" views and "serious" analysis.

Outside of serious analysis, outside of our critical protection rackets, we shall find a choir of angels, the pealing bells of a childlike Germanic Christmas. They gesture towards the infinitude of texts, the gay science of implication which helps us to rediscover the world in each work of music, helps us to conclude, with Friedrich Schlegel, that "a classic is a writing that is never fully understood".

References

Derrida, Jacques (1974). *Of grammatology.* Translated by Gayatri Chakravorty Spivak. Baltimore: Johns Hopkins University Press.
- (1981). *Dissemination.* Translated by Barbara Johnson. Chicago: University of Chicago Press.
Franklin, Peter (1991). *Mahler: Symphony No. 3.* Cambridge: Cambridge University Press.
Gasché, Rodolphe (1986). *The Tain of the Mirror: Derrida and the philosophy of reflection.* Cambridge, Mass.: Harvard University Press.
Hjelmslev, Louis (1961). *Prolegomena to a Theory of Language.* Translated by Francis J. Whitfield. Madison: University of Wisconsin Press.
Meeus, Nicolas (1991). "Apologie de la partition", *Analyse Musicale,* 24/3, pp. 19–22.
Monelle, R. (1991). "Structural semantics and instrumental music", *Music Analysis* 10(1–2): 73–88.
- (1992). *Linguistics and Semiotics in Music.* London: Harwood.

- (1995). "Music and semantics", *Musical Signification: Essays in the Semiotic Theory and Analysis of Music*, E. Tarasti (ed.), pp. 91–108. Berlin, New York: Mouton de Gruyter.
- (forthcoming). "BWV 886 as allegory of listening", *Musica Significans: proceedings of the Third International Congress on Musical Signification, Edinburgh*, 1992. Chur: Harwood Academic Publishers.

Pople, Anthony (1983). "Serial and tonal aspects of pitch structure in Act III of Berg's *Lulu*", *Soundings* 10: 36–57.

Samuels, Robert (1994). "Music as text: Mahler, Schumann and issues in analysis", *Theory, analysis and meaning in music*, A. Pople (ed.), 152–163. Cambridge: Cambridge University Press.

Whittall, Arnold (1987). "The theorists's sense of history", *Journal of the Royal Musical Association* 112: 1–20.

SEMIOTICS AS "SOCIAL PSYCHOLOGY"

Quelles perspectives sociologiques pour une sémiotique de la musique?

JEAN-MARIE JACONO

Les différentes sémiotiques et la sociologie de la musique n'ont rien eu en commun jusqu'ici. La sémiotique a privilégié l'analyse des structures internes de l'œuvre musicale et de ses significations. Les travaux de sociologie de la musique, très divers eux-aussi, ont mis en valeur ses dimensions sociales. Ils ont été le plus souvent considérés de manière suspecte par les sémioticiens. Ainsi Nattiez, en quatre pages seulement (1975: 413–416), ridiculise quelques études maladroites de sociologie; il en conclue que seule sa sémiologie a de l'avenir. Peut-on se satisfaire de cette coupure entre sémiotique et sociologie ? L'étude de la signification d'une œuvre peut-elle se passer de l'étude de son contexte social et historique ? Peut-elle aussi se passer de l'étude de sa réception, c'est à dire du sens qu'elle a pris pour différents groupes sociaux, à des époques différentes ? Ces aspects n'ont pas été pris en compte jusqu'ici par la sémiotique. Or l'évolution des disciplines et des champs de la recherche musicologique permet de penser des approches nouvelles, pluridisciplinaires, comme l'a montré tout récemment Vecchione (1992). Il est possible de définir de nouvelles sémiotiques qui abordent aussi des questions sociologiques. Ces nouvelles disciplines ne s'opposent pas aux sémiotiques existantes. Elles permettent de mieux cerner l'étude du sens et de la signification de l'œuvre. C'est le cas de ce que nous nommerons la sémiotique de l'institutionnalisation, c'est à dire l'étude de la reconnaissance d'une œuvre dans une société. Nous prendrons ici notre travail sur les révisions de *Boris Godounov* de Moussorgski (Jacono 1992) pour définir ces perspectives.

Sémiotique et sociologie: abattre les murs

Parler de"émiotique de l'institutionnalisation", c'est tenter de définir un domaine qui relève à la fois de la sémiotique et de la sociologie de la musique. On peut d'abord se demander si cette tentative est légitime dans le champ de la sémiotique. Il faut, en fait, partir de la réalité particulièrement complexe de l'œuvre musicale. Elle nécessite, pour être déchiffrée, plusieurs approches différentes.

Toute œuvre musicale ne se réduit pas à un système formel et à une structure. La sémiotique de la musique l'a bien sûr montré, par exemple dans la théorie de la tripartition reprise par Nattiez (1975, 1987) ou dans l'étude des modalités (Tarasti 1985). La sémiotique a laissé cependant de côté les aspects sociaux pour privilégier surtout l'étude de l'interprétation. Fondamentalement, pourtant, l'œuvre musicale peut être considérée dans sa réalité anthropologique. Elle ne dépend pas en effet seulement de la conscience de son créateur. C'est aussi une production marquée historiquement, socialement et culturellement à l'intérieur d'une société. Elle est soumise à l'appréciation d'individus et de groupes sociaux non seulement dans la société où elle est créée mais aussi auprès d'autres publics, surtout depuis l'essor considérable des moyens de diffusion qui permettent d'apprécier instantanément les œuvres du passé. Ces individus, ces groupes sociaux lui donnent un sens. En tant que signe tout à fait particulier, en tant que forme de pensée, l'œuvre s'inscrit dans des réalités qui conditionnent sa création et sa diffusion. En se référant au sociologue de l'art Pierre Francastel (1967) on peut ainsi définir l'œuvre musicale comme un objet de civilisation. L'œuvre renvoie au monde qui l'a vue apparaître. Elle renvoie aux conceptions esthétiques, aux conceptions intellectuelles, aux mentalités et aux structures psychiques des groupes sociaux de son temps, ainsi qu'à la réalité sociale et politique de cette époque. En même temps, elle est le départ d'une nouvelle expérience dans la conscience de ceux qui la réceptionnent et qui ne cessent de lui donner un sens.

Le matériau musical n'échappe pas à des déterminations sociales qui peuvent être décisives dans le choix même des éléments musicaux. Blacking l'a bien montré dans ses études d'ethnomusicologie (1967, 1973). Certes, les conditionnements historiques et sociaux sont généralement admis dans l'étude des musiques de tradition orale. Ils sont même souvent évoqués dans la musicologie traditionnelle occidentale avant de passer au second plan devant l' étude des aspects formels de l'œuvre. Ils n'ont pourtant pas été pris vraiment en compte dans le champ de la sémiotique dans la recherche du sens et de la signification.

La sociologie, de son côté, a porté son attention sur ces dimensions sociales. L'étude des publics et de la consommation musicale a cependant prédominé. Des approches fécondes, dont Supičić (1985) a fait le bilan, ont permis de cerner bien des conditionnements socio - historiques. Les travaux sociologiques ont souffert cependant de leur diversité et de l'éclatement de leurs méthodes. Le poids d'interprétations discutables a ensuite terni la recherche. L'ombre du marxisme stalinien et de la 'théorie du reflet' plane toujours sur toute étude sociologique. Les interprétations mécanistes, réduisant l'œuvre à une simple dimension idéologique, ont été néfastes à la mise à jour de rapports complexes avec la société. Le compositeur, dans la 'théorie du reflet' n'est, de plus, qu'un simple relais de forces sociales déterminantes.

Malgré les perspectives intéressantes tracées en partie par Adorno, malgré des travaux apparus par exemple en France ces dernières années[1], la sociologie de la musique n'est généralement pas prise au sérieux par les musicologues. Ainsi Carl Dahlhaus (1975) a t-il pu mettre même en question la possibilité de la sociologie de l'œuvre musicale au profit de l'histoire de la musique. On comprend, dans ces conditions, que les sémioticiens se soient surtout préoccupés d'étudier ses composantes internes. Les récents développements de la recherche musicologique permettent néanmoins de jeter de nouvelles perspectives.

Chercher à déterminer la signification de l'œuvre musicale a provoqué la naissance de travaux pluri-disciplinaires et l'apparition de nouvelles disciplines. Etudier la réalité anthropologique de l'œuvre, c'est se confronter à des problèmes relevant de l'histoire, de la sociologie, de l'esthétique, de la psychologie mais aussi de la sémiotique, ce que Bernard Vecchione nomme des réseaux d'intersciences (1992: 285). L'étude de la réalité de l'œuvre musicale passe par son déchiffrement, par l'indispensable analyse musicale pour mettre à jour sa problématique. Ce déchiffrement préconisé par Francastel à propos des peintures du Quattrocento (1967), mais aussi par Adorno (1968), débouche sur de nouvelles perspectives. Ainsi, on peut distinguer deux types complémentaires de sémiotiques: la sémiotique de l'instauration et celle que nous nommerons la sémiotique de l'institutionnalisation.

La première se donne pour but d'étudier la problématique mise en place par le compositeur dans son œuvre. Elle se consacre essentiellement au déchiffrement[2]. Elle peut donner lieu à l'emploi de techniques différentes. L'énorme travail de Christine Esclapez sur l'expression temporelle dans les Quatuors à cordes de Beethoven (1993) ne fait pas appel aux mêmes méthodes d'analyse que celui de Fabienne Desquilbé dans l'étude de la narrativité au début de l'opéra italien. La sémiologie de l'institutionnalisation prolonge ce type d'études. Il s'agit d'étudier non seulement les processus d'instauration mais aussi la réception de l'œuvre dans une société. L'œuvre est en effet pensée en fonction des attentes d'un groupe social. Le compositeur peut répondre à ces attentes ou au contraire choisir d'aller plus loin. On le voit: la sémiotique de l'institutionnalisation a une grande parenté avec l'étude de la réception développée en littérature par Jauss (1978). La réception des œuvres joue un rôle capital. *Elle agit sur leur sens.* Les réactions peuvent être très différentes selon le contexte socio-économique et la forme de la diffusion. Ainsi, une œuvre peut prendre un sens différent de celui instauré par un compositeur lors de sa création et être même adaptée aux goûts du public. L'opéra *Boris Godounov*, révisé à plusieurs reprises, fournit un excellent exemple pour comprendre ces phénomènes. Abordons-le avant de faire de nouveaux développements théoriques.

Le problème *Boris Godounov*

Le plus célèbre opéra russe est un cas unique dans l'histoire de la musique. Il a d'abord fait l'objet de deux versions de la part de Moussorgski (1869, 1872). Seule la seconde a été représentée, avec des coupures, à partir de 1874 à Saint-Pétersbourg et éditée sous forme de partition pour chant et piano. L'opéra a été peu joué jusqu'à la fin du XIX° siècle tout en obtenant beaucoup de succès. Il a donné lieu à six révisions qui ont modifié considérablement son orchestration et sa structure. Ce sont celles de Rimski-Korsakov (Saint-Pétersbourg 1896 et

1908), Melngailis (Riga 1924), Ippolitov-Ivanov (scène de Saint-Basile intégrée ensuite à l'orchestration de Rimski — Moscou 1926), Chostakovitch (Leningrad 1940), Rathaus (New York 1953). Ce n'est que depuis 1975, année de la parution de l'édition de l'orchestration originale par David Lloyd-Jones[3], soit *plus de cent ans* après la création de l'œuvre, que l'on a commencé à jouer *Boris Godounov* tel que l'avait voulu Moussorgski. L'opéra a surtout été connu jusqu'ici dans la seconde révision de Rimski-Korsakov alors qu'une première édition de la partition pour orchestre originale avait été réalisée à Moscou en 1928.

La musicologie traditionnelle n'a jamais expliqué vraiment pourquoi le plus grand opéra russe avait été si souvent transformé sous des régimes différents, à des époques différentes, en Russie et en Occident. Elle s'est contentée de comparer les travaux de Rimski-Korsakov et de Chostakovitch à l'écriture de Moussorgski (Le Roux 1980). L'explication des révisions a reposé jusque là sur des raisons musicales et psychologiques. Il aurait fallu remanier *Boris Godounov* en raison de l'ignorance des techniques d'orchestration pour Moussorgski. C'est l'acharnement de Rimski-Korsakov à rectifier les 'fautes' qui aurait entraîné la restructuration de l'opéra. On justifie aussi maintenant les révisions par le caractère 'ouvert' de l'œuvre (Kandinskij 1990), en raison de l'existence de deux versions originales de Moussorgski.

Reprendre les éléments ou la totalité d'une œuvre d'un autre compositeur fait certes partie des processus de composition. Cela ne concerne pas seulement la musique savante occidentale où des thèmes ont toujours été réutilisés dans des contextes différents. Le jazz, le rock et le rap l'illustrent aussi. Les réorchestrations sont fréquentes au XIXème siècle, y compris pour les opéras de Verdi souvent aménagés pour des théâtres désireux de les représenter. D'un point de vue sémiotique, il est alors tout à fait possible de considérer la réorchestration comme faisant partie du réseau de modalités de l'œuvre. Dans un remarquable article sur les *Tableaux d'une Exposition* de Moussorgski (1992), Eero Tarasti évoque ainsi les différentes orchestrations de cette œuvre pour piano. Celles-ci peuvent l'affaiblir par le mauvais choix des instruments ou en révéler de nouvelles dimensions. Il serait possible de traiter des réorchestrations de *Boris Godounov* comme d'une remodélisation de sa structure au terme d'une analyse poussée qui dégage les isotopies de la partition. Le problème dépasse cependant le cadre des modalités. Réviser un opéra comme *Boris Godounov* n'est pas un travail technique. C'est en fait en transformer le sens et l'adapter pour de nouveaux publics en créant de nouvelles problématiques.

Un fait est en effet particulièrement troublant. Les réorchestrations de *Boris Godounov* se produisent à chaque fois au moment où la Russie connaît des profondes mutations sociales et historiques. Entre la création de l'œuvre (1874) et la première révision de Rimski-Korsakov (1886) une transformation considérable a lieu dans la société russe. La Russie passe du stade d'une société agraire, émergeant du féodalisme (le servage n'est aboli qu'en 1861), à une économie capitaliste. L'industrie se développe à partir du début des années 1880. Une bourgeoisie dynamique joue un grand rôle dans ce développement économique, tout comme dans la vie culturelle. Elle crée même des théâtres privés qui vont concurrencer les institutions traditionnelles, les théâtres impériaux. C'est dans ce cadre que la première révision de Rimski-Korsakov connaît un grand succès à la fin du siècle. C'est après un autre moment décisif de l'histoire russe, la révolution de 1905, qu'est réalisée la seconde révision de Rimski (1908), compositeur opposé au régime tsariste. Elle consacre l'œuvre sur les scènes internationales. La révolution d'octobre 1917 entraîne un bouleversement de la vie musicale et un développement des courants d'avant-garde. Dans l'URSS des années 1920 Moussorgski est célébré comme un précurseur en raison de ses audaces musicales et de son engagement aux côtés du peuple. La découverte des manuscrits pour orchestre de la partition originale amène la critique du travail académique de Rimski. L'opéra est représenté dans son écriture initiale en 1928, dans une ambiance passionnée. Le développement du pouvoir de Staline aboutit cependant à son rejet. L'orchestration originale est jugée peu efficace pour assurer la réussite du spectacle auprès du peuple. On confie à Chostakovitch le soin de faire une nouvelle révision en 1939. Elle ne sera pourtant jouée que sous Krouchtchev, en 1959 ! En 1946, en effet, au plus fort du Réalisme socialiste, c'est l'orchestration de Rimski-Korsakov qui est à nouveau employée en URSS. Elle n'avait d'ailleurs pas cessé d'être utilisée en Occident. Il faut attendre la mort de Brejnev et le déclenchement de la perestroïka pour voir apparaître le premier enregistrement soviétique de l'orchestration de Moussorgski (1985)[4] et le développement de ses représentations.

Cette correspondance entre l'histoire de *Boris Godounov* et l'histoire de la Russie impose de rester prudent. Cette relation ne constitue qu'un point de départ, pas un aboutissement. Il faut d'abord examiner la problématique posée par chacun des deux *Boris* de Moussorgski. Ce sont bien deux œuvres différentes comme l'a montré Taruskin (1984). La seconde version est une œuvre radicale qui suscite des réactions contradictoires de la part des différents groupes sociaux composant le public du théâtre Maryinski de Saint-Pétersbourg en 1874. Il s'agit ensuite d'établir les modifications de l'orchestration et de la structure effectuées, notamment, par Rimski-Korsakov et Chostakovitch. Celles-ci se font non seulement pour des raisons esthétiques mais aussi pour des raisons sociales, afin d'adapter l'œuvre trop audacieuse de Moussorgski aux goûts d'un nouveau public.

Pourquoi *Boris Godounov* n'est-il pas repris dans sa forme originale à la fin du XIX° siècle ? L'opéra avait pourtant connu un grand succès lors de ses représentations à Saint-Pétersbourg de 1874 à 1882 comme l'a prouvé Iakovlev (1930). La problématique de l'œuvre demandait pourtant un haut niveau de conscience pour être comprise, ce que Lucien Goldmann (1966) nomme le maximum de conscience possible d'un groupe social. En plein mouvement populiste les étudiants applaudissent un opéra qui met en valeur le peuple russe et se termine par sa révolte contre le tsar. Ils ne comprennent pas sa problématique esthétique. Celle-ci n'est d'ailleurs pas plus comprise par les membres de l'intelligentsia liés au Groupe des Cinq. César Cui fera une mauvaise critique de *Boris* (Orlova 1983: 378–383). Quelques scènes sont appréciées mais non l'opéra dans son ensemble. Moussorgski conçoit en effet une œuvre trop nouvelle pour son groupe social, l'intelligentsia. Il s'agit, avec des moyens musicaux originaux, notamment un nouveau type de déclamation lyrique et une structure symétrique, de renverser le cadre du grand-opéra symbole de la culture nationale, *La vie pour le tsar* de Glinka (1836) . Cette œuvre avait pour cadre la fin de la période historique où débute l'action de *Boris Godounov,* le Temps des troubles (1598–1613). Elle célébrait l'union du peuple russe et du tsar et se terminait par le couronnement de Mikhaïl Romanov. *Boris Godounov*, lui, marque la coupure entre le peuple russe et son souverain. Il se termine par la prédiction des malheurs qui vont toucher la Russie. Apprécié pour certaines de ses qualités musicales, pour son interprétation et pour son sujet, l'opéra ne connaît qu'une *institutionnalisation partielle* après sa création.

Il serait trop long, ici, de traiter de toutes les révisions. Nous ne parlerons que de celle de Rimski-Korsakov (1896). Que fait Rimski dans *Boris* ? Trois choses. Il transforme totalement la structure de l'œuvre en inversant les deux dernières scènes: dans sa révision l'opéra se termine par la mort de Boris et non plus par la révolte du peuple. Il réorchestre presque toute la partition en embellissant la couleur sonore. Il procède, enfin, à des rectifications harmoniques, mélodiques et rythmiques de caractère académique. Sa révision transforme *Boris* en grand-opéra à l'opposé des conceptions de Moussorgski. Sur le plan esthétique, cette transformation correspond aux attentes d'une classe sociale qui n'existait pas en 1874, la bourgeoisie. Rimski, par sa position sociale, ses positions libérales et son opposition à l'aristocratie, peut y être rattaché. C'est dans l'opéra privé du riche mécène Mamontov, le théâtre Solodovnikov de Moscou que *Boris* connaît un grand succès en 1898 auprès de l'intelligentsia libérale. Ce public est particulièrement intéressé par le thème d'une œuvre où le tsar n'est plus un souverain légitime. Il est cependant avant tout sensible à l'interprétation du rôle de Boris par un jeune chanteur, Chaliapine, et par une mise en scène somptueuse. En mettant au centre de l'œuvre le tsar Boris, la révision de Rimski crée les conditions de ce succès. Chaliapine va en effet faire triompher l'opéra en Russie et à l'étranger au point que son nom reste encore aujourd'hui attaché au rôle de Boris. L'interprétation est donc un facteur décisif de l'institutionnalisation de la version de Rimski. *Boris Godounov* est transformé plus tard en raison de son thème fondamental, une réflexion sur la légitimité et l'essence du pouvoir, mais aussi de son statut d'opéra symbole de la culture nationale. Même aujourd'hui, alors qu'on sait que la seconde version (1872) correspond exactement aux choix de Moussorgski, l'œuvre n'est pas encore institutionnalisée sous cet aspect. Alors que l'orchestration originale est de plus en plus employée, la présence de la scène de Saint-Basile de la première version (1869) détruit l'équilibre instauré par le compositeur.

Quel champ d'étude, quelle méthode ?

Si *Boris Godounov* est bien sûr un cas particulier, toute œuvre est cependant caractérisée par des processus d'institutionnalisation. Etudier ces dimensions sociologiques met l'étude du sens dans une perspective synchronique et diachronique . Cela donne également tout son poids à la notion de chaîne d'interprétants donnée par Peirce dans sa définition du signe. C'est dans la réalité des sociétés humaines que l'œuvre prend son sens et sa valeur, au point de susciter l'interprétation dans des contextes très différents de celui de sa création. Reste alors à définir quand il faut parler d'œuvre et quand il faut parler de production, c'est à dire d'œuvre sans originalité, qui peut disparaître après avoir connu le succès. Nous nous contenterons ici de donner quelques pistes de recherche pour préciser le vaste champ d'études de l'institutionnalisation.

L'étude du contexte historique de l'œuvre ne suffit pas. Nous proposons une série de critères interdépendants pour étudier ce que devient l'œuvre dans la société où elle est créée et dans les sociétés où elle continue d'être jouée. Il faut distinguer ce qui relève des processus d'instauration, d'une part, et ce qui appartient en propre à l'institutionnalisation, d'autre part. Examinons ces critères.

– le groupe social à l'origine de l'œuvre. Nous nous référons ici aux travaux de Goldmann (1956, 1966) pour éclairer cette notion. Une œuvre ne naît pas simplement de la volonté d'un artiste. Elle est aussi générée par un groupe social qui lui confie, de manière explicite ou implicite, le soin de réaliser une forme en rapport avec ses valeurs morales et ses conceptions esthétiques. Jusqu'à la fin du XVIII° siècle le phénomène de la commande permet de bien saisir la dépendance des créateurs par rapport à d'autres groupes sociaux. La libération sociale de l'artiste ne l'a pas isolé. Il reste membre d'un groupe dont il représente consciemment ou inconsciemment les valeurs et les aspirations à travers la réalisation d'un univers imaginaire. Il convient donc de cerner la place de l'artiste dans la société, de le relier à un groupe social dont les contours (classe sociale, couche sociale, groupe particulier) doivent être précisés. Il faut enfin, comme dans toute étude historique, examiner le contexte de production de l'œuvre.

– le sujet et le genre de l'œuvre. Il faut relier ces notions traditionnelles aux valeurs des groupes sociaux. Nous parlons de sujet au sens littéraire dans un opéra ou une œuvre vocale. Le choix d'un sujet est très significatif ; c'est un facteur fondamental de la reconnaissance de l'œuvre par une société. Le genre musical l'est aussi. On peut entendre ce terme dans son sens commun. Certains genres sont plus significatifs que d'autres d'un point de vue esthétique et social. Le fait que *Boris Godounov* soit un opéra le rattache à une forme qui a une importance primordiale pour les sociétés européennes.

– la structure. Par ce terme nous entendons l'étude des moyens littéraires ou musicaux utilisés par le compositeur dans son œuvre. Il faut établir s'ils sont conformes aux lois du genre ou s'ils s'en distinguent. Le déchiffrement, par une analyse musicale poussée, doit le déterminer. Cette étape est fondamentale dans la recherche.

Ces trois premiers critères font partie du processus d'instauration. Ils constituent la première partie de l'étude de l'institutionnalisation. D'autres voies d'approche s'imposent alors.

– l'attitude du pouvoir politique. En autorisant ou en censurant l'œuvre, les autorités politiques déterminent son existence. Ce n'est cependant qu'un facteur parmi d'autres dans l'institutionnalisation.

– le rôle des institutions. Les institutions musicales jouent un rôle important dans la réalisation de l'œuvre. Il convient ainsi de déterminer dans quel cadre l'œuvre est représentée. Pour un opéra, le fait d'être joué dans la capitale ou en province, dans une institution d'état ou une institution privée est significatif. Toute institution a des règles de fonctionnement spécifiques qui entrent en jeu dans l'adoption ou le rejet d'une œuvre.

– l'interprétation. Bien évidemment l'interprétation est fondamentale. Il faut entendre ce terme au sens large. Il ne concerne pas seulement les chanteurs et les musiciens mais tous les éléments qui entrent en jeu dans la représentation de l'œuvre. Dans un opéra la mise en scène, les décors, les costumes en font partie. Il faut alors examiner si l'interprétation correspond à l'attente du public. La qualité des interprètes est déterminante dans ce domaine. Les interprètes peuvent améliorer ou fausser la perception du sens de l'œuvre.

– la réception par un public. Il faut cerner les groupes sociaux qui réceptionnent l'œuvre et voir, là aussi, si l'œuvre correspond à ce que Jauss nomme l'horizon d'attente du public (Erwartungshorizon). Cela impose de confronter la vision du monde du créateur, dégagée par le déchiffrement, avec les conceptions des groupes sociaux qui réceptionnent l'œuvre. Cette réception peut aboutir à la transformation de l'œuvre pour le propre usage de certains groupes sociaux, comme le montre l'histoire de *Boris Godounov*. L'écart qui a pu se manifester entre l'œuvre et le public lors de sa création peut être comblé au fil du temps. L'œuvre est alors institutionnalisée si... elle a été diffusée.

– la diffusion est un critère décisif de l'institutionnalisation. Il ne faut pas entendre ici les représentations seulement mais l'édition des partitions, les éditions de disques, les films, les émissions de radio, etc... Ce critère de diffusion s'évalue en chiffres: nombre de représentations, de spectateurs, chiffre de recettes, nombre de disques vendus.

Tous ces paramètres s'articulent au sein des transformations économiques, sociales, culturelles et historiques, même s'il faut se garder d'expliquer directement l'existence et l'origine de l'œuvre par des facteurs économiques ou idéologiques. L'étude de la reconnaissance de l'œuvre par une société ne peut se passer d'étude historique.

Tous ces critères fondent donc pour nous la sémiotique de l'intitutionnalisation. Ce nouveau champ de recherches ne s'oppose pas aux sémiotiques existantes. Il reconnait leur intérêt et s'en veut complémentaire. L'étude de la narrativité a ainsi donné lieu à de riches travaux en sémantique structurale et permis de dégager la signification de certaines œuvres. La tâche de cette nouvelle sémiotique est de tenir compte de ces travaux tout en replaçant l'œuvre dans sa réalité anthropologique, au coeur des sociétés humaines. Loin de vouloir aboutir à une signification figée, notre projet est de développer de nouvelles liaisons entre des disciplines séparées pour mieux expliquer le fait musical.

Janvier 1993

Notes

1. Cf. les travaux du séminaire d'Histoire Sociale de la Musique de Paris (IRCAM — CNRS — Ecole Normale Supérieure), édités par Hugues Dufourt et Joël-Marie Fauquet (1987, 1991). Un troisième volume doit paraître en 1993.
2. Sur la sémiotique de l'instauration, cf. les contributions de nos collègues d'Aix-en-Provence Fabienne Desquilbé et Christine Esclapez dans ce volume.
3. Deux volumes, Oxford: Oxford University Press.
4. Boris Godounov, dir. V. Fedosseiev, orchestre et choeurs de la radio télévision d'URSS, Philips, 1985.

References

Adorno, Théodor W. (1968). *Einleitung in die Musiksoziologie*. Hamburg: Rowohll-Verlag.

Blacking, John (1967). *Venda children's songs*. Johannesburg: Witwatersrand University Press.

Blacking, John (1973). *How musical is man?*. Seattle: University of Washington Press.

Dahlhaus, Carl (1975). "Vorwort", *Texte zur Musiksoziologie*, Tibor Kneif (ed.). Köln: Gerig.

Dufourt, Hugues et Fauquet, Joël-Marie (1987). *La musique et le pouvoir*. Paris: Aux amateurs de livres.

– (1991). *La musique: du théorique au politique*. Paris: Klincksieck.

Esclapez, Christine (1993). Sémiotique musicale et figuration. La complexité temporelle des Quatuors à cordes de Beethoven. Thèse de Doctorat, non publiée, Université de Provence (Aix-Marseille I).

Francastel, Pierre (1967). *La figure et le lieu*. Paris: Denoël-Gonthier

Goldmann, Lucien (1956). *Le dieu caché*. Paris: Gallimard.

– (1966). *Sciences humaines et philosophie*. Paris: Gonthier.

Iakovlev, Vassilij (1930). "Boris Godunov v teatre", *Musorgskij Boris Godunov: stat'i i issledovanija*, 166–246. Moskva: Gosudarstvennoe Izdatel'stvo Muzykal'nyi Sektor.

Jacono, Jean-Marie (1991). "Boris Godounov: un enjeu culturel et politique", *Moussorgski Boris Godounov*, Michel Beretti (ed.), 39–51. Paris: Opéra de Paris-Bastille.

– (1992). Les révisions de *Boris Godounov* de Moussorgski: transformations musicales et transformations sociales. Thèse de doctorat, non publiée, Université de Provence.

Jauss, Hans-Robert (1978). *Pour une esthétique de la réception*, Tr. de C. Maillard. Paris: Gallimard.

Kandinskij, Aleksej (1990). "Les visages de *Boris*", *Le monde de la musique* 129: 57–60.

Le Roux, Maurice (1980). *Moussorgski Boris Godounov*. Paris: Aubier-Montaigne.

Nattiez, Jean-Jacques (1975). *Fondements d'une sémiologie de la musique*. Paris: Union Générale d'Editions.

– (1987). *Musicologie générale et sémiologie*. Paris: Bourgois.

Orlova, Alexandra (1983), *Musorgsky's days and works: a biography in documents*, Trad. de Roy J. Guenther. Ann Arbor: UMI Resarch Press.

Supičić, Ivo (1985). "Perspectives pluridisciplinaires: difficultés d'approche", *IRASM* 16 (2): 125–151.

Tarasti, Eero (1985). "A la recherche des modalités musicales", *Exigences et perspectives de la sémiotique*, H. Parret & H. G. Rupprecht (eds.), 649–659. Amsterdam- Philadelphia: John Benjamins.

– (1987). "On the modalities of opera", *Semiotica* 66 (1–3): 155–168

– (1992). "Pictures and promenades. An excursion to the semiosis of Mussorgsky", *Festschrift for Juri Lotman*. Tartu: University of Tartu.

Taruskin, Richard (1984). "Musorgsky versus Musorgsky; the versions of *Boris Godunov*", *Nineteenth Century Music* 8 (2): 91–118.

Vecchione, Bernard (1992). "La recherche musicologique aujourd'hui: questionnements, intersciences, métamusicologie", *Interface* 21 (3–4): 282–311.

A model of development of the socio-cultural sphere

O. DANILOVA AND YE. POKORSKAYA

The notion of a strong correlation between processes occurring in many fields of the *socium* has arisen repeatedly in the minds of scientists of various kinds, including culturologists and natural scientists, mathematicians and ecologists, art theorists and biologists. In cultural studies the phenomenon of artistic consciousness has mostly been treated as the embodiment and implementation of a general "spirit of the epoch" or *Zeitgeist*, which is reproduced in various kinds of art and visible in a diversity of artistic forms. G. Velfi noted the tendency of art historians to draw parallels between stylistic and cultural epochs: "to explain a style means no more than to relate it to general history and to prove that its forms present in their own language the same things that are expressed in other voices living in the same time." In other words, artistic consciousness is traditionally considered to be in direct relationship with other factors of social development. However, recognizing the relationship between art and the spirit of the epoch, we should take another step toward understanding the essence of this phenomenon. We should try to envision (at least generally) the causes that bring about the spirit of the epoch, a spirit that determines all spheres of mental life, politics, science, and art.

Obviously, we are faced with the search for a certain invariant that would be equally important for the development of both culture and *socium*. Such an invariant can be found only at a rather high level of abstraction that would allow us to bring together the diversity of the spiritual sphere and demonstrate this diversity by means of some general principles. As a result, one might reveal those regularities that have impact on the evolution of both culture and *socium*.

As one way to study the problem of spiritual-sphere development, we suggest information analysis. The general theory of information processing by complex self-developing systems (including an individual and a society as a whole), in our view, can become a key to unification of artistic and socio-psychological spheres. To do that it is necessary to project the main principles of information processing onto the area concerned.

The work of S. Y. Maslov, a prominent Soviet logician and culturologist, played a leading role in shaping a theoretical model of socio-cultural sphere development. Some of Maslov's latest work, devoted to the application of an information model to natural and human sciences, constitutes a qualitatively new stage in the treatment of this problem. Maslov's model is based on the assumption that two opposite principles of information processing take place. Any sufficiently complex self-developing system requires two ways of processing information that enters the system from the outside: (1) The first, conventionally called "analytic", is characterized by rationalism and appeal to logic. Here occurs sequential processing of small pieces of information; these processes are developed in time, characterized by high accuracy and objectivity, and easily modified. (2) The second type of processing, conventionally called "synthetic", is characterized by intuition, reference to feelings and emotions. Here occurs processing of large pieces of information. These processes work in the form of instant action. They are not practically cognized and are characterized by subjectivity and approximation.

Both types of processing are necessary for normal functioning of any of the above systems. Actually, analytic and synthetic types of information processing are none other than two different strategies used by both human intellect and the joint intellect of society in the course of mastering and cognizing reality. In other words, humanity possesses two symbolic models of the world, by means of which a surrounding reality is interpreted.

Each of the two types forms a complex of well coordinated characteristics, due to which we can speak of a consciousness that can dominate in informational, spiritual, and social processes. It is domination (not complete suppression) of one type over the other that ensures a stable state of these systems. Why do we speak of domination, not combination, of the two types of consciousness? First, because society always strives to have a single spirit and a single language. Second, the "parity" of both types is impossible due to incompatibility of a number of principles of analytic and synthetic types of consciousness.

But while societies, people, cultures gravitate towards one type of consciousness, the potentialities of each type, taken separately, are rather limited. Therefore the striving for a comprehensive cognition of the world inevitably causes a change in orientation and a transition to domination of a polar type (exceptions occur in cases of a cultural development leading to deadlock or to clinical human pathology). In culture this change manifests in a society's disappointment in artistic styles, directions, and schools that prevailed earlier. In the social and psychological spheres a change of mind-set takes place as well, leading to a change in concrete forms of political structure, with authoritarian or democratic features as the overwhelming majority.

Thus, in light of the concept being suggested, social and cultural development appears as an undulating phenomenon: alternation of the two types of consciousness, that is, gravitation towards either analyticity or syntheticism. These two types have conflicted with and replaced each other throughout the history of mankind, influencing not only the process of cognition, but the whole complex of human deeds, the formation of tasks, ideas, and aspirations in diverse spheres of life.

This concept was experimentally tested on the following material: the evolution of social and psychological climate in Russia and in a number of West-European countries throughout the 18th–20th centuries; the evolution of architectural styles in the 18th–20th centuries; and the evolution of musical art of the 17th–20th centuries. Indeed, in all three spheres there appeared an undulating process, that is to say, the alternation of two opposite types of consciousness.

Social and psychological climate

We first developed a technique that made it possible to estimate quantitatively the extent of gravitation of each time-period towards either the analytic or synthetic pole. Further, certain features were formulated that reflect the manifestation of these two types of consciousness in *socium*: (1) the domination of the spirit of optimism in society (typical of analytic consciousness) or, on the contrary, of the spirit of pessimism (a feature of the synthetic type); (2) openness of society to outside factors (A-type) or, on the contrary, isolation, separation (C-type); this aspect of social and psychological climate can be easily traced via the character of foreign policy of the state, its foreign relations, customs politics (for example, through the dynamics, growth or drop, of imports and exports); (3) the domination in society of voluntary and contractual elements (A-feature) or tough authoritarian style (C-feature); (4) high (A-type) or low (C-type) status of knowledge; the role of culture and knowledge is traced, in particular, through the dynamics of the number (growth or reduction) of students in the country.

Figure 1a provides a graph showing changes in social and psychological climate in 19th–20th centuries. Quite obvious are the "analytical" waves (1860s, first decades of the 19th century, etc.) and "synthetical" waves (for example, 1830s and 40s, 1880s and 90s, 1930s and 40s). A complete period of such variations is equal to about 50 years.

Let us try to see how the mind-set of the epoch changed in the 20th century, of which many events are still fresh in the memory of our contemporaries. In the 1930s and 40s a synthetic surge occurs, characterized by irrationality, reserve, deep pessimism, and growth of a number of totalitarian states having antidemocratic and authoritarian styles of power. In Russia it was related to Stalinism, with its senseless and bloody repressions. In the countries of Western Europe this synthetic tendency appeared in fascist ideology. It was not by chance that World War II (with its millions of victims) became the culmination of this period, which resulted finally not only in disintegration of the fascist coalition, but in the formation in Europe of two antagonistic camps. And only the next, "analytical wave" led to shaking the "iron curtain" between them. This latter wave started at the beginning of 1950s and lasted for a shorter time than normal — somewhat over 15 years.   During this time democratic tendencies strengthened, resulting in international relations in many fields, including science and culture. In social climate, a "common-sense" ideology and the presence of reason in world structure prevailed. In Russia it was called "thaw", and in Europe ideas of a "common home" were pronounced for the first time. In the mid 1960s this wave broke sharply (remember how the careers of some progressive political leaders were terminated: a number of attempts on Charles de Gaulle's life, Nikita Khrushchev's dismissal, and in the USA the murder of John Kennedy, who undoubtedly implemented analytical trends in American society).

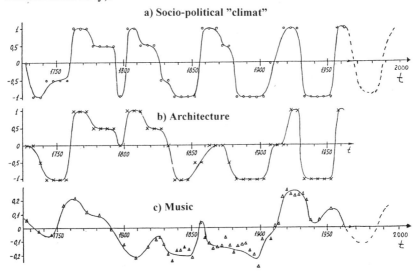

Figure 1.

In the foreground of 1960's political life one again sees a synthetic wave with its authoritarian features of aggressiveness, atmosphere of conflict, and tension in relations (recall the events in Ulster, the occupation of Czechoslovakia, student disturbances in France, etc.). For Russia it is a time of "stagnation", social numbness; for Europe it is characterized by the intensification of conservative trends that slow down integrative processes.

The next shift happened literally before our eyes, at the end of 1980s. The start of "perestroika" in the USSR, peaceful revolutions in the countries of Eastern Europe, unification of Germany, realization of common-home "ideas" in Western Europe — these are just some of the events that signified the advent of a new historical epoch. And while, as we see, the logic of shifting reference points in the social mind is definitely confirmed by all the development of history — which is why we can with high probability predict an imminent analytical wave in *socium* — we would nevertheless note that at present we are experiencing a special situation. It is a so-called "zero period" — a special time when the two polar trends are in a peculiar state of equilibrium and confrontation. The scales are chaotically oscillating, causing a sense of instability and higher tension in society. Such brief (3–4 years) "boundary" periods can be illustrated by the following statistical data: higher crime rate, increased number of suicides, spread of psychological diseases. It is not by accident that at this time society holds the pessimistic convictions that progress is impossible and that the course of history can be reversed. During such zero periods, social tension reaches its climax and may result in clashes both within and outside a country. (The latest events in the USSR and the Persian Gulf War reflect precisely these law-governed processes.) However, the final outcome of the struggle manifested in the zero period is determined by the inevitable logic of complicated self-developing systems, that is, by which of the two types of consciousness should prevail in the *socium* following this period. The future analytical wave will last not less than two decades. Its realization (main features: humanization, democratization of all aspects of social life, reasonable and voluntary relations, etc.) will not be simply the consequence of somebody's will nor an accidental phenomenon, but the result of fundamental, immanent laws of social development.

The most surprising conclusions following from the concept of two types of consciousness can be made when studying the dynamics of art development. This analytic/synthetic concept provides a means for explaining the mechanism of the shifts in cultural traditions in art. The concept of two types of domination and strict quantitative analysis of the dynamics of the shift were applied to architectural styles and musical art (at present, similar studies are being carried out on the material of fine arts and history of drama).

The evolution of architectural style and musical art

Systems of features reflecting the manifestations of A- and C-types of consciousness have been formulated for architecture and music. In the domain of artistic activity, Maslov developed specific features that make it possible to attribute the work of some artist to a certain type of domination. The domination of A-type consciousness is conditioned by the following features: optimism, inclination to "invention", schematization and modelling, pragmatism and rationalism, domination of the "general" over the "particular". Here beauty is understood as high expediency, and the main cognitive categories are treated in a rational way. By contrast, the domination of the C-type consciousness is determined by such features as pessimism, looking to the past, striving to be natural, antipragmatism, and individualism in artistic activity. Beauty is perceived as a result of "free and agonizing creative work".

Hence specific architectural features of A-type: strictness and logic of structures, the desire to bring the structure to the foreground, pragmatic conditioning of parts; whereas typical manifestations of C-type consciousness in architecture are the inclination to fancifulness and the grotesque, exaggerated decor and pretentiousness, the desire to "veil" the structure. The analytic style of thinking in architecture is represented by High Renaissance, Palladio style, Empire style, engineering style, constructivism, styles of the 1950s and 60s. The synthetic style of thinking includes mannerism, Baroque, Rococo, romanticism, eclecticism, modernism, and retrospection.

In Figure 1b an evolution curve is shown for the architecture of the 18th–20th centuries. One can also observe waves with a fluctuation period of about 50 years.

For musical art we also developed specific features characteristic of the A-type creative work: optimism, single timbre domination, graphic nature of music notation, strictness of form, logical development of musical material, and so on; C-type creative work is characterized by tragic disposition, harmonic and timbral richness, picturesqueness (colorfulness), free form, improvisation (spontaneous, impromptu character). By means of these features the experts (musicologists) evaluated the creative work of 102 of the most outstanding composers of West

European and Russian music of the 17th–20th centuries. With the help of a technique specially developed for this purpose, we obtained a quantitative index of the extent of each composer's bias towards one of the types of consciousness. This index was calculated by the sum total of features characterizing various orientation of creative workers to the two types of consciousness. On the basis of the data obtained, a music evolution curve was also plotted, shown in Figure 1c.

Comparison of all three curves revealed a very interesting fact: their waves are practically synchronous, they rise and fall at the same time! These curves refer to various spheres of human activity and thus have different natures and material. This surprising fact is a convincing proof of the reality of periodic alternation of analytic and synthetic trends both in culture and in *socium*.

In recent years, strong support for the concept of two types of consciousness has come from studies in the field of functional asymmetry of human brain hemispheres; these studies present a concrete psychophysiological explanation of this phenomenon. In the light of modern assumptions about functional difference of the mechanisms of the left and the right brain hemispheres, analytic processes can be related to the domination of the left hemisphere in cognition; the synthetic process relates to the processes characteristic of the domination of the right hemisphere.

Thus the existence of two types of consciousness, the orientation of an individual (or society as a whole) to one of them, the fact of alternation of A- and C-types of consciousness — all this can now be treated as more than a hypothesis that successfully explains startling coincidences in history: these are phenomena well-grounded in fact. Moreover, with the help of the suggested model, we can not only clearly represent the logic of social and artistic development, explain the mechanism of shifts of cultural traditions and social systems, but with great assurance forecast the future in quite various aspects — the way art will look in the nearest coming decades, the type of political leaders, the character of future social conflicts and the means of resolving them.

Analysis and fantasy from the viewpoint of the interpersonal hypothesis of musical semantics:
An attempt at analysis

JARMILA DOUBRAVOVÁ

Interpersonal hypothesis of music

The interpersonal hypothesis of musical semantics has been verified at several stages of research, and the results have been evaluated statistically by Knobloch (1968). The hypothesis runs as follows: "In musical compositions from different periods, there appear interpersonal tendencies, which can be determined by independent observers with an agreement that cannot be accidental." The hypothesis was formulated on the basis of the interpersonal concept of spiritual life and on the basis of research on group processes. It originated from the assumption that every individual passes through various social groups during his lifetime. The social group in which his experience and his personality are formed is small, his family in most cases. The individual generalizes his experiences concerning the small social group in a *group scheme*. Unrecognized, and later recognized, this scheme, which motivates and guides the motion of an individual in a group, accompanies him not only in his conscious life, but also in his fantasy, day-dreaming, and dreams. It manifests itself also in a work of art and is an important factor of its perception.

A *work of art* then represents, among other things, a *fictitious manipulation of the group scheme* of the author, and creates the interpersonal space of a similarly fictitious manipulation in the listener. This is made possible by the common features of group schemes. The listener may identify himself with the group scheme of the author, but he may also have more complex needs; for example, he may wish to find a supplementary scheme or to appropriate other schemes, either because he looks for the solution to some unsatisfactory interpersonal situation or for reasons of intellectual exercise.

To illustrate, we shall use three examples that contain the same expressive intention, while representing a very wide palette of meanings: (1) *Nasloucháme přírodě* (Sounds of Nature), recorded by the Originální pražský synkopický orchestr (Original Prague Syncope Orchestra), Supraphon DV 15293; (2) "Bombay", sung by Tiny Parson, Supraphon Stereo 1115 2654 H; (3) Ivan Moravec: *F. Chopin — 24 preludií pro klavír* (24 Preludes for Piano), Supraphon Stereo 1112 1396. The expressive intention — the content of which is the exhibition of a non-quality of weakness — appears in the crying of a chimpanzee, in a blues song, and stylized in the Prelude in E minor by Chopin. Neither in terms of expression nor of other tendencies are these examples comparable. Even the representation of the tendency to exhibit non-quality differs among the three examples. The *Sounds of Nature* express this tendency in intention, "Bombay" demonstrates it, and the Chopin manipulates it as a mastered sorrow. Still less are the illustrations comparable in the sphere of structure. Yet they are comparable as expressions of certain behavior.

The *interpersonal tendencies* are represented in a *circle*, with the use of two orthogonal factors (see Figure 1). The opposite of exhibition by non-quality is exhibition by quality, force, beauty, and intelligence; the opposite of dominance is submission; the opposite of affiliation is resistance; the opposite of aggression is flight. These eight tendencies, internally differentiated, are testified to in expert literature. Interpersonal tendencies are linked to two basic roles, "ego" and "non-ego", and in a more differentiated way to the following roles: authorities, coordinate subjects, subordinate subjects, and erotic object. They are presented on the levels of conscious behavior, recognized behavior, on the fantastic level, on the uncognized level, and on the level of the ideal "ego" — the level of values.

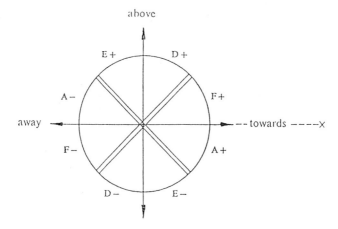

Figure 1. (Knobloch 1968: 374).

Musicological application

For musical-analytic purposes, this rough classification of interpersonal tendencies has been found valuable precisely on account of its roughness, which combines typological similarity with morphological difference. A number of compositions by Janáček, Bartók, Stravinsky, and others were analyzed by means of this scheme (see Doubravová 1981a). It was found that the criterion of interpersonal tendencies is probably related to the criterion of musical form. On the basis of an analysis of all types of musical forms it is possible to formulate the following hypothesis about the correspondence between the interpersonal and musical-formal levels: the formal schemes probably represent model situations, which became stabilized and generalized in the development of music and were absorbed into the sign system of music. Musical forms represent generalized and stereotypical chains of interpersonal patterns of behavior. The term "chains" is related to the fact that the interpersonal tendencies group into units of various orders, patterns, and sequences of patterns and chains. Musical forms, then, probably represent the most effective models for manipulating the expressive possibilities of music;

that is, they represent the most communicative models of musical communication.

The criteria of interpersonal tendencies were further analyzed as an instrument of musical analysis oriented towards the explanation of musical composition. Even if this application of the criterion of interpersonal tendencies is not very proper to the interpersonal hypothesis, still it furnishes certain information about the relationship of the author to musical themes and the like, and also to his own work. A fantastic occurrence, which can be verbalized by means of the interpersonal hypothesis, represents a fictitious manipulation of the interpersonal tendencies. Musically, it presents the motion of a subject in a group whose primary members have been specified: superior authorities, coordinate and subordinate subjects, and an erotic object. The results obtained by means of this analysis on the whole confirm the explanations that appear in musicological literature, but on a more general level. (This issue has been dealt with especially in my analysis of the Alban Berg's Violin Concerto; Doubravová 1972a.)

Some results of the interpersonal hypothesis in musicology

It appeared that the work of every author represented a specific "palette" of interpersonal tendencies and ways of dealing with those tendencies. This problem was studied closely in my analysis of the works of Leoš Janáček (see Doubravová 1972b). A *representative palette* was demonstrated by a sequence of twelve illustrations from the work of Bartók, in a paper read at the Semiotics of Culture Symposium 1974 in Hungary (in Doubravová 1981b). From the interpersonal viewpoint, the work of Béla Bartók stands for a very outstanding type, by the intensity of its representation of individual tendencies and by its characteristic patterns and chains. The manipulation of interpersonal tendencies is conscious; the "roles" are differentiated and objectified. The dramatic action of the characters and textures of early works such as *Bluebeard's Castle* and Dance Suite, for example, is outstandingly different, on an interpersonal level, from the characteristics of the works of his middle and last periods (Concerto for Violin and Orchestra, Concerto for Orchestra). Some outstanding patterns "manneristically" pervade the compositions of the three periods; these include elegant aggression, in the fourth movement of the Dance Suite, third movement of the Fifth String Quartet, and first movement of the Concerto for Violin and Orchestra; robust defiance, in the first movement of the Dance Suite, second movement of the *Music for Strings, Percussion, and Celesta*; other patterns appear in the arrangements of folk songs as well as in the culminating artistry of *Music for Strings, Percussion, and Celesta.*

Differing from Bartók, Janáček, from the interpersonal viewpoint, represents a "world" in which rapid variation of the presentational level of interpersonal tendencies, together with most pregnant patterns of the sequence of interpersonally opposite tendencies, overrule the conscious and the recognized. Janáček's work culminates in his final style period, in which the composer discovers myth; for example, the Perunian myth. Perun was a Slavonic god of rain and storm, also combining birth and doom, or the divine and the human, as do most mythological characters (see Doubravová 1981a); the level of brotherly equality and of compassion with the most miserable ones, such as *Zápisky z mrtvého domu* (Notes from the Dead House) (1927–28); and also the level of the consonance of human propinquity, in the String Quartet "Listy důvěrné" (Intimate letters, 1928).

To approach the work of Jean Sibelius, we make the following assumption: that which can be said about Sibelius's work on the basis of the interpersonal hypothesis will probably confirm that which is known about him. At the same time, it may be expected that the statement about the interpersonal tendencies will underline typological similarity amidst morphological difference.

An attempt at conceptualizing the work of Jean Sibelius

For study of the compositions of Sibelius in their historical continuity, special attention should go to the Fourth Symphony in A Minor (Op. 63, 1910). The autobiographical features of this composition of four movements cannot be ignored: dramatic characters related to Sibelius's personal life (illness), to the oppressed situation of the Finnish nation, or to both. The significant role of the cello as a solo instrument in the first and third movements; the opening motive (the motto) of cellos and double basses; the unique tension of the entire composition, appearing in the harmony by abundant chromaticism and tritone usage; a form that modifies the exposition and the development of traditional sonata form to suit its own dramatic end — these are the fundamental structural characteristics of the Fourth Symphony.

(The dramatic character of the Fourth Symphony is most poignantly expressed in the second movement, *Allegro molto vivace*, which brings elegant, playful dance music, all the while pervaded by a sequence of chords bearing the tritone as a tragic reminder.)

The internal dialogue of this music is carried out on the "ego" level, the ego being identified with affiliative tendencies and with the exhibition of quality; and on the "non-ego" level, menacing, hostile, authoritative; this opposite pole may be identified rather with a gradually dawning recognition of illness than with that of general distress.

The menacing cello theme of the opening is a prominent and clearly defined motive — a symbol. Such a motive appears as early as *Finlandia* (Op. 26, 1899). The domination of evil, with which the latter begins, is of a kind other than that in the Fourth Symphony. It is an external, menacing force, which, however, can be fought, as shown in the middle part of the work, and which can be overcome, as expressed in the prayer and thanksgiving of the third part, the subsequent song of victory, and the concluding hymn.

Tapiola (Op. 112, 1926) is also a work of dialogue. The ego and non-ego roles, however, are cast differently this time: the submissive ego and the dominant, aggressive non-ego. The dialogue in this work develops from the primal, natural lyricism of an individual lost in the unknown, into the bewitchment of man by humanized nature, until it changes again into the dialogue of an individual full of sorrow, powerless before the voice of nature. The individual eventually becomes reconciled with natural law, with the powerful voice of chaos, as infinite as it is inchoate, levelling all differences, and simultaneously expressing the beginning and the end.

The second movement of the Violin Concerto (Op. 47, 1905) contains idyllic lyricism. The representation of interpersonal tendencies, their patterns and variations — affiliation, dependence and sorrow, personal tragedy, affiliation and exhibition of a quality, affiliation and sorrow — refer to the experience of an intimate relationship, probably not a happy one. These tendencies, however, also indicate a type of dialogue less characteristic for Sibelius than the earlier mentioned type: while non-ego manifests itself in a friendly way, ego reacts submissively and suffers.

The dialogue of the first type — ego as submissive, and non-ego as threatening authority — is very characteristic of the personality of Sibelius. Not by accident does such a dialogue permeate his work, beginning with *Finlandia*, through the Fourth Symphony, and up to the symphonic poem *Tapiola*. Further explanation would require special interpretation. Here, it may be suggested that the relationship to his father played a key role in Sibelius's life. The originally paternal authority absorbed more and more signs until it became a sort of law, the voice of fate.

From the interpersonal viewpoint, the Sixth and Seventh Symphonies are altogether different. They are balanced, non-dialogic, and their interpersonal world is one of the consciously recognized motion of an individual in human society. The cultivated and elegiac atmosphere, elegance and robust vitality, all this is presented from a knowing, positive, and superior perspective whose balanced state includes the tremors of tragedy, heard at the conclusion of the first movement of the Sixth Symphony (Op. 104, 1923), in the dancing Scherzo of the third movement, or in the second theme of the concluding movement (the symbol mentioned earlier). Also the symphonic fantasy of the single-movement Seventh Symphony (Op. 105, 1924) contains tragic implications, but here one finds the objective, friendly, and majestic atmosphere of a world as seen by a strong and balanced individual.

The incidental music to Shakespeare's *Tempest* (Op. 109, 1925) is of the same family. The romantically, but objectively, conceived image of nature, of human inward character and relationships, has the quality of dramatic exposition, whose musical resolution appears in an augmented triad — a dissonance.

About Sibelius's elegiac intonations little new can be said. Eero Tarasti (1978), in this connection, discusses *The Swan of Tuonela* as a kind of music in which the timbre of the instrument is the bearer of mythological meaning. This music has outstanding *Jugendstil* features: stylization, mystic atmosphere, sensitivity, mystery. The similarity of expression of the *Swan of Tuonela* to the opening of the first movement of the First Symphony (Op. 39, 1899), characterized as a gestic *lamento* by Tarasti (1978: 163–164) and lamentation of the rune singer by Krohn (1942), leads Tarasti to note the similarity with the Largo in the second movement of Dvořák's Ninth Symphony of the New World (Op. 95, 1894) originally inspired by an American Negro spiritual (Sychra 1959: 343–345).

Also the second movement of the First Symphony brings elegiac music, in which personal and impersonal sorrows intermingle in varia tions. The interpersonal background is probably formed by a deeply experienced personal conflict. It is to be noted that the initial theme of the first movement resounds also in the fourth movement and that elegiac tones are heard also in the coda of this movement. We have already mentioned the peculiar sorrow of *Tapiola*, in connection with the dialogic music of Sibelius.

If the interpersonal spheres produce a highly original music, then both other spheres indicate that, to communicate at all, the originality of a great and powerful creative personality must also be necessarily expressed in the interpretative sphere, as a definite measure of invention. Exhibition by quality appears in an outstanding generic likeness among the first and third movements of the Violin Concerto, in the third movement of the First Symphony, and in the first and fourth movements of the Sixth Symphony. Also the world of power, with its pre-image in the first themes of the sonata movements of the symphonies, occurs with Sibelius in its typical form in the first theme of the First Symphony. It has the distinct character of friendly dominance and condescension in the third part of the single-movement Seventh Symphony, and has several levels in *Finlandia*, as discussed earlier.

The interpersonal hypothesis then led us to processes as shown by the analysis of Sibelius's music. As stated by Knobloch (1968: 368): "the dichotomy [of] intra-psychic processes / interpersonal processes disappears. The intrapsychic processes are understood here as models of the interpersonal processes." One of the many ways opened by this hypothesis would be, for example, its utilization in music therapy or pedagogy, or in general semiotics.

Let us now define the interpersonal tendencies: they represent the designates of musically objectified interpersonal relationships. As such, they can be known, experienced as being in common with the composer, and verbalized by means of the interpersonal hypothesis. They explain the fact of common sharing of a work of art at its perception. Interpersonal tendencies establish the special character of the musical sign in general. In music as in other arts, such an activity of the designating subject towards the designated object appears, which takes part in the structure of the sign. This common share in music, however, differs from that in objective arts and in verbal arts. Designation realized on the basis of "thinking by music" (Osolsobě 1973) is more closely, latently and intersubjectively, connected with motion in music than in other arts. Even verbal designation belongs to the music, such as the designation of the mode of performance, of genre, form-type, or style. It is probable that the latent, "motional" participation in the structure of the sign is the fundamental part of designation, preceding designation by language.

Notes

1. See the program of Finnish Culture Week in Czechoslovakia in the spring of 1976; also in a paper of Erik Tawaststjerna entitled "Jean Sibelius und Claude Debussy: Eine Begegnung in London 1909; in the Proceedings from *L. Janáček et musica Europea* (Brno: 1968), 307; and Eric Nils Ringbom, *Jean Sibelius: Symphonies, Symphonic Poems, Violin Concerto, Voces intimae* (Helsinki: 1955).
2. See Doubravová 1984a (below); and Jean-Jacques Nattiez, *De la sémiologie de la musique* (Montréal: Université de Québec, 1988).

References

Doubravová, Jarmila (1972a). "Houslový koncert Albana Berga z interpersonálního hlediska" [The Violin Concerto by Alban Berg from an interpersonal viewpoint], *Hudební věda* 9 (2): 117–139.

- (1972b). "Interpersonální aspekt v hudebním vyjadřování a sdělování" [The interpersonal aspect in musical expression and communication], *Opus musicum* 4 (8/9): 254–256.
- (1975). "Interpersonální význam hudby a hudební sémitoka" [The interpersonal meaning of music and musical semiotics], *Hudební věda* 12 (1): 154–164.
- (1981a). "L. Janáček: Glagolitic Mass — I. Stravinsky: Symphony of Psalms: Semantic confrontation of two orientations", *Music of the Slavonic Nations*. Brno: Çeská hudební spoleçnost.
- (1981b). "A zenei kommunikácio jel — aspektusának elemzése" [Sign aspect in musical communication], *Semiotic Studies* 68. Budapest: Académiai Kiadó.
- (1984a). "Musical semiotics in Czechoslovakia and interpersonal hypothesis of music", *International Review of the Aesthetics and Sociology of Music* 15 (1): 31–38.
- (1984b). "Musical forms as models of communication", *Semiotic Unfolding*, 1613–1618. Berlin: Mouton.
- (1988). "The symbol of the tree in Musical *Jugendstil*", *Musical Signification* (1995), ed. E. Tarasti, 565–574. Berlin-New York: Mouton de Gruyter.
- (1991). "Czech semiotics: Recent past and foreseeable future", *Proceedings of the Symposium about the Object*. Perpignan.
Doubravová, Jarmila—Anna Sochorová (1975). "Testing Interpersonal Hypothesis of Music Using the GUHA Method", *Languages of desing* [forthcoming].
Knobloch, Ferdinand et al. (1968). "On an interpersonal hypothesis of the semiotics of music", *Kybernetika* 4 (4): 364–382.
Krohn, Ilmar (1942). *Der Formenbau in den Symphonien von Jean Sibelius*. Helsinki.
Osolsobê, Ivo (1973). "Funkce hudby v prožitku myšlení aneb myslíme hudbou" [The function of music in the experience of thinking; or, we think in music], *Opus musicum* 5 (9): 258–264.
Sychra, Antonín (1959). *Estetika Dvořákovy symfonické tvorby* [Aesthetics of Dvořák's Symphonic Work]. Prague: KLHV.
Tarasti, Eero (1978). *Myth and Music*. Helsinki: Suomen Musiikkitieteellinen Seura.

Survie ou renouveau?
Imagination structurelle dans la création électroacoustique récente

MÁRTA GRABÓCZ

Cet article est, en quelque sorte, la présentation de "la table des matières" d'une étude à rédiger sur les différents types d'idées structurelles (et de leur contenu référentiel ou non-référentiel) dans les musiques électro-acoustiques créées, pour la plupart, dans les studios français de la recherche et création musicales (GRM, IRCAM, UPIC, GMEM etc.). Ce travail d'étude et d'analyse a commencé en Hongrie en 1988 lors d'une série d'émissions de Radio sur certains chapitres de l'histoire de la musique électroacoustique.[*]

Ensuite, il a été repris sous plusieurs formes, telle une étude sur la narrativité en électroacoustique[**], puis, même actuellement, sous forme d'une typologie plus complexe embrassant toutes les approches formelles-structurelles d'une trentaine d'œuvres caractéristiques répertoriées depuis les années 70. Ces pièces choisies offrent un éventail de quêtes et d'investigations sur la structure depuis les idées toutes neuves jusqu'à la reprise des pensées structurelles les plus anciennes, en passant par les catégories intermédiaires.[***]

---

[*] travail soutenu en Hongrie par l'aide de la Fondation SOROS.

[**] sous forme de communication présentée lors du 2e Colloque International de la Signification Musicale à Helsinki en 1988, publiée en français dans le No. 51. de MUSICWORKS Magasine, en anglais: dans les actes du Colloque *Musical Signification*, Eero Tarasti (éd.). Berlin & New York: Mouton de Gruyter, 1995.

[***] projet d'un livre dont certains chapitres ont été élaborés dès 1990 en France, grâce à une bourse de la Direction de la Musique du Ministère de la Culture accordée au CIREM en vue de publications sur la musique électroacoustique.

L'idée initiale de mon travail était d'affirmer que les musiques électroacoustiques ou mixtes, malgré l'apparente nouveauté de leur matériau, ont souvent recours aux anciennes méthodes de structuration, telles que la forme cyclique, la forme énumérative, la forme symétrique ou les formes descriptives, voire musiques à programme.

Dans la plupart de ces cas, c'est justement la conception entièrement nouvelle du matériau même, qui pousse le compositeur à appliquer les principes de structuration connus du passé, pour pouvoir établir l'équilibre, le juste milieu entre éléments inconnus et traditionnels, en vue de la réception aidée et facilitée de l'œuvre de la part du public.

Mais au cours de la dernière décennie, on observe pourtant l'émergence de nouveaux types de structuration au sein de la création électroacoustique et des œuvres "mixtes" et, depuis quelques années, dans la création assistée par ordinateur. Ces nouveaux principes structurels relèvent souvent des modèles extra-musicaux choisis par le compositeur ou des processus ayant leurs origines dans la technique électronique même ou dans l'acoustique.

En ce qui suit, je vous présente les trois groupes des idées structurelles principalement exploitées et, en partie, une typologie des éléments d'une sémantique, c.-à-d. des références du contenu décelées dans les œuvres, tout en partant des types expressément nouveaux , en passant par les constructions intermédiaires proposant un compromis, jusqu'aux plus traditionnels.

1. Parmi les idées nouvelles de structuration, on connaîtra 1. les différents modèles extra-musicaux, puis 2. les structures du statisme, de la stasis, et, enfin, 3. les œuvres dont l'articulation suit un diagramme, un dessin graphique (où les axes vertical et horizontal du schéma dessiné, correspondent à l'évolution des hauteurs/ambitus dans le temps.)

1.1. Utilisation de modèles extra-musicaux

Les modèles extra-musicaux sont très variés: le compositeur peut se servir des lois des phénomènes naturels, de la théorie des catastrophes ou de la théorie des prototypes dans le domaine de la psychologie cognitive ou bien des analyses structurales des mythes.

1.1.1. Dans l'œuvre de Magnus Lindberg *Action-Situation-Signification* (1982, pour quatre musiciens et bande), le mot "situation" du titre correspond à *l'utilisation des bruits de la nature* (= ceux de la mer, de la pluie, du feu et du vent).

> Les différentes sections de l'œuvre débutent par une situation confuse dans laquelle sont mélangés différents objets sonores classés par éléments de la nature. En approchant de la fin d'une section, la texture s'affine, se concentre au point de ne présenter — en dernier lieu — que des sons se référant au symbole en question; une fois parvenue à cet instant, l'action devient situation et le matériau concrêt passe au premier plan.[1]

Les différents mouvements sont les suivants: I: Terre/1; II: La mer; III: Interlude: Bois; IV: Pluie; V: Interlude: Métal; VI: Feu; VII: Vent; VIII: Terre/2.

> La base de l'œuvre fut constituée par deux livres: le *Traité des objets musicaux* de Pierre Schaeffer et *Masse und Macht* d'Elias Canetti. Le premier démontrait un lien avec la musique concrète française et offrait de plus un modèle pour grouper les bruits et les autres sources sonores. Le livre de Canetti fut important d'un autre point de vue. Lindberg fonda l'élaboration de sa pièce sur les modèles de Canetti concernant certaines analogies dans le comportement entre les phénomènes de la nature et des groupes humains. /. . . / Pour Lindberg, la composition s'apparente aux mathématiques: elle consiste dans la résolution d'un problème donné. Dans ce cas précis, le problème était l'édification de liens entre la mise en mouvement des musiciens (=action) et l'utilisation de sons naturels, statiques, concrets (=situation). De l'activation de cette situation naquit la signification de l'œuvre et de la réunion de ces trois mots (action-situation-signification), le titre de l'œuvre.[2]

Dans l'œuvre écrite pour six percussionistes et bande magnétique, intitulée *Maraé* (1974) de François-Bernard Mâche,

> les sons bruts de la nature (= de la mer, du vent, du feu, d'une grotte) sont enregistrés et montés sans manipulation. Mais ils sont

colorés par une écriture instrumentale qui en est pour l'essentiel *une transcription* en synchronisme rigoureux avec son modèle. [3]

Le message caché concerne l'abolition des frontières entre nature et culture. Le compositeur a consacré beaucoup d'essais, d'articles et son livre (voir note 8 plus bas) à l'exposition de ses idées concernant l'esthétique "du naturalisme sonore". (Son énoncé est donc en contraste avec l'idée d'arrière-plan de Lindberg qui, en utilisant les mêmes modèles, voulait souligner l'interaction et la transformation réciproque des deux mondes: celui du "statique" /=nature/ et celui du dynamique /=culture/.)

La macrostructure, l'évolution interne de *Maraé* correspond à un voyage initiatique à travers le vent, la mer, une grotte, de nouveau le vent et, pour finir, le feux.

Beaucoup d'autres œuvres créées au GRM (Groupe de Recherche Musicale de l'INA) et dans d'autres studios français au cours des deux dernières décennies, se servent du modèle du "paysage sonore" de toutes sortes. Voir par exemple *De natura sonorum* (1975), *La création du monde* (1984) de Bernard Parmegiani (GRM); *Heterozygote* (1964) de Luc Ferrari /GRM/; *Abyssi symphonia* (1980) de Georges Boeuf /GMEM/; *Hyperion* (1981) de F.-B. Mâche /UPIC/, *Sud* de Jean-Claude Risset (1985) /GRM/; *Pacific Tubular Waves* (1979) et *Immersion* (1980) de Michel Redolfi /GRM-GMEM/; *Océane. . . ou troisième passage de la baleine* (1984) de Pierre-Alain Jaffrennou /GRAME/; *Sphaera* (1987/1990) de Daniel Teruggi /GRM/; *Opéra d'eau* (1991) de Jacques Lejeune (GRM) etc.

1.1.2. Chez d'autres compositeurs qui ont une réflexion profonde sur le sens de la forme musicale, on trouve *l'application de certaines théories scientifiques*.

Costin Miereanu a fait appel à la théorie des catastrophes en suivant les idées de René Thom et Jean Petitot[4] ainsi qu'à la théorie des narra-tions, des labyrinthes depuis le nouveau roman. Dans l'œuvre intitulée *Labyrinthes d'Adrien*, il crée

des personnages d'une narrativité musicale qui, en fait, ne sont rien d'autre que les structures musicales elles-mêmes: des structures étales, pelliculaires, passées au rouleau compresseur, des structures mouvementées, abyssales, ainsi que de nombreux modèles issus d'une morphologie de la théorie des catastrophes.[5]

(Voir par exemple "les catastrophes de conflit" ou les "catastrophes associées dites de bifurcation" etc. qui peuvent correspondre en musique à l'alternance de l'explosion et du statisme, aux changements brusques et aux états internes stables etc.)

Marco Stroppa, après avoir composé *Traiettoria* pour piano et sons synthétisés par ordinateur (au Centro di Sonologia Computazionale de Padou en 1982–84), s'est rendu compte de l'utilisation "mi-consciente" de *la théorie des prototypes (appliquée dans le domaine de la psychologie cognitive)*, à l'intérieur de son 3e mouvement de *Traiettoria* appelé *Contrasti* (voir: cadence du piano). Ces convergences lui ont permis d'élaborer sa théorie sur "les organismes de l'information musicale".[6]

La recherche d'une virtuosité adéquate doit s'inspirer du travail de 'synthèse instrumentale' qui gère le développement compositionnel des matériaux pianistiques. Synthèse dans le sens où l'organisation des 'morphèmes' (=sons isolés, résonances, fragments gestuels, figures primitives etc.) en groupements générateurs d'événements sonores plus complexes (que le compositeur appelle 'les organismes de l'information musicale'), compose la structure et l'évolution temporelle du matériau sonore pur et fonde le discours de la pièce. Il faut donc 'concevoir' une virtuosité fonctionnelle et cohérente. *Ces 'organismes d'information musicale', sorte de correspondant compositionnel aux familles de sons synthétiques, constituent la base du langage musical.* Leur forte identité morphologique les dote de caractères très différenciés qui les rendent très distincts et très reconnaissables. Chacun d'eux porte en lui-même sa propre évolution qui décrit une trajectoire concernant l'espace des registres, la durée de vie de chaque 'organisme', la fréquence et le déroulement de ses interventions, etc. La cadence pour piano de 'Contrasti' est un exemple d'évolution de sept 'organismes' selon des trajectoires contrastées qui influent sur chacun d'eux au point d'en transformer l'identité. Certains passages de cette cadence explicitent dramatiquement le jeu des tensions générées par la présence de pôles d'attraction qui infléchissent la courbe temporelle des trajectoires de chaque 'organisme'.[7] (C'est moi qui souligne, M. G.)

1.1.3. Dans certaines œuvres de François-Bernard Mâche — comme dans *Aliunde, Danaé, Iter memor* — c'est *l'analyse structurale des mythes* révélant le rôle magique et rédempteur de la musique joué dans la vie d'un héros, qui sert de modèle structurel-dramaturgique. Le premier chapitre du livre du compositeur (*Musique, mythe, nature. Ou les dauphins d'Arion*, Méridiens Klincksieck, 1991), présente les résultats de ses recherches approfondies sur 'La musique dans le mythe'.

> On voit que le rapprochement de ces quelques mythes grecs — /. . . / — ramène inlassablement les mêmes images. Schéma-tiquement: après un plongeon initial, le sujet (ce n'est pas vraiment un héros) accomplit une traversée dangereuse. Des ennemis pervers essaient de le détourner. La magie musicale intervient alors, entraînant le plongeon décisif. Des divinités, ou leurs serviteurs animaux, se portent au secours du plongeur qui accomplit heureusement la seconde partie de sa traversée. Les méchants sont punis, parfois par pétrification, et les bons sont récompensés, sur terre ou au ciel.[8-9]

1.2. Le deuxième groupe des processus nouveaux est représenté par *les œuvres du statisme*: par la stabilité et la transformation lente des matériaux sonores.

En 1981, Tristan Murail décrivait déjà le changement de pensée des compositeurs dits "spectraux": le changement survenu grâce aux nouveaux moyens d'analyser le son.

> Parallèlement à l'apparition de nouveaux instruments, les techniques instrumentales se sont renouvelées et offrent maintenant au compositeur toute une catégorie de sons aux caractéristiques imprévues — sons-limites, sons paradoxaux, sons instables, complexes sonores qui défient la description traditionnelle par l'harmonie et le timbre, car ils se situent à la lisière des deux concepts. . .
> Les nouveaux moyens d'analyse auxquels je faisais allusion nous permettent, dans le même temps, de porter un regard différent sur les sons, de voyager à l'intérieur du son et d'observer sa structure interne. On découvre ainsi, immédiatement, qu'un son n'est pas une entité stable et toujours identique à elle-même, comme les notes abstraites d'une partition peuvent le laisser croire, et toute notre tradition musicale est basée sur cette assimilation par son symbole de la chose réelle, mais que tout son est essentiellement variable, d'une fois sur l'autre bien sûr, mais aussi à l'intérieur de sa propre durée. Plutôt que de décrire un son à l'aide de 'paramètres' (timbre, hauteur,

instensité, durée), il est plus réaliste, plus conforme à la réalité physique et à celle de la perception, de le considérer comme un champ de forces, chaque force ayant son évolution propre. *Cette étude des sons nous donne le pouvoir de mieux agir sur les sons, de perfectionner les techniques instrumentales en comprenant les phénomènes sonores. Elle nous permet aussi de développer une écriture musicale basée sur l'analyse des sons et de faire des forces internes des sons l'un des points de départ du travail du compositeur.*[10] (C'est moi qui souligne, M. G.))

C'est cette pensée compositionnelle qui a conduit à la naissance des œuvres comme *Désintégrations*, de T. Murail, *Saturne, Antiphysis* de Hughues Dufourt, de *Stria* de John Chowning, et à toute une série d'œuvres créées dans le studio de CRM à Rome (créations du "Centro de Ricerche Musicali" à la fin des années 1980 et dans les années 90: de Laura Bianchini, Michelangelo Lupone et de Luigi Ceccarelli et son l'Electravox Ensemble.)

En 1982, lors de la création de *Saturne*, H. Dufourt formulait ses idées de transformation continue et de ses matériaux créés à partir de masses fluentes, de la manières suivante.

La convergence de ces technologies se traduit, dans le domaine de la composition, par le renversement des rapports traditionnels du son et de l'écriture. *Au lieu d'organiser les sons entre eux, on tire une organisation du sonore lui-même.*

De ce fait, l'écriture musicale, au cours de ces dix dernières années, s'est profondément modifiée. Elle a dû tenir compte de l'allure essentiellement évolutive du nouveau matériau. Dans cet esprit, j'ai cherché à transcrire et maîtriser des caractéristiques d'ordre dynamique en constante interaction: transitoires, bruit, résonances, sons complexes. . . *La principale difficulté réside sans doute dans la conversion de mentalité qu'impose cette discipline d'écriture. Car au lieu d'avoir prise sur des configurations stables, il faut s'aventurer dans les franges obscures du son.*

Au plan formel, l'exercice est double. *Il vise à donner une dimension esthétique aux formes acoustiques nouvelles, qui sont des formes en croissance. Il tend à doter ces formes d'une syntaxe appropriée de transformations continues.* 'Saturne' est ainsi construit autour des centres de forces, *avec une nette préférence pour les masses fluentes, les situations de tension, les formes allongées, étirées, sans résolution à la normale, et un parti-pris d'indétermination.* Les timbres instrumentaux jouent un rôle prépondérant. J'ai cherché à obtenir des teintes livides et une lumière blafarde.[11] (C'est moi qui souligne.)

A ce type d'approche de la pensée structurelle appartiennent certaines œuvres de Jean-Claude Eloy *(Shânti, 1973; et Gaku-No-Michi, 1978; Anâhata, 1984–86;)*; les procédés microscopiques de F.-B. Mâche dans les *Quatre phonographies de l'eau* (1980); *Mortuos plango, vivos voco* (1980) de Jonathan Harvey; *Verblendungen* (1984) et *Io* (1987) de Kaija Saariaho etc.

1.3. Le dernier type des conceptions macro-structurelles nouvelles est *la forme qui serait engendrée par un graphisme, un diagram — tout en suivant un dessin géométrique-spatiale.*

1.3.1. Probablement, elle doit ses origines aux transcriptions de certaines musiques concrètes, effectuées surtout au GRM dans les années 1970, afin de produire une partition de suivi, de l'écoute, permettant la diffusion d'une œuvre sans la présence de son compositeur. (Voir par ex. partitions de suivi de *F. Bayle: Jeîta,* 1970; *Pour en finir avec le pouvoir d'Orphée 1972,* de B. Parmegiani , *Symphonie* de Jean Schwarz etc.) Il est vrai, que les premiers graphismes d'œuvres électroacoustiques ont été dessinés dans le studio de Cologne et de Varsovie (voir *Studie II*, 1954; *Kontakte*, 1959 de Karlheinz Stockhausen, transcription d'*Artikulation* (1958) de György Ligeti réalisée par Rainer Wehinger, éditée chez Schott; puis les partitions de Boguslaw Schäffer et de V. Kotonski réalisées sous forme de diagramme en Pologne etc. partitions de Boguslaw Schäffer, V. Kotonski etc.) (Exemple 1).

Dans ces graphismes qui succèdent à la création, chaque compositeur utilise ses propres symboles, créant ainsi un système d'hieroglyphes, parfois évoquant l'utilisation des neumes. Dans la transcription parlante et joliment pictographique de différents mouvements de *Jeîta* (1970), François Bayle a créé les symboles récurrents de l'œuvre: celui du cluster électronique de 18 sons, des murmures ou des clapotis d'eau, des glissandi électroniques ou "vocaux", celui des cloches stalagmites ou des cloches stalactites.

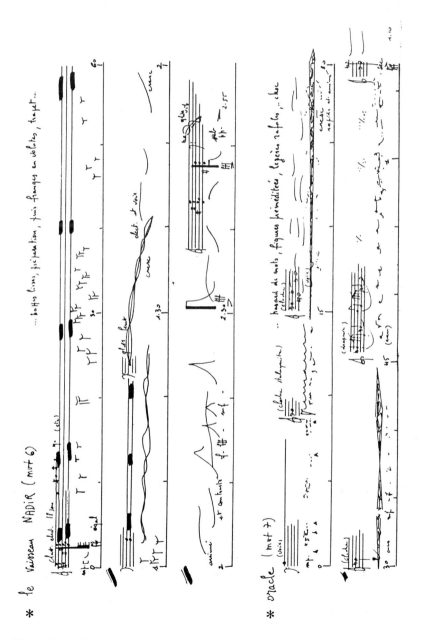

Exemple 1. François Bayle: *Jeîta*.

Si le matériau de la musique contient plusieurs couches complexes, la notation devient moins picturale, signalant surtout le changement du matériau et la superposition des strates (Exemple 2).

1.3.2. La transcription indispensable et consciente d'une bande magnétique voit le jour avec les œuvres orchestrales accompagnées d'une couche de musique électroacoustique (=électronique ou concrète). Dans *Volumes* (1960), F.-B. Mâche se fixait le but de prolonger la musique instrumentale à l'aide de la bande à 12 pistes synchrones (Exemple 3).

> La partie électro-acoustique est elle-même pour une grande part d'origine instrumentale, et son rôle est d'amplifier l'orchestre, hors de tout esprit concertant.
> Réciproquement, la partition instrumentale est sans doute le premier exemple d'écriture systématiquement adaptée des notions et des sonorités familières à la musique 'concrète', à tel point que *les mêmes symboles ont pu servir à noter celle-ci et celle-là*.
> . . . L'auteur a essayé d'utiliser le manque de souplesse des maniements de la bande magnétique *comme un tremplin pour l'imagination de formes nouvelles de masses,* parfois proches des conceptions (mais non des sonorités) de Varèse.[12] (C'est moi qui souligne, M. G.)

L'œuvre intitulée *Librations* (1983) de Fernand Vandenbogaerde écrite pour bande au CERM, montre bien les associations spatiales-visuelles de points, de grains, de courbes, de trames aux impulsions et motifs musicaux, aux clusters et glissandi lors de la transcription graphique (Exemple 4).

1.3.3. Une dernière étape conceptuelle dans l'utilisation d'un schéma géométrique et visuelle est née dans certaines œuvres de I. Xenakis, J.-C. Risset, M. Lindberg, K. Saariaho et de T. Murail.

Je pense au moment de l'évolution historique où *le dessin graphique précède la composition d'une œuvre en reflètant l'articulation de sa macrostructure.* On a déjà démontré l'articulation "spatiale" tripartite de la forme de *Songes* (1979) de Jean-Claude Risset.[13] Cette fois-ci je présente — sans entrer dans les détails — deux structures "dessinées" respectivement par Magnus Lindberg et par Tristan Murail.

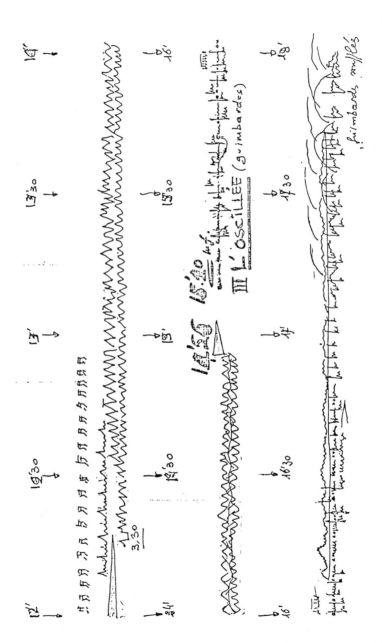

Example 2. Bernard Parmegiani: *Pour en finir avec le pouvoir d'Orphée II*, 1972, Mouvement III: "L'oscillée".

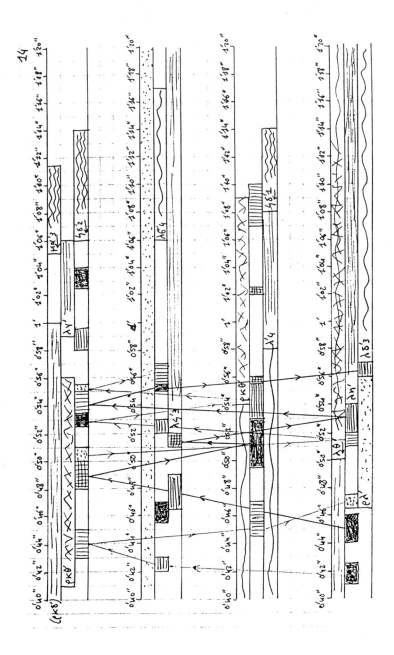

Exemple 3. F.-B. Mâche: *Volumes (Sphères)*.

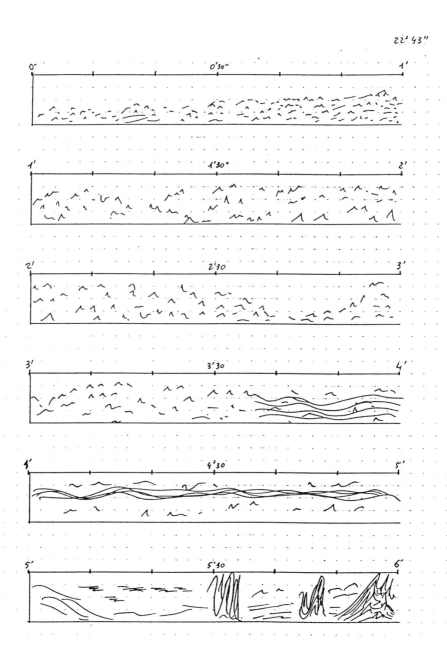

Exemple 4. F. Vandenbogaerde: *Librations*.

Depuis *Ur* (1986), Magnus Lindberg expérimente les différentes dispositions "spatiales" d'une chaconne (= série d'accords dans son acception): les montées et les descentes de ses accords, leurs progressions rétrécissantes et croissantes en ce qui concerne le remplissage de l'espace, voire la superposition de ces processus.

Dans *Joy* (1990), les catabases/anabases, les élargissements et les contractions de textures s'érigent à un niveau supérieur de la structuration: ils se trouvent aussi bien à l'intérieur d'une chaconne que dans les grands intermèdes (appelés "processus" par Lindberg) qui articulent, — par les vastes gestes d'une montée, d'un remplissage de l'espace etc. — la grande forme, tout en reliant les variations de la chaconne.

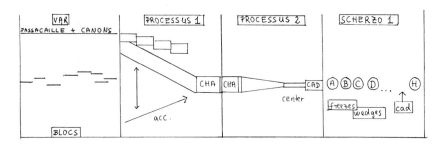

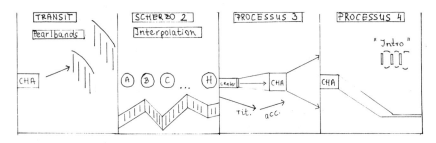

Example 5.   M. Lindberg: *Joy* (esquisse de la macrostructure, réalisée d'après le croquis du compositeur).

Allégories (1990) de Tristan Murail est construite sur la métamorphose d'une idée musicale de départ: sur "le processus du processus". On assiste à des transformations d'"un objet de base" par différents processus, grâce à une hypersyntaxe appliquée au-delà d'une syntaxe élémentaire.

L'objet de base est composé d'un arpège suivi d'une résonance se prolongeant en trille. Il peut être transformé plus tard en un bloc sonore ou en un nuage de sons. Certains éléments de cet objet seront développés, superposés, juxtaposés, ou plus tard, même inversés.

L'ensemble instrumental d'*Allégories* comporte flûte (+petite flûte), clarinette en si bémol, cor, violon, violoncelle, percussions (un instrumentiste) et un dispositif de synthèse.

Dans cette pièce, T. Murail cherche à mêler intimement le son électronique et la musique instrumentale afin qu'il soit difficile de distinguer l'un de l'autre.

La plupart des sons sont construits selon la technique de synthèse additive à l'aide des modules Yamaha TX816 (deux groupes de quatre mudules). La "simulation" et/ou la "prolongation" des spectres instrumentaux se passe en temps réel par l'interprète jouant sur un clavier MIDI. Ce dernier est relié aux modules de synthèse par l'intermédiaire d'un ordinateur Macintosh (à 2 MO de mémoire au minimum) utilisant le programme MAX et le programme *Allégories* écrit en MAX.

Ce dispositif instrumental et électroacoustique permet au compositeur de pouvoir calculer et réaliser les distorsions progressives des spectres choisis. L'utilisation des sons de synthèse permet également de "prolonger" les sonorités intrumentales dans des registres inaccessibles aux instruments réels et d'amplifier ou de faire ressortir les partiels des spectres dans les registres où ils perdent normalement leur l'audibilité. C'est de cette manière que dans *Allégories*, le compositeur arrive à réaliser une forme qui s'inspire de la géométrie fractale: on retrouve les mêmes contours d'un objet (et de ses modifications) au niveau des spectres, au niveau des motifs musicaux, au niveau du schéma graphique des sections et, enfin, au niveau de la macro-structure de l'œuvre.

On observe une démarche semblable utilisant un schéma graphique global, préalable à la composition musicale, dans certaines œuvres de Kaija Saariaho (*Verblendungen*, *Lichtbogen*) et dans d'autres œuvres de M. Lindberg et de T. Murail.[14]

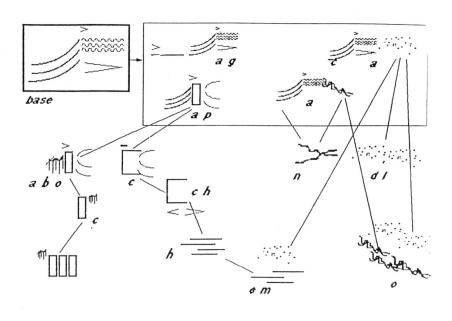

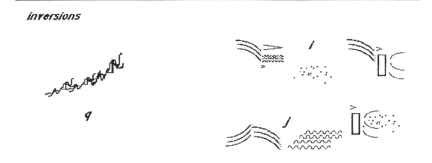

Exemple 6. "objets" dans *Allégories* (représentation du compositeur).

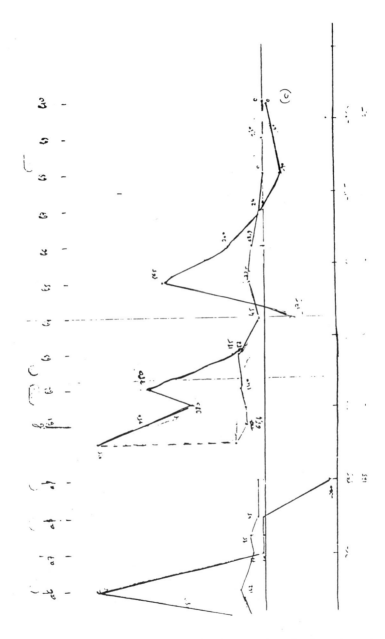

Exemple 7. Tristan Murail: *Allégories* (progressions de distorsions, section 1: a, b).

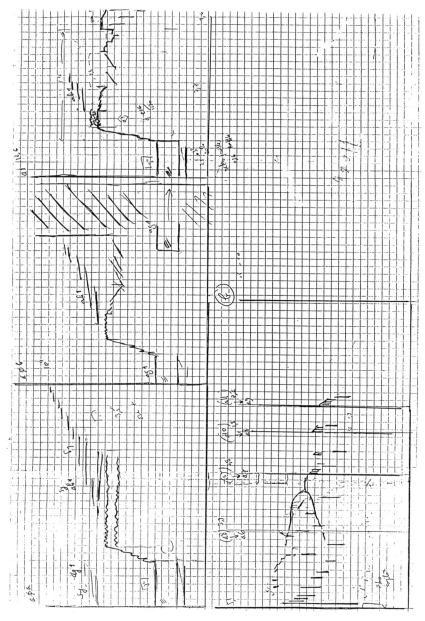

Exemple 8. T. Murail: *Allégories*: section 1: a, b.

2. Entre l'inconnu et le connu: les structures musicales intermédiaires

En parcourant la nature du déroulement d'un grand nombre des œuvres mixtes, des œuvres écrites pour bande ou des pièces utilisant l'ordinateur en temps réel, il faut constater la réapparition de quelques principes très anciens de la construction musicale: de principes nécessairement modifiés à cause du caractère nouveau de leur matériau sonore.

Sans trop entrer dans les détails cette fois-ci, je présenterai les trois sous-groupes les plus fréquents.

2.1. Forme à variations dans la musique électroacoustique

L'idée éternelle de la variation est exploitée ces temps-ci à l'aide de sons de synthèse ou des techniques sonores diverses de la musique concrète ou encore, du traitement de son par ordinateur. Le plus souvent, ces sources sonores inouïes sont mises en rapport, sous forme d'un dialogue, avec un instrument acoustique. Grâce au contrôle, au traitement de son et au suivi de partition dans le cas des instruments MIDI, les moyens de variation sont démultipliés d'une manière considérable.

Parmi les musiques utilisant le support d'une bande magnétique — même si les sons sont créés à l'aide de l'ordinateur -, j'évoque deux pièces où le recours à la variation n'est pas arbitraire: il fait allusion aux traditions d'un passé lointain, notamment à la tradition orale des chants populaires dans certains pays de l'Europe de l'Est.

En 1983, Tamas Ungvary a réalisé des variations sur un thème d'une danse des enfants tziganes connue en Hongrie. Au départ, il s'est servi d'un ordinateur PDP-15/XVM du studio EMS à Stockholm, en élaborant son propre logiciel et une liste d'interactions appelée "ILI" (Interactive List Interpreter). Plus tard, il a eu recours — pour les transformations sonores — à un programme de Paul Pignon, appelé "Giant Fourier Transform Program" (= "Transformation Fourier à fenêtre géante"), appliqué déjà sur un ordinateur VAX-11/750.

D'où le titre de son œuvre: *Danse géante d'enfants tziganes avec ILI Fourier.* (En anglais: *Gipsy Children's Giant Dance with ILI Fourier.*)

Ces techniques nouvelles des années 80 ont permis à Ungvary de créer des matériaux complètement nouveaux tout au long de la série d'une dizaine de variations (groupéées en quatre sections), — en exploitant toujours le même thème de base.

Le travail de transformation/déformation progressives des spectres autour d'une autre mélodie de chant populaire hongrois a été développé par Lászlo Dubrovay sur le Synclavier II du studio électronique de Technische Universität de Berlin dans son *Symphonia* en 1981.

Dans le domaine de la musique concrète, je me réfère à *L'arbre et caetera* (1972; forme à refrains et au développement/variation) d'Alain Savouret, à *Variations en étoile* (1966) de Guy Reibel, à *Courir* (1989) de Christian Zanési, aux certains mouvements de *Pour en finir avec le pouvoir d'Orphée II* (1972) de B. Parmegiani et aux mouvements de *Fabulae* (1990–92) de F. Bayle.

Dans son œuvre intitulée *Red bird (Oiseau rouge. Ou le rêve d'un prisonnier politique*, 1977), Trevor Wishart utilise la transformation et la variation des "Leitmotifs" musicaux traditionnels ou d'origine "concrète" ou encore, d'origine "électronique", à la manière dont les opéras de R. Wagner les exploitent.

P. Manoury dans *Pluton* (1988, écrite pour piano MIDI et ordinateur, actuellement: la Station d'Informatique Musicale de l'IRCAM), fait varier certaines idées de base à l'aide de l'interactivité et du concept "des partitions virtuelles" élaboré par lui-même. Grâce au suivi de partition, le jeu de l'instrumentiste crée des événements multiples, comme par exemple: sons de piano échantillonnés; sons de synthèse additive; réverbération infinie; matrices de Markov ou séquences markoviennes mises en mouvement à partir de motifs du piano échantillonnés; effet de phasing etc. Les possibilités d'intervention de l'ordinateur (développées à partir du programme MAX de Miller Puckette) permettent que la structure de cette œuvre d'une durée de 45', reprenne souvent le même élément de la première section appelée "toccata" et que les idées de cette dernière soient variées tout au long des cinq grandes parties de *Pluton*:

I. Première Toccata
II. Antiphone (seconde toccata)
III. Séquences

IV. Modulations (à partir dela IIe partie)

V. Variations (à partir de la première toccata)

2.2 Le deuxième groupe des types intermédiaires est *la forme dite "évolutive" ou "téléologique"*. C'est le cas de beaucoup de formes musicales "romantiques" de la deuxième moitié du 19e siècle quand le processus de développement et de variation construit à partir d'un ou de deux éléments de base, aboutit à un nouvel état, à une vraie métamorphose des matériaux.

Les œuvres contemporaines appartenant à cette catégorie sont par exemple: *Intervalles intérieures (1981)* de Péter Eötvös ou *Préfixes* (1991) de Michael Levinas, ou encore *Music for Guitar and Tape* (à partir de sons synthétisés par ordinateur) de Cort Lippe de 1990, et *Aulodie (1983)* pour hautbois (ou saxophone) et bande de F.-B. Mâche etc. Dans l'œuvre de P. Eötvös, la nature cachée d'un matériau sonore se révèle au fur et à mesure en avançant par le développement et les variations de la même idée, pour qu'à la fin de la pièce on la retrouve sous forme de références nettes à la musique populaire de la tradition instrumentale connue en Transylvanie.

Dans *Préfixes* de M. Levinas, on assiste à la naissance d'une "strette" à la Beethoven: une stretta et une ascension variées et amplifiées à l'aide de sonorités rares (échantillonnées et traitées, "hybridées") afin d'exprimer une accélération et un accroissement de la tension.

Dans *Lichtbogen* (1986) de Kaija Saariaho, la partie de la flûte, c'est-à-dire celle du protagoniste de l'œuvre est transformée par un dispositif électroacoustique à tel point qu'elle évoque des souffles d'un être surréel ou surnaturel qui, tout en jouant, prononce aussi des phonèmes. Ceux-ci sont tirés du poème de Henry Vaughan: *J'ai vu l'éternité l'autre nuit.* Selon Kaija Saariaho, il y a là une vision de lumière infinie et de l'espace: "sous la lumière et la paix éternelles, avance le temps par heures, par jours, par années."[15] La fin de *Lichtbogen* est censée évoquer cette image, tandis que le reste de l'œuvre n'est qu'une préparation progressive à l'amplification du souffle surnaturel.

2.3. Le dernier groupe des structures intermédiaires serait *l'ancienne forme-sonate ou la forme dite "d'équilibre"* selon la terminologie allemande (=Gleichgewichtsform). D'après cette dernière acception, on constate à la fois une symétrie interne de la structure (ABA') et une symétrie à l'intérieur de ses membres: la partie *A* est constituée d'un contraste, *B* est l'évolution de ce dernier, tandis que la partie *A'* apporte le dénouement en mettant l'accent sur un des éléments constrastants pour résoudre le conflit.

Ces formes "cathartiques" ou "dramatiques" seront investies de nouvelles qualités du matériau musical et d'un nouveau sens du conflit dans les œuvres comme *Sud* (1985) de Jean-Claude Risset, dans *Jupiter* (1987) de Philippe Manoury, dans *Théâtre d'ombres — Ombres blanches* (1988–89) de F. Bayle, dans *Rambaramb* (1973) de F.-B. Mâche etc.

Dans *Jupiter* pour flûte et ordinateur de P. Manoury, les éléments porteurs de forme et de conflit se placent au niveau du timbre. Ce qui veut dire que tout ce qui se manifestait autrefois dans les thèmes, motifs et degrés de tonalité comme contraste (voir les "expositions" de sonate), confrontation (voir le "développement"), puis comme dénouement (voir la "réexposition") de la musique classique-romantique, se trouve aujourd'hui incarné par, ou dans le timbre.

Grâce au suivi de partition (Programme MAX et Station de l'Informatique Musicale) et aux modules de traitement (comme les harmonizers/transpositions; la réverbération; le Frequency Shifter; les effets de spectres de synthèse additive filtrés par la flûte etc.) et aux sons de la flûte enregistrés et traités ainsi qu'aux autres sons de synthèse pré-enregistrées et déclenchés par la flûte, l'œuvre possède toute une gamme de timbres à partir de sons bruités à travers les différentes sonorités de type "son normal de la flûte", jusqu' aux sons de la "flûte idéalisée" c'est-à-dire aux sons éthérés, cristallins dérivés de la flûte.

A l'aide de ces trois catégories, trois grandes classes de timbres, Manoury arrive à créer un parcours constitué d'une exposition, d'une partie conflictuelle où les sons de la flûte "se perdent" — submergent — dans les sonorités bruitées des cloches graves et dissonantes (voir: développement), jusqu'à ce que dans la partie "réexposition" les sonorités aériennes, brillantes et argentines prennent le relais et dominent le monde sonore des cloches ténèbres.

Dans cette œuvre aussi, il s'agit donc de la présentation d'un problème, d'une intrigue, et le reste du parcours est consacré à la quête d'une solution afin de liquider le conflit et d'apporter une réponse, un apaisement. Depuis Aristote, on connaît cette stratégie de catharsis. De nos jours, elle revient d'une manière renouvelée mais les modes d'exploitation des jeux de tension/détente et de collision/dénouement ne perdent rien de leurs forces suggestives.[16]

Dans l'œuvre de Jean-Claude Risset (*Sud*, 1985), on découvre également l'existence nouvelle, le vêtement nouveau d'une hiérarchie des éléments. Les trois catégories de timbres désignant trois mondes sont les suivants:

1. sons de la mer, de la bouée, des oiseaux, des vagues, des ressacs, de l'orage;

2. sons du monde humaine: bruits des pas, sons d'instruments, etc.

3. sons synthétisés par le programme (MUSIC V), capables de représenter un monde imaginaire, surréel ou idéel grâce aux trames aériennes, au retentissement d'un orgue ou de cloche, aux sonorités quasi cosmiques etc.

Le va-et-vient, le conflit s'installe entre les éléments appartenant à ces trois univers différents, à l'aide de la technique de hybridation et de l'utilisation de l'ordinateur *SYTER*, et à l'exploitation de sons de synthèse faits par MUSIC V. A la fin de l'oeuve, on assiste à la naissance d'une qualité nouvelle, d'une sonorité de l'orgue imaginaire évoquant le sublime.[17]

3. Formes traditionnelles

A ce dernier groupe appartiennent les structures dans lesquelles le nouveau matériau électroacoustique n'exige pas de compromis au moment du recours à un cadre traditionnel de construction musicale.

3.1. Œuvres cycliques ou énumératives (la construction se crée par la juxtaposition libre de différents mouvements formant un cycle ou une suite; ou bien la structure se fait par l'énumération libre de différents petits mouvements.)

Œuvres appartenant à cette classe: François Bayle: *Expérience acoustique* (1970–72), *Jeîta ou le murmure des eaux* (1970: œuvre à 17 mouvements), *Théâtre d'ombres — derrière l'image* (1988–90); Bernard Parmegiani: *De natura sonorum* (10 mouvements, 1972), *La création du monde* (1984); Michel Chion: *La ronde* (suite, 1982), *On n'arrête pas le regret* (-scènes d'enfant, 1975); Jonathan Harvey: *Bhakti* (1982, cycle de 12 mouvements pour bande faite à l'IRCAM et pour un ensemble instrumental); D. Teruggi-J. Schwarz: *Mano à mano* (1989), Jean Schwarz: *Symphonie* (1974), *Erda* (1971) etc.

2. Œuvres de musique descriptive ou, à programme

Les œuvres qui se servent d'un programme littéraire, biblique ou mythique pour articuler leur structure ou qui se servent d'un texte pour guider et inspirer certaines couches de la composition, sont connues depuis les débuts de notre histoire de la musique occidentale ou même orientale. Leur réapparition semble tout à fait normal et légitime dans le contexte de la composition avec les moyens électro-acoustiques. C'est peut-être le genre musical le plus exploité et développé dans les domaines de la musique concrète, de la musique mixte et de la musique faite par ordinateur.

Voici quelques exemples sélectionnés parmi le grand nombre d'œuvres qui illustrent cette catégorie:

F. Bayle–B. Parmegiani: *La Divine Comédie* (GRM: 1972–74); Michel Chion: *La Tentation de Saint-Antoine* (GRM: 1984); K. Saariaho: *Stilleben* (YLE Experimental Studio, Helsinki: 1988), Morton Subotnick: *The Double Life of Amphibians — Ascent into Air* (IRCAM:1981), Pierre Henry: *Le Livre des Morts égyptien* (IRCAM: 1990); Gilbert Amy: *Une saison en enfer* (GRM: 1979); Jean Schwarz: *Quatre saisons* (GRM: 1983); Marco Stroppa: *Proemio* (IRCAM, 1990), *In cielo, in terra, in mare* (opéra radiophonique, IRCAM:1992), Pierre-Alain Jaffrennou: *Océane ou troisième passage de la baleine* (GRAME:1984) etc.

La présentation de ces trois grandes catégories des concepts de la structure musicale au sein des créations électro-acoustiques récentes, est fondée sur mes expériences personnelles. Cette classification ne contient aucun jugement de valeur. De toute évidence, elle permet l'existence d'autres systèmes de vue d'ensemble parallèles, établis ou à établir par la réflexion d'autres experts ou compositeurs.

L'argumentation actuelle recevrait sa forme réelle à travers les analyses approfondies et illustrées (à l'aide des exemples sonores ou graphiques ou de ceux de partition), interrogeant les œuvres évoquées ci-dessus. Ces analyses ou études, pour une partie, ont été déjà préparées et partiellement publiées, tandis que pour l'autre partie du corpus, elles sont en cours de réalisation.

Notes

1. Etude de Risto Nieminen sur l'œuvre, publiée comme texte de présentation, accompagnant le disque FINLANDIA (FACD 372) consacré aux œuvres de M. Lindberg, pp. 11–12.
2. Ibid: pp. 10–11.
3. F.-B. Mâche: notice de présentation, publiée lors de la création de *Maraé*, 1974.
4. René Thom: *Stabilité structurelle et morphogenèse*, Amsterdam, Benjamins-Ediscience, 1972, René Thom: *Modèles mathématiques et morphogenèse*, Christian Bourgois, 1980, (2e éd.), Jean Petitot: *Pour un schématisme de la structure: quelques implications sémiotiques de la théorie des catastrophes*, Thèse, 4 vol., Ecole des Hautes Etudes en Sciences Sociales, 1982.
5. Texte de présentation du compositeur, accompagnant le disque de la série *Salabert Actuels*, consacré aux "Espaces électroniques", 1988, SCD 8801, pp. 4–5.
6. voir l'article de Marco Stroppa: "Les organismes de l'information musicale: une approche de la composition", in: S. McAdams – I. Deliège: *La musique et les sciences cognitives*, Pierre Mardaga éd., Bruxelles, 1989, pp. 203–234.
7. Version française du texte de présentation du compositeur, écrit pour le cahier accompagnant le disque CD WERGO 2030-2, 1992, (dans la série *Computer Music Currents*, No. 10).
8. F.-B. Mâche: *Musique, mythe, nature. Ou les dauphins d'Arion.* 2e éd. Méridiens Klincksieck, 1991, p. 15.
9. pour une analyse plus détaillée, voir l'article de l'auteur publié dans le No. 22–23. des *Cahiers du CIREM*, (1992) sur "L'esquisse typologique des macrostructures dans les œuvres de F.-B. Mâche", pp. 128–130. (Voir la présentation des analyses de *Aliunde*, de *Iter memor*, et de *Danaé*, en fonction de ce schéma mythique mentionné

ci-dessus.) La version complète de ces analyses se trouve dans l'article: "From the Naturel Model to the Ideal Model", in: *Music, Society and Imagination in Contemporary France*, série: *Contemporary Music Review*, Harwood Academic Publishers, London, 1993.

10. Tristan Murail: Révolution des sons complexes, in: *Darmstädter Beiträge XVIII*, 30, Ferienkurse 1980, Schott, Mainz, 1980, pp. 78.

11. Texte de présentation de H. Dufourt sur *Saturne* lors de sa création, Concert d'Itinéraire, nov. 1982.

12. Extrait de la notice de présentation écrite par le compositeur sur *Volumes*.

13. voir présentation du digramme graphique du déroulement spatial-temporel dans "Songes" dans le No. 52 de *Musicworks*, (1991), page 63, comme complément (erratum) ultérieur apporté à l'article de M. Grabocz, intitulé "Narrativité et musique électro-acoutique" publié dans le No. 51 de *Musicworks*, pp. 47–50.

14. Voir nos analyses (entamées) sur *Lichtbogen* de Saariaho et sur *Ur* et *Joy* de Lindberg dans le No. 26–27. des *Cahiers du CIREM*, "*Musique et geste*", 1993, — sous le titre: "Conception gestuelle de la macrostructure dans la musique contemporaine finlandaise: K. Saariaho et M. Lindberg", revue citée, pp. 155–168.

15. texte de présentation de Risto Nieminen; voir dans le cahier accompagnant le disque FINLANDIA FACD 374, 1989, consacré aux œuvres de K. Saariaho, page 15.

16. Voir l'analyse détaillée de *Jupiter* faite par l'auteur de cet article, dans le cadre des études de la *Documentation Musicale de l'IRCAM*, 45 pages, 1991.

17. Voir la présentation un peu plus détaillée de cette œuvre dans un compte-rendu écrit en Hongrie par l'auteur de cet article, et publié en français dans le No. 14–15. des *Cahiers du CIREM*, décembre 1989, pp. 261–263, (sous la titre: "Créations de M. Battier, F.-B. Mâche et J.-C. Risset en Hongrie").

A semiotic approach to computer assisted composition

FRANCESCO GIOMI AND MARCO LIGABUE

The project concerns the application of semiotic principles to computer assisted composition. Starting from a theoretical basis belonging to semiotics and linguistics, it tries to offer, through artificial intelligence techniques, a generally reformulable framework capable of assisting contemporary composition.

Problems of music and linguistics

The problems concerning the relations between music and linguistics are several and they date back quite a while. The linguistic nature of the musical phenomenon has been long debated, with positions ranging from absolute denial to total affirmation. But the problem of whether music can be considered a language, and to what extent, concerns neither linguists nor musicians. It is a truly semiotic problem to understand if and how an eventful process of semiosis can exist in music, as well as to clarify the possibility that music functions as a symbolic system.

For the moment, apart from all questions, we can say that many criteria derived from transformational linguistics have demonstrated their applicability in music with satisfactory results. As we go deeper into the matter, we can say that the functional structure of a linguistic proposition can be summarized through a tree diagram. A musical proposition, for example the harmonic structure, can be summarized in the same way. It should be made clear that a linguistic proposition, going through different levels of a syntagmatic marker, has an actual generative structure. The musical proposition, passing in its turn through the different levels of the tree structure, has more precisely a *derivational* structure: the different elements have a relationship of functional derivation following the structure of the marker from top to bottom (Lerdahl & Jackendoff 1985).

In this way we have a sufficiently definite, formal method to describe musical structures and processes: through series of derivational tree markers, we can gain knowledge of the organization of the several levels of the piece. Such methodologies, even if used mainly from the aesthesic perspective, can also be successfully applied from the poietic point of view.

The semiotic basis

While on the one hand music seems to allow definition in a linguistic sense, on the other hand it is very difficult to qualify music as a sign. There are, in fact, many difficulties in locating an actual process of semiosis in music: finding musical reference to something other than itself and defining its levels of articulation. (These kinds of problem are better explained in Ligabue 1989.)

By attributing the ability to describe other systems only to verbal language, we may say that today we really can reveal, from a semiotic as well as an experimental point of view, that there exists an actual process of semiosis in the musical phenomenon, too, and that its levels of articulation can be made explicit. The problem is not to apply willfully and literally a linguistic model to music, but rather to understand that the process of semiosis, like the concept of multiplication, manifesting itself as the levels of articulation, is one of the basic structures of human cognition. Thus, not a linguistic model, but a general one can be established, with due differences, to depict the specificities of verbal, musical, gestural, and other kinds of expression. Simply put, one can develop a descriptive model, in order to represent the process of symbolic construction with a sufficient degree of generality and adaptability.

Therefore, one is permitted to speak about "musical grammars", "double articulation", "sense" and "meaning" in music. Thus from a strictly heuristic point of view, it is completely justifiable not only to apply methodologies derived from transformational linguistics, but also to integrate different levels of language: phonemes, monemes, grammar, and text.

General strategies

The application of linguistic methodologies to music has, as its principal aim, the reconstruction of a set of rules that govern the grammar of a given style. The question is how to clarify grammatical connections and modalities through which different lexical components are organized for the production of sense.

When carrying out the analysis, we understood that it was necessary to examine the creative strategies of a musician during a performance. This meant trying to understand the general, underlying macrostructures of a creative process, that is to say, the mental behavior of a musician. The latter would be independent of the outcome these structures would have, from a grammatical point of view; that is, independent of the form they would have assumed and the sense the grammatical chaining would have given.

For practical reasons we had to hypothesize a possible cognitive model for the process of musical creation, a model capable of holding a large number of variables in due consideration and, at the same time, suitable for our purpose. Starting from the above-mentioned semiotic assumption, the process of semiosis was considered to be a valid, general cognitive model. Thus, music became a symbolic system in all respects, capable of producing sense by organizing meanings of its own. So, the phonemes constitute the level of distinctive features (in this case the sound parameters). The monemes, again composed of phonemes, form the level of meaningful units (in this case the notes). Afterwards come the grammatical and the textual levels. In this way we can develop a series of abstractions, very useful from the programming point of view, about the musical process.

A single note (moneme) may be considered as consisting of several distinctive features (phonemes), which allow one to distinguish one moneme from another. These features are in this case the sound parameters: pitch, duration, intensity, space, and timbre. Every note is experienced as a whole, as in the case of a word. To understand the moneme it is not necessary to break it down to the level of the phonemes: the process develops in a highly cultural way at a deep, nearly unconscious level.

The "phonemic" representation is transposed to the upper levels, excluding the process of global comprehension of the moneme. This means that, at the grammatical level, we consider the rules separately for every set of features: all the rules pertinent to the durations, all the rules pertinent to the pitches, and so on. Only afterwards — and this is the accomplished abstraction — did we reintroduce the criterion of unity pertaining to the level of the moneme. In this way we safeguarded the integrity of the descriptive model. The several modules were made completely interactive among them through series of control/rejection rules.

Applications to automated composition

The semiotic approach allowed us, starting from a functional and adequate theoretical model, to make explicit some general structural categories of musical thought. As a matter of fact, the several levels can be used for the creation of general sound structures, taking the sound phenomenon into consideration from a poietic point of view .

The first aim of the project is to make explicit, from a theoretical point of view, the levels, as well as to verify the possibility of other levels of description. In fact, the "phonemic" description of sound events is functional also in the case of sound events more complex than the notes of the traditional system: it is possible to extend the number of distinctive features considered pertinent in order to differentiate sounds. These features are marked as "present" or "absent" (+ or -), according to a system of binary opposition on the model of that used in phonology. The traditional categories of features, such as durations or intensities, are integrated with those developed by Schaeffer in his *Traité des objets musicaux* (1966) for describing musical objects.

These categories are applied to the phoneme level as distinctive features to differentiate sounds. This allows us to describe exactly and construct the following level of monemes, that is, the level of actual sound objects. Once constituted starting from the minimal units, they can be easily handled as meaningful units, when all their features have been made formally explicit.

Practically, this means that if a composer wants to create an underlying universal strategy inside the composition — for example, a special sequence of durations or sound textures — it can be easily done merely by controlling the state of one or the other feature and, at the same time, by following the structural unity and the variety of sound objects. This brings us to the next level, where the sound objects (monemes) are grammaticalized.

Some general, underlying compositional principles can be formulated to describe a fundamental structure that can be covered differently each time: a sort of metagrammatical frame, therefore capable of supporting the organization of specific grammars.

The last level, that of text, works mainly according to principles derived from textual semiotics. It tries to control, at the syntagmatic level, the organizing macrostructures of the composition, by means of a "top-down" control on the several signification areas and "meaning nebulae" of the text.

Computer assisted composition

These theoretical bases can give adequate support to the implementation of a program for computer assisted composition (CAC) and provide it with a degree of generality sufficient to allow reformulation according to a user's needs. The underlying idea of the project is precisely the following: to create a set of previously arranged structures that can receive data on different levels, and allow reformulation in accordance with the exigencies of the user.

We have a definition level for the minimal units, where the basic material of meaningful units can be organized; this is the level of the phonemes. The following level concerns actual meaningful units, that is, the sound objects used in the composition. Here, the user can control precisely the constitutive elements, and therefore several significations, of composition; this is the level of the monemes. The level of grammatical organization interacts necessarily with the others, allowing organization of the several signification processes, which can be either superficial or represent deeper signifying structures. The textual level allows to organize in a general form, through a comprehensive view, several signifying areas of composition. It offers a surface control on the results of the deeper organization of the elements.

The implementation on an expert system is based upon the construction of open tree structures that support both the organization of the lexicon and the grammatical rules defined by the user. These markers furnish us with the basic structure for the next phases; for example: constitutive features of sound objects; sound objects; structural relations among objects; sequence of objects; simultaneity of objects; changing of position; movement; density; rarefaction; tension and relaxation on the text level.

The user can insert and develop his own compositional intentions on each preset marker. At the same time he has a certain amount of completely open structures that he can reformulate according to particular exigencies. Thus the system offers not only a frame for making explicit the several variables of the compositional process, but it also allows the composer — as in all the CAC processes — to attain a high degree of clarity in the research of his own strategies. Besides, he can easily produce a large number of variants, including ones not foreseen but nevertheless grammatical. The interaction between the composer and the system generates a sort of feedback that can prove to be very interesting for compositional purposes.

As regards implementation, there are not many examples where artificial intelligence techniques are applied to computer assisted composition. A very good historical survey concerning automatic composition can be found in Ames (1987), while more specific remarks about applications of artificial intelligence to musical composition are in Camurri (1990).

The present system distinguishes itself from those because it offers a high degree of flexibility, primarily from the user's point of view; it can be used as a "general purpose" program that can be reformulated and adapted to different compositional needs of the user. This main characteristic permits one to include different compositional repertoires and each one with different stylistic approaches.

Artificial intelligence techniques can lead to models concerning musical entities such as general sound objects, chords, clusters, sets of melodic lines, and so on; for example, by means of frame-like structures, where *frames* are particular complex-structured objects of artificial intelligence programming on which we can do global operations or change specific attributes. And artificial intelligence techniques can also lead to processes that operate on such objects; for example, by means of inference rules or backward and forward chaining. Therefore, we are oriented towards a knowledge-based system building, which tries to combine several knowledge-representation methods.

According to what we have already explained, concerning the reformulation of rules and entities and their adaptations to different styles and genres, the system can be seen as a plurality of systems instead of a single unit, working alternatively in accordance with the choices made by composers. For every style and composer, a sort of database, which can be used again by the system or by new users, can be generated.

References

Ames, Charles (1987). "Automated composition in retrospect: 1956–1986", *Leonardo* 10 (2), 169–185.

Camurri, Antonio (1990). "On the role of artificial intelligence in music research", *Interface* 19, 219–248.

Lerdahl, Fred and Jackendoff, Ray (1985). *A Generative Theory of Tonal Music*. Cambridge, MA: MIT Press.

Ligabue, Marco (1989). Mezzo espressivo e segni di memoria musicali. Thesis, University of Florence.

Schaeffer, Pierre (1966). *Traité des objets musicaux*. Paris: Seuil.

Narratives of self-consciousness in Proust and Beethoven

Michael Spitzer

Introduction

The question of representation in a non-referential, temporal medium such as music is partly answered by what can be termed 'art about art', painting "which refers", as Charles Rosen says, "not outside itself, but directly to the medium of paint". Rosen sees the *Hammerklavier* as a work "about its own technique", displaying a "paradoxical interchange of form and content". A work, however, can be self-reflexive without being totally abstract, for self-referentiality is not necessarily a corollary of a symbolist aesthetic of *l'art pour l'art*. It can also be a means for realism, countering the depletion of out-worn imagery by defamiliarizing them or alienating them from their normal contexts and associations. Since familiarity desensitises our impressions of the world, the artist's role, according to Bergson, is to strip away the deadening veneer of habit and routine. The process is actually one of the century's chief concerns. Brecht draws attention to the mechanics of his dramaturgy in order to impress upon his audience the contingency of history and the freedom of individuals to change it. The Russian formalists thought that the history of art was propelled by the dissolution of old genres and the shock of the new: over-familiarity devalues the meaning of codes, requiring new codes to be put in circulation. The Surrealist technique of shock, derived from the poetry of Baudelaire and Mallarmé, was installed by Walter Benjamin at the heart of his esoteric theory of art. Following Bergson, Proust warns us, in his discussion of the sea-scapes of his fictional painter Elstir, that we see not what there is but what we want to see. Vision is generally a matter of of recognising familiar patterns, what Proust calls 'intellectual notions', which filter out our 'true impressions'.

The painter sets forth the content of his figures in their true reality only by stylising their form. Paradoxically, the object is apprehended in a new vividness the more unrealistically, or 'metaphorically', it is portrayed. The question of representation, then, ultimately bears upon the relationship between the material and the concept into which it is subsumed: its 'name', as Proust calls it, or, in musical terms, its *genre*.

Likewise, Beethoven counters the depletion of the classical language by defamiliarizing or estranging it. His late compositions are not only *in* a form but also *about* form. In cyclical works such as the sonata op.109 or the Ninth Symphony, the finale's return to the first movement's point of departure represents the last stage of an on-going process of self-examination, whereby the work addresses the foundations of its own thinking. With this turning inwards, the subject of the musical narrative does not consist in "the operations and works of history," as Derrida puts it, but rather in "the history of this consciousness *itself*". Beethoven thereby follows a tendency, begun by Hegel's *Phenomenology of Mind* and culminating with Proust's *Remembrance of Things Past*, of discourses propelled by self-consciousness.

But what of the *music* ? The sonata op.109 in E simply and clearly reveals both the reification of musical convention and its alienation. It is *about* the cadenza. Ritornello and cadenza, time and timelessness, exchange roles in a way which challenges everything we mean by meaning. Op.109 thereby points beyond itself, as an allegory of non-meaning. Op.109 is everything which is NOT op.109.

1. Background

Some time in April 1820 Beethoven interrupted work on his Mass in D to sketch a little piano sonata. In its origins, op.109 in E major is a parenthesis between a Credo and a Benedictus of a great and solemn mass. With its two sister works, the sonatas opp.110 and 111, op.109 marks a break between two choral masterworks, the *Missa Solemnis* and the Ninth Symphony. So between two overtly programmatic works which cross the boundary from music to meaning, Beethoven lapses into absolute music. Wherefore Beethoven's silence?

In as much as these 3 sonatas are a cadenza between the ritornellos of Beethoven's two main ideological statements, they are also, in body and spirit, 'about' the very principle of cadenza. Each sonata asks the same question: how is a cadenza different from a ritornello? Beethoven deconstructs our notions of time and stasis, structure and parenthesis, ariticulate and abstract meaning. Ultimately, music and text.

These sonatas, I argue, are narratives of self-consciousness. As cyclical works, their ends go back to criticise, recompose and redeem their beginnings. I interrupt my own examination of op.109 to consider an exerpt from Proust's *A la recherche de temps perdu*, the most remarkable of narratives of self-consciousness. Marcel's first encounter with the painter Elstir at Balbec both remodels Beethoven's technique in a textual medium and takes a plastic art as its subject. And Proust suggests some interesting parallels between painting and music, representation and temporality.

Op. 109 has been the subject of 3 major studies by Heinrich Schenker, Allen Forte and Nicholas Marston. They all take as their starting point the relationship between the upbeat to the first movement and the structure of the entire sonata. The skip form G# to B is composed out by the modulation, via A#, to B (Example 1).

Example 1.

The peak of the progression is then projected to a top register at the climax of the development. In Beethoven's initial version, B descends back to G# at the retransition with a complementary falling progression. The first movement therefore traces a broad arch pattern, an expansion of the motive G#-B-G#. In the final version, however, Beethoven suspends this falling progression and leaves the movement hanging in mid air unresolved. It is up to the 3rd movement to provide the descent of the arch. The theme of the variations rehearses the rise from G# to B more concisely, and answers it with a fall back to G#. It is in this respect that Marston calls the 3rd movement a recomposition of the 1st.

But this is all far too neat; a familiar narrative of incompletion and eventual closure, dissonance and resolution. In reality, the finale supplies a shock which overturns the premise of the first movement. The overall effect of the sonata is problematic and critical of convention. One could say that it defies analysis. Significantly, Schenker, Forte and Marston are all pitch-orientated. They ignore the most characteristic idea of op.109, which involves a contrast of texture. It is thanks to Leonard Ratner and Kofi Agawu that rhetoric and topic have re-entered the analytical discourse over Classical Music.

One is struck by an alternation of Vivace, mechanical figuration with Adagio, improvisatory material. These don't so much succeed as interfere with each other. The Vivace climbs to A#, striving to modulate to B. But it is cut off by the Adagio, which enters on an A natural and pulls the music away from its goal. B is only fulfilled by the return of the Vivace material, initiating what looks like the development section. This shades into the reprise of the opening phrase, interrupted, once again, by a da capo of the Adagio.

This is a conventional reading of the form. In reality, the intercutting of Vivace and Adagio textures destroys the form. The 8–bar opening Vivace phrase is of course impossibly short to function as a first subject by itself. Thus, what we took to be the start of the development is really the continuation of the first subject, inspite of the new key. And what had seemed to be an Adagio second subject is therefore an interruption, a parenthesis, within the tonic group. So the Adagio functions as a cadenza which, strictly speaking, belongs outside the true structure of the movement. Beethoven is making a value-statment about style here. He is saying that there are two kinds of musical discourse:

1) A structured, symmetrical, tonally goal-orientated style.
2) A free, improvisatory music without form or direction.

In the classical sense, this cadenza is not music at all, and, as a classical composer, Beethoven is obliged to endorse the ordered, dynamic style over the free and static one.

Ratner groups cadenzas with fantasies, capriccios and recitatives as the great unknown quantity of classical music.

These genres, according to Heinrich Koch, are "not bound by the forms and modulations of ordinary compositions". They are signs of the unique, embodying one aspect of the idea of genius. With very few exceptions, fantasies and cadenzas were not recorded and enshrined in score. But Mozart and Beethoven were celebrated as much fom their creative improvisation as for their notated composition. Music as performance succumbed to music as form, and the prestige of the fantastical retreated before the logocentric musical text. There are two points to note here:

1) Theorists such as Schenker and Reti get round this historical injustice by simply assimilating improvisation into their notion of compositional process. The composer's originating conception is a fluid energy or line over which he superimposes a grid of bar lines and durations. Or it is a non-temporal idea or Ursatz, a simultaneity which is unravelled into real time through the compositional process. In chapter 1 of *Der Freie Satz*, Schenker writes: "The ability in which all creativity begin — the ability to compose extempore, to improvise fantasies and preludes- lies only in a feeling for the background, middleground and foreground". Schenker's denunciation of the jelly-mould formalism of the so-called 'composition school' in favour of a more fundamental organicism echoes Ruskin and Bergson's impressionistic stance in painting, to defend the primal freshness of reality from a stultifying iconography. There will be more to say about *visual impressionism* later. But Schenker and Reti's own equation of fantasy with inspiration is a signal instance of analytical bad faith.

2) The second point is that op.109 is Beethoven's unilateral response to a compositional bad conscience. In this work, he problematises the distinction between true music and non-music, i.e., fantasy; the opposition between his Vivace ritornello and Adagio cadenza. Rather than assimilating improvisation into composition, like the theorists, he does the opposite. Now the whole structure will become an aspect of the

cadenza. Furthermore, the entire sonata will be transformed into a parenthesis within a bigger but unstated structure. Op.109 is therefore everything outside of op.109. Whether this background structure is the group of three sonatas, the surrounding choral works, the late style as a whole, all of music, or simply silence, is not important.

The Adagio cadenza is lacking an essential feature: the trill which, next to the cadence, is the most potent signal of closure in classical music. Cadenza trills are interesting because their conclusive function is independent of tonality or pitch. The cadenza-cum-trill topic is unique: unlike all the topics Kofi Agawu considers, it has no direct bearing on the Schenkerian beginning-middle-end model.

The trill in op.109, missing in the first movement, arrives in the final movement. We will see that it is used in such a way as to turn the cadenza inside out. Where the cadenza had first seemed to be outside the movement, it is now interiorised. The sonata becomes all cadenza, and it is the Vivace ritornello which is exiled to the realm of non-music. The work turns back upon itself in a critical, self-conscious way. It is about itself, taking itself as its own subject. This narrative of self-consciousness is instituted via a process of alienation or dispossession. Beethoven concretises the cadenza by taking away its conventional role as parenthesis. The functions of cadenza and ritornello are thereby reversed. This idea of 'taking away' a name or function is actually a Proustian conceit.

2. Proust

Consider Elstir's technique as a painter: Naturally enough, what he had in his studio were almost all seascapes done here at Balbec. But I was able to discern from these that the charm of each of them lay in a sort of metamorphosis of the objects represented, analogous to what in poetry we call metaphor, and that, if God the Father had created things by naming them, it was by taking away their names or giving them other names that Elstir created them anew. The names which designate things correspond invariably to an intellectual notion, alien to our true impressions, and compelling us to eliminate from them everything that is not in keeping with that notion.

We can identify three main factors here:

1) Proust celebrates the impressionist painter's gift of reproducing the original freshness of reality as seen in a first glance, before the viewer knows what it is he sees. Elstir has a direct and immediate access to reality, unimpeded by intellectual notions or habit.

2) Elstir's art is animated by ambiguities and metaphors in which everything is depicted in terms of what it is not. The most frequent metaphor in Elstir's seascapes is one which makes land seem sea and sea seem land. Or which confuses land, sea, and sky. In this Proust has Turner in mind, as seen through the eyes of his revered Ruskin. "Turner," Ruskin writes in his *Harbours of England*, "was never able to recover the distinction between sea and sky, or sea and land". An example of Turner's visual metaphors is his sketch of "Venice: The Piazzetta, from the Water" of 1835 (Plate I). Here sea, sky and land alternately reflect each other or collapse into a single element. We see now why the water-bound city of Venice is such a load-star to Proust throughout his book. Just as Italo Calvino's *Invisible Cities* are all variations on Venice, Proust's novel is one vast metaphor around this simultaneous and static city.

3) The third implication of the text is that impressionistic truth can be brought about, paradoxically, by the clash or mediation between oppositions. It is such clashes, according to Bergson, which rip the veil of habit and let reality through. Ruskin's metaphors are intensified into Magritte's visual paradoxes. His "Le soir qui tombe" is a neat example (Plate II). In a single gesture, Magritte smashes window, picture and reality, and simultaneously strengthens them all. It is precisely by stripping the pipe of its name that Magritte intensifies its pipeness (Plate III). In Proust's terms, Magritte the father creates the pipe anew.

The narrative in which this tract about painting is situated is itself an allegory of the painterly metaphor. By the end of the scene, the oppositions which support the argument are neatly inverted. The oppositions within the painting are between land, sea and sky. In the discourse, they are between painting and life, representation and reality, space and time.

Plate 1. Turner, "Venice: The Piazzetta from the Water", 1835.

Plate 2. Magritte, "Le soir qui tombe", 1964.

Marcel is forced by his grandmother to abandon his pursuit of Albertine, his obsessive object of desire, and to visit instead the studio of the great

Plate 3. Magritte, "Ceci n'est pas une pipe".

painter Elstir. Elstir's studio represents an enclave far removed from the course of time and the pressing concerns of life. It is the cadenza which regrettably interrupts Marcel's preoccupation, his eternally recurrent *idée fixe*. But Proust will demonstrate that the studio, far from being a withdrawal from the moto perpetuo of the chase, is actually the womb which offers Marcel a point of penetration.

Suddenly, on walking to the end of the studio to gaze through a window, which of course is always a substitute picture in Magritte's vocabulary, Marcel sees the band of girls. Albertine smiles at Elstir and comes to shake his hand. "Do you know that girl, Monsieur?" Marcel asks, and suddenly Elstir becomes a passport to his future mistress.

"Not a day passes but one of them comes by here and looks in for a moment or two, Elstir told me, plunging me into despair at the thought that if I had gone to see him at once, when my grandmother had begged me to do so, I should in all probability have made Albertine's acquaintance long since."

Marcel wants to run after the girls, but Elstir detains him with a painting of a young actress in a bowler hat. This portrait, of an as yet un-named woman, will prove to be pivotal. As an actress and as a hermaph-rodite, she echoes Barthes and Balzac's La Zambinella (a male castrato posing as a female singer), from *Sarrasine*, bridging world and stage, and the two sexes. In the da capo of this narrative, she will be given her name, and the identification, ironically, will also name the painter.

Now Elstir and Marcel go for a walk, a transition in a real sense. From Marcel's view-point, they are looking for a girl, so they are em-barked upon a sexual hunt; from Elstir's angle, they are off to view a picturesque beach — as if on a genteel promenade through a picture gallery. Thus, what begins as a 'hunt' becomes a 'promenade'. This walk will be the pivot of the substitution, whereby painting and reality ex-change function.

They bump into the band of girls. Marcel waits for Elstir to introduce them; nothing happens; Marcel is too paralysed by his neurotic inhibi-tions. He is, after all (and this turns out to be Proust's funniest irony), *impotent*. They return to the studio. The da capo- another cadenza. The emphasis shifts. Proust's focus on the painter sharpens; conversely, Albertine is converted into a painting.

"What did I know of Albertine? One or two glimpses of a profile against the sea, less beautiful, assuredly, than those of Veronese's women."

"Those girls, who only that morning had been to me merely figures in a picture with the sea for background".

We note two crucial developments:

Proust's discourse begins to reverse the conventional relationship between representation and reality. Now painting is seen as not just recording but also constituting. It is just by disturbing and estranging what we take to be the photographic image of a subject that the painter breaks through to its true essence. A portrait by the hand of genius dislocates a woman's type. It is by taking away her type that Elstir names the figure in the bowler hat as *Odette de Crecy*.

This naming is most significant. Elstir is thereby integrated into the metanarrative of the episode, the background, paradigmatic adventure between Swann and Odette, the theme to Marcel's variations.

Furthermore, Elstir himself is named as the buffoon Biche, the idiot painter of the Verdurin salon. The true subject of the *Bildungsroman* shifts from Marcel to Elstir. The allegory centres, ultimately, on the painter's growth from foolishness to genius:

> "There is no man," says Elstir, "however wise who has not at some period of his youth said things, or lived a life, the memory of which is so unpleasant to him that he would gladly expunge it. And yet he ought not entirely to regret it, because he cannot be certain that he has entirely become a wise man — so far as it is possible for any of us to be wise — unless he has passed through all the fatuous or unwholesome incarnations by which that ultimate stage must be preceded. I know that there are young people, the sons and grandsons of distinguished men, whose masters have instilled in them nobility of mind and moral refinement from their schooldays. They perhaps have nothing to retract from their past lives; they could publish a signed account of everything they have ever said or done; but they are poor creatures, feeble descendants of doctrinaires, and their wisdom is negative and sterile. We do not receive wisdom, we must discover it for ourselves, after a journey through the wilderness which no one else can make for us, which no one can spare us, for our wisdom is the point of view from which we come at last to regard the world."

This speech would have done credit to a Wilhelm Meister. Note, in particular, that wisdom is here a *painterly* wisdom, a *visual* 'point of view' upon the world.

Thus two elements that had seemed to be exiled from the studio are readmitted: reality and time.

Where painting had seemed to be secondary to life and love, it is now revealed as primary. And time is introduced with the revelations of Elstir's history as Biche.

The motion of the narrative from studio to beach and back to studio reverses the paradigm of ritornello and cadenza. Now it is the chase which functions as interruption. And because it is the cadenza which returns, it assumes the function of ritornello. The real world is now extrinsic to the interiority of the studio. Proust has renamed painting by taking away its original name.

After this intermezzo, let us pick up Beethoven's trill, to signal our own closure.

3. Beethoven

It grows out of a double dominant pedal within the sixth variation and climaxes with the return of the cadenza figuration from the first movement.

Note the various manipulations of convention here:

1) The variation set should have ended with the fugal fifth variation, since the last variation is conventionally contrapunal. Counterpoint is a sign of a finale. See, for example, the fugal finales of Haydn's Op.20 Quartets.

2) Occasionally, the fugue is penultimate, and a set closes with a da capo of the original theme. Variation VI begins this way. Beethovens 'Eroica' and 'Diabelli' Variations also have a penultimate fugal movement.

3) This finality is in turn undermined by the growing trill, which ushers in the true climax, the cadenza of bar 169.

4) But the cadenza is still underpinned by the trill, which resolves, ultimately, on a truly final da capo of the theme.

Through the convolutions of this semiotic dialectic, two things stand out:

1) The variations return cyclically not to the Vivace material of the first movement, but to the Adagio cadenza figurations.

It is the *cadenza* which returns, not the mechanical ritornello.

Material which had been originally parenthetical is revealed, finally, at the heart of the structure. Beethoven has inverted the relationship of cadenza and ritornello. The sonata as a whole occupies the space between two cadenzas.

2) This turn around is prepared in a subtle process which parallels Proust's walk from the studio to the beach. The cadenza interruption is implicit in the second half of the theme (Example 2).

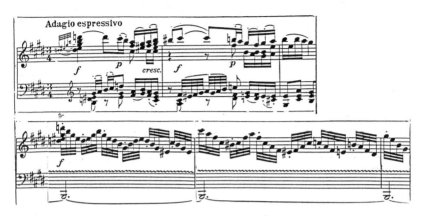

Example 2.

The theme of the Finale variations is related to the exposition of the first movement. The first half moves (repeatedly) to the dominant in eight bars, corresponding to bars 1–8. The second half, like the Adagio, traces a VI-II-V-I progression (Example 3).

Nevertheless, there is no sense of interruption between bars 8 and 9, neither is there yet much material relationship between the theme and the first movement. The first note of bar 9 is unharmonised, and one infers a continuation of the preceding dominant. This is corroborated by the bass D# on the second beat. Nevertheless, the first bass note of bar 9 is implicitly a C#, and the D# is actually a passing note linking C# to E#. At the present moment, however, the bar unfolds not a chord of C# but a chord of B. The theme promotes textural and harmonic continuity between its two phrases. But the subsequent variations gradually widen the breach between the phrases, as they approach the harmony and the texture of the cadenza (Example 4).

Example 3.

The unisono D naturals of bar 57 in variation 2 (implying the dominant ninth of F#) rudely correct the impression that the dominant harmony is sustained accross the divide. The corresponding point of the fourth variation, bar 105, enhances the interruption; Variation VI clinches the textural relationship of the interruption to the first movement Adagio.

The arrival of the cadenza of bar 169 is thus fairly inevitable, but not without a struggle. It is stiking that the interruption is realised only in alternate variations, variations II, IV, and VI. The intervening variations, I, III and V smooth over the break between the two phrases of the theme. And their material looks back not to the Adagio but to the Vivace.

In particular, their through-composed textures, a two-part invention and a fugato, disguises the bipartite structure of the theme.

Example 4.

The same alternation of ritornello and cadenza we see in the first movement recurs therefore within the variations. But now the cadenza gains the upper hand and has the last word.

Beethoven creates a remarkable interchange between outside and inside, interruption and continuity, exactly as in Proust's episode (Example 5). If the essence of op.109 is cadenza, then the work points beyond itself and is an allegory of the inscrutability of musical meaning. It is not surprising, therefore, that this reversal of function between cadenza and ritornello is the basis for Beethoven's structural gambits in the Ninth Symphony. The symphony plays the same game as the sonata, but with verbal counters. The birth of the Ode to Joy out of an instrumental recitative is achieved via the same techniques. Beethoven's leap into language in the symphony is predicated on his silence in a trifling piano sonata. Op.109 was a vital interruption and paid the highest possible dividends.

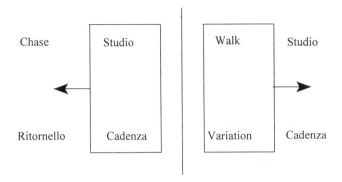

Example 5 .

One can read this either way. Either Beethoven's meaning is essen
tially musical, or his music is inherently meaningful. Either way, his
compositions are self-reflexive.

References

Barthes, Roland (1970). *S/z*. Paris: Seuil.
Forte, Allen (1961). *The Compositional Matrix*. New York: Baldwin.
Marston, Nicholas (1986). "Schenker and Forte Reconsidered: Sketches for
    the Piano Sonata in E op. 109", *19th-Century Music*, x.
Rosen, Charles (1972). *The Classical Style*. New York: Norton.
Schenker, Heinrich (1913). *Die letzten fünf Sonaten von Beethoven*. Vienna.

Some Greimasian concepts as applied to the analysis of film music

ENNIO SIMEON

L'hypothèse selon laquelle la forme du contenu des discours musicaux serait de nature pathémique et susceptible de ce fait d'être décrite comme une syntagmatique des dispositifs modaux d'un langage semi-symbolique semble on ne peut plus prometteuse. (Greimas 1983: 16)

A. J. Greimas postulated a close analogy between narrativity and the organization of every discourse; according to him the fundamental structure of signification is based on polemic-contractual relations that we can find in every kind of utterance. The semiologist attained such a level of abstraction in his theory that it seems able to answer for the whole universe of signification, for the "sense of life". One must stress, however, that the strong hypothetical-deductive form of his thought is not always easily applicable to every enunciational situation. These difficulties are particularly present in music analysis, where attributing Greimas's various modal and thymic categories to the different musical themes or syntagmatic moments is not easy to do. In spite of these problems — and apart from all questions concerning the application of semiotic concepts to music — the musical enunciation, too, can evidently be seen in the light of Greimas's principles. In other words, musical discourse can no doubt "être décrite comme une syntagmatique des dispositifs modaux d'un langage semi-symbolique". Actually there have been various rapprochements between musicology and narratology. Eero Tarasti has applied Greimasian principles to music in the most complete and convincing way (e.g., 1984; 1987; 1992). Other scholars have made such applications using single facets of his complex semiological thought. Ivanka Stoianova (1986), for example, in her analysis of Hans Werner Henze's *El Cimarrón*, convincingly reveals the development of the opera in three stages of Qualifying Test, Decisive Test, and Glorifying Test defined by Greimas as the basic structure of every narration. Yet at a macro-structural level the "story" of the protagonist, El Cimarrón, is viewed as being the same in every other form, such as theater piece, novel, cartoon, and so on; thus when she considers the "significant fusion" (1986: 280) between sounds, words and gestures, her analysis, however interesting, has little to do with the Greimasian method. At the opposite end of the spectrum, Michal Bristiger (1990) has approached the micro-structural level of the relationship between music and text, showing how any element of music can take into account any seme of a certain word, even the least direct, and clarifying so many cases of apparent contradiction between music and verbal images.

In the study of film music Greimasian concepts have been applied rarely (Larsen 1988), yet the method of the great French semiologist can perhaps be used to good advantage in that field, where one does not meet with the difficulties that arise when we confront "absolute" music. The possibility of giving to a film a precise semantic content lets us confer upon the music a certain function, in a much more detailed way than when we deal with a merely instrumental piece. Let us think of the modalities of 'will' (*vouloir*), 'know' (*savoir*), 'can' (*pouvoir*); and let us think of more essential categories of signification such as contrariety, contradiction, and presupposition. In most cases, music in film can express the above-mentioned basic categories of signification and modalities, and be their vehicle in a clear, functional manner (in the sense of being well codified and open to investigation). I speak here both of music as such and of music as symbolisation of extramusical referents. Of course not all film music can contribute in such a manner to the basic signification of a film. But precisely this inability might be a criterion by which to judge if certain film music is more or less "significant". If music can "activate" the process of signification on the same level as images, we should be able to insert the visual and the musical elements into the semiotic square, since the latter shows every logical articulation of a semantic category. If, for example, the presentation of a character at the beginning of a film asserts the semantic category "good vs. evil"

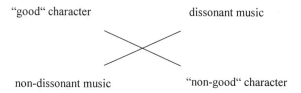

"good" character   dissonant music

non-dissonant music   "non-good" character

Figure 1.

through the friction between image and music, we can place our terms in the following semiotic square (Figure 1).

This taxonomic description must then be seen in syntactical terms, in order to understand how the situation is going to develop. We find that music and images can be in actantial syncretism (and thus serve the same dramatic requirement) or that they can be two autonomous actants and actually create the signification and even the narration on the same level. Music can "belong" to a character, who in the case of Figure 1 is marked at the same time by "positive" (visual) and "negative" (musical) semes but who in other cases can be marked by semes that are not contrary or contradictory. On the other hand, music can be the vehicle of a sense not "belonging" to the character, as a second "negative" character or as a future situation that will be difficult to solve.

Of course the case of actantial syncretism is by far the most common, these being cases where images and music "say" the same thing ("good" character with "positive music"); but this does not mean that the role of music is merely dilatory or redundant. Here music adds signification at other levels, influencing the semic content of the character. For instance, in the case of a "friendly image" + "modal organ phrases", the music adds the seme "religiosity" through the instrumental timbre and the particular non-tonal scale, and it could add the seme of "vitality" by speeding up of rhythms, by major keys, and so on.

To pursue such relationships, we cannot avoid the problem of music semantics. In order to understand thoroughly the role of music in film signification, it is indispensable to take into account researches on the "meaning of music", or more precisely, on the existence of a kind of film-musical *Affektenlehre*. Musical signification in cinema is mostly based on pre- and para-cinematographic expressive standards (Cooke 1959; Imberty 1981; Stefani 1987). In addition to a century of cinema, television and video have brought new film-music conventions with highly signifying power (Tagg 1979). This relation between music and images based on semantic exteroceptive references is not the only one. For example, one can find a purely rhythmical-motory relationship, or a sensorial function of music as neutralization of silence, but usually a more or less explicit semantic valence of every musical insert emerges. One can find musical inserts functioning as "episodic markers", which, according to Tagg's subtle classification of the musical sign, are pieces eliciting "lots of associations like 'has just', 'after that', 'after a long time', 'about to happen', 'leading to', etc." (1992: 377). From our point of view, in these last examples we can apply the Greimasian concept of temporal engagement and disengagement. Deictical, anaphorical, and cataphorical functions of music are very frequent in cinema. Spatial engagements and disengagements can be obtained through the evocation, in music of different places, through the use of heterogeneous style elements (in this case we have exteroceptivity) or through musical elements already presented in the film and bound to particular places (interoceptivity). Style elements can also be at the service of temporal engagements and disengagements in the case, very frequent in cinema, of music evoking a particular epoch.

Let us now see briefly how the above-mentioned concepts may be used in the analysis of a definite film. *The Mission* (1986) by Roland Joffé, music by Ennio Morricone, has been widely appreciated as a film where music is very important and where Morricone's contribution has been particularly successful. In *The Mission* music plays an important role in the whole signification of the film at a manifest level: "The noble souls of these *indios* have talent for music"; "With an orchestra the Jesuits could conquer all the continent", says the papal envoy at the beginning of the film.[1] Father Gabriel overcomes the Guaranys' aggressiveness and suspicion by playing the oboe. Building musical instruments is a primary activity of the natives. And at the end the only survivors are some children who go away bearing a violin. To judge only by the screenplay, therefore, one can expect music to have particular importance in the story. Of course the main signification of the film is given by images and/or words, as almost always occurs in films, and music is not absolutely necessary: "The noble souls of these *indios* have talent for music", says the papal envoy. And we *see* some natives playing stringed instruments, so that even without any soundtrack we would understand that Father Gabriel is gaining the Guaranys' confidence by means of his peaceful attitude (playing the oboe in the middle of aggressive people). But the strength of signification is quite different with Morricone's musical contribution. The music of *The Mission* is not intrusive, seeking a role of primary, active importance; one finds much of the music used as background and a lot of it used for syncretic, strengthening purposes: the "wicked" papal envoy is presented with menacing, dissonant sounds; the geographical ambience is underlined with ethnic musical semes such as Latin American flutes and percussion instruments; a hint of European, eighteenth-century string music is inserted when the natives' ability in constructing instruments is mentioned; the true first theme sounds when Father Gabriel appears. In all these places one can point to a semiotic valence of the music, according to the categories proposed above. From the very beginning music constitutes an "enunciate of state":

$$S1 \wedge O1$$
The Guaranys (S1) possess a highly musical soul (O1).

In *The Mission*, music creates spatial disengagements (eighteenth-century European string music juxtaposed with images of *indios*) and engagements (Latin American music with the *indios*' images). But from the actantial point of view the most interesting moment of the film is where Father Gabriel overcomes the Guaranys' aggressiveness and suspicion by playing the oboe. The oboe theme seems in every respect to drive the sequence (Example 1).

Example 1.

Example 2.

After a reluctant waving (here rendered with grace-notes)[2] (Example 2) the melody shows an initial, energetic leap of an ascending fourth (A–D) followed by a gradual course in the opposite direction, all repeated twice (Example 3) only to "leave again" in a more resolute manner with the interval of an ascending sixth (A–F♯) (Example 4).

Example 3.

Example 4.

The ascending sixth interval, with its euphoric tension, is also twice repeated, and in its last orchestrated form in this sequence it appears, perhaps accidentally but for us significantly, together with an image of the Virgin Mary offered to an *indio* (and to the spectators).

But the theme shows a further stage, transposing a fourth higher the two previous thematic nuclei. The fourth A–D becomes D–G (Example 5)

Example 5.

and the sixth A–F♯ becomes D–B. The melody, in its more complete version, has its most affirmative character in the note B, followed by a descending phrase (Example 6).

Example 6.

One may say that the oboe theme is so effective because its structure has a course somehow isotopic to that of the visual sequence. Considering the three sections into which we divided the theme (bars 1–7, 8–10,

11–13) we may say that the trajectory Uncertainty-Conquest-Achieve-ment is common to the two components (musical and visual), save the very different levels of abstraction. And since here the dramatic verbal content is absent and the visual one is very limited (Father Gabriel says nothing and there is little movement), it is precisely the music that "drives" the sequence. A possible analogy between this tripartite devel-opment and the three stages of the "qualifying", "decisive", and "glori-fying" tests is as suggestive as ever. Besides, the music constitutes here an "enunciate of doing":

Music (the oboe theme) can put in conjunction the Jesuits (S2) with the Guaranys (O2).

It is possible to follow a whole film in conformity with the principles discussed above, although there is still much to do before application of Greimasian theories to the analysis of film music produces a less frag-mentary view of structure. Here we hope to have made some headway in that direction.

Notes

1. We based our work on the Italian dubbing of the film, so it is possible that the sentences are not exactly the same as in the original.
2. Because we had no score, we transcribed the melody, with some possibly subjective interpretation of time-values. Moreover, the melody appears

$$M \longrightarrow (S2 \wedge O2)$$

a few times in this first sequence and many other times in the film, and never exactly alike as regards both time-values and notes. So our tran-scription purports to be nothing more than an indicative, "average" version of the theme.

References

Bristiger, M. (1990). "Le unità elementari del significato nel campo delle relazioni fra testo e musica", *Rivista italiana di musicologia* 24 (1).

Cooke, D. (1959). *The Language of Music*. London: Oxford University Press.

Greimas, A. J. (1983). *Du sens II: Essais sémiotiques*. Paris: Seuil.

Greimas A. J. and Courtès, J. (1979). *Sémiotique: Dictionnaire raisonné de la théorie du langage*. Paris: Hachette.

Imberty, M. (1981). *Les écritures du temps: Sémantique psychologique de la musique*. Paris: Bordas.

Larsen, P. (1988). *Beyond the narrative. Rock videos and modern visual fictions: Readings, experiences*. Unpublished typescript. University of Bergen.

Stefani, G. (1987). *Il segno della musica*. Palermo: Sellerio.

Stoianova, I. (1986). "Strategie narrative nel *Cimarrón*", *Henze*, E. Restagno (ed.), 270–293. Torino: EDT.

Tagg, P. (1979). *"Kojak": 50 Seconds of Television Music. Toward the Analysis of Affect in Popular Music*. Göteborg: Studies from the Department of Musicology.

– (1992). "Towards a sign typology of music", *Secondo Convegno Europeo di Analisi Musicale*, R. Dalmonte and M. Baroni (eds.), 369–378. Trento: Università degli Studi. Dipartimento di Storia della Civiltà Europea.

Tarasti, E. (1984). "Pour une narratologie de Chopin", *International Review of the Aesthetics and Sociology of Music* 15 (1): 53–57.

– (1987). "Some Peircean and Greimasian semiotic concepts as applied to music", *The Semiotic Web 1986* (Approaches to Semiotics 78), Sebeok—Umiker-Sebeok (eds.), 445–459. Berlin: Mouton.

– (1992). "A narrative grammar of Chopin's G Minor Ballade", *Minds and Machines* 2: 401–426.

Spatial soundings: Aalto and Sibelius

SARAH MENIN

1. Introduction

> Nature, biology, offers profuse and luxuriant forms with the same
> constructions, same tissues and same cellular structure it can produce
> millions of flexible combinations, each of which is an example of a
> high level of form. (Aalto, 1935)

> Tapiola represents something that can be called organic process form,
> a kind of total variation form. (Salmenhaara, 1970)

The first quotation is from an article by Aalto, and the second from Prof.
Salmenhaara's analysis of *Tapiola*.

This article represents the beginning of my doctoral research, and is
therefore not a definitive essay on the proposed subject.

It is important to state that my research grew out of an experience of
a spatial dimension in Jean Sibelius' late music during a visit to Finland
to experience Alvar Aalto's buildings. This sense grew as I was drawn
into Sibelius' sound world and became more familiar with the genesis of
Aalto's buildings. I began to explore the creative roots of the two artists,
their environment, their lives and their motivation. The synthesis of this
sensory experience became deeper as I experienced more of Finnish
culture.

What I had experienced in the music and the architecture I also felt
while I wandered in the Finnish forests. The experience was deeper than
one of the pastoral romanticism of Nature familiar to me in "England's
green and pleasant land". I began to see that the process of Nature, and
one's response to experiencing this process, seemed to be the level at
which the correlation between Sibelius' and Aalto's work affected my
senses. The synthesis initiated a process of sensory modulation.

Finland seems not to be a land of monumental views, but rather an experience of little vistas, fragments of forest and lakes. There are few hills, yet the terrain is never exactly flat. The forests appear dark and foreboding. However, once one dares to approach they offer security and, when one's eyes have adjusted to the colours within the darkness, a surprising quality of light. All these experiences are translated by Sibelius and Aalto into their work.

I began to examine the scores of Sibelius' late works, and discovered they comprised tiny fragments of sounds which were gradually permuted, varied and amalgamated through the composition. The structure of the piece seemed to grow with these germs of sound. They are treated like cells of a living creation.

Jean Sibelius was born in 1865, in Hämeenlinna, and grew into the Finnish equivalent of the Arts and Crafts Movement, which had found political determination in the struggle for national independence. Alvar Aalto, on the other hand, was born in 1898. He grew into the progressive Modern Movement of the Twentieth Century. The longevity of their careers creates a chronological overlap, and their positions as national heroes ensured that they were discussed in the same patriotic breath, yet little correlative analysis of their work has been undertaken.

Aalto's association with Nature is widely known, yet seems often to be based on the misunderstanding that his buildings are, 'irrational-organic'. To Aalto, Nature primarily meant "the complicated system of checks and balances that supports biological life on earth — a system in which all components affect one another, man being but one component." (Schildt, 1991)

Examples of Aalto's thoughts, such as this, began to provide evidence of the roots from which the synthesis between his work and the late music of Sibelius grew, and helps to explain why their forms were so unusual in the world of the machine aesthetic.

"Contact with Nature and the variety Nature always provides is a life form which gets on very uneasily with over — formalistic ideas." (Aalto, 1935)

This article will explore the environmental and cultural contexts in which Sibelius and Aalto worked, before moving to explore the comparable compositional techniques they employed. A discussion of the unity in their work completes the thesis that a shared, 'profound logic', under girds their work, and is of universal relevance, beyond the field of creativity.

2. Finnish context

2.1. Finland suppressed

It is helpful to make a few observations of Finnish history in order to illustrate the context in which Aalto and Sibelius grew. The political, cultural and economic oppression vilified the advancement of the Finnish race, but failed to eradicate the indigenous, folk culture, which was fed by the agrarian subsistence eked out from the floor of the forest. It seems that what have been called the backwoods Finns knew what opportunities raw Nature offered for survival.

When independence was grasped from the Russian Empire at the moment of the Revolution, and the ensuing Civil War was over, the suppressed energy of the Finns was channelled into the growth of towns and Cities. In 1935 Aalto projected that the Industrialisation which fed Finland's growth also held the key to the alienation or destruction of her roots in Nature. His solution was to bring their roots in his buildings.

2.2. Finland emerging

Again, in the Winter War, the instinctive knowledge of the Nature of the forest more than doubled the strength of the small Finnish army against the Russian Bear. The passion and pathos of Sibelius' live broadcast of *Andante Festivo* at the opening of the New York World Fair in the same year represented the agony of Sibelius' own creative journey, and the struggle of the Finnish nation. This is the only moment when the work of Finland's cultural protagonist coincided. Aalto designed the *Finnish*

Pavilion at the World Fair, which has been described as "a Symphony in wood" (Pallasmaa, 1987).

2.3. Natural roots and forest culture

The conventional Finnish wisdom is that the untouched wilderness is the ideal setting — "the place to be" (Schildt, 1991). Here, Aalto's biographer, Göran Schildt, elucidates what is quite outside the experience of most Europeans. Certainly, for the English, wilderness is beyond reach. We are always safe, never far from civilisation. Finnish philosopher Juhani Pietarinen has distinguished four basic attitudes to the forest amongst Finns: The Utilitarian (using the resources of the forest), the Humanist (using the forest to educate ideals), the Mystical (experience of unity between man and Nature through sensory or spiritual experiences), and the Primitivist (denying all human privileges in Nature). (Pietarinen, 1984)

Arvid Järnefelt (1922), the Finnish painter and Sibelius' friend and brother in law, observed that "Sibelius didn't look at the forest like other people, he entered into it and became part of it", and Sibelius himself wrote, "Today I have melodies like God. . . rejoiced and revelled and trembling as the soul sings. . . the mysticism of Nature and the agony of life".

2. 4. Aalto and the forest

"Nature. . . offers millions of flexible combinations Human life comes form the same roots. . . cells and tissue are the building components of which human life is composed." (Aalto, 1938)

Aalto experienced close observation of the continually changing and infinitely varied nature of the forest as a child, while surveying with his father. After courting the pure white rationalism of the International Movement, Aalto's functionalism found its roots in the forest. Aalto encouraged people to 'be' in his buildings as they would 'be' in Nature. Schildt writes that,

Insight into the wood of the forest — forest wisdom — is at the heart of everything Aalto created. . . a biological experience which never allows itself to be overpowered by tectonic civilisation or short-sighted rationalism. This is not a matter of rationalism or mysticism, but of their opposite, an extreme sense of reality, a sharing in Nature's own wisdom and rationality. (Schildt, 1984)

2.5. Sibelius and the forest

Wide spread they stand
The dark forests of the North
Ancient, Mysterious, brooding savage dreams
And in the gloom wood sprites weave their magic secrets

This passage, which Sibelius supplied with the score of *Tapiola*, heralds life-controlling gods like Tapio. This paganism speaks of Nature's indifference to Man, and the forest's great power against which Man can rage and scream. Tawaststjerna pointed (pers. com.) that Sibelius' last piece for piano, *Song of the Forest*, offers fascinating insight into his Nature stimulation.

Sibelius battled with the sacrament of creation, of creativity and the human condition. Only when he withdrew from the drinking bouts in Helsinki, and faced solitude could his creativity which was both his life blood and his torment, flow. "My art demands a different environment. In Helsinki all my melody died within me." The multi-sensory experience were intricately recorded in his imagination. "I drank in the cries of the budding spring, full of air, haze and mist. . . fortissimo scent of earth. I got a wonderful theme and sailed through the air on a strong wind."

3. The threat of the new

3.1. The new

The New culture of Modernism was the opening up of new modes of perception. The process of discovery and expression are often inseparable: entering into creativity expands perception at the same time as attempting, through the chosen idiom, to communicate this experience, by grappling with the bounds of an old language, or the necessity to strive to invent a new language. Schöenburg exploration of a new language of music was greeted by antagonism. This was largely the case for Sibelius as well as Schöenburg. Sibelius was enlarging the empire of sound within a given form.

Conflicting feelings so often accompany new experiences, which, in good art, are invited into synthesis at the cost of, often painful, inner revelation. Despite the gradual enfeeblement and eventual abandonment of functional tonality and perspective, the public saw the New aesthetic movement as a destructive abjuration rather than a creative assertion. The New Music aroused feelings of hostility, as if the music touched the audiences' inner anxiety, and threatened to whip up a storm in their unconscious.

3.2. Sibelius, Aalto; The new sound and space

History has shown that some 'new modes of perception' manifest in art find swifter acceptance than others. Perhaps it comes down to those which affirm and those which threaten.

Sibelius' epic works, which strive towards heroic power and dominance, stirred and confirmed audiences. But the inspiration, or in Freudian terms new at the time, the unconscious, which we hear through every moment of his later works, seem to engender panic and fear within, and also fear regarding the withdrawal of the structural lifeboats of known musical form.

In the work of both Sibelius and Aalto there was no desire to shock, or revolt, but a deep tuning to the logic of Nature, and, by creating their own language of composition, in their respective fields, were challenging the aesthetics status quo; whether it be Romanticism or the New. They both saw and felt a massive untapped potential in the natural systems around themselves, and coupled this with their passion for inventive creativity.

In his article "The Trout and the Stream" Aalto explained his method of designing, to illustrate the way in which time for development, in creativity, can integrate, and make sense of seemingly unrelated internal processes. (Aalto, 1947) He moved away from Modernism when he saw technology and rationalism ignore humanity and Nature, and when it came against something instinctive in himself. Sibelius perceived pressure to dismiss the logic of classical form in music. However he set out to explore symphonic form within the bounds of classical tonality. This was not blind reverence of an old master clinging to vestigial forms, nor was it a neo-classical recapturing of a genre, but rather a delving into the undiscovered and paradoxical potential of both harmony and chaos in the accepted musical forms of the last two hundred years, by confronting the harmony and chaos in himself. He believed that tonality and form had both communicative potential and a rich, and as yet unspoken, vocabulary. The ascetic, uncompromising, and often aphoristic language of these new sounds ironically found life through what seemed like abjuration, but was actually deeper exploration of tested, musical forms, such as polyphonic dissonance. His sound world demands a measure of understanding and a gesture of commitment.

It appears that Sibelius was to the New music of Schöenburg what Aalto was to the International Modernism of Le Corbusier. Despite the pull of the New Movements' belief in the Method for composing and the Module for designing, Sibelius and Aalto explored new modes of perception in ways which went against the tide of the International culture. They sought the roots of themselves and the potential of their chosen idiom and their natural environment.

4. Nature's process

4. 1. Compositional structure

Sigfried Giedion's understanding that Aalto's work is "illogical and organic", (Giedion, 1950) and the critique of Sibelius by Walter Niemann, in which he criticises the lack of "concentration of form, . . . organic and logical inner development and proportion", shows no insight into the reality and inherent logic of Nature's ordering process. (Gray, 1931) These critics lacked the motivation to explore the ever-new potential of the creative system, which Sibelius and Aalto developed and in which they were both most creative.

4. 2. Nature's growth process and creativity

Aalto believed that "Proximity to Nature can give fresh inspiration both in terms of form and construction". (Aalto, 1953)

The "new modes of perception" Aalto and Sibelius developed were different from those of their contemporaries in Europe. It is as if they had independently developed a shared creative language, not exclusive, yet one which remained foreign to other artists working in culture's far removed from essential Nature. The language used what Aalto called "continual renewal and growth" and what Tawaststjerna called the "strong organic cohesion" of creation to bring the material and sensory world, as Aalto said "into harmony with human life" through creativity.

What Aalto called 'the process of crystallisation', Sibelius spoke of as 'the crystallisation of ideas from chaos', and the integration of fragments into something wholly organic. He describes the transparency and improvisatory structure of his *Fourth Symphony* as "A theme slowly grows, an improvisation in three phases", wherein the process of metamorphosis reflects different aspects of a basic idea. Aalto spoke of the "profoundest property of architecture being the a variety and growth reminiscent of natural organic life". He continually explored the permutations and elasticity of combinations of "the smallest possible units" in any creation he undertook.

Sibelius' friend, Rosa Newmarch, wrote that from the scintillating fragments "the germ motifs need time to coagulate and form an organic whole". This describes a compositional process in Aalto and Sibelius' mature works. Nature's infinite capacity for nuance is explored in Aalto's wood experiments, for example the overlapping of cells and the intermingling of germ motifs. The use of motific fragments as textural trig points is apparent in the *Sixth Symphony* where the timpani is pulling towards D minor, with the determined C sharp motif, against the orchestra's D Dorian mode headed by the C natural monolith.

Yet Aalto also wanted to imbue cells of awareness of human functions, inflecting towards a priority of life to be reflected at all scales of form.

> The importance of variability. Nature, biology, offers profuse and luxuriant forms; with the same tissues and same cellular structures it can produce millions and millions of combinations, each of which is an example of a high level of form. Human life comes from the same root, The objects that surround man are hardly mere fetishes and allegories with some mystical eternal value. They are more likely to be cells and tissues, alive just as cells and tissues are the building components of which human life is composed. They cannot be dealt with in a different way from biology's other units, otherwise they would be in danger of becoming unsuited to the system, of becoming inhuman. (Aalto, 1938)

4. 3. Flexible standardisation

The concept of standardisation had developed with industrialisation, becoming a tenet of the design philosophy of Modernism. Aalto was determined to explore the natural derivation of standardisation. He said "Nature herself is the best standardisation committee," and that standardisation must go deep "into the inner system of building components and elements. . to form an infinite number of different combinationsa system in which variable entities of almost infinite function and form can be produced out of the same parts." (Aalto, 1941)

Aalto and Sibelius explored how Nature builds on this serial principle, producing nothing but unique individuals, "Even though the building materials, the cells are massed produced, the answer is flexible combination potential." (Schildt, 1988) This equates with "continual variation form", a phrase used to describe Sibelius "handling of germ motifs", using the "natural variability of theme" (which, incidentally, are Aalto's). The motific dialogues in the *Fourth Symphony* illustrate this.

Prof. Salmenhaara believes *Tapiola* "represents something that can be called organic process form, a kind of total variation form" (Salmenhaara, 1970), where the starting point is not a small theme, but even smaller germ motifs, which, with total variation process, proceed as a way of building music.

Aalto's multi-cellular buildings are formed in such a way that the smallest possible units are each uniquely formed to avoid the powerful and inhuman monotony. *Baker House Dormitory* at MIT well illustrates this.

There are other aspects of Aalto and Sibelius' composition which are drawn from Nature's growth process. There is not time here to explore all these in detail. However it is helpful to briefly illustrate them.

4. 4. Fragmentation

An impression of incompleteness and even dissonance is understandable if the creation is seen as a static *objet d'art*. If however it is experienced as an unfolding creation, which requires the person to enter into the experience of its unfolding, the fragmentation can be perceived as parts interacting in the process towards wholeness, rather than a finished, chaotic object or entity. The first movement of the *Fourth Symphony* shows fragments of sound interleaving to comprise the musical whole.

In many of his buildings Aalto allows large mass fragment-like fan-forms to break from the more rectilinear portions of his libraries. Spatial differentiation is intensified by these fragmented or incomplete geometry's, and by sculptural manipulations of light and level change. *Rovaniemi Library* manifests good examples of this.

4. 5. Economy

The deliberate reduction of their means of expression, actually enhanced and clarified Aalto and Sibelius' work through a process of distillation. As Sibelius famously put it, "While other people offer the public cocktails of various hues, I offer pure spring water." Their work was essentially highly selective, and therefore economic in formal terms.

4. 6. Mediation

The capacity to reconcile forces acting on the outside of a creation with those working from inside out, is central to both Aalto's and Sibelius' creative technique. The points of transition, or change, are articulated with great skill, drawing the user or listener through the change, with sensory awareness, yet without necessarily making a conscious note of it. This surreptitious leading on is the inflecting nature of growth. Tapiola is a complete experience of this.

Entering Aalto's *Vuoksenniska Church* one is led from the external barn-like impression, through a low, dark portico to a flowing sinuous cave-like interior. The drama of the transition continues to live in the transmission of light through the extraordinary double glazed windows which mediate between inside and out.

Robert Layton expresses Sibelius' mastery of mediation:

> It is impossible to say where on movement ends and the other begins. Sibelius' mastery of transition and control of simultaneous tempi is a continuously growing entity in which the thematic metamorphosis works at such a level of sophistication that the listener is barely aware of it. (Layton, 1970)

The mastery of mediation and the points of change facilitate a complex ambiguity in which wholes may grow from a great variety of formal and emotional fragments, into a unity.

4. 7. Plasticity and Undulation

Undulation is often a mediating element, acting simultaneously between different functions, programmes or spaces, edging and enfolding at the same time. Both Sibelius and Aalto use undulation at different scales. In music it may be a slight tremolo in the strings and in architecture a textural indentation, as on the wall of the *House of Culture* in Helsinki. On the other hand there are the gradual surging and diminution in the breadth and volume of sound over a ground bass and the undulating ceiling in Viipuri or whole building, like *Baker House*. Aalto maintained that the undulating forms were always functional. An understanding of his philosophy illustrates quite how broad his definition of function was. "Technical functionalism is only right if extended to the psychological field too. It is the only way to humanise architecture." (Aalto, 1940)

4. 8. Spatial Manipulation

The shared methodology of approach to spatial manipulation comprises the static and the dynamic spaces. In the static space there seems to be a suspension of movement (which incidentally facilitates inner or interpersonal dialogue). For example Aalto's sunken wells in the *Rautatalo* building in Helsinki and the virtual stasis, which coalesce all the tensions of the preceding passages, as in the first movement of the *Fourth Symphony*.

The dynamic spaces are tools for compositional movement or unification. These busy, dashing, spaces are often rushing to or from a void.

The counter motion elements in Aalto's sections and elevations create highly charged dynamics. In Sibelius this counter motion seems to entangle the listener, as in the first movement of the *Sixth Symphony*. However, when the pace, in many of Sibelius' late works, seem to be active, the deep progress is actually very slow. The superficial dashing is underpinned by long pedal points, thus the whole musical space holds the seemingly contradictory phenomena of activity and a deeper, almost grieving stasis.

Having surveyed the compositional structure and techniques which are common to Aalto and Sibelius, and which I believe derive from their experience of Nature, it is important to explore the motivation for the wholeness of their creations.

5. Wholeness and Universality

Lional Pike said of Sibelius, "The unity of each work is complete, and derives from the total integration of all aspects of the composition." (Pike, 1978)

Sibelius' clear and painful vision was that his life's mission lay in his uncompromising will to forge musical ideas into unified wholes. Aalto strove to unite the different realms of existence he experienced, and with which he saw little man struggle.

5. 1. Symphony

The musical phenomenon which so enthralled Sibelius was the symphony. The word derives from the Greek word, meaning an agreement of sound, in which there is a concerted, or harmonious collection of utterances of the sound. Exploration of this led Sibelius to the quest for unity, economy and the reconciliation of different and contrasting ingredients. Eventually this led to the *Seventh Symphony*, wherein the symphonic form is reduced to its essentials. For Sibelius the symphony was the mirror of complete man, a microcosm of the human experience. "I look to the development of the first movement, trembling. The symphony is not a composition in the ordinary sense of the word. It is an inner confession at a certain stage of one's life."

Perhaps the ideal symphony, would comprise a constantly growing entity through an inter-relatedness of germ themes and movements, a paring down of expression to achieve an economy whereby all is essential form, and a continuity which demands mastery of transitional passages. Within organic cohesion each idea dictates the flow of the music and establishes its own disciplinary logic. Sibelius' dedication to such form forged completely new sound worlds, where melody and harmony are united, creating a unified sound space.

In Tapiola Sibelius synthesised his symphonic technique. Prof. Salmenhaara writes that "In *Tapiola* expression — content — and structural thinking — form — are an integral part of one another." (1970)

Sibelius held the essence of classical precedents at the heart of his work, then went on to develop them beyond anything known. He believed "new and transforming ideas must come from within, not from exterior form". In reporting a conversation with Mahler about the symphony Sibelius said that he "admires its style and severity of form, and the profound logic that created the inner connection between all the motives. This is my experience in the course of my creative work. Mahler's opinion was just the opposite."

Sibelius found great stimulation in the logic of symphonic form. It seemed to draw the fragmented musical subject matter, which his roaming in Nature offered him, into a symbiotic relationship.

The word symphesis is helpful to draw Aalto's work into this discussion. It means the growing together of elements, by forming or involving a coalescence, or fusion. This describes what otherwise might be referred to as their symphonic determination,

5. 2. Synthesis

In "Concerning the Spiritual in Art", Kandinsky wrote, "And so the arts are encroaching one upon another and from a proper use of this encroachment will rise the art that is truly monumental." (1914)

Traditional analogies between the arts, and particularly between architecture and music, have divided into two categories; mathematical and poetic. This division illustrates the way western society has tended to be split off from the holistic view, either neglecting the logical or the inspirational faculty. Architecture like music, is both scientific and artistic. Both disciplines are experienced in the dimension of time. The unfolding essence of the music (or the building) is a process in which the art is revealed through our sensory perception. We are often unaware of drawing our senses into the realm of the music (or building), of consciously assenting to the affectivity of the art, but our autonomic sensory system is at work at an unconscious level.

The theory of harmonic proportion developed by Pythagoras, and followed in the works of Vitruvius, Alberti, Palladio and more recently the module systems of Le Corbusier, propounds the mathematical system of absolute formal and proportional creation. The Poetic approach, on the other hand, refers to a common spiritual unity in different art forms. By its nature, this is less of a system of analysis than a way of perceiving.

These different models must be drawn into synthesis for a correlative analysis of the arts to be effective, since together they enable an understanding of the structure within which the universe (and the particular piece of art) was conceived, and the poetic narrative of the spiritual entities conceiving it. An understanding of the whole experience of life can begin to emerge, and particularly, as Kandinsky described, the "spiritual life to which art belongs and in which she is one of the mightiest elements,"

> I believe, in fact, am convinced that in their beginnings architecture and other art genres have the same starting point, which is, admittedly, abstract but at the same time is influenced by all the knowledge and feelings that we have accumulated inside us. . . Construction — in this case intelligence, reason or what ever you choose to call it, is at one with creation. . . Someone who has not the constructive intelligence indispensable to the creative artist, is nevertheless enabled to receive positive impressions, . . simply with the aid of that indefinable thing called sentiment. (Aalto, 1959)

Here Aalto is demonstrating that the scientific and the poetic are inextricably linked, and that the observer can appreciate this synthesis quite naturally. Aalto is showing that the 'sentiment' in 'little man' the often powerless eventual user of his architecture, can unite the realms of logic and spirit which, as we have seen, are often cut off from each other in purely cerebral, academic, analysis of art and creativity.

Central to a correlative analysis between the work of Sibelius and Aalto is the balance, inherent in the works' creation and in their reception, of qualities of the left and right hemispheres of the brain: Works which achieve sensory affectivity and functional effectiveness, and require exploration in both structural and poetic, (logical and sensory) terms. As is well known, the left hemisphere of the brain controls the logical, reasoning, thinking, language and analytical faculties, tending to formulate things in linear terms. The right side of the brain, however, controls the creative, visual, rhythm, recognition, feeling and intuition, tending to formulate in synthesis

It is difficult to separate these elements in Sibelius' and Aalto's work. The study of the logical (structural) and inspirational (poetic) basis of their work in the preceding chapter, reveals their profound rootedness in Nature, and their experience of human life. Unfortunately, in art the phenomenon of Nature is usually associated solely with the poetic realm

A synthesis has emerged between the creative process in man and Nature. Cézanne said, "I would like to unite them (art and Nature). It is my opinion that by taking Nature as your starting point you attain art." Göran Schildt has explored Cézanne's influence on Aalto, explaining that the overlapping concrete forms in his paintings, (the fragmentation of Nature), shows how space grows directly out of Nature's forms. In a letter to Bonnard, Cézanne was drawn to express the essence of the "logical development of everything we see and feel through the study of Nature". The emergent synthesis is between the root inspiration, Nature, and the art this inspires.

5. 3. Architecture. . . frozen music?

The most familiar, romantic, phrase which associates architecture with music dates from 1802, when Friedrich Schelling referred to architecture as frozen music. Goethe challenged his simplification by commenting, "Architecture is not so much frozen music", but "music fallen silent", referring to the myth of Orpheus singing and playing his lyre to summon stones to build the city.

Goethe believed in the mathematical harmony of proportions, and used his poetic sense to indicate that, both (music and architecture) are referable to a higher formula; both are derivable, though each for itself, from a higher law. They are like two rivers that have the same source in one mountain, but subsequently pursue their own way.

The source, in the case of Aalto and Sibelius, was Nature's whole organic system, a higher law which is intrinsically both poetic and logical.

The appraisal of Sibelius and Aalto needs to be drawn towards a correlation in which the modulation of the senses is explored.

Kandinsky believed that, "(The) borrowing of method by one art from another, can only be truly successful when the application of the borrowed methods is not superficial but fundamental." (1914) Indeed, it is in the common root of the two artists' spiritual, sensory and analytical experience of Nature that, through their artistic inspiration, sensory modulation and their compositional structure, there is an audio-spatial congruence. This congruence resides in valid harmonic interrelation, equally applicable to sound and image, and arguably, to all aspects of life. This harmony was intrinsic to the processes of Nature which Sibelius and Aalto observed.

5.4. A space within: The merging of artistic experience through sensory perception

I want to explore the possible correlation between sensory experiences of architecture and musical activity. I do not intend to form a new theory of comparative analysis, but rather that the synthesis of sensory modulation in Aalto's designs and Sibelius' music may be explored.

Art speaks to the soul through sensory perception, creating movement within our inner world. However, as Sibelius believed, "We human beings need much more than the kind of reality that is accessible to the five senses. If there is a reality, greater than sensation, being translated from the artist, via his art to the observer, which cannot be transmitted by the senses, a gestalt occurs, what is received is greater than what was sensorially transmitted, and the "limits set by the field of an art" (David, 1968) are expanded, liberating the bounds of narrow artistic disciplines, and opening up new modes of perception.

5.4.1. Time and space. . . and the unconscious process of the arts

The interpenetration of space and time adds a fourth, dynamic, dimension to the three which had held court since the Renaissance. Sigfried Giedion believed this was the essence of the modern perception which motivated, and was a liberating phenomena in the arts of the early twentieth century. The phenomenon of space in architecture is established with our perception of three dimensions, relative to a moving point of reference, the observer. In modern architecture Giedion saw this most strongly demonstrated in Aalto's work.

It is in the co-operation of the phenomena of space and time that Sibelius and Aalto are most closely related, yet in a most tantalisingly intangible way. In their work there is both a relativity and a wealth of detail which grows, so, their patterns of behaviour coincide at too many important points for the creative concurrence to be brushed aside.

5.4.2. Sound Spaces

"Music is enriched by spatial thinking" (David, 1968)

An understanding of the correlation between the later works of Aalto and Sibelius is enhanced by an exploration of the phenomenon of musical space forms. There are two kinds of space in music. The space that sound travels through has been explored in the study of acoustics. However, the space-forms, created by the different musical parts (instruments) in relation to each other, has received little attention.

On hearing Sibelius' *Seventh Symphony* Vaughan Williams wrote to the Finn, "You have lit a candle in the world of music that will never go out". The 'sound spaces' and 'the new sound world' which have been identified through experience of Sibelius' music, have "opened up clairvoyant vistas into a future world" of sound.

Gianmarco Vergani, of Colombia University, recently described two ways of attempting to correlate the antithetical natures of music and architecture, (Vergani, 1987) through an exploration of our perceptions of these arts, rather than of their formation, (the poetic rather than the structural, the right rather than the left side of the brain). First he uses the concept of synchrony to describe the elements of architecture fixed in space; synchrony being a description of a subject as it exists at one moment in time. The synchronic approach reduces music to its architectonic dimension outside of time. Structural relationships are then extracted from music and applied to architecture; diachrony, on the other hand, describes the way music derives from the vitality of change and its continuous permutation in the medium of time: Diachrony being concerned with the historical development of a subject. Vergani thus describes it as "The reading of architecture unfolds through time." The observer is required to move to set the composition in motion by investing his/her time, and enlivening a fourth dimension: The process of the experience.

The diachronic mechanism establishes a taxonomy of elements in music (tone, timbre, duration, pitch, dynamics) and architecture (texture, material, light, colour, scale), and thus relevant events in music can be transposed into architectonic space-structures. For example musical dynamics would be transposed into spatial contraction and dilation. The range of high and low pitch or frequency, or 'up' and 'down', and the duration of time, can be envisaged as a lateral movement or progression.

The diachronic approach assists the correlative analysis, because it helps identify Sibelius' sound spaces, which can then be compared with Aalto's spaces. It is the more inclusive approach of Vergani's two, and, for the purposes of this particular analysis, moves in the direction of sensory modulation, by engaging time and the process of experience.

Earlier research, undertaken in the sixties, enables further exploration of the existence of musical spaces. The German scientist Fritz Winckel was exploring the hearing process as "a perception through the senses, which is subject to a complicated psycho-acoustical transformation occurring before the real psychological area of perception is reached." (Winckel, 1967) In his introduction Winckel states that, "In the field of music theory and musicology both simple and compound sound are treated as concrete building material having differing valences. (A valance being the a unit of combining or replacing power of an atom) In this way a function is ascribed to each building block with respect to the others, whereby a distinctive architecture is formed, possessing a singular tonal character. Music, however, is a multiform complex function of sound series, only certain aspects of which have been known to us up to this time.

As Sibelius is acknowledged to have explored a 'new sound world', it is reasonable to credit him with offering a new acoustic experience, and an auditory glimpse of what Winckel calls the 'multiform complex function of sound' which was unknown to that point, and which has not been explored in relation to his music since. Exploration of the relationship between this field of music and architecture has, up to recently concentrated largely on acoustics, and on the musical works and the Methods of Webern and Schöenburg, ignoring Sibelius' inimitable music.

Winckel too explored the space relationships in music, through the information implicit in the tonal body (pitch and tone colour, dynamics and the development of these in time). Yet, as John Whitney, in his book Digital Harmony explains, "The ear resides at the centre of a spherical domain. We hear from all around. We hear music as patterns of ups and downs, to and fro in a distinctly three-dimensional architectonic space — a space within." (Whitney, 1980)

In music the listener senses the flow of the whole. The flow, because, as Winckel believed, the link in the chain of hearing, between the outer ear and the cortex, provides a reciprocal relationship between place and time, enlivening the fourth dimension. Music, though experienced in a static position by the listener, is itself a dynamic phenomenon, intrinsically related to the unfolding of time. Winckel believed. In an acoustic perception, space and time. . . play complementary roles. . . there is no difference.

At any one moment a section, or splice, taken vertically through a score of music, is perceived as a synthesised whole. The quality of the whole is spatial. Its form is a unique synthesis of the composer's imaginative composition of the various musical elements of theme, or in Sibelius' case germ motifs, tone rhythm etc. During the course of a musical audition, the vertical line (for the free movement of variation of pitch) and the horizontal line (the degree of extension of time) are never at a standstill. As soon as this concept is placed in relation to the listener, another dimension becomes evident: Time. Winckel verifies this by saying, "The whole is a gestalt in the sense of Gestalt psychology; it is perceived instantaneously, independent of time, just as thought."

The process of unfolding music, is therefore a process of the synthesis of millions of such whole spaces.

If it were possible to place an elevation or cross-section of a spatial element experienced within an Aalto building adjacent to a cross-section of a musical moment within a Sibelian sound, the spatial correlation between Sibelius' music and Aalto's architecture could be elucidated. It is however possible to abstract the two-dimensional score into graphic form and place it adjacent to a building section, to encounter something of the spatial synthesis. This exploration introduces the idea of vertical syntax in which Sibelius and Aalto discover the freedom to stack. There is little homogeneous vertical structure in their work.

It is clear that the coherence of Sibelius' music does not emerge from the linear tonal direction, but rather from a synthesis of the horizontal and vertical disposition of motifs, drawn from the principle melody, and reassembled in continually changing orders and textures.

5.5. Synesthesia

This exploration of our sound system illustrates how our sensory perception is rooted in the physiological synthesis, or the cross fertilisation, of our senses. In his book *The Unity of the Senses*, Lawrence E. Marks explores the concept of unity among the arts is supported by a parallel theory of unity of the senses proposed by Aristotle. (Marks, 1978) This was known as the 'sensus communis, ' in which the activity of all the senses was integrated into one higher level mechanism (what Sibelius referred to as the reality not appreciable by the senses). This doctrine led to the development of the psychological phenomenon of synesthesia, which investigates the involuntary transposition of sensory images from one modality to another. This Hellenic understanding further verifies the potential for a synthesis of inter-artistic sensory experiences. Incidentally, it is no accident that one discovers that a Hellenic concept assists in an understanding of the synthesis between Aalto and Sibelius, since they were both stimulated by the Ancients holistic view.

In his book Marks highlights, "The universal synesthetic capacity to appreciate the closeness and richness of similarities among visual, auditory, and other sensory qualities, a capacity that is strongly aroused in particular by powerful sensory-aesthetic experiences."

It is logical to find oneself perceiving a synthesis of sensory stimulation from different idioms of music and architecture, (a sense of déjà vu), if what inspired the form and content of Sibelius' musical space is the same, as that which stimulated the Aalto's spatial creativity. Nature's growth process.

5.6. The Profound Logic

Sibelius said, "Music. . . is brought to life by means of the logos, the divine in art." He believed this phenomenon of the divine in art, brought analysis and synthesis into harmony, with the "profound logic that created an inner connection between all the motives". This stimulated Sibelius "to allow the musical thoughts and their development in (his) spirit, determine the form of (his) music". Gerald Abraham believed that the organic unity of Sibelius' music stimulated by Nature's growth process is far in advance of the music of classical Vienna, "the general architecture is held together in a way that had classical precedents but had never before been so fully developed." (Abraham, 1949)

Sibelius believed that it is, "that wonderful logic (let us call it God) which governs a work of art, that is the important thing." In Sibelius, the Hellenic scholar was closely linked with the creative musician. Julian Herbage has written that,

> Like the Greeks of antiquity, (Sibelius') closest companion was Nature. It was Nature and the forces of Nature which had shaped the poetry of Finland. . . Throughout his music one is conscious of this direct contact between Man and Nature. (Herbage, 1949)

Sibelius' mastery of symphonic logic was a means to the end of explorative musical poetry. The relationship between the logical and the poetic is a symbiotic one. The process of exploration of his art, what Aalto called 'experimentation', was a gestalt means of exploring and expressing deep personal issues of doubt and concern. Both artists had experienced the profound logic of nature as children, and followed this creative pattern in their own creativity. I believe that having both lost a parent in their childhood both men would have known, from experience of the Nature in which they had surrounded themselves, that there was something vital and real which continued to nurture them through their creativity as adults.

"We have admitted, and probably agree, that objects which can, with justification, be called 'rational' often suffer from a considerable lack of humanity." (Aalto, 1935) Aalto, too, was a passionate adherent of ancient Greek cosmology in an age thirsty for technology. His writings "Rationalism and Man" (1935) and "The Humanising of Architecture" (1940), explore how technology can, and must, be subordinate to humanistic ideas and enable Man's harmonious interaction with Nature. Aalto knew that this was to be a vital ingredient and setting for a whole and balanced experience of life. "Truly functional Architecture must be functional primarily from the human point of view" (Aalto, 1940)

Göran Schildt draws attention to a key to much of Aalto's form.

> If we go on to note that the stair motif merges in form with the (classical theatre) we see that we have arrived at the nuclei of Aalto's architecture. We have every reason to see something more in Aalto's

stairways than the mere ways of getting from one level to another. They are symbols of man's correct relationship with Nature; they are the most genuine expression of practical humanism. (Schildt, 1984)

What may appear to be irrational form in strict Euclidian terms can be quite the most rational solution because of the nature of, for example, the inspiration, the motifs, the site, or a desire to root something of the human experience in the biological growth of other species.

The profound logic which Sibelius and Aalto used is not what might be considered to be Man's logic. They had adopted a different set of principles.

5.7. Organic, Living Art

Aalto's research "into the health needs of the individual right up to the frontiers of psychology and beyond" (Aalto, 1935), illustrates that, "Architecture is not merely finished buildings, but rather a variegated process of development that, thanks to the internal reciprocal action, constantly leads to new solutions." (Aalto, 1938)

It is clear that for Aalto, the process of creating architecture, was closely related to the process for which it was created: the process of living, moving and interacting. The architecture evokes an immediate response in the user, as if he is drawn into the process of the building.

"Architecture should always offer a means whereby the organic connection between a building and Nature (including man and human life as an element of greater importance than others) is catered for." (Aalto, 1941)

The reality, or one could say the themes, with which Aalto and Sibelius are concerned, draw the user or the listener through the process of a specific experience of the music or form, and through this to broader fields of existence. Aalto said that the built milieu needs "to meet psychology's demands for continuous renewal and growth." Here too we can see why openness to truly organic art requires the audience or user to participate in the unfolding creation. Truly organic art, such as Sibelius' *Tapiola* and Aalto's *Baker House Dormitory* is a process of creation. It is, and continues (as it is experienced) to be as relevant to spiritual and psychological growth, as to the physical growth, with which it is usually correlated, since the growth process has universal application.

Nature is a state of 'becoming', in which the creation comes into 'being'. Participation in the process is called Life. Nature's tendency for growth, enriching and healing (as Aalto saw it), is obvious. This growth is a phenomena of process, which requires time. The mature works of Aalto and Sibelius create a micro-environment into which the user, or listener, is drawn, and in which they give time to the growing and changing reality of the music or building. However unsettling the experience, if the listener or user is open, she may experience the life boat of patterning and organic procedures inherent in the form and content of Sibelius' and Aalto's creations.

The richness of Aalto and Sibelius' work, lies in their ability to draw the participant, who comes in contact with the work, in one dimension, (for example the physical succour of shelter or gentle musing), surreptitiously, deeper into themselves and life.

Intrinsic simultaneity of the biological, psychological and spiritual dimensions of creativity, draw the attention of the user's unconscious, and stimulate the inner movement or growth. Experience shows that users' psycho-social sensitivity key into dimensions of the secret life of Aalto's buildings, beyond mere ergonomic functioning.

The growth of the mind's arena and the expansion of life that comes from it, is based, Aalto believed, on both "knowledge and analyses stored in our subconscious." (1947) This is intrinsic to the creative work of Sibelius and Aalto.

In recognising, and working from the simile between the standardisation of the machine and that in Nature, Aalto seemed to know (perhaps from his childhood experiences of the forest), that Nature's creative process had the key to all subsequent creative processes; recognition of the application of Nature's biological creation of Life, to the perennial physical, psychological and spiritual problem of keeping Life alive. His deep concern for humankind, and his sense of the universal need for exposure to creativity, be it in Nature or in the life of a building, was part of his understanding of the profound logic. At the time they were working, biology was concerned only with dissection, rather then the current exploration of the interaction of living organisms, eco-system analysis, and the tending towards interdependency. Now we have the insight into Quantum processes too, with which we can draw analogy between our deep Quantum Nature and our life experiences.

Sibelius seems not to have been able to grasp the significance and fecundity of his creativity in his own life, although he believed so vitally in the profound logic which joined his musical fragments, as Nature's creative process. The organic unity of *Tapiola* is complete. It is said that Sibelius could go no further with his journey to musical unity, without lapsing into complete silence. Perhaps if he had applied the profound logic to personal, as well as musical growth, he may have discovered a way of facing the desperate doubt of his suspended musical voids, by means of a process inherent in his own work: The correlation between biological, psychological and spiritual growth.

5.8. Harmony and Chaos

The harmony which most concerned Sibelius and Aalto was not conven-tional tonal, but cosmic and spiritual harmony. Indeed they were both drawn to a residual harmony of the Ancients. So the fact that the mature works of both Sibelius and Aalto have been widely described as a 'Uni-versal' is not suprising. This universality can be said to be a state of being where the overarching patterns of creation and existence become clear, and indeed themselves provide both the motivation and the form for creative exploration.

Their work has also been somewhat derogatorily judged to be illogical and chaotic. However Sibelius and Aalto compose a harmony of irregular forms, which come from an experience of Nature's processes within the mind and beyond, in the context of the Natural environment. There is a discipline in this Natural irregularity, which has been explored, and which can not, on close study, be said to be chaotic nor ad hoc.

The creative process of continual renewal and growth (Aalto) comprises an inherent self- motivation and propulsion to explore new sound or spatial worlds, which extrapolate Sibelius' inner experience of both order and chaos. During the writing of his *Fourth Symphony* Sibelius wrote, "Everything is in chaos. I come closer and closer to heaven. My heart is full of sadness and adoration for Nature."

Man has glibly mused that there may be order in chaos, to reassure, or, in a phrase, to dismiss the irregular, doubtful or chaotic features of his experience of life. There are clear ways in which the process of the creation of Sibelius' and Aalto's work, and the process of the creations' unfolding to the user and the listener, intuitively exposes the system of Nature which the new Chaos theory propounds.

"Self-criticism grows to impossible proportions". Sibelius and Aalto both experienced colossal depths of self-doubt which were manifest in different ways. This inner chaos motivated fragments of light, or insight, to "grow out of the mythical, primeval gloom", into ever-evolving creativity. In her book Rosa Newmarch describes how the "initial pages (of the *Seventh Symphony*) give the impression of entrance into a mysterious forest, intersected by numerous small paths which appear momentarily to lead nowhere" (Newmarch 1964). However, the music does not end there. These sometimes uncomfortable moments of stillness are only part of the whole process of the music.

> The oft-despised philosophy of doubt is an absolute necessity for anyone who would contribute to culture. This naturally calls for the transformation of doubt into a positive phenomenon, an unwillingness to 'drift with the current'. At a higher level doubt is transformed into its apparent antithesis, love with critical awareness. This is a love which endures, since it rests on the foundation of the critically proven. It can give rise to such love of little man that will stand guard whenever the mechanised forms of our time threaten to stifle individual and organically harmonious life.

Here again, Aalto describes Nature's creative process changing from the tangible, physical realm found only in animals, to the spiritual realm of human creation. It is the point at which one pushes through doubt and fear, to the edge of oneself, that one comes to a moment of paradox in which one either moves forward into the unknown, or one retreats to the safety of the familiar.

Aalto mused, that people wish to replace the knowledge of life's uncertainty with absolute certainty and some kind of truth. The English writer and broadcaster, Gerald Priestland, believes that in his sound of silence, the vastest of sound-space, Sibelius had found the essence of the symphony. Those suspended musical spaces demand a willingness to be alone with the universal questions and doubts. Being in and with creation, instead of living outside and despite it, becomes the central theme of Sibelius music in its fully integrated form and content. It was just this ascetic, uncompromising language which baffled audiences. His silences were pregnant with searching through "life, a hard struggle for existence". His work was concerned with the human psyche and inner state of being, but he never failed to apply the discipline of profound musical form. There is no doubt that Sibelius created an "entirely new sound world", just as Aalto created new spatial entities, neither of which found congruence with current stylistic trends. Aalto's use of what has been considered to be primitive, illogical, irregular form, was a challenge to those who believed that the right angle is the preference of advanced, civilised man. One might rightly ask how whole such civilisation is.

Sibelius and Aalto did not seek to overthrow past forms, but rather sought, often through uncertainty, to discover their roots anew, and forge ahead towards new ways in which what is worthy of the old might flourish.

6. Conclusion

Having established that Sibelius and Aalto shared motivation, sensory modulation and compositional structuring, it is necessary to realise that it is not the "successive contrasting of reiterated units" which is the important essence of their creativity, but rather, as Professor Salmenhaara has put it "the process which takes place within these units and which also transgresses their clear, or not so clear, boundaries."

"Dynamics freed at last from the shackles of order and predictability. . . systems liberated to randomly explore their every dynamical possibility. . . Exciting variety, richness of choice a cornucopia of opportunity" (Gleick 1989). If the phenomenon of dynamics is replaced by those of music and architecture, this quotation, celebrating the young Chaos theory, describes Sibelius' and Aalto's work, made inimitable by their determined translation of the process of 'continual renewal and growth' which they observed in Nature, into their own creative process.

Sibelius and Aalto had a genius for structure and form, and a quest for truth in their art. Through their condensed expression and cogent argument they made Nature's growth process manifest in the worlds of sound and form, in entirely new ways.

Their work has a quality of timelessness. The formal and sensory roots of their creativity are universal and Natural, yet sensitivity to these has been lost in virtually all western cultures. Through their Nature-rootedness, Sibelius and Aalto exemplify something essentially Finnish. Their art emerged into a world of the often iconoclastic New art, yet they consistently drew attention to the organic process without which they believed life was incomplete. Now their work can serve to remind Finland and the world of its roots, at a time when the world is recognising the cost of ignorance of the processes of Nature.

Sibelius' and Aalto's work has enshrined a vibrant sense of the potential of living contact with natural processes. The organic principle, which has been explored through the study of the correlation between the work of Sibelius and Aalto, ensures the change, growth and transformation which are an intimate part of life-processes.

References

Aalto, Alvar (1935). "Rationalism and Man, Swedish Craft Association", *Alvar Aalto Sketches*, Schildt (ed.). Cambridge: MIT Press, 1985.
– (1938). "The Influence of Construction and Materials on Modern Architecture", *Alvar Aalto Sketches*, Schildt (ed.). Cambridge: MIT Press, 1985.

- (1940). "The Humanising of Architecture", *Technology Review*, MIT Press.
- (1941). "The Reconstruction of Europe", *Arkkitehti*, vol. 5.
- (1947). "The Trout and the Mountain Stream", *Alvar Aalto Sketches*, Schildt (ed.). Cambridge: MIT Press, 1985.
- (1953). "Experimental House, Muuratsalo", *Arkkitehti-Arkitekten*.
- (1959). "Art and Technology", *Domus* 2.
Abraham, Gerald (1949). *A Hundred Years of Music*. London: Duckworth.
David, Avram, (1968). "Thoughts on Spacio-Acoustic Analysis", *Connection*. Harvard: Summer 1968.
Giedion, Sigfried (1950). "Alvar Aalto", *Architectural Review* 2.
Gleick, James (1989). *Chaos*. London: Cardinal.
Gray, Cecil (1931). *Sibelius*. London.
Herbage, Julian (1949). "Sibelius", *The Symphony*. Ralph Hill (ed.). London: Penguin.
Kandinsky, Vasily (1914). *Concerning the Spiritual in Art*. Republished New York: Dover 1977.
Layton, Robert (1970). *Sibelius and his World*. London: Thames and Hudson.
Marks, Lawrence E. (1978). *The Unity of the Senses*. New York: Academic Press
Newmarch, Rosa (1964). *Sibelius*. London: Goodwin and Tabb.
Pallasmaa, Juhani (1987). "Metsäarkkitehtuuri", *Silva Fennica* 21(4). Helsinki.
Pietarinen, Juhani (1987). "Ihminen ja metsä", *Silva Fennica* 21(4). Helsinki.
Pike, Lional (1978). *Beethoven, Sibelius and the 'Profound Logic'*. London: Athlone.
Salmenhaara, Erkki (1970). *Tapiola: The tone poem as representative of Sibelius' late music*. (English summary.) Acta Musicologia Fennica 4. Helsinki.
Schildt, Göran (1984). *Alvar Aalto, The Early Years*. New York: Rizzoli.
- (1991). *Alvar Aalto, The Mature Years*. New York: Rizzoli.
Vergani, Gianmarco (1987). "Questions of Unification and Musicalisation in Art", *Precis*, spring 1987.
Whitney, John (1980). *Digital Harmony*. New York.
Winckel, Fritz (1967). *Music Sound and Sensation*. New York: Dover

VOCAL MUSIC

The analysis of a holy song

WILLEM MARIE SPEELMAN

On this holy day we start with a most unholy analysis of a holy song.[1] However, what is holy? How is it that we speak of holy days and holy songs and even holy people. Carl Jung is rumored to have said: "I have met a man, so remarkable that I thought he was holy, . . . until I met his wife in psychoanalysis." But the fact remains that there are days, people, and songs we call holy. They have a certain aspect or aura which leads us to attach the word holy to them. This aura must have something to do with the content of these holy people, days, and songs. I believe that it is Heaven that makes ordinary people, days and songs *holy*, but I *know* that it is Earth that gives form to holiness. And this giving form to a holy Sense by human beings can be analyzed without fear of blasphemy.

Introduction

Recently I have become a member of a group of theologians, called SEMANET, which stands for "SEMiotic Analysis by NEtherlandisch Theologians". For some years this group has been involved in a research program, which has reference to the semiotics of Greimas and his Paris School, in relation to Christian forms of utterance. SEMANET has analyzed parts of the Scripture, parts (mostly texts) of the liturgy and sacraments. The question is always *how is meaning generated in this particular utterance*? And when you ask the question how meaning is generated, the question of *what meaning is being generated* is also touched. In plain English: *how does it say what it says*? Now this approach is very much like reading. When you read a book your eyes are constantly asking *what is being said and how is it being said*. Actually, the only difference between our practice of analysis and normal reading practice is that we read very slowly. The advantage of doing things slowly is that it fills your life with joy. But there is also another advantage, namely that you can communicate in an intelligent and responsible way about the discourse that is being analyzed. In this way the Greimassian semiotic approach can bring scientists together, can make them actually communicate with one another.

What is a syncretic object?

The Greimassian approach makes it possible, not only to gather scientists of different disciplines, but also to relate different manifestation-languages. And that possibility is very important when you want to analyze liturgy. Liturgy is constituted of different manifestation-languages, so, when you analyze a liturgy, you have to analyze music, text, architecture, vestments, icons, et cetera, and finally relate them to one another. To analyze different manifestation-languages in relation to one another is to approach liturgy as a syncretic object (*sun-krinein* — bringing together)[2]. In my project I confine myself to liturgical songs. But a song is in itself also a syncretic object, that is, it consists of two different manifestation-languages which are mutually related, namely music and text. There are several opinions about the relation between music and text in song. Some people say that every song is music without words, that is, the words of a song are swallowed by the music. This is the case when a sixteen year old girl, who suddenly becomes aware of the meaning of a song she has been singing for years, cries out: "Gee, this is a *dirty* song!" Another opinion is that in a song the music does not really matter, a song is its text. I bet that when you read an article on liturgical song, you will not find *one* musical note in it. Here the music is swallowed by the text. Neither of these two opinions is true of course. I myself hold that, to put it very neatly, a song does not consist of two separate manifestation- languages, but that a song is the com-position, the togetherness, the syncretic relationship that two manifestation-languages hold mutually.

How can I describe this relationship which is the song?

Influenced by Ferdinand de Saussure and Louis Hjelmslev, Algirdas Julien Greimas made the following distinctions in the analysis of the sign (Figure 1).

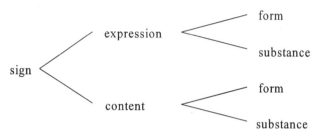

Figure 1.

All semiotic manifestation-languages are to be analyzed in this way. I confine myself to music and text. When we look for the relationships between music and text in song, we find the following terms:

musical expression form
musical content form
musical expression substance
musical content substance
linguistic expression form
linguistic content form
linguistic expression substance
linguistic content substance

Only that which is form can be analyzed (or read, or perceived). We cannot analyze the substance unless it is formed. Therefore I will confine myself to the form. In Figure 2 the field of analysis is represented (by the way, this is not a semiotic square).

There are theoretically six possible relationships between these four terms, but I confine myself to four: the relationships between the forms of musical expression and musical content, the forms of linguistic expression and linguistic content, the musical and linguistic expressions, and the musical and linguistic contents.

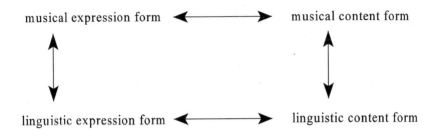

Figure 2.

I will try to make the four terms imaginable. The form of linguistic expression is when you hear a Dutchman speak without understanding his words, while nevertheless hearing some kind of organization in the sound stream: "wat u mij nu hoort spreken is voor u volkomen onverstaanbaar, terwijl de fonemen toch hoorbaar georganiseerd zijn." The form of linguistic content is the specific organization of what is meant in a given language. Take for example a color continuum between blue and green. Now I can have an argument with you about a specific color, which I call green and you call blue. It is one and the same color, so we do not have an argument about the color itself. But we have organized the color continuum in a different way, so it is an argument about different forms of linguistic content. The form of musical expression is what you hear when you hear an Eskimo woman sing. In one way or another you can hear that she is singing, but you do not understand the music. Maybe she sings out her sorrow, I only hear a specific sound organization. The form of musical content is the specific organization of Sense in the musical manifestation-language. Another Eskimo will understand the song of the woman and tell me that she is sad; whereupon I reply, "How can she be sad, she is singing beautifully?"

How am I going to analyze?

Greimas constructed a generative trajectory for the form of linguistic content. The underlying thought is that meaning is a product of a generation process, and the generation of meaning follows a trajectory. In French the terms are *parcours* and *discours*. The process of generation of a specific meaning is called a *discours*, but the system in which this generation process takes place is called a *parcours*. Take a student's curriculum. You follow a certain route to become a PhD. Everyone who is a PhD has followed structurally the same route, but it is also true that every PhD has realized this route in a different way. That is why there are Doctors of Theology and Doctors of Music. That is why there are Doctors who think they are Greimas and Doctors who think they are Peirce. Every *discours* is a generation of a unique meaning, but the structure according to which these unique meanings are generated is the same. There is only one structure and that structure is called the generative trajectory.

This trajectory consists of three levels and two components. The levels (which are in fact levels of abstraction) are called deep level (the most abstract level), surface level, and discursive level (the most concrete level). All these levels can be divided in two components: the syntactic component and the semantic component (Figure 3).

(manifestation level)		
	syntactic component	semantic component
discoursive structures	discoursive syntax	discoursive semantics
surface level	narrative syntax	narrative semantics
deep level	fundamental syntax	fundamental semantics

Figure 3.

We can follow the generation of meaning in a specific discourse by going from the deep level via the surface level to the discoursive level. But in analysis we go the other way round: from the discoursive level to the deep level.

Greimas constructed this generative trajectory which gives the route by which all meaning is generated in all manifestation-languages. But actually he only constructed the trajectory for the form of linguistic content. This means that, when I want to interrelate all the terms that constitute a song, I have to apply this generative trajectory to the form of linguistic expression, the form of musical expression, and the form of musical content. I hope that I have made clear that this generative trajectory has only one structure for all the manifestation languages. But I think this is also true for both the forms of the sign function, namely the form of expression and the form of content. So, there is one and only one generative trajectory for all the manifestation languages and for both the form of expression and the form of content. Now I can work! Now I can apply the given generative trajectory for the musical expression form, the musical content form, and the form of linguistic expression.

What are the results?

So far I have only made operational the generative trajectory to the forms of musical expression and musical content.[3] I started with the plane of musical expression. The substance of musical expression is Sound. We cannot analyze Sound, unless it has been given form. Take for example the environmental sounds in a work of John Cage called *4´33´´*. This piece has three movements, and every movement has a specific duration, the total of which is four minutes and thirty-three seconds. In these three movements the musicians are prescribed to remain silent. In performance, however, you will hear sounds, environmental sounds. These environmental sounds themselves are not musical sounds and thus cannot be analyzed as music. But then John Cage has given them form through the organization in musical time: he gave durations to the environmental sounds. The only thing we can analyze is thus the duration of the piece. The rest is, musically speaking, silence. And that is why *4´33´´* is called the silent piece. Of course there are sounds, but they are not musical sounds, only musical durations, durations of silence.

Let us leave the piece of Cage, and try to describe the path which goes from the Sound substance to a musical work. The first step on this path is to make Sound perceivable as musical sound. The first condition of the musical perception is that there are differences, so Sound has to be differentiated in musical ways. We know these categories as parameters: pitch, duration, loudness, and timbre.

(A) The musical categories differentiate Sound in the oppositions high/low, long/short, loud/soft, complex/simple. These are the musical phemes at the deep level. The next step towards a musical work is the differentiation of these categories in intervals. For example the opposition high/low will only be musically perceived when it is a relation. You do not perceive high as /high/ if you do not also perceive /low/. If you listen to a solo of an octave-flute, you will only hear high sounds. But when you listen to the melody, you will differentiate high-octave flute sounds from low-octave flute sounds. This relation is known as the interval, but I use the term interval for all musical categories (although I cannot imagine something like a coloristic interval). The interval is also a musical pheme when it is considered as an opposition large/small.

(B) At the surface level the musical phemes are actualized and realized as musical phonemes. That is, the oppositions become virtual in specific intervals, actualized in specific scales, and realized in specific curves. The pheme interval becomes a phoneme when it is specified as "a fifth" or "a major third". From specific intervals we go to scales. Scales are not constructed out of notes but out of intervals. From a specific scale we go to curves. Curves are not organizations of notes, but of interval relations (scales). We still do not hear a musical sound, because curves are abstractions: you cannot hear a melodic curve without also hearing loudness, duration, and timbre.

(C) In order to become perceivable we have to relate the curves of the different categories. Now we are at the discursive level, where the curves of the different categories are related to become musical figures of expression.[4] Now we hear something. For example, let us relate the curve in which the opposition high/low is realized in a descending major third; the curve in which the opposition many/few is realized in three to one; the curve in which the opposition short/long is realized in the eighth-note value to the whole-note value: and you get "Tatatataaaaaaam". Finally the composer has to do something with this figure, put the things in a specific syntactic order, and there you have a symphony.

Next, I postulated a musical content form. I used to hold that there is no such thing as musical content. Music, I thought, is only expression, and maybe not even that. But having left the concert hall several times with the tiresome feeling: "Nice notes, but the composer has nothing to say", I started to rethink my own dogma. And I think this is the most difficult matter of the project, because I can hardly imagine a thing like musical content. So I worked in an abstract theoretical way. In the combination of the given generative trajectory of the linguistic content form and the found generative trajectory of the musical expression form I tried to construct the generative trajectory of the form of musical content.

Let us follow the path again. The musical content substance is Sense. Musical sense differs from linguistic sense in that it is always formed by a musical content form. Remember that I said the same thing about Sound. Musical sound differs from linguistic sound in that it is always formed by a musical expression form. And musical sense differs from linguistic sense in that it is always formed by a form of musical content. Sense is made musical by the articulation of musical semes. Think of them as moods or concepts (like /integration/ or /loveliness/) and think of them in terms of tension oppositions. The generative trajectory of the musical content form runs a path along which musical semes are invested in tension relations, tension curves, figures and thematizations of content until their discoursivization in a specific discourse. Please, follow me again step by step.

(A) Sense is articulated at the deep level (of the content form) in musical semes: moods and concepts such as /musical love/ vs. /musical hatred/ or /musical community/ vs. /musical individuality/. Parallel to the intervals on the expression plane we can articulate tension relations on the content plane. It is very important to distinguish tension as measured by a physician from tension on the content plane. These last tension relations are based upon the musical moods or concepts; so it is a tension between /musical love/ vs. /musical hatred/. We can only understand something like /musical love/ if we also know /musical hatred/. Now, the tension between musical moods can be related (semi-symbolically) to the tension between interval relations, but they are not identical.

(B) At the surface level the tension relations become tension curves (parallel, but not identical to the categorial curves on the expression plane). Those curves of musical tension can be musical actants in a narrative program. Let me explain these last new words: actant and narrative program. Consider for example this little story: A woman expresses her love to a man by giving him a ring. The syntactic description of this little story is a narrative program. The narrative program of this story is that the seme /love/ is invested in the giving of the ring, and the woman realizes /love/ by giving the ring to the man. In this syntactical function /love/ is a seme (or value) and the woman, the man, and the ring are actants. As actants they are the terms of a syntactical function, namely subject of doing (woman), subject of state (man), and object of value (ring). Back to music.

If we take for example the first measure of Chopin's *Marche funèbre* we can interpret the metric curve (crotchet, dotted quaver, semi-quaver, half) as a musical actant in which a musical seme (/musical death/) is invested. This musical seme, invested in the metric curve, is realized by the conjunction of the metric actant with the melodic actant (B♭, B♭, B♭, B♭). This realization of the musical seme in the conjunction of two actants is in fact a step in the construction of a musical figure of content: the figure of death in the musical manifestation-language.

(C) When we talk about musical figures of content we are already at the next level, the discursive level. A figure of musical content is what we remember. It is what the composer Morton Feldman called an image, what Eero Tarasti calls an intonation, what Boris Asafiev called a memorandum. A friend of mine asked Feldman what he meant by an image. Feldman asked him, "What do you think when I say Anton Webern?" The interviewer replied by singing three notes. "That's an image", said Feldman. That is a figure of content. Another important term at this level is the thematization. When Greimas talks about thematization he does not mean the first or second theme in a sonata. The meaning of the term thematization is more like the thematicity of the musicologist Rudolph Réti: it is a thought underlying the structure. In his analysis of the Fifth Symphony of Beethoven, Réti calls the motive Ta-ta-ta-taaaam "Thus knocks fate on the door", and analyzes what is happening with that figure of fate: it is being integrated into life. Well, in Greimassian terms that would be: the figure is ta-ta-ta-taaaam; the thematic is integration.

Finally the musical discourse comes into being by the syntactical organization of the actors, that is, of the figures that have an actantial role. This is called discoursivization. The difference between the discoursivization on the expression plane and the discoursivization on the content plane is like the difference between a form-scheme and a genre, the difference between ABA and a Lied.

How do I make this operational in a song?

In my analysis of the *Exsultet* (a shortened Dutch version called *Paasjubelzang in korte vorm*) I tried to apply the model mentioned above. (See Appendix 1.)

(A) I started with the form of musical expression on the level of discoursivization (see Appendix 2). The syntax of the discourse can be abstracted as in Figure 4.

A [123]	A [123]	x	A [123]
A [123]	A [123]	x	A [123]
A [123]	A [123]	x	A [123]
A [123]	A [123]	x	A [123]

Figure 4.

In the phonemic component of the discoursive level we find the figurative isotopy of the psalmodic arch structure, which can be found in every syntactic unit (A [123]); see Appendix 3. The thematic of the expression plane can be found when we abstract the trajectories of the figures themselves: the trajectory of figure 1, the trajectory of figure 2, and the trajectory of figure 3. We can formulate the thematic isotopy in the terms lowering and lengthening.

(B) In the syntactic component of the surface level we look at how the expression values are invested in the programs of the curves (in this case only the metric and diastematic curves can be analyzed). These values can be formulated in analyzing the variation of the curves: lowering, lengthening, and change of scale (larger intervals). Now we see that the two curves that constitute figure x are active in the programs of the curves that constitute figures 1, 2 and 3. See Appendix 4. Next we look at the diastematic scales constructed by the diastematic curves and the dominant notes therein. We see that the figurative isotopy of the psalmodic arch structure first constructs the scale g´-a´-b´-c´´-d´´, with a´ and c´´ as dominant notes; at the end of each couplet the psalmodic arch structure constructs the scale d´-e´-f´-g´-a´-c´´, with e´ and a´ as dominant notes.

In the phonemic component of the surface level we describe the nuclear phemes and the contextual phemes. The nuclear phemes are abstractions of the expression figures; the contextual phemes are the abstractions of the thematizations on the expression plane. The nuclear phemes of the psalmodic arch structure can be described in the oppositions /low/ vs. /high/, /change/ vs. /repetition/. The contextual phemes invested in the variation of the psalmodic arch structure can be described in the oppositions /high/ vs. /low/, /short/ vs. /long/; the contextual phemes of the intervals in /small/ vs. /large/ and /few/ vs. /many/.

(C) The deep structure of the form of musical expression in this discourse can be drawn by putting the contextual phemes into a semiotic square, as done in Figure 5.

Having analyzed the form of musical expression in the *Exsultet* I move towards its form of musical content.

(A) In the syntactic component of the discursive level we look for the actors. An actor is a combination of a thematic and an actantial role. In our discourse, figures 1, 2, 3, and x have a thematic and actantial role and are thus also actors. This means that on the content plane we can describe the discoursivization parallel to the discoursivization on the expression plane (Figure 6).

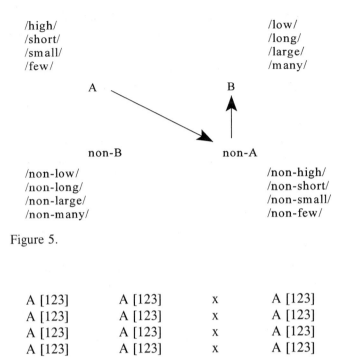

/high/   /low/
/short/   /long/
/small/   /large/
/few/   /many/

A   B

non-B   non-A

/non-low/   /non-high/
/non-long/   /non-short/
/non-large/   /non-small/
/non-many/   /non-few/

Figure 5.

A [123]	A [123]	x	A [123]
A [123]	A [123]	x	A [123]
A [123]	A [123]	x	A [123]
A [123]	A [123]	x	A [123]

Figure 6.

In the semantic component of the discoursive level we describe the
figures by substituting them for linguistic figures. The figurative isotopy
of the psalmodic arch structure can be described as "a sacred platform",
or "speaking in an exalted tone", and figure x is on the content plane a
figuration of "descending". So, on the content plane we can read in the
music a figurative isotopy of a sacred platform coming down. When we
look for the thematization on the content plane we interpret this figurati-
vization: what is said about this sacred platform descending? The lowering on the expression plane can be understood as a movement from
heaven to earth. But when we look deeper we can see that the pitch scale
in the first two arch structures is not yet realized and only becomes
realized in the third arch structure. So, the realization of the pitch scale

goes from partly realized towards fully realized. And when we give the thematization of lengthening a second look, we see that the first two arch structures are carried by quarter notes, while the third arch structure is carried by an alternation of quarter notes and half notes. This can be interpreted as an articulation of time by the differentiation of durations. In the same way the differentiation of intervals at the end of the couplet can be interpreted as an articulation of space. What actually happens in the musical discourse under examination is that a message, sung in an exalted tone, is coming down from heaven to earth and becomes articulated in time and space: becomes realized in the world we are living in, is a becoming.

(B) In the syntactic component of the surface level I analyzed the utterance of state as the actualization of the value /heightened position/ in the tenor c´´ as actant-object, and its realization in the conjunction of the tenor c´´ with the arch structure as actant-subject. The utterance of doing is described in the formula:

$$F (Sd) \Rightarrow [(O1 \wedge S \vee O2v) \rightarrow (O1 \wedge S \vee O2v)]$$

F = function
Sd = subject of doing, the diastematic actant of figure x
S = subject of state, the actant of the arch structure
O1 = object, the actant of the tenor c´´
O2 = object, the actant of the tenor a´
v = value, lowering of the heightened position

In the semantic component of the surface level we formulate the nuclear and contextual semes. /Heightened position/ is a nuclear seme invested in the arch structure; /coming down/ is a nuclear seme invested in figure x. As contextual seme I formulated /heavenly promise/ vs. /worldly realization/.

(C) Again, the contextual semes form the terms on the semiotic square, which is framed in the figurative isotopy of the sacred platform coming down (Figure 7).

Relation between the musical expression form and content form

Let me finally answer my first question, "How is holiness given form in a song?" When we compare the semiotic square on the expression plane and the semiotic square on the content plane we see a parallel; that is, the relations on the expression plane are related to the relations on the content plane. In semiotic terms, there is a semi-symbolical relation between
the form of musical expression and the form of musical content. The differentiation of the musical categories on the expression plane is related

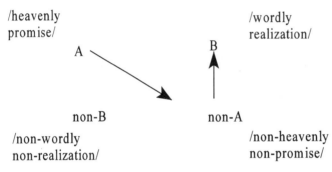

Figure 7.

semi-symbolically to the becoming of a promise on the content plane. A promise is given and the music has given form to that promise. Now that is what we call holy: to the world a promise is given and this promise is given form so that it can be fore-tasted, fore-felt, known already. The form as a foretaste of the promise is what we call a holy form. That is why the *Exsultet* is a holy song.

Notes

1. This lecture was held on a Sunday morning at Imatra in September, 1991.
2. Another etymology connects the world with sun — *crescĕre*, which means 'growing together'.

3. In the meantime I have finished a book called *The Generation of Meaning in Liturgical Songs* (Kok: Kampen, 1995), in which five liturgical songs have been analyzed in their musical *and* literary expression and content forms.

4. I am afraid this thought needs to be readjusted, because in the analysis I will find a psalmodic arch structure as expression figure. But the psalmodic arch structure is in fact a diastematic curve. So, a curve can also be an expression figure. My mistake is probably that I too easily identified the terms of musical organization (for example "curve") with the terms of the generative trajectory (for example "actant"). The term "figure" can be used for anything that bears a phonemic value, whether that is an interval, a scale, a curve, a motto, or a form scheme. Bearing a phonemic value it is concretely perceivable.

Appendix 1. The discourse.

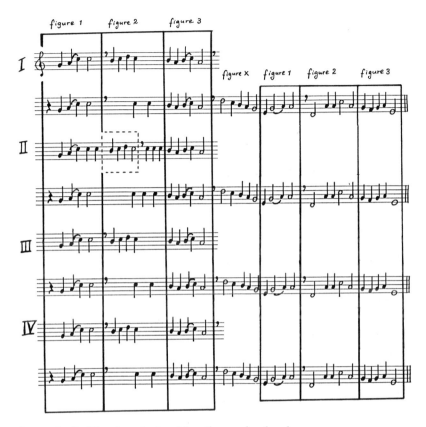

Appendix 2. Visual analysis of the discoursive level.

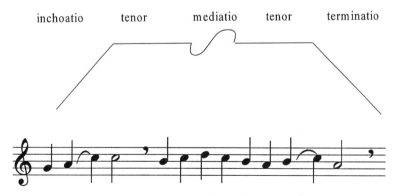

Appendix 3. The figurative isotopy of the psalmodic arch structure.

Figure 1.

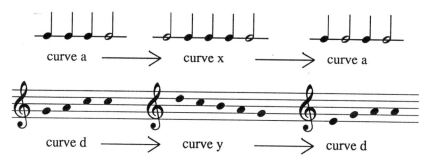

Figure 2.

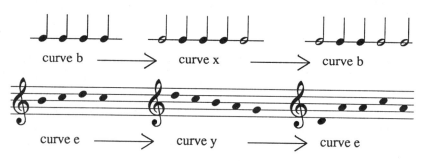

Figure 3.

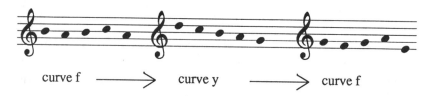

Appendix 4. "Narrative" programs of the curves on the expression plane.

Opera Translation: Charles Peirce Translating Richard Wagner

DINDA L. GORLÉE

The manifold sins committed against the word-music synthesis, the trials and tribulations suffered by opera translators skilled in language yet ignorant of music, and the resulting tongue twisters facing opera singers (whether singing in their native language or in a foreign language) have been the target of bitter criticism, and indeed ridicule, by Richard Wagner (1813–1883), the greatest musico-dramatic genius of his time. Wagner not only composed romantic, monumental operas; he was also deeply concerned with their textual components and, in contrast to composers (such as Vivaldi) who took a more nonchalant position on this, he also wrote the libretti, aiming at a harmonious unity between all the components of his operatic *Gesamtwerk*. These and related ideas were not only close to Wagner's heart as an opera "practician" (so to speak): they also revolved in his mind when he composed much of his theoretical work.

Wagner developed his ideas on the theory of opera, which were to revolutionize the history of opera, during the years he had to spend abroad (first in Zurich, then in Paris), following the 1849 revolts in Dresden. While living in political exile, and free from his former duties as a Royal Saxon *Hoffkapellmeister*, Wagner wrote a number of theoretical works: *Die Kunst und die Revolution*, *Das Kunstwerk der Zukunft*, and *Oper und Drama*[1]. *Oper und Drama* (Wagner 1984), written in 1851 and first published in 1852, offers the contours of Wagner's *Gesamtwerk* and elaborates on its central feature, the nature and union of music and words. It is commonly, yet not generally[2], considered to be Wagner's main essay, the theoretical counterpart of the tetralogy from his mature period, *Der Ring des Nibelungen*[3].

Curiously, perhaps, for a composer, Wagner was a self-declared non-musicocentrist, at least in his mature view as reflected in *Oper und Drama*. For Wagner, the goal of the operatic performance is not, as in the traditional view, the music. Yet neither should Wagner be considered an adherent to logocentrism. The music is for him not the message but the medium, or rather one of the media acting in combination. This is one reason why Wagner's music is, in and for itself, often rather trivial and even banal[4]. While the meaning-potentialities of the poetic words in themselves rank above those of the music, the music-drama is, according to Wagner, above all drama, in the etymological sense of *action*: dramatic action. Through this dramatic action, music and words together are instrumental in achieving their specific goal and mission: the artistic synthesis in which the music, with its special ability to express what, in Wittgenstein's words (1988: 3), "we cannot talk about"[5], is called upon to develop the poetic intent of the words into melody and harmony, in interaction with text, gesture, and stage action. The *Gesamtkunstwerk* is in this sense the perfect drama — Wagner's *das vollendete Drama* (1984: 308) — as it unfolds itself, serially and structurally, on stage and in the orchestra, as a massive and polysensuous symphonic poem[6]. In Ostwald's words,

> The music-dramas of Richard Wagner played upon the primitive association between sound and magic. For example, the power of a sword was symbolized by a musical theme whose sounding invariably reminded the listener of the inanimate object and myths associated with it. Incoherent words, in the mouths of fantastically disguised stage apparitions, transcended specific meanings, thus further charging the emotional tension produced by dramatic harmonies, vivid orchestration, and theatrical hocus-pocus. (1973: 25)

In his aesthetic endeavor, Wagner's *Leitmotive* have become, in tandem with his device of the *unendliche Melodie*, the trademark of his art. *Leitmotive* are short, flexible orchestral themes marked by their high concentration of emotion associated with a person, a situation, a mood, or an idea. Concerted with words equally expressing condensed feeling, they were transformed into powerful musical phrases, which, once introduced, were repeated many times, and modified by modulation and interpretation ("further developed" in Peirce's semiotic terminology) to explore the full meaning-potential of the poetic-melodic-harmonic universe in all its mythical proportions and depth. Wagner frequently used these recurrent melodic symbols, in particular in his *Ring* dramas[7]. At times the motifs are interwoven into extended themes, thereby leading to an "unending melody" such as the love music of *Tristan und Isolde*. Consequently, the discrete and the continuous can no longer be neatly delimited in the Wagnerian discourse, which is marked by intertextuality as well as intermediality. The systematic use of the above-mentioned musico-dramatic devices, with their (in Peirce's semiotic jargon) iconic-indexical overtones, serves to blur the boundaries between what is the whole and what a fragment, thereby generating the continuous flow of music, that is typical of Wagner's melos.

From the above it should be obvious that Wagner's *Gesamtkunstwerk* can only hold the audience's attention, let alone have on it the "almost hypnotic impact" (Tarasti 1994: 149) to which it owes much of its mystique and popular acclaim, if the overall text (that is, the key words, the storyline) can be grasped and understood:

> . . . *was hat eigentlich ein Engländer in der Covent Garden Opera, ein Italiener in der Mailänder Scala von Wagner's "unendlicher Melodie" und ihrem Sinn verstanden, wenn er, ohne den psychologischen (oft tiefenpsychologischen) Kongruenzen oder Spannungen von Gesang und orchestralen Leitmotiven folgen zu können, fünf Stunden lang auf die Bühne der "Götterdämmerung" starrt?* (Honolka 1978: 10)

This implies that, except for a native, German-speaking audience, translated lyrics play a crucial role in correctly understanding Wagner's operas in performance. In *Oper und Drama* (Wagner 1984: 385 note) Wagner himself underscored that the audience should be able to enjoy the musical drama easily and unintellectually: unencumbered, that is, by lack of special knowledge — including knowledge of foreign languages. In comparison with the Italian language, rich in vowels, the notion of singability has relative value in German libretti, thereby relieving to some extent the translator's burden. Yet Wagner added a number of particular constraints upon the translation of his music-dramas. Not only do his lyrics have a distinct poetic value, in contradistinction to many other libretti in Italian, French, German, or other language; also, particularly in *Oper und Drama*, Wagner expounded at length on the role in poetic verse of rhythmicity, melodic flow, and rhyme. Since these and related ideas must necessarily be reflected in any translated singing version of his opera libretti, they deserve to be briefly described here.

As librettist as well as composer, Wagner imposed upon himself a triple role. Twice utterer and once interpreter, he embodies the sender of the primary, verbal message, its privileged addressee, and the sender of the secondary, musico-verbal message[8]. As writer of the lyrics and composer of their intersemiotic translation[9] into music, the opera in its finished form, Wagner is a dual agent; and as interpreter of his own primary sign, he is a (relative) patient. The sign-manipulative status through which Wagner monopolized the whole composing process, is reminiscent of what I have elsewhere described and analyzed as the (rather problematic) role of the translator in the process of translation (Gorlée 1994: 188-194). Logically and methodologically, my argument was built on Peirce's doctrine of signs. "[T]wo minds in communication are, insofar, 'at one', that is, are properly one mind in that part of them" (*MS* 283: 107), Peirce wrote; and "In the Sign they are, so to speak, *welded*" (*CP*: 4.551). Wagner's own theoretical position on this issue, as expounded in *Oper und Drama*, seems to confirm my argument. As joint sign makers, Wagner, the poet, and Wagner, the musician, have chosen to act in unison, in a creative continuum. Therefore both "halves" should not be viewed separately. Unsurprisingly, therefore, Wagner's sexual metaphor of the *Liebesbund* between his two *personae*, sounds remarkably Peircean. In it, Wagner characterized the cooperative action between poet and musician as a labor of passionate love, in which

> . . . *der Musiker zum notwendigen Gebärer des Empfangenen würde; denn sein Anteil an dem Empfängnisse ist der Trieb, mit warmem, vollem Herzen das Empfangene wieder mitzuteilen. An diesem, in einem anderen erregten Triebe würde der Dichter selbst eine immer steigende Wärme für sein Erzeugnis gewinnen, die ihn zur mittätigsten Teilnahme auch an der Geburt selbst bestimmen müßte. Gerade die Doppeltätigkeit der Liebe müßte eine nach jeder Seite hin unendlich anregende, fördernde und ermöglichende künstlerische Kraft äußern.*
> (Wagner 1984: 370)[10]

In *Oper und Drama,* Wagner advanced strong and revolutionary views on topics such as prosody and rhyme: views which he put into full practice in his music dramas from his middle period on. He was scornful of the conventional iambic verse with end-rhyme and four or five accents on each line. Instead of such "antiquarianism" he advocated and used in his libretti (particularly from *Lohengrin* onwards[11]) a novel poetic language which was, paradoxically, at the same time both free and forced to a great extreme. All this was, rather intuitively, argued by him in the name of German language and historical linguistics.

Wagner's verse is free because he abandoned traditional verse forms, metric norms, and rhyme patterns, which in his view represented and overemphasized reason and logical thought, to the exclusion of emotion and feeling — which were what poetic verse should be about. However, Wagner's defense of what may be assimilated, within semiotics, to free, spontaneous, and poetic Firstness, together with his critique of conventionalism (i.e., rule-bound Thirdness), which was overly prosaic to his free poetic mind, are more apparent than real, because Wagner forced the German language back to the musical qualities of its monosyllabic roots which, still in his intuitive view, distinguish the German language from other languages used in operatic verse (here, Wagner made particular mention of Italian and French). Unhampered by knowledge of linguistics in the modern sense, Wagner, the romantic, positively stated (1984: 373) that the accent in German words (which more often than not are polysyllabic, with several unstressed syllables) is on the root syllable, which is also the semantically pregnant part, because in the root, the *tönende Laut* (Wagner 1984: 278) lie the music and the feeling. In this way, Wagner argued, the emotional content of the German word typically exemplifies the *Gefühlswerdung des Verstandes* (Wagner 1984: 215), the harmonic whole uniting cognitive and emotional meaning. In the creation of melodic poetry, the *Gefühlsverständnis der Sprache* (Wagner 1984: 371) was, to Wagner, an essential element.

The alleged superiority of the German language, which Wagner somehow intuited but was unable to convincingly explain, lay for him in its special expressivity, musicality, and rhythmicity. He took an equally controversial stance on rhyme, which deeply concerned him. He rejected standard end-rhyme; in its stead, he favored the so-called *Stabreim*

(Wagner 1984: 287ff. and *passim*), a typically Wagnerian technique consisting of alliteration (rhymed consonants) and assonance (rhymed vowels), occurring irregularly, in stressed syllables anywhere within the verse-line or adjacent verse-lines[12].

Wagner's *Stabreim* may be found in identity, similarity, or correspondence on the level of the signifier and/or the signified, and is always a matter of degree. We may distinguish various types: it is either based on iconicity, indexicality, or both; and it involves either denotative (referential) meaning, connotative (associative) meaning, or both. One exemplary instance given by Wagner (1984: 288) is *Auge und Ohr*, in which the limited consonance (the dual open vowel) suffices to produce rhyme, contributing to the related meaning of both words. Examples of alliteration also involving meaning are *Lust und Leid* and *Wohl und Weh*, which may again be combined with assonance: *Die Liebe bringt Lust und Leid* and/or *Die Liebe gibt Lust zum Leben*, and further complexified and enhanced in successive verse-lines such as *Die Liebe bringt Lust und Leid / doch in ihr Weh webt sie Wonnen* (Wagner 1984: 305f). Wagner's musical settings serve to further bring out the manifold "family resemblances" (in Wittgenstein's sense) within the word-music synthesis. Through the musical phrasing, the words become even more strongly connected and rooted in their iconic and/or indexical correspondence, thereby weaving a dense web of cross-references. This is Wagner's standard procedure in a nutshell: further examples may be found throughout his libretti.

In a personal and rather pungent vein, Wagner in *Oper und Drama* criticized translated opera as performed in his days. Quotation of the following, somewhat extended passage is in order here, because it wraps up Wagner's expert opinion on this issue beautifully:

Bei diesen Übersetzungen ist nie weder ein dichterischer noch musikalischer Verstand tätig gewesen, sondern sie wurden von Leuten, die weder Dichtkunst noch Musik verstanden, im geschäftlichen Auftrage ungefähr so übersetzt, wie man Zeitungsartikel oder Kommerznotizen überträgt. Gemeinhin waren diese Übersetzer vor allem nicht musikalisch; sie übersetzten ein italienisches oder französisches Textbuch für sich, als Wortdichtung nach einem Versmaße, welches als sogenanntes jambisches unverständerweise ihnen dem gänzlich unrhythmischen des Originals entsprechend vorkam, und ließen diese Verse von musikgeschäftlichen Ausschreibern unter die Musik so setzen, daß die Silben den Noten der Zahl nach zu entsprechen hatten. Die dichterische Mühe des Übersetzers hatte darin bestanden, die gemeinste Prosa mit läppischen Endreimen zu versehen, und da diese Endreime selbst oft peinliche Schwierigkeiten darboten, war ihnen — den in der Musik fast gänzlich unhörbaren — zuliebe auch die natürliche Stellung der Worte bis zur vollsten Unverständlichkeit verdreht worden. Dieser an und für sich häßliche, gemeine und sinnverwirrte Vers wurde nun einer Musik untergelegt, zu deren betonten Akzenten er nirgends paßte: auf aufgedehnte Noten kamen kurze Silben, auf gedehnte Silben aber kurze Noten; auf die musikalisch betonte Hebung kam die Senkung des Verses, und so umgekehrt. (Wagner 1984: 374–375)[13]

Needless to say, the interlingual reproduction of Wagner's operatic lyrics from the original German into another language is a Herculean and little-rewarding task. The cumulation of musico-rhythmic devices constantly threatens to overburden the conscientious translator, who needs to mobilize all his linguistic skills, musical knowledge, and poetic creativity in order to produce a translation which "works" on all levels, both microscopically and macroscopically. That is, a translation with an equivalent (or at least similar) musico-poetic patterning, and with equivalent (or at least similar) intermedial cross-references.

Peirce as translator of Wagner

Unfortunately, Charles Sanders Peirce (1839–1914), the patriarch of Anglo-American semiotics, would later join the ranks of the opera translators, whose failures (musical, literary, and otherwise) Wagner had denounced in his *Oper und Drama*.

The fields of Peirce's encyclopedic learning included first chemistry, and then logic, philosophy, astronomy, biology, as well as the social sciences — particularly psychology and sociology, then emerging. Though not a linguist, Peirce had a keen gift for languages, and wrote a great deal on language-related issues.[14] However, one field Peirce seemed to have little interest in, at least as a scholar, is art. Though he did not develop any specific thoughts on artistic communication, his conceptual apparatus can be applied successfully to analyze artistic or aesthetic signs as well. This is why there is, within applied Peircean studies, a lively and growing interest in a semiotics of music, literature, dance, cinema, and many other art forms, including opera.

Despite the wide scope of his learning, Peirce was never able to secure a tenured academic position. He lectured for some years at Harvard University and Johns Hopkins University, but was never offered a tenured position and, as a matter of fact, dismissed. Instead, he earned his livelihood for nearly thirty years as a scientist employed by the United States Coast and Geodetic Service. In 1887, after having inherited some money, he retired to Milford, Pennsylvania, where he lived in relative isolation and continued his philosophical work on his own. To ease his financial stringencies, he wrote book reviews (particularly for *The Nation*) and dictionary entries (for *The Century Dictionary*), while also doing some translations[15]. Seen from today's perspective, Peirce was at that time perhaps the greatest philosopher in the world; but since he worked in almost complete isolation, his work became more and more speculative and obscure. In 1914, Peirce died, at the age of 74, in poverty and without recognition.

In 1896, Peirce (*MS* 1517[16]) translated William Hirsch's *Genie und Entartung: Eine psychologische Studie* (1894), a refutation of the ideas on genius, criminality, and the decline of moral standards developed by Max Nordau and Cesare Lombroso. According to the latter, Wagner was an insane person, a "degenerate"[17]. The English translation of Hirsch's book, *Genius and Degeneration: A Psychological Study*, appeared in the following year (Hirsch 1897) and was reviewed by Peirce under the title *Genius and Insanity* (*MS* 1402)[18]. Although in Hirsch's *Genius and Degeneration* no mention is made of the name of the translator or translators (be it Peirce's and/or anyone else's name), Peirce's handwritten translation must have formed the basis of it, albeit in heavily edited and changed form, almost beyond recognition[19]. Such a procedure is, of course, not exceptional in the world of translation, and Peirce's case here illustrates the sad saga of how the professional skills of translators are often freely used, and indeed abused, in the publishing world.

The penultimate chapter of Hirsch's book is on "Richard Wagner and Psychopathology" (Hirsch 1894: 264–329 and 1897: 249–319; *MS* 1517: 1–116). Peirce was a fervent admirer of Wagner, whom he admitted in three versions of the (unfinished) *Study of Great Men* (*W*: 5: 30, 34, and 35), which he composed in the years 1883–1884 to test the usefulness of statistical methods and his own categorial scheme for comparative biography[20]. Peirce's affection for Wagner makes it particularly interesting to study one aspect of his translation: some renderings into English of key passages from several libretti by Wagner, which are quoted in Hirsch's book, and reproduced and interlingually translated in the English versions. Some of Peirce's translations will, in the next paragraphs, be compared with the original texts and with the printed translation.

Unfortunately, Peirce's manuscript pages referring to Wagner's later works, *Siegfried* (1856–1876), *Götterdämmerung* (1869–1876), and *Parsifal* (1877–1882), are lost, and *Tristan und Isolde* (1857–1865) and *Die Meistersinger von Nürnberg* (1862–1868) were not treated by Hirsch. Therefore my analysis shall concentrate on the earlier music-dramas: *Tannhäuser und der Sängerkrieg auf Wartburg* (1843–1845), *Lohengrin* (1846–1850), and the first two operas of the *Ring* cycle, *Das Rheingold* (1853–1854) and *Die Walküre* (1854–1856). My comparison of selected fragments of the original libretti and their translations shall also take into account the incidence of Wagner's ideas about the musical and rhythmical qualities of opera lyrics as put forth in *Oper und Drama*, which Wagner wrote in 1851 after finishing *Lohengrin*, the transitional work, and before starting on *Das Rheingold*.

In Peirce's translation of Hirsch's observations on *Tannhäuser* it is surprising to see Peirce's ignorance of Wagner's music-drama. E.g., Peirce leaves the word *Sängerkrieg* (or song contest) from the title of the work, untranslated, and adds in parentheses: "(What is that?)" (*MS* 1517: 33). Wagner's lyrics, themselves quoted in fragmentary and decontextualized form, are meaningfully embedded in the context of Hirsch's text. To judge from the relatively few erasions in Peirce's handwriting, he seemed to have had no trouble making sense of them. Yet, as Freadman points out, "Peirce evidently knew precious little about music" (1993: 90); and "Peirce was a philosopher, not a linguist, and he was not used to attending to vowels and consonants and intonational and rhythmic patterns. He was brought to such things by dwelling on pen-strokes, tinctures, and printing fonts" (1993: 89–90).

Tannhäuser still belongs to Wagner's earlier works[21]: its arias relate it to traditional opera, while the declamatory recitative and the dramatic dialogue, e.g., approach it to the later, modern Wagner. The verse form is mostly conventional, iambic, with (in the examples) four or five accents to the line and regular end-rhyme. In addition, however, there is a fair amount of internal rhyme both in consonants and in vowels, thus heralding Wagner's later *Stabreim*. Tannhäuser, knight and minstrel, has sought refuge from the griefs of the earth in the hill of Venus, or *Venusberg*. After living with Venus a whole year, he is weary of love's monotonous delights, and longs for the ups and downs of earthly life:

(1)
Tannhäuser:
Nicht Lust allein liegt mir am Herzen,
Aus Freuden sehn' ich mich nach Schmerzen;
Aus deinem Reiche muss ich flieh'n,
O Königin, Göttin! Lass mich zieh'n!
(............................)
Doch hin muss ich zur Welt der Erden,
Bei dir kann ich nur Sklave werden;
Nach Freiheit doch verlange ich,
Nach Freiheit, Freiheit dürstet's mich;
Zu Kampf und Streite will ich stehen,
Sei's auch auf Tod und Untergehen: —
Drum muss aus deinem Reich ich flieh'n, —
O Königin, Göttin! Lass mich zieh'n!
(*Tannhäuser*: I,ii: 40–41, 58–59; quoted in Hirsch 1894: 278–279)

Not pleasure alone concerns my heart,
I long to pass from joys to pains;
From thy realm must I flee,
O queen, goddess, let me go.
(......................)
Yet I must go on to the world of earth,
With thee I can become only a slave;
I hanker for freedom,
For freedom, freedom I am athirst;
In battle and combat I am ready to stand,
Be it even to death and overthrow: —
Therefore I must flee thy realm
O queen, goddess! Let me go!
(*MS* 1517: 95, 97)

There's more than joy affects my heart,
'Midst my delight I seek for smart;
Far from thy realm I must hie,
O Queen! O Goddess! Let me fly.
(.......................)
Nay, I must off the earth to see,
With thee I can a slave but be;
For liberty I still do crave,
For full free liberty I rave;
To toil and strife I must be near,
Though 'tis to die and disappear;
So from thy realm I must me hie —
O Queen! O Goddess! Let me fly!
(Hirsch 1897: 263, 264)

Only a few characteristics of the original verse are reproduced in Peirce's translation. Not only do his verse lines count a varying number a syllables alternating freely (which makes them, for all practical purposes, unsingable); also, the stresses are unevenly divided, and both end-rhyme and internal rhyme are missing. Peirce's prosaic translation is in sharp contrast to the published version, produced by the anonymous translator. The latter is metrically and rhythmically regular, and makes an effort to reproduce the sound effects, directly, or by compensation. While the striking alliteration of the first line (*Lust, allein, liegt*) is lost in the translation, in the second line *sehn'* and *Schmerzen* is successfully (more so than Peirce's *pass, pains*) translated as *seek for smart*. The assonance in the third line: *deinem Reiche* is lost in Peirce's version, while the anonymous translator creatively transposed it into an alliteration (*Far from*). The assonance in the fourth line (*Königin, Göttin*) is reproduced in both translations, but it is a long way from Peirce's *O queen, goddess, let me go* to the more poetic solution: *O Queen! O Goddess! Let me fly*. The key word of this passage, *Freiheit*, is sung three times and receives special stress. Peirce chose to translate the triplet literally: *freedom, freedom, freedom*; yet *liberty*, followed by *still*, and subsequently duplicated in *full free liberty*, is perhaps a more inventive solution, since it is a word-play on vowels as well as consonants, all in one stroke.

In the story, Tannhäuser wins the heart of the virtuous Elisabeth in a song contest, then leaves her to join a group of pilgrims headed for

Rome. On Tannhäuser's return, his (and Elizabeth's) good friend, Wolfram, appeals to him not to return to Venus's joys:

(2)
Wolfram:
Ein Engel bat für dich auf Erden —
Bald schwebt er segnend über dir;
Elisabeth! Elisabeth!
(*(Tannhäuser*: III,iii: 334–335; quoted in Hirsch 1894: 278–279)

An angel besought for thee on earth
Soon hovers he benignant over thee:
Elizabeth! Elizabeth!
(*MS* 1517: 96)

An angel prayed for thee on earth —
All blissful did she soar o'er thee:
Elizabeth! Elizabeth!
(Hirsch 1897: 264)

This musical fragment shows pronouncedly modern elements, antici-
pating the compositional structure of the *Ring*. The lyrics are the dominant element, while the music is subordinated to the rhythm and nuances
of the dramatic dialogue (in which the voice of Wolfram is intertwined
with those of Tannhäuser and Venus, as well as the chorus's). Yet in this
ensemble singing, music and words are in agreement. In tandem with
regular end-rhyme, we also see a flexibilization of the musical beat to
fully exploit breath as a vehicle of meaning. For instance, in the dual
exclamation, "*Elisabeth! Elisabeth!*" the stressed vowel is lengthened to
prolong the climactic moment and intensify the emotional effect. Rhythmically, Peirce first line is hop, step, and jump rather than iambic, as in
the original. Lexically, it complexifies what is, in the original, a perfectly transparent sentence. In the second line, Peirce misconstrues the
German adverb *bald*. Moreover, the masculine form of the pronoun in
this line, though quite common in German with reference to a female
person, is confusing to an English-speaking audience.

Next comes Wagner's *Lohengrin*, an audience-pleasing Romantic
opera. While it is still a reflection of traditional opera, it also points
towards Wagner's new operatic forms. Once again, the Peirce hand-

writing contains a parenthetical apology, deleted by Peirce himself but still quite readable. To translate Hirsch's *"Aber bald regen sich Neid und Missgunst, denen es gelingt, Zweifel und Eifersucht in der Seele des geliebten Weibes zu erregen"* (1894: 282), Peirce wrote: *"But soon envy* [the variant, *jealousy* is deleted] *and ill will are astir. (The translator, not being acquainted with the drama, does not know what* Neid und Missgunst *here signify.) and succeed in kindling doubt and jealousy in the soul of the beloved woman"* (*MS* 1517: 100). The published translation reads as follows: *"But soon jealousy and envy set to work, and awaken doubt and suspicion in the soul of the beloved woman"* (Hirsch 1897: 267).

Lohengrin is, as remarked above, a transitional work[22]. It is characterized by the tonal fixation of situations and persons (Wagner's *Leitmotif* technique, later systematically exploited in the *Ring*), alongside a relatively simple musical phrasing (with its four and eight bar phrases), and a rhythmical monotony (the music consists mostly of triads). The vocal parts are no longer separate arias or recitatives, but are integrated into the flow of dramatic lyrics. In addition, there is fair amount of choral singing. The vocal parts in *Lohengrin* are governed by a "normal" speech rhythm approaching declamation. In this way Wagner felt and created in *Lohengrin* the right musical speed for his German polysyllables. Still following the traditional pattern, he used regular rhymed iambic verse throughout.

Lohengrin, a supernatural creature, drawn by a swan, comes to save the honor of Elsa von Brabant, an innocent maiden in distress, who, according to Wagner's libretto, *"seitdem sie Lohengrin erblickte, wie in Zauber regungslos festgebannt war, sinkt, wie durch seine Ansprache erweckt, in überwältigend wonnigem Gefühle zu seinem Füßen"* (*Lohengrin*: 25):

(3)
Elsa:
Mein Held, mein Retter! Nimm mich hin!
Dir geb ich alles, was ich bin!
(*Lohengrin*: I,iii: 45; quoted in Hirsch 1894: 282)

My hero, my deliverer! Take me!
To thee I give all I am!

(*MS* 1517: 100)

Take me! Hero, saviour mine!
All that I am deem thou as thine!
(Hirsch 1897: 267)

Both translations of this fragment are, for different reasons and to different degrees, unsingable and incongruent with Elsa's original words, in
which the words match the music in speed, accent, meter, vocal register,
and, particularly, in overall tone, or mood, Peirce's quality of Firstness,
which is dreamy, devotional, almost orgastic[23].

Peirce himself seems to have been unaware of this: his own translation lacks poetic quality. The first line runs a syllabic surplus, the second
is shorter than the original. Again, no rhyme. The inversion, in the first
line of the published translation, results in a seemingly good translation,
which is, however, unsuited to be sung, because the accents fall on the
wrong words. To maintain the rhyme, which consists of a single stressed
end-syllable, the translator changed the linguistic register in the second
line. A serious shortcoming in both translations is that no attempt was
made at reproducing the conspicuous sound structure of the original,
which builds on the vowels *e* and *i*.

The Knight of the Swan makes it a condition of their eternal love that
Elsa (who was Wagner's favorite female creation) must never inquire
about his name, birth, or descent:

(4)
Lohengrin:
Nie sollst du mich befragen,
Noch Wissens Sorge tragen,
Woher ich kam der Fahrt,
Noch wie mein Nam' und Art!
(*Lohengrin*: I,iii; 46 and 47; quoted in Hirsch 1894: 282)

Never must thou question me,
Nor care to know
Whence I travelled,
Nor what my name or condition.
(*MS* 1517: 99)

Ne'er venture to inquire,

Nor proof from me desire,
Whence I my journey trace,
And what's my name and race!
(Hirsch 1897: 267)

Elsa lives with the secret three days before she puts the fateful question to Lohengrin, and has to watch her lover as he leaves her.

This is the famous *Frageverbot* motif, the central one in the drama[24]. Not only is this the only vocal motif in *Lohengrin*, it also shows the perfect marriage of lyrics and music. The content of the four-line stanza is divided into two parts: the first and second line, the second line re-phrases the first one; and the third and fourth line, in which the forbid-den question is specified: *(kam)-Fahrt-Nam'-Art*. Note the alliteration of *a*, and the placement (end-rhyme), which is foreshadowed in the rhymed first lines: *befragen-tragen*. Other characteristics are the repetition of the *ie/i* in *Nie-mich-Wissens-mich-wie*, as well as the triplet of correlative coordinators, *nie-noch-noch,* all negatives and placed in anaphoric position. About the use of the latter, negative items in this passage, Stein remarks:

> It is of interest to note that for melodic purposes the word *noch* must bear an emphasis which it is not important enough to warrant. Wagner was apparently conscious of this discrepancy. While he has added weight to the entire first half of the phrase by the unusual expedient of putting a stress mark over each note, he carefully omits the mark over *noch*. This is, of course, not sufficient to prevent it from receiving a very strong accent by virtue of its position on the strongest beat of the measure and at the beginning . . . (Stein 1973: 58)

Again, Peirce's translation does no justice to the complex texture of this key passage in *Lohengrin*, while the anonymous translator again did a better job, although he was only partially successful in reproducing the sound and meaning structure of the original. The rhymed triplet *trace-name-race* (the triple taboo) has no connection with the rhyme in the first and second lines, *inquire-desire*. The anonymous translator's *ne'er-nor* is, however, a crippled version of Peirce's fine triplet *never-or-nor*, which is as pregnant with meaning as the original.

Der Ring des Nibelungen (written between 1853 and 1976) is Wagner's central masterpiece. The difference between its first music-drama,
Das Rheingold (1853–1854) (which serves as prologue to the cycle), and
Lohengrin is striking and quite dramatic. *Oper und Drama* (first edition
1852) may serve as a vademecum for the new compositional and lyrical
structure. Accordingly, the orchestral music and vocal parts of *Das
Rheingold* are fully subordinated to the poetic text, which is the more
expressive element; while the versification is "highly alliterative, com-
pact, with root syllables predominating, and with irregular rhyme" (Stein
1973: 82).

The overall topic of the *Ring* is power, love, and gold. As the title of
the first drama, *Das Rheingold*, suggests, the three Rhine-daughters
(Woglinde, Wellgunde, and Flosshilde) are the custodians of a golden
treasure which, if forged into a ring, possesses a secret power. As they
are merrily swimming about in the river Rhine, the nymphs are hotly
pursued by Alberich, a troll-like figure:

(5)
Wellgunde:
Der Welt Erbe
Gewänne zu eigen
Wer aus dem Rheingold
Schüfe den Ring,
Der masslose Macht ihm verlieh.
(*Rheingold*: I,i; 40; quoted in Hirsch 1894: 287

He of the universe
Winneth his own
Who from the Rhine-gold
Maketh the ring
Which measureless might must lend him.
(*MS* 1517: 106)

He gains the world
As his own inheritance,
Who from the Rhinegold
Creates the ring
Which measureless might doth bestow.
(Hirsch 1897: 272)

In this fluvially orchestrated fragment we hear and see Wagner's new ideas at work. Sound and meaning of the key syllables/words are severally connected through pitch, stress, and "rhyme": *Welt-Erbe, Rheingold-Ring, masslose-Macht.* End-rhyme has disappeared in favor of *Stabreim.* Peirce as well as the anonymous translator were unsuccessful in the first two lines, but gave a better shot at reproducing the internal rhyme in lines three and four: *Rheingold-ring, (maketh-)-measureless-might.*

For the sake of comparison it is tempting and instructive to quote here from the radically modern (1983) translation composed by the American libretto translators, Mark Herman and Ronnie Apter:

> The whole world will belong to the one
> who forges the Rhinegold into a ring,
> And he will be lord of us all. (Wagner 1983: 5)

This is a simplified, extremely singable version. The translators have taken a novel, yet genuinely Wagnerian, look at the poetic-melodic synthesis. The result is as creative as it is refreshing. The verse lines correspond with the grammatical units as well as the singer's breath. Note the pervasive assonance, evenly distributed over the verse lines, of variations of the vowel *o* in *whole-belong-forges-gold-lord-of-all.* The chiastic *lord of us all,* with its building up towards the highly-pitched dramatic climax, is a particularly felicitous rendering of the original German.

(6)
Woglinde:
Nur wer der Minne
Macht versagt,
Nur wer der Liebe
Lust verjagt,
Nur der erzielt sich den Zauber,
Zum Reif zu zwingen das Gold. (Rheingold: I,i; 42; quoted in Hirsch 1894: 287

Only who Eros's
Power denies,
Only who love's delights
Chases away,

Can attain to the magical power
To bend round the gold to a hoop (*MS* 1517: 106)

Only who Love's might
Doth withstand,
Only who Love's joys
Drives away,
None but he gets the secret power
The gold to force into a ring. (Hirsch 1897: 273)

This passage, sung with emphasis, yet *legato*, is crucial to the musico-semantic structure and development of *Das Rheingold* and the whole *Ring des Nibelungen*. It hinges, of course, on the parallelism between *der Minne Macht* on the one hand and *der Liebe Lust* on the other. This parallelism is beautifully expressed in both media involved: linguistically, by the alliteration, and melodically, by the repetition of exactly the same musical phrase. Further reinforced by the anaphora of *nur wer* and the end-rhyme *versagt-verjagt*, this is a perfect example of what Wagner called a musical alliteration. Note, in the last two lines, the fivefold alliteration of *z* in *erzielt-Zauber-zu zwingen*.

Somewhat disappointingly for a key passage in the dramatic structure, little of this is recognizable in the English texts. Consequently, both translations fail to produce the desired emotional effect on the verbal side, thereby relying too heavily on the meaning-potentialities of the music. This shift of emphasis is at variance with all of Wagner's intentions and beliefs. To illustrate the possibility of a translation which is, paradoxically perhaps, both free and faithful to Wagner's ideas as a composer and librettist, quotation of Herman and Apter's translation is in order here:

He must reject the fact of love,
He must renounce the act of love,
to be imbued with the power,
the magic to master the gold. (Wagner 1983: 5)

Seized with new desire, Alberich steals the gold and disappears into the depths of the river Rhine. Later, the giants Fasolt and Fafner claim Freia, goddess of youth and beauty, as recompensation for building Wotan's new castle, which is named Walhalla, or Hall of the Slain

Heroes. But Wotan, as god of justice, is reluctant to relinquish Freia. Erda, the wise earth goddess (who later bears to Wotan the nine Valkyrs), intervenes, whereupon Wotan offers the magic ring to the giants as a substitute for Freia:

(7)
Erda:
Wie Alles war, weiss ich,
Wie Alles wird,
Wie Alles sein wird,
Seh' ich auch:
Der ew'gen Welt
Ur-Wala,
Erda mahnt deinen Mut.
(*Rheingold*, IV,iii: 203; quoted in Hirsch 1894: 289)

How all was, know I,
How all becomes,
How all will be,
See I also:
The everlasting world
Ur-Wala,
Erda warns thy courage.
(*MS* 1517: 108)

How all was,I know,
How all is,
How all will be,
I see too:
Th' eternal world
Ur-Wala,
Erda puts in your mind.
(Hirsch 1897: 275)

Ur-Wala means primeval wisdom (Huber 1988: 166). Yet it is at best doubtful whether both translators are aware that Ur-Wala *is* Erda; nor, for that matter, that *Mut* here means as much as *Übermut*, the Greek notion of ὕβρις.[25] These grammatico-lexical misconstruals make Erda's warning — which is sung strictly *ritenuto* — more opaque than it really is.

   Erda's ominous words echo her earlier *Weiche, Wotan, weiche!* as well as Wotan's *Wer bist du, mahnendes Weib*, in that they build acoustically on repetition of the semiconsonant *w*, with its strong tone and voice vibration. Its counterpart, *How all*, in both translations, is no more than a weak reflection — as well as a dubious translation — of Wagner's original, which expresses this dramatic quality with a particular emotional impact.

Finally, Peirce's version of *Die Walküre* — which he translates alternately as *The Valkyrae* and *The Valkyries* (*MS* 1517: 111) but is commonly called *The Valkyrie* in English. In Act I of this drama, dealing with the love of Siegmund and Sieglinde, the music is more prominent than it was in *Das Rheingold*. The word-music parallelism is pervasive and continuous, the use of *Stabreim* is consistent with the ideas put forth in *Oper und Drama*, and the leitmotifs occur frequently but functionally, as keys to emotional reminiscence. In *Die Walküre*, "Wagner's new *Gesamtkunstwerk* approaches perfection" (Stein 1973: 99), forming a single, all-inclusive poetico-melodic alliterative unit.

The story of *Die Walküre* is too complex to be told here in its entirety. A few brief indications will suffice to illustrate our study examples. Wounded, Siegmund seeks refuge in a hut, where he is given shelter and refreshment by Sieglinde, wife to cruel Hunding. Siegmund and Sieglinde fall in love, discover they are brother and sister, and escape together. As goddess of matrimony, Fricka is enraged by their adulterous as well as incestuous relationship and comes to her husband, Wotan, to whom the love and flight of Siegmund and Sieglinde is at first less repugnant:

(8)
Wotan:
Unheilig
Acht' ich den Eid,
Der Unliebende eint;
Und mir wahrlich
Mute nicht zu,
Dass mit Zwang ich halte,
Was Dir nicht haftet:
Denn wo kühn Kräfte sich regen,
Da rath' ich offen zum Krieg.
(*Walküre*, II,i: 89; quoted in Hirsch 1894: 293–294)

Unholy
Deem I the oath
That unites the unloving;
And to me truly
Impute not
That I hold with compulsion
What affects thee not.
For where bold powers raise in
There I openly counsel war.
(*MS* 1517: 114)

Unholy
Deem I the oath
Which without love unites;
And of me in truth
Do not require
That by force I hold
What doth not cling to thee.
For where bold powers themselves array,
I must counsel open war.
(Hirsch 1897: 281)

In response to Fricka's defense of *der Ehe heiligen Eid*, the stress in Wotan's words and musical accompaniment is on the negative prefix *un-* in *unheilig* and *Unliebende*, while echoing the diphthong (or rather digraph) *ei* (*unheilig-Eid-eint*) in meaningful combination with its reverse, *ie*, in *Unliebende*[26]. The next sentence shows the end-rhyme *halte-hafte* blending with the *u* of *mute-zu* into the emphatic *Zwang* and ending with an interesting *k-r-kr* climactic sequence: *kühn-Kräfte-regen-rath'-Krieg*.

For Wagner's meaningful poetico-melodic union, no clear parallelism can be detected in the sound-meaning structure of either translation. True, *war* can only make a poor substitute for its expressive German counterpart, *Krieg*. Yet once again Peirce translates for an audience of readers, not listeners. His felicitous pair, *unholy-unloving*, is repeated graphically, if not vocally, in *unites*, while remaining unsupported by contextual rhythm and rhyme. Peirce's own acute awareness of his inability to understand — let alone translate — the rest of this passage, is made plain by the big question mark which he has scribbled next to his translated version. The anonymous translator improves slightly on

Peirce's performance, but without even beginning to do justice to the original's intricacies of sound and meaning.

One last fragment from *Die Walküre* must suffice to exemplify the points I want to make here. Brünnhilde, Wotan's daughter and his favorite Walküre, disobeys her father by protecting the sinful lovers, Siegmund and Sieglinde, and by helping Sieglinde, who is pregnant by Siegmund (she will give birth to Siegfried). Toward the end of this musical drama, Wotan, angry and heartbroken, punishes Brünnhilde for her disobedience by condemning her to slumber on the Walküre Rock surrounded with flames, so that only a fearless yet mortal hero will dare cross the fire, wake her from her enchanted sleep, and become her husband:

(9)
Wotan:
Ein bräutliches Feuer
Soll Dir nun brennen,
Wie nie einer Braut es gebrannt!
Flammende Glut
Umglühe den Fels;
Mit zehrenden Schrecken
Scheuch' es den Zagen;
Der Feige fliehe
Brünnhildes Fels: —
Denn Einer nur freie die Braut,
Der freier als ich der Gott!
(Walküre, III,iii: 300–303; quoted in Hirsch 1894: 295[27])

A nuptial fire
Shall now burn thee,
As never a bride it burnt!
Flaming fire
Glow round the rock,
With consuming terror
Scare it the coward;
Fainthearted flee
Bruenhilda's rock: —
Let he only free the bride
Who is freer than I the god.
(*MS* 1517: 115)

A true bridal fire
Shall burn now for thee,
As ne'er hitherto for bride it has burned!
Let flaming glow
Warm the rock around;
With consuming terror
Let it cowards scare;
Let faint heart avoid
Brünnhilde's rock:
For one alone woos the bride,
Who is freer than I, the god!
(Hirsch 1897: 282–283)

Wotan's adieu has a high concentration of emotion, which is given an singularly eloquent expression, both musically and verbally, by Wagner. Musically, by a nervous rhythm marked by galloping syncopation, suggestive of the burning flames of the god's anger and clearly imitative of the magical fire separating his beloved daughter, as another Sleeping Beauty, from her godly kin. Verbally, Wotan's angry plaint builds on two ingeniously intertwined alliterative series, involving the rhyming consonants *br* and *f*, in addition to the use of secondary, supporting alliteration of *gl (Glut-umglühe)*, *z (zehrenden-Zagen)*, and *sch (Schrecken-scheuch')*, always in the stressed root syllables placed at the beginning of the word, and always instrumental in constructing different aspects and levels of meaning: *bräutliches-brennen-Braut-gebrennt-Brünnhilde-Braut* and *Feuer-flammende-Fels-Feige-fliehe-freie-freier*.

Note the change of tone and mood in the last two lines, in which Wotan brings his point home to Brünnhilde with authority and emphasis, yet in a more lyrical vein. The final word, *Gott!*, which in Wagner's *Stabreim* scheme "rhymes" with *Braut* in the previous line, serves as climax and apotheosis.

In contrast to his earlier transpositions of Wagner's libretti, Peirce here produces an adequate singing version. Alas, by mistaking *freie* for *befreie*, he misses the erotic point of Brünnhilde's situation. Yet this is not a vital error. Peirce makes an interesting attempt at reproducing at least some of the alliterations, and he finds support for his endeavor in the sound correspondences between both Germanic languages involved: *Feuer* becomes *fire*, *brennen* becomes *burn*, *Braut* becomes *bride*, *der*

Feige fliehe becomes *fainthearted flee*, and *freier* becomes *freer*. Inexplicably, after a felicitous beginning, it is the anonymous translator who goes completely astray in terms of number of syllables, rhythm, stress, and sound pattern of the translated material.

Concluding remarks

It is difficult to be complimentary about Peirce's renderings of Wagner. Even though the space allotted to me here does not permit a thoroughgoing study of each of Peirce's translations of Wagner, it is clear that they are decontextualized chunks of text; mere reading versions, unsuited to be sung in a real performance. They are often longer (that is, have more syllables) than the original German lyrics. Besides, they are unable to tune into the lyrical mood and are hardly evidence of artistry and poetic sensitivity. A self-declared admirer of Wagner's work, and an accomplished linguist though Peirce was, as an opera translator he lacked an easy flow of language set to music. Peirce's aim, in everything, was the top. Here, the result of his hard work is poor and disheartening. All this is in pointed contrast to the anonymous translator, who, as I hope to have persuasively argued, shows that he/she is more knowledgeable about poetry, music, and the interface between both. The anonymous libretto translator (and a fortiori, Herman and Apter) has a voice which is melody itself. He/she deserves kudos for his/her performance.

Notes

1. The fourth work, *Über das Judentum in der Musik*, written in 1850, and the fierce debates about Wagner's antisemitism which it still arouses today, fall outside the scope of my article and must remain undiscussed here. For a recent contribution, see Weiner 1995.
2. See, e.g., Stein 1973: 163 and *passim*.
3. *Der Ring des Nibelungen*, Wagner's central masterpiece, was written between 1853 and 1876. Its parts are: *Das Rheingold* 1853/1854, *Die Walküre* 1854/1856, *Siegfried* 1856/1876, and *Götterdämmerung* 1869/1876. In this essay I shall also make references to two operas

preceding the *Ring*: *Tannhäuser oder der Sängerkrieg auf Wartburg* 1843/1845 and *Lohengrin* 1846/1850. The composing process of the *Ring*, which lasted more than two decades, was interrupted by *Tristan und Isolde* 1857/1865 and *Die Meistersinger von Nürnberg* 1862/1868. *Parsifal*, Wagner's last opera, was written 1877/1882.

4. For the sake of clarity, what is meant here is that when taken *in isolation*, Wagner's music lacks the richness of, e.g., music in the Beethovenian symphonic tradition.

5. The whole quote refers to the need for clarity and precision in language use, away from meaningless concerns such as metaphysics: "what can be said at all can be said clearly, and what we cannot talk about we must pass over in silence. Thus the aim of the book is to draw a limit to thought, or rather — not to thought , but to the expression of thought" (Wittgenstein 1988: 3).

6. For a different view on the *Gesamtkunstwerk* as the work-of-all-arts, see Langer 1953: 160ff.

7. More on this in Orlando 1975.

8. In my argument here, abstraction needs to be made of the visual, scenic aspects of the opera performance.

9. For this, see Wagner 1984: 127–131, where he opposed Lessing and defended, among other mixed art forms, the music drama as synthetic union of the arts.

10. It is tempting to draw a parallel between the erotic image used by Wagner and Peirce's concept of "evolutionary love" (*CP*: 6.287ff), and to extrapolate character traits common to both men, such as, e.g., genius, a revolutionary spirit, and a keen sexual interest in women.

11. For the chronology of Wagner's operas, see note 3.

12. Not coincidentally, Wagner's contemporaneous, the Norwegian Henrik Ibsen was the first playwright who used prose (that is, everyday language) instead of the traditional use of rhymed poetic verse.

13. Wagner added to this the following footnote: "*Ich hebe diese gröbsten Verstöße heraus, nicht weil sie in Übersetzungen gerade immer vorkamen, sondern weil sie — ohne Sänger und Hörer zu stören — oft vorkommen konnten: ich bediene mich daher des Superlatives, um den Gegenstand nach seiner kennlichsten Physiognomie zu bezeichnen*" (1984: 375 note).

14. As Fisch reminds us, while Saussure was a linguist, "Peirce was a chemist and his first professional publication was in chemistry, but his second was on the pronounciation of Shakespearian English, and he was a lifelong student of comparative linguistics. In 1870, during the first of his five European sojourns, he wrote home that he had heard eighteen distinct languages spoken, seventeen of them (including Basque) in places where they were the languages of everyday speech" (Fisch 1986: 430).

15. For a catalogue of his translations, see Robin 1967: 160–161. For Peirce as a translator, see also Gorlée 1994: 115–118.

16. Robin (1967: 161) notes that the pages of *MS* 1517 are numbered as high as 347, but that it has survived in incomplete form, with many pages missing.

17. See also Peirce's review of Lombroso's *The Man of Genius* in *The Nation* 54, 25 February 1892 (*N*: 1: 139–144), where Wagner is also mentioned, albeit in passing and on rather trivial grounds.

18. *MS* 1402 is a 7-page, incomplete draft of the review, which was published in *The Nation* 64, 29 April 1897: 326–327 (but not reproduced in Peirce's *N* 2). Towards the end of the manuscript, Peirce makes some shrewd remarks about Wagner's art. Given their interest for musicological and narratological studies of Wagner, as well as for semiotic studies, especially of Peirce's categorial scheme as connected with the forms of reasoning, quotation of this somewhat extended passage is in order. In it, Peirce blames Hirsch for not perceiving "the diametrical contraries of his [Wagner's] Flying Dutchman, Tannhaeuser, and Lohengrin, which, as their great composer said, can be understood by the heart alone. On would imagine that nothing could be more detestible to Wagner's warm nature than allegory. At any rate, if he did use such a scaffolding to help his construction of his later dramas, he had the good taste to keep it well in concealment from the public eye. Allegories and emblems are just the reverse of that Ideal of primitive, heroic man, which others than Dr. Hirsch have conceived that Wagner endeavored to kindle in the hearts of his fellow-men. The former start with a doctrine admitted on all hands, and proceed to fit it with a handsome suit of clothes; the other begins by presenting a picture which he to whom it appeals must recognize as answering to something in his heart, and then proceeds, by the development of the action, to lead that interpreting heart to recognize other things of which it had scarcely been aware before" (*MS* 1402: 8). In this passage, the deductive course of reasoning, typically based on binary oppositions, a doctrine later revived by European structuralism, is pitted against abductive-inductive thought, which approaches the phenomenon from the opposite side. Further on this in Gorlée 1992.

19. To complexify this state of affairs, *MS* 1517 is, in the form in which it has survived, occasionally and lightly corrected by a handwriting other than Peirce's own.

20. Peirce's references to Wagner are from *MSS* 470, 471, and 475, all three written between Fall 1883 and Fall 1884. Richard Wagner had died on 13 February 1883.

21. More on this opera in Stein 1973: 39–49.

22. On the treatment of words and music in this opera, see, e.g., Palm 1987 and Stein 1973: 51–60.

23. Elsa's state of mind as she falls in love with Lohengrin, typically embodies Peirce's notion of *Musement* (*CP*: 6.455 ff).

24. More on this passage in Palm 1987: 99–101.

25. This has also been misunderstood by Herman and Apter, who translate Wagner's *mahnt deinen Mut* by *measure of all* (Wagner 1983: 21), a strange *faux pas*.
26. For an interesting analogy to this, see Wotan's later words of despair: *"In eig'ner Fessel / Fing ich mich: — / Ich unfreiester Aller!* — " (*Walküre*, II: 110; quoted in Hirsch 1894: 294), "In my own fetters / I caught myself: / I unfreeest of all!" (*MS* 1517: 114), "In my own fetters / Am I caught: / I, the least free of all! (Hirsch 1897: 281). Harking back to a key passage in *Das Rheingold*, Alberich's *Bin ich nun frei? / Wirklich frei?*, Wotan pits freedom against unfreedom, the latter term a neologism used by Peirce in his translation and eschewed by the anonymous translator. Note the alliterative use of the *f* in *Fessel-fing-unfreiester*.
27. Both versions differ on minor points. *Soll dir nun brennen* in Hirsch 1894 vs *soll dir nun brennen* in *Walküre*; in Hirsch 1894 the apostrophe after *Scheuch'* is omitted; *Glut, einer,* and *Freier* in Hirsch 1894 vs *Gluth, Einer,* and *freier* in *Walküre*.

References

Fisch, Max H. (1986). *Peirce, Semeiotic, and Pragmatism: Essays by Max H. Fisch*, Kenneth Laine Ketner and Christian J.W. Kloesel (eds.). Bloomington: Indiana University Press.
Freadman, Anne (1993). "Music 'in' Peirce", *Versus* 64 (January-April), 75–95.
Gorlée, Dinda L. (1992). "Symbolic argument and beyond: A Peircean view on structuralist reasoning", *Poetics Today* 13/3: 407–423.
– (1994). *Semiotics and the Problem of Translation: With Special Reference to the Semiotics of Charles S. Peirce* (=Approaches to Translation Studies 12). Amsterdam and Atlanta, GA: Rodopi Editions.
Hirsch, Dr. William (1894). *Genie und Entartung: Eine psychologische Studie*. Intro.: Prof. Dr. E. Mendel. Berlin and Leipzig: Oscar Coblentz.
– (1897). *Genius and Degeneration: A Psychological Study*. Transl. from the 2nd ed. of the German work. London: Heinemann.
Honolka, Kurt (1978). *Opernübersetzungen. Zur Geschichte der Verdeutschung musiktheatralischer Texte* (=Taschenbücher zur Musikwissenschaft 20). Wilhelmshaven: Heinrichshofen.
Huber, Herbert (1988). *Richard Wagner, Der Ring des Nibelungen: Nach seinem mythologischen, theologischen und philosophischen Gehalt Vers für Vers erklärt* (=Acta Humaniora). Weinheim: VCH.
Langer, Susanne K. (1953). *Feeling and Form: A Theory of Art Developed From Philosophy in a New Key*. New York: Scribner's Sons.

Orlando, Francesco (1975). "Propositions pour une sémantique du leitmotiv dans L'anneau des Nibelungen", *Musique en jeu* 17: 73–86.

Ostwald, Peter F. (1973). *The Semiotics of Human Sound* (=Approaches to Semiotics 36). The Hague and Paris: Mouton.

Palm, Helga-Maria (1987). *Richard Wagner's "Lohengrin": Studien zur Sprachbehandlung* (=Münchner Universitäts-Schriften Philosophische Fakultät, Studien zur Musik 6). München: Wilhelm Fink Verlag.

Peirce, Charles Sanders (1896a). *Genius & Degeneration: A Psychological Study*. Manuscript. Peirce Edition Project. Indiana University-Purdue University at Indianapolis. [Transl. of Hirsch 1894] [In-text references are to *MS* 1517, followed by page number]

– (1896b). *Genius and Insanity*. Manuscript. Peirce Edition Project. Indiana University-Purdue University at Indianapolis. [Draft of a review of Hirsch 1897] [In-text references are to *MS* 1402, followed by page number]

– (1905–1906). *The Basis of Pragmaticism*. Manuscript. Peirce Edition Project. Indiana University-Purdue University at Indianapolis. [In-text references are to *MS* 283, followed by page number]

– (1931–1966). *Collected Papers of Charles Sanders Peirce*, Charles Hartshorne, Paul Weiss, and Arthur W. Burks (eds.). 8 vols. Cambridge, MA: Belknap Press, Harvard University Press. [In-text references are to *CP*, followed by volume and paragraph numbers]

– (1975–1978). *Contributions to The Nation, vol. 1 and 2 (1869–1893 and 1894–1900)* (=Graduate Studies Texas Tech University 10 and 16), Kenneth Laine Ketner and James Edward Cook (eds.). Lubbock, TX: Texas Tech Press. [In-text references are to *N*, followed by volume and page number]

Robin, Richard S. (1967). *Annotated Catalogue of the Papers of Charles S. Peirce*. Amherst, MA: University of Massachusetts Press.

Stein, Jack Madison (1973). *Richard Wagner & the Synthesis of the Arts*, Westport, CO: Greenwood Press Publishers. [Rprt. of 1960 ed.: Detroit: Wayne State University Press]

Tarasti, Eero (1994). "Brünnhilde's choice or a journey to the Wagnerian semiosis: Intuitions and hypotheses", *Signifying Behavior* 1/1: 148–175.

Wagner, Richard (n.d.). *Tannhäuser und der Sängerkrieg auf Wartburg* (=Wagners Werke). Vocal score. Piano score: Karl Klindworth. Mainz, Leipzig, London, Brussels, and Paris: B. Schott's Söhne. [In-text references are to *Tannhäuser*, followed by page number]

– (n.d.). *Lohengrin*. Vocal score. Piano score: Felix Mottl. Leipzig: C. F. Peters. [In-text references are to *Lohengrin*, followed by page number]

– (n.d.). *Das Rheingold* (=Wagner's Werke). Vocal score. Piano score: Karl Klindworth. Mainz, Leipzig, London, Brussels, and Paris: B. Schott's Söhne. [In-text references are to *Rheingold*, followed by page number]

– (n.d.). *Die Walküre* (=Wagners Werke). Vocal score. Piano score: Karl Klindworth. Mainz, Leipzig, London, Brussels, and Paris: B. Schott's Söhne. [In-text references are to *Walküre*, followed by page number]
– (1983). *Der Ring des Nibelungen/The Ring of the Nibelung: Das Rheingold/The Rhinegold*. English-Only Libretto. Transl. from German into English by Mark Herman and Ronnie Apter. [MS provided by the translators]
– (1984). *Oper und Drama*, Klaus Kropfinger (ed. & comm.). Stuttgart: Philipp Reclam Jr. [First published in 1852 by J.J. Weber's *Verlagsbuchhandlung* in Leipzig]
Weiner, Marc A. (1995). *Richard Wagner and the Anti-Semitic Imagination*. Lincoln, NE: University of Nebraska Press.
Wittgenstein, Ludwig (1988). *Tractatus Logico-Philosophicus*. Transl. D.F. Pears and B.F. McGuiness. London: Routledge and Kegan Paul. [First published in 1921]

Les techniques de la narration aux origines de l'opéra: isotopies et stratégies narratives dans *l'Orfeo* de Claudio Monteverdi

Projet d'une approche interdisciplinaire de la naissance de l'opéra en Italie

FABIENNE DESQUILBE

Ce travail, qui s'inscrit comme première étape de notre recherche doctorale, est une tentative d'application d'analyse sémantique structurale au domaine de l'opéra pour une étude des formes de la narration de l'œuvre de Claudio Monteverdi.

Notre problème de départ est celui de l'unicité ou de la multiplicité des formes de narration et nous avons choisi *L'Orfeo* comme terrain d'application parce que cette oeuvre marque une période charnière dans l'histore des formes musicales et des modes de représentation.

En effet, l'Italie au début du XVIIème siècle voit naître une nouvelle forme qu'est l'opéra. Claudio Monteverdi en est un brillant illustrateur.

Nous avons donc fait l'hypothèse que la musique de *L'Orfeo* était narrative outre le fait bien entendu que nous avions affaire à un langage textuel, gestuel et pictural qui fournit une "intrigue" toute faite. La musique a-t-elle une fonction narrative propre? De plus, comment Monteverdi procède-t-il musicalement pour nous présenter et nous compter ce mythe?.

Nous avons adopté une analyse de type greimassienne (*Sémantique Structurale*, 1966, nouvelle édition 1986). Partie de l'exploitation de la thèse pour le Doctorat de troisième cycle de Márta Grabócz sur l'étude des stratégies narratives dans les oeuvres pour piano de Liszt[1], cette étude de la narrativité chez Monteverdi s'inscrit dans la lignée des travaux d'analyses sémiotiques musicales d'Eero Tarasti.

Ce que Greimas propose, c'est une méthode pour l'étude du plan de la signification: "le but que propose la sémantique consiste à réunir les moyens conceptuels nécessaires et suffisants en vue de la description d'une langue naturelle quelconque considérée comme un signifiant" (Greimas 1966: 13). Voici les différents niveaux de description donc d'observation définis par Greimas.

1) Le premier niveau d'observation porte sur les éléments sémiques et consiste à déterminer des classes de sèmes. Le sème c'est l'unité minimale du signifié: "dans notre système de typologie sémantique, les unités minimales signifiantes seront apellés sèmes" (Greimas 1966).

En musique, les unités minima sont définies selon les critères suivants: ce sont les unités porteuses de fonctions et de signification qui correspondent au niveau du motif ou de la figure musicale. Dans un sens plus large, les sèmes correspondent au "symbolisme" musical historique qui peut être porté par un motif mélodique ou un trait caractéristique dans l'enchainement harmonique ou bien par une texture musicale.

Les sèmes correspondent aussi à ce que Márta Grabócz appelle "associations musicales". Ce sont des associations aux mouvements, à l'espace, aux couleurs, à l'imitation des instruments, des gestes humains, respiration etc...[2] Nous avons observé de nombreux passages dans *L'Orfeo* où les éléments musicaux reflétaient l'influence associative des situations et du texte donné par le livret comme:
– Une instrumentation propre à certaines scènes, par exemple les familles de violons et de flûtes utilisés systématiquement dans les scènes pastorales ou les cuivres de manière aussi systématique dans les scènes souterraines.
– Les tempi établit par Monteverdi sont propres à certaines situations ou à l'état psychologique des personnages (tempo vif quand il s'agit du pastoral, du climat pastoral par exemple).
– Une écriture caractéristique, verticale ou horizontale selon le sujet abordé.

A la fin du premier acte par exemple, le choeur ramène l'attention sur le bonheur d'Orfeo. L'écriture qui caractérise ce passage est tout en accords calmes et substanciels, en succession d'harmonies purement verticales. En revanche les moments de désarroi, de panique et d'angoisse des personnages correspondent musicalement à une écriture horizontale, plus contrapuntique.

– Les tonalités sont spécifiques aux personnages, aux lieux et situations des scènes (cf. tableaux)

– Les figures musicales telles des figuralismes ou des chromatismes en association avec le texte du livret ou des intervalles caractéristiques de quarte, de quinte ou de quinte augmentée. Certains éléments de la nature ou des saisons ont des figures représentatives comme cet exemple de l'hiver et du printemps (Exemple 1).

L'analyse sémique se fait toujours par l'intermédiaire d'associations.

Nous avons distingués dans *L'Orfeo six* grands types de signifiés (tous les éléments sémiques regroupés en six classes de sèmes) portés par les récitatifs, les choeurs, les ritournelles et sinfonies instrumentales c'est à dire toute les formes que l'on trouve dans l'opéra, aussi bien vocales que purement instrumentales. Ces six classes de sèmes sont: Les sèmes pastoraux, les sèmes religieux, les sèmes funestes, les sèmes d'angoisse, les sèmes de bonheur et les sèmes infernaux.

2) Le deuxième niveau des unités signifiantes sera dénommé par la catégorie des classèmes. Greimas utilise ce terme en désignant comme classème les sèmes contextuels, c'est à dire ceux qui sont récurrents dans le discours et en garantissent l'isotopie. Les classèmes étant des sèmes récurrents ils doivent constituer en principe des catégories d'une grande généralité. Le contexte a un rôle principal puisqu'il est considéré comme unité du discours. Nous avons désigné comme classème les sèmes contextuels proprement dit. C'est le phénomène de récurrence (récurrence des différents types de sèmes ou récurrence de périodes musicales) qui nous a permis de définir les catégories de classèmes. Nous retrouvons donc les mêmes thèmes que pour les sèmes mais observé à un second niveau d'ordre plus général, au niveau des périodes en association avec le livret. Les six groupes de classèmes sont les suivants:

Pastoral, tragique, échec, bonheur, religieux et infernal.

Exemple 1. Acte I: mesure 518. Représentation musicale de l'hiver et du printemps.

3) C'est à partir de là que nous sommes en mesure de dégager une ou plusieurs isotopies sémantiques. Greimas a emprunté le terme d'"isotopie" au domaine de la physique-chimie et l'a transféré dans l'analyse sémantique en lui conférant une signification spécifique, eu égard à son nouveau champ d'application. Voici la définition de Greimas: "Par isotopie nous entendons un ensemble redondant de catégories sémantiques qui rend possible la lecture uniforme du récit,

telle qu'elle résulte des lectures partielles, des énoncés et de la résolution de leurs ambiguités qui est guidée par la recherche de la lecture unique". Appliquée au domaine musical, par isotopie sémantique nous entendons les catégories des signifiés qui embrassent plusieurs classèmes pour faire ressortir une catégorie sémantique esentielle et reconnaissable dans plusieurs oeuvres à l'aide de classèmes et sèmes divers. Eero Tarasti parle de "champs de signification" à propos des isotopies, "ce sont les structures profondes de la signification qui garantissent la cohérence interne d'une pièce musicale" (1989. Analyse Musicale 16).

Nous avons dégagé cinq isotopies et deux bi-isotopies: sept signifiés de grande unité comme les fonctions narratives les plus importantes de L'Orfeo:

L'isotopie pastorale, l'isotopie religieuse, l'isotopie infernale, la bi-isotopie funeste et de la douleur, la biisotopie pastorale et de bonheur et enfin deux isotopies typiquement baroques qui sont l'isotopie de l'Allégorie et l'isotopie du triomphe et de la gloire.

L'isotopie de l'Allégorie: l'Allégorie initiale du prologue est à lui seul une isotopie, il introduit la notion de récit et non de discours. L'Allégorie est le narrateur et *L'Orfeo* est un personnage narré à la troisième personne; la réalité est alors ici racontée sur le mode de la fiction a un second niveau de signification. L'isotopie du triomphe et de la gloire, pose le problème de l'homme face aux divinités. En effet le cinquieme acte se termine dans la gloire, Orfeo est appelé au ciel par Apollon et accède à la contemp]ation éternelle d'Euridice parmi les étoiles contrairement au mythe d'Orphée où le héros meurt déchiré par les Bacchantes.

Le dégagement des isotopies constitue le premier palier de toute étude de la narrativité. Les stratégies narratives s'étudient à partir de ces isotopies mais il faut pour cela suffisamment de résultats sur une partie importante de la production d'un même compositeur.

Une interprétation sémantique est réalisable si, après une synthèse des isotopies définies dans les oeuvres analysées, on peut conclure des isotopies dominantes et déterminantes de l'oeuvre.

Tableaux acte par acte des isotopies dominantes de *L'Orfeo* Ordre d'apparition: Acte I, acte II, acte III, acte IV, acte V.

Table 1. Acte I.

Numéros	Style	Instruments	Forme	Tonalite	Sèmes ou Classèmes	Isotopies
Ritournelle		Violes	unique de 8 mesures	ré min.	Unique Allégorie	Allégorie
Berger I	air	chant + gravicembalo (?)	A.B.A.	mineure		∧
Choeur A "Viesi Imeneo"	Choeur polyphonique Ballo (?)	5 voix + violes et flûtes	A.B.B'.	mineure (sol)	Funeste	Bi-isotopie *Pastorale* et de *Bonheur*
Nymphe	Récit	chant + gravicembalo viole basse (?)		majeure		
Choeur B "Lasciati i Monte"	"Choeur polyphonique en forme de balletto"	5 voix + cordes et flûtes	AA. BB'	majeur (sol)	Pastoral	
Ritournelle a/	danse	paroles–flûtes	aa	majeure	Pastoral	
Choeur B	danse	paroles–flûtes	AA	majeure	Pastoral	
Ritournelle a/					Pastoral	
Berger II	Récit	Chant: ténor + gravicembalo		majeure		
ORFEO	Arioso	chant + chitarrone	unique	mineure	Bonheur	
EURIDICE	Arioso	chant + orgue (?)	unique	mineure	Bonheur	
Choeur B "Lasciati i Monti"			AA BB		Pastoral	
Ritournelle a/			aa		Pastoral	∨
Choeur A Imeneo			A B B'		Funeste	
Berger I	Récit	voix + gravicembalo				∧
Ritournelle b/		violes	ab		Religieux	Isotopie
Bergers I–II	Air –duo écriture contrapuntique	2 voix + gravicembalo violes ?	unique	majeure		*Religieuse*
Ritournelle b/	"	"	"	"	Religieux	

Numéros	Style	Instruments	Forme	Tonalite	Sèmes ou Classèmes	Isotopies
Nymphe, IIe et IIIe bergers	séquence vocale en trio – style contrapuntique	3 voix + basse continue	unique	majeure		
Ritournelle b/					Religieux	V
Bergers I & II	séquence à 2 voix contrapuntique	2 voix + basse continue	unique	majeure	Pastoral	
Choeur C "Ecco Orfeo"	madrigalesque harmonie verticale	5 voix + cordes	A	majeure (do et sol)	Bonheur	

Table 2. Acte II.

Numéros	Style	Instruments	Forme	Tonalité	Sèmes et Classèmes	Isotopies
Ière partie						∧
Symphonie	danse	cordre		mineure (sol) m	Pastoral Bonheur	Bi-isotopie *Pastorale* et *Bonheur*
Orfeo	air	voix + cordes	A.B.A.	"	Pastoral Bnheur	
Ritournelle a/ Berger I Ritournelle a/ Berger I	air (reprise sur le 2ème couplet)	2 petits violons	a A a A	passagés mineure majeure	Pastoral Bonheur	
Ritournelle b/ Bergers I et III Ritournelle b/ Bergers I et III	air à 2 voix homorythmiques "reprise" sur le 2e couplet	cordes	b A b A	mineure	Pastoral Bonheur	
Ritournelle c/ Bergers I et III Ritournelle c/	air à 2 voix nouveau	flûtes	c B c	majeure	Pastoral Bonheur	
Choeur A nymphes et bergers	Funestepolyphonie à 5 voix	voix et violes	unique	Do majeur Sol Majeur	Pastoral Bonheur	
Ritournelle Air d'Orfeo	air accompagné	voix et violes	dAdA dAdA	mineure sol majeur	Pastoral Bonheur	
Berger I	air accompagné	voix + gravicembalo			Pastoral Bonheur	V

Numéros	Style	Instruments	Forme	Tonalité	Sèmes et Classèmes	Isotopies
IIème partie						$\wedge$
La messagère Berger III Messagère Berger II Messagère Orfeo Messagère Orfeo Messagère Orfeo	dans le style "recit" échange de phrases rapides	orgue + chit. viole + chit. +gravicembalo orgue + chit. orgue violes orgue + chit. violes orgue violes		nombreux change-ments	Funeste Tragique	Bi-isotopie *funeste* et de la *douleur*
Messagère	récit	orgue + chitar-rone		multiples	Funeste Douleur	
Berger I Berger II Berger III	récit, même air que messagère n° 1, puis dia-logue	gravicembalo			Funeste Tragique	
Orfeo	Air	orgues, violes, chitarrones		sol mineur	Douleur	
Choeur B des nymphes et des bergers	Madrigal	5 voix + cordes	A B		Funeste Tragique	
IIIème partie					Funeste	
La Messagère	récit	orgue et chitar-rone		la mineur	Douleur	
Sinfonia		cordes		sol mineur	Funeste	
Bergers I et III					Douleur	
Choeur B des nymphes et des bergers	Madrigal	5 voix + cordes	A (reprise du choeur précédent)		Funeste	
Bergers I et III	récit, air à 2 voix				Douleur	
Choeur B			A seulement		Funeste	$\vee$
Ritournelle					Pastoral	

Numéros	style	Instruments	forme	tonalité	sèmes ou classèmes	Isotopies
Sinfonia a/		5 trombones + cornets	unique	sol majeur	Infernaux	∧
Orfeo	récit	clavecins ou chitarrone ?		do m (?)		
La Speranza	récit			majeure mineure		
Orfeo	récit	chitarrone		mineure	Angoisse	
Caron	récit	orgue regale			Infernaux	
Sinfonia b/		cuivres (5 trombones)	unique	mineure (sol)	Infernaux Echec	i n f e r n a l e
Orfeo ritournelle a/ Orfeo	Airs	chitarrone + violons, violons + trompettes, trompettes, Harpe double	A a B c C		Douleur	
ritournelle c/ Orfeo		Harpe double Orgue –violes puis orgue + chitarrone puis cordes ajoutées	c D D' D''		Douleur	
Caron	récit	orgue regale		Fa majeur	Infernaux	
Orfeo	arioso	orgue + chitarrone		mineure (sol) chromatismes	Douleur	
Sinfonia b/		cordes	unique	sol mineur	Echec	
Orfeo	arioso	orgue + chitarrone		sol majeur		
Sinfonia a/				sol majeur	Infernaux	
Choeur	madrigal			sol majeur	Espoir	∨

Table 3. Acte III.

Problèmes et limites de cette approche

Cette étude a porté essentiellement sur les influences associatives du texte ou des situations de la dramaturgie, c'est une étude immanente qui reste une application d'analyse sémantique structurale sur une oeuvre étudiée comme telle en dehors de tout contexte social et historique. Notre approche est restrictive dans la mesure où elle ne tient compte que de la partition et des indications manuscrites données par le compositeur.

Numéro	Style	Instruments	forme	tonalité	sèmes ou classèmes	Isotopies
Proserpine	récit	gravicembalo + viole(?)basse	unique	mineure		
Pluton	récit	origue - chitarrone		majeure		
premier Esprit deuxième Esprit	récits	gravicembalo - violes + chitarrone				
Proserpine	récit	gravicembalo - violes + chitarrone		mineure		
Pluton	récit	orgue + chitarrone		majeure		
Choeur des Esprits Infernaux	polyphonique à 5 voix - madrigalesque	5 trombones		la majeur		
ORPHEE ritournelle 1 couplet I ritournelle 2 couplet II ritournelle couplet	Air	chitarrone orgue	a A a B' a C	majeur chromatismes	Bonheur / Angoisse	
récit	récit	.		mineure		/\
Esprit						
Eurydice	récit	orgue		mineure	Funeste Douleur	Bi-isotopie *Funeste* et de la *Douleur*
Esprit					Funeste	
Orphée	récit	violes gravicembalo				
Symphonie		violes			Infernaux Douleur	
Choeur des Esprits Infernaux	polyphonique à 5 voix Madrigal	violes clavecin luth	A B C	la mineur la majeur majeure la mineur la majeur		\/

Table 4. Acte IV.

De plus, c'est une approche sémantique littéraire appliquée au domaine musical, qu'il a fallu réadapter et qu'il faut réadapter à chaque fois. Ce type d'analyse n'est pas applicable de manière aussi systématique et aussi sûre que sur un texte littéraire. Il faut tenir compte de l'aspect polydiscursif de l'opéra. Il semble que dans le cadre de l'opéra

Numéros	Style	Instruments	Forme	Tonalité	Sèmes ou Classèmes	Isotopies
Ritournelle					Pastoral	∧
Orfeo	récits	orgue + chitarrone		mineure	Douleur	Bi-isotopie *funeste* et de la *douleur*
Echo Orfeo Echo Orfeo Echo Orfeo Echo Orfeo	entrecoupés d'intervention d'écho qui répéte le dernier mot de chaque partie					
Symphonie		violes cuivres		mineure	Echec	
Apollon	récit	cordes chitarrones		majeure		∨ ∧
Orfeo	récit	cordes chitarrones		mineure		Isotopie du *Triomphe*
Apollon Orfeo Apollon Orfeo	récits récits récits récits			majeure		
Apollon et Orfeo	Duo	orgue − cordes			Bonheur	
Ritournelle		cordes	a	majeure	Bonheur	
Choeur	polyphonie 5 voix		A a A	majeure	Bonheur	
Moresca	danse			majeure		∨

Table 5. Acte V.

tout reste à faire en matière de méthodologie car en sémiotique l'opéra est un sujet d'étude particulièrement complexe puisqu'il fonctionne avec plusieurs processus de signes. Il faudrait pouvoir effectuer la synthèse de tous ces procesus de signes.

Orientation de nos recherches

Notre projet de recherche est de développer cette application selon les grilles de modalités greimassiennes et prendre comme base d'observation les quatre catégories suivantes: le lieu, la figure, l'action et le temps c'est à dire spatialité, temporalité, actorialité auxquels s'ajouterait une notion de figure à travers une étude de la notion de personnage et de personne.

Les formes de la narration et les techniques de narration sont des éléments qui peuvent être utilisés et abordés sous des angles d'études différents et sont des éléments d'analyse précieux pour l'étude d'une période charnière qui voit naître une forme musicale nouvelle: l'opéra. Cette approche permet d'aborder des questions fondamentales qui deviennent l'objet de notre recherche. Tout d'abord y-a-t-il historicité des modes de la narration? Cette question relève du cadre de l'anthropologie historique, les modes de la narration étant sujets à variations historiques, sociales et culturelles. Notre problématique implique que, une fois les constats faits, nous cherchons à les comprendre.

Comme autres questions fondamentales se pose le problème de l'apparition de l'opéra. Pourquoi y-a-t-il apparition de l'opéra? L'opéra intervient-il dans une période de transition? Cette transition est-elle essentiellement esthétique?. L'apparition de la notion de personnage dans la nouvelle forme de l'opéra est-elle en relation avec la transformation de l'idée de personnage à la Renaissance? (au sens philosophique du terme. Nous faisons ici référence à un ouvrage de psychologie historique d'Ignace Meyerson: *"La Notion de Personne"*). Un aspect intéressant de cette recherche consiterait à réélaborer la notion de personnage telle qu'elle a été abordée en psychologie historique.

Le problème du lieu est également une notion de grande importance (en référence à l'analyse de Pierre Francastel: *"La Figure et le Lieu"*). Ainsi que l'action dramatique, nous essayons de "comprendre" le sens social du lieu, du personnage et du temps narré dans le récit (en tenant compte bien entendu des aspects du temps narré par le texte et du temps narré par la musique).

Cette recherche tiendra compte, du mieux possible, du caractère polydiscursif de l'opéra et de sa nature intersémiotique, l'opéra étant la réunion de plusieurs systèmes de signes différents qui évoluent ensemble. Aussi, nous nous attacherons également à l'articulation narrativité/figurativité en essayant de déterminer ce qui relève précisément de la narrativité puis de la figurativité et comment l'une et l'autre s'articulent.

Les résultats que nous venons de présenter ne sont bien entendu pas définitifs mais ils sont un premier tremplin pour une approche interdisciplinaire et donc plus complète du problème de la naissance de l'opéra et des modes de narration de l'opéra. Une approche sémantique conduit et donne des éléments pour une étude pluridisciplinaire et interdiscilplinaire du problème. c'est une base pour une dimension sociologique de ce sujet. Une approche pluridisciplinaire est considérée comme nécessaire puisqu'elle permet une approche cognitive de la musique aussi vaste que possible et puisqu'elle ne réduit pas cette approche à de simples considérations formelles. Le déchiffrement de l'opéra au début du XVIIème siècle en Italie n'est pas le résultat d'une seule analyse mais de plusieurs analyses qui diffèrent suivant leur projet (analyse des techniques d'inscription, des techniques et modes de la narration, analyse de l'éco-forme, analyse de la réalité sensible). Note démarche actuelle d'étude de la narration, des techniques de narration et des stratégies narratives s'inscrit dans un projet de déchiffrement[3].

Notes

1. Grabócz, Márta, 1985. *L'influence du Programme sur l'évolution des formes instrumentales dans les oeuvres pour Piano de Liszt*, Thèse pour le Doctorat de IIIème cycle, Université de Paris I-Sorbonne, 440 p.
2. Toutes ces associations ont été répertoriées par Joszef Ujfalussy et l'on peut s'y reporter dans la thèse pour le Doctorat de IIIème cycle de Márta Grabócz.
3. DÉCHIFFREMENT: Le déchiffrement vise à expliciter et à rechercher le sens de l'objet musical civilisationnel qu'il actualisera et qu'il tentera de comprendre en tant qu'objet de civilisation. Le déchiffrement se définit comme une étude interprétative, explicative, musicologique et foncièrement pluridisciplinaire.

Références

Courtes, Joseph (1976). *Introduction à la Sémiotique Narrative et Discursive*. Paris: Hachette.

Francastel, Pierre (1967). *La Figure et le Lieu*. Paris: Eds. Gallimard.

Grabócz, Márta (1985). L'influence du Programme sur l'évolution des formes instrumentales dans les œuvres pour Piano de Liszt, Thèse pour le Doctorat de IIIème cycle, Université de Paris I-Sorbonne, Paris.

– (1987). "Liszt — sonate en si mineur: une stratégie narrative complexe", *Analyse Musicale* 8: 64–70 .

– (1986). "Modernité des œuvres pour piano", *Silences* 3: 211–221.

Greimas, A. (1974). *Sémantique Structurale*. Paris: Larousse.

Greimas, A. J. & Courtes, J. (1979). *Sémiotique, Dictionnaire Raisonné de la Théorie du Langage*. Paris: Hachette Université.

McAdams, Stephen & Deliège, Irène (éds., 1989). *La Musique et les Sciences Cognitives*. Liège/Bruxelles: Pierre Mardaga.

Mélétinski, Evguéni (1969). "L'étude structurale et typologique du conte", in: V. Propp (1970). *Morphologie du Conte*, 201–254, traduit du Russe par Claude Kahn. Paris: Seuil.

Meyerson, Ignace (1948). *Les Fonctions Psychologiques et les Œuvres*. Paris: Librairie Philosophique J. Vrin.

– (1973). (Sous la direction de) *Problème de la Personne*, Colloque du Centre de Recherches de Psychologie Comparative, Ecole Pratique des Hautes Etudes. Paris: Mouton & Co.

Mounin, G. (1975). "Sémantique", *Encyclopedia Universalis* 14: 846-854. Paris.

Propp, Vladimir (1969). *Morphologie du Conte*. Traduit du Russe par Marguerite Derrida, Réed. remaniée. Paris: Seuil. (Ed. orig. Morfologija Skazki; Transformacii Volshebnykh Skazok. Leningrad: Akademia, 1928.)

Ricœur, Paul (1983). *Temps et Récit: 1 L'intrigue et le récit historique*. Saint-Amand: Seuil.

– (1984). *Temps et Récit: 2 La configuration dans le récit de fiction*. Saint-Amand: Seuil.

– (1985). *Temps et Récit: 3 Le temps raconté*. Saint-Amand: Seuil.

Tarasti, Eero (1987). "On the modalities of opera", *Semiotica* 66/1–3: 155–168.

– (1989). "L'Analyse sémiotique d'un prélude de Debussy: *La terrasse des audiences du clair de lune*", *Analyse musicale* n° 16: 67–74.

La lecture du sens dans les œuvres polysémiotiques

PATRICK FARFANTOLI

1. Introduction

Depuis quelques années, on a tenté de transférer dans le domaine musical un certain nombre de théories issues de la linguistique, de la sémiotique et de la théorie des textes littéraires. Le transfert a souvent été fait pour des raisons méthodologiques indépendamment de la spécificité sémiotique ou de la réalité même de l'œuvre musicale. En effet, la plupart du temps, les œuvres musicales ont été analysées en considérant leur fonctionnement comme homogène du point de vue sémiotique. Si ce type d'analyse a pu s'appliquer facilement aux œuvres purement instrumentales de type concertos, sonates ou symphonies, le problème est en revanche différent pour les œuvres mixtes: musiques à texte; opéras; ballets; poèmes symphoniques; musiques de film ou de publicité, qui sont de caractère polysémiosique, et qui, au-delà de la question des relations entre texte et musique que soulève Ruwet en 1972 posent le problème des relations entre sémioses de type différent. Il apparaît alors nécessaire de s'interroger plus particulièrement sur les mécanismes de la coopération des diverses sémioses au sein de ces œuvres, dans les domaines de la production et de la lecture du sens (Vecchione, 1992).

Pour éclairer ce problème, nous prendrons pour exemples deux œuvres illustrant des cas de fonctionnements différents de la coopération intersémiosique au sein de l'œuvre musicale. Il s'agit d'une part du *Don Giovanni* de Mozart, dans lequel les sémioses musicales et littéraires sont simultanément présentes. D'autre part la *Symphonie Fantastique* de Berlioz, dans laquelle la coopération s'effectue entre une sémiose "in præsentia" (la musique), et une sémiose "in absentia" (le programme).

2.1. Spécificité de l'œuvre

Postulat I— Spécificité des œuvres polysémiosiques.

Les théories traditionnelles de la littérature et de la musique ne traitent habituelllement pas le problème de la signifiance dans une perspective de coopération intersémiosique, car elles étudient le fonctionnement du sens dans des œuvres monosémiosiques, ou qu'elles considèrent comme telles.

Postulat II— Indépendance de fonctionnement et coopération des sémioses au sein des œuvres mixtes.

Nicolas Ruwet (1972), avait imaginé le fonctionnement indépendant du texte et de la musique dans les œuvres faisant coopérer ces deux dimensions. Généralisant cette hypothèse méthodologique, nous postulerons qu'il s'agit de deux dimensions complètement hétérogènes possédant chacune un fonctionnement spécifique. Le problème a résoudre est donc celui des mécanismes de la coopération de ces dimensions sémiosiques au sein d'une même œuvre pour produire le sens (Vecchione 1993).

2.2. Réalité de l'œuvre musicale

Postulat III— Sens et configuration dans les œuvres polysémiosiques.

Compte tenue des travaux de B. Vecchione (1984,85) et de A. Boucourechliev (1993), nous considérerons que la configuration de l'œuvre dans laquelle le sens s'inscrit ne se réduit pas simplement au schéma formel. Celui-ci n'est qu'une composante de l'œuvre prise en tant que discours. En effet, il existe une infrastructure, une dialectique entre matière et temps grâce à laquelle la "kinésis" de l'énoncé musical va engendrer la signifiance. La configuration du sens dans une œuvre polysémiosique doit donc être étudié en fonction et à partir de la résultante des diverses sémioses qui la constituent.

Postulat IV— L'opéra et le poème symphonique comme discours.

Nous nous sommes basés sur les travaux de Paul Ricœur (1983; 1985) pour considérer, sur un plan général, l'œuvre musicale comme discours, et plus particulièrement dans l'opéra et dans le poème symphonique, comme récit de fiction.

Sur les travaux d'Umberto Eco (1979; 1990) concernant les problèmes d'interprétations des œuvres littéraires.

Et enfin sur les travaux de Bernard Vecchione (1992–1993) concernant l'œuvre musicale prise comme discours dans le cadre des polysémioses de type argumentatif, et dans le cadre de la polydiscursivité.

Postulat V— L'opéra et le poème symphonique comme polysémioses de type discursif.

A partir des travaux sur les polysémioses de type argumentatif, nous avons développé le concept de polysémioses d'un type discursif particulier, qui n'est pas nécessairement seulement narratif ou argumentatif pour caractériser d'une part l'opéra et d'autre part le poème symphonique.

Postulat VI— Spécificité du propos d'une œuvre.

Le problème du déchiffrement tel que nous l'entendons, c'est à dire dans la perspective du récit, du discours s'instaurant lors de la réalisation sonore de l'œuvre sous entend une démarche spécifique pour chaque œuvre.

3. Le problème du sens

Le but de notre étude est de restaurer pour chaque œuvre l'intentio autoris. Cependant, victime de réécriture, de ré-interprétation celle-ci ne nous parvient jamais sous sa forme originelle. C'est d'autant plus ennuyeux qu'à chaque nouvelle réécriture il y a réinstauration d'un sens différent. L'œuvre se présente donc, la plupart du temps, comme le résultat d'un processus sociologique transformationnel, un objet de civilisation issu de manipulations successives. Ainsi, reprenant le concept de réplicabilité proposé par Eco (1985), nous pouvons affirmer que dans le cas du Don Giovanni de Mozart on ne joue que des "Faux" depuis le XIX siècle. Il est donc important d'effectuer au préalable un travail de restauration permettant de mieux cerner l'œuvre originale.

Le premier constat à effectuer dans le cas de cet opéra c'est qu'il a été rapidement considéré comme la mise en musique du mythe littéraire de Don Juan. Partant de là on ne s'est pas posé la question de savoir si la volonté de Mozart était différente comme tendent à le montrer certaines scènes par exemple celle du cimetière. En tout cas, à partir d'Hoffmann, il y a eu assimilation systématique du mythe de Don Juan avec le personnage de Don Giovanni. D'autre part il est facile de constater qu'aucune des représentations ne correspond exactement soit à la version de Prague soit à celle de Vienne. Nous sommes donc en présence d'une troisième "version collective" ou plus exactement d'une voie d'interprétation se définissant à travers une rhèse interprétative que nous reconnaissons comme étant *Le Don Giovanni* de Mozart.

Dans le cas de cet opéra le facteur de transformation est lié en grande partie à l'idéologie romantique. Ainsi, le mythe de Don Juan va subir une importante métamorphose, il va être la négation de ce qu'il avait été jusque là. Le héros n'est plus un libertin cynique et frivole qui se dresse contre Dieu, mais représente entre autre l'incarnation idéologique d'une quête sans fin de la femme idéale. De plus il est petit à petit contaminé par son "demi frère" Faust et bien que Don Juan n'ait jamais pactisé avec le diable, les commentateurs lui prêtent une situation satanique qu'ils voient dans son cynisme et sa sensualité. La liaison que l'on fait entre les deux personnages se concrétise d'ailleurs en 1829 avec la tragédie *Don Juan und Faust* de Christian Dietrich Gragge.

Le problème que l'on rencontre est donc que le sens attribué généralement à l'opéra provient d'une tradition de lecture datant du début du romantisme, et issue d'une visée littéraire ne concordant pas nécessairement avec la volonté de Mozart. Partant de cette constatation il nous semblait nécessaire d'étudier l'opéra tel qu'il a réellement été écrit. A ce stade, on pourra nous objecter que le manuscrit qui nous est parvenu est trop embrouillé, seulement cette objection contient en substance le fait d'étudier toutes les transformations de cet opéra, or, ce qui nous intéresse, c'est uniquement la version de Prague du 29 octobre

1787 et non pas les différentes versions de circonstances écrites par la suite. De fait quand un compositeur remanie une de ses œuvres, sa problématique initiale s'en trouve altérée.

Ce problème se pose aussi, mais dans des termes légèrement différents, à propos de la *Symphonie Fantastique*, pour laquelle il existe deux versions originelles, mais dont, aujourd'hui, une lecture unique (et univoque) du sens s'est institutionnalisée. Ainsi donne-t-on couramment la deuxième version de l'œuvre sans sa suite *Lélio*, ce qui engendre des erreurs de sens dans le processus d'actualisation discursive.

4. Analyse

4.1. Don Giovanni

Dans *Don Giovanni*, les deux dimensions littéraire et musicale sont énoncées in præsentia. Il s'agit alors d'étudier comment deux énonciations coopèrent, et particulièrement dans les moments privilégiés où elles inscrivent des configurations qui divergent. L'ouverture de l'opéra représente un cas particulier au sein de laquelle la production de sens fonctionne, relativement au reste de l'opéra, de façon purement intratextuelle, par des mécanismes d'évocation, et par une sensibilisation aux principaux éléments signifiants, mis en système par le reste de l'œuvre.

Nous considérerons l'œuvre dans sa totalité, et donc comme un type de discours très particulier. Ceci nous permet de prendre quelques distances avec les théories des signes élémentaires ou complexes se réduisant dans le domaine musical à des structures composantes de l'œuvre et non pas à une structure d'ensemble.

Dans ce type d'analyse l'important est tout d'abord d'isoler le ou les éléments fonctionnant dans le système d'ensemble que représente le discours. Nous verrons que selon le type d'œuvre ils peuvent être différents. Pour l'opéra le livret représente naturellement un des éléments. Quant aux autres éléments on peut penser qu'ils sont contenus dans la musique elle-même, or tous les composants musicaux ne remplissent pas les conditions exigées. En effet il ne s'agit pas seulement pour l'élément de signifier ponctuellement mais aussi de pouvoir acquérir à l'intérieur du système une valeur d'opposition spécifique. A partir du moment ou il y a œuvre musicale, celle-ci s'inscrit structurellement dans le temps et la temporalité qui en découle peut être rapprochée de celle du discours, c'est à dire qu'à des moment différents du discours il peut y avoir une série d'occurences d'un même terme, mais le sens de ce terme peut avoir évolué par le fait de la narration.

4.1.2. Système des champs de signifiance

Un des seuls éléments musicaux qui puisse être inscrit dans un système fondamental sur le plan du sens c'est l'emploi des tonalités et plus particulièrement l'emploi de ces tonalités à travers un système spécifique à l'œuvre étudiée. Pour effectuer ce codage le compositeur utilise, entre autres, les différentes règles communicationnelles, culturelles, sociales, fonctionnant dans son environnement. Il va donc construire son œuvre autour de signes connus: la forme, les règles d'écritures harmoniques ,etc , mais va agencer les éléments de façon à organiser un sens particulier. L'auditeur, de son coté, possède certaines clés qui lui permettent d'appréhender des signes communs autour des propriétés de la matière sonore. L'auditeur ne peut pas appréhender, à la différence de l'analyste, l'œuvre dans sa totalité. Son approche se fait au même rythme que se forme la réalité de l'œuvre. Cette approche, pour qu'il y ait déchiffrement, implique donc que l'émetteur-compositeur utilise une chaîne "d'artifices expressifs" devant être actualisés par le destinataire-auditeur. Ceux-ci vont nous aider dans la recherche et la détermination du système. Cependant l'auditeur n'est pas toujours à même de reconstruire ce système, tout d'abord par le fait que la narration peut volontairement induire le lecteur à activer de faux éléments, ensuite, dans le cas des œuvres possédant un lourd passé littéraire, il arrive souvent que l'auditeur ne fasse pas l'effort de rechercher les éléments signifiants au sein de l'œuvre.

4.1.3. Configuration des champs de signifiance

Dans un premier temps il faut considérer que nous avons affaire à un type de récit narratif instaurant une réalité fictionnelle et symbolique qui ne requiert pas les mêmes propriétés que les récits possédant une prétention à la vérité, comparable à celle des discours descriptifs ayant cours dans les sciences. Comme le fait Ricœur, nous suivrons Aristote quand il désigne la composition verbale constituant un texte par muthos, c'est à dire l'assemblage des actions accomplies, non pas dans le sens d'une structure statique, mais dans celui d'une structuration issue de la sélection et de l'arrangement des événements et des actions racontés. Ce qui permet à Ricœur d'employer le concept de "mise en intrigue" plutôt que celui d'intrigue. Celle-ci représente donc l'ensemble des combinaisons à travers lesquelles des événements sont transformés en histoire. L'intrigue est donc le médiateur entre l'événement et l'histoire.

Ricœur conclut donc que tout événement contribue à la progression d'une histoire et donc qu'un événement n'est pas seulement une occurence mais une composante narratrice. Notre propos est d'essayer de voir si l'on peut généraliser cette problématique 1) à des sémioses autres que littéraires, 2) à des œuvres polysémiosiques. Comme postulat de départ nous considérerons que ce transfert est possible, du moins en partie.

4.1.4. Structure du processus de codage

La recherche du système de signification utilisé par Mozart se fait sur plusieurs niveaux et en plusieurs étapes. La première étape consiste à relever les tonalités correspondant à des séquences discursives complètes (Fig. 1), par exemple l'introduction qui a comme tonalité générale Fa majeur.

Acte I		Personnages	Tonalités
N⁰ 1 Introduzion	Notte e giorno faticar	Leporello / D Anna / D Giovanni/Commendatore	Fa M.
N⁰ 2 Duetto	Fuggi, crudele	D Anna/ D Ottavio	ré min.
N⁰ 3 Aria	Ah chi mi dice mai	D Elvira	Mi♭ M.
N⁰ 4 Aria	Madamina, il catalogo	Leporello	Ré M.
N⁰ 5	Giovinette che fate	Masetto / Zerline	Sol M.
N⁰ 6 Aria	Ho capito	Masetto	Fa M.
N⁰ 7 Duettino	Là ci darem la mano	D Giovanni/Zerline	La M.
N⁰ 8 Aria	Ah fuggi il trator	D Elvira	Ré M.
N⁰ 9 Quartetto	Non ti fidar, o misera	D Anna/ D Elvira/ D Ottavio/ D Giovanni	Si♭ M.
N⁰ 10 Aria	Or sai chi l'onore	D Anna	Ré M.
N⁰ 11 Aria	Fin ch'an dal vino	D Giovanni	Si♭ M.
N⁰ 12 Aria	Batti, Batti	Zerline	Fa M.
N⁰ 13 Finale	Presto Presto	Masetto	Do M.
Acte II			
N⁰ 1 Duetto	Eh via buffone	D Giovanni/ Leporello	Sol M.
N⁰ 2 Terzetto	Ah taci, ingiusto core	D Giovanni/ Leporello D Elvira	La M.
N⁰ 3 Canzonetta	De vieni alla finestra	D Giovanni	Ré M.
N⁰ 4 Aria	Metà di voi quà vadano	D Giovanni	Fa M.
N⁰ 5 Aria	Vedrai Carino	Zerline	Do M.
N⁰ 6 Sestetto	Sola, sola in bujo loco	Leporello / D Ottavio / D Anna / D Elvira	Mi♭ M.
N⁰ 9 Duetto	O statua gentilissima	D Giovanni / Leporello	Mi M.
N⁰ 10 Aria	Non mi dir	D Anna	Fa M.
N⁰ 11 Finale, Scène 13	Già la mensa	D Giovanni / Leporello	Fa M.

Figure 1. Tableau 1: Niveau 1.

Nous obtenons une série de tonalités principales qui confrontées à leurs caractères situationnels acquièrent pour certaines un premier potentiel signifiant général qui devra être affiné au fur et à mesure. C'est le cas par exemple pour le Fa Majeur qui semble être affecté à un champ de signification centré sur la "vie physique", la "comédie" et du Sib Majeur qui marque la "tragédie", mais aussi toutes les scènes correspondant au mythe et que Mozart n'a pas modifiées. Pour d'autres tonalités, il faudra attendre une analyse plus profonde. Ce tableau représente simplement un premier système de champs généraux de signification mais il n'indique pas comment le sens est instauré ni comment il est utilisé dans la narration.

A ce stade du déchiffrement de la signification de la pièce ce qui est important c'est de voir comment se développe la relation entre sémiose littéraire et musicale. Nous partons de l'hypothèse que si la signification du texte littéraire et de certaines figures signifiantes musicales peut être appréhendée immédiatement il n'en va pas de même pour les tonalités. Ainsi, dire que la scène 1 est en Fa Majeur apparaît comme une indication relativement secondaire, parce que, dans la perspective du récit s'instaurant (c'est à dire dévoilant progressivement la réalité signifiante de l'œuvre), le Fa Majeur ne représente rien tant qu'il n'a pas encore été relié au système de ses occurences et donc tant que n'a pas été défini son potentiel signifiant.

Ainsi, dans un premier temps, chaque tonalité utilisée par le compositeur va acquérir un potentiel par connotation avec un ou plusieurs éléments immédiatement identifiables, sur le plan du sens. Ces éléments ne sont d'ailleurs pas forcement uniquement d'ordre textuel. Nous voudrions faire toutefois une remarque à propos des tonalités auxquelles on ne peut pas attribuer de signification a prioriste pour l'ensemble de la production du compositeur, chaque œuvre recréant son propre système.

D'autre part il est bien évident que la première occurence significative d'une tonalité, c'est à dire l'occurence permettant la codification ne pourra être très éloignée du sens des figures signifiantes immédiates, mais ce n'est pas obligatoirement la première rencontrée sur le plan temporel. Pour des raisons de mise en intrigue le compositeur a pu décaler la révélation d'un sens particulier.

Le processus de codification dépend de plusieurs facteurs:

A) La structure "mécanique" conçue à partir d'éléments "encyclopédiquement reconnus" c'est à dire les lois régissant, au moment de la composition, l'écriture musicale. On ne peut toutefois pas considérer que la structure agit en tant qu'élément porteur de sens, au même titre que la structure sujet-verbe-complément en linguistique ne donne pas (la plupart du temps) un sens particulier à la séquence émise, mais nous sommes obligé de l'utiliser comme support communicationnel pour véhiculer des lexèmes dans un ordre déterminé et pour un environnement social précis. Nous nous trouvons donc en présence d'opérateurs formels, qui ne sont pas forcément signifiants sur le plan narratif, mais peuvent le devenir si leur occurence renvoie à une isotopie voulue par le compositeur.

B) Des éléments musicaux, faisant partie de l'encyclopédie générale de la sémiotique communicationnelle. Entre aussi dans cette catégorie une série de "séquences sonores" pouvant être perçues par l'auditeur comme la représentation d'un scénario.

C) La signification que donne le compositeur à ces éléments. Celle-ci est défini contextuellement, co-textuellement mais aussi de façon pragmatique.

La scène 1 de l'acte I de *Don Giovanni* donne un exemple simple de coopération intersémiotique "in præsentia". Leporello peste contre son maître pour lequel il fait la sentinelle pendant que celui-ci prend du bon temps, puis déclare qu'il veut lui aussi "fare il gentiluomo". Cette situation renvoie bien évidement aux divers scénarios hypercodés de la comédie et peut être interprétée comme une inférence de scénarios connus ou "frame" (Eco 1985) et de scénarios intertextuels du type [récriminations d'un valet à l'égard de son maître]. Peu d'élément dans le texte littéraire, indique que l'action est "comique". En revanche, le texte musical va faire ressortir par un système complexe de codification, le coté " giocoso" (Fig. 2).

Dans cette introduction les premières mesures peuvent êtres décrites comme des sèmes musicaux (Fig. 3).

On peut dissocier ici deux actions distinctes (a) et (b) représentant l'arsis et la katalexis. La première, (a), est saccadée, très marquée, elle peut être caractérisée par deux séquences X0 et Y0 . La séquence X0 repose sur la succession tonique-dominante (I–V), ce qui fait apparaître l'enchaînement X0/Y0 comme une cadence, une brève rupture dans la continuité du temps informé par la matière de X0. La perception est d'autant plus forte que la dernière note est plus longue donnant ainsi une

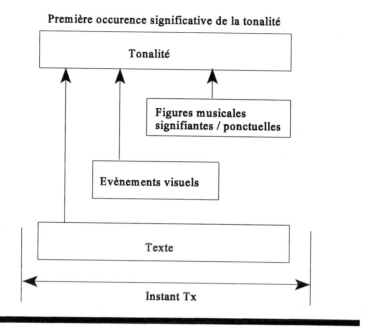

Figure 2. Structure générale du processus de codage des tonalités.

impression de repos, ceci pouvant traduire le temps d'arrêt avant le demi-tour pour revenir sur ses pas.

La deuxième, (b), est plus rapide et plus liée. Elle produit un mouvement furtif. Cette séquence va être modifiée plusieurs fois par la suite sans que cela influe sur son sens général, en revanche ces modifications vont donner une "couleur" plus ou moins marquée à l'action.

La duplication de ce lexème musical implique donc une action répétitive contenant elle-même un processus répétitif, on peut donc inférer que, contextuellement et co-textuellement, ce lexème "iconise" l'action "faire les cent pas" de Leporello. Nous que, contextuellement et co-textuellement, ce lexème insistons sur le fait que ce lexème, dans un autre contexte aurait pu tout aussi bien traduire une action répétitive différente.

Figure 3. Don Giovanni. Acte 1, Scène 1.

Le phénomène n'est pas statique, l'espace sonore est en mouvement chaque fois que l'on répète le lexème (a), son déplacement (se traduisant par un mouvement de spirale sur la figure 2) est caractérisé par une montée d'un ton à chaque répétition. Ceci étant également une "séquence sonore" reconnue, prépare, de plus, l'entrée de la voix.

L'aria de Leporello est basé sur des signes musicaux faisant partie de l'encyclopédie (qui nous est encore familière) donnant à celui-ci une connotation "giocoso". Par association, la tonalité de Fa Majeur va être connotée de la même façon. Il est bien entendu que, pendant le déroulement de l'œuvre, la sphère de sens va pouvoir être affinée, réorientée, mais toujours autour de cette signification première créant ainsi une dialectique complexe entre les deux sémioses (Fig. 4). C'est ce que nous appellerons la découverte ou l'apprentissage du système de signification de l'œuvre.

Autre exemple: la modulation en Si♭ Majeur introduisant Donna Anna et Don Giovanni après l'aria de Leporello. Le drame est signifié, dans un premier temps, sur le plan discursif, par le texte musical. Remarquons ici que le texte littéraire ne sert pas à définir le drame, puisque celui-ci sera décrit plus loin par le livret. L'effet dramatique survient en même temps qu'une modulation de Fa Majeur à Si♭ Majeur. Ce n'est pas une modulation très éloignée (de 1b à 2b) et l'effet dramatique ne vient pas de cette seule opération, mais aussi du traitement de la matière sonore. De toutes manières, l'encyclopédie de l'auditeur ne contient pas (ou pas encore), comme information, le fait qu'une modulation (X) représente le drame, sinon cela impliquerait que dans toutes les autres œuvres (non seulement du compositeur, mais de tous les compositeurs de cette époque) la modulation (X) correspondrait à une situation de drame. L'auditeur réagit en fait à un crescendo de l'orchestre, une figure signifiante ponctuelle, qui est reconnu comme signe dramatique dans son encyclopédie.

En poursuivant l'analyse de cette manière on arrive à décomposer chaque plan discursif (Fig. 5).

Les niveaux 1, 2 et 3 de l'analyse ne présente pas de difficultés sur le plan du déchiffrement parce qu'il s'agit seulement de relever les tonalités donnant un éclairage général et introduisant une scène où une action. En revanche à partir du niveau 4 nous sommes confrontés à deux problèmes importants parce que l'analyse porte sur des fragments musicaux de plus en plus petits qui peuvent se chevaucher et contenir un texte littéraire différent. C'est d'ailleurs la première grande différence d'avec un texte littéraire pur puisque dans ce dernier cas nous n'avons qu'une surface lexématique à analyser.

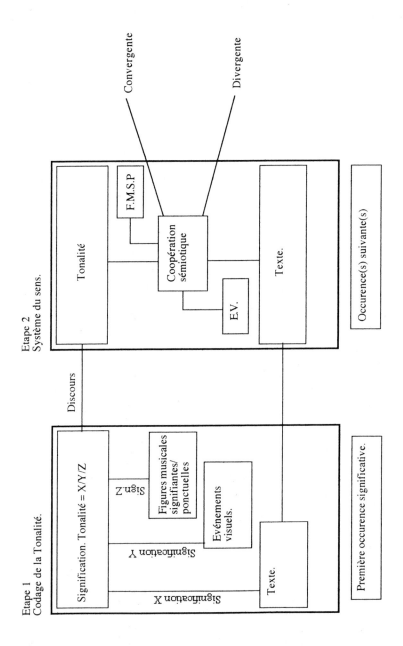

Figure 4. Système de signification.

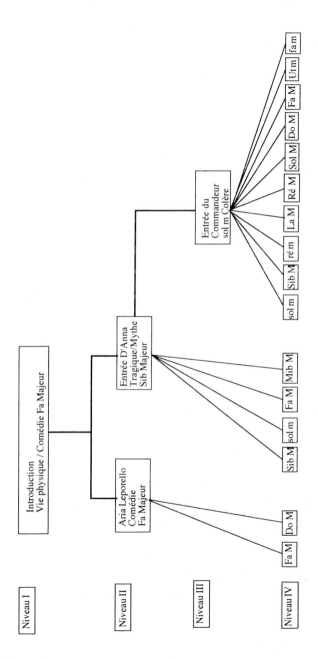

Figure 5.

Le premier problème consiste à pouvoir faire, en l'absence d'événements codificateurs évidents, la distinction entre le système des tonalités et le système narratif, c'est à dire définir à quel moment une tonalité à une fonction technique et non plus narrative dans le cas par exemple d'un accord de passage ou d'une modulation rapide nécessaire pour répondre à la cohésion de l'écriture tonale. En extrapolant, on pourrait considérer que plus un idiome musical sort de la norme d'écriture plus il est signifiant. Cependant on ne pourra faire une vérification définitive qu'en le comparant à toutes ses occurences. En effet, comme nous l'avons déjà dit une tonalité n'a pas de signification particulière, en revanche une fois qu'elle a été codifié son sens général ne peut pas être changé parce que le système de signification autour des tonalités est beaucoup moins maniable que les éléments textuels qui s'y superposent.

L'autre problème est posé par le chevauchement des textes des personnages. En effet sur un segment temporel donné même si le compositeur veut faire ressortir plusieurs colorations différentes à l'aide du système des tonalités il ne peut le faire qu'en utilisant la succession, ce qui n'est pas le cas pour la partie textuelle lorsqu'il y a plusieurs personnages. Cependant étant donné le postulat que nous avons déjà ennoncé tout à l'heure définissant le discours musical et textuel comme spécifique nous ne sommes pas tenus de réaliser une signification terme à terme, sauf dans les cas où la volonté de superposition est évidente, soit pour un seul personnage soit pour plusieurs.

En procédant ainsi, et en opérant une vérification systématique au sein de l'œuvre nous obtenons un système d'interprétation basé sur la dialectique texte/musique.

Ce type d'analyse est important surtout en ce qui concerne l'évolution psychologique des personnages et le sens du discours voulu par le compositeur. Par exemple, Donna Anna qui évolue tout au long de l'opéra entre haine, tragédie, colère et douleur va intervenir pour son dernier aria en Fa majeur, elle accède ainsi pour la première fois au concept de vie, de comédie et se détache ainsi du mythe. Autre exemple tout aussi intéressant est le moment où Don Giovanni disparaît dans les flammes et pour lequel on invoque généralement la tonalité de ré min. En fait, c'est une modulation en Ré Majeur qui accompagne la fin de

Don Giovanni ce qui, sur le plan du sens, est très différent si l'on tient compte des différentes occurences de cette tonalité tout au long de l'opéra.

4.2. Le cas de la Symphonie Fantastique

Ici le problème est très différent puisque la dimension musicale seule est énoncée, l'autre n'est qu'évoquée, et la dialectique n'est pas entre deux énonciations qui coopèrent pour la production de sens mais entre évocation et énonciation. Le cas est très intéressant sur le plan sémiotique, car, dans la *Symphonie Fantastique*, pour "agir" le sens que propose le programme, la musique s'inscrit comme évocation de celui-ci et fonctionne dans une dépendance au texte "in absentia", la question étant de comprendre comment ce que la musique "énonce" se rapporte à ce que la musique "évoque". Précisons que pour cette œuvre il n'existe pas de système de codification spécifique, mais que tous les éléments sont étroitement liés à un éco-système particulier, celui du fantastique littéraire qui apparaît, en France, après la parution des *Contes Fantastiques* d'E.T.A Hoffmann en 1829.

Nous dirons plus précisément que la forme donnée par Berlioz au récit peut être comparée à celle des nouvelles fantastiques littéraires de Gautier ou de Mérimée à ceci près que certaines constantes telles que la notion de modification temporelle liée en littérature à la découverte d'un objet antique sont ici présentées musicalement. Dans une large majorité, tous les éléments font partie d'une encyclopédie que possède déjà l'auditeur. La fin du troisième mouvement, intitulée: Scène aux champs, illustre bien le phénomène de dépendance au texte, même si celui-ci n'est pas "in præsentia". Dans la partie littéraire proprement dite, on s'aperçoit qu'il existe une recherche de l'espace mais aussi une volonté de suspendre la continuité temporelle. Les dernières phrases sont entrecoupées par des points de suspension et s'espacent petit à petit en se réduisant à de simples mots. Sur le plan musical, Berlioz, pour évoquer le texte, va créer une profondeur, un espace sonore en jouant notamment sur le roulement de timbale qui symbolise l'orage grondant dans le lointain, mais aussi l'éloignement par rapport au monde extérieur caractérisant la prise d'opium ainsi que le passage à une réalité différente. On remarquera d'ailleurs que le grondement lointain du tonnerre est pris comme passage et prétexte sonore pour la marche suivante.

Dans le premier mouvement "Rêveries Passions" le passage qui commence à la mesure (232) montre clairement comment Berlioz va "altérer" le temps musical grâce à une désagrégation rythmique (Fig. 6).

Le passage débute par trois mesures en valeurs longues et tenues au cor seul, on s'installe donc dans un temps qui dépend étroitement de la matière sonore puisqu'il n'y a plus d'élément rythmique (1). L'information du temps T0 (la désagrégation rythmique) se fait par rapport à la partie qui précède et la partie suivante (T$-1 <>$ T0 $<>$ T$+1$).

Sur le troisième temps de la mesure (234), les violons II font leur apparition mais avec l'indication PP et diminuant jusqu'à PPP. Le rythme [DPause Noire Croche DSoupir / noire croche dsoupir noire croche dsoupir] repris sur trois mesures et demie, en diminuant, donne, par rapport aux notes tenues du cor, l'impression d'un élément essayant de s'imposer timidement par rapport à la pédale du cor solo. Mesure (237) les violons I et II jouent sur le premier et le troisième temps, mesure (238) les violoncelles et les contrebasses entrent à leur tour, mais sur le deuxième et quatrième temps tandis que les violons alto entament un trémolo se poursuivant jusqu'à la mesure (269). L'élément timidement introduit par les violons II va se métamorphoser et prendre plus de puissance, il va y avoir à cet instant altération du temps précédemment informé par la matière sonore. Les valeurs longues tenues aux cors vont être reprises par les bois et divisées en cellules rythmiques plus courtes dont les temps faibles seront liés aux temps forts annulant ainsi les appuis de la mélodie. Il y a ainsi superposition de deux courants temporels antagonistes, l'oreille ne perçoit donc plus d'appuis stables sur lesquels elle puisse se fixer(2).

Le rôle de l'altération temporelle dans les récits fantastiques littéraires est primordial. Ici cette altération va être contenue dans le discours musical. Tout ce passe comme si Berlioz introduisait petit à petit l'idée de fantastique. On rejoint la nouvelle littéraire dans laquelle le récit devient étrange par l'accumulation de détails sortant de la norme

Figure 6. Berlioz: Symphonie Fantastique. "Rêveries. Passions", mesure 232.

établie, comme dans *La Cafetière* de Gautier. Ainsi le compositeur, par les propriétés phénoménales de la matière sonore, crée un espace instaurant lui-même un temps en suspens. Dans ce cas, les sémioses musicales et littéraires n'étant pas simultanément présentes, il ne peut y avoir évocation du texte que si le destinataire possède une pré-connaissance de ce texte.

Notes

1. Dans ce cas précis le terme "matière sonore" concerne la texture du son lui-même et non son utilisation dans une structure rythmique.
2. Il existe déjà une pédale aux violoncelles/contrebasses qui commence à la mesure (46) et finit à la mesure (60), mais il n'y a pas cette impression de désagrégation rythmique car les parties supérieures, elles, ne sont pas décalées. On ressent toutefois la superposition de deux temps différents mais qui ne s'altèrent pas entre eux. A la mesure (72), le thème repris par les bois à la mesure (240), est joué par les flûtes et les violons I. Mais contrairement au passage que nous avons analysé, l'accompagnement se place sur le temps fort.

Références

Berlioz, H. (s.d). *Symphonie Fantastique*, Op.14. Paris: Heugel & Cie.
Boucourechliev, A. (1993). *Le Langage Musical*. Paris: Fayard.
Eco, U. (1979). *Lector in Fabula*. Milan: Bompiani. (Trad. 1985 Paris, Grasset & Fasquelle, le livre de poche coll. biblio essais.)
– (1990). *I Limiti dell' Interpretazione*. Milan: Bompiani. (Trad. 1992: *Les Limites de l'Interprétation*. Paris: Grasset.)
Mozart, W. A. (s.d). *Don Giovanni*. Opéra K.527. London, Mainz, New-York, Tokyo, Zürich: Ernst Eulenburg Ltd, N° 918, Livret de Lorenzo Da Ponte.
Ricœur, P. (1983). *Temps et récit: 1. L'intrigue et le récit historique*. Paris: Seuil, coll. Points. Série Essais.
– (1984). *Temps et récit: 2. La configuration dans le récit de fiction*. Paris: Seuil, coll. Points. Série Essais.
– (1985). *Temps et récit: 3. Le temps raconté*. Paris: Seuil, coll. Points. Série Essais.
– (1986). *Du texte à l'action*. Paris: Seuil.
Ruwet, N. (1972). *Language, musique, poésie*. Paris: Seuil.

Vecchione, B. (1984). *Pour une science de la réalité musicale: Eléments d'épistémologie musicologique nouvelle.* Thèse de IIIéme cycle, Aix en Provence.

– (1985). La Réalité Musicale. Eléments d'Epistémologie Musicologique. Thèse pour le doctorat d'état es-lettres Option musique, Université de Paris VIII, Dpt.de Musique.

– ( ). "Eléments d'analyse du mouvement musical", *Analyse Musicale* 8: 17–23.

– (1992). *Sémiotique, Anthropologie musicale historique, Pragmatique du sens. La figurativité dans le motet "Nuper Rosarum Flores/ Terribilis est locus iste" de Guillaume Dufay.* Aix-en-Provence: C.R.S.M, Dactyl.

– (1993). Séminaire Doctoral. Aix-en-Provence. Notes personelles.

Musical signs in *Death in Venice* by Benjamin Britten

ANNELI REMME

This paper, the essence of my diploma thesis at the Tallinn Conservatory, is my first attempt to do something in the field of musical semiotics. Some specific features of the opera *Death in Venice* led me to the domain of musical semiotics when looking for a way to analyze the musical ideas of the work. The first strong impulse to regard *Death in Venice* as a complex of signs sprung from the note combination D–C–E–E♭/D♯, both musically and visually the sign of the cross associated with death throughout the piece. Its role in the opera is remarkable. Using some general terms of musical semiotics it is possible to classify musical ideas of the opera according to the way they express their meaning. In other words, it is possible to talk about *Death in Venice* taking into account the relationship between the content and expression of its musical ideas.

Some light on the opera

Death in Venice, as the novella by Thomas Mann, an opera, or a film by Luchino Visconti, has interesting biographical backgrounds connected not only with Mann, Britten, and Visconti but also with Gustav Mahler and others. In addition, the introductory part of my diploma study — *Musical Signs in "Death in Venice" by Benjamin Britten* — has a chapter about parallels between novella and opera; it deals with *Death in Venice*, *Faust* by Goethe and *Doctor Faustus* by Christopher Marlowe (it would not be an exaggeration to include Thomas Mann's *Doctor Faustus* in this group). Coincidences between *Death in Venice* and the Faust tale occur in the action as well as the verbal expression of these three works. From more or less strong connections arise pairs of thoughts: Faust and the German writer Gustav von Aschenbach; Mephistopheles and The Messenger of Death in *Death in Venice*; the beautiful Polish boy Tadzio in a role parallel to that of Margarethe.

The Messenger of Death in the opera has seven different faces: Traveller, Elderly Fop, Old Gondolier, Hotel Manager, Hotel Barber, Leader of the Strolling Players, and Voice of Dionysus. Britten connects them with one musical sign that varies according to the nature and speech manner of each person. This half-real, half-unreal character accompanies Aschenbach throughout the opera. Still, Aschenbach himself feels much stronger the influence of Tadzio, whose Greek, sculpture-like beauty makes him think about life and creative work in a different way than he is accustomed. Because of Tadzio the question of Apollonian and Dionysian mentality, that is, the problem of the relation between reason and passion, arises for Aschenbach.

In order to classify the musical signs of *Death in Venice* I have combined sign categories of semiotic theories by Juri Lotman and Charles S. Peirce. In Lotman's conception there are two kinds of sign: conventional signs and icons. In Peircean theory signs in relation to an object are symbol, icon, and index. The conjunction of these sign categories results in a triple symbol-icon-conventional sign; where *symbol* is a musical sign which in a certain musical tradition conveys some meaning; *icon* is an imitation of natural sound (Tarasti 1990: 136); and *conventional sign*, according to Lotman (1990: 44), is a sign such as a word in natural language. Consequently, the content and expression of the sign are identified only within the limits of a certain language, thus also within the musical language of a certain piece.

The most effective sign in the present work is the symbol of death or cholera: the sign of the cross (D–C–E–E♭/D♯). C (major and minor) is the key associated with death everywhere in the opera. The pitch combination D–C–E–E♭/D♯ may be a quotation from the incidental music to *Orestes* by Euripides, although authorities on Britten's music usually refer only to the quotation from the "First Delphic Hymn to Apollo", which in Britten's opera signifies The Voice of Apollo.

The sign of death (or cholera) acts as a turning-point or critical event in the piece; sometimes it gives the context of cholera to everything taking place in the opera. The sign of death first appears in The Traveller's monologue, but its real meaning is as yet concealed. The Traveller's narrative about exotic oriental marvels is, as Patrick Carnegy says, like an enticing travel brochure (1987: 176); it must entice Aschenbach to begin a journey that holds the possibility for him to emerge from his creative crisis. The real meaning of the sign becomes clear much later. Concealment is reflected also in the structure of the sign. The pitch combination D–C–E–E♭/D♯ contains a minor third within a major third. Peter Evans calls it a "canker"-structure (1987: 77); it is tonal ambiguity according to Eric Roseberry (1987: 86). Hiding a minor third within a major third represents the principle of ambiguity or concealment of meaning in the smallest unit of the piece. Still, the principle that something has more than one meaning dominates each level of the work.

Examples of the sign of death as a critical musical event in the work

In scene 7, after the long Apollonian idyll and his observation of Tadzio in athletic games, Aschenbach decides to contact the boy, but he cannot. Aschenbach blames the heat of the sun for his powerlessness, but he does so through the medium of the sign of cholera. An appearance of the sign of death is a critical event which dissipates the idyllic Olympian atmosphere of the scene and causes the formation of a new sign — the sign of pursuit. Having missed the opportunity to speak with boy, Aschenbach can only look at him from afar and pursue him. In the same scene Tadzio passes Aschenbach on the way to the hotel, and his smile in connection with the sign of death creates another new sign — the sign of love. Upon its inception, the sign of love occurs both in Aschenbach's vocal part and in the orchestra. Later in the opera the sign reveals itself only in the orchestra, without text. The purpose of the sign of love is to give reasons for Aschenbach's activity; the pursuit, in turn, is an indicator of love. The sign of death gives both of them the structure of a "canker". A total of five signs in the opera have a "canker"-structure, consequently, they are connected with the concealment of something. (The first three are also pointed out in Evans 1987: 77, but without particular comments.)

Example 1.

Symbols

(1) The sign of death. The sign of the cross, occurring at first with counterfeited text, is really identified with the words "death" and "cholera" only in scene 11; the infectious disease spreading in Venice, therefore the danger of death, remains unknown to Aschenbach for a long time.

(2) Serenissima, the sign of Venice in the opera. Serenissima is the Italian nickname for the city: bright, splendid, magnificent. It is always connected with water, especially with Aschenbach's journeys by gon-

dola; some authorities call it a barcarolle (White 1983: 272; Evans 1987: 78). Bright and magnificent Venice is scourged by fatal disease, while the city fathers try to keep secret the news of its spreading. Serenissima, as well as the sign of death, has the shape of the cross; for Aschenbach, Serenissima also symbolizes death.

Conventional signs

(3) The sign of The Messenger of Death. Throughout the opera Aschenbach is accompanied by different characters of the same person, who helps conceal the danger of death: The Traveller displays the sign of death with, it may be said, false text. The Hotel Barber and The Leader of the Strolling Players do not answer Aschenbach's questions about disease. The Hotel Manager does not warn his guests.

(4) The sign of love. Aschenbach's affection for Tadzio is a forbidden love; it must be concealed.

(5) The sign of pursuit. Activity that indicates a forbidden feeling is also predisposed to hiding.

About icons in *Death in Venice*

Many imitations of natural sounds do not have great importance in the dramaturgy of *Death in Venice*; mostly they act in the opera as signs of the background. Gondoliers's shouts and church bells form part of the everyday life of Venice; laughter and calls belong to the communication of hotel guests. The song of The Leader of the Strolling Players, with the assistance of all the hotel guests except Aschenbach and Tadzio, is based mainly on the laugh-icon.

Some icons function in the opera as adverbs of place: the ship's engine and whistle indicate the stay on the sea; the voices of gondoliers refer to the canals nearby. Still, two icons have an essential position in the dramaturgy of *Death in Venice*: (1) The Children's cry imitating the sound of the name of Tadzio is transformed into the hoots of the followers of Dionysus in the orgy scene in Aschenbach's dream. (2) In a narrow street of Venice Aschenbach suddenly finds himself face to face with Tadzio and his family whom he is following; frightened, Aschenbach gives out of breath. It is musically marked as a rest within the conventional sign of pursuit; the rest gets its impressiveness from what precedes and follows it.

Sign universes; influence fields of signs; Aschenbach's journey

Signs in the opera can be divided into four sign universes between the characters. These are the sign universes of Aschenbach, Death and The Messenger of Death, Tadzio, and the sign universe of secondary characters (hotel guests, boatmen, citizens of Venice, etc.). Aschenbach's sign universe is the only continuously developing universe. Aschenbach experiences messages from other sign universes, sometimes on the level of reality, sometimes on the level of myth or unreality, depending on his state of mind. With regard to Aschenbach each musical sign in the opera has a sphere of influence. *The opera may be regarded as Aschenbach's journey throughout the influence fields of different signs towards his death*. Different characters of the same person — The Messenger of Death — constitute the escort on his journey; they assist in the fulfillment of the myth-like, predetermined fate of Aschenbach.

Signs in Aschenbach's universe fall into three groups: (1) signs characterizing Aschenbach's personality before his start on the fatal journey; (2) signs adding to Aschenbach's universe during the action, the results of his passing through the influence fields of different signs; (3) signs from other sign universes in Aschenbach's world as messages or codes.

The description of Aschenbach's journey towards death may be arranged according two temporal categories: before and after, following the example of Eero Tarasti's *Myth and Music* (1979: 191–192). Adapting the model of the life of the mythical hero to Aschenbach's journey, it is as follows: (1) *before*, prehistory (sc. 1); Aschenbach's personality before the start of the action; the first contact with The Messenger of Death who starts the action; the exposition of the sign of death, the meaning of which as yet remains obscure for Aschenbach as well the audience; (2) Aschenbach's journey and its summary in the so-called Phaedrus-aria (sc. 2–16); (3) *after*, posthistory — Aschenbach's death (sc. 17).

Unlike the model of the life of the mythical hero, in Aschenbach's story the physical death of the leading character may be regarded as a part of posthistory or epilogue; psychically his journey ends with his own summary of life at the end of scene 16. In scene 17 even the sign of the cross is not so much a tragic announcement of death as an indicator of diagnosis. (Incidentally, Lotman notes that in the nineteenth century the word "semiotics" was understood as a science of the symptoms of disease [1990: 3].) In the role of funeral march, Tadzio's music sounds at the very end of the piece.

Most important events on Aschenbach's journey towards death have their climaxes in scenes 7, 13, and 16, entitled *The Games of Apollo*, *The Dream*, and *The Last Visit to Venice* respectively. Each culmination has a significant role in the opera. Scene 7 is an exaltation of Apollonian mentality. Aschenbach has always thought of himself as a rational person, an admirer of reason and self-control. After all, the glorification of Apollo, the symbol of reason and pure form, becomes an apotheosis of the beautiful boy Tadzio. His love for Tadzio, which Aschenbach later must confess to himself, is a passion which becoming stronger leads him to exalt the antagonistic, Dionysian disposition. The first and second climaxes are contrasts such as order and chaos, reason and passion, idyll and orgy. The build-up of the two scenes is similar: (1) scene with the participation of mythological character (or characters, in scene 13); (2) triumph of the mythological character who represents the elevation of mentality; (3) consequences for Aschenbach — in scene 7 the confession of his love for Tadzio; at the end of scene 13, resignation to fate; both adding new signs to Aschenbach's sign universe. The third climax (sc. 16) is a general culmination serving as both musical and dramatic recapitulation.

Inner iconicity

As mentioned above, ambiguity (the principle that something has more than one meaning) dominates the work. Likewise this principle influences the form of the inner organization of *Death in Venice*. Thus some significant signs of the opera occur only twice; the second time they appear in a different context and may have an opposite meaning. Here we shall point out nine examples of inner iconicity.

(1) E — Aschenbach's visiting-card, his expression of self-consciousness on a repeated E, his key-note from which the abbreviation of the sign is given in this treatment. Still, E is under the influence of F; it is one manifestation of tonal ambiguity in the opera. The symbolism of the keys E and F becomes evident when the voices of Apollo and Dionysus join the action. The juxtaposition of E and F represents Aschenbach's being of two minds, between two antagonistic forces, Apollonian and Dionysian. On first appearance, the sign E represents Aschenbach, who tries to find balance (being in a creative crisis) and declares himself as a famous, successful, and honored writer whose strength lies in his self-discipline. The second appearance of the sign E is Aschenbach's addressing himself in the second person, his bitter self-mockery at the end of his journey, a shadow of his lost dignity.

(2) The Traveller's monologue in scene 1 exposes the sign of cholera with counterfeited text. With no word about death, The Traveller's description of oriental marvels provokes Aschenbach to start on a journey southward, towards death. In scene 11 The Traveller's monologue recurs as a whole (in cello and double bass), which becomes a basic structure for the narrative of the English Clerk who tells Aschenbach about the oriental origins of the cholera spreading in Venice. Thus the sign of the cross is identified with the words "cholera" and "death". So far it has appeared under the pseudonym "plague", accompanying Aschenbach's complaints about his bad health or the bad weather. In scene 11 The Traveller's monologue acts as an inner monologue of Aschenbach, while everything connected with death finds its place in his mind. The musical sign of Tadzio's Mother flashing into the monologue is a message about the idea to warn the Polish Family of the "sickness" growing in Aschenbach's head.

(3) Decision ("So be it"). Aschenbach decides to go to Venice, taking The Traveller's suggestion. In scene 6 Aschenbach decides not to leave Venice but to stay and "dedicate his days to the Sun and Apollo himself". Both decisions are made under the influence of the sign of The Messenger of Death.

(4) The song "Piazza". In scene 2, "Piazza" is sung at the time of the trip to Venice, by the youth and by the second character of The Messenger of Death — The Elderly Fop, whose make-up disgusts Aschenbach. In scene 16 Aschenbach himself has the appearance of an elderly fop, and he also tries to sing "Piazza" as a certificate of youthfulness. (For a musicologist this is not a certificate of juvenility but a precondition for recapitulation.) In scene 16 Aschenbach has to pass through the fields of influence of several signs, once again being a copy of The Elderly Fop. In order to do so he must sing "Piazza", which marks the beginning of his journey. (The Hotel Barber, who also gives him the appearance of a fop, reminds Aschenbach of the song.)

(5) The Strawberry Seller's song. When Aschenbach hears it for the first time he is in high spirits watching Tadzio's games on the beach; the song seems to him as clear as Tadzio's music. On second occurrence, the strawberries are overripe, and the sign of death disturbs the song as a warning of cholera.

(6) In *Death in Venice*, extensive reference to Plato occurs twice. In scene 7 (*The Games of Apollo*) the choir creates an atmosphere of antiquity, rendering Plato's conception of beauty. In scene 16 the same music accompanies Aschenbach's aria in the form of a dialogue between Socrates and Phaedrus. By the medium of Plato's thoughts Aschenbach summarizes his journey.

(7) In the climax of *The Games of Apollo*, praise of Apollo becomes glorification of Tadzio, the victor of all athletic games. The song of praise started by The Voice of Apollo is continued by Aschenbach, who in his exultation moves from the influence field of the sign of Apollo to the sphere of influence of the sign of Tadzio. One section of that process is repeated in the final scene, after the death of Aschenbach, simultaneously with the "pure" music of Tadzio, as confirmation of the relationship between Tadzio and Apollo.

(8) The combination of the signs of death and love express Aschenbach's thought of himself and Tadzio as the only living persons in Venice after the cholera epidemic. The result of the first appearance of this combination is Aschenbach's vision of Dionysian orgy; the second occurrence is to Aschenbach a bitter reminder of his loss of self-control.

(9) Surrender. After the vision of orgy Aschenbach confesses his moral decadence to himself and decides to "let the gods do what they will with him". The musical sign of surrender is inverted when Aschenbach in the next scene, instead of giving himself up to the powers of the gods, submits himself to the superiority of The Hotel Barber who gives him the appearance of a fop.

Briefly, although the third is a leading interval in *Death in Venice* (Roseberry 1987: 88), the number two rules everywhere in the opera. Inside of signs it dominates in the form of tonal ambiguity; between signs it is expressed as a presentation of the sign and its icon in the piece, or the sign and its variant (as it is on the occasion of some signs not mentioned in this paper). Unquestionably, the primacy of the number two was inscribed by Thomas Mann, in the literary basis of the opera.

References

Carnegy, Patrick (1987). "The novella transformed: Thomas Mann as opera", *Benjamin Britten, Death in Venice*. Cambridge: Cambridge University Press.

Evans, Peter (1987). "Synopsis: The story, music not excluded", *Benjamin Britten, Death in Venice*. Cambridge: Cambridge University Press.

Lotman, Juri (1990). *Kultuurisemiootika*. Tallinn: Olion.

Roseberry, Eric (1987). "Tonal ambiguity in *Death in Venice*: A symphonic view", *Benjamin Britten, Death in Venice*. Cambridge: Cambridge University Press.

Tarasti, Eero (1979). *Myth and Music*. (Approaches to Semiotics No. 51.) The Hague: Mouton.

– (1990). "Semiotics as a common language of musicology", *Music as a Universal Language*, Pozzi (ed.). Firenze: Olschki.

White, Eric Walter (1983). *Benjamin Britten, His Life and Operas*. London: n.p.

Structures and symbols in Tormis's music:
An introduction to the *Estonian Ballads*

URVE LIPPUS

Introduction

Crucial to analyzing a piece of music is the choice of a proper method, of the right method of analysis. This intriguing topic — analysis of analysis or meta-analysis — has already prompted some interesting discussion. Often the resulting texts form an introduction to a new analytic approach (e.g., Narmour 1977) in which the object of observation is the method itself, rather than the adequacy of different methods to different kinds of music. It is clear that some analytic systems are designed for a particular kind of music (e.g., set theory for the description of atonal music), but most advocates of a new strategy like to show its scope to be as wide as possible.

In a discussion on meta-analysis, however, it would perhaps be useful to concentrate more on what aspects of the music would be best revealed by this or that analytic strategy. The semiotic approach is certainly one of the most universal methods of description, and it can be successfully applied to music of different styles and composition techniques. At the same time, it reveals more about the contents of music, its place in culture, its emotional and associative aspects, and less about its structural constituents, composition technique, and the like. If we look at the examples of music analyzed in the works of semioticians, we can also see their preference for music where some kind of immanent narration is quite evident (the list of their favorite composers includes Liszt, Wagner, Debussy, and so on; but even quite an abstract sonata form with its contrasting themes and development can be easily represented as a "story" with acting characters).

In the case of Veljo Tormis's music it is clear that by describing the construction, the architectonics of a piece, we discover only one, though very important aspect of the composition. The real impact of his music is produced by the wonderful cooperation and balance between this constructive aspect and the multiple layers of symbolic structures deriving from text, tradition, musical material and composition, and cultural context.

In my analyses of Tormis I have not followed an established analytical method. My aim has been to demonstrate the possibilities this music offers for different semiotic approaches, but I do not feel myself expert enough in semiotics to attempt a full analysis according to those routines. Over the years I have developed a very personal way of describing Tormis's music (*Towards* 1976; Lippus 1983 and 1985) that is a symbiosis of structural analysis (looking for the constituents of the composition and describing the relations between the constituents) and semantic or semiotic analysis (describing the internal, external or even extramusical meanings and associations the elements or the structures may carry).

In this paper the second approach dominates, for I consider it more important for the present audience. That does not mean that the musical structures, textures, and the like, i.e., the architectonic aspect, in the *Estonian Ballads* should be considered less important.

Tormis and his *Estonian Ballads*

Veljo Tormis (b. 1930) is an Estonian composer. He is particularly famous for his song cycles in which ancient Estonian and Finnish (Baltic-Finnic) folk songs have been used as basic material. His internationally most well-known composition is probably *The Curse on Iron* (*Raua needmine*, 1971), a large-scale piece for mixed choir. The *Estonian Ballads* (*Eesti ballaadid*, 1980) is called a cantata-ballet and was performed in the opera theater *Estonia*, with the choreography of Mai Murdmaa. However, this music for soloists, mixed choir, and symphony orchestra can be performed also as a cantata or oratorio without any staging, and it has had several successful concert performances as well. The *Estonian Ballads* consists of six epic songs (ballads): "A Chaste

Girl" (Karske neiu), "A Girl in the Wrong" (Eksinud neiu), "The Husband-Killer" (Mehetapja), "The Wife-Killer" (Naisetapja), "The Wife of Gold" (Kuldnaine), "The Bride From the Grave" (Kalmuneiu).[1] As a frame, the seventh song, "The Daughters' Fate" (Tütarde saatus) is used for prologue, epilogue, and for transitions (Epigraphs I-IV).

The music of Veljo Tormis has recently found wide international resonance. His success is all the more remarkable considering that his abundant use of old Estonian (Finnish, Izhorian, Karelian, et al.) texts makes it extremely hard for singers unfamiliar with the peculiar prosodic structure of Baltic-Finnic languages to learn his songs. As is often the case with ancient (ritual) poetry, retelling the contents doesn't help much in understanding. Such things as the flow of the words with their sounds and rhythms, the metaphors, and stereotypical formulas are much more important than the story. Certainly, it is possible to make a good translation of the whole text, but that is a job of translating an epic, *Kalevala* or *Iliad* or the like, not an opera libretto. There are 998 eight-syllable verses in the *Estonian Ballads*.

Tormis has said: "It may seem paradoxical or illogical, but the descriptive content of the *Kalevala* is not as important to me as its structure. By this I mean everything characteristic of the *Kalevala* — of metrical rune, runic song: suggestive monotony, repetition of thought, which coheres well with ancient tunes" (1985). We are quite safe to consider not only Tormis and *Kalevala*, but also the relation of Tormis the composer to the whole runic song tradition. That is, we should not look for the story in the music. Although the contents of the text, its metaphors and associations, are reflected in the music, the relationship is much more intricate.

At the same time, Tormis has also confessed that he has trouble with writing "pure" music, he *must* have some song, some text, something meaningful for him to start with (as I could not find that statement in any of his printed texts it must belong to some conversation). In fact, he has written almost no instrumental pieces. The use of material that already has a complicated semiotic structure and the ingenious exposing and transforming of such material into his own structures are reflected in several circles or layers of associations we can discern in his works.

Some of those associations are graspable for every musician; some demand a good knowledge of culture context.

Sources and associations

Tormis is a composer, not an ethnomusicologist studying traditional music. He is quite free in his choice of source materials, although his devotion to the runic song is so dominating that we often forget about the other possibilities that he has also used. However, the methods of treating the sources and the webs of associations the source material can evoke will be revealed better if we compare some very different works. Some examples: *Laulu algus* (The Beginning of the Song, 1968), a cantata written for the centenary of the Estonian Song Festivals, is built on several famous and beloved choral songs that have had a special function in the history of song festivals, songs that every Estonian recognizes and associates with the history of national awakening; "Rahvaste sõpruse fantaasia" (Rhapsody of the Friendship of Peoples, 1982) is a witty and ingenious musical commentary on the Soviet tradition of commissioning works for celebrating some official anniversary; these include a number of popular songs of several Soviet peoples, put together with great symbolic strength.

Several compositions seem to have been prompted by a given text. These include cycles on texts by Juhan Liiv: *Dialektilisi aforisme*, 1978; *Juhan Liivi sarkasmid*, 1979; and by Hando Runnel: *Lojaalsed laulukesed, Eestlase laulukesed, Vindised laulud, Mõtisklusi Hando Runneliga*, all from 1981; and also quite a strange composition, *Mõtisklusi Leniniga* of 1982, to passages from Lenin's writings. The musical texts of these songs are full of descriptive passages, clear paraphrases, and hidden symbols; enough so that Toomas Siitan (1991) has analyzed the musical semantics in these songs according to principles of the *musica poetica* of the sixteenth and seventeenth centuries.

The runic songs, *Kalevala* songs, and folk songs in general are certainly the most important source of ideas, associations, and musical building material for Tormis, but not the only one. Tormis's treatment of the material reflects very precisely his attitude to the sources. Being sometimes ironical, even sarcastic, he is always very serious and sincere when using runic songs or other ancient folk music.

I would like to point out the following layers of associations important for the reception of compositions by Tormis: (1) the background of the song tradition, the whole culture to which the source material belongs, including its religion and way of life (*Kalevala*-world, Runnel and present-day Estonian life, and so on); (2) the particular song or text used as building material or the starting point, its content, function, etc.; (3) musical comments provided by Tormis on the arrangement of the material, ideological and emotional interpretation inherent in the musical structure, sound symbols, and the like.

Tormis and folk song

I must cite here probably the most popular statement by Tormis:

> Not that I make use of folk song, folk song makes use of me. To me, folk music is not an instrument through which I can express myself. On the contrary, I feel it my duty to present folk music as it is, its essence, spirit, idea and form. To my understanding, Runic song is the most outstanding and original phenomenon of Estonian culture of all time. Since today it has lost its form of existence as a once inseparable part of the way of life, what I am trying to do is to link it with modern art forms, and to bring out the uniqueness of Runic song and the message it conveys.[2]

People often forget that Tormis is a composer, that even his most simple folk song arrangements are still compositions, not folk songs. This is all the more easy because Tormis himself likes to stress his role of chanter or medium (wise man or shaman).

Speaking about the widest circle of associations connected with this music we should differentiate between two points of view. First, to a member of the community (congregation) the meaning of this music contains a strong ideological charge (it is certainly open to discussion as to what criteria make one a member of the community; though it is probably not only nationality and/or knowledge of the language). In Estonia Tormis's music has fulfilled two related ideological functions:

(a) supporting the identity of a member of the Estonian community by suggesting the feeling of participation in an ancient ritual, showing the authentic or "right" way of life (singing and listening to this music is one of the many activities in the general search for one's roots); and (b) supporting the ideas of environmental movements by the singing of songs of a pre-Christian traditional community (whose way of life is the ideal model of relations between man and nature).

The second point of view is that of an outsider, who listens to Tormis against the background of European musical traditions. The same circle of associations connected with the use of folk song may be analyzed from three perspectives: (a) Tormis as a phenomenon of folklorism, (b) as a representative (like Béla Bartók) of a national school, (c) as exotica in Western music, such as bird song and Indian ragas in Messiaen.

The background of the *Estonian Ballads*

The Estonian runic song repertory contains a very limited number of epic songs. This is in stark contrast to the Karelian and Izhorian tradition where Elias Lönnrot transcribed all his source material for *Kalevala*. In the introduction to one of the first published collections of Estonian songs Walter Anderson (1926: lxvi) argues that Estonians do not have epic songs at all:

> . . . die sogenannten epischen Lieder der Esten enthalten meistens nicht einmal einen *an sich* interessanten Erzählungskern, der sich auch in prosaischer Form noch von Mund zu Mund fortsplanzen könnte. Im estnischen epischen Liede ist die Form, die Stimmung, das poetische Bild das Wichtigste, der Erzählungsinhalt völlige Nebensache: wie eine Reihe phantastischer Traumbilder zieht er meist am Hörer vorüber und zerflattert in nichts, wenn er in prosaische Form umgegossen werden soll.

However, Herbert Tampere (1964: 8), who prefers speaking about narrative songs instead of epics or lyro-epics, has stressed that the small group of ballads has clear features of epics: these songs have a plot, different characters, a conflict, some development, and usually a tragic end. Yet even in ballads the story often remains fragmentary, the conflict obscure. For example, the song "Husband Killed" consists of an extensive description of the heroine Meeli fleeing and asking various trees for shelter. We do not learn much about the conflict, in most of the folk variants the exposition is missing altogether and the story begins with telling that one of the three women (sisters) has blood on her apron and a knife and that she has killed a young man. In the variant chosen by Tormis and the librettist, the folklorist Ülo Tedre, there is a concise exposition: a newly married couple is riding home, the bride discovers that the chest with the presents for her in-laws has been left at home, but the bridegroom refuses to turn back. Still, the arrival at home and the murder itself is passed over very quickly to proceed with the description of Meeli fleeing from one tree to another and in the end drowning herself in a lake.

One reason why epic songs are so rare in the Estonian repertory is certainly the female character of the whole tradition, for epics in general mostly concern men's activities (stories about heroes, wars, hunting, fishing, etc.). As early as the eighteenth century the author of an extensive topographic study of Estonian life, A. W. Hupel, considered it remarkable that in Estonian villages it is the women and, in particular, young maids that are the main singers while the men sing only when drunk (Tampere 1935: 20–21). In some cases of ritual singing, and above all at weddings, the singers had to be elderly (married) women. In contrast, although the performances of some great female singers have been recorded in Karelia, in the Finnish song tradition male singers were much more important (Virtanen 1968: 8–15).

In this context we must also think of the central figure of the *Estonian Ballads* — the Mother. By singing the framing song "The Daughters' Fate", acting in the last ballad "The Bride from the Grave", commenting on the ballads in the Epilogue, she becomes much more important than any one of the characters. In view of the role of an elderly woman, who often must be a mother herself, as a singer in Estonian wedding rituals (one of the few surviving pagan rituals), the Mother acquires great dimensions as a symbol. As some of the meanings of this symbol we might list: everlasting life, perpetual birth and death, love and mercy, fate and bearing the fate, ancestors watching the life of their family and tribe. It is probably not incidental that the framing song is the one containing the most ancient and, I think, the wildest subject ever found in Estonian runic songs: the Mother had to kill her newborn daughters if the family could not bring up so many children (or whatever the motives were). This is not only a story about fate, but also about an old, traditional society together with its old and wise women, closeness to or unity with nature, with all its long-lost way of life.

Tormis's structuring of the material

In the *Estonian Ballads*, the conception of fate and the heavy symbolic weight of the Mother's role certainly cannot derive from the song texts of folk tradition. The songs normally do not have titles and even in folklorist use the text that Tormis has called "The Daughters' Fate" is usually referred to as "The Daughters' Killer", "Daughters into the Water/Spring", or "Daughters Changed into Birds;'. Thus, the stress on fate is strongly intentional. Tormis has also pointed out in program of the *Estonian Ballads* (1980) that for him the main idea of the cycle as a whole is fate guiding one's decisions in life, the need to choose between (two) opposite ways of behaving. The framing song "The Daughters' Fate" and the musical motif symbolizing Fate are not only a structural link between different ballads, but also the uniting element projecting all the stories onto a common background, that of the different fates of daughters. The ballads are chosen and arranged to form pairs describing the opposite behaviors of young girls, or their opposite fates (Figure 1).

Tormis also writes in his introduction that he was not intrigued by the bloody stories of the ballads, but by the human state of mind, the emotional and ethical assessments inherent in these songs. I agree completely with his statement that these songs contain very primeval moral norms and a system of values that are still valid (the feeling of guilt and responsibility, the relationship of a man with another man, with nature, and with the whole universe). But I think that the problem of moral evaluation is quite complicated, since there is no unambiguous pointing to what is right and what is wrong. In the Epilogue verses composed by Tormis/Tedre some morals are pointed out for each song. Yet it is evident even from the titles of the pairs of songs that they do not form a

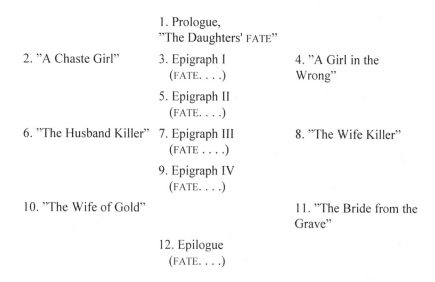

Figure 1.

group of "white" songs opposed to that of "black" songs, one with positive and another with negative heroes. Only in one song is the hero, a young man, directly condemned for his crime ("The Wife Killer"). In other cases the assessment is either avoided or only hinted at (for example, the trees refuse to hide the maid who has killed a young man). In "The Girl in the Wrong" the problem is that the mother and father of a newborn baby should take care of the child, should confess that it is their baby; the maid is not condemned for being "wrong". But the most important aspect is that in folk tradition the mother who has drowned her daughters is an object of compassion, not of contempt. This in its turn reinforces the role of fate, together with the possibility of mercy that is particularly stressed in the repeated concluding lines of the Epilogue: "the winds will have mercy and the sun will caress" (Tuleb tuuli, annab armu,/ paistab päeva, pead silitab).

The musical symbol of fate, a simple melody moving on the interval of the (major) second, is derived from the Mother's song (Example 1). This motif would have been important merely due to its contextual force.

In addition, it is used in the music as a strongly constructive and unifying element. Tormis himself has pointed out that in all the melodies chosen for different ballads the interval of the (major) second is very prominent and, thus, a melody moving by seconds enables one to link them smoothly and unite them by stressing their common feature (Example 2). But the constructive role of the second is expressed on every scale up to the largest: the tonal plan of the whole cycle is also derived from the same major second, D-E.

Example 1a.

Example 1b.

Example 2a.

Example 2b.

In the Prologue the fate motif moves on D-E, but the tonal center is E (bass, that tone dominating in pedals and chords). Both the tonal center and the second start to change at the end of the first Epigraph (see Example 2b). This change (tonal development) is illustrated in Example 3. Mostly, the dominating bass is one of intervals of a second; only the tenth song ("The Wife of Gold") has a melody with a very prominent fifth, strengthened even more by the bass that reaches one of the tones of the second (E♭-F in this case) only at the very end. In every sense the last ballad ("The Bride from the Grave") is the center or culmination of the cycle, since it is the most dramatic, the most complicated, and longest ballad in the cycle. At the beginning of this ballad the bass again reaches D, the tone of the initial major second. But the second itself has changed, alternating between major and minor versions. I think we are quite safe relating the minor second to the "black" forces and, as the story unfolds, we notice that the passages where the hero Peeter sings consist of alternating seconds while the passages of the grave-dwellers are accompanied with extremely intense minor seconds. The most important point in any tonal development is certainly the end. The last ballad ends after very dissonant sounds with the bass E and the second D-E. It would be almost as if it were the more important of the two, the "right" choice. But the Epilogue is written entirely on the bass D. Tormis has said about the fate motif alternating between two notes, that this is as in life: you can go either this way or another. In the Epilogue it seems that D, the final tone of the fate motif, would remain the final tonal center, the final choice in this story. Yet at the very end suddenly E sounds rather penetratingly in the chord with strong D bass (Example 4).

I have described here only some aspects of the use of the most important symbol in Tormis's *Estonian Ballads*, the fate motif. It is possible to find many other symbols, such as other expressions of the same fatal second. But I am convinced that such an analysis would be much more fascinating for each to carry out on their own, for many of the clever associations so enjoyable to discover may become quite boring to read about.

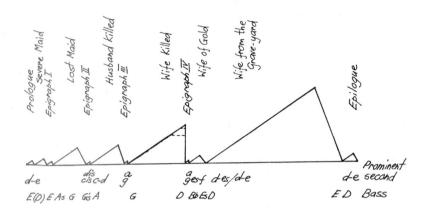

Example 3.

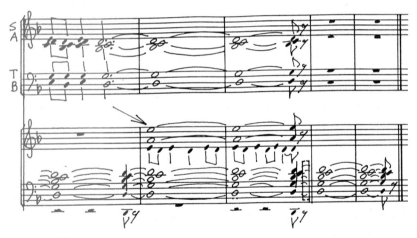

Example 4.

I would like to conclude this discussion by pointing out some of the very attractive symbols that have little to do with the structure of the composition but that contribute to the interpretation of the songs according to Tormis's intentions, and certainly create a specific exotic atmosphere. In addition to the normal symphony orchestra, a number of folk music instruments are used: a kantele (psaltery), a jew's harp, a buzzle, and a frame drum (shaman drum). Those instruments are used mainly for particular symbolic functions; much less important is that they give some specific sound or add color to the usual orchestral instruments. It is a very old custom of opera, dating back to sixteenth-century plays, that strings accompany "white" forces, innocent heroes, angels, while trombones, brass, drums, and the like are used to create the excitement of infernal scenes, of danger and wickedness.

The most important instrument in the folk tradition of all Baltic-Finnic peoples is the kantele, a holy instrument (along the lines of Apollo's lyre or that of Orpheus). Part of its symbolism has been acquired during the last hundred and fifty years, the time of the Estonian (and Finnish) national movement. In *Kalevala* songs the kantele was the magic instrument of Väinämöinen, the prototype of the Estonian Vanemuine, a pseudomythological figure that became so famous a symbol in Estonian cultural activities in the second half of the nineteenth century that it is hard to explain that it is not our genuine god, that it has nothing to do with Estonian folk beliefs. In modern times, an archaic type of kantele has been reintroduced into Finnish folk music as the Väinämöisen kantele (a small trapezoidal, almost triangular psaltery with five strings). In the score Tormis has written Väinämöisen kantele, designating this particular five-stringed instrument to be played. We hear it in the introduction of "The Girl in the Wrong" and in the culmination of the same ballad, when the newborn baby suddenly speaks out. Similarly, chords and tremolos in the strings and harp arpeggios accompany the young woman going to be killed in "The Wife Killer", while the story about planning the murder is told on the long drones of trombones. In the same ballad, the wicked atmosphere grows more and more ominous with the monotonous drumming of the jajai (the Korjak shaman drum; it would have been much better to have a drum of some Finnish-related tribe, since the drum is much more of a symbol than a musical instrument, and a similar sound could just as well have been made by another type of drum). Further, the buzzle, claves, beating against a log, all resemble the noise-instruments used in shaman rituals and witchcraft. The same arsenal is used in the last ballad, "The Girl from the Grave". In addition, the singing of the grave-dwellers, a glissando-like sound on the minor second, gives an astonishing imitation of the jew's harp. This long discussion might end by answering the question, Why has Tormis made the shaman attributes a symbol of "black" forces, of wickedness? But that will form the topic of a new treatise.

September 1991

Notes

1. The English translation of the titles and an abridged introduction to the contents of the songs are published in Veljo Tormis, *Eesti ballaadid. Klaviir* (Leningrad: Sovetskij kompozitor, 1987), 4–5: (1) "The Fate of the Daughters" (Tütarde saatus); (2) "Severe Maid" (Karske neiu); (4) "Lost Maid" (Eksinud neiu); (6) "Husband Killed" (Mehetapja); (8) "Wife Killed" (Naisetapja); (10) "Wife of Gold" (Kuldnaine); (11) "Maid from the Graveyard" (Kalmuneiu). Later a different version in English was printed on the cover of the recording on Melodiya Records (STEREO C 10 29679–82, 1990): (1) "The Daughters' Fate"; (2) "A Chaste Girl"; (4) "A Girl in the Wrong"; (6) "The Husband-Killer"; (8) "The Wife-Killer"; (10) "The Wife of Gold"; (11) "The Bride from the Grave". It seems to me that the latter translation is better.
2. This comes from a newspaper article published in 1972 and is quoted in the program of the *Estonian Ballads* in 1980. The translation was published on the cover of the recording.

References

Anderson, Walter (1926). "Plan des Werks. Editionsgrundsätze", *Eesti rahvalaulud Dr. Hurda ja teiste kogudest I*, edited by various hands, lxvi–lxviii. Tartu: Eesti Kirjanduse Selts.

Lippus, Urve (1983). "Ringist ringi", *Teater, Muusika, Kino* 1: 14–20.

– (1985). "Analüütiline etüüd", *Raua needmisest. Teater, Muusika, Kino* 2: 20–29.

Narmour, Eugene (1977). *Beyond Schenkerism*. Chicago: University of Chicago Press.

Siitan, Toomas (1991). "Veljo Tormis — *musicus poeticus*", *Teater, Muusika, Kino* 3: 34–38.

Tampere, Herbert (1935). *Eesti rahvaviiside antoloogia I* (= ERA Toimetised 5). Tartu.

– (1964). *Eesti rahvalaule viisidega IV*. Tallinn: Eesti Raamat.

, **(1985)**. "*Kalevala*, the Estonian perspective", *Finnish Music* 1/2: **20–24**.

6). = ***Towards a Monographical Analysis of Some Folk-Song** nts*. **J. Sarv, L. Se**mlek, U. Lippus, J. Ross, M. Remmel **Preprint KKI–6. Tal**linn: Academy of Sciences of the Estonian

a **(1968)**. *Kalevalainen laulutapa Karjalassa* (= Suomi 113, lsinki: **SKS**.

The role of text in meaning formation[*]

INGA JANKAUSKIENĖ

Among living Lithuanian composers Bronius Kutavičius[1] is preeminent. His music has influenced a new generation of composers, and his oratorios have enjoyed popularity in Lithuania among those who do not like modern contemporary music at all. What is the reason for that popularity? Is it caused by inner features of the compositions or by the other things? It is necessary to examine the structure of his oratorios and the situation in which one or another composition was written in order to answer these questions. The problem can be formulated differently: How does the oratorio text express (or show) the idea and content of the composition, and how do textual elements help form the meaning of the piece? It is also interesting to ascertain what models of culture can help us better understand the oratorios. At the same time it is important to compare the conclusions of the compositions in the process of perception.

Two oratorios by Kutavičius will be examined here: the *Last Pagan Rites* (Paskutinės pagonių apeigos, 1978) and *From the Jatvingian Stone* (Iš jotvingių akmens, 1983). These oratorios have some mutual similarity in that both have a ritual-like character and both appeared at the time of the Soviet occupation of Lithuania, at the period then communists were in the phase of stagnation in their creation of socialism. The *Last Pagan Rites* and *From the Jatvingian Stone* are especially well known in Lithuania, because they were something of a manifesto or declaration of independence for the Lithuanian people. Though the oratorios contained no political words, people understood what the composer wanted to say. What did the listeners-receivers hear in the oratorios at that gloomy time?

The *Rites* were seen to mirror the Lithuanian past. The scenic space and time of the oratorio were related to the history of Lithuanians, to ancient days when they were pagans. The pagan Lithuanians were turned

to Catholicism by force in 1385. That religion had no tra
the ordinary people until approximately the end of eighte
and a few centuries ago in Lithuania was considered an
paganism. The invasion of the organ into the vocal musi
Pagan Rites was understood by Lithuanians as the repressio
pagans by the Catholic church, a very real thing indeed.
time and space of the oratorio recalled the history of when I
occupied by the Soviet army in 1940. This occupation was in
time the *Rites* was written (1978). There was a real dan
Lithuanian national and cultural identity, and escape from th
was made with some other pagan Baltic tribes such as Jatvii
sians, and others. So for Lithuanians this oratorio became a
the recent times of the 1980s. The oratorio *From the Jat*
(1983) was perceived as a picture of Lithuanian linguistic
formation from ancient Baltic tribes, for the purpose of sho
back this formation dates.

How do these ideas of content manifest at the textual le
sition? This question common in music semiotics; it is f
Eero Tarasti, in his *A Theory of Musical Semiotics* (1994
lows: "How can the influence of these models can be felt i
discourse itself, in the very structures of music?" This qu
pertinent to the analysis of oratorios. As Mikhail Bakhti
What unites the bottom with the top?

There are several ways of answering this question, but
the analysis of the above-mentioned oratorios was taker
Greimas (1991) and Giroud and Panier (1991). It consists of
discoursive, narrative, and logico-semantic. But first we sh
the main characteristics of the oratorios.

The *Last Pagan Rites* was written for chorus, soprano,
quartet of horns (a kind of woodwind). The verse by
Lithuanian poet Sigitas Geda is used as text for the work. It
oratorio and thus requires special conditions of the concert
should not be large because the chorus surrounds the liste
soprano is in the center of the audience. The quartet of I
rated from the other performers, preferably on the balco
listeners.

s **consists of six** sections, with all but fifth having a closed
ginning **and the end** are instrumental sections (horn fanfares
.ng **and organ chords** at the end) that frame the mostly vocal
'n.

Kutavičius, 1984, *Paskutinės pagoniṷ apeigos,* score.
;a.) **The first section,** played by the horn quartet, has a
.cter **(Example 1),** with stereotypical rhythms of the same.
layer **begins his own** motif forte, and each successive entry
y **longer than the** preceding. This culminates in a major
iised **fourth degree** (C–E–F♯–G). This first section serves
iction **and an invita**tion to the rites signalled by the title of

.lle **part of the comp**osition (sections 2–4) is the rites them-
second section is intonationally related to the first. It is
horus and organ, which supplement each other, the organ
intonations of the chorus. The verse of this section tells of
r **who once walked** through the sky in summer, when the oat
g. **But harsh orders** follow this poetic image:

cut **the green stem** of the green oat of yesterday of the
reen.
ireak **the green stem** of the green oat, the green grasshopper
en **God.**

section **is more** complicated musically, making use of
:, **and organ.** Theoretically, the main instrument here is the
st **this seems strange** because the organ plays only a single,
chord, **which grows** louder throughout the entire third sec-
treme **tones of the** organ serve as a frame for all the tonal
iis **section, includi**ng that of the horns quartet and chorus.
nd **the chorus have** separate pitch organization here, con-
each **other by only** one note, G♮. But the organ as a main
n **be treated only** theoretically. In fact, the chorus prevails
for the very end of the section, because only it has the
. **The chorus's pitch** material is based on the intervals of
ds **and major thirds.** The picture is different with the dy-
re **is an opposition** between the organ on one hand, and the

ŽIOGE ŽALIASAI

Vasarų vasaružės žalia aviža
žalia aviža vakar žydėjo
vasarų vasaružės žaliai žydėjo

Vasarų vasaružės vasaružės danguj
žiogas žaliasai vasaružės ilgai
Vasarų vasaružės per dangų ėjo

Vakar vakaro vasaružės vakar
žaliai aviža vasaružės žaliai
žioge žaliasai vasaružės žalio

Nekirsk žalio stiebo žalios avižos
nekirsk avižos vasaružės stiebo
žalios avižos vasaružės kelio

Vasaružės vakar vasaružės žalio
nelaužk žalio stiebo žalios avižos
žioge žaliasai žioge dievo žalio

GYVATES UŽKEIKIMAS

Nekirsk mano brolio,
nekirsk mano sesers,
nekirsk mano motinos,
nekirsk mano tėvo,
tu gyvate gyvatėla,
tu gyvate gyvatėla, oj!

Nekirsk mano namų,
Nekirsk mano saulės,
Nekirsk mano javo,
Nekirsk mano dievo,
tu gyvate gyvatėla,
tu gyvate gyvatėla, oj.

MEDVEGALIO PAGARBINIMAS

Kalnelis kalnasai,
kalnalėlis kalnasai,
kalnelis kalnelio,
kalnulėlis kalnėlio,
kalnolis kalnuosai,
kalnuolėlis kalnuolio,
kalnulis kalnusai,
kalnusėlis kalnusio,
kalnylis kalnylio,
kalnylėlis kalnylio,
kanlylio kanlylio,
kalnuolėli liuole-lio...

ĄŽUOLO PAGARBINIMAS

Tu ąžuole, tu ąžuole,
Tu ąžuole ąžuolasai!
Tu ąžuole, tu ąžuole,
Tu ąžuole, ąžuolranki!
Tu ąžuole, tu ąžuole,
Tu ąžuole, ąžuolgalvi!
Tu ąžuole, tu ąžuole,
Tu ąžuole, ąžuolkoji!
Tu ąžuole, tu ąžuole,
Tu ąžuole, ąžuolburni!
Tu ąžuole, tu ąžuole,
Tu ąžuole, ąžuoliausias.

Example 1. Bronius Kutavičius (1984): The Last Pagan Rites.

chorus and horns quartet on the other hand. The latter two always have the same dynamic (forte). The organ, as mentioned, grows in intensity (from pianissimo to fortissimo). Finally, an onomatopoeic game is played here, with the Lithuanian word meaning "mountain" or "hill" in the various diminutive forms in the verse.

A new interpreter, solo soprano, appears in the fourth section of oratorio. She sings from the middle of the hall, surrounded by listeners. The soloist, after singing every two strophes, turns to the east, south, west, and north. As she sings, the words sound like plaints or requests because the melody has a downward direction except for the rising perfect fourth at the end. The same motif repeats with every "request" of the verse. Only the end of strophe, the words "Oh, snake", is merely ornamental. The verse, encompassing the whole world, runs:

> Don't cut my brother,
> Don't cut my sister,
> Don't cut my mother,
> Don't cut my father,
> Oh, snake!
>
> Don't cut my home,
> Don't cut my sun,
> Don't cut my crop,
> Don't cut my God,
> Oh, snake!

The soprano sings her part forte and the other performers serve as background for her (organ and chorus pianissimo). The main intonation of the soloist is the interval of a fourth, surrounded by major seconds above and below. The organ and chorus project the same three tones, G–A–B♭; the B♭ alone connects them with the soprano part.

The fifth section is the only one that has an open form, and it leads straight to the last section; Example 2 shows the end of section 5 and beginning of section 6. The fifth section has cyclic form with many repetitions (sections 2–5 are in cyclic form). It is performed by chorus and the horn quartet. They all play mezzo forte, and all have the same main body of intonations, a diminished seventh chord (C♯–E–G–B♭). The verse portrays the image of the World Tree:

Oh, oak tree,
Your hands, oak tree,
Your head, oak tree,
Your legs, oak tree,
Your mouth, oak tree,
Oh, oak tree.

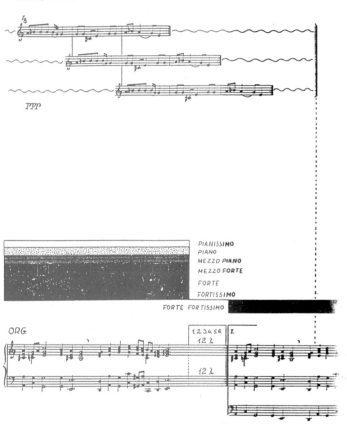

Example 2. Bronius Kutavičius: The Last **Pagan Rites.**

At the beginning of the sixth section the choral counte
chorus, singing *ppp*, is covered by the chords of the organ
chorale grows from pianissimo to fortissimo, and becomin
intense with triads and diminished seventh chords.

From the Jatvingian Stone is also a chamber oratorio. It can be performed by a small group of performers who sit in a circle on the floor, with faces turned inward. The hall is usually darkened. The oratorio consists of two different sections but is usually perceived as a whole. Intense rhythmic development is the main feature of the first section, itself in ABA form. Here the composer designates no fixed temporal values for the instruments, which are stones, small clay drums, whistle, straw pipe, and an instrument resembling a bow. The short cries of the performers are in the dead language of Jatvingian (one of the Balt tribes); the vocals serve as rhythmic and timbral instruments, as do the others. Every performer has his own rhythmic formula of four motifs, which is always repeated. The rigid and periodic rhythm pattern and tempo in this first section of the composition (Example 3) create the picture of active movement or stepping forward. And, at the same time, this elemental rhythm produces a mythical effect. As mentioned, this first main part of the oratorio is in an ABA form; the B section provides the space for other rhythmic formulas.

In the second main part of the work, rhythmic development is supplemented by intonational imitation and development. The principle of performance remains the same: each player repeats his own intonation with the characteristic rhythm formula of four motifs, with the instruments entering successively with short intonational and rhythmic formulas. Pitched instruments enter, playing lines of fixed temporal length: flute, violin, concertina, vocalists, kanklés (resembling kantele), panpipes, skudučiai, and tuned bottles. The rigid and periodic rhythm pattern and tempo are the same as in the first part but the music development, it seems, rises to a new and higher level (Example 4). A small episode occurs here where the language changes from Jatvingian to Lithuanian. The Lithuanian song, "The Wind Blew", is performed by a female soloist, in the folk manner. The song is rhythmically free and has a fanciful, active forward movement (Example 5). It seems that the music has turned round and that the ultimate purpose is attained.

Example 3. The rhythmic motifs in the first part.

Example 4. The rhythmic motifs of the second part.

There are two types of discourse in the *Jatvingian Stone*: (1) the discourse of the first two sections until the Lithuanian folk song enters; (2) the discourse of this song. The first is a minimalistic style of music; the folk song seems to be a new level of development. The narrative analysis of the song shows a conjunctive transformation as a realization (Greimas 1989: 249–257). The song can be treated as supplemental, as a continuation of developments before it entered, or as a result of this development. The discursive and narrative analysis of the *Last Pagan Rites* shows the opposite: There is a disjunctive transformation in the latter oratorio, which Greimas might call a "virtualisation" (1989: 249–257). The intrusion of the organ into the chorus's discourse can be treated as such.

Example 5. Lithuanian folk song, "Pūtė vėjas" (The Wind Blew).

These two oratorios are in minimalist style. Sections 2–5 of the *Rites* are based on repetitions of motifs. The first large section of *From the*

Jatvingian Stone has an ABA form, with each subsection consisting of the repeated material. Kutavičius uses mostly on repetitive techniques, which leads to the following question: What kind of narrativity can be seen in Kutavičius's oratorios? Seemingly, it can be called a macro-narrativity because it is not possible to talk about it in every section of the composition (because of the minimalist character); yet this macro-narrativity is real in terms of the logic of the entire oratorio. Indeed, there is pure durativity, without precise beginning or end, in every part of the oratorio. Further, every section of the *Last Pagan Rites* (except the fifth) has a cyclic form; this means that there is a constant return to the initial situation. On the other hand, the *Rites* has a quite clear musical logic, with beginning, development, and end. The beginning can be identified with the first, fanfare-like section; the development, with the ritualistic middle sections; and the end, with the final, chorale-like music.

It is easier to understand this logic of music development by identifying the vocals and musical instruments with the four actors at the so-called macro-discoursive level. The first actor (a1) is music by horns, horn-like wooden music instruments; the second (a2), choral music; the third (a3), organ music; and the fourth (a4), the soprano solo. We can see the relations of these "actors" throughout the composition. The development proceeds slowly because of a repetitive techniques and minimalist style in nearly every section. By contrast, the importance (significance) of actors changes during the all composition. Actor a1 (horns) is most important at the beginning, but is deadened during the following development. Contrarily, the importance of actor a3 (organ) gradually grows, and becomes predominant at the end, after being covered by the other instruments. Thus "archaic" instruments (horns and voices) are supplanted by "civilized" organ, and simple, consonant intervals of counterpoint transform into verticals of harmony.

After this macro-segmentation, we can talk about the phases of narrative analysis. Macro-narrative analysis makes it possible to reveal the main conflict of the composition, which is based on confrontations.

The *Last Pagan Rites* is a nearly perfect example of the narrative scheme. Actor a1 is actant A1; actors two and four (a2, chorus; a4, soprano solo) are actant A2; and actor a3 (organ) is actant A3. Actor a1

composition as an Addresser; actant A2,
, an Anti-Subject.
's can be identified with the manipulation
·sser (A1, horns) helps create the atmo-
ares). The second section is the phase of
he oratorio. We can see the Subject (A2)
onforms to the Subject in this part. The
ond section. The first three strophes can
ation and the last two strophes as a phase

of oratorio correspond to the phase of
e -être) in the narrative analysis. We can
t and Anti-Subject in the sound intensity
n; there is no conflict between them in
ict of Subject versus Anti-Subject occurs
on of the oratorio; there is no opposition
ject in the music of this section. This
(false) because it takes place inside the
orus (a2) and soprano solo (a4).
e de l'être) is in different places in the
roblem is solved in the verse of the fifth
ure of the World Tree and the harmoni-
music of the fifth section exudes the same
f conflict. There are relations of confor-
dresser in the fifth section. (The return of
sanction phase of narrative analysis, and
Addresser.) But this picture of harmoni-
an, the Anti-Subject in the sixth section.
s place in the music but not in the verse.
in the music was untrue. The Anti-Sub-
nger) at the end of oratorio, and it denies
out all the instruments and vocals). Thus
Realized Subject. "The text produces an
is a mistake" (Giroud & Panier 1991:
these levels the kind of main transforma-
nas 1989: 249–257) may be conceived. It

leads to the following chain of opposition
Subject vs. Anti-Subject, Vocal vs. In
Harmony, Horizontality vs. Verticality.

It is possible to go deep into the oppos
The verse is inseparable from the voca
symbolizes the harmoniousness of the pa
of the World model in the fourth section
the fifth. The verse shows that the Subject
meaning the victory of order in the worl
World Tree. But in the music, at the end
organ gains in strength. Above all this in
Catholic church in Lithuania, giving the fo
Catholic, Harmoniousness vs. Chaos. Th
the immanent analysis of the three level
idea of the *Last Pagan Rites*.

The macro-segmentation and macro-
Jatvingian Stone also helps disclose the m
can talk about three actors on the level of
an unusual super-macro-segmentation, bec
fied with the actors here: section 1, with
up to the soloist, with the second actor
song, with the third actor (a3). This is s
music, as a rule, changes very slowly
helps us to show the essence of the orat
From the Jatvingian Stone appears as in

As noted above, regular rhythm prev
The strict rhythmic formulas and regular
opposite of the third actor (a3), which is
Wind Blew". So one can speak about the
in the oratorio.

But the essence of this composition
narrative analysis as a tool. The first act
the instrumental parts of oratorio, with s
and a2); the second actant (A2), by the so
sis reveals some special features of this
of manipulation, because no Addresser c

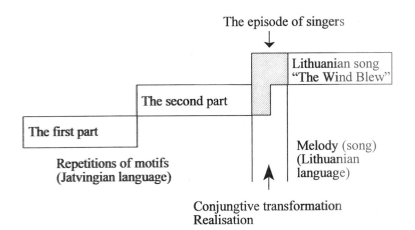

Example 6.

clearly defined beginning, which is quite typical of minimalistic compositions based on repetitive techniques. It is nevertheless possible to speak of a Subject-actor at the beginning of the *Jatvingian Stone*. The Subject-actor (a1 and a2) is connected with the modalities "to be obligated to" (*devoir*) and "to be able to" (*pouvoir*). This can be seen in the continuous, unbroken development, the active movement forward. This movement leads to the (conjunctive) transformation of the composition. This transformation can be identified with the above-mentioned Lithuanian song. The transformation begins a little earlier than when the song appears. There is a small episode during which all the instruments are silent and only the vocalists sing. Some intonational material from the song "The Wind Blew" and the Lithuanian language, which appears for the first time in the oratorio in this episode, shows that the transformation has begun. This phase can be called an "unbending" phase. The action of the Subject (a1 and a2) ends in the transformation of state. The appearance of the Lithuanian song "The Wind Blew" is a phase of sanction in the composition. Thus the narrative program is appreciated and transformed. The Appreciated Subject can be treated as a Realized Subject here: $S \rightarrow S\text{-}R$ (S = Subject, $S\text{-}R$ = Realized Subject). There is no logico-semantic opposition between actants A1 and A2, and A1 leads to A2: $A1 \rightarrow A2$. This change can be appreciated as positive, and the

In the text

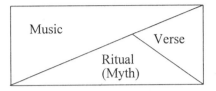

In the interpretation

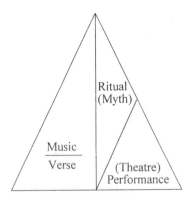

Example 7.

As mentioned, Kutavičius's oratorios are not real ritual but only ritual-like (and only the middle section of the *Last Pagan Rites*). Noske has ascertained the features of ritual in the ritualistic scenes in Verdi operas (1977: 241–270), mentioning indirect relation to a supernatural element as one important feature of ritual scenes. The *Last Pagan Rites* has a good example of such a relation: the second section deals with conjuring or invocation (features mentioned by Noske) and the chorus as a community acts in the ritual appeals to God. In the fourth section we find the same picture of appealing to God. The soprano solo can be treated here as an individual from the group, and she struggles against a supernatural power — the snake that in Lithuanian pagan mythology is the sacred goddess of the Water of the World. Also according to Noske's theory, the scene (or section of the oratorio in our case) tends to be symmetrical, governed by an arithmetical formula. All the sections of the middle of the *Last Pagan Rites* are symmetrical. They are of rounded formal design (except the fifth section); the round (or circle) can also be treated as a geometrical symbol here.

According to the theories of van Gennep (1960), Lévi-Strauss (1962), and Turner (1969), the transformation or passage from one state to another is the most important element of ritual. For Lévi-Strauss it is a bridge between Nature and Culture; for van Gennep it is a passage from one position or station to another; for Turner it is a "connection between known and unknown territory", the connection of "structured and ordered as against the unstructured and chaotic" (1969: 15).

The *Last Pagan Rites* represents the transformation from pagan to Catholic, i.e., from affectivity to intellectuality, from Nature to Culture, in Lévi-Strauss's terms (1962: 101). For the pagan this is a passage from the known to the unknown; for pagans it meant the transformation to a dangerous, unstructured, and chaotic world. This is why the transformation in the *Rites* was mentioned earlier as a negative event. It is an opposition of structure and anti-structure because it does not fit the model
of pagan structure

From the Jatvingian Stone stresses the processive character of rites and shows the passage to the transformation and the transformation itself. So the transformation can be seen in the composition as an expected goal or end. The transformation of this oratorio can be called a transformation from one state to another, in van Gennep's terms. As mentioned, it is a passage from music limited rhythmically and melodically to music that undergoes development. This passage leads to a qualitative change (the song "The Wind Blew") and can be understand as a solution. Thus the transformation in *From the Jatvingian Stone* was called positive in the narrative analysis above.

Here we may conclude that the various methods of analysis supplement each other and give more information about the content-level of compositions, especially about the kinds of transformations in Kutavičius's oratorios.

Karbusicky, Vladimir (1988). "The anthropology of semiotic levels in Music", *Essays on the Philosophy of Music*, 54–63. Helsinki: Philosophical Society of Finland.

Kavolis, Vytautas (1986). *Sąmoningumo trajektorijos*. [The Trajectories of Consciousness]. Chicago: AM & M Publications.

Lévi-Strauss, Claude (1991). *Mitas ir prasmė* [Myth and Meaning] (translated by Vytautas Karpas). Abstract in *Proskyna 2*: 91–101. Vilnius: Lietuvos Aidas.

– (1991). *Totemism* (translated by Rodney Needham). London: Merlin.

Noske, Frits (1977). *The Signifier and the Signified*. The Hague: Martinus Nijhoff.

O'Sullivan, Tim et al. (1983). *Key Concepts in Communication*, John Fiske (ed.). London: Routledge.

Saussure, Ferdinand de (1990). *Zametki po obščej lingvistike* [The Annotations to the General Linguistics] (translated by B. P. Narumova). Moscow: Progress.

Schwarz, K. Robert (1981). "Steve Reich: Music as a gradual process part 1", *Perspectives of New Music* 19: 374–392.

– (1982). "Music as a gradual process", part 2, *Perspectives of New Music* 20: 226–286.

Stoianova, Ivanka (1981). "Die 'Neue Einfachheit' in der heutigen Praxis: Repetitive Musik, Klangenvironments und Multimedia-Produktionsprozesse", *Zum "Neuen Einfachheit" in der Musik*, Otto Kollerisch (ed.). Vienna: n.p.

Szacki, Jerzy (1964). *Durkheim*. Warszawa: PW Wiedza Powszechna.

Tarasti, Eero (1978). *Myth and Music*. Helsinki: Acta Musicologica Fennica.

– (1986). "Music models through ages: A semiotic interpretation", *International Review of the Aesthetics and Sociology of Music* 17 (1).

– (1988). "On the modalities and narrativity in music", *Essays on the Philosophy of Music*, 110–131. Helsinki: The Philosophical Society of Finland.

– (1994). *A Theory of Musical Semiotics*. Bloomington, IN: Indiana University Press.

Turner, Victor W. (1969). *The Ritual Process: Structure and Anti-Structure*. Chicago: Aldine.

INSTRUMENTAL MUSIC

Un essai d'étude anthropologique du temps musical

ISABELLE SERVANT

Introduction

On ne sait pas avec exactitude ce que le temps musical peut être réellement, mais il semble raisonnable de se le représenter comme un mélange subtil d'au moins trois composantes: le temps physique, tel qu'il peut être défini par les scientifiques, les temps sociaux, et le temps psychologique, ou personnel. Naturellement ces composantes ne doivent pas être considérées comme indépendantes les unes des autres: le temps physique est obstinément sous-jacent à toutes nos perceptions, en tant que l'objet duquel nous déduisons notre sens de la durée, et nous espérons parvenir à convaincre plus bas par nos exemples que le temps psychologique ou personnel est aussi largement influencé par nos habitudes sociales de pensée.

Un point commun intéressant entre ces trois composantes est qu'aucune d'entre elles n'est absolue. Psychologiquement et socialement, il semble évident que nous n'apprécions pas la durée ou la position dans le temps d'un événement musical de la même façon que notre voisin, ou que quelqu'un de complètement étranger à notre culture. Ceci n'est parfois démontré qu'indirectement, par exemple dans un groupe d'expériences sur la mémoire réalisées par Clarke et Krumhansl (1990), où les auditeurs sont invités à repérer la position dans le temps de segments musicaux extraits d'une œuvre musicale: leurs résultats montrent un schéma de déviations par rapport à la réalité, des segments situés vers le commencement et la fin de la pièce apparaissant localisés plus près du centre de cette pièce qu'ils ne sont réellement, et bien sûr pas au même endroit selon les sujets. De la même façon, des divergences culturelles peuvent être découvertes dans ce que James Kippen (1992) nomme

usico-cognitive", lorsqu'il analyse le très
ion des 'tablas' d'Inde du Nord. "Quand
t-il, et il semble bien qu'il y ait un réel
cte position de la fin d'une chaîne de
u refrain final, chez les experts des 'tab-
s tous la même solution pour cette posi-
indiquer deux positions différentes selon
ce qui nous apparaît, mais il est probable
ement l'énorme effet du contexte dans ce

e, nous devrions de la même façon
tricte dans le contrôle absolu que nous
es modèles physiques du temps dérivent
iques de l'univers. Bien après Aristote et
687 ses "Philosophiae Naturalis Principia
idee religieuse d'un espace absolu et fixe,
lui, comme absolu, linéaire, dont les
t contrôlables, et qui est complètement
à notre époque l'une des grandes théories
hysique, la relativité, met précisément
solu. Nous voyons donc que, même en
st loin d'être si simple.
oyons autorisé à suggérer l'hypothèse que
emps humain, vécu, est une construction
partir de certaines donnees, écrites,
qui tend à nous faire appréhender une
la plus satisfaisante pour nous, alors que
né personnel, physique et social.
e dans le champ encore mal connu des
it le musicologue à faire un choix, et à
des composantes du temps: par exemple,
psychologue expérimental, il choisira
hysique et personnel, et ainsi d'examiner
un sujet musicien ou non-musicien à tel
, et ses éventuelles predictions. Notons,
réel objet d'étude est davantage le sujet

lui-même que le fait musical auquel il
sommes convaincu que l'existence de ce f
de l'existence du sujet. Cette considé
éloignent les musicologues de la métho
musique des lors qu'ils étudient la mu
nous n'avons aucun droit de poser comm
l'époque de Louis XIV, par exemple, av
de percevoir.

L'anthropologie musicale historique
même, d'une certaine manière, exactemen
préalable que nous avons justement une
moins partiellement différente d'appréh
passé. Son but consiste donc à déchiffrer
œuvres qui sont issues d'un environ
historique qui est complètement différent

Nous avons en effet l'habitude de dire
de manière complexe, du temps, et que se
de même vers 1700, mais en réalité no
variable: le fait que les compositeurs util
1700 des signes tels que des rondes ou de
quantite à laquelle ils pensaient avait tou
de la concevoir.

La difficile interprétation de la musiqu
un exemple éclatant. Prenons, par e
Couperin datant de 1660 (Figure 1).

Une première lecture montre aisémen
temps se posent au musicologue cont
manière, ces rondes n'ont pourtant pa
connaissance livresque des préludes, à t
nous assure en effet qu'il s'agit de pièc
rapides et imprévisibles. D'autre part, c
en 1989, il ne s'agit pas non plus d'imp

Figure 1.

Paradoxalement, la notation apparemment libre de ces préludes est en fait une indication plus exacte pour l'interprète qu'une notation plus conventionnelle puisque, comme pour le prélude non mesuré au luth, elle montre précisément le nombre de notes dans un accord, les additions dissonnantes, et s'il y a des accaciaturas, des ports de voix, des notes de passage etc... La notation des préludes non mesurés, à certains égards non négligeable, donne à l'interprète des instructions exactes, plus qu'une base pour l'improvisation, de la même manière que la tablature de luth. (Ledbetter, p 93, notre traduction).

Il s'agit donc d'une qualité de temps aussi efficace et exacte que la nôtre, mais qui de toute évidence ne fonctionne pas avec les mêmes règles.

Tout se passe donc comme si, dans la musique française de clavecin, la construction d'une interprétation se faisait a l'intérieur d'un ensemble de représentations différent du nôtre, une sorte de schéma complexe des sensibilités temporelles. Les temps simples s'agenceraient selon un équilibre dont on peut penser qu'il reflète les plus fréquentes et significatives conduites de création de la société.

Nous avons donc considéré qu'un corpus de partitions qui aurait l'avantage de présenter une certaine distance entre la partition écrite et le résultat sonore aurait toutes les chances d'être significatif si l'on veut tenter de mesurer les différentes manières de concevoir le temps musical. D'autre part l'instrument à qui ce corpus est destiné, le clavecin, possède lui aussi quelques caractéristiques intéressantes: d'une part son rôle social est extrêmement grand à l'époque dont nous parlons, ce qui lui donne à notre avis une incontestable valeur de représentation des goûts de la société baroque; d'autre part la lutherie du clavecin présente la particularité de ne permettre pratiquement que des changements temporels: En effet, selon la classification de Hornsbostel et Sachs, le clavecin fait partie d'une des quatre grandes catégories organologiques, celle des cordophones, c'est-à-dire des instruments dont l'une ou plusieurs cordes sont tendues entre des points fixes. La tension des cordes sur toute la surface de l'instrument et leur passage sur des chevalets en font une cithare, que complètent pour une définition plus précise le mode de production du son-corde pincée par un bec- et la présence d'un clavier actionnant mécaniquement le producteur du son, en l'occurrence le mécanisme complexe appele 'sautereau'.

Cet élément mobile, mince lame de bois qui repose sur l'extrémité arrière de la touche, est en effet la pièce essentielle de l'instrument.

Le haut du sautereau est constitue d'une large gorge verticale occupée par une languette pivotante. Cette languette à son tour porte un plectre de plume ou de cuir, le bec. Lorsqu'on appuie sur une touche, le sautereau s'élève, le plectre pince la corde. Lorsque la touche est relâchée, le sautereau tombe, le bec touche la corde et oblige la languette à pivoter en arrière jusqu'à ce que le bec puisse éviter la corde, après quoi un ressort léger, en soie ou en en cuivre fin fait retourner la languette dans sa position originale.

Pendant ce temps, un étouffoir de tissu doux mais raide maintenu dans une fente à côté de la languette entre en contact avec la corde, étouffant les vibrations.

Une planche de bois placée au dessus de la rangée de sautereaux-le chapiteau- empêche ceux-ci d'être éjectés de l'instrument lorsque la touche est enfoncée. Quelle que soit la force avec laquelle la touche est enfoncée, la corde est pratiquement déplacée de la même façon par le bec.

On peut cependant placer plusieurs rangs de sautereaux l'un derrière l'autre, mais l'intensité sera très peu augmentée. En effet, dans la zone des intensités et des fréquences moyennes, la loi de Weber-Fechner, nous indiquant que la sensation croît approximativement comme le logarithme de l'excitation, peut être appliquée. On a donc: $S = \text{Log } I2/I1$, où S est la sensation perçue, K une constante, et I2 et I1 les intensités acoustiques dont la comparaison crée la sensation relative S. Par exemple si deux jeux de huit pieds sont joués ensemble, on n'aura guère qu'une augmentation d'intensité perçue de l'ordre de 0,3. (En fait, cette utilisation de plusieurs registres simultanés a surtout la particularité de modifier le timbre.)

Le corpus étudié est un ensemble choisi parmi les suites françaises de danses pour clavecin à leur période de floraison principale, c'est-à-dire entre 1660 et la fin du XVIIIème siècle, environ 1750. La forme de ces suites reste relativement constante pendant cette période, bien que le nombre de pièces descriptives qui ne sont pas des danses cryptées, c'est-à-dire que l'on peut reconnaître meme si leur nom n'est pas indiqué, tende à augmenter largement. Certaines des suites de la fin de la période sont presqu'exclusivement composées de pièces de caractère, donc descriptives.

Rappelons brièvement que la suite se compose des pièces suivantes:

Prélude: pièce qui doit donner une impression de souplesse et de liberté, en général non mesuré, c'est-à-dire écrit uniquement en rondes.

Allemande: danse binaire;lente, mais allante ;le futur andante.

Courante: danse assez rapide, avec passage de ternaire et binaire et réciproquement.

Sarabande: danse ternaire, lente et de tessiture grave, au rythme caractéristique, avec un accent sur le deuxième temps.

Gigue: danse ternaire rapide.

Chaconne ou passacaille: danse avec refrain et couplets.

Souvent s'intercalent entre sarabande et gigue diverses autres danses comme la gavotte, la passepied, le menuet, etc...

Les partitions qui forment notre corpus d'étude ont donc été choisies parmi les tres nombreux compositeurs français qui ont écrit pour le clavecin à ce moment-là. Il s'agit en particulier de l'imposant manuscrit Bauyn, date de 1660, dont les deux volumes sont répertoriés Res. Vm7 674–675 à la Bibliotheque Nationale, et qui comprend surtout des pièces de Chambonnières, la quasi-intégrale des pièces connues de Louis Couperin, et des pièces de Gilles Hardel, Jean Henri D'Anglebert, Nicolas Lebègue, Etienne Richard, Joseph de la Barre, Nicolas Monnard. Nous avons également étudié: le petit manuscrit à but pédagogique rédigé par une certaine Mlle de Lapierre, en 1680; puis, en 1689, l'édition des trois suites de D'Anglebert, suivies de ses nombreuses transcriptions. Au XVIIIème siècle, les pièces de Marchand en 1702 et 1703, les sept suites de Leroux en 1705, les suites de Rameau en 1706, 1724, 1728. Du monument que constitue l'œuvre de François Couperin, nous avons choisi L'Art de toucher le clavecin en 1717, puis les sixième, septième et huitième ordres. L'ensemble plus récent est constitué des suites de Corrette, 1734, de Royer, 1746, et de Fouquet, 1751. Le tout est loin d'être exhaustif, mais donne une idée de l'evolution du répertoire.

Il nous est ensuite nécessaire, puisque nous partons d'un point de vue à dominante sociologique, de découvrir parmi les théories existantes sur les temps sociaux, celle qui part du même point de départ intuitif que le nôtre, c'est-à-dire que le temps est une construction abstraite et complexe, et qui dépend du milieu social et de l'époque dans laquelle nous existons. Il est ensuite facile de suggérer que le parallèle entre cette théorie de société et le corpus musical étudié, qui est lui-même une production sociale, doit donner un utile outil d'observation et de lecture des œuvres considérées.

La théorie des milieux temporels

William Grossin, en 1988, a défini de manière précise ce concept de construction abstraite du temps, qu'il nomme 'milieu temporel': c'est un temps complexe qui peut être décomposé en éléments plus simples. Il dépend de la société, et réunit des temps naturels comme les saisons ou les marées, et des temps construits comme les temps de travail, les emplois du temps, les programmes. Il peut être polychrone, lorsque tous les types de temps ont autant d'importance les uns que les autres, ou monochrone, quand un type de temps est fortement dominant.

Un examen du milieu temporel entre 1650 et 1720 en France semble montrer que la population d'alors ne considérait pas le temps comme nous le faisons, ni même comme Newton ou d'autres théoriciens l'ont fait après 1720: le temps du XVIIème est mou, souvent non gradué, mesuré imprécisément, et très faiblement orienté. Le résultat est une société très fortement considérée comme confuse, ce qui est précisément, selon l'anthropologue E.T. Hall (1984), la caractéristique principale d'un milieu polychrone, vu par les yeux d'un observateur monochrone.

Grossin définit au moins trois manières de se représenter le temps, chacune d'entre elles etant affectée de plusieurs caractéristiques. Par exemple le temps dit chronologique est extérieur et universel, gradué, orienté, ordonné etc... Il va de soi que pour des raisons d'analyse musicale, nous avons été obligé de scinder ces grandes catégories en de plus nombreuses propriétés temporelles. Pour reprendre l'exemple cité plus haut, un enchaînement harmonique fortement orienté comme la cadence de la dominante a la tonique V-I devait pouvoir être examiné séparément d'une éventuelle extériorité ou graduation.

Enfin nous avons rapidement perçu les interactions entre les propriétés simples d'une catégorie et celles d'une autre. Ainsi le croissant intérêt que connaissent les modulations au XVIIIème siècle, lorsque s'établit la musique tonale, s'examinent a la lueur d'une simultanéité entre l'orientation, propriété chronologique, et la répétition, propriété analogique.

CATÉGORIES DE W. GROSSIN

Temps chronologique	*Temps plastique*	*Temps analogique*
Universel	Imprévisible	Récurrence
gradué	Mou	Sans orientation
orienté	Non Quantifié	
ordonné...		

PROPRIÉTÉS TEMPORELLES

Extériorité	Imprévisibilité	Similitude
-Universalité		
Orientation	Plasticité	
Ordre		
Quantification		
Graduation		
Homogénéité		

Figure 2.

Explication sommaire des propriétés temporelles

Plasticité:

Le musicien lit un signe temporel, dont il doit traduire la valeur selon les contextes intérieur et extérieur à l'œuvre, et selon le goût de son temps.

Dans nombre de pièces, par exemple, les croches ou les double-croches sont écrites égales, et jouées inégales. Il est pratiquement impossible de savoir à l'avance leur exacte durée, qui peut aller d'un mouvement très souple aux notes surpointées, où la deuxième note est extrêmement rapide. Un autre exemple de plasticité est la notation en rondes des préludes non-mesurés et semi-mesurés.

Similitude:
Il s'agit de répétition ou d'imitation sans obligation de produire quelque chose de différent d'un modèle. Les compositeurs de la fin du XVIIème siècle évitaient de répéter ou d'imiter dans le but d'un développement musical ou en relation avec les modulations. Une autre manière d'étudier la similitude est d'examiner la floraison des pièces de caractère au cours du XVIIIème siècle, telles que les portraits musicaux et les descriptions.

Imprévisibilité:
Cette propriété est peut-être l'une des plus importantes, dans la mesure où elle traite de la pertinence du fait musical. La dissonnance est considérée par Rameau, Saint-Lambert et Quantz comme un problème d'imprévisibilité.

Extériorité–universalité:
Le besoin d'extériorité est général au début du XVIIIème siècle. Il peut être observé aussi bien dans les travaux des scientifiques que dans ceux des musiciens, et est particulièrement pertinent lorsqu'on se rappelle le fait que la musique est entièrement à l'epoque considérée comme une science. Il existe de nombreuses publications sur une théorie générale et universelle de la musique, des inventions comme le métronome, ou du moins son ancêtre, le chronomètre de Loullier, l'usage grandissant du tempérament égal et une généralisation du système tonal avec Rameau.

Quantification:
Des raisons économiques rendent la quantification du temps de plus en plus nécessaire. Les musiciens trouvent également utile de mesurer leurs pièces avec des termes de mouvement comme Allegro assai, Adagio cantabile etc...

Graduation:
Un événement est situé le plus précisément possible sur une échelle temporelle. En musique, cela signifie que ce que l'on joue est le réel

début de l'œuvre, d'où la disparition graduelle des préludes non-mesurés, et des autres traits traditionnels de ce qui peut être nommé le temps hors de l'œuvre, avant et après. Cela signifie également que les événements musicaux sont plus distincts et clairs que ce qu'ils n'étaient dans les pièces pour luth de Gaultier et Pinel. Les agréments sont très significatifs de ce point de vue, surtout dans la musique de D'Anglebert et de François Couperin. De manière générale, l'intelligibilité devient préponderante.

Homogénéité:
Cette graduation du temps devient bientôt homogène et influence certainement assez fortement les compositeurs du XVIIIème siècle dans leur manière de diviser les mesures ou les périodes musicales.

Orientation et ordre:
Ces deux propriétés semblent devenir une manière obligatoire de penser au moment où Descartes fonde sa méthode sur la décomposition de tous les problèmes en une séquence de problèmes plus petits. Dans le manuscrit Bauyn, les danses pour clavecin ne sont pas ordonnées en suites, comme elles le seront plus tard. Le mot lui-même, suites de clavecin, n'apparaît que graduellement. Quant à François Couperin, il utilise même le mot d'ordre.

Je pense que le changement fondamental de doigté que l'on constate avec Rameau autour de 1728 peut être expliqué par cette notion d'ordre. De plus, l'orientation dans la musique tonale après Rameau semble une évidence et beaucoup de principes harmoniques sont basés sur ce principe.

Activations simultanées et interactions

Dans l'analyse sommaire du milieu temporel d'une œuvre ou d'un ensemble d'œuvres que nous effectuerons, ces neuf propriétés pourront prendre différentes valeurs, par exemple: –1, 0, 1/2, 1 (la valeur 1/2 est utilisée dans le cas d'interaction suivant: lorsqu'une propriété A, présente dans un trait musical, entraîne la perception d'une autre propriété B, nous pensons que A est plus importante que B parce que sans elle, B n'existerait pas, et d'autre part B n'est toujours qu'une interprétation de notre part. D'où la valeur moindre, arbitrairement 1/2). L'imprévisibilité, la similitude, la plasticité, et l'extériorité sont indépendantes les unes des autres et indépendantes des cinq autres propriétés. Par contre, la graduation, la quantification, l'homogénéité, l'ordre et l'orientation sont liées entre elles de la façon suivante:

si Quantification=1, alors Graduation=1
si Quantification= 1/2, alors Graduation= 1/2
Si homogénéité=1, alors quantification= 1
Si homogénéité= 1/2, alors quantification= 1/2
(ce qui fait aussi que la propriété graduation est également activée);
Si ordre= 1, alors graduation=1
Si orientation=1, alors ordre=1 (ce qui fait que la graduation est également activée)
Si orientation=1/2, alors ordre= 1/2

Les propriétés temporelles citées précédemment peuvent être activées de deux façons différentes: Elles peuvent être présentes en même temps dans un fait musical, sans réelle interaction entre elles, ou bien l'une d'entre elles peut être utilisée par le compositeur pour en exprimer une autre. Troisième cas, deux des propriétés peuvent être présentes simultanément et donner naissance à une troisième.

Par exemple, dans les rondeaux et les chaconnes, similitude et orientation sont présentes simultanément, alors que dans 'le moucheron' de François Couperin — sixième ordre-, l'homogénéité de la graduation — groupes de croches égales — est utilisée pour produire la similitude — imitation d'un insecte.

D'un ensemble de traits caractéristiques à la musique de clavecin, traits d'analyse musicologique relativement conventionnelle, on peut déduire une image du milieu temporel d'une œuvre ou d'un ensemble d'œuvres.

Voici par exemple un ensemble de questions qui pourraient être posées à propos d'une pièce, prise dans le corpus et analysée par un musicologue de manière traditionnelle:

1. Cette pièce correspond-elle à un schema de danse, cryptée ou non?
2. Distingue-t-on une incohérence des signes?
(extériorité)
3. Y a-t-il un éloignement par rapport au signe écrit?
4. Les notes sont-elles inégales?
(plasticité)
5. Quel est le rôle de la clarté et de l'intelligibilité?
6. Existe-t-il du temps hors de l'œuvre, avant ou après?
(graduation)
7. Constate-t-on une tendance vers l'égalisation?
(homogénéité)
8. Y a-t-il une ambiguité modale?
9. Les harmonies sont-elles dissonnantes?
(imprévisibilité)
10. La composition tend-elle à être séquentielle?
11. Y a-t-il des indications de doigtés? (si oui, anciens ou nouveaux?)
(ordre)
12. Cette pièce est-elle écrite en style français ou italien?
13. Les deux sections sont-elles unies par une formule?
14. Constate-t-on la présence d'un au moins des éléments suivants:
14.1. usage fréquent des accords de 9èmes, 7èmes, sixtes
14.2. changement de mode d'un accord
14.3. usage dans la même mesure d'un dièse et d'un bécarre sur la même note
14.4. importance de l'accord du quatrième degré
14.5. utilisation des altérations accidentelles à un position autre qu'à gauche de la note.
14.6. rythmes lombards
(orientation)
15. Y a-t-il une indication de tempo ou de mouvement?
(quantification)
16. est-ce une œuvre copiée?
17. est-ce la copie d'un caractère ou de la nature?
18. la mélodie tend-elle è se répéter par fragments?
19. y a-t-il des imitations?
20. y a-t-il des répétitions de sections?

21. y a-t-il emploi du même incipit légèrement modifié (en général dans le ton de la dominante) au début de la deuxième section de la danse?
(similitude)
22. trouve-t-on des batteries?
(similitude homogénéité)
23. le style brise est -il employé?
(plasticité non graduation)
24.le temps est-il cyclique?
(orientation similitude)
25.y a-t-il usage d'un accord six trois à l'endroit où une quinte est attendue?
(imprévisibilité orientation)
26.le tempérament est-il égal?
(homogénéité universalité)
27.y a-t-il développement, double ou variation?
(similitude orientation)
28.y a-t-il modification d'un rondeau durant le déroulement de la pièce?
(similitude orientation)
29.y a-t-il usage d'un accord de dominante avec cadence au milieu de la pièce?
(symétrie orientation)
30.peut-on constater la présence du mot fin, dessin de fin de morceau, indication du début de deuxième section, présence du mot suite?
(graduation non extériorité)
31. Y a-t-il des indications par des mots ou par des notes du recommencement de la pièce?
(similitude non graduation)
32. Comment se situe la pièce dans l'évolution vers le système universel sol2 fa4 pour les claviers?
(universalite symétrie (similitude))
33. Utilisation de l'homogénéité pour suggérer un objet ou un caractère?
(homogénéité / similitude 1/2)
34. Emploi d'adjectifs ou de noms de caractère avec l'idée adjacente d'indiquer un tempo?
(similitude /quantification 1/2)
35. La pièce est -elle tres modulante?

(similitude orientation extériorité)

36. Y a-t-il des cadences?

(ordre plasticité imprévisibilité)

37. Le style brisé est-il utilisé pour décrire un caractère et non plus par lui-même?

(plasticité non graduation / similitude)

38. Le style brisé est-il utilisé pour obtenir un mouvement régulier?

(plasticité non graduation /homogénéité)

39. Utilise-t-on une note altérée imprévue pour moduler?

(imprévisibilité similitude /orientation)

40. Utilise-t-on une cadence rompue pour répéter une formule?

(imprévisibilité orientation / similitude)

Conclusion

La réponse au questionnaire précédent permet d'établir à l'aide d'un calculateur de type informatique (Baccino, 1993 — communication personnelle) une image graphique du milieu temporel de la pièce étudiée. Si l'intérêt de cette image n'est certes pas négligeable, il est encore plus intéressant de faire une comparaison systématique entre plusieurs images, pour voir s'y dessiner des évolutions soit chez les compositeurs, soit a l'intérieur d'une époque. De plus, et en extrapolant les possibilités de généralisation de l''outil milieu temporel', l'étude systématique tant longitudinale que transversale d'un groupe d'œuvres pourrait être, pensons-nous, élargie avec profit à d'autres répertoires musicaux, et faciliterait dans ce cas une ouverture analytique de la musique vers les autres arts, dans la mesure ou l'étude des sensibilités au temps plonge encore plus loin dans les conduites de création artistique.

Références

Baccino, T. (1993). Logiciel "Image des milieux temporels", communication personnelle.

Benoît, M. (1982). *Les musiciens du Roi de France*. Paris: PUF collection "Que sais-je?", n° 2048.

Couperin, F. (1961). *L'Art de Toucher le Clavecin*. Wiesbaden: Breitkopf. (facsimile of original edition: Paris, chez Boyvin, 1717.)

Francastel, P. (1970). *Etudes de sociologie de l'art*. Paris: Denoël, Collection Tel.

Grossin, W. (1988). "Pour une écologie temporelle", *Les temps sociaux*, D. Mercure and A. Wallemacq (éds.). Editions Universitaires de Boeck Université.

Hall, E. (1984). *La danse de la vie: temps culturel et temps vécu*. Paris: Le Seuil.

Kitchen, J. P. (1979). Harpsichord Music of Seventeenth-century France, with Particular Emphasis on the work of Louis Couperin. Doctoral diss. University of Cambridge.

Kuhn, T. S. (1983). *La structure des révolutions scientifiques*. Paris: Flammarion, collection Champs.

Lavisse, E. (1988). *Louis XIV*. Paris: Laffont.

Ledbetter, D. (1987). *Harpsichord and lute music in XVIIth century France*. Indiana University Press.

Le Goff, J. (1977). *Temps et travail au Moyen-âge*. Paris: Gallimard.

Quantz, J. J. (1975). *Essai d'une Méthode pour Apprendre à Jouer de la Flûte Traversière*. Paris: Zurfluh (facsimile of the French edition of 1752).

Rameau, J. Ph (1968). *Traité de l'harmonie*. Paris: Méridiens Klinksieck (facsimile of the edition of 1722).

Vecchione, B. (1985). "La Réalité Musicale, Eléménts d'Epistémologie Musicologique". Thèse pour le doctorat d'état ès-lettres, Université de Paris-VIII.

Servant, I. (1992). How was Time represented? French Society and its Harpsichord Music. Third international Congress on Musical Signification, Edinburgh (UK), 1–5 September (to be published).

Servant, I. (1993). "Milieux temporels et musique du passé", *Temporalistes*, n° 24.

Les quatuors de Beethoven
Un cas de l'expression temporelle

CHRISTINE ESCLAPEZ

Introduction

Depuis deux décennies, la recherche musicologique connaît une véritable 'révolution de paradigme'[1] qui affecte sa problématique, sa méthode et son objet. Longtemps tributaires de l'histoire, ses progrès ont été dépendants des méthodes de la recherche documentaire, archivistique ou biographique.

La compréhension de son objet — le fait musical — a été liée à l'hypothèse d'une musique symbolique, fait d'expression et de communication de sentiments, de concepts ou plus généralement d'idées extra-musicales.[2]

La signification musicale, au centre de toutes ces propositions esthétiques, est considérée comme le résultat d'un décodage de la part de l'auditeur ou de toute personne participant à sa réception. Elle est, ainsi, comparée au langage parlé qui 'exprime'. Comparaison inévitable, source des recherches, nées au XXème siècle sous l'impulsion du structuralisme.

Cette 'révolution épistémologique' se manifeste par l'intégration, dans notre culture musicologique occidentale, de disciplines considérées habituellement comme extérieures à l'objet même de la musicologie. Informatique et Sciences Humaines rejoignent le champs de la recherche en musicologie et réforment les objectifs de ses travaux en complexifiant la représentation du fait musical. Celui-ci, sous l'impulsion de telles disciplines, devient un fait complexe, un objet de culture[3], un fait musical total (Molino 1975) impliquant une appréhension pluridisciplinaire.

L'apport théorique des 'humanités' permet de considérer l'activité musicale comme une production essentielle à l'être humain vivant en société. Elle est désormais définie comme une forme de pensée spécifique, un moyen de connaissance aussi fondamental que le langage parlé.[4]

Si le langage parlé s'occupe essentiellement de décrypter le message sonore émis; la musique, pour sa part, s'intéresse à la matière sonore, à sa plasticité et à ce qu'elle peut informer, éventuellement, comme conception du monde et de l'homme sans utiliser toutefois la médiation d'un message organisé, conceptuel et décryptable de façon univoque. Son objet est ainsi l'information — au sens d'une 'mise enforme' ou d'une 'formation' — d'une matière et d'une combinatoire musicales. Ou bien comme le dirait le compositeur Luciano Berio, "la formation de la forme" que l'auditeur n'a pas l'habitude de prendre en compte lors de la signification linguistique; attentif, par contre, au décodage du message qui doit se réaliser avec plus ou moins de succès et de fiabilité.[5] Parallèlement, l'étude du processus de signifiance — objet de la sémiotique musicale — est largement influencée par ces changements épistémologiques, théoriques et méthodologiques. Elle considére, désormais, le fait musical dans sa réalité la plus complexe et la plus délicate à saisir.

Les sciences de l'instauration

Aperçu épistémologique

En calquant le signe musical sur le signe linguistique, la sémiotique structuraliste[6] étudie la fonction sémiotique dans des fonctionnements constitués, véritables artefacts épistémologiques.

Elle recherche le partage optimum des codes entre émetteur et récepteur et fait l'hypothèse d'une œuvre statique, message invariant lors de ses processus de signification quelque soit les temps et les lieux de production ou de réception.

Le schéma de la communication[7] est reproduit de façon implicite et l'on assiste à une comparaison injustifiée entre deux systèmes a priori éloignés. Langage et musique sont considérés, tout particulièrement sur un plan épistémologique, comme deux entités semblables, comme deux systèmes au fonctionnement sémiotique identique.

Ce que l'on appelle la sémiotique de l'instauration ou sémiotique anthropologique cherche à étudier le signe musical de façon spécifique, comme le résultat de l'équilibrage de plusieurs conduites: compositionnelles mais aussi perceptives, analytiques et plus généralement instauratrices...

Si le compositeur est toujours ressenti, de par sa fonction de créateur comme le centre de gravité de l'œuvre, il n'est plus considéré comme le seul personnage ayant des relations privilégiées avec elle. L'analyste, l'auditeur, le(s) commanditaire(s) et bien d'autres acteurs de la création, jouant des rôles fondamentaux, intègrent, de fait, la chaine sémiotique.

Le signe musical est conçu comme le résultat d'un processus complexe d'objectivation où l'activité compositionnelle n'est plus une alchimie mystérieuse, ni même l'œuvre d'un génie inexpliqué.
Système de significations ou de ramifications, le signe musical est un lieu particulier d'inscription ou d'instauration du procès compositionnel.

La sémiotique de l'instauration se situe en amont des divers projets sémiotiques que l'on peut recenser: la sémiologie de la communication (Ruwet 1972), de la signification (Barthes 1953), de la tripartition (Nattiez 1976 et 1986), de la compétence (Stefani 1986) et la sémiotique structurale d'Eero Tarasti (1979).

Considérant l'œuvre comme le prolongement de plusieurs conduites et la définissant comme un objet de culture, spécifique mais connectée à l'environnement qui l'a produite ou appréhendée; ce projet sémiotique aborde le fait musical à travers l'intégration de diverses approches anthropologiques: sociologie, psychologie, sémiotique, histoire...

Si la spécificité du fait musical doit être revendiquée, spécialement sur un plan cognitif (comme le fait Ivo Supicič, en 1985, dans un de ses articles), son autonomie face à l'environnement culturel ne peut être que partielle.

Psychologie historique et sémiotique de l'instauration

La psychologie historique d'Ignace Meyerson est fondamentale dans ce cadre de recherche. Elle postule la spécificité et la variabilité historique des formes de la pensée (artistiques, religieuses, verbales...) (Meyerson, 1948). Différente de tout behaviorisme, de tout mentalisme ou de toute psychologie abstraite supposant l'invariance du psychisme humain, elle accorde une place fondamentale aux activités humaines dans tout ce qu'elles ont de "changeant", de complexe ou de multiple...

L'homme se définit par ce qu'il a construit, achevé, transmis...Son activité aboutit à des œuvres, formes organisées, combinatoires complexes, objectivations conscientes et/ou inconscientes de ses conceptions du monde et de sa pensée.   Dans   cette   optique   épistémologique, plusieurs options de recherche et de reflexion se dégagent:

Au niveau de l'objet musical, l'œuvre n'est plus une simple forme immanente et immuable. Système ouvert, elle est un aboutissement, un travail, une composition. En perpétuelle transformation, elle est virtuellement inachevée; soumise aux multiples interprétations successives dont elle a fait et dont elle fera l'objet.

Au niveau de la fonction sémiotique, on postulera la variabilité des fonctions psychologiques de l'homme. Ces variabilités ne sont pas seulement des variations du contenu mais aussi des variations de la fonction psychologique qui a crée les œuvres.

Histoire des mentalites et sémiotique de l'instauration

Lucien Febvre et Marc Bloch ont participé à la rénovation de la science historique et ont forgé une histoire des mentalités et des représentations qui a donné naissance à l'anthropologie historique. (Le Goff, 1986.)

Avec le XXème siècle, la critique de la notion de fait historique apparait, corrélativement à celle de document. Le fait historique n'est plus un objet donné; il est le résultat du processus, désormais créateur, qui est à l'œuvre lors de l'analyse historique.

Et réapparait alors toute la dualité entre passé/présent, frontière fragile, paramètre particulièrement pertinent, lors du déchiffrement de l'objet de culture.

Febvre et Bloch ont conçu l'histoire comme un procès ou une problématique dont la lecture la plus juste est possible avec un minimum de conscience méthodologique par rapport à la subjectivité de l'historien et à l'utilité d'un comparatisme historique. Avec ce courant de la nouvelle école historique française est née une histoire des représentations ou des mentalités dominantes qui a pris des formes diverses mais qui a eu le mérite de positionner statégiquement l'imaginaire dans le processus de création. Le symbolique est définitivement connecté à la réalité historique.

L'histoire anthropologique cesse de travailler sur l'axe rigide et syntagmatique d'un déroulement temporel idéal: le temps mesuré, chronologique, 'historique', pour s'intéresser à un temps paradigmatique et pour retrouver les temps réels des hommes et de leurs représentations.

Les productions humaines ne sont plus considérées comme des représentations immuables, préformées, universelles, comme cela a été le cas dans bon nombre de psychologies. Elles évoluent en même temps que l'esprit humain, lui-même soumis aux changements historiques....

L'objet de la Psychologie Historique et de l'Histoire anthropologique sera l'étude de la variabilité des fonctions psychologiques et des modes de représentations à travers l'histoire de l'esprit humain et celle des mutations des sociétés.

Sociologie historique de la culture et sémiotique de l'instauration

La sociologie historique des formes de la pensée plastique de Pierre Francastel (1951, 1965 et 1967) représente un ensemble de concepts importants pour cette recherche.

Elle considère l'œuvre comme un objet de civilisation, creuset culturel et inscription du contexte anthropologique dans lequel elle a vu le jour. Ce que l'on peut encore définir par le concept relativement opérant d'Eco-Forme.

Ce terme vient de l'écologie et est apparu dès 1866 avec les travaux de Haeckel pour désigner la science — l'écologie — qui étudie les rapports entre les organismes et le milieu où ils vivent.

Le modèle éco-formel conçoit les différents niveaux d'intégration du sens comme des réseaux interactifs qui optimalisent la forme en tant que système d'inscriptions à déchiffrer.

La sociologie historique de la culture étudie, plus particulièrement, les cadres mentaux de la représentation tels que (pour Francastel) la spatialité et ses diverses formes de représentation, replacés dans leur contexte de production et observés sous le signe de l'invention, comme des facteurs déterminants d'instauration d'un sens dans l'œuvre. [8]

Poïétique et sémiotique de l'instauration

Dans un tel courant épistémologique, la notion de création devient un concept transversal de grande importance.

Avec la sémiotique de Julia Kristeva, la distinction capitale entre l'œuvre en train de se faire — qui pourrait renvoyer à la conduite instauratrice du compositeur: le travail compositionnel et l'œuvre une fois faite -objet d'analyse- revient à l'ordre du jour. [9]

Pour Julia Kristeva, la mise au jour de systèmes de signes relève d'une étude structurale (démarche taxinomique) mais cette visée demeure incomplète; le sémioticien doit rapporter les sytèmes qu'il étudie à leur production par un sujet situé dans un lieu dont la topologie est spécifique.

Autrement dit, il convient de replacer tout procès de création et de signifiance dans un cadre, défini comme relatif et variable, dépendant — hic et nunc — du sujet produisant.

Avec les sciences de l'instauration, le niveau d'immanence tel que le supposait Nattiez pert de sa rigidité et de son universalité. [10]

La réalité musicale de l'œuvre comme objet de civilisation implique un processus de signifiance tenant compte de l'objet instauré et de ses réinstaurations multiples tout au long de la chaine de l'échange musical qui comprend l'activité de composition, d'appréhension ou de déchiffrement... et la liste n'est bien sûr pas exhaustive.

Le mot de création (revenu à la mode en 1970) se met à polariser l'attention que l'on porte aux œuvres qui deviennent des 'choses à faire' en même temps que des 'choses à déchiffrer'.

La création est autant l'affaire du compositeur que celle de l'analyste. L'instauration existe chez ces deux acteurs de la signifiance musicale.

L'activité d'appréhension ou d'analyse est un contact interactif avec un objet — l'œuvre musicale — définie comme un objet de civilisation, une éco-forme, produite par un compositeur, homme historique évoluant dans un certain cadre de pensée et de réprésentation et reçue par une chaine sémiotique aux multiples facettes.

Dans cette optique, seul, un déchiffrement permet l'instauration de son 'sens' ou du moins d'un de ses 'sens'. La théorie du déchiffrement ne revendique pas la découverte d'un sens enfoui de façon univoque au plus profond de l'œuvre, dans le but implicite de restaurer sa vérité absolue. Le concept de découverte du sens suppose, en effet, un signe statique dont la signification s'impose de façon irréfutable lors de l'acte d'appréhension.

A l'inverse, le concept de déchiffrement met en valeur toute la polysémie et la variabilité du signe dans une appréhension interactive entre le sujet analysant et l'œuvre analysée...

Problématique

Le concept de mutation des formes de la pensee musicale

Par extension aux travaux réalisés par Francastel sur la notion d'espace en peinture, cette recherche travaille sur la notion de temporalité et sur sa manifestation et sa représentation dans l'œuvre de chambre de Beethoven, peut-être la plus connue, du moins la plus déroutante: les Quatuors.

Ce cadre temporel de référence est lié à un second concept: celui de mutation.

En effet, le temps du discours beethovénien est considéré, comme un cas parmi tant d'autres, de génération d'une nouvelle expression de la temporalité musicale, instauration induite en partie par des changements sociologiques, précurseurs de la société contemporaine.[11]

Ce concept de Mutation est capital dans le cadre d'une approche instauratrice puisqu'il suppose une vision originale de l'histoire. Celle-ci ne constitue plus un axe syntagmatique, linéaire, à complexification continue où l'idée de progrès est constitutive de celle de chronologie mais un axe dépendant directement de la variabilité de l'histoire des fonctions psychologiques humaines.

Les mutations représentent des périodes de transformations conscientes et/ou inconscientes de la pensée musicale mais aussi de transformations des cadres mentaux de référence (comme l'espace et le temps par exemple) ou des structures implicites de la société contemporaine.

La sémiotique de l'instauration n'étudie pas des systèmes préconstitués où la communication a été institutionnalisée par une acculturation progressive mais des périodes où des nouvelles combinatoires sont expérimentées, où le langage se cherche. Des périodes de création intenses où un imaginaire nouveau est instauré. Bernard Vecchione a étudié dans quelques uns de ses travaux, une mutation particulière, celle du milieu du XIIIème siècle à la fin du XVème siècle en Italie ainsi que celle de la fin du XIXème siècle au début du XXème siècle. (Vecchione 1984.)

Cette recherche étudie une autre mutation celle qui, débutant dès le milieu du XVIIIème siècle, a conduit au langage contemporain du XXème siècle.

L'hypothèse de recherche retenue est que le changement du langage contemporain est déjà en germe dans le discours beethovenien et se manifeste par une expérimentation de la part du compositeur sur les différents modes de représentation du temps. La représentation classique ne satisfaisant plus.

Considérer Beethoven comme l'un des intaurateurs d'une nouvelle forme de pensée temporelle musicale ne sous-entend absolument pas qu'il a été le seul instigateur d'un tel changement.

Mozart et Haydn et d'autres encore bien avant lui, ont proposé des conceptions temporelles très originales. Et que dire de la période d'expérimentation particulièrement riche d'où sont issus le Moyen-âge ou certaines musiques extra-européennes...

Nous attirons simplement l'attention sur un compositeur,en particulier, certainement important pour notre culture occidentale; avec le sentiment que cette mutation se réalise de façon plus systèmatique dans son procès compositionnel que dans celui d'autres compositeurs issus de la même culture.

Mais il est bien évident qu'une innovation n'est jamais un acte gratuit et isolé; elle prend racine chez des groupes sociaux particuliers, s'appuie sur des compositeurs plus anciens et instaure de nouvelles structures compositionnelles imaginées à partir de combinatoires existantes.

La marge entre l'innovation individuelle et collective est mince et il est réducteur de croire que la création est uniquement l'œuvre d'un seul individu...

La temporalite musicale

L'objectif principal est d'appréhender la musique à travers les fluctuations de temps qu'elle décrit. Cette attitude est typiquement culturelle, elle est une disponibilité d'accès que se donne l'auditeur, conscient qu'il perçoit, selon les époques et les langages, des processus musicaux différemment organisés quant aux rapports de durées et au cadre formel. (Deliège, 1986)

La pensée musicale a un cadre de représentation bien particulier qui n'est pas la représentation d'un message à communiquer où d'une réalité à découvrir mais la représentation d'une certaine organisation et sensibilité temporelles, cadre de pensée historique évoluant avec l'histoire de l'esprit humain. La signifiance de la musique ne résiderait pas dans l'expression d'une idée, d'un sentiment ou de toute autre forme de discours conceptualisable mais -entre autres- dans l'instauration d'une temporalité musicale ou dans la combinatoire temporelle d'une matière musicale .

Les quatuors de Beethoven: un cas de l'expression temporelle

Beethoven apparait être un auteur privilégié pour appréhender la temporalité musicale (Boucourechliev 1963). En effet, les libertés prises par Beethoven par rapport aux traditions musicales trouvent leur sens et leur justification dans la manière dont est traité le temps musical, non comme un cadre chronologique et compositionnel pré-établi mais comme un évènement solidaire et spécifique d'une œuvre donnée.

Comme se construisant dans l'œuvre et par l'œuvre, comme résultat d'une combinatoire musicale particulière. Comme un espace-temps venant complexifier le déroulement chronologique de l'œuvre par une mise en relief de sa forme.

> L'âge classique disposait — en musique et hors de la musique — d'une conception du temps qui en faisait le simple ordre de la succession, mais la force organisatrice de cette succession était elle-même hors du temps, antérieure et supérieure à lui. (Revault d'Allones, 1982: 77)

La temporalité classique véhicule une certaine fonction rhétorique et c'est dans ce sens qu'elle a mis en place un système basé sur une discursivité et une compréhension claires, voire facilement déchiffrables.

A l'inverse, la représentation du temps plus contemporaine que nous propose Beethoven, intègre tous les paramètres du discours musical. Le temps n'est plus simplement rythme et métrique mais il devient mouvement et dynamique.

> Le temps musical du discours de Beethoven a créé les normes de perception de tous les auditeurs européens pendant près d'un siècle et bien au delà (...). (Deliege, 1986)

Les quatuors ont toujours été pour Beethoven et selon ses 'dires' (cf. certaines lignes des carnets de conversation) un lieu d'expérimentation privilégié où le compositeur pouvait se permettre les plus folles incursions dans l'original.

A ce titre, ils représentent un laboratoire expérimental de premier choix. La texture particulière de cet effectif instrumental permet une écriture plus fine qui créé une épaisseur particulière, des interférences entre les quatre instruments riches de potentialités sonores et des tensions propices à toutes sortes de divagations. Le mode de composition de ce genre chez Beethoven est différent de l'écriture des symphonies, pensées comme des grands blocs de temps successifs et induisant ainsi une mise en temps travaillant sur l'axe syntagmatique de la temporalité.

Beethoven — tel que le démontre Boucourechliev — est l'un des premiers esprits modernes, au moins en ce qui concerne l'instauration d'un nouveau cadre temporel. Un des premiers compositeurs à s'essayer consciemment à des techniques nouvelles au risque de paraître déroutant ou de choquer.

Un des premiers compositeurs à être réellement autonome, non asservi à une commande obligatoire, libre d'innovations gratuites. Un des premiers compositeurs à distordre la forme classique (forme sonate) sans toutefois la détruire. Il rend la morphologie perceptible en y intégrant l'accident, l'événement et en leur donnant une densité inégalée lors du parcours temporel. La structure ne peut plus être considérée comme un modèle architectural préformé.

Méthodologie

Remarques générales

Il parait intéressant, de tenter de dégager des techniques d'inscription du temps employées par Beethoven au sein de la production des quatuors. Techniques d'écriture bien entendu mais aussi techniques perceptives jouant avec la mémoire de l'auditeur et débordant le cadre de la simple discursivité mélodique et harmonique.

Ceci, dans le dessein évident, d'en établir une taxinomie, une description et de modéliser une représentation de ces techniques au niveau du quatuor mais aussi au niveau des dix-sept quatuors. Dans le but évident, de tenter de comprendre quelles ont été les techniques les plus utilisées et s'il est possible de dégager une progression compositionnelle dans leur formalisation. Structurer cette taxinomie de façon à dégager des types de techniques temporelles et à étudier leur utilisation par le compositeur en relation avec la chronologie de composition de ces œuvres. [13]

Le cadre d'investigation se situe au niveau de l'inscription de l'éco-forme dans la forme. Il s'agit de l'étape préalable à tout déchiffrement: la découverte des réels constituants musicaux de cette inscription. Démarche méthodologique indispensable qui permet d'éviter les écueils rencontrés par les diverses approches sociologiques qui ont tenté de rapprocher sociologie et musique. Réalisant, souvent, de grossières applications de l'une vers l'autre, elles ont considéré la situation musicale comme le miroir d'une situation sociologique donnée.

L'observation de ces catégories temporelles permet de réaliser une analyse des représentations temporelles directement connectées à la réalité musicale.

Leur observation[14] et leur caractérisation a permis de même, de constituer un recueil de données assez important (plus de 270 indices temporels relevés, décrits et caractérisés) qui représentent des moments temporels saillants, des configurations signifiantes annoncés par des indices divers tels que: indices formels, rythmiques, matière problématique , instrumentation originale, intégration de l'accident ou de l'incident dans la forme...

Ces moments, relevés et caractérisés à l'aide d'un vocabulaire original[15] deviennent des éléments de signification ou des systèmes d'inscription fondamentaux pour tenter, après un traitement et une comparaison, de déchiffrer des techniques relativement stables d'instauration du temps au sein des quatuors. Et par la suite, d'établir une étude comparative avec les autres modes de représentations en vigueur dans la société contemporaine.

Ces sèmes temporels sont de nouveaux instruments de segmentation du discours musical tout comme l'étaient les critères structuraux de l'analyse paradigmatique ruwétienne ou tout autre critère issu des théories des grammaires qui ont vu le jour après les années soixante.

A ce stade, aucune élaboration de résultats définitifs. Ce qui suit est libre de modifications, de changements et peut-être de renversements. Voici un état de l'interprétation des résultats.

Essai d'interprétation

Voici, donc, quelques types d'indices temporels relevés après étude ainsi qu'un aperçu de ce que pourrait être un traitement de ces données, recueillies après audition, confrontation de diverses interprétations et analyse.[16]

Après étude des dix-sept quatuors, il semble que l'action beethovénienne sur le temps musical s'exerce à plusieurs niveaux:

* au niveau de l'instauration d'un moment temporel par l'utilisation d'une technique déterminée

– quelques exemples de techniques: superposition, suspension, arrêt, rupture de directionnalité.

Ces techniques, dès qu'elles sont employées de façon unique, créent des moments temporels saillants.

* au niveau de l'instauration d'un moment temporel par l'utilisation d'une combinatoire de différentes techniques.

Niveau supérieur de construction qui donne naissance à des parcours complexes.

Les techniques temporelles s'organisent, à ce stade de l'interprétation, en trois niveaux déterminés par la complexité du moment temporel relevé. Deux critères se dégagent: le degré de combinatoire et la durée du moment.

* Niveau 1: une seule technique est instaurée.

Elle constitue une arête saillante dans le déroulement de l'œuvre musicale et, en général, est clairement délimitée dans l'espace du quatuor: elle ne dure que quelques mesures. Bien que cette remarque ne puisse constituer, bien sûr, une règle stricte de fonctionnement.

* Niveau 2: niveau plus complexe qui est basé sur le concept de dualité.

En effet, à ce stade, deux types de techniques apparaissent connectées et fonctionnent souvent sur le principe de l'opposition.

Ce niveau 2 constitue un nœud temporel, carrefour privilégié dans le déroulement de l'œuvre. Le niveau 2 est un moment temporel privilégié d'instauration du schème tension/détente.

Celui-ci, à la base du langage tonal classique, est représenté de façon originale. Au lieu d'être uniquement symbolisé par la relation harmonique Dominante/Tonique, comme c'est bien souvent le cas; il s'ancre directement dans la matière sonore en y intégrant tous les paramètres musicaux: hauteur, durée, intensité, timbre.

* Niveau 3: une combinatoire de niveau plus élevé.

Il s'agit d'une interrelation entre différentes techniques, au nombre variable (toujours plus de deux) et qui représente un véritable parcours ayant une action dans le déroulement de l'œuvre: bien souvent après cette structure processionnelle, la morphologie de l'œuvre change et épouse une toute autre dynamique que celle qui était, primitivement, exposée.

C'est en ce sens que ce niveau apparait, souvent, à des endroits stratégiques: avant la réexposition, en préparation du développement, avant la coda.... Cette mise en valeur — dramatisation, spatialisation — rend ces moments saillants même s'ils deviennent, du fait de leur apparition originale, moins compréhensibles pour l'auditeur contemporain de l'œuvre qui réagit plutôt par rapport aux conventions formelles mises en place par des codes sociaux très précis en cette fin du XVIIIème siècle.

Par contre ils deviennent des entités beaucoup plus perceptibles à un niveau plus sensible. L'œuvre musicale n'est plus simplement une architecture, elle devient une morphologie à la plasticité variable.

* Niveau 4: niveau le plus extrëme, dans le sens des bouleversements temporels induts: une ou plusieurs techniques temporelles sont utilisées sur une plage sonore beaucoup plus longue: à l'échelle d'un mouvement ou du quatuor dans son entier.

Il s'agit, ici, du niveau le plus fertile en bouleversement, du niveau le plus avancé dans la mutation. Beethoven y prend les risques les plus incontrolés en proposant à l'auditeur une nouvelle conception du temps exposée longuement et de la façon la plus claire possible.

Ceci est très intéressant au niveau de l'audition: Beethoven propose des conceptions musicales originales et prend le temps de les exposer....

Les techniques relevées s'organisent en deux grandes familles
* Celles qui travaillent sur un axe syntagmatique et qui ont comme ordre: la successivité.

Elles ne remettent pas en question le déroulement linéaire de l'œuvre en tant que cadre chronologique mais tentent de le déstabiliser en insérant des noeuds temporels saillants, des moments temporels détruisant toute stabilité chronologique Rupture de directionnalité, suspension avec ou sans résolution différée, arrêt, interruption, fragmentation, atomisation, accélération, ralentissement, fixation, statisme, incertitude temporelle, densification dynamique... Cette liste n'est, bien sûr, pas exhaustive.

* Celles qui travaillent sur un axe paradigmatique et qui ont comme ordre la simultanéité.

Elles instaurent un temps multiple, en superposant des couches temporelles complètement indépendantes les unes des autres. Une polyrythmie est créée, une polytemporalité de même. Cette technique est directement issue de l'emploi du contrepoint par Beethoven, simplement celui-ci intègre cette technique d'écriture ancienne dans un autre contexte compositionnel.

Pour l'instant, une seule technique temporelle a été répertoriée: la superposition et sa technique corrélative: la spatialisation.

Le traitement qui consiste à comparer tous ces moments temporels est en cours; il n'est pas possible de formuler des conclusions explicites quant aux techniques, à leur utilisation et à leur complexification tout au long de la production beethovénienne.

Il semble que Beethoven bouleverse les habitudes temporelles des auditeurs de l'époque. Non pas en réalisant une innovation constante et destructrice mais plutôt en expérimentant progressivement une nouvelle combinatoire de la matière musicale. Beethoven n'est pas un réformateur usant la technique de la table rase: il utilise des techniques anciennes qu'il reformule dans un cadre différent et qu'il distord. Ces techniques sont utilisées et rendues suffisemment puissantes pour instaurer dans un contexte différent une nouvelle conception du temps. L'instauration se produit par la constitution d'une combinatoire de niveau plus élevé que celles déjà en place. Ce niveau est l'amorce de changements plus radicaux qui seront expérimentés de façon systèmatique par d'autres.

Le temps n'est plus égal à rythme mais à mouvement, morphologie, densité...Plasticité. Ce n'est plus un temps métrique mais un temps physique, un temps multiple, un temps sensible...La sensibilité est exprimée par la matière musicale elle-même, dynamique et mouvante et non pas par les structures syntaxiques.

> Chez Beethoven, le temps de l'œuvre se construit au fur et à mesure de son déroulement chronologique, une figurabilité du sonore y est instaurée. "Chez Beethoven, le son ne se mesure plus, ne se confronte plus qu'à lui-même, la transgression devient un passage, la rupture devient un moment, l'irruption une entrée, la destruction un déploiement, le paradoxe une évidence et même le silence, un événement." (Revault d'Allones, 1982: 42–43)

Septembre 1991

Notes

1. Ce concept est employé pour la première fois par Bernard Vecchione dans son article de 1990 (cf. références bibliographiques).
2. On se rappelera, ici, les diverses théories qui ont participé à ces croyances esthétiques comme la théorie des affects ou les nombreuses théories expressionnistes...
3. Le terme d'objet de culture a été utilisé par Pierre Francastel (1970) dans le cadre de ses études sur la Peinture.
4. Nous faisons, ici, référence au langage parlé en accord avec les diverses études comparatives entre Musique et Langage qui se sont développées dès les années 60, en appliquant les concepts structuralistes aux objets des sciences humaines
5. Nous évoquons uniquement et de façon très grossière le fonctionnement du langage parlé.
6. Pour référence, citons les travaux de Umberto Eco, Roman Jackobson, Nicolas Ruwet, Claude Lévi-Strauss, Roland Barthes dans la lignée des travaux structuralistes appliqués en musique.

7. On fait référence, ici, au schéma instauré par la Théorie de la Communication mise au point par Shannon et Weaver en 1949. Le schéma de la Communication peut être modélisé comme un message stable entre un émetteur et un récepteur. Il a été conceptualisé à partir du modèle des messages téléphoniques. Emetteur. Message. Récepteur.

8. Pour ce problème du temps, on peut faire référence aussi à un article de William Grossin (1989).

9. Kristeva 1969. Et en référence aux premiers travaux portant sur cette distinction, citons les formalistes russes et le Cercle de Prague ainsi que les concepts de phénotexte et de génotexte.

10. On fait référence, ici, au schéma de la tripartition de Nattiez tel qu'il est présenté dans ses deux ouvrages: Nattiez 1976 et 1986.

11. On fera référence, ici, à l'impact et aux influences de la révolution française dans la société allemande et sur Beethoven, le définissant, dans nombre de littératures et biographies, comme le représentant d'une idéologie progressiste.

    On pensera également au mouvement philosophique de l'Aufklärung que l'on peut traduire sommairement par "L'âge des lumières" et qui constituait un nouveau cadre de pensée face à une économie et une politique attardées. Ce Renouveau de l'Allemagne du XVIIIème siècle est un renouveau philosophique universitaire qui touche une petite élite constituée en majeure partie par des professeurs et des penseurs. Mais après extension, il est aussi un renouveau philosophique populaire. Hostile au langage technique et à l'ordre abstrait des traités, la philosophie populaire souhaite une clarté toute littéraire dans l'argumentation des références concrètes et un recours au sentiment. Elle s'élabore surtout dans les salons bourgeois. Et que dire de Vienne qui a exercé sur Beethoven, fascination mais aussi répulsion. Une ville qu'il ne s'est jamais résolu à quitter et qui a vu la naissance de toutes ses créations sans vraiment le comprendre. Que de prospectives comparatives...Peut-on comparer cette situation avec celle que connu Schönberg confronté lui aussi à cette même ville. Ces considérations plus sociologiques constituent un cadre de référence de grande importance mais qu'il n'est pas dans notre propos de développer au sein de cet article.

12. On peut citer, aussi, le numéro 40 de la Revue Arc rédigée sous la direction d'André Boucourechliev, publiée en 1970 et consacrée entièrement à Beethoven.

13. Bien que ceci ne soit pas évident: les dates exactes de composition étant relativement incertaines.

14. Relevé d'après partition: plusieurs éditions sont prises en compte ainsi que plusieurs versions. L'instauration du temps dépend aussi des interprètes, ceux-ci sont des acteurs privilégiés dans la chaine de l'échange musical.

15. Bien souvent le traditionnel vocabulaire musicologique ne possède pas de termes assez précis pour permettre une réelle caractérisation de ces éléments.

16. Je ne rentrerais pas plus en détail sur ce problème de l'interprétation mais cette notion fait partie intégrante d'une sémiotique de l'instauration: l'interprète joue un rôle tout particulier dans la chaine de l'échange musical et il s'agit de se demander si ce que l'on étudie est du Beethoven ou le Quatuor Julliard, par exemple.

Références

Barthes, Roland (1953). *Le degré Zéro de l'Ecriture suivi de Nouveaux Essais Critiques*. Paris: Seuil.

Boucourechliev, André (1963). *Beethoven*. Paris: Seuil.

Deliège, Celestin (1986). *Invention Musicale et Idéologie*, 96. Paris: Bourgois.

Francastel, Pierre (1951). *Peinture et Société*, réed. 1977. Paris: Denoël/Gonthier.

– (1965). *La Réalité Figurative*. Paris: Denoël/Gonthier.

– (1967). *La Figure et le Lieu*. Paris: Denoël/Gonthier.

– (1970). *Etudes de Sociologie de l'Art*. Paris: Denoël.

Grossin, William (1989). "Les Représentations temporelles et l'émergence de l'histoire", *L'Année Sociologique* 39: 233–254. Paris.

Kristeva, Julia (1969). *Séméiotiké. Recherches pour une sémanalyse*. Paris: Seuil.

Le Goff, Jacques (1986). *Histoire et Mémoire*. Paris: Gallimard.

Mandrou, Robert (1985). "Histoire des mentalités", *Encyclopédie Universalis* 17: 366–368. Paris: Encyclopedia Universalis SA.

Meyerson, Ignace (1948). *Les Fonctions Psychologiques et les Œuvres*. Paris: Vrin.

Molino, Jean (1975). "Fait Musical et sémiologie de la musique", *Musique en Jeu* 17: 37–62. Paris: Seuil.

Nattiez, Jean-Jacques (1976). *Fondements d'une Sémiologie de la Musique*. Paris: Bourgois.

– (1986). *Musicologie Générale et Sémiologie*. Paris: Bourgois.

Revault d'Allones, Olivier (1982). *Plaisir à Beethoven*, 77. Paris: Bourgois.

Ruwet, Nicolas (1972). *Langage, Musique et Poésie*. Paris: Seuil.

Stefani, Gino (1986). "La Compétence musicale: un cadre de référence pour l'analyse, la pratique et la pédagogie musicales", *Analyse Musicale* 5, 7–13. Paris: Société Française d'Analyse Musicale.

Supicic, Ivo (1985)."Perspectives pluridisciplinaires. Difficultés d'approche", *Irasm* 16(22): 125–151. Zagreb: Institut de Musicologie, Académie de Zagreb.

Tarasti, Eero (1979). *Myth and Music. A Sémiotic Approach to the Aesthetics of Myth in Music, especially that of Wagner, Sibelius and Stravinsky.* La Haye, New York: Mouton.

Vecchione, Bernard (1984). Pour une Science de la Réalité Musicale. Eléments d'Epistémologie Musicologique Nouvelle. Thèse de IIIème cycle, Aix-en-Provence.

– (1990). "Les Sciences et les technologies de la Musique: la révolution musicologique des années 1970–1980", *Actes du 2ème Colloque International "Musique et Assistance Informatique".* Marseille.

ANNEXE

Quelques indices temporels
Niveau 1
Quatuor n °2 op 18 en Sol Majeur
1er mouvement (Mes 233-240)
Coda
Dilatation du temps
* Enchaînement d'accords de septièmes non résolues
Septième diminuée en Do mineur / Septième de dominante en Mi / Septième diminuée en Mi mineur / Septième diminuée en Sol mineur/
* d'où une ligne mélodique supérieure chromatique où chaque septième, traitée mélodiquement, est mise en valeur par une indication de nuance "Crescendo/Decrescendo" et un point d'orgue, le tout dans une nuance générale "Piano".

    Remarque: Ici, un exemple de Niveau 1: Technique unique employée, bien délimitée dans le temps et qui, visiblement joue un rôle dans le déroulement du quatuor au niveau formel: préparation de la Coda.

    La coda qui est le moment de terminaison, de fin, est ici symbolisée clairement par la matière musicale (Exemple 1).

Exemple 1. Quatuor n°2 op 18 en Sol Majeur (Niveau 1).

Niveau 1
Quatuor 7 op 59 n °1 en Fa majeur
2ème mouvement (Mes 1-8)
Scherzo (thème principal)

Spatialisation de la matière
Deux plans sonores visuellement perceptibles: le concept de mélodie (et la conception du temps qu'il supposait: la linéarité) est remis en cause: fragmentation de la matière.
– Violoncelle: antécédent du thème principal en ostinato 'staccato'.
– Violon 2: conséquent: thème populaire 'staccato'.
Le matériel expérimental utilisé dans ce mouvement est mis en place de même que la technique de spatialisation.

Remarque: Fragmentation de la matière. Destruction du concept de mélodie (Exemple 2).

Exemple 2. Quatuor 7 op 59 n°1 en Fa majeur (Niveau 1).

Niveau 2
Quatuor 3 op 18 en Ré mineur
1er mouvement (Mes 151-159)
Fin développement (vers la réexposition)

– *Mes 151-156 (1er temps):*
Débute par un martèlement de croches à l'alto (annonciateur).
Intensification harmonique de cet élément mélodique, soutenue par une nuance 'Fortissimo'.

Densification de la matière musicale (modulation en Fa dièse mineur) qui aboutit à un 'Sforzando' sur l' accord de dominante de Fa dièse mineur.
– *Mes 156–159:*
Brusque disparition de la matière: résonnance de l'accord ci-dessus.
* notes tenues
* Retour d'une nuance 'Pianissimo'
* modulation en Ré Majeur (6/4) pour le retour de la réexposition. Noeud temporel. Tension/Détente

Remarque: joue sur l'opposition de matière...met en valeur le retour de la réexposition.
Schème: Intensification dynamique / Suspension (Exemple 3).

Exemple 3. Quatuor 3 op 18 en Ré mineur (Niveau 2).

Niveau 2
Quatuor 7 op 59 n °1 en Fa Majeur
1er mouvement (Mes 76–90)
Exposition (cadence avant développement)

– Mes 76–85: Intensification dynamique:
* triolets perturbateurs qui explorent toute l'étendue de la matière * Accord-de +6 en Sol Majeur
* aboutissement à une formule cadentielle homorythmique et 'Fortissimo' concluant la réexposition Intensification dynamique de la matière.
– Mes 85–90: Interruption de cette formule et Incertitude discursive...
* accords dissonants (7+ alternant entre Ré mineur/majeur et Do mineur/majeur) fragmentés et entrecoupés de silences.
* nuance "Pianississimo"

Bouleverse habitudes des auditeurs.

Remarque: moment d'incertitude discursive rendu grâce à l'effet harmonique et à la fragmentation extrême de la matière. Ici, l'effet est d'autant plus surprenant.

Schème: Intensification dynamique + Interruption / Incertitude discursive (pas simple suspension) (Exemple 4).

Exemple 4. Quatuor 7 op 59 n°1 en Fa Majeur (Niveau 2).

Niveau 3
Quatuor 7 op 59 n°1 en Fa majeur
1er mouvement (Mes 185–217)
Développement (Fugue en Ré b Majeur)

Moment temporel en plusieurs phases:
– *Mes 185–210*: interruption de la formule cadentielle du développement par une double fugue en Ré b majeur. Processus de 'mise en abîme' du discours par la référence explicite à un genre stylistique très éloigné de l'esthétique du quatuor.
* Ré b Majeur: tonalité éloignée de Fa majeur

* Dissonances
* Crescendo
Tension qui atteint un certain paroxysme
– *Mes 210–217*: Pulvérisation de la fugue
Suspension du temps
* brusque 'diminuendo' après une nuance bloquée
* accord de septième diminuée en Do majeur/mineur arpègé aux quatre instruments en valeurs longues.
  Le développement reprend ensuite normalement.

Remarque: il s'agit, ici, d'une véritable parcours dynamique de la forme qui évolue, se transforme…
  Beethoven rend la forme perceptible: l'incursion que représente la fugue est ici clairement audible; son échec au sein de ce mouvement est rendu perceptible temporellement.
Schème: Interruption / Mise en abime + Intensification dynamique / Suspension + Résolution différée (Exemple 5).

Niveau 3
Quatuor n°1 op 18 en Fa Majeur
1er mouvement (Mes 84–101)
Exposition (coda)

Moment temporel en plusieurs phases:
– *Mes 84–87*: antécédent homorythmique suspendu (mes 87) par une quinte diminuée (Vème degré de Do Majeur/mineur)
– *Mes 88*: une mesure de silence
– *Mes 89–92*: conséquent réalisant la résolution en Do majeur à la mes 89
– *Mes 92–95*: reprise intégrale du passage homorythmique une octave plus haut. Suspension sur la quinte diminuée (Vème degré de Do majeur/mineur)
– *Mes 96*: une mesure de silence
– *Mes 97–101*: réduction harmonique et rythmique (érosion) du conséquent réalisant la résolution en Do mineur à la mes 97.
Remarque: processus tout à fait intéressant qui joue encore sur la perception de l'auditeur. Jeu entre le passé, le présent et le futur de l'œuvre et de son déroulement.
Schème: Suspension / Résolution différée en Majeur / Suspension / Résolution différée en Mineur + Dépouillement
Macro-structure — Réversibilité: plusieurs solutions temporelles sont adoptées. La répétition n'est pas gratuite; elle a pour fonction de rendre le temps réversible (Exemple 6).

Exemple 5. Quatuor 7 op 59 n°1 en Fa majeur (Niveau 3).

Exemple 6. Quatuor n° 1 op 18 en Fa Majeur (Niveau 3).

Niveau 4
Quatuor n ° 6 op 18 en Si b Majeur
4ème mouvement (Mes 1–44)
Le mouvement dans son entier.

Mise en cause du discours et de sa linéarité. Aucun repère temporel classique n'est proposé à l'auditeur. La discursivité classique est remise en cause
* Mes 12–20: Mes 37–42:
Enchaînement de 7ème diminuées utilisées comme de véritables plaques tournantes du discours.
* Mes 1–20:
Opposition de masse et de poids rendue par une écriture concertante: soli (mes 1–4; mes 9–12): tutti (mes 5–8: mes 17–20)
* Mes 13–16:
dialogue équilibré entre les instruments; opposition alternée de nuance.
* Opposition de nuance 'Forte / Piano' et de registre 'Grave / Aïgu' Destruction de toute discursivité classique: registres distendus, dynamiques opposées, harmonies fluctuantes.

Remarque: ce mouvement est très connu, prémice de la Grande Fugue.
Schème: Fluctuation temporelle (Exemple 7).

Exemple 7. Quatuor n° 6 op 18 en Si♭ Majeur (Niveau 4).

Niveau 4
Grande Fugue en Si♭ Majeur op 133

Est-il besoin pour ce niveau de citer la grande fugue op 133 comme
l'exemple le plus abouti: la technique de superposition de couches

temporelles y est poussée à l'extrême générant une matière problématique ainsi qu'une polytemporalité (Exemple 8).

Exemple 8. Grande Fugue en Si♭ Majeur op 133 (Niveau 4).

B.53.

Signs, symbols, and expressive elements in the String Quartets of Dmitri Shostakovitch

ESTER SHEINBERG

Questioning methodologies: A proposal for a new un-methodology

Music is a complex and compound phenomenon — an emulsion of emotional, biological, and rational ways of communication and perception. In spite of that, we are used to approaching it only with rational, one-tracked, statistical-experimental, or purely philosophical research tools. We try to do it using ways of rational discursive thinking, and are sometimes so fascinated by the beautiful and reassuring integrity of these thinking techniques that we tend to forget the basic complexity of our very material, the musical phenomenon itself.

I believe that music requires not only the above-mentioned research tools, but others, too, ones that in certain ways are subtler and richer: our emotional, perceptive, and intuitive immediate responses. Unfortunately, there as yet are no definitive criteria on which we can base such appropriate research tools, and perhaps these criteria are undefinable by their very nature. I am aware of the apparent methodological impossibility that arises from using these immediate, intuitive responses; nevertheless, I think that this constant search for clear-cut definitions deflects us from our main issue and gets in our way when we try to understand music.

We who belong to the humanistic field of research tend to suffer from the "Wissenschaft-complex": in our efforts to be considered "serious researchers", we develop some almost pathologically scientific aspirations. These scientific claims which bind us to certain methodological ways of thinking, this fear of being called "non-scientific", which means being unworthy of so-called scientific respectability, is an impediment to our search for the humanly meaningful truth reflected in the wholeness of the communicational potential of music.

We must begin to use these other tools, unreliable as they may seem. We must do so because our so-called "purely scientific" tools, even those of psychology and philosophy, no longer suffice. Therefore I would like to suggest that our methodologies should be built eclectically, on the basis of an intercalation of existing methodologies, selecting from each one only the elements proven relevant to music, and adding to them our musical intuition. I think we must dare to risk our so-called "scientific respectability" and our insured place, our methodological cradles, and open ourselves up to new data. This will contribute to true scientific communication, in that it will be open to all kinds of facts, and not only to those presently considered provable.

2. A basis for musical-semiotic inquiry: General psychological assumptions and findings about human perception

Music-perception studies deal mostly with questions of recognition and memorization of patterns, i.e., of relative perception; and almost all psychological art theories deal with the relativity of perception, especially, of course, the well known Gestalt theory. When dealing with "absolute" items such as pitch, volume, timbre, and rhythm, most of the studies focus almost exclusively on physical boundaries: the limits of high-pitch perception, aural differentiation between two notes, and so on. Other studies examine the biological implications of music listening, such as the change in rate of heartbeat, increase of perspiration, and so on.

Musical-meaning studies, dealing with semantic messages transmitted by music, analyze semantic interpretations mostly on the basis of learned, conventionalized associations, presented as statistical, basically unexplained phenomena.

Even if it is a proven fact that our perception can react only to relations between elements (be they vibrations of sound waves, light waves, space or surface dimensions, and the like), it is almost amazing how little, if anything at all, has been said about our reaction to isolated auditory phenomena, regarding them as *absolutely* "high", "long", or "weak". The truth is that we *do* react to isolated musical phenomena as bearing certain absolute attributes. We do hear bird song as "high pitched", even if we don't hear bass notes with or before it. Of course it can be stated that we did hear bass notes sometime before, and that we interpret, thus, the bird song as "high" on the basis of some remembered point of reference. But this statement is not the only possible explanation: I think it is clear that we have a certain "normal sound-scope", and that this "normal sound-scope" is based primarily on our own voice range, or, more generally, on the human voice range.

My assumption is that at least one aspect of the meaning that music acquires for us is based on the relation it bears to a constant, fixed point of reference: our human body, its physical attributes, and its situation in time and in space. Our primary reaction to any visual or auditory stimulus is, first of all, a test of empathy or identification. Failing to do so, the perceived item will be classified as "absolutely" high, low, loud, fast, etc.(the point of reference being, of course, our human nature). This assumption is in accordance with the "projection theory" advanced by Ernst Gombrich in regards to visual arts (1959), and is based on our tendency to "project" human features, wherever possible, on any visually perceived object.

I believe that we use the same "projection technique" on music, which, lacking visually concrete features, is expressed by musical features bearing analogy to human psycho-biological aspects. Thus, if the tempo of a certain musical piece is faster than the average heartbeat or walking tempo — for instance, more than 80 MM — we define it as "absolutely fast"; if the pitch is higher than the average human speaking voice — say, higher than c2 — we perceive it as "absolutely high". I want to stress that this perception will be primarily sensed as "absolute", for taking ourselves as point of reference is quite unconscious.

This is why we should consider the basic states and functions of the human body and human mind as fundamental, primary points of reference for musical meaning, and why we should measure, treat, and understand music first of all in reference to them. These basic parameters are, first of all, the normal rate of heartbeat, normal pitch of the voice, normal timbre (not too nasal, not too harsh), and normal span of breath.

Accordingly, our interpretations of meanings transmitted in a musical message must also relate to natural, biologically comfortable states such as "stability", "constancy", "sense of gravity", etc. These are the basic features that define the human situation in the universe in terms of human perception and self-evaluation, and therefore should be considered as natural and primary points of reference for interpretation of any humanly transmitted message, whatever the specific medium used.

3. A definition of musical sign and musical symbol

In order to communicate my ideas, I have to clarify what I mean by "musical sign" and "musical symbol". If we look into the many existing definitions of sign, symbol, musical sign, and musical symbol in semiotic literature, we meet with an overwhelming wealth of definitions, each one correct and convincing in its own context, and each one despairingly insufficient from a more general perspective; for not one of them is applicable to *all* the existing (and/or possible) semiotic systems. Thus, in the present state of things, every semiotician has either to accept one of the already existing definitions, with all of its limitations when applied to his own work, or dedicate time and energy to a long (and seemingly hopeless) struggle in trying to reach better general definitions.

As it is now, there are either exact but narrow definitions that will not be applicable to *all* semiotic systems, or definitions that are so general (so "universal") that they become trivial and insignificant when applied to any specific semiotic analysis.

Therefore I suggest my own definitions of musical sign and musical symbol, which I find appropriate to my present research. These definitions are open, of course, to debate and criticism, but I think it should be made clear that they are meant only and solely to be applied to this very project, of deciphering Shostakovitch's musical code and of finding and understanding the meaning of his musical messages.

In the present study, a MUSICAL SIGN will be any combination of musical convention and/or musical imitation of a non-musical phenomenon, be it physical, emotional, or conceptual. Examples would be cuckoo calls; fanfares; any musical topic such as "scherzo", "marche funèbre"; musical anagrams; and so on. A MUSICAL SYMBOL will be any musical phenomenon that, by synaesthesia or analogy to a certain human condition or situation in space or in time, will represent a non-musical phenomenon, be it physical, emotional, or conceptual. Examples would include a solo part appearing in a middle of a sparse musical texture, creating an analogy to a subject's situation in space; a constant, steady beat analogous to an assured feeling; an ostinato analogous to an obsessive idea; and so on.

4. Dmitri Shostakovitch's music — A subject for semiotical research

Far beyond its aesthetic qualities, Shostakovitch's music has a communicational power. An agonized message of pain mixed with bitter, sarcastic irony cries out of it. Moreover, much of this music is characterised by a feeling of a double message, of signs that cannot be interpreted in a one-to-one translation of any particular idea or emotion. There is a strong feeling of the existence of a code, a sign-system that needs to be decoded and learned in order to understand the complete meaning of the message. It feels like a dense network, a kind of a grid, an iron web through which only sparkles of a hidden "something" managed to shine. This is a much more challenging task than defining and analyzing an overtly "gay", "sad", or "pastoral" piece of music; in the special case of Shostakovitch's music, hidden symbols can be heard through the mask of signs.

Solomon Volkov's book of Shostakovitch's memoirs, *Testimony* (1979, which I found only later to be controversial), confirmed the messages I felt in the music, and urged me to understand the process by which musical messages — even hidden and forbidden ones — are communicated. In some loose, unsystematic experiments made with musically competent and uncompetent students, it was obvious that even the double message, the face behind the mask, reached the attentive listener.

In one of those experiments the second movement of Shostakovitch's Tenth Symphony was played to a class of uncompetent music-listening students, without any background remarks on the piece or the composer. I asked them what feeling was communicated by the music. Their reactions were usually "it is like running" or "it is threatening"; others said that "it is gay". Thus, the music seemed to convey contradictory messages: how can a message be gay and threatening at the same time? Then said one of the students, "It is as if someone is forcing a smile, or pretending to be happy". The apparent "smile" in the music, then, was perceived as an "unnatural, false smile".

How might music convey such a complex message? Even if we feel "sadness" or "happiness" in music, how can we know that someone is forcing a smile and not smiling sincerely? I then turned again to the recording and asked the students to stop me when we arrive at the point at which they could really get the "unnatural" quality of that apparent smile, the very point in the music at which they feel as if somebody is "being forced to smile". The music was played again, and the listeners signaled a certain point in the music: rehearsal number 72 (bar 21). [1] What happened at this very point that made this message to turn up so clearly? And how could a "musically uncompetent" listener know that the gaiety was not true, but only *apparent* happiness? How could he decipher the "lie" in the music?

The answer seems to be that at this moment a sudden acceleration of rhythm occurred which could not have been expected. It remains unexpected even after repeated listenings. Because of its asymmetrical structure, one must learn that fragment by heart in order to know when exactly the acceleration will occur. This asymmetry and unexpectedness, contrary to the deeply rooted human psychological structures of stability and symmetry, give us the feeling of something illogical, something weird, unnatural. This "unnatural behavior" of the music leads one to think that what the music says is not true.

I want to stress again the subtleties of messages that music can convey. It can be violent, it can even be angry, but it was this unexpected burst that gave the message of a *lie*; something that is only allegedly dancing, even if "a violent dance" but which actually *really* is frightening, really weird: the message of insanity. It is an interesting fact that Shostakovitch himself, on a certain occasion, called this very movement "a portrait of Stalin" Volkov 1979: 107). He was speaking, on that occasion, about Stalin being insane. Obviously, there is "insanity" — in the sense of "unnaturalness", absence of "logic", "asymmetry" — in this unexpectedly violent, accelerated change of rhythm.

4.1. The 'Yurodivy' image of Shostakovitch

According to Volkov, Shostakovitch claimed that he had chosen "to play the role of a Yurodivy" (Volkov 1979: xxi). A Russian "Yurodivy" (God's fool) is also a kind of "king's fool". Half insane, half village idiot, between the lines of his nonsense-talk emerges, now and then, a piece of astounding, harsh truth.

The Yurodivy, very much the same as the king's fool, can say whatever crosses his mind. No one will do him any harm because of what he says. In a certain way he is even "sacred". For example, in Mussorgsky's *Boris Godunov* the Yurodivy is the only one who can say that the Tsar is a murderer, and the Tsar does not let anybody punish this man for what he says. He is holy, and so are his insane sayings. He has gained his holiness through his insanity, and only thanks to that can he openly say whatever he wants. This role has political, historical, and cultural connotations. Many cultural phenomena deal with a similar kind of figure; they all have something in common, which may lead to the assumption that we are confronted here with a "cultural archetype" of the Outsider. The King's Fool, the Village Idiot, the Sacred Total Fool, the Virgin, the Whore, the Blind who sees the future, the Handicapped — all are outsiders.

Art, literature, and music deal almost obsessively with this archetypal figure: Rigoletto; the Hunchback of Notre-Dame; Pierrot (and Petrouschka, of course); Charlie Chaplin; Wozzeck; Parsifal; Jenny the Whore in *Die Dreigroschenoper* of Brecht and Weill; the Yurodivy in *Boris Godunov*; Theresias the Blind in the Greek tragedies (and even Oedipus who blinds himself after he has seen the truth, or Wotan who gives one of his eyes after he had learned the Secret of Life); Alberich in Wagner's Ring; Loge in *Das Rheingold*; and even Hamlet, who discovers the truth only after he has spoken with a ghost. The motif that unites all these otherwise totally different figures is their being outsiders in their own society; and precisely because of their being outsiders, they have the ability to see the truth, to see that very society as it really is. Likewise, because they can see and speak that truth, they are condemned to constant humiliation and, finally, to insanity.

But what if the society itself is insane? We have already seen, several times in history, a whole society become insane. It happened in Nazi Germany in the Thirties and Forties, and in Stalinist Russia at about the same time. In those cases, the Outsider who can see and speak the truth turns out to be the only sane one. This, of course, makes no difference; he, as everything and everybody, is measured by his context. In any case, *he* is the one who will turn out to be insane; he is the abnormal one, the one who exists outside the norms of society.

The logical conclusion at which Shostakovitch apparently arrived, is that in order to be truthful, and yet remain, in a way, inside society, he should "lose his mind"; he should become, in a certain way, insane. The "real" world becomes, then, a world of masks, of constant carnival, a circus of real insanity, of dances, smiles, polite small-talk, of "Pagliacci's laughter"; while the hallucination-world, the inner-world, is the only truthful, even if lonely and painful, realm. The real world turns out to be a place in which the truth about human nature hurts so much that it can be accepted, or even heard, only if it is not taken seriously, only if it is said as a joke, or if uttered seriously, then only by the insane.

Shostakovitch was accused (and still is) by musicians as being a "simplistic" musician. However, Shostakovitch claimed that works such as his Fifth Symphony, for example, which disappointed many musicians, were really part of the clown's mask that he wore in order to please the Soviet authorities, so that they would not prevent his expressing his true message in other works such as his string quartets. Moreover, he said that the true message of the Fifth Symphony is hidden behind the clownish mask of "happy music", and that if we listen carefully we shall hear and comprehend its true, underlying, painful message. (Volkov 1979: 140)

How could such a thing be done? What was that "musical mask" made of? One of the major artistic tools used by Shostakovitch for this end was his constant use of extremes of expression. In his overt musical declarations he reached, usually, such exaggerated extremes that they cannot be taken seriously. His so- called "optimistic", proletarian marches, for example, are so simple, so gay, so straightforward, so expected, that we cannot believe they are true. This is one of the ways in which through this tight, carefully knitted mask of clownish, almost vulgar musical laughter, we can hear — if we listen carefully — the true, sincere message of his weeping.

In order to understand exactly — not only by intuition and feeling, but also on the basis of more concrete evidence — the messages in Shostakovitch's music, I examined some of his early works, written before January 1936. On that date an article, supposedly written by Stalin, was published in *Pravda*, denouncing Shostakovitch's opera, *Lady Macbeth of the Mtsensk District* (1934). The article, called "Chaos Instead of Music", marked the opening of a new period in the composer's life, in which he was literally persecuted as an "individualist", "formalist", and "modernist" composer. The works I concentrated on were his non-absolute, "referential" works, such as his lieder, his first opera *The Nose*, and the music he wrote for plays and films.

In these works I found that Shostakovitch had used constantly and consistently some specific musical devices when referring to particular subjects, and my thesis is that these musical devices became, for him, a code system of signs and symbols for these same subjects in his later, absolute musical works.

As a matter of fact, it seems that in all of his works Shostakovitch makes use of musical material in order to convey ideas, thoughts, opinions, feelings, moods and atmosphere.[2] In the last decade some very interesting works were written about expression in Shostakovitch's music. Not denying the importance of these recently published studies about the expressive musical tools that he used in his music (for example, the studies of E. Roseberry, 1989, and B. Longman, 1989), I must point out some weak points in them, namely that they deal almost exclusively with questions of pitch, such as melodic intervals (based on Deryck Cooke's theory of melodic conventions and symbols), scale structures (dealing mostly with questions of modality, atonality, and dodecaphony), and harmonic issues of the same kind.

However, when we actually listen to Shostakovitch's music, these items are not the first ones that we become aware of. Other, much more primary and basic musical features stand out; such as long, asymmetrical phrases; hollow textures (mentioned in a more "journalistic" book like Ian MacDonald's *The New Shostakovitch* (1990), that is often ignored by more formally analytical musicological studies); characteristic composing techniques, linked consistently with the same non-musical ideas, like fugues for crowd-music, "circus" gestures (from "realistic" trombone-glissandos to deliberately simplistic "oom-pah oom-pah" accompaniment); very low basses contrasted with extremely high registers of shrieking violins and melancholy oboes; lone solo parts, usually given to a violin, cello, bassoon, or clarinet; and oscillating movement between two notes, in intervals ranging from a minor second to a fifth.

Shostakovitch certainly did use obvious and direct signs, as for example his anagram D-S-C-H, which appeared for the first time in his Tenth Symphony, dated 1953, and then in some of his later works, such as the first violin concerto and the String Quartet No. 8, which was described by the composer himself as "autobiographical" and for which this anagram serves as a main theme. But he used, as well, much more subtle musical tools, which will be classified, in this research project, as *symbols*. For example, the constant use of certain musical textures, mainly those hollow textures mentioned earlier; manipulation of phrase lengths; and ambivalent musical messages communicated through sophisticated counterpoint or through changes of tempo, meter, and rhythm.

As mentioned earlier, sometimes the painful, truthful messages are almost totally hidden behind sarcastic webs of musical gestures; as, for example, in his film music and in some of his symphonies. Sometimes they are exposed and more accessible, as in his string quartets.

My purpose here is to understand those messages, as they appear in what I consider to be Shostakovitch's most personal and intimate channel of musical expression: his string quartets. Since all of his string quartets were written after the *Lady Macbeth* scandal of 1936, I believe that he deliberately chose to reveal his true feelings through them. The only place in which the King's Fool can be himself, can express his true feelings, is in his own home (or if you like, in the Jungian symbol of his soul). Rigoletto's first burst of anger — "O rabbia! . . . Esser difforme!

. . . O rabbia! . . . Esser buffone. . ." — occurs near the doors of his
own house, and Petrouschka's hallucinations happen in the night, when
he is alone, closed in his own room. Shostakovitch's spiritual home,
after Stalin's condemnation of his opera, lay in his string quartets. This
is the only place in which he could express himself with considerable
safety, without the risk of being heard in the big concert-halls, while still
reaching his fellow-musicians and the relatively small public that listens
to chamber music, understands it, and is capable of perceiving his
musical messages. The Russian intellectual and artistic elite is culturally
accustomed to and well practiced in discovering and perceiving such
double-messages. (MacDonald 1990: 11) This public is used to censor-
ship and, consequently, to deciphering hidden messages in all kinds of
publications, including works of art.

5. An unmethodological methodology

The methodology I propose is based, first of all, on personal reactions to
the music and on musical intuition. Once these are grasped, the reason
for these reactions is sought for in the musical elements themselves.

My first step therefore was to study and understand my own perceptions and emotional reactions to the apparent emotional messages in the
music of Shostakovitch's string quartets. This step was taken in accordance with my previous definitions of musical SIGNS and SYMBOLS,
which considered as a basic point of reference the human biological
construction and way of perception, as well as our conceptual, physical,
and emotional self-placement in time and space. According to those
features I built parameters based primarily on a stability/non-stability
axis and, further, on any other comfortable/uncomfortable human criteria.

Musical time is examined in relation to the normal span of one
breath (inhalation and exhalation), to the normal tempo and rhythm of
the human pulse, the normal rate of heartbeat, the normal tempo of
walking and of speaking. *Musical space* is examined in relation to the
natural range of the human voice, of the normally comfortable singing
intervals, of the usual pitch and dynamics of the speaking voice, and the

natural pitch contour of a spoken sentence. As an additional criterion of musical space I will consider the basic, average, balanced, culturally and generally accepted proximity between objects and people in our environment; suggesting and pointing to the degree of isolation, proximity, intimacy, or comfort, and finding the musical analogy for them in musical texture, melody, harmony, and orchestration.

Besides the above-mentioned criteria of musical analogues for our perception of time and space, several additional musical features will be considered. These will be general, psychological perception principles such as symmetry, continuity, expectability, and repetition.

As can be seen, all these criteria are based on one common denominator: the basic operation of primary identification we perform unconsciously with every perceived sensation. This basic psychological function was defined by Ernst Gombrich (1959) as the "projection principle", namely, our tendency to identify in every perceived object a human figure, or at least its closest possible simulacrum.

6. An application of the suggested methodology to Dmitri Shostakovitch's Quartets

In his early referential compositions I found that Shostakovitch had used, constantly and consistently, the same musical elements in similar dramatic or emotional situations. I could easily discern two basic emotional messages, which are communicated by two different and characteristic "groups" of musical elements, each of them defining and/or referring to a certain, consistent, non-musical idea, feeling, or emotion. These two basic emotions were Pain and Fear.

Pain

Shostakovitch's musical works express two different kinds of pain: the cry of anguish and the feeling of despair. In the first way of expressing pain — by a cry of anguish, a desperate cry of pain as if from a very bad injury — the musical elements that characterize such expressive moments are always a dynamic of fortissimo, use of the whole range of the instruments with emphasis on the extremely high register, a full texture mostly chordal, with a very clear beat. The instruments will almost always be instructed to play with down-bow strikes, and then will often use double and triple stopps. Such instances happen in literally all the 15 quartets, and have become a stylistic sign of Shostakovitch. Yet they are particularly prevalent in his first quartets; from Quartet No. 7 they begin to occupy a smaller place, while the second kind of musical expression of pain — that of despair —takes priority.

There are many examples of this kind in Shostakovitch's symphonies, too; for example, one instance in the first movement of the Babi-Yar Symphony (1962) describes the capture of Anna Frank. While the German soldiers are breaking down the door to the Franks' refuge, the text speaks of the terrible noise of ice-breaking, and we hear human pain in the music, evoked by the same musical elements, supporting the correlation of this combination of musical gestures to the subject of Pain.

Another salient musical feature of Shostakovitch's musical works is a constant, almost obsessive repetition of a melodic or rhythmic motif. This musical idea is not only one of the most outstanding features in Shostakovitch's music, but it was known and referred to by some of his acquaintances, as characteristic of his everyday way of speaking (Vishnevskaya 1984: 226). In his musically referential works we find this element connected not only to human pain but also to the idea of insanity, which will be discussed later.

The second kind of painful musical expression is a feeling of despair. This arises out of the general feeling of loneliness. Here Shostakovitch uses mostly the dynamics of *pianissimo*, a rather slow tempo, and a melodic line played on one instrument only; this line is sometimes distributed in the general musical space in a way that places it far from the other instruments' sounding register, thus creating a feeling of "hollowness", of emptiness surrounding the lonely melodic line. Often, such a texture begins as a monody; after some time, other instruments join in the musical texture, transforming it into homophony.

In other instances the same emotional message is transmitted by a basically contrapuntal texture, in which several melodic lines — sometimes in imitation and sometimes not — create a special sensation: the different parts that sound together seem never to meet, never really to relate to each other. Somehow they continue, each at its own pace, in its own lonely path. This phenomenon becomes more and more prevalent in the late quartets: the opening of the last one, No. 15 Op. 144, is particularly telling: apparently the texture is imitative, it even follows the rule of imitation at the fifth, as well as sticks to all the traditional rules of dissonant handling: yet the four parts sound totally unrelated to each other.

Another characteristic feature is the loss of musical direction in spite of a seemingly obvious tonality. This feature stems not only from the characteristic melodic figure of oscillation between two notes, but also from the extremely long and asymmetrical musical phrases, coupled with atonality which is used here in its most obvious meaning: lack of musical "gravity" or center. In spite of that, a paradoxically contrasted feeling of melodiousness is always present, even in the 12-tone opening of the 12th Quartet.

As stated before, these two facets of pain are often coupled with a strange purpose of insanity, something that can be characterized as "musical obsession", expressed by constant repetitions of a note, a motif, or arhythmic gesture. Again, the extreme high register is often used in this context as a sign of abnormality, of insanity (reminding us also of the pathological phenomenon of aural tinnitus, which happens in times of psychic hypertension or extreme fatigue).

To summarize, the feeling of pain is expressed in Shostakovitch's string quartets in two main ways: a cry of anguish, which is usually in a very high register, fortissimo, with a clear beat and full texture; and as a message of loneliness, which uses a single melodic line in a generally hollow texture, pianissimo, in a slow tempo, and with apparent loss of tonal direction.

Fear

The second basic emotional message manifested in Shostakovitch's music is fear. Again, it acquires two main ways of expression.

In the first the music "tells" us *about* fear. The general dynamic is *piano*; the articulation is mostly pizzicato or tremolo, with special effects such as mutes or playing sul-ponticello; the melodic and/or harmonic direction is often unclear (mainly by the constant use of melodic oscillation), and so is the metric and/or rhythmic pattern. All these musical elements are also signs of hesitation and instability.

A sul-ponticello technique is widely used in the first movement of Quartet No. 10 (see rehearsal number 11). A few bars before (m. 16) another feeling is transmitted here, one of illness, or nausea, as if from sea-sickness. This is rooted in the parallel chordal progression, which is based, apart from the "falling" melodic direction, on the use of a real sequence (in contrast to a tonal one). It adds the disconcerting, "anti-gravitational" meaning of atonality to the above-mentioned feeling of "unhealthiness". This description of fear is overt and even obvious, and stands almost in the category of a *musical sign*.

A totally different message involving fear is transmitted by musical passages that don't "describe" fear, but rather seem to be aiming at frightening the listener. I want to stress the difference between these two types of fear. In the first, the music is telling us about fear; in the second, we the listeners actually *feel frightened*. I find this last type of message much more effective and interesting, from the point of view of musical semiotics. Here we are confronted with new technical means that Shostakovitch uses for expressing feelings and ideas through music.

The opening of the third movement of the String Quartet No. 3 is similar to the opening of the the second movement of the Tenth Symphony, discussed above. Both begin with violent, short, harsh, and sudden chords. Nevertheless, here the music is governed by yet another musical element, the "oom-pah oom-pah" accompaniment gesture, with all its connotations and associations with vulgar, popular, and simplistic music. The coupling of this populistic and simple musical gesture with violent, harshly dissonant chords appears in Shostakovitch's referential musical works — operas, lieder, incidental and film music — in association with fear caused by the violence of a mob. This frightening musical message always bears, in Shostakovitch's music, a connotation of the vulgarity of the masses. For example, in his first opera, *The Nose*, when the crowd gathers (as in the jetty scene in Act I or in the public-garden scene near the end of the work), we feel scared. Always, in instances like these, Shostakovitch uses the above-mentioned accompaniment figure, usually with dissonant chords, fortissimo dynamics, and a full, thick instrumental texture.

In the opening of the third movement of the Seventh String Quartet, all of the musical features mentioned above are present: it is violent, vulgar, repetitive, obsessive, insane. In addition, and again very much like in the above-mentioned scenes of *The Nose,* he uses the technique of imitation, in a contrapuntal, fugal texture. This technique, which appears in almost all of the crowd scenes in *The Nose* (and, for example, in similar moments of the incidental music he wrote for Mayakovski's play *The Bedbug*), stresses the impact of a perpetual, mechanised, cumulative process, which seemingly cannot be stopped.

Another effect is achieved by the independence of the melodic lines in the contrapuntal musical texture. In String Quartet No. 15, as seen above, Shostakovitch uses this imitative technique to convey the basic noncohesion of the different parts of the general texture, and also the basic, existential loneliness of each member of the crowd, united and massive as it may seem.

This brings up another problematic issue concerning Shostakovitch's nature and message, and points to a new side of the composer's personality, not obvious until this moment: his sense of irony. This particular side of him has much to do with his peculiar position on the Russian-Communist stage of the late Twenties, and his attitude toward "the Russian people", which is clearly ambivalent.

Shostakovitch was apparently a real, committed communist, as was everyone educated by an intellectual, liberal family at the beginning of the century; the Shostakovitches were communists because they were open-minded. Nevertheless after the revolution, and especially in the late Twenties, under the terror of Stalin's government (which made itself unequivocally explicit during the Shakhty trial) nobody could continue being naively convinced of the rightness and justice of the communist regime.

Another point lies in Shostakovitch's elite education and upbringing in one of the most cultured families of Petrograd. To an educated, refined artistic taste like his, even the mere thought of writing populist music, in order to be understood by everyone, was almost absurd, and certainly repelling. This schizophrenic role as a communist artist who despised the artistic taste of the people, might have contributed to this fear of the masses which, I think, is also something very personal and characteristic, distinguishing him from his fellow composers and artists. The masses seem to provoke in Shostakovich a paradoxical reaction that combines empathy with their cause, despisal of their uneducated taste, and fear of their violence. As paradoxical as it may seem, all these sentiments are conveyed by the same musical techniques.

Of course, such declarations must be built on more solid ground. Here I wanted just to point out some of the musical clues that led me to the observations I have made concerning the emotional messages in Shostakovitch's string quartets, and to give some preview of the methodology (or, should I say, unmethodology?) which I use in my present research.

Notes

1. This happens to be the very same point signalled by the listeners in the Helsinki presentation.
2. This affirmation fits completely with the theoretical influence of Asafiev and his theory of intonation on Shostakovitch's musical aesthetics.

References

Gombrich, Ernst (1959). *Art and Illusion*. New York: Pantheon.
Longman, Richard (1989). *Expression and Structure: Processes of Integration in the Large-Scale Instrumental Music of D. Shostakovitch*. New York: Garland.
MacDonald, Ian (1990). *The New Shostakovitch*. London: Fourth Estate.
Roseberry, Eric (1989). *Ideology, Style, Content and Thematic Process in the Symphonies, Cello Concertos, and String Quartets of Shostakovich*. New York: Garland.
Vishnevskaya, Galina (1984). *Galina: A Russian Story*. London: Hodder & Stoughton.
Volkov, Solomon (1979). *Testimony: The memoirs of Dmitri Shostakovitch, as related to and edited by Solomon Volkov*. London: Hamish Hamilton.

Modalities and intonation in music analysis:
Some observations on the Fourth Symphony of Alfred Schnittke

SVETLANA BAUER

> Music is more than art, it is a work directed to-
> wards the active cognition of the world, although
> one cognizes by music not things, but relation-
> ships.
>
> Boris Asafiev

The study of the modalities holds interest for ethnomusicologists and other scholars who deal with the elaboration of a general theory of music expression. Their researches concern the specific nature of musical semantics, musical idioms, and musical thinking.

The term "modalities" is often used in musicological essays and music analysis as a fundamental analytic concept connected with imma-nent qualities of the musical system. On the other hand, modalities are also considered as extra-musical or, rather, musical-aesthetic categories — the emotional-psychological character connected with processes of creating and perceiving the musical work.

Modalities in terms of modern musicology

My research centers on refining the concept of "modality" in modern musicology, and on using the principal bases of modality theory as a methodological tool for the characterization of evolutional processes in art-music culture, especially that of the 20th century. Such a goal pres-ents a number of particular tasks (subproblematics of the research), to be carried out along two lines: the first involves studying the concept of "modalities", its theory and history; the second, the phenomenon of the modalities themselves. The aim of this work is to isolate the problem, to analyze the views, and as far as possible to make predictions.

As known, the "modalities" are understood in two senses: (1) as a central category of melodic-scalar, metrical-rhythmic, and compositional-structural relations of the elements of musical systems (see Powers 1980); (2) as an important concept in the semio-linguistic branch of musical perception theory, starting with Aristotle's theory of modal ethos and ending with the Greimasian semiotic concepts as applied to music (see, for example, Greimas 1987; Tarasti 1987b).

This indicates that there are two traditions and two levels in the comprehension and treatment of the "modalities". The most important is the interpretation of modalities proposed by Evgeni Nazaikinsky in his work on musical psychology and logic of musical composition (1973, 1982). In his article "On the constantness [*sic*] in perception of music", modalities are an integral part of the dichotomy Constancy / Modality, wherein the modalities deal with expression of the author's attitude (Nazaikinsky 1973: 87). In Nazaikinsky's work on the logic of musical composition, the modalities are considered as an all-embracing principle or musical universal (1982: 236–249). In this sense, modalities are "general attitudes or approaches by which a subject evaluates an object, takes possession of it, and 'humanizes' it. It is through modalities that a speaker is able to instill in his enunciation his wishes, beliefs, wills, emotions, etc." (Tarasti 1987b: 452–453).

Theoretically, the two approaches to modalities — author attitude and subject evaluation — do not exclude each other; rather, they represent various levels of interpretation. In practice, however, these aspects are considered as separate, probably polar opposites within an analytical situation where the modalities, in reality, have very limited possibilities to take part in the music analysis. Consequently, it is necessary to define a modal level that can comprehend the entire music analysis. In such a case, the modalities of a musical object would be principally determined by correlation of the two levels mentioned above, through the mediation of semantic modalities. In this connection, two important ways of construing the modalities have been outlined by Eero Tarasti (1982; 1987a and b). These follow two directions:

(1) modalities as the inner qualities of a musical text, as connected with aspects of the musical process (Asafiev) and the concept of musical tension;

(2) modalities as a notion that comes very close to Asafiev's concept of the intonation (see Tarasti 1987b: 453).

The aim of my research is thus to explain the modalities by the correlation between a specifically musical level and an extra-musical (emotional-psychological) level, and by extension, to clarify the deeper meanings of the concept of "modalities". In other words, it is necessary: (a) to consider the modalities as an element of the general system of music expression and music perception; (b) and to explain the phenomenon of the modalities as a self-dependent, integrated hierarchic system that might include a multitude of various approaches.

The modalities are central to the expression of every tradition and can be examined from a variety of perspectives. The key to modern understanding of the modalities is to see them as an integral system of components that concern form and purpose, as well as meaning.

Modalities as a methodological problem

Modalities as an object of theoretical investigation are closely connected with the problem of the formation and functioning of the terminological apparatus of music theory as a whole. The movement of forces and trends in scientific knowledge at every stage of development necessitate changes and corrections in the determination of possibilities and approaches to the analysis of musical phenomena. These shifts in scientific knowledge periodically call for more precise definition and elaboration of each item of music theory — from very elementary concepts to concepts of the categorial level. The "modalities" belong to the latter inasmuch as: (1) they involve a complex system of connections and relations; (2) the whole history of the musical thought is reflected in their content.

The polysemy of the concept "modalities" shows up in the humanities, where many-sided operational modal functions can be researched from the perspectives of musical philosophy, musical psychology, semio-linguistics. The factors providing the "vitality" of the *modus* in modern science, can produce dialectically a more flexible comprehension through searches for new relations and interdependencies and through releasing the general aesthetic potentials of the modalities. There is one important summary tendency, which is connected with searching out different universals in the infinite variety of ways to reflect the universe. This tendency is evidenced by the complex views of the musical reality's phenomena, stated in terms of general scientific concepts. Such approaches attempt to create universal systems such as general theories of musical expression and of interaction of arts. Such systems would allow one to study a situation at some historical stage, without having a mature theory (or having lost one).

One theoretical problem is to determine the most effective methodological criteria for examining the various elements, functions, and levels of the functioning of the musical system. Here we should lay bare the immanent musical essence, but only by establishment of flexible mechanisms of extrapolation and reflection of connections and relations of one level (intonational-melodic, rhythmic-metrical) on the other (for example, compositional or structural). In this context, it is necessary to take into account the nature of the historical and analytical works by musicologists in Russian and other national fields of musicology.

Modalities and *lad* in Russian musicology

In Russian music theory, systematic thought about the modalities is characterized by fragmentation, in the sense of heterogeneity of observations and information. This situation is explained by traditional conditions of development of Russian theoretical knowledge in which the term "modalities" appears in the background of an all-embracing category called *lad*. This category, specific to Russian music theory, usually assumes a great part of the semantic load of the concept "modal". This is both a major problem and an advantage for research. The wealth of semantic-syntactic possibilities that attach to *lad* makes for extreme unevenness in various conceptions of the modalities. This unevenness can be observed in certain schools and tendencies in non-European cultures, and also to a layer of the Old-Russian culture.

It is necessary to construct a system of ideas in *lad* by defining its genetic connections with *modus*, in terms of a restoration of the age-old sense of this generative, immanently Russian category of culture. In this regard, it is important to make an analysis of all interpretations of the term "modalities" by determination of its genetic connections with the ancient comprehension of *lad*.

One may use this principle as a methodological tool to study the process of evolution of primary *lad*-intonational ideas of Orthodox culture, from their origin and crystallization, to their existence in the arts in the 20th century. The genetic method of analysis, by semiography, of the Osmollasny Church chants draws nearer to the authentic notions about the concept of musical style in Orthodox worship. Further, it allows us to located a contemporary composer's archetypal principles of organizational thinking.

Deep connections between the existence and the creative wisdom of a master are concealed in the semiographical nature of the Russian *glas* script. The indivisibility and syncretic wholeness of *Znamenny* notation defines its sign and essence based on delicate interconnections — direct and mediated — between a person's existence and the soul, between logos and pathos. In other words, that sign is rooted both in the ontology of Russian religious philosophical and in the musical style of Orthodox worship. There are foundations and sources of mythological ideas and the nature of the religious art symbol, somewhat in the manner of Sanskrit. At the present, study of the origin and influence of extra-musical notions upon the polymorphic reality of cult music is possible through the use of the genetic method of research.

On the problem of modal functions: Functional-processual approach

Elaboration of Asafiev's ideas entails unification of the functional typology of the musical system on the semiotical level. The functional approach to the music, in some cases, has become exclusively a probability-statistical method, while evaluation of the semantic factor lies beyond the scope of the methods of exact sciences. Here, at the moment of transition to the aspect of expressiveness, music analysis usually resorts the intuitive "translation" (see Milka 1982: 141).

In this case, the semantic aspects of the analytical apparatus of music theory is "deprived" of the chance "to take part" in the process of the functioning of the system because of a lack of the necessary modal correlate. On the semiotic level, to study the dialectics of relations in the dichotomy of the "langue-parole" concept leads to underestimation of semantic factors.

To follow Victor Bobrovsky: at the analysis of the work on the *langue* level ("form as a principle", in Bobrovsky's terms; 1978: 29), the correlation of dramaturgic and compositional functions has distinct criteria of a general logical and general compositional character. The level of *parole* ("form as a given fact"; 1978: 29), which is always inimitable and unique, demands introduction of an additional concept that can give notions about the strength and degree of the relationships between dramaturgic and compositional functions.

The modalities provide this special concept or category, inherent in language in action, that is, in speech. This concept can be neither "before" nor "after" the function; it is a force that perfuses the entire system. The modal meaning is peculiar to the syntax and inheres only in the construction as a whole, according to linguistics. This force seems to define an "inclination" of the system in relation to a functional scheme, and imparts a certain "mood" that on the whole is subordinated to the artistic idea and dependent on the author's attitude ("a modus as a condition of the system, a mood of the system"; Yujack 1986: 1–2).

The "communicative validity" of the musical composition is determined by the modalities of the system, which are formed through the particular relations between the syntax and the semantics, the compositional and dramaturgical functions (Bobrovsky 1978: 71–78), or semantic and communicative syntax (Medushevsky 1976). Thus, some modalities might be considered a missing link between the "function" and the "structure" in Bobrovsky's scheme (1978: 17), that is: function — modus — structure.

The transitive nature of the modalities (as a moment of transition) confirms the notion of the art modus that views a mode (way) of the translation of the "artistic text" as a substantial semantic feature of the text. It forms part of the three levels (three phases of formation and development) of the system: functional, modal, and compositional.

This approach to the analysis of the movement of the musical entity holds great methodological possibilities in terms of systematics. Two axes of the system — the axis of selection (paradigm) and the axis of combination (syntagm) — are two important principles of the composition; that is, they are bases of the given speech act, and they have the maximum formal and, at the same time, the maximum mobile nature. Their intersection forms the general system of the functional "measure".

For the time being, this is only the framework of a system. In other words, this generative view of the musical idiom, based on stereotypical connections, is both stable and open to variation. Mark Aranovsky defined such a system as a "system of invariants", or "intra-musical semantics" (1974: 113). This system has open, potential characteristics; its meaning consists in the orientation of the functional gravitations. At that stage, the system is that of functional possibilities.

The "open" system finds a "support-point" as soon as the context appears and is somewhat out of the ordinary in terms of functional correlations; here we are in the presence of the author's attitude or some emotional-psychological purpose. At this stage, the context assumes decisive significance, and dictates a mode (way) of the existence of the system. This points to the variable-combinatory essence of the modalities: here the modus appears as a particular principle of the correlation between the paradigmatic and syntagmatic axes. Within the bounds of the modus, the process of "mastering" the functional connections of the elements and levels is complicated by the correlative modal dependence.

In short, the modalities are that "medium" (the context) where functionality "germinates". A monosemantic-formal, adjusted connection of the idiomatic elements of system, enriched by contextual connections, is beginning to function, having produced the complicated indicator of musical wholeness: the intonation. The interpretation of the functional relationships means a process of their mastery (assimilation) and modification.

The result of this process is a unique quality. Thus, a mode of expression — the modus — is the way of mastering the musical reality; it is artistic interpretation, broadly speaking. It follows that the modus is the actualization (realization) of the functional relationships; a unique connection of the components of the system, at the moment when each of them, having lost a monosemantics, becomes a means of reflection.

The specific features of modal functions are connected with the concept of "conditionality". Here we observe the principle of "functional co-significance", proposed in Kushnarev's theory of *lad* (1958: 412–413). As known, the function, which normally has a "purpose" or "setting" (the paradigmatic level), is also a particular kind of determinism with respect to the interrelations of each stage of the musical process (syntagmatic level). The latter corresponds to an aspect of function, with regard to the kind of dependency (connections by contiguity or association) within the bounds of a given system, wherein alterations in a syntagmatic link at one level are derived (is functioning) from alteration of the others. The modal characterization of expressive means, in this sense, is first of all a gauge of correlative dependency; that is, the estimation of the extent of their intercorrelation with other phenomena and concepts of the whole context.[1]

Thus, the modalities, born of a particular contextual nature, depend directly on situational conditions and contain qualitative characterizations of the intonational totality. So, if the organization of "tonal-system thinking" is determined by principles of functional isotopy, then the principle regulating modal functions may be determined by the correlative functional dependency of elements. The interaction of functional isotopy and functional correlation in music analysis ensures the completeness of evaluating a musical system. Probably both the strategy and tactics of organization of the functioning and the perceiving of a musical discourse consist of the relation "modality–functionality". The extrapolation of this system of principles into all kinds of artistic communication opens many important lines for further study.

On the principles of modal logic

We continue the characterization of modal and tonal functions. The logic of tonal thinking is intimately connected with the dramaturgy of action; whereas modal logic deals with the expression of certain conditions: *inversio* (introspection, intuition, and meditation) and *extraversio*.

The functions of modal thinking are a centrifugal force connected with the intertextual sphere; in other words, modal principles function "before" and "after" the system, on both infra- and meta-levels. These two principles of the formation of the musical system (the modal and tonal functions) correspond with two fundamental principles of thinking: the principles of "identity" and "contrast" (Asafiev 1963: 104).

The logic of modal thinking as a specific type of artistic thought is connected with the poetics of confession, mystery, piety, prayer, sacraments; it is the poetics of symbol, ceremony, canon and anti-canon, metaphor and other rhetorical figures. Here such textual-poetic devices as "estrangement" (*ostranenie*), model, implication, commentary, inversion, and so on — the main moduses of anonymous and pseudonymous author's positions — might be considered by means of modal logic as a logic of the "probabilities".

Each facet of the functional mobility of the system, each factor of its unforeseen fluctuations are studied in terms of the logic of "instability" — a latent mechanism of control of the deepest levels of the musical thinking. One can likely propose the existence of a particular logic of the modalities, containing a set of all points of view on the subject and proposing any modifications within the bounds of the given "measure". This feature is similar to phenomenon of a "plural correlation", noted by Aranovsky, where the element has a many-sided interpretation and turns to be the intersection of many semantic fields, which are formed by the structures of various levels (1974: 118).

The dialectics of the modal principles consists in the correlation of the deep, genetic functional connections (objective measure) and the actual connections where the peculiar individual quality (modus of being) is "grasped" in this concept. Such modal logic serves the heuristic function of revealing the single unique mode of all possible modes of musical expression.

The composition, performance, and perception of such music ("music about music", "work on the model", "music of self-appraisal") are experienced transcendently and immanently; that is, they are connected with the primitive arts, folklore, modern art of the contemporary period, and, in general, with the tendencies of cosmology and mythology.

The phenomenon of modality has a communicative nature connected with a technique of being in some state (Medushevsky 1988: 13). It relates to a particular kind of mentality, one of the moduses of thinking: a suggestive modus. In this sense, variation form, in contrast to sonata form, could be considered a basis of modal logic wherein every variation (or rather, variant) is a deeper penetration but not a motion forward. Here it is important as an effect of "being" in the same state, or the same modus (see Nazaikinsky 1985: 19–27).

Hence the modal aspect of music reflects not only different phases of the evolution of musical thinking but also different kinds of thinking in the arts as a whole. (There is an important problem of transmission of modalities in the tendencies of the modern avant-garde and post-avant-garde.) It is important to note that the differentiation of modal and tonal functions is only a methodological device for the purpose of the maximum elucidation of differences. One thing is certain: the essence of musical thinking consists in the logic of the interaction of the tonal and modal principles (the principles of identity and contrast in Asafiev's sense; for one principle, with the inevitability of dialectical logic, provokes another, and the predominance of one of them provokes a certain category of the form, but does not destroy or revoke the other one; 1961: 104–105).

Modalities and intonation in music analysis: The psychosemiotical aspect of study

The ethos of the modal functions (modal poetics) is closely connected with a characterization of the style aspects of music analysis. This touches on the problem of approaching intonational dramaturgy by way of modalities; that is, the modalities as a means of realizing "expressive-dramaturgical functions" (Bobrovsky 1978: 56–58), and as a factor of a style-foundation.

Such a comprehension of the modalities, having become one of the connecting links between the general scientific method and special sciences through a systems-approach, is directed to gaining a total vision of an object. On the other hand, it is also connected with a search for more flexible (correct) methods for constructing various style models: intonational, structural, compositional, spatial-temporal, and so on. Fundamental to this search is Nazaikinsky's interpretation of the modalities, mentioned above (1982: 236–249).

Specific to an approach to the object of study is an attempt to establish the typology of manifestations of the modal factor as one of the essential factors of functional connection that provide compositional wholeness; this is one aspect of the intonation phenomenon as proposed by Eero Tarasti (1982: 510; 1987a: 567). The effect of complex interaction of all levels of the system is connected with the establishment of the decisive properties in the characterization of the whole picture of the "life" of the musical image, and of the types of functioning of the artistic system.

A more important approach is perhaps connected with the psycho-philosophical understanding of the modality: "A 'mode' is the expression of a psychophysiological state through sound. . . . A state, a mood (for example, anxiety, wrath, joy, jubilation, courage, internal peace, etc) is, of course, psychosomatic. Through the voice it has a sound characteristic, a precise sound expression, and therefore also musical expression" (Tarasti 1987a: 567).

It is interesting to consider the problem of the relations between the modalities and the intonation in the psycho-semiotical terms of the theory of musical perception. For instance, Medushevsky hypothesizes the unique phenomenon of "proto-intonation", which becomes a key to the scientific conception of the duality of musical form (1980). According to the Medushevsky, the mobile, sounding and sensible image can be "compressed" and "expanded" (1980: 184). If we take "a birth of the intonation from the proto-intonation" (Medushevsky) as the basis of the mechanism of signification or "doubling" — "Sign is the doubled existence", says Hegel — then a subject of the creative act must be in the position of an interpreter. Moreover, if one follows the principles of "wrapping" and "unwrapping" then it is easy to overcome all contradictions arising from the characterization of the triadic process, described above. The importance of the idea of the duality of musical form is that it touches the direct connection between the psycho-semiotical aspect and the spiritual-personal domain (the attitude to the perceptible content).

The complex approach (the system-structural method) to the problem of the modalities results in the discovery of the focus or nucleus of the modal conception: it is the concept of "attitude" or "relationship". It is a position from which we come to the notion of intonation as a sacred object, the Holy of Holies of art music.

In this regard, it is interesting to read Aranovsky's "Intonation, relationship, process" (1984). This research throws new light on the nature of musical thinking as well as on such important matters as interpreting Asafiev's intonational theory. It elucidates broadly and profoundly the greatness of intonational theory, an original concept of Asafiev which long went unnoticed. The concept of "relationship" plays the most important role in Aranovsky's attempt to solve some of the most vulnerable and mysterious moments of intonational theory. The "relationship" allows the concept of intonation to be recognized more specifically and precisely. Thus, a concept of "expression" bifurcates in two directions of meaning: a "way" and "significance".

On the one hand, it is an artistic image, that is, the "sensible sounding" in Asafiev's sense (1963: 198). The relation to a tone which is manifested at the moment of its pronunciation, multiplied by the relations between the tones in the micro-structure, form a "saturated solution" such that we perceive and experience all properties arising under those conditions as its "significance" (Aranovsky 1984: 84). According to the Aranovsky, this is the starting-point for studying the semantics of intonation.

On the other hand, the intonation is also understood as a mode of expressing musical sounds. The relations, as a peculiar field of values of the music, "carry the responsibility" for a musical structure as well as for semantic processes in it (Aranovsky 1984: 85). However, the relationship is not the whole intonation, but only one aspect — the modal aspect — of its functioning in a musical text (a musical message). It seems that the "intonation" is not only a way but also an image-structure, as a non-formal linguistic projection of lively human emotions. Thus an important rejuvenation of this research comes from the concept of "relationship": correlation of all existent points of view on the subject and, as a result, exposure of a maximum general (philosophic-aesthetic) sense and, at the same time, a maximum and precise meaning in its applied sense.

Towards a metatheory of music analysis

In the course of analysis, the search for precisely determined characteristics of the musical system, as determined by structural description, has intensified the antinomy in views about theoretical constructions in our post-structural period of musicological researches. This antinomy is less pointed on the level of metalanguage structures. The application of more flexible criteria to interpreting the linguistic structure of myth avoids the "hardening" of the concept of structure in a particular theory. There is need to raise questions about a metatheory of music analysis based on the structural study of myth (narration, discourse) by means of the modalities. Such study evinces two basic tendencies: a search for genetic methods of analysis, and for general ways of reflecting and cognizing the universe.

It is an idiom elaborated by Lévi-Strauss through the structural study of myth, and through the studies on the semiotics of myth, symbol, religion, and culture by Florensky, Bakhtin, Losev, Lotman (see the works on semiotics by the authors at Tartu State University). Indeed, this idiom of analysis may be used as a logical method for study of deep semantic levels and structures. One of the fundamental researches in this direction is Eero Tarasti's *Myth and Music* (1979).

The idea of myth as one aspect of a universal cognitive process has a direct relation to the metatheoretical level of thinking. New paths of research open up in searching the inner structure of the consciousness itself for traces of musical and scientific thinking. It is a starting-point for the formation of a metatheory of the modal analysis of styles and forms.

Modern semiotic investigators of textual-linguistic messages try to avoid both the decoding of the significance of the art work and the establishing of a truth as regards its content. They rather seek to re-create the rules and conditions for generation of significance; they search for the principles of system organization that by coherence imparts sensibility to the "utterance". Therefore, it is necessary to admit that the art work is a semantic system, according to Roland Barthes, that intro-duces in the world "du sens" but not a single sense — "un sens" (1989b: 274). Proceeding from the notion of "fluidity", fluctuation in the sense of the sign itself, one can state that the strength of a sign or the sign-system depends not on its completeness (presence of signified and signi-fier in complete form), nor on its genetics, but first of all on the those connections which the sign has with its environment (Barthes 1989a: 287). This is even more important with respect to musical contents, where the nature of the "signification" peculiarly reflects all elements and levels of the musical totality. One can say that wholeness is "grasped", as it were, at a particular degree of coherence or comprehen-sibility.

Thus the highest function of the modal factor is to connect, whichsaid connection being responsible for the measure of functional coherence of the musical totality. The modalities may be construed as one of the methodological criteria by which musical wholeness is made comprehen-sible. The modalities, as one of the principles of sound-pitch organiza-tion, can at the same time be used in the analysis of specific musical phenomena.

The theory of the modalities therefore becomes to some extent an aspect of metatheory as regards the language-object, that is, according to the logic of the musical idiom. This not only allows definition of the degree of wholeness of the musical work, but also permits us to come nearer to revealing the nature of this coherence, that is, the specification of style factors. As regards style, the metatheory of musical modalities will be concerned with the "poetry of substances" — the deepest level of the artistic system.

So, the modality is one of the most important properties of the musical utterance, its qualitative characteristic as determined by the quality of the functional concordances/non-concordances through a complex system of relations between syntax and semantics, dramaturgy and composition, function and structure, language and speech, sign and meaning. In other words, the modality is the "measure" as an equivalence of the organics and the entirety of the system, whose qualitative peculiarity is the expression of the author's attitude in a specifically encoded form — the intonational form.

Possible only at the level of "speech", the modality, which is a systematic and contextual category, depends directly on situational conditions. It is simultaneously an indication, a peculiarity, and a natural result of the organization of a creative process. The modalities "appeal" to the interaction of the functions not in their invariant relations but in the course of functioning with regard to contextual circumstances. These relations sometimes take place outside or even against a norm, causing deviations, transformations, and modifications of the norm. For instance, with the help of the modalities, hollow, bloodless models are turned into intonations. This semantic function is the primary function of the modalities.

The modal "measure" is the only correct criterion for determining the quality of the system; it is the main correlate of genetic and actual relations of all elements and levels of a structure. The modal parameters have a separate, individually embodied status in the musical utterance. Proceeding from the general notion of "modalities", we can try to specify some concepts derived therefrom.

The modus interconnects syntax and semantics. It regulates their relationship in each specific mode of realization in accordance with the emotional purpose of an author's disposition (tastes and ideas). Hence the modus is an emotional-estimative factor. However, the modus does not mean some emotion, but represents a "mode" or way to attain it.

This category is "in charge" of the "predicative" function because it directly participates in the formation of predicative units of a musical utterance (tune, phrase, sentence, theme, and the composition in general). It would be more proper to designate "modus-schemes" — such as those enumerated by Nazaikinsky: moduses of rhythm, movement, pitch, performance logic, dialogue, and so on (1982: 242–246) — as a notional "model", or a sign of modus.

A third element of the modal system is the "modulation". It is a process of the linear development of musical texture, connected with "a change of purpose" (Medushevsky) when a "horizontal" movement (in time) entails the dislocation of the whole system in the "vertical" dimension (mood). If the modulation is understood as a "change of purpose" — which is an essential and principal scientific discovery — then purpose is the modus itself, as confirmed by Nazaikinsky in his study of musical logic (1982).

Hence a modulation is a notion derived from a modus, i.e., a modus of an extended action, or a modus of development. With the help of the modus the process of interpreting the general language functional code is realized. In other words, a model turns into the intonation whereas the modulation means something different; this is a process of recoding ("a secondary act of selection and combination"). In these terms the modulation is not an incidental phenomenon, but the result of the interaction of the two functional axes of selection and combination. All this permits to treat the modus in its poly-functional meanings, as a sequence of three functions: forecasting, modeling, and representing.

Thus, such a many-sided category as the modality proposes a most complex conceptual apparatus, and a threefold conception underlies its bases: modus — modulation — model. The causative-effective connections between these comprise the essence of the dialectics of musical development.

The modalities are not a local problem. All modern justifications of the particular nature of musical semantics depend on this problem. For example, attempts to assimilate the "semiotical triangle" in the field of the art music result in the process of reformulating the sign system of verbal languages into the musical idiom; and this complicates the typology of musical signs. The modal principle in its new interpretation — as the way of translating the emotional-psychological attitude into a complex hierarchy of relations of elements and levels of the musical system — is a more immediate, spontaneous, flexible principle.

The modalities are an integral part of the whole phenomenon of the intonation, a point of intersection of all modern conceptions of artistic thinking. Probably, musical psychology will have to elaborate this problem. It is this discipline, indeed, that can make manifest the mystery of processes of our spiritual life (Aranovsky 1984: 87). Perhaps modalities are that musicological "term", the use of which is necessary to express a close connection (relationship) of the artistic intonation with the surrounding reality, and to relate it to a field of musical semantics (Asafiev 1963: 208).

In connection with the present matter, one can survey several aspects of analysis of Schnittke's Fourth Symphony that are primarily connected with the modal aspects of musical thought (for example, the modalities of composition, musical text, musical system, and so on). The problem of searching out the faith of a person (listener, composer, analyst), in the modern spirit of religious ecumenism, is connected with the realization of one's own place in the universe. From this position one might explain the phenomenon of Schnittke's style, which appears at the intersection of traditions of Eastern and Western (oriental and occidental) cultures of thinking. The genetic nucleus of this style concentrates in itself a colossal force of antinomy of the different kinds of psychology of a consciousness.

The creation of the Fourth Symphony "grasps" the main sign of the time as a crisis. In the course of a new search, this continues and develops the moral-philosophical type of symphonism one finds in Shostakovitch and Mahler. The Christian awareness of social problems and the spiritualization and Christianization of personality are at the basis of the Fourth Symphony's creation. Its sense contains, in attempts at understanding, an idea of person as the Christian idea; its highest purpose is' the aspiration to expose the Christian doctrine in a person. The Fourth Symphony's re-creation of a religious, even archaic world outlook, through certain style transpositions, exhibits a particular comprehension of contemporariness: the personality is the center of all dramaturgic events.

Poetics of genre

The genre model of the work proceeds from the idea of commentary, which relates to the genre of Schnittke's Second Symphony (Epifanova 1989; Vartanova 1989). This is a "dialogue-duel" of liturgical and secular genres, an aspiration to unite, to synchronize the "voices" of the various epochs by common moral-aesthetic problems (Vartanova 1989: 16). Here, a symphony is also a "commentator" for a Mass. The main principle of form-building and development cantus firmus composition, as a way of a detailed investigation of the initial material, such as its thematics, form, canonical organization, harmonic outline.

From this perspective one can view this genre as a paradoxical combination of ritual and symphony, whose core (symphonic dramaturgy) is historically determined by rhetorical skill and drama. In this connection, we take into consideration rhetorical function and narrative principles of organization of the musical text (discussed further, below).

The beauty of the genre solution and its intrinsic justification are, broadly speaking, determined by way of the relations between two fundamental principles of thinking: "canonical" and "uncanonical" (improvisation, commentary, lyricism). It is necessary to make few remarks on the etymology of the concepts "canon" and "commentary". According to the Explanatory Bible (1987) the Greek word "canon" means a reed stick, a straight stick; figuratively, it means everything that may be used to rectify other things. "Canon" is used in the meaning that can serve as a rule, norm, a pattern for life, ("A canon of the truth is God's words"; 1987: v). In addition, as known, the genuineness of the Holy Writ, the degree of its authoritativeness, and God's spirituality in it reflect its canonical nature.

By contrast, etymological examination of the Latin word "commentary" reveals its rhetorical meaning as "entimema": compensating for past failure (Latin-Russian Dictionary 1976: 209). Thus, the uncanonical area in the genre's model belongs to a lyrical, confessional plan of the work.

The canonical principle of organization is realized by the direct and inverted paradigm of the relations of theme A to themes B, C, D, where the functions of cantus firmus and commentary were recognized as interchangeable (see Examples 1–4). In terms of the process of development, the synagogue theme (A), as expression of a personal, confessional feature, appears in the role of a counterpointing voice of commentary in relation to each theme, as the symbol of different kinds of faith.

A final coda reveals another truth, another way of interpreting this model — an inverted way. Here, in the fourth macro-phase of a cycle, all themes form an ecumenical polylogue by interacting and conjoining in four-part counterpoint (see Example 5). It is nonetheless a united polymelodical texture where three tunes are orientated to a tenor (the cantus firmus, theme A), and depart from the initial tunes of this synagogue theme which serves to support the four-part counterpoint. From this point of view, the themes of three branches of Christianity indeed reveal their origins in melisma. Thus, we can see their functions in this context as a commentary on the unique synagogue theme; each of them appears as a certain interpretation of the only united faith, the faith in the one God. Probably, this confirms the idea that in the structure of culture there is only one, true, deep text, and all others play the role of commentary in relation to it.

Thus the principle of the canon is used here as judgment on certain law, and at the same time, a way of manifesting this judgement. In this sense, the canon is a system of moral-aesthetical principles resulting from a generalization of emotional and spiritual-intellectual experience. It is not only a type of world outlook, spiritual attitude, or ideology, but also a principle of artistic thinking, i.e., a system of connection between a process of perception and features of the work's internal structure. An artistic image gains extra-musical sharpening through canon (see Losev 1973: 12).

Lastly, one of the features of the Fourth Symphony is the lack of a specific genre model of the Mass, though it does project the conditions of heightened concentration emblematic of liturgical music (Vartanova 1989: 12). This is not incidental; on the contrary, this greatly relies on the spiritual-psychological system of music and the more important role of extra-musical factors. Therefore, the presence of the bivalent directness of the process of perception, mentioned above, is connected with a principle of re-comprehension of the model. Now, it is not a merely

Example 1. Schnittke, Symphony No. 4.

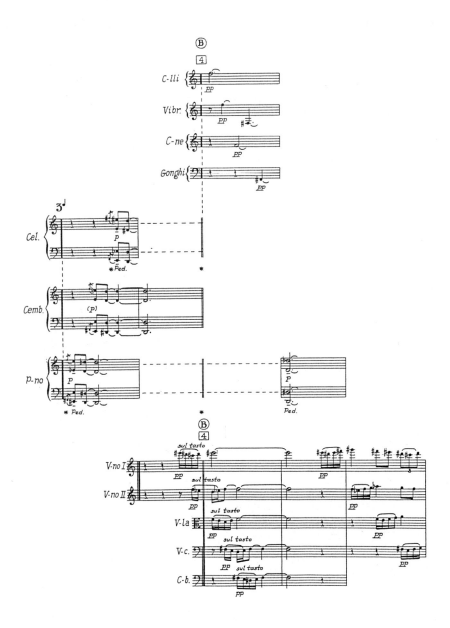

Example 2.

Example 3.

Example 4.

Example 5.

canon alone, nor merely interpretation of a canon, but, rather, the anti-
canon that is also one of the main means of modal thinking. Moreover,

it is not a modus, but a sign of modus (or the sign of sign).

Here, we see the principle of "alienation". This phenomenon, quite typical of Schnittke, is an analogue of the principles of Brecht's conventional theater. It is caused by the necessity to search for a specific mode of transmitting "information", where an unusual semantic layer arises between the levels of the text and the context; and through this layer a sign-intonation is perceived not in a direct but in an indirect meaning. Therefore, metaphor becomes the main means of modifying signification. The modalities, arising in the particular quality as an implication, regulate a process of the polyphony (dialogue) between the expressional and other levels of the text. This polyphony provokes to action the secondary sign-systems that allow us to define a system, as a whole, as the "structure of the structures", whose main semiotic unit is the "sign of sign".

The system of themes-symbols as a basis of the musical discourse

According to the composer, an aesthetic task of this work relates to an attempt to represent the interaction between three branches of Christianity and the latter's common source — the Old Testament (Schnittke 1988: 20–21). The general thematic idea constitutes a synagogue melody that acts as the generative model from which originate all three intonational spheres: the Catholic (B), Lutheran (C), and Orthodox (D) tunes. These themes assume the expression of a specific program, having become an embodiment of the eternal values and moral imperatives of religions in different historical times and national-ethnic regions (Vartanova 1989: 18). They are also the signs of metonymy — parts substituting for the whole. So, the purpose of the work is to set a person thinking about how Christianity, born into the entrails of Judaism, connects with another relation to God and the world (Vartanova 1989: 17).

Each of these symbol-signs, with their intertextual significations, assimilates aspects of the whole culture such as its world outlook and mentality (Vartanova 1989: 18). In general, the musical language of the Fourth Symphony has been viewed precisely as referring to the mentality of medieval culture. The concept of the artistic canon, in this case, defines not only the principle of artistic thinking, but also a certain system of the connections between the process of perception and features of the internal structure of a composition.

Each of the themes is created according to the laws of tonal thinking, yet all the strategies of the thematic development are supported by the modalities; in other words, here the modalities have a generative function. The synagogue choral melody, as canonical thematic support of a musical composition, is the subject of artistic evaluation in the subsequent interpretation of each macro-phase of a gigantic monoform. It is the generating model and genetic code: firstly, the scale (motive-intonational continua); secondly, a source and means of functional connection. The mission of this theme (A) is identical to a "way of reading the musical universe" (Yujak 1986: 1–2). It contains a capacious melodical-intonational summary of the whole musical content, and as such is a condensed image, prototype, "proto-intonation" (Medushevsky 1987).

All other themes originate from this source and are linked with each other by a very strong connection — genetic and intonational — through a modality. The paradigm of the relations between theme A and themes B, C, D is formed on the vertical axis according to the principles of melismatic organum (cantus firmus and commentary). Thus, the type of thematic connection has a transcendent character. Each of the themes arises in chronological and narrative succession, according to the increase of its social-historical importance in world history.

On the face of it, these themes seem to be independent, each having its own type of expression; yet they also go beyond this individualized sense. Probably, in this polymodal picture of the universe there is only one text: the archetype that in every age should be decoded in a particular way for each particular culture. This way is a search for beauty, for true faith; such are the attempts of humanity to express the truth in one's own way, to represent the unique picture of the universe in one's own interpretation, according to a given ethnic type and system of thinking. At the same time, it is a tragic understanding of its inexpressiveness. It is a test of the faith and a test by the faith. A result of dramaturgic development is not merely climax, but catharsis and transition into a new quality, i.e., reincarnation; it is the Great Transfiguration's Eve.

The sign-symbol is crucial to the complex hierarchy of the sign-system of dramaturgic contrasts. These contrasts find expression in the form of a symbol; it is based on the de-actualization of the significance of a sign through the dissonance between textual and extra-textual information, which semanticizes the oppositions of external / internal, superficial / deep, false / truthful, and so on (Vartanova 1987: 27). Here we are interested to know: (1) the nature of the religious-mythological symbol, its magic and mysterious strength, which takes part in the transformation of the expression form, the usual business of the ear; (2) that symbol's principle of construction, its singularity and phenomenological endlessness.

There are factors that determine the symbolic function of each theme. In the exposition, two textual-thematic layers — two dramaturgic themes, or "macro-themes" (Valkova 1978: 186) — represent the specific oppositions of "upper / lower", "communal / personal". In terms of the musical lexicon, however, one sees a paradox of both spheres retaining for themselves the value-orientated functions of the "cantus firmus" and "commentary", although they are in a sense reversed: syllabic organization of commentary and melismatic for cantus firmus (Vartanova 1989: 21–22). Thus the macro-theme A, in the function of cantus firmus, objectifies the "eternal" values, and, at the same time, it is expressed similarly by a melismatic line (see Example 4). In contrast, the macro-theme B, serving as commentary, has a processive, unstable nature; but it imitates the principle of syllabic organization of a choral melody, where a sense of each pronounced syllable is important (see the detailed analysis in Vartanova 1989).

A deformation of these symbol-signs provokes difficulties for their identification: the forms of expression are so conventional that, apart from the whole context, a listener could hardly correlate them with the reality of perception and notions. The effect of the "sign's sign" arises not only as a sign of the real object, but above all as a symbolic indication of its place in the represented universe (Uspensky 1971: 195). It is a coda of each macro-phase that is a version appearing in specific religious sources of themes (Vartanova 1989: 20).

One can understand a true meaning of these themes only from the perspective of the coda, wherein the same themes sound in the warm timbres of the human voice. There thematic sections are independent micro-universes, each having its own micro-space and temporal dynamics. Nevertheless, the separate fragments of the whole correlate with its conditional denotatums not in an immediate sense; rather, the true role of each theme appears only in retrospective terms as viewed within a general context.

Poetics of a text

1. The artistic model and its interpretation

The signs of dramatic contrast determine not only a kind of a dramaturgic model of composition, but also a certain type of artistic communication employed in the system of the culture. The peculiarity of the fourth-phase development — a macro-cycle with indications of a gigantic monoform — is that this one phase combines in itself the function of prologue and exposition. This phase is the first "event" (text) and has within itself the key contrasts (dramaturgical, intonational, thematic, semantic) of the piece; at the same time, it is the model of a text (model of contrast), invariant. This is the first and, probably, the only "event" — a sacred event. While all following phases expand with the inner movement, in an artistic text their developments are only interpretations of a given model. Here we find a principle noted by Yuri Lotman, whereby a text is functionally applied not as a message but as a code (1973: 238). For example, there occurs a simultaneous combination of two macro-themes that have contrast relations at both the "vertical" and "horizontal" levels (A, A/B).

The concept "canonical model" is, indeed, a key by which to decode the complex and multi-faceted dramaturgy of a symphony. Each successive "text" is like the model of re-comprehension of an artistic reality. As is known, polysemantic interpretation of the same text is an inalienable quality of the Middle Age's language. In the latter, new meanings appear not by way of adding other "information" to preexistent ones. On the contrary, an invariant of the text-model transforms the understanding of the person who generates the texts, and transfers a given message into a new system of meanings (Lotman 1973: 238).

2. Organization of time and space: Modalities of a form

Nevertheless, from an invariant (model) to its interpretations is only one direction of musical expansion. There is also a reverse movement: from each of the variants to the basic model. In other words, an aesthetic effect arises not at the moment when the code is used as a message, but, on contrary, when a message is used as a code (Lotman 1973: 240).

The interaction of centripetal and centrifugal tendencies in current music form certain self-intersecting surfaces that resemble the inner-spherical perspective which Pavel Florensky discovered in Byzantine architecture and Old-Russian painting. The effect of comprehension of signification arises at the moment of intersection or self-crossing of the planes. This is analogous to the perception of symbolic space in icon-painting. It is the inside-outside represented as the universe: a sphere where the center is anywhere, but the circle is nowhere (Kedrov 1989: 236).

According to cosmological consciousness, there exists a center of a spatial-temporal model of the composition, where and when an act of creation is realized. That central point in dramaturgy has the highest value (maximum sacredness) as "center of the universe". From the viewpoint of the psychology of perception, such a center has a migrating nature; the dynamics of the migrating, perceiving look combines the outside and inside images of the universe. In this way we can describe the "universe / person" dichotomy and the notations of spatial-temporal relations within ontogenesis. In other words, here feelings of distance and of highest concentration arise simultaneously. On the other hand, the center is the bewitching effect of a distance that encloses a person (listener, performer, or composer) within its area.

The beginnings of the sign-symbol, and the signs of metonymy and metaphor, depend in each case on a parallel or contrary movement of the semantic and syntactic levels, their transposition (inversion) such that the macro-themes appear in the role of each other. On the other hand, while the dramaturgic levels intersect, the distance comes into focus. This phenomenon characterizes the type of auto-communication typical of the arts, where the subjects, taking and transmitting a message, combine in one and the same person (Lotman 1973: 237). This is a process of self-knowledge of existence, a personal process of reforming consciousness.

So, the viewpoint of the listener (or composer) moves with and accompanies a migrating center. The effect of a transmission of message by two communicative channels ("I-I" and "I-You") is effected through a peculiar "swing" of these structures (Lotman 1973: 240–241). From the viewpoint of meditation and mono-dramaturgy, it is a monologue, which Mikhail Bakhtin recognizes as a dialogue, but as an interior dialogue (see Ivanov 1973: 21). Intercorrelation of these communicative levels in each case is unique and represents a specific kind of dramatur-gical contrast, for example, of a distanced, close, or diffused nature, according to Vartanova's typology of contrasts (1987: 6). Still, in all cases they function as symbol-signs.

We can consider the temporal-spatial model in light of the psychology of perception of church-painting. According to Pavel Florensky's theory of inverted perspective, there is a peculiar system of transmission of the spatial characteristics of reality. Here it is important to distinguish the concepts of direct and inverted perspectives as two principles of the attitude to life — inside and outside — as two cognitive experiences of the universe, or as two kinds of thinking (of a culture) that endlessly and periodically alternate throughout history (Florensky 1967: 391).

One can consider the operating of these principles by analogy to the functioning of tonal and modal principles of organization in systems of thought. Probably, this aspect of the formation and functioning of the compositional system could be conventionally defined as a modality of the form or of the composition. In this situation, one should proceed from interrelation of functions not only in their invariant relations, but also in the process of their functioning, taking into account the contex-tual conditions.

Hence according to the principles of linear or direct perspective, here are some attributes of different musical forms in the Fourth Symphony:

(1) Principles of a sonata-symphonic cycle: the dialectics of contrast and connection between two macro-themes; presence of the dramaturgical story; the attributes of development and recapitulation. For example, the four phases of the macro-cycle correspond with the semantic-syntactic functions of the symphonic cycle as described by Yelena Vartanova (1989: 18): Phase I, a predominance of meditative modality; Phase II: going outside into the area of vital reality (the outside world); Phase III is connected with the development section; Phase IV is the coda-repentance (catharsis) in Mikhail Bakhtin's sense (1986: 128–129), that is, the postcommunicative phase of meditation.

(2) Principles of concerto form: existence of soloist (piano-celesta-cembalo), double-exposition, complex cadence-system.

(3) Principles of variation form (this cycle may be considered a system of the double-variations, or simultaneous variations), but also of a variant and a monoform or "intonational-phase form" (Pertrikov 1988: 5).

From the viewpoint of directness to the listener's perception, all the aforementioned principles are potentiality and actually acting, according to the laws of linear perspective or of a tonal system. However, there is only one possible mode of interpretation of the universe — "the perspective interpretation of the universe" (Florensky 1967: 384), connected with the presence of one viewpoint, of one suppositional center.

At the same time, one observes an opposite tendency in the contrary functioning of the inverted perspective laws. Hence in the moment of transition to a next macro-phase, the operation of the principles of linear development instantly "wraps" into focus, similar to the principle of quantum jump, changing the point of view to a process of development and producing new dramaturgic quality.

The effect of an aesthetic comprehension arises only as a result of a summary moment. This phenomenon relates to the aforementioned concept of "dynamics of a perceiving view" (Uspensky 1971: 194), as a way of embracing and understanding the artistic wholeness and a way of deforming the artistic images. Identical to the principle of summing up the aural impression of a listener is the way of perceptually organizing a picture: views from within and from without are combined. This becomes the way of conceiving the artistic work's wholeness. Here we can speak of an original redistribution of perspective by the operation of modal principles of organization.

Poetics of rhetorical figures

The genre-intonational allusions and motives of medieval culture demand judicious use of analytical criteria on the musical-semiotical plane. The principle of canonic organization of the musical material and the importance of the implied verbal level ("intoned words of a prayer") — a factor of narrative organization of a text — are concerned with an attachment of the rhetorical level to the structure of a text, which could be considered in terms of appropriateness to the musical discourse.

In this context, the term "rhetoric" will be used taking into account its three traditional aspects, as represented by Yuri Lotman: (1) from a linguistic point of view, as a structure of narration (the rules of construction of speech at the supra-phrase level); (2) as a discipline, studying the "poetical semantics", i.e., the kinds of figurative meaning or the so-called "rhetorical figures"; (3) as a "poetics of the text" which deals with the intratextual relations and social functioning of a text as an integral semiotical formation (Lotman 1981: 8–9). In addition, we shall also use the rhetorical figure or "metabola" as a concept from Antiquity and also of "general rhetoric" (see M. Groupe 1986).

The main reason for use of the rhetorical function is the immanent dependence of any artistic (including musical) phenomenon on *ethos*. In this context, the concept of ethos is borrowed from a field of rhetoric: the ethos is the affective state of a recipient that arises as a result of a message in him, the specific features of which vary according to several parameters (M. Groupe 1986: 264). In this connection, the rhetorical function becomes especially important to define the nature and conditions of generation of specific kinds of ethos.

Here, one should mean the field of the communicative aspect as a result of interaction between syntax and semantics. As in the domain of traditional rhetoric, the purposeful forming of the ethos is realized through an introduction of breaches into the codes of the language levels.

In other words, what concerns us is that level of analysis connected with study of the metalinguistic code. Hence, a rhetorical figure is a bridge by which to establish equivalences in the case of untranslatability of a text from one language into an another (see Lotman 1981: 11). From the viewpoint of referred connection (a psychology of perception), one can say that it is the laws of reverted perspective, in their summarizing meta-meaning, that seem to be concerned with generation of the ethos. Quite another aesthetic function is outlined in the conditions of perception of linear perspective — the pathos of a creative expression for the purpose of exciting an emotion, a feeling, a sympathy.

The generative model of the rhetorical figure concerns an implicit verbal substance in the structure of a musical text, a substance that refers to an infra-structural level rather than to an extra-musical one. Therefore the focus of our attention shifts to the systemic evolution of the norms of conjunction between verbal and musical means of perception. Such an aim, in this case, allows semiotical principles to enter more suitably into the system of musicological analysis, by way of a theory of figures and of rhetoric as a whole.

A means of determining the rhetorical status of a figure and of de-scribing its functioning is concerned with the concept of "sign". As is known, a sign function of a rhetorical figure manifests by the interre-lation between a substance of the expression (the morphological, gram-matical, syntactical aspects) and a substance of the content (semantic, logical aspects).

It is now necessary to dwell on the description of "trope". According to Lotman, the trope is always a semantic transformation, a semantic transposition from a sign of one language to the sign of another. A troping effect is based on construction a certain content that is impossi-ble to construct within the bounds of one language (Lotman 1981: 18). We can see an analogy to a trope-figure in theme A. This theme may be described as a contradiction between melodic-scalar, rhythmical-intonational arrangement and textural-timbral devices of expression. Here occurs a principle of collision and paradoxical coexistence of two styles, of two cultures: a medieval or mythological consciousness connected with ancient-archaic traditions, and the modern type of ex-pression typical of the poetics and aesthetics of avant-gardism and post-avant-gardism. Here, the trope-figure appears at the juncture of two languages; and in this respect, a trope is iso-structural to the mechanism of creative consciousness as such (Lotman 1981: 18).

The functioning of a trope-figure leads to "exfoliation" of a semantic space of the textual universe and emergence of a semantic "break". A rhetorical effect arises through a clash of signs referring to different spatial-temporal registers. This is typical not only for the first macro-theme, however, for the whole text may be perceived as a trope, that is, as a rhetorically active figure in non-rhetorical culture (Lotman 1981: 18).

It is important to consider the factors that take part in forming the ethos of a given figure. The first macro-theme turns out to be alienated from the stylistic environment it usually "inhabits", which provokes notions about a certain style. The normal melodic-motivic organization of the theme through its own immanent *lad*-intonational potency has the "ability" to provoke a notion about a certain level of the language. A peculiar coloration of meaningfulness of the language unit springs from the connections that the sender (or receiver) establishes with the identified environment(s) (M. Groupe 1986: 264). In this context the synagogue theme, representing "in the modus of quotation" or the "quotation mood" (Nazaikinsky 1982: 173), sounds on the verge of losing its stylistic integrity and even artistic meaningfulness.

There is a "semantic field" of perception connected with the concept of "contextual ethos" (M. Groupe 1986: 274): it is the presence of a minimum meta- and socio-cultural basis of a given sign-type, which demands knowledge of the language of the culture. The common context of work ("stylistic field") is formed from a sum of musical-aesthetic meaningfulness. A difficulty of study of such a field lies in the fact that it is created not instantly but as late as decoding of the message (M. Groupe 1986: 277); that is, one must take into account the dynamics of the process of perception.

Thus ethos as a special aesthetic effect is a real object of the artistic communication. It relates to the fact that the influence of a rhetorical figure is not contained in the figure itself but arises in response to a certain stimulus in the listener (M. Groupe 1986: 264).

Musical discourse: The narrative aspect

Now it is necessary to focus our attention on the relationship "discourse" to "narration" (or expression figures to content figures). That narrative sign is constituted by a relation between the form of narration (*récit racontant*) and the content of narration (*récit raconté*) (M. Groupe 1986: 301–302).

As to the expansion of a discourse, this involves formation of two universes: the universe of narration and the universe of discourse, where the latter subordinates the former to its own order. In this case, the discourse has its own dynamics, which is opposed to the dynamics of the narration. It is the discourse that assumes representation of past, future, or times. Moreover, the discourse opposes its own intrigues to the reproduction of events in a listener's imagination.

On the micro-level, theme A "comments" on each new theme (B, C, D), and undergoes modification through them (its own modus-variants), as if it would "experience" their birth. On the level of dramaturgy, as mentioned above, each of the chants is considered in its capacity as modal commentary on theme A. Hence the same text, or model of text, and the same signs serve to express different contents on various structural-semantic levels. That is, at each stage of expansion we can observe a second or re-codification of the basic model and, therefore, the "variant's variation" or "sign's sign". In this analytical situation, we can regard as more acceptable the application of principles from the field of semiotics of an artistic text, recalling Lotman's principle of "transformation of a figure into figures that are summarized in time" (1973: 384).

The deviation (figure) appears here because the musical text has an inherent internal antinomy: the narrative develops in an area whose existence is concerned with the time. In fact, the narration itself may be considered as a rhetorical device. Moreover, it is important to take into account the fact that transformation is the main method of expansion in indiscrete texts such as musical ones. By internal permutation of elements, according to the modal principle, there occurs a transformation of one figure into another.

Thus, the modal principles characterize in this case a kind of syntagmatic relation of a narrative text in music, which is defined as a text based upon a temporal junction of synchronously organized structures that are transformed into each other (Lotman 1973: 384). Hence, one can observe by this method the functioning of the principles of mono-dramaturgy.

The internally mobile relations between textual elements (as material for selection and combination) are, indeed, the main factors realized in the course of the narrative of a text — its musical expansion by transformation into a figure. However, the result of that syntagmatic expansion turns out to be more than unexpected.

From the structural point of view, the narration is made up of phrases, but may never add up to their sum. Hence, according to inverted perspective laws, a listener faces the paradoxical fact that a main concluding (general) transformation takes place in the post-communicative phase of comprehension, i.e., on the logical level. The whole series of successive transformations is in one turn transformed into a metalogism-figure: the essence of the logical transposition (permutation) consists in the inter-turnover of substances. Its mechanism is a logical or temporal inversion; its purpose is to change the meaningfulness of the whole syntagmatic succession from the viewpoint of the assertion expressed in it. We could call that metalogism a parable of religious content (a similitude).

There is another factor of that inversion mechanism: in the coda of each macro-phase, a figure-metalogism appears at the moment of switching over from a plot-topical plan to a moral-philosophical, evaluative plan, which is connected with the appearance of the human vocal timbre (Vartanova 1989: 12). The figure-metaphors are summarized into a meta-metaphor. Thus, the reduction of a deviation (figure) is realized on the level of the highest unit, in which preceding rhetorical devices are integrated (M. Groupe 1986: 275). Each stage of the semiotical organization increases the dimensions of a semantic structure. Each next step may be expressed by means of a preceding one; each new step in regards to subordinate ones is a semiotical sacrament (Lotman 1973: 21–22).

The ethos of a given figure is formed through several factors; for example, (1) an inadequacy (insufficiency) in a "literal" sense of the events that occurred; (2) an impetus to search for another sense in the narrative organization, rather than the organization of discourse, for its sacred secrets (M. Groupe 1986: 250). Chiefly, the meaningfulness attributed to a musical fact is a function of an individuality that is integrated into a certain social and cultural context (ibid.: 273). If preceding figures (deviations) appear through violation of a code, that given metalogism is formed by re-comprehension of an extra-musical context. The parable as a rhetorical figure of thought is an estimated judgment and is concerned with such fields of rhetoric as meta-stylistics, which logically follows after perception ethos, being formed by a text as a whole (ibid.: 278).

Hence, the meaning of the parable formed "after" a metaphor-sign of the coda-cadence consists in the fact that the final coda of each macro-phase, despite maximum effort, still is not a resolution of contradictions, which can be realized only from the perspective of the whole; because, according to Russian philosopher Nikolai Berdyaev, a true sense of history consists not in that all contradictions should be solved at some moment in time, but in the fact that internal movement of a tragedy of history leads to the all-solving truth only in the end. Then, its final solution casts retrospective light upon all preceding periods of history. The highest mission of a human being and humanity is supra-historical, and the only possible only solution of all fundamental contradictions of history is supra-historical (Berdyaev 1990: 215). A main mechanism for formation of a "meta-metaphor" is transposition that arises in source — the macro-theme and first model of a text (macro-phase). This transposition has as its basis temporal and spatial inversion. That main, and possibly only, "event" simultaneously symbolizes the cause and the effect. Therefore, all other events are considered in direct and reversed successions: their temporal lines are closed into the sphere of the text, i.e., the space of a conventionally-staged ritual action.

In a narrative plan, each link of the development (macro-phase) is not only a continuation of the preceding one, but at the same time is the cause and the effect of the following. That is, each event is estimated by a system of the complex contextual connections. That phenomenon in the field of *rhétorique générale*, "transposition having as its basis the temporal inversion is accompanied by causal-effectual inversion: the effect generates the cause" (M. Groupe 1986: 326). Taking into account the temporal and causal successions in Schnittke's Fourth, one should note that the chronology of narration and the chronology of discourse disagree in their directions: the narration is from the beginning of the Judaic religion while the discourse is from a viewpoint of the present time.

A chronological succession, thus, is distorted solely for a caprice of discourse, for the organization itself (M. Groupe 1986: 321-322), in order to give its own version, to create its own discourse. A single moment of life is not self-valuable, for a sense of each instant of life is always exposed only with respect to eternity; a moment of time by itself is meaningless (Berdyacv 1990: 215).

One should point out the increasing polysemantics of the language according to Lotman's principle of the informational paradox in the artistic canon (1973c). So, it requires a surplus number of images, including such ones that reflect an origin illusorily and pervertedly in order to create an integral, more objective picture of the universe.

It is interesting in this context to consider another rhetorical figure — a twelve-voice fugue (see Example 6). The mechanism of this figure is based on the permutation of elements: it is a motive-intonational transformation of elements of the first macro-theme; however, in its further development it is perceived as a complete substitution. Such figures are related to rhetoric if they violate convention and deceive the listener's expectations (M. Groupe 1986: 299). The sudden intrusion of the fugue is perceived as a tragic opposition to the meditative sphere. Nevertheless, its serial organiza tion, thematic limitation, the lack of intermediums, prove that it is the "rotation on a closed circle", "absolute lack of purpose", "movement to nowhere", as a symbolization of anti-movement, anti-wholeness, as "annihilation of matter" (Vartanova 1990: 34-35). The action turns out to be inaction; so, semantically opposed phenomena form a sense of unity, identical to the rhetorical figure of oxymoron. However, at the logical level, i.e., in the whole context, such a device is perceived as a figure of metalogism, such as antiphrasis or paradox. In contrast to the previous ritualistic and sacramental development, this figure seems to be the real subject of a symphony, even a surreal one. Such new reality of action oversteps the limits of the semantic universe, "pretends" to change it, and also "presses" its own conditions on the language consciousness. The paradox of the language situa-

tion consists in the language postulating the reality and at the same time crossing it. The fetishism of an idea of the super-order of the universe, the "dictatorship"
of order, turns on the parody of that order: constructivism and mathematical calculation result in fanaticism and then chaos.

Representation of space in discourse: The figure of "point of view"

The concept of "point of view" is defined, according to Todorov, as a way by which the event is perceived by a narrator and a potential listener (see M. Groupe 1986: 328). Todorov distinguishes in the concept of point of view two fundamental aspects: "more or less marked presence of a narrator in the discourse and his more or less near, more or less intimate attitude to the personages, to their inner life" (M. Groupe 1986: 328).

In terms of rhetorical organization, transparency of point of view is considered a norm; whereas the omniscience and omnipresence of a narrator, as objective description "from without" are deviations in the perception of a contemporary listener (M. Groupe 1986:329). In this analysis of the Fourth Symphony we shall use several modifications of the figure "point of view", proposed by authors of *Rhétorique générale* (M. Groupe 1986: 329):

(1) The figure of "looking from without" (figure of abridgement). There is objective narration when a narrator does not show his presence; he avoids external commentary and value judgments and reports only facts and thoughts of personages, leaving it to the reader to judge the characters and "events" (M. Groupe 1986: 329). From the viewpoint of functions of the ritual action, here ellipsis is important, a device of omission. That figure of omission (or abridgement) appears in the junction of macro-phases (codas) and obliges the listener to search for causes and motives for these events.

(2) The figure of omniscience (figure of addition) relates to interference of a narrator. For example, the synagogue theme as a solo part is represented as one of three timbral roles (see Example 1), but whose

Example 6.

unity is contradictory: it is division into three — a person in a discordant spiritual sphere. That sign symbolizes degradation of the human image, decomposition of a person who was shaped in Christianity (Berdyaev 1990: 214), who lost the internal support of a spiritual center. However, the cadences are true semantic indications of happening "events". The system of the cadences reveals interaction of the rhetorical categories of "pseudo-person" and "ortho-person". The mechanism of transformation of a figure into a figure is connected with ritual as a "self-contained phenomenon where the objects momentarily take over changed identifies in order to play out sacred roles" (Wheelock 1987: 444). Nevertheless, the counterpoint of all themes, in the final coda of the post-communicative phase, represents the polyvalent viewpoint. A metalogism such as allegory is the brightest expression of the author's omniscience. In that polylogue from the author's person comes forward a non-person (or super-person) who performs here. The final coda could be considered as a device "minus-rhetoric" (Lotman 1981: 18); that is, the rhetorical situation, in the context of the preceding one, defines this device rather not as a trope but rather as a meta-trope (Lotman 1981:18). Therefore, one would think that its new, purified and ideal harmony corresponds to the stylistic norm for religious parable — as idyll. However, it turns out to be a deviation in respect to the whole preceding development. This is a case when rules of the lexical code are not broken, and only lack of isotopy indicates the presence of a figure, isotopy being one of the factors of coherency of the text on the supra-phrase level of the language structure.

(3) The figure of "joint-vision" (figure of abridgement with addition). This is a discourse in the first person, in which the composer's presence (his point of view) is always a feeling for his own discourse connected with a thorough development of the synagogue macro-theme. Its dramatic fate manifests at the most painful points of the whole paradigm, in its relations with the other themes. By that meditative sphere the author projects the presence of himself in his own discourse. The figure of joint-vision is evidenced by the fact that the author/composer penetrates into the secrets of his "personages" and "betrays" them to the listener. This rhetorical device of the syntagmatic level forms the discourse of the inner monologue: it is commentary-experience. However, the "inner speech" never hides the narration.

(4) The figure of the "intersection of the viewpoints" (figure of transformation or inversion). We can conventionally call this a look "from within-from without". It is connected with the presence of an effect of polylogics and polystylistics, but also of a semantic break between the levels of content and expression. The sense placed in the area of "distance" (see M. Groupe 1986: 268) is the main essence of the sign-metaphor (or trope). The revealed distance is not only an indication of violation of the norm, but also a tool of auto-correction, i.e., of narrowing the perception. It is distance that allows a listener to keep in the "field of vision" the musical-semantical current and to perceive a dialogue. The direction of the distance in its depth has a centrifugal-centripetal nature. The concept of "shifting point of view", mentioned above, is the principal concept for formation of the final effect of a figure.

Conclusions

Having considered the modal factors of the organization of a given musical work, we have several observations:

(1) Modalities as a probabilistic logic of musical development. The modal system of thinking may be considered as a totality of the viewpoints on the object, which are a possible range as fixed by modal measure. So, the first macro-theme is a way to combine the multitude of all its possible interpretations and attitudes or into it — all its moduses. Each model (interpretation) is at the same time a deviation from and approach to it. Here a conceptual "norm" is conventional and established in the process of perception. Another feature of the modal logic is connected with the fact that the selected point of view on the object always seeks to be a norm; however, having reached relative stability, a given emotional-psychological "purpose" could be observed departing from that point.

(2) The type of functioning of the musical system. The type of thinking in Schnittke's Fourth Symphony, one can define, very schematically, as interaction of two principles of thinking: modality and tonality, and the atypical interchange of their functional essences. This interchange

corresponds to the fundamental principles of organization: the poetics of identity and of contrast. Moreover, if the tonal principles of organization function as a measure of the linear development, then the modal principles function at infra- or meta-levels of the system.

The tonal thinking, connected with dramaturgy of action, develops in real, historical time, while the modal thinking relates to a state and is connected with an "unwrapping" of a temporal instant in space, in another type of imaginary temporality ("eternal time"). If the tonal principles are subordinated to the tonic center (centripetal tendencies), then the modal principle come in the intertextual spheres, in the intra- and extraversio. Lastly, the mechanism of development: in the tonal organization the motivic power is the principle of modification, while in modal organization such power is the principle of mutation (transformation of a figure into a figure).

Thus the dialectics in the correlation of the modal and tonal parameters gives an idea of how a level of artistry of the musical work depends on its systematic regularity. There are two principles that have important significance for functioning of the system and for structuration of the spatial-temporal organization: the principle of actualization of functions (a term borrowed from systems-theory) and a mechanism of temporal and spatial inversion. Then the viewpoint of a composer (or listener) is not "I am in the world" nor "the world is in me", but it is we who are in the conventional center of the world — "within-without" (see Kedrov 1989: 236). Here the "external becoming internal" (and vice versa) conforms to fundamental notions in modern cosmology, folklore, and primitive arts.

The whole spiritual way of the Fourth Symphony, its internal content, is the Christian work on the human image that expresses a return to some elements of the Middle Ages (although New Age spirituality experiences life not transcendentally but immanently; Berdyaev 1990: 214). The pattern of this symphony is interesting as not only a "meeting" of several kinds of culture, but also of several types of thinking. As such, this symphony perhaps demands a transformation of the system of principles and approaches to music analysis into a new system of correlations.

Note

1. On the relative nature of significances in the musical semiotical system, see Lotman (1965: 24). This idea is further developed by Aranovsky (1974: 112).

References

Aranovsky, Mark (1984). "Intonation, relationship, process" [in Russian], *Sovetskaya muzica* 12: 80–87. Moscow: Sovetsky Kompozitor.
- (1974). "Thinking, idiom, and semantics" [in Russian], *The Problems of Musical Thinking*, Aranovsky (comp. and ed.), 90–128. Moscow: Muzgiz.
Asafiev, Boris (1963). *Musical Form as a Process* [in Russian]. Vols. 1–2. Leningrad: Muzgiz.
Bakhtin, Mikhail (1986). *Aesthetics of Literary Creation* [in Russian]. Moscow: Iskusstvo.
Barthes, Roland (1989a). "Literature and meaning" [in Russian], *Selected Works*, trans. and introduction by G.K. Kosicov, 276–296. Moscow: Progress.
- (1989b). "What is criticism?", *Selected Works* (above), 169–275. Moscow: Progress.
Berdyaev, Nikolai (1990). "The end of the Renaissance and the crisis of humanism" [in Russian], *Novyi mir* 1, S.P. Zalygin (ed.), 207–232. Moscow: Izvestiya.
Bobrovsky, Victor (1978). *The Functional Bases of Musical Form* [in Russian]. Moscow: Muzgiz.
Dvorzhetsky, Iosif (1976). *Latin-Russian Dictionary*. Moscow: Russky Yazyk.
Epifanova, L. (1989). "The idea of commentaries in Alfred Schnittke's Second Symphony", *Theses of the Young Musicologists' Scientific Conference*, 56–57. Gorki: Volga-Vyatka Press.
Explanatory Bible (1987). [in Russian]. Vol. 1. Stockholm: Institute of Translations of the Bible.
Florensky, Pavel (1967). "Reversed perspective" [in Russian], *Works on Semiotics* 3 (198), Yuri Lotman (ed.), 381–416. Tartu: Tartu University Press.
Greimas, Algirdas J. (1987). "Toward a theory of modalities", *On Meaning: Selected Writings in Semiotic Theory*, trans. Paul Perron and Frank Collins, 121–139. London: Frances Pinter.
Ivanov, Vyacheslav (1973). "The importance of M. Bakhtin's ideas on the sign, utterance and dialogue for modern semiotics" [in Russian], *Works*

on *Semiotics* 6 (308), Y. Lotman (ed.), 5–44. Tartu: Tartu University Press.

Kedrov, Konstantin (1989). *Poetical Cosmos* [in Russian], preface by V. Gusev. Moscow: Sovetsky Pisatel.

Kushnaryov, Christofor (1958). *Problems of the History and Theory of Armenian Monodic Music* [in Russian]. Leningrad: Muzgiz.

Losev, Aleksei (1973). "On the concept of artistic canon" [in Russian], *The Problem of Canon in Antique and Middle-Ages Art of Asia and Africa*, I. F. Murian (ed.), 6–15. Moscow: Nauka.

Lotman, Yuri (1965). "On the problem of meanings in secondary modeling systems" [in Russian], *Works on Semiotics* 2 (181), Lotman (ed.), Lotman (ed.), 22–37. Tartu: Tartu University Press.

– (1973a). "Canonical art as informational paradox" [in Russian], *The Problem of Canon in Antique and Middle-Ages Art of Asia and Africa*, I. F. Murian (ed.), 16–22. Moscow: Nauka.

– (1973b). "One the dual model of communication in the system of culture" [in Russian], *Works on Semiotics* 6 (308), Y. Lotman (ed.), 227–243. Tartu: Tartu University Press.

– (1973c). "Notes on the structure of the narrative text" [in Russian], *Works on Semiotics* 6 (308), Y. Lotman (ed.), 382–386. Tartu: Tartu University Press.

– (1981). "Rhetoric" [in Russian], *Works on Semiotics* 12 (515), Y. Lotman (ed.), 8–28. Tartu: Tartu University Press.

M. Groupe (1986). *Rhétorique générale par le groupe* [in Russian], trans. E. Razlogova, B. Narumov (ed.), preface by A. Avelichev. Moscow: Progress.

Medushevsky, Vyacheslav (1980). "Duality of music form and musical perception" [in Russian], *Perception of Music*, V. N. Maximov (ed. and comp.), 178–194. Moscow: Muzgiz.

– (1979). "Musical style as semiotical object" [in Russian]. *Sovetskaya Muzika* 3: 30–39, Y.S. Korev (ed.). Moscow: Sovetsky Kompozitor.

– (1988). "Musical Work and its cultural-genetic basis" [in Russian], *Musical work: Essence, Problems of Analysis*, I. A. Kotlyarevsky and D. G. Terentiev (comp.), 5–18. Kiev: Muzichna Ukraina.

– (1976). *On the Principles and the Means of the Artistic Effect of Music* [in Russian]. Moscow: Muzgiz.

Milka, Anatoli (1982). *Theoretical Bases of Functionality in Music* [in Russian]. Leningrad: Muzgiz.

Nazaikinsky, Evgeni (1982). *Logic of Musical Composition* [in Russian]. Moscow: Muzgiz.

– (1973). "On constancy in the perception of music" [in Russian], *Musical Arts and Science* 2, comp. E. Nazaikinsky, 59–98. Moscow: Muzgiz.

– (1985). "Preface: Theory of interaction of the music forms" [in Russian], in: P. Stoyanov, *Interaction of the Music Forms*, trans. K.N. Ivanov, 5–30. Moscow: Muzgiz.

Petricov, Sergei (1988). "Non-typical compositional structures in B. Tishchenko's instrumental works" [in Russian], *Soviet Music: The Problems of Symphonism and Musical Theater*, E. Durandina (comp. and ed.), 96, 5–22. Moscow: Gnesins' State Musical and Pedagogical Institute.

Powers, Harold S. (1980). "Mode", *The New Grove Dictionary of Music and Musicians*, Stanley Sadie (ed.). Vol. 12. London: Macmillan.

Schnittke, Alfred (1988). "Reality that I waited for life . . ." (Dialogues with Yulia Makeyeva and Gennadi Tsypin) [in Russian], *Sovetskaya Muzika* 10: 17–28, Y.S. Korev (ed.). Moscow: Sovetsky Kompozitor.

Tarasti, Eero (1987a). "Intonation and modality in the music of oral tradition and Antiquity", *The Semiotic Web 1986* (= Approaches to Semiotics 78), Thomas A. Sebeok and Jean Umiker-Sebeok (eds.), 567–570. Berlin: Mouton de Gruyter.

– (1987b). "Some Peircean and Greimasian semiotic concepts as applied to music", *The Semiotic Web 1986* (= Approaches to Semiotics 78), Sebeok and Umiker-Sebeok (eds.), 445–459. Berlin: Mouton de Gruyter.

– (1979). *Myth and Music*. Berlin: Mouton.

– (1982). "Peirce and Greimas from the viewpoint of musical semiotics: An outline for a comparative semiotics", *Semiotics 1980* comp. M. Herzfeld and M. D. Lendart. New York: Plenum.

Uspensky, B. (1971). "On the icon's semiotics" [in Russian], *Works on Semiotics*, Y. Lotman (ed.), 5 (284), 178–222. Tartu: Tartu University Press.

Valkova, Vera (1978). "On the concept of the musical theme" [in Russian], *Musical Arts and Science* 3: 168–190, E. Nazaikinsky (ed. and comp.). Moscow: Muzgiz.

Vartanova, Yelena (1989). On the problem of genre in A. Schnittke's Second and Fourth Symphonies. Unpublished manuscript, Saratov Conservatory.

– (1987). On the typology of the style contrasts in contemporary music. Unpublished manuscript, Saratov Conservatory.

Wheelock, Wade T. (1987). "Language: Sacred language", *The Encyclopedia of Religion*, vol. 8, 439–446. New York: Collier Macmillan.

Yujak, Kiraina (1986). *Lad*: Type of order — dynamical and evolving system. Unpublished manuscript, Leningrad Conservatory.

Analyzing *Arabescata*, Rautavaara's multiserial symphony
A semiotic interplay between the title and the musical structure

ANNE SIVUOJA-GUNARATNAM

Einojuhani Rautavaara (b. 1928) is a Finnish composer with a vast production of compositions belonging to various genres and to different stylistic periods. *Arabescata*, written in 1962 for a full symphony orchestra, represents a qualitative climax to Rautavaara's twelve-tone period, and it is the only work where Rautavaara rigorously applies integral serial principles. *Arabescata* is since 1986 Rautavaara's Fourth Symphony, the previous Fourth Symphonies (1964 and 1969) having been withdrawn by the composer. Originally, *Arabescata* bore no genre indications, just its title. This was for ideological reasons, says the composer, because in the 1960s it was out of date to compose symphonies, especially by (multi-)serial methods (Rautavaara 1989: 230, 239).

After a short introduction to *Arabescata*, I will present two interpretation strategies, both arising from a semiotic interplay between the musical structure and the name of the composition. The analysis of the form and the contents of the title, *Arabescata*, offers keys for a possible reading. At the level of the form phonetic symmetries are juxtaposed with symmetrical musical solutions. At the level of contents the signified of *Arabescata* (*arabescare*, arabesque) also appears to be relevant to interpretation.

Introduction to *Arabescata*

Faithful to the demands of (integral) serial aesthetics, *Arabescata* is relatively short: its total duration is about 16 minutes. It has four parts, each lasting from three to five minutes. The first three parts have been generated by more or less classical multi-serial methods, but the last part takes quite a distance even from serial writing.

Part One could be well described as "point-serial". In accordance with structuralist thinking of the 1960s, in each tone different musical parameters or composites meet: besides pitch and duration, also timbre, register, dynamics, density, articulation, etc. need to be considered. As a spiritual forefather of *Arabescata*'s first part could be mentioned, e.g., Pierre Boulez's *Structures I* for two pianos.

Part Two contains five miniatures: (1) Quadratus, (2) Zigzag, (3) Figurae, (4) Dedicatio, and (5) Rotatus. Rautavaara generated the sonorous events from these graphic designs, which he drew upon coordinates on millimeter-paper. Instrumentation, duration, density of simultaneous events, dynamics, and indirectly also the total duration have been pre-established in the coordinates. The structure of the coordinates for all five miniatures of the second part remains basically the same. Yet each individual design realizes this pre-established diagram in different ways.

Part Three is governed again by a deductive matrix, not very different from the first part. Unlike these first three parts which are composed by integral serial means, *Part Four* escapes rigorous dogma and approaches aleatory organization. It is composed of 10 groups or segments, which are to be performed according to the pre-established order from one to ten. None of the groups can be deleted or repeated. Each group consists of five subgroups or five instrumental colors: brass, woodwinds, strings, percussion, and chordal instruments (like celesta, piano, and harp). The performance order of these five subgroups is free. They can be played in any order, and they can overlap each other partly or even totally. There is only one limitation: repetition of subgroups is forbidden (except for groups 7 and 10). The composer has thus left the fourth part somewhat open, to be completed by the performer, in this case by the conductor. Thirty years later, in his autobiography *Omakuva*, Rautavaara is very critical of his aleatory approach in *Arabescata*. He writes that there the liberty was no greater than in a furnished room, where you can only change the order of the furniture, but nothing else (Rautavaara 1989: 154; see also Aho 1988: 90–97 and Heiniö 1986: 101–106).

"Serial" listening — an unsolved problem?

I spent two months trying to understand the serial genesis of *Arabescata*; that is, what kind of serial equations or principles Rautavaara had used for the organization of forms, pitches, timbres, dynamics, etc. Excluding a couple of unclear bars in the third part, I succeeded in tracing the surface events to the series and abstract equations with the help of a printed score (Rautavaara 1988/1962), composer's program notes (Rautavaara 1962), some of his sketches, and Kalevi Aho's book *Rautavaara as Symphonist* (1988).

However, my intention is *not* to present here Rautavaara's multiserial manipulations in *Arabescata*, because they are not very interesting from the point of view of a listener. In the best or worst case, as you like, these serial manipulations may remain the composer's private secret. One cannot really hear serial operations in detail; even recognizing aurally in a real musical context a single twelve-tone row and its mirror forms is complicated and requires previous ear training (cf. Krumhansl et al. 1987). Instead, the *results* of the serial operations can be received as acoustic events, but the point is that the listener does not hear the series or abstract equations. She or he hears only acoustic events and structures them by other than (multi-) serial compositional strategies, maybe even by strategies unforeseen by the composer.

The aesthetics of integral serial music demanded constantly new, unheard acoustic objects, to be used sometimes just for one piece. It aimed at new forms, new sounds, new morphology, new syntax, a new conception of music. This newness of everything was not unproblematic. The situation is formulated by Tarasti from a semiotic point of view as follows: "The problem of so-called modern music . . . is that the listener cannot be forced to receive at the same time a [new] message and a [new] code. The modernists . . . thought they could create an active audience by constructing works of art which concealed the rules for interpretation within themselves. . . . But instead the audience grew absent-minded and distracted . . ." (1986: 3; and cf. Subotnik 1991). Composers' program comments usually did not orient the listening, because their main emphasis was on the technology and complex genesis of the piece, not how you could listen to it. This holds true also for *Arabescata*.

In the following I will present two strategies for interpreting *Arabescata*, both initiating from a semiotic interplay between musical structure and the name of the composition. It is obvious that they don't exhaust the work. My heuristic inspiration comes mainly from three sources: Grabócz (1986), Genette (1987), and Escal (1990).

First reading of /arabescata/ (based on the form of the expression)

The first strategy is called mirroring or mirror symmetry. There are no hints of this strategy in the composer's program comments. Still, the keys for this interpretation are given before a single tone has been heard — in the name of the piece.

Arabescata is an Italian word with a precise signified, but what is important here is the form of the expression. If you segment the name in the following way, hidden symmetry based on phonetic repetition will be revealed: *ARA-BESC-ATA*. The first and last segments are similar in their arrangement and thus refer to each other in this limited context, the second one being different from the two others. It should be noted that the first and last segments are not only symmetrical with reference to each other, but also within their one structure (both *ARA* and *ATA* are symmetrical).

These embedded mirror symmetries of the name made me wonder if there really were symmetrical structures within the piece, if they were just my fiction, or merely "innocent" play on the composer's part. My answer now is that they are all this, at least partly. Indeed, I did find many symmetrical solutions in the piece, but I began to read them differently only after I had segmented the name of the piece in a symmetrical way. And of course this playful title is given by Rautavaara himself, whose innocence can be questioned, since he is known to be obsessed with symmetries. His first published piece, *Three Symmetric Preludes* for piano (1949), carries symmetries not only in the title but also in the rhythm, texture, and pianistic technique. And in the late 1950s the composer changed his artistic name from Eino Rautavaara to Einojuhani Rautavaara, as he started using his second Christian name spelled together with his first name. The reason for this was only his desire to have both first and last names contain symmetrically ten letters.

According to Rautavaara (1962), *Arabescata* refers to an Italian marble stone (see, e.g., *Marmi italiani*). This is true, but apparently not the whole truth. *Arabescato corchia*, *Arabescato cervaiole*, and *Arabescato orobico rosso* are indeed Italian marbles. What is important is that the grammatical form used for these marbles is *arabescato*, not *arabescata*. These Italian words are masculine and feminine forms of a verb, *arabescare*, which means to ornament with bizarre figures or arabesques. Now the question is, why did Rautavaara reject the masculine, grammatically correct form *arabescato* and choose instead a feminine one, *arabescata*? My guess is that the grammatically proper form for marble, *arabescato*, would have destroyed the mirror games suggested by *arabescata*. Whether this was so or not, it is obvious that at the level of expression, the form of the name is thematically motivated.

Like its name, *Arabescata*'s first and fourth parts are symmetrical within themselves, and they do bear some references to each other. The first part forms a large dynamic curve. The texture at the beginning and the end is very thin, almost transparent (see Example 1). Towards the middle of the first part (e.g., bars 19–23) the texture becomes extremely dense, to the extent that it is almost impossible to hear events. What is perceived is rather a sound mass. After this dynamic climax, the texture gradually begins to thin out. There are less and less overlapping events, and the number of instruments also decreases. In the end, only the strings and the brass remain. This curve-like global form of the first part is based on the density of the simultaneous events and instruments. The "phonological" factor (see, e.g., Ruwet 1972: 39–40) here is not a pitch or harmonic configuration; it is density, arranged in a symmetrical curve form.

Interestingly enough, this symmetrical curve manifests itself not only in a global form, but also at a micro-level. The regular movements of the strings actually form miniature curves. Always during three bars (e.g., bars 1–3) the strings move upwards, and during the next three bars (e.g., bars 4–6) the movement goes down. This string figure remains constant during the 36-bar first part, and it is perceived as small curves or arabesques (Example 1).

Example 1. Rautavaara: *Arabescata*, Arabescata I, bars 1–5.

Like the first movement, the last movement of *Arabescata* is also symmetrical, mirror-like: A (groups 1-3) — B (groups 4-7) — A (groups 8-10), and this can be easily perceived without a score. Mirror writing also controls local events. As an example could be mentioned the percussion in groups one and two (Rautavaara 1988/1962: 56-57), which are each other's retroversions (see Example 2).

Example 2.   Rautavaara: *Arabescata*, Arabescata IV, percussion groups 1 and 2.

Second reading of *«arabescata»* (based on the form of the content)

For my second interpretation strategy, the semantic content of the title is relevant. As mentioned before, *arabescata* is the feminine form (*participio passato*) of the Italian verb *arabescare*, which means to ornament a surface with arabesques. *Arabescata* would also mean a surface embellished by arabesques. In this form of decorative art, essentially a two-dimensional surface (without depth) is covered with intertwining symmetrical figures. These figures, most often different kinds of curves, are usually non-figurative. They do not refer to anything beyond themselves. Thus arabesques do not represent familiar objects, persons, animals, or plants, or if this happens, representation is distorted with strong stylistic effects.

In arabesques, it is quite possible for the same geometric motive to repeat in different sizes. For example a star or circle motive may be multiplied from macro-level to micro-level. The situation is analogous within Rautavaara's *Arabescata*: the symmetry "motive" is reflected innumerable times from symmetrical formal structures of the macro-level to micro-level, manifesting as a mirror-like organization of the texture or its parts (for further examples see Sivuoja-Gunaratnam 1993: 174–177, 201–204). I will just recall as an example the first movement, where the curve motive governed not only the background setting, but also small surface motives of the strings.

Symmetry is reflected also in the serial technique of *Arabescata*. For instance, the two original all-interval series and their fifth-rows[1] (*Quintenreihen*) used in *Arabescata* are both symmetrical in many ways.[2] Also, a comparison of sets to each other clearly reveals symmetrical details (Sivuoja-Gunaratnam 1993: 135–184).

The aesthetics of multi-serial music (and more generally so-called absolute music) and arabesques share a common interest: they all put great emphasis on the purely formal properties of an object. What is essential is an abstract play of forms and formal relationships, not any expressive, sentimental, or figurative connotations. According to Hanslick's famous formulation "Der Inhalt der Musik sind tönend bewegte Formen" (1874: 45; see also pp. 45–46, where Hanslick uses arabesques as a metaphor for the abstract play of beautiful forms in music).

Single arabesques in decorative art and in Rautavaara's *Arabescata* form a dense textural network, where it is impossible to perceive all the possible ties and links between the units. And it is not even necessary. One can start deciphering arabesques from any part and continue in any direction. There are no fixed directional rules for reading arabesques.

Each bunch of arabesques is important, and besides the aspect of size, there are no privileged or hierarchical units, which would be emphasized one over another. Arabesques form a rather stagnant and multi-directional network of relationships, not a narrative with chronological salient events. This description of arabesques is valid also for integral serial music in general and naturally for Rautavaara's *Arabescata*.

Umberto Eco wrote quite a lot about serial music during his early career (see, e.g., "Series and structure" in Eco 1989 or "Necessità e possibilità nelle strutture musicali" in Eco 1990/1968). He argues that the epistemological background for serial music is strongly linked to an Einsteinian conception of the world. Eco writes: "In this kind of universe, relativity means the infinite variability of experience as well as the infinite multiplication of possible ways of measuring things and viewing their positions" (1989: 18). In an Einsteinian world there are no privileged points of view, as in multi-serial music or in the art of arabesques. All the perspectives are at least potentially equally valid, as in Deleuze and Guattari's rhizomatic structure (1976). The lack of a dominant principle does not, according to Eco, lead to chaos but instead to alternative ways of reading the world and objects, including works of art. Following Eco's line of interpretation of integral serial music, one encounters an obvious paradox: a seed of pluralism and postmodern aesthetics is embedded in the strictest and most rigorous modernism of music, if not in its genesis, at least in the reception and interpretation of complex structures in multi-serial music.

Notes

1. In American music theory the operation is also known as M7 or multiplication by 7; see Eimert 1952: 26–28, and Rahn 1980: 98–105.
2. See, e.g., Aho 1988: 91 for analysis of the series used in the first and last movements.

References

Aho, Kalevi (1988). *Einojuhani Rautavaara as Symphonist*, trans. J. Parsons. Helsinki: Sibelius Akatemian julkaisusarja nr. 5 and Edition Pan 131.

Deleuze, Gilles and Guattari, Felix (1976). *Rhizome*. Paris: Minuit.

Eco, Umberto (1989). "The poetics of the open work", *The Open Work*, trans. A. Cancogni, 1–23. Cambridge: Harvard University Press.

– (1990/1968). *La definizione dell'arte*. Milano: Mursia.

Eimert, Herbert (1958). *Lehrbuch der Zwölftontechnik*. Wiesbaden: Breitkopf & Härtel.

Escal, Françoise (1990). *Contrepoints: Musique et littérature*. Paris: Méridiens Klincksieck.

Genette, Gérard (1987). *Seuils*. Paris: Seuil.

Grabócz, Márta (1986). *Morphologie des œuvres pour piano de Liszt: Influence du programme sur l'évolution des formes instrumentales*. Budapest: MTA, Zenetudományi Intézet.

Hanslick, Eduard (1874). *Vom Musikalisch-Schönen: Ein Beitrag zur Revision der Ästhetik der Tonkunst*, 4th ed. Leipzig: Johann Ambrosius Barth.

Heiniö, Mikko (1986). "12-säveltekniikan aika. Dodekafonian ja sarjallisuuden reseptio ja Suomen luova säveltaide 1950-luvulta 1960-luvun puoliväliin", *Musiikki* 3–4.

Krumhansl, Carol L. et al. (1987). "The perception of tone hierarchies and mirror forms in twelve-tone serial music", *Music Perception* 5 (1): 31–77.

Marmi italiani. Guida tecnica. (s.a.). Istituto commercio estero. Roma-EUR: F.lli Vallardi editori.

Rahn, John (1980). *Basic Atonal Theory*. New York: Longman.

Rautavaara, Einojuhani (1962). *Arabescata*. Composer's program notes on the premiere, The Finnish Radio Symphony Orchestra, 26 February 1962.

– (1988/1962). *Arabescata: Symphony No. 4*. Helsinki: Edition Pan.

– (1989). *Omakuva* [A Self-Portrait]. Juva: WSOY.

Ruwet, Nicolas (1972/1959). "Contradictions du langage sériel", *Langage, musique, poésie*, 23–40. Paris: Seuil.

Sivuoja-Gunaratnam, Anne (1993). Rautavaaran sarjallinen projekti. Unpublished licentiate's thesis, University of Helsinki, Department of Musicology.

Subotnik, Rose Rosengard (1991). "The Challenge of Contemporary Music", *Developing Variations: Style and Ideology in Western Music*, 265–293. Minneapolis: University of Minnesota Press.

Tarasti, Eero (1986). "Musiikkitiede humanistisena tutkimusalana", *Musiikki* 1: 1–8.